THAILAND and BURMA

THE TRAVELLER'S GUIDE

GW00671275

THAILAND and BURMA

THE TRAVELLER'S GUIDE

BY STEFAN LOOSE, RENATE RAMB, RICHARD DORING,
URSULA SPRAUL-DORING
TRANSLATED BY PETER CONOLLY-SMITH

SPRINGFIELD BOOKS LIMITED

THAILAND and BURMA

The Traveller's Guide

Published by

SPRINGFIELD BOOKS LIMITED
NORMAN ROAD, DENBY DALE, HUDDERSFIELD HD8 8TH
WEST YORKSHIRE, ENGLAND

First edition 1988

TRANSLATED FROM THE 2ND GERMAN EDITION BY
Peter Conolly-Smith

PRINTED AND BOUND
in Hong Kong by Colorcraft Limited

MAPS AND LAYOUT BY
Klaus Schindler

PHOTOGRAPHY BY
South East Asia Picture Archives Renate Loose

© 1988 Stefan Loose

British Library Cataloguing in Publication data

Loose, Stefan
  Thailand and Burma, the traveller's guide.
  1. Burma - Visitors' guides 2. Thailand - Visitors guides
  I. Title II. Ramb, Renate III. Thailand Burma handbuch.
  English
  915.91'045

ISBN   0-947655-39-5

TABLE OF CONTENTS

PREFACE

Who doesn't want to go on a holiday, and the further away from home, the better? Lying beneath palm-trees on sandy, white beaches, discovering the magnificently colourful underwater world of coral reefs, exploring the mysterious life of the jungle, and getting to know peoples hitherto untouched by western society - the perfect holiday.

Most people secretly associate visions of a better, different life with countries such as Thailand and Burma. Different, in this sense, means mainly not like at home, where the sun is only seldom seen, where lakes and rivers are polluted, where life is dull and boring, and where civilizational diseases seem to be gaining the upper hand.

Travel brochures would have you believe that all you need do to get what you want is board the next eastbound aeroplane; you'll be in the country of your dreams only a day later.

Those landing in Bangkok with such visions will quickly become disillusioned as they fight their way through the chaotic traffic of Thailand's capital. The technical feats of western society are being introduced in Thailand and Burma, and with them pollution and the gradual destruction of the environment. Modern western cultural export articles, from Dynasty to Dire Straits, have an almost unbelievable impact on far eastern countries, and those wishing to discover the genuine Thai and Burmese culture should be prepared to invest quite some time and much patience.

But do not panic: Bangkok doesn't equal Thailand, and you will be able to find dense jungle, fine, white beaches, wildly romantic waterfalls, and colourful coral reefs only a few hours from the capital.

With over 3 million tourists visiting Thailand yearly, it seems improbable that you will ever discover the proverbial, secluded, and totally uninhabited 'Robinson Crusoe' island. But such places do exist; many of Thailand's beaches and islands are still virtually undiscovered in terms of tourism. You won't find airports, comfortable hotels, or restaurants there, though, nor will you find such islands and beaches listed in this book - if they were, they would not remain undiscovered for long.

And then, after you finally have found your personal, tropical paradise, you will start missing the comforts of western society. You'll find that it isn't really as much fun as you'd always thought; where are those cool, refreshing drinks, showers, and people to talk to? In addition, a life without electricity or communications is not everyone's cup of tea.

Few tourists ever really go exploring; most simply relax and enjoy the security and comfort of some tourist ghetto. Package-deal tourists usually stay at the hotels of Phuket, Pattaya, and Chiang Mai, while individual travellers choose to spend their time lazing about on the beaches and in the guesthouses of Ko

Samui, Krabi, Ko Samet, Chiang Rai, Pai, and Mae Hong Son. You'll always be able to find an English-speaking person in the above places, and there'll always be plenty of restaurants serving fried eggs for breakfast.

Trekking tour organizers have adapted perfectly to western demands. Those setting out to discover the 'primitive' villages of the hilltribes, where western civilization has also already left its mark, will feed on food their guides have brought along from their base. For only those who do not have to live it can possibly find a 'primitive' life romantic. If you walk through the hilltribe villages with open eyes and register the poverty and squalor, however, you will find yet another vision of the tropics crumbling - that of the 'happy savages'.

You will always be something special in a hilltribe village. People will approach you spontaneously, and you may even find yourself being invited into homes. Always remember that you are much richer than most people here. For this reason it is very important to accept the simple lifestyle of the tribes as well as their often (to us) incomprehensible customs and traditions without acting with typical western presumption. Try to understand and respect their culture.

One used to speak of developing countries, a typical symptom of the egocentricity of western society, which simply presumes that no country is fully developed until it has reached the standards of Europe or America. The white race used to be mainly characterized by an arrogant attitude (and still is today, though not quite as badly) - one always wanted to advise, better yet tell, other countries how to do things, instead of letting them do them in the way they felt best. With the end of colonialism now in sight, this attitude has finally been more or less eradicated.

Along with their visions of a tropical paradise, most travellers also carry a set of values and standards around with them, usually formed back at home. You will quite unconsciously start comparing the two worlds you know, and you'll find yourself thinking "we do it better" more and more frequently. Some people start longing for a soft bed all of a sudden, more order, western food etc. If you're one of the kind of people who like everything to be the way it is back home, then stay there!

Try ridding yourself of your prejudices and values whilst travelling around Burma and Thailand. Take the time to observe and listen; you will gain a much more genuine image of the country. And maybe then you'll be able to question your own, western values, and to understand a different culture.

It would be ridiculous to claim that the observations made in this book are not influenced by our personal experiences and subjective opinions. Even though we have done our best to handle each of the regions objectively and with equal attention to detail, we cannot deny that we, too, have our preferences. Every traveller sees Thailand and Burma through different eyes. We have therefore not attempted to set universally acceptable standards in our book, but simply to give you a little help when it comes to discovering a brand new country.

Since we have not restricted ourselves to describing only monuments and temples, which have been standing in the same place for centuries, but also want to give some good practical information as to where to stay, eat, and go, you may find that many of the prices and facts listed have already changed. We have tried to research everything as thoroughly as possible. Our special thanks goes to all those readers who sent us detailed letters with information and up to date corrections. Please, continue sending us letters telling of your experiences, giving new information, corrections, and criticism!

Finally, we wish you open eyes and ears whilst travelling in Thailand and Burma, and - of course - lots and lots of fun and sunshine!

Berlin, spring 1988
Richard Doring
Stefan Loose
Renate Ramb
Ursula Spraul-Doring

LANDSCAPE & GEOGRAPHY

THAILAND

as it is seen when approaching Bangkok by air, seems like an endless plain of ricefields, sometimes of a glistening green, a rich yellow, or an earthy brown, depending on the time of year. Shimmering canals and rivers criss-cross the land. Along their banks one sees the houses of occasional villages lined up next to one another like pearls on a string, each framed by a palm-studded garden. Ah yes, typically Thailand...

But is there anything typical about this elephant-head shaped country? Travellers who have explored its 514,000 km^2 will swear that the country defies typification. Thailand is easily twice the size of England. The distance between its northernmost and southernmost tips equals the distance between the Shetland Islands and Plymouth, approximately 1600 km. At its widest point Thailand measures 800 km, the distance between London and Aberdeen. In contrast, the elephant's trunk, more commonly know as the Isthmus of Kra, measures no more than 15 km at its narrowest point. Lying just south of the Tropic of Cancer, between 6°N and 20°N and 97°E and 106°E, Thailand reveals itself to the traveller as a country of many landscapes, some of them contrasting, all of them appealing.

CENTRAL THAILAND consists mainly of a huge river delta, divided into sections by the various arms of the Menam Chao Phya, Thailand's largest river. Its name, incidentally, consists of two components, with 'Menam' meaning mother of water or river, while 'Chao Phya' is a title only given to the nobility. The river winds its way through wide lowlands, which lie between 0 and 80 metres above sea level. Over the milleniums the river's water flooded vast quantities of sand, gravel, and other decaying materials into the lowlands, depositing layer upon layer. These days, a number of large dams situated around the upper course of the river keep it under control. Now the water rarely floods the river banks as dramatically as it used to, when the level of water during the rainy period would rise to 100 times that of the level during the dry period. All the same, large portions of land are still flooded with water for months each year, and large quantities of sedimentary rocks and fertile minerals are constantly being washed from the mountains in the north to the sea. The waterways for inland navigation have to be re-dug every year, and the coastline itself shifts out into the sea by a few metres yearly. The outer edges of this fertile plain, which is used intensively for the cultivation of rice, merges with a hilly landscape, consisting in part of old rock deposition.

NORTHERN THAILAND, with its wild hills and mountains, makes up a completely different landscape. The mountain chain here could be seen as an extension of the Himalayas, the mountain range stretching from India through

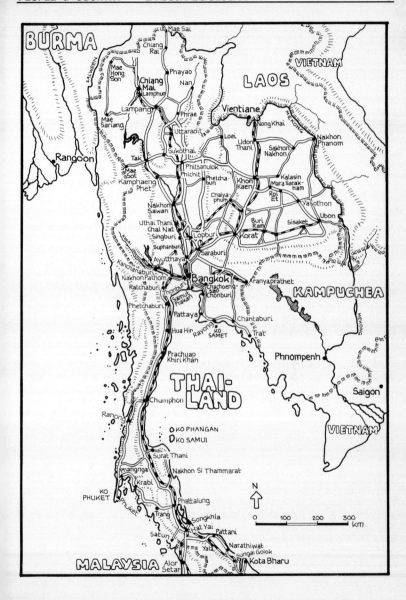

Burma to China, along the western border of Thailand, and all the way to the Malay Peninsula. There are few Thai mountains exceeding 2000 metres in height. Doi Inthanon, 60 km southwest of Chiang Mai, is Thailand's highest mountain with 2595 metres. The mountain range is divided into segments by deep valleys which were channelled by rivers and subsequently filled with deposits. The tributaries of the Mekong flow through the valleys in the east (Menam Kok, Chiang Rai etc.), those of the Salween in the west (Menam Pai, Mae Hongson etc.), and the headstreams of the Menam Chao Phya irrigate the centre of the country - the Ping in the west (Chiang Mai) merges with the Wang (Lampang) a little north of Tak, while the Yom in the east (Phrae, Sukhothai) flows into the Nan (Nan, Phitsanulok) further south. All these rivers meet at Nakhon Sawan, forming the Menam Chao Phya. The alluvial river-valleys are used intensively for agriculture. Humans have lived here for centuries, among them the early Thai settlers who started colonizing the country from Yunnan in the north.

NORTHEAST THAILAND is made up of a bowl-shaped, hilly area, the so-called Korat plateau, which lies 100-300 metres above sea level. It is enclosed by the Petchabun mountain range in the west, the Phanom Dongrak mountain range in the south, and the Mekong river in the east and north. Sediments which were later geologically raised and folded were deposited here during the Reptilian age. The ground has few nutrients and cannot store water for a long period of time. This makes the area unfit for agricultural use. There are floods here during the rainy period, when the Menam Mun and its tributaries are barely able to hold the water masses, while only a few months later the landscape is completely dry and arid.

SOUTH- and SOUTHEAST THAILAND are closely connected to the sea. All in all, Thailand's coast measures more than 2600 km, most of it bordering on the Gulf of Thailand, some on the Indian Ocean (Andaman Sea). In the southeast of the country the foothills of the Cardamon mountain range reach the coast. During the Tertiary period much sandstone was deposited here, which was later covered with magma coming from deep within the earth. The gem deposits of Chanthaburi's sapphire mines can be traced back to the volcanic activity of this period.

In the south, Thailand reaches well into the Malay Peninsula, where the echelon formation of the various mountain chains (Tenasserim-, Phuket-, Nakhon-, and Kalakiri mountain range) distinctly separates the east coast from the west coast. Steep karst cliffs border on the sea at the west coast, where they sometimes form bizarre limestone island groups (the Bay of Phang Nga). In the east, the mountains merge into a wide coastal plain.

THAILAND'S REGIONS - PROVINCES, POPULATION, AREA

Central region: Bangkok, Thonburi, Ang Thong, Ayutthaya, Chai Nat, Lopburi, Nonthaburi, Pathum Thani, Saraburi, Singburi

Eastern region: Chanthaburi, Chachoengsao, Chonburi, Nakhon Nayok, Prachinburi, Rayong, Samut Prakan, Trat

Western region: Kanchanaburi, Nakhon Pathom, Prachuap Khiri Khan, Phetchburi, Ratchaburi, Samut Songkhram, Samut Sakhon, Suphanburi

Northern region: Chiang Mai, Chiang Rai, Kamphaeng Phet, Lampang, Lamphun, Mae Hongson, Nakhon Sawan, Nan, Phayao, Phitchit, Phitsanulok, Phetchabun, Phrae, Sukhothai, Uttaradit, Uthai Thani

Northeastern region: Buri Ram, Chaiyaphum, Kalasin, Khon Kaen, Loei, Maha Sarakham, Nakhon Phanom, Nakhon Ratchasima (Korat), Nong Khai, Roi-Et, Sakon Nakhon, Sisaket, Surin, Ubon Ratchathani, Udon Thani, Yasothon

Southern region: Chumphon, Ranong, Surat Thani, Phang Nga, Phuket, Krabi, Nakhon Si Thammarat, Trang, Phattalung, Satun, Songkhla, Pattani, Yala, Narathiwat

Region	area in km²	population in millions (1986)	density of pop./km²
Bangkok and Thonburi	1540	5,61	3642
Central region without Bgk/Thonb.	18610	3,67	197
Eastern region	37328	3,80	102
Western region	46092	4,15	90
Northern region	170003	0,84	64
Northeastern tregion	70226	18,75	110
Southern region	70189	6,72	96
Thailand - total	513988	53,54	104

AKHA PEOPLE WORKING IN THE FIELDS

BURMA

Since only 7-day visas are issued for Burma, there is not much time for the average traveller to discover this interesting and manifold country. People with plenty of energy and a little luck will just be able to manage the Rangoon - Pagan - Mandalay - Lake Inle - Rangoon round trip. If you take a look at a map of Burma, you will see that the above route seems like a smaller, more central version of the entire, almost kite-shaped country. The distance from its northernmost to its southernmost tip (which reaches all the way down into the Malay peninsula) is 1500 km, the distance between London and Rome. At its widest point the 'kite' has a span of 900 km (= Paris-Prague). This 678,000 km² sized country, lying between 10°N and 28°N and 92°E and 101°E, is easily three times the size of the United Kingdom. Quite similarly to Thailand, the central region of the country is criss-crossed by the large Irrawaddy river and its many tributaries. There are large mountain ranges in the north and the west of the country, while an elevated plain rises in the east. A long coastline makes up the south of the country.

The northern mountains of the Kachin state, which reaches to beyond the Tropic of Cancer, are quite inaccessible to tourists. The entire area is rugged, with mountain peaks measuring an average height of 900 - 2700 metres. Mount Khakaborazi in the north of Burma, near the Chinese border, measures 5881 metres and is the country's highest mountain. This is the head-waters region of the Irrawaddy, separated from the river valleys of the Salween, Yangtze, and Mekong, which work their way through the rough cliff formations of China in a north-to-south direction, by high mountain ridges. Once its various sources have joined to form the Irrawaddy river, between the Kumon mountains and Myitkyina, the river's current decreases in speed. As it works its way through wide valleys formed by sedimentary deposits, the river gradually becomes slower. The towns of Bhamo and Putao lie on wide plains enclosed by mountains. Spectacular canyons, sometimes no more than 50 metres wide and with steep cliff walls, were formed at those points at which the river had to work its way through the Kaukkwe mountains, southerly foothills of the larger mountain ranges (north and south of Bhamo). Burma's largest lake, the Indawgyi, 26 km long and 10 km wide, was formed in an area where the earth sank due to an earthquake.

The western mountains rise to form a semi-circular mountain range along the border with India and Bangladesh. Mount Victoria (3120 metres) is the highest peak of the Chin mountains, which lie in the northern part of the Chin State and have an average height of 1500 - 2700 metres. The range merges into the Arakan Yoma (Yoma = main back) further south, where the mountain peaks reach a height of over 1200 metres, even near the coastline. This mountain chain continues beneath the surface of the ocean, forming small island groups, among them the Andaman Islands (India). In contrast to the north of the country, there are only narrow canyons in the western mountains.

Wide plains can be found near the coast, especially in the delta areas of the Mayu, Kaledan, and Lemro rivers, near Akyab, the capital of the Arakan state.

The eastern plateau (Shan State and Kayah State), is a large, raised, hilly plateau, consisting in part of ancient, hard, eruptive rock (gneiss, granite), in part of more recent alluvial deposits and limestone. The plateau, which has an average height of 900 metres, rises rather abruptly from the central plain just east of the Sittang river. (This becomes plainly visible when taking a bus to Lake Inle.) The Salween and its tributaries run through the valleys, which were formed by tectonic folds, in a north-to-south direction. Lake Inle lies in one of these depressions, at a height of 875 metres. The lake's main claims to fame are the floating gardens upon its surface and the so-called 'leg-rowers', who row their boats standing up, with one leg wrapped around an oar. Other lakes of the Shan plateau have dried out during the course of time. The landscape gradually becomes more level towards the south, where various caves (Pindaya and Padalin caves), grottoes, and small lakes can be found in the limestone formations.

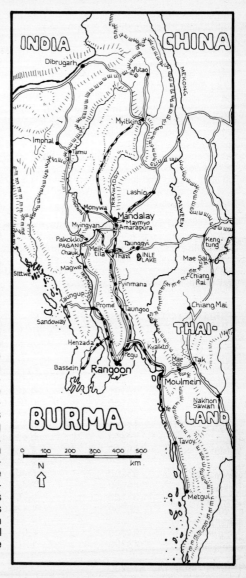

The highest density of population in Burma can be found in **the central plain.** As in Thailand, this is also the main area used for the tillage of rice. The deposits of the Irrawaddy river, over 2000 km in length, are responsible for the forming of this wide, level plain. During the dry season some of the river's tributaries are completely dried out (Yaw, Salin), while others are only a few centimetres deep (Pin, Yin). The mangrove-overgrown coastline of the 33,670 km^2 sized delta is constantly shifting towards the sea due to the mud deposits of the Irrawaddy. Various ridges run through the plain from north to south, forming a watershed for the Irrawaddy in the west (Chin and Arakan Yoma) and in the east (Pegu Yoma). The Pegu ridge ends with Mount Popa, 1495 metres in height, which once rose like a huge hat out of the otherwise rather flat landscape after an earthquake. To the south, the ridge peters out into a hilly landscape characterized by laterite stone formations. The Shwedagon Pagoda stands upon one of these hills. In the west ancient river deposits were geologically folded and later washed away. The remaining sandstone formations make up the foothills of the Arakan Yoma.

The coastal region is mainly mountainous except for the delta areas - the delta of Akyab in the west, the vast delta area of the Irrawaddy, the river mouth of the Sitang, the Salween (which flows into the sea at Moulmein), and various smaller rivers coming from the Tenasserim mountains further south-east. Travellers looking for a typical beach holiday will find what they're after at the popular Ngapali Beach near Sandoway.

BURMA'S STATES AND DISTRICTS, THEIR POPULATION AND AREA

State/area	area in km^2	population in million (1986)	density of pop./km^2
Arakan	36900	2,227	60,3
Chin	36100	0,421	11,7
Kachin	89100	0,957	10,7
Karen	30500	1,115	36,5
Kayah	11900	0,164	13,8
Mon	12400	0,934	75,3
Shan	155900	4,136	26,5
Irrawaddy	35200	5,405	153,5
Magwe	44900	3,426	76,3
Mandalay	37100	4,766	128,5
Pegu	39500	4,132	104,6
Rangoon	10300	4,148	402,7
Sagaing	94800	4,055	42,8
Tenasserim	43500	1,709	39,3
Burma - total	678100	37,595	55,4

FAUNA & FLORA

These days few travellers will ever get to see elephants and teak woods, probably the most 'typical' representatives of Thai fauna and flora, in their natural habitat. Instead, domesticated water buffaloes and cultivated ricefields dominate the landscape.

The wide variety of flora in Thailand and Burma is due in part to the different soil conditions and - particularly - to the specific geographical location and its respective climate. Both of these South East Asian countries reach from the ever-humid, tropical regions to the subtropical zones along the Tropic of Cancer. While tropical rainforest dominates the landscape in the south, the flora of the north has had to adapt to recurring seasons of drought, during which the temperatures climb unceasingly. A completely different type of flora, one adapted to cold weather, has developed in the mountain areas, where temperatures may sink close to freezing point.

Of all tropical regions in the world, South East Asia has the widest variety of fauna and flora. One reason for this is the long history of climatic stability in this area. One assumes that the same climatic conditions have existed for the tropical rainforests of the Malay Peninsula for the past 150 million years. Although the jungle areas in the south of Burma and Thailand keep shrinking, they still make up the two countries' most important ecological systems.

George Maxwell described the **tropical rainforest** in his wonderful book 'In Malay Forests' in 1907 - "Though it is midday it is very dark and very sombre. The sun cannot pierce the dense foliage of the branches of the giant trees, and so heavily do shadows lie upon shadows that the very green seems almost black." Enormous, 70 metre tualang trees join with other large trees to form the rainforest's roof of leaves. It is not rare for single trees to rise well above this roof. In the primary jungle one can see various 'floors' of distinctly different plants. The leaves of the highest trees are exposed to the most intense rays of sun as well as the daily change of temperature (from 32°C at midday to 22°C at night). At the same time the humidity drops from 100% to 60% at nights. There is hardly any variation of temperature or humidity beneath this uppermost roof of leaves. Thus one could speak of two different climatic zones within the primary jungle.

A second roof of leaves, belonging to trees competing for the life-giving light of the sun by trying to outgrow each other, rises to a height of about 10 - 20 metres. A large variety of shrubs and bushes that need little light but a high humidity thrive down below, between the roots and lianas, in the jungle's twilight. Foliage and other organic substances are broken down and converted into humus by the many insects and micro-organisms of the jungle. A fine layer of this humus covers most of the mainly unfertile, loam ground. It is the earth's main source of nutrients in Thailand and Burma. The green of the jungle floor is only rarely broken by colourful flowers. On the upper levels there are many kinds of orchids and epiphytic plants that grow on top of other plants like parasitic creatures. Should you find yourself in a clearing in the jungle, you will see how the vegetation suddenly changes due to the direct sunlight - high grass, shrubs, and other plants merge to form a sheer impenetrable thicket.

When the primary jungle is cut down the natural cycle of plant growth and humus production is broken. The remaining vegetation may seem very fertile, but the further supply of organic substances has been cut off. In addition the loose humus, no longer protected by roots and plants, is quickly washed away.

If the earth is not cultivated, a secondary jungle will gradually develop, consisting mainly of low trees and bushes, and with fewer species.

Mangrove forests sometimes form a thick seam at the coast, making it extremely difficult to actually reach the water. The various kinds of trees of these forests, some of them growing up to 20 metres in height, are supported by many tangled roots which rise above the muddy swamps in which they grow. Sandbanks, pushing these swamps inland, are often formed just off the shore, in front of the mangroves. Nipa palms (nipa fruticans), whose large palm leaves are used for making roofs and mats, also grow in the large and swampy delta regions.

The further one moves away from the coast, the less precipitation. This means that plants have to be able to handle annual periods of drought. During these periods many trees shed their leaves, as in Europe during the autumn. If these *monsoon forests* receive an adequate supply of water during the rainy period they will develop a thick foliage similar to that of the tropical rainforests. In December and January the leaves already start taking on autumnal colours. Were it not for a few trees blooming early, the forests of the central plain and the north would seem completely barren in April and May. As there is no roof of leaves at all during this, the hottest of all seasons, only plants able to adapt to the yearly change in climate are able to survive on the lower levels of the forest. In contrast to many trees, the low bushes and plants do not shed their leaves as they are shielded from dehydration by a fine protective film.

The variety of species in these dry monsoon forests is far less extensive than in the evergreen rainforests. Dipterocarpus trees with sweet-smelling, leathery leaves dominate the landscape. Thick, impenetrable *bamboo forests* can be found in many river valleys. This unique, tree-like form of grass is used for the production of various items, the construction of houses, as well as food. Acacias and thornbush savannas dominate in the drier areas. *Teak trees* (Tectona grandis) are a typical representative of the leaf-shedding trees in this region. Their fine, durable wood which even thrives in tropical climates, has been highly valued for centuries. These trees can be found in the lower mountain forests of Burma, Thailand, and India, where the water is quickly drained out of the ground. They thrive best at an average yearly temperature of 24^0C - 27^0C and a yearly precipitation of 1500 mm. These days the trees, which bear only few seeds, are artificially recultivated with their leaves (which can grow up to 50 cm in size) on plantations. Under ideal plantation conditions, the straight, high trunks can reach a height of 20 metres within 15 years, a process which takes up to 200 years under natural conditions.

The variety of *fauna* in the subtropical and tropical rainforests depends largely on the varying climatic conditions, as does the variety of plants. Enclosed by India, China, the Malay Peninsula, and the ocean, Thailand and Burma have a particularly large variety of species. Nevertheless, sixteen species of animals are endangered, while eight further ones are already (or just about) extinct. Even though an increasing number of national parks has been opened since 1961 for the protection of animals, large mammals are highly endangered, e.g. the Sumatra rhinoceros (which can only be found in the Umphang district of the Tak province), the tapir, leopard, and tiger. Predators and other big game are only seen extremely rarely. The relentless pursuit of the rhinoceros, whose horn is an aphrodisiac according to ancient Chinese traditions, is one of the factors which has led to this species' disappearance. The fact that the natural habitat of the animals (the rainforest) is reduced in size year by year is another factor contributing to the endangerment of all species.

Even the elephant, long-honoured by the Thais for its strength and size, is endangered. It is predicted that wild elephants will be extinct 30 - 40 years from now if nothing is done to protect the species. Less than 4000 elephants live in all of Thailand, most of them in the Tenasserim mountains along the border with Burma. In addition there are approx. 5000 trained elephants, whose main job is to carry wood out of the jungle (in 1955 there were still over 13,000). Approx. 3000 wild and 4000 trained elephants live in Burma. If you wish to see what kind of work these magnificent creatures are able to perform, there are training-camps for young elephants in north Thailand. A fully grown, strong elephant can lift about 400 kg with its tusks or pull 1 1/2 tons. Though the tusks of Asian elephants are smaller than those of African ones, a pair of the 80 cm long and 24 cm wide tusks goes for 20,000 Baht. A fully grown, fully trained elephant can be sold for up to 100,000 Baht.

Banteng and Kating, wild forms of cattle, are animals one can still frequently see. Wild deer, among them the Sambar (Cervus unicolor), a dark brown, rather large creature, can be found living in the leaf-shedding forests. The mouse deer (Tragulus), no more than 20 cm tall, is the world's smallest hoofed animal. It can also be found in India.

You will frequently come across monkeys, mainly Gibbons and Macaques. One type of Macaque, reddish brown with a short tail, moves about the jungle ground on hands and feet. Young males of the species are frequently caught and trained to help with the coconut harvest. They climb to the top of the palm-trees better than any expert, and once there they twist the coconuts off with their feet until they drop to the ground. Well trained animals can harvest up to 700 coconuts a day.

So-called 'gliders' can also frequently be seen. The largest, the giant flying squirrel, has a wing-span of almost 1 metre, while the body is only approx. 50 cm long. One also gets flying lemurs, which can grow to the size of the common housecat, as well as flying lizards and flying frogs. The fact that these creatures have learnt to glide enables them to move about the jungle more rapidly than other animals.

Not only fishes live in **Thailand's waters** - tortoises and crocodiles can be found here, too. The largest reptile of the country is the estuarine crocodile, measuring up to 10 metres in length. The smaller Siamese crocodile is more common by far. The mud skipper, a 15 cm fish, is able to survive on land as well as in water; it stores liquid in its gills and moves about on its arm-like fins.

There are roughly 100 different species of **snakes** in Thailand. Sixteen are poisonous, six of these are deadly - the King Cobra (Naja hannah), Cobra (Naja naja), Russell's Viper (Vipera russelli), the Banded Krait (Bungarus fasciatus), and the Malayan and the Green Pit Viper (Ancistrodon rhodostoma and Trimeresurus popeorum). Some species of sea serpents are also extremely dangerous. The poison of a cobra attacks the nervous system of its victim, while that of a viper affects the blood and blood vessels.

The longest snake in the world, the Reticulated Python, can also be found in Thailand. It can grow to a length of ten metres and may weigh as much as 140 kg. These snakes twist themselves around their victims and squeeze them to death. They usually prey on small mammals, monkeys, and birds. Sometimes pythons even find their ways into towns.

The multitude of *insects* is quite staggering - crickets, grasshoppers, and praying mantis are equally common as the less agreeable and sometimes even dangerous ants, Anopheles mosquitoes, wasps, hornets, centipedes, millipedes, and maggots. There are 500 different species of butterflies in Thailand.

The Rhinoceros Beetle, which can grow up to 5 cm in length, is most impressive. There are also tiny beetles which live among the ants in a symbiotic relationship. The giant ants that can often be seen on jungle paths can reach a length of over 2.5 cm. Red Weaving Ants construct their nests out of leaves and fragments of leaves, which are held together by a thread-like secretion. If one accidentally disturbs one of these nests the ants will react in a most aggressive manner.

Birds are rarely seen - they stick to the top of the trees. One can usually hear them from afar, though - the Rhinoceros Birds like clapping their huge wings, which may reach a span of 3 metres. Green and blue shimmering kingfishers can be seen chasing insects and small fishes along the rivers, while the white herons like to perch on top of water buffaloes. These birds hunt for food in the ricefields, where cranes and storks are also frequently to be found.

ECOLOGY

South East Asia's main food product is rice, and rice tillage has been the basis for Burmese and Thai society for many centuries. During the course of the centuries the lowlands were gradually cultivated, while the annual floods kept providing the ricefields with fresh nutrients.

Siam began exporting rice in the middle of the 19th century. This meant a re-structuring of the entire agricultural system which had - up until then - been solely self-sufficient. Although the country quickly became one of the world's principal rice-exporting countries, the traditional methods of cultivation have remained - only half-hearted attempts were made to intensify the agricultural system, so that the earnings and profits per hectare remained the same and in many cases even sank. This, in turn, led to a considerable expansion of the areas used for cultivation.

At the same time, Thailand experienced a population boom, resulting in the fact that areas rather less suitable for rice tillage were suddenly being culti-vated, too. Here, of course, the output sank to an even lower level. In addition, new cultivated plants were introduced (sugar cane, corn, cassava, kenaf), so that even mountain slopes and other unsuitable areas were cultivated.

During the past 25 years the area of land used for agricultural cultivation has grown from just below eight million hectares to over 20 million hectares. Dur-ing the same time Thailand's wooded areas have decreased from over 30 mil-lion hectares to below 15 million hectares. Because of this the complex eco-logical system of the tropical and the subtropical rainforests is gradually being destroyed. The consequences can already be seen everywhere.

Scientists, using satellite pictures as the basis for their findings, estimate that 1.2% of the world's remaining rainforests are cut down yearly. This would mean that approximately 21 hectares of rainforest disappear per minute, and that 38% of the originally wooded areas in South East Asia have already been destroyed. Although rainforests only cover about 13% of the world's land-masses, they are of much more vital importance than one might suspect; here solar energy is converted to organic materials, while superfluous water is stored and released during periods of drought. Basically, these rainforests and the animals and micro-organisms that live within them (fungi and bacteria that mineralize organic substances) constitute our planet's main and most efficient natural ecological system.

Regular doses of sunshine and the high humidity are responsible for the rapid growth of plants here. The fact that the fauna and flora is not exposed to clearly defined seasons as, say, in central Europe, also contributes to their unhin-dered development. These are only two of the reasons why South East Asia's tropical rainforests were able to bring forth such a variety of species.

Scientists predict that by the year 2002 one third of the area of the South East Asian countries will have been lost to agriculture. This will mainly be due to the blatant misuse of the soil in these countries, as well as the relentless development of lalang grass steppe on what was once fertile ground. Due to the ever-rising population, even the last forests will have been cut down and converted to areas fit for agricultural cultivation. Since many forms of animal and plant life are highly endangered if not already extinct, the structure of the still-remaining forests will have to change drastically. The timber industry will move into the few remaining forests, as will local villagers, searching for wood. The hilltribes of the north will have burnt down all remaining mountain forests by then, too, seeing as they periodically shift their areas of cultivation into clearings by burning down the forest (slash-burn agriculture).

More than simply the forests are destroyed through this form of clearing woodland, though; the earth's main water reservoir is drained, and the soil can more easily be washed away during the rainy season because of the absence of roots. Erosion, floods, and periods of drought will be the result, seeing as lalang grass and small plants are far less suitable for storing water and protecting the earth from erosion than the rainforest is.

DEFORESTATION IN THONG PHA PHUM

The higher the living standard and the more the industrialization of the country progresses, the more the Thai people themselves could be said to be contributing to the problem; the so-called developing countries are already taking on distinct characteristics of our disposable way of life. Rubbish is disposed of in the simplest way - the junk surrounding railway tracks, beaches, and hiking trails is visible proof. The rubbish from hotels, factories, and homes is thrown into the sea and the rivers without a second thought. Bangkok's klongs are gradually turning into sewers. Organic waste needs the water's oxygen in order to decompose - little is left over for fish and other organisms for whom rivers are the natural environment. The paper and the petrochemical industries also do their part in contributing to the general contamination of the water, as does the food industry, particularly in connection with the processing of tapioca and sugar cane. The increasing use of pesticides and fertilizers constitutes a further problem, as do the heavy metals polluting the waters, especially in the Gulf of Thailand.

The general consciousness concerning these ecological problems has, however, been raised in recent years, particularly among students. Protesters are beginning to actively challenge the increasing pollution due to industrialization. In 1986 for example, Asia's first tantalum factory on Phuket was stormed and burnt to the ground by irate protesters. Tantalum is made out of the residue of tin and is used, among other things, for the production of silicon chips, machines, and atomic power plants.

The Thai government - especially the King - is promoting afforestation programmes in order to check the further development of wasteland. The regenerated forest areas cover considerably less ground than those areas in which forests have been destroyed, however. A move has been made to try to convince the hilltribes to employ different methods of cultivation and to start planting fruits, vegetables and other foods instead of poppy. Even though the country exports far less fine woods than it used to, forests are still being cut down illegally.

We as visitors can also contribute to the preservation of nature;

❑ all you should leave on footpaths are your footprints, and all you should take with you are memories and photographs.

❑ Do not buy souvenirs of endangered plants or animals (e.g. tortoises, crocodile leather) - according to the agreement over the preservation of species the import of such items into Europe is in any case forbidden.

❑ Divers who break off corals are in part responsible for the slow death of many coral reefs. This also endangers scores of fish, crabs, and other molluscs.

❑ Do not eat frogs - they are the natural enemies of many insects that live in paddies, and they are more effective and less dangerous than pesticides.

POPULATION

53.5 million people lived in Thailand in 1986, 37.5 million lived in Burma. As the Thai population increases by 1.9% per year (Burma 2.2%), one can assume that in 36 years (Burma - 32 years) the population will have doubled in size. Due to bad medical care in Burma the death rate of infants is high - 1% of all children die before they reach 1 year of age, and 40% suffer from malnutrition. The family planning projects promoted by the Thai government, meanwhile, have started to show definite results. While the death rate of infants has sunk to 0.5 % the increase of the total population has also receded; in 1970 16.5% of the entire population was beneath 5 years of age, today this figure has dsropped below 12%. The average life expectancy in Thailand is now 63 years, in Burma at 55 years (1960: Thailand 52 years, Burma 44 years, the average life expectancy in western Europe today lies at 72 years).

A large percentage of the population of both countries still lives on the verge of starvation, especially those living in rural areas (Thailand: 34%, Burma 40%). In spite of the family planning schemes of the Thai government, the rural population here as well as in Burma still believes in the old, traditional way of thinking; children are a sign of high social status and the only available security for when parents reach an old age. One does not become a fully accepted member of a village community until one has become a father or a mother. Hardly anyone is insured against illness or accidents, and children are expected to contribute to their family's income from an early age. Children play a central role in the village community, and you will be able to see how well Thai and Burmese people are disposed towards children if you travel through their countries with a child of your own.

In Burma and Thailand the major portions of the population live in rural areas. The global tendency of moving to town is noticeable here too, though. Bangkok's population has increased to twice its size during the past fifteen years. The city has an almost magnetic effect on young, out of work Thais. Often, the dream of a better life ends in dirty factories or sleazy massage parlours. The density of population lies at 3642 people per km^2 in the Greater Bangkok and Thonburi area, which is roughly the same as in London. Most inhabitants of Bangkok live in one or two-floor houses, just like the rural population. Apart from the two capitals, Rangoon (just below 4 million inhabitants) and Bangkok (including all suburbs 8 million inhabitants), there are no cities with populations exceeding one million inhabitants in either of the two countries. The principal towns: Mandalay (approx. 500,000), Moulmein (approx. 200,000), Pegu and Bassein (approx. 150,000) in Burma, Korat (205,000), Chiang Mai (137,000), and Hat Yai (130,000) in Thailand. People began settling in the river plains long ago, and these regions still belong to the most densely populated areas of the two countries today. The mountain regions stand in marked contrast - here, only few people are able to live off the land.

82% of Thailand's total population is *Thai*, making the population reasonably homogeneous, in contrast to Burma and Malaysia, where there is a high diversity of ethnic groups. 80% of the inhabitants of the four southern Thai provinces bordering on to Malaysia (Pattani, Yala, Narathiwat, and Sadao) are Muslim Malays. There are different underground guerilla groups in these provinces fighting for autonomy and, in part, even for independence from the Thai government. This constitutes quite a problem for Malaysia and Thailand, seeing as both countries are allies in the ASEAN community.

For centuries the Thai people migrated further and further south from the Chinese province of Yunnan. While the 'big Thai', today's Shan, moved to eastern Burma, the 'small Thai' settled in the present northern Thailand area. The first independent principalities were founded in the 13th Century. The Thai people acquired their own cultural identity under King Rama Khamhaeng. Artisans and artist came from China, the Ceylonese Theravada-Buddhism was adopted as the national religion, and the old alphabets of the Mon and Khmer people were converted into a new, Thai alphabet. Bec ause Thailand was never colonized by foreign powers, the country has kept its specific cultural identity to this day.

During the Ayutthaya period the role of the king as sovereign became increasingly important. Although the constitutional monarchy was introduced in 1932, the king still plays an extremely important role in the life of the average Thai. He is respected and honoured by all his subjects. Just as Buddhist temples are one of the main features of Thai towns and villages, the Buddhist ideology strongly marks the social life in Thailand. These days people are educated at state-run schools, true, but Thai men still go to live at a Buddhist monastery for a certain period of time (usually three months) at least once during their lives. Next to these Buddhist traditions, there are several Hindu and animistic customs that play an important role in the lives of Thais. The family is of utmost importance. Younger members of the family are expected to obey and respect their elders. The construction of irrigation systems, roads, and temples is undertaken by the entire village community, as are all other important projects.

The approx. 500,000 members of the *hilltribes* in the north of the country constitute a further ethnic minority. Their number is increasing due to rising life expectancy and the fact that many people are entering Thailand illegally from Laos and Burma. The seven most important tribes are the Lawa, belonging to the ethnic group of the Mon-Khmer, and the Karen, Meo, Yao, Lahu, Lisu, and Akha, all of whom belong to the Sino-Tibetan groups. While the Lawa were pushed into these mountain regions by the immigrating Thai people as early as the 11th and 12th century, it seems that the Karen did not settle here until the 17th and 18th century, when they came from northern China and southeast Burma.

Since the mid-19th century, other groups have started settling in Thailand, too. Problems in the internal politics of China were one reason for this general migration south. In 1880 the first Akha tribes settled on Thai ground. The Meo

SCHOOL EXCURSION TO THE RIVER KWAE

had managed to move as far south as the province of Tak by 1920. Immigration into the country increased after the end of World War II. Remainders of the beaten Kuomintang troops came from south China and it is estimated that about 10,000 of them are still living in Thailand today. Another wave of immigrants came from Laos in 1975. In this case it was mainly Yao and Meo who left their country to settle in Thailand.

The older tribes (Lawa, Karen) have mainly settled in the valleys, where they live in village communities and cultivate rice. The tribes that arrived more recently live on the various mountain slopes, at heights lying between 800 and 1200 metres. They grow mountain rice and opium, and in order to gain new space for cultivation they frequently burn down large portions of mountain forests. The villages of a particular tribe may lie quite far away from one another, with several villages of other tribes sprinkled in between.

The Thai government did not formulate a state policy concerning the hilltribes until the 1950s. These days, the government is mainly concerned with replacing opium with other 'cash crops' (coffee, flowers, vegetables, fruits), an improvement in the methods of cultivation, and the prevention of erosion. The slash-and-burn agriculture has led to irreversible damage.

A further, economically influential minority is made up of the 3.5 million *Chinese* living in Thailand. A recent survey of the Thammasat university has shown that 63 of the country's 100 main industrial firms are run by Chinese. In addition, 23 of the 25 most influential economical 'brains' of the country are also Chinese. Even though economic relations have existed between the Thai and Chinese people since the 13th and 14th century, Chinese immigration on a grand scale did not really start until the mid-19th century. After the People's Republic of China was founded in 1949 emigration from the country gradually petered out. The Thai government has repeatedly tried to limit Chinese influence can have on the economy through legislation, but the Chinese seem to be as adept at finding a way around these laws as they are at earning money.

Roughly 3/4 of the Burmese population really is Burmese. They are mainly settled in the central plains of Burma (Mandalay, Pegu, Rangoon) near the lower course of the Irrawaddy. The raised plateau in the east of the country (the Shan State with its capital Taunggyi) is mainly populated by Shan, who make up approx. 9% of the country's total population. The *Karen* (7%) live near the Thai border, in the river delta and the Tenasserim mountains, east of Rangoon. The *Chin* (2%) live in the wild mountains of the west, along the borders with India and Bangladesh. The *Kachin* (1%), who have settled in the northern mountain regions near the Indo-Chinese border, constitute a further minority, as do the *Kayah* (also known as Karenni or Red Karen) who live south of the Shan State along the Thai border.

The *Pyus* and the *Mon*, belonging to the Mon-Khmer group, had developed an extremely advanced culture with their own alphabet and language at an early stage. They adopted Buddhist beliefs as early as the 5th century. The beautifully decorated temples and flourishing market-places of their former capital, Pegu, evoked the admiration of their neighbours, but also their jealousy. Even though the Burmese people, who started settling in Burma in the 9th century, readily adopted many of the cultural mannerisms of the Mon, they were an aggressive people and gradually managed to drive the Mon further and further out of the country. In contrast, the ethnically related Pyu, belonging to the Tibeto-Burmese group, mingled with the Burmese. Most of today's Mon (including the Wa, La, and Riang people) live in the Tenasserim mountains in the south of Burma. Many also live in the west of Thailand.

The *Burmese* people, belonging to the ethnic group of the Tibeto-Burmese, have been living in the present national territory of Burma since the 9th century. Originally, they came from central Asia via Tibet. As in Thailand, a neighbour the Burmese are not especially partial to incidentally, rice tillage forms the basis of Burma's economy.

Even though today's socialist government does not exactly approve of religion, Theravada-Buddhism is still one of the most significant influences in Burmese society. The temple ruins of Pagan, Mandalay, and Ava, as well as the imposing Shwedagon Pagoda in Rangoon, can be seen as a testimony to the uninterrupted tradition of Buddhism in this country. The Burmese people were able to retain many Asian traditions in spite of British colonialism. Even in recent times, western influences have hardly had any effect on Burmese society. This is in part due to the self-imposed isolation of the country. In the rural regions houses are still supported by stilts and covered with palm leaves. Two wheeled ox-carts, pulled by water buffalo, can frequently be seen rumbling down dusty, country paths. With the sole exception of a few city-dwellers, Burmese men wear chequered wrap-arounds ('longyi'), while women wear single- or multi-coloured wrap-arounds ('htamein'), with a blouse which is buttoned from the side.

In the 15th century, **Shan** principalities were widely spread all over the present national territory of Burma. During the course of time, however, conflicts arose within the Shan community. The Burmese took advantage of this disunity and managed to drive the Shan back into the mountains. The Shan territories were granted an extended autonomy by the British in their main area of settlement, the eastern Shan plateau. After the country had gained independence in 1948, the entire area was given the special status of an independent federation. Bloody conflicts that continue to this day arose when the government tried to limit the rights of the respective Shan leaders in the early fifties. The fact that much of the country's opium-output is cultivated in the Shan territories also contributes to the conflict. Caravans bringing raw opium

BURMESE WOMEN ON THEIR WAY TO THE MARKET

to the Thai border are frequently ambushed by armed bandits.The various rebel armies are willing to 'loan out' armed fighters to protect these caravans. Getting hold of modern small arms does not constitute a major problem in South East Asia, since there is much money floating about due to the opium business. In addition, American weapons have been available in abundance ever since the end of the Vietnam war.

Since May 1986, when nine nationalistic groups of the already existent NDF (National Democratic Front) and the BCP (Burmese Communist Party) agreed to work together, political as well as military cooperation seems to be developing between the various rebel forces. This means a union of approximately 40,000 well trained, armed guerillas, something which hasn't occurred in Burma for 40 years. The most important units are the 10,000 guerillas of the BCP and the 8000 soldiers of the KIA (Kachin Independence Army), which has been controlling two thirds of Kachin State for years. They have founded a civil administration in their sphere of influence, with schools and even hospitals. The huge influence of the KIA (or their civil army, the KIO = Kachin Independence Organization) and its legendary leader Brang Seng cannot be denied, not even in those territories of the Kachin State controlled by the Burmese Army.

Some *Indians* and *Chinese* came to the country during the period of British colonialism. Most of them, however, left the country after it had gained independence. Today, they make up 1% of the entire population. The official statistics concerning the population are intentionally deceiving - the Arakan and Mon people are included in the 75% of Burmese people even though they had settled here well before the Burmese even arrived. There are further ethnic minorities in Burma - the official statistics speak of 67 different ethnic groups.

You will rarely meet non-Burmese people because the areas in which they live are for the most part not opened up to tourism. Some of these tribes have been openly revolting against the central government for over 20 years. The guerilla armies of the Shan, Karen and Kachin have total control over certain parts of the country. In addition there are several units of the BCP (Burmese Communist Party) operating in the northeast near the Chinese border.

Even the Burmese Army, on which one quarter of the state's yearly budget is spent, is unable to control the entire country. Many of the regions are just too remote and extremely difficult to reach. Guerilla actions rarely make the international press unless 'whites' are somehow involved. In 1978, for example, a BAC plane on an inland flight was shot down, most probably by guerillas. Several Europeans who were aboard died. Trains travelling from Mandalay to Rangoon were bombed in 1985 and again in January 1988. For an outsider the whole problem seems very difficult to understand - tourists hardly ever experience violence in Burma. To you, Burma will seem a peaceful country with inhabitants who are even more peaceful.

PHOTOGRAPHS: Working for tourists. *top:* Dancing group, Bangkok; *bottom:* Making deliveries to beach restaurant. Phuket

HISTORY

THAILAND

Early history

In contrast to all other countries in South East Asia, Thailand has never been put under direct colonial rule. Lying between the British spheres of influence in the west and south (British India, Burma, Malaya) and the French colonies in the east (Laos, Cambodia, Vietnam), Thailand had to follow a well balanced course of politics. Various territories had to be sacrificed to the two colonial powers in the 19th century. In return, the two rival powers guaranteed the everlasting neutrality of central Siam - as Thailand was then officially called - though not without having ensured that they were to have access to important strategic points, of course. Still, Thailand has never been subjected to military invasion in recent history.

Discoveries of ancient pieces of ceramics and weapons in **Ban Chiang** and near Kanchanaburi are conclusive evidence that Thailand was populated over 7000 years ago. The actual origin of the Thai people is a question of some controversy. Its migratory movements can be historically reconstructed to the beginning of the Christian era. By the 8th - 11th century Thai settlers coming from southern China had already advanced to an area stretching from Assam in the far west all the way to Vietnam. They frequently came into contact with groups of Hindus. The Thai people had sufficient social unity and political order to found their own principalities, though. The first significant Thai settlements were founded in **Chiang Mai** and **Chiang Rai,** as well as in northern Burma and the Chinese province of Yunnan. The importance of these principalities increased during the 13th Century, when the Thais, as allies, shared in the spoils of the Mongolian victories over Burma and Champa.

Sukhothai

Two of the peoples inhabiting the Indo-Chinese peninsula were strongly influenced by India. The **Khmer** in the Mekong valley and the **Mon** in central Thailand and lower Burma had developed distinct cultures and powerful empires. Their influence receded during the course of the 13th century, however. The Thai people took advantage of this vacuum of power, defeated the Mon state **Haripoonchai** (Lampun), and founded Chiang Mai in 1296. The Khmer had already been driven out of the central plain in 1220, and Sukhothai was founded in 1228.

Both of these new Thai states were still strongly influenced by the Mon and the Khmer, though. Most importantly, they adopted the Theravada Buddhism of the Mon, which was also heavily influenced by old animistic beliefs. Sukhothai experienced a cultural flowering under King **Rama Khamhaeng** (1275-1317) in the late 13th century. The oldest written record in the Thai language, imprinted on a stone tablet, tells us that the King was wise and just. Apart from

---

PHOTOGRAPHS: Beach scenes: fish, sea, fishermen in South Thailand

one or two regal exaggerations, the Thai form of government proved vastly superior to the former government of the Khmer, which was based on slave labour and a god-like sovereign. King Rama Khamhaeng combined an efficient government with military strength, as well as being a patron of the arts and a supporter of Buddhism. Today he is considered the 'father' of Thailand.

Ayutthaya

Ayutthaya was the next great Thai kingdom to develop after Sukhothai. The city lay in the middle of the fertile Chao Phya plain, the most important area of rice cultivation in the country. It was founded around 1350. Sukhothai was overthrown at the beginning of the 15th century. The Khmer were also overthrown, or rather degraded to being mere vassals. From this date all Khmer kings were appointed by the Ayutthayan leaders. Several wars were waged against the northern states of Chiang Mai and Laos under *King Trailok.* As a result Phitsanulok became the capital of Ayutthaya for a while, because of its superior strategic position. Overthrowing Chiang Mai was no easy task, though, as the town had formed a temporary alliance with the Burmese kingdom, Thailand's greatest rival. Not until the end of the 18th century did Ayutthaya finally manage to conquer Chiang Mai.

A number of changes in society reflect the influence Cambodia had on the country during the first century after the founding of Ayutthaya. Thai society changed considerably due to these influences. While the role of the sovereign in Sukhothai had been one of a father-figure who gave his people wealth, justice, equality, and spiritual guidance, the Ayutthayan leaders gradually came to think of themselves as god-like leaders. This marked the advent of absolute monarchy in Thailand. The greatest social changes took place in the administrative body. Members of the royal family who had - up until then - been ruling the various regions of the country as if these were their own dukedoms, were replaced by Thais of the nobility, appointed by the king. An order of rank for all members of the royal family and the nobility was set, with the social function of each member clearly defined. The king stood at the top of this hierarchy. The common people were divided into two classes - free and enslaved. Those free were allowed to buy and cultivate up to 25 rai of land (1 rai = 1600 m²). Taxes and services had to be submitted to the local patrons. Most of the slaves were actually prisoners of war. The term 'slave' is actually rather unfitting, as they could usually buy their freedom and frequently even owned land of their own. The social 'worth' or prestige (sakdi na) of members of society was defined by the amount of land they possessed. The king's worth was immeasurable, that of an average free farmer 25 'sakdi na', that of the crown prince 100,000 etc. Basically, the 'sakdi na' concept could be compared to today's concept of "on a scale from one to ten I would give you eight".

Compared to other South East Asian states of the time, Ayutthaya was powerful and had an efficient administration. All the same, conflicts within the royal family and the nobility did arise. Some of these have been historically documented. One of the bloodiest events took place when a minister of one of the southern provinces had two kings murdered and 3000 members of the ruling class executed during a coup d'état. Ayutthaya's strongest rival in the struggle for military supremacy on the Indo-Chinese peninsula was the Burmese kingdom. In 1569 the Thais were defeated by Burma. Garrisons were founded and a new king was appointed by the Burmese. Ayutthaya was Burma's vassal for the next 15 years. **Prince Naresuan** mounted five military expeditions (1584 - 1592) before he was able to shake off the Burmese rule. His armies had up to 250,000 foot soldiers, 3000 war elephants, and 20,000 cavalrymen. Today Prince Naresuan is honoured as a national hero. Ayutthaya's relationships with other South East Asian countries were mainly of a business nature.

Le Manifique et Superbe Roy de Siam, auec l'Auguste Princesse Reine de Siam allant a leur Chasteau Royal de Louuo. qui est vne fois lan. Cette Reine est angée de 28 ans. Sa Cour est composée des femmes des principaux mandarins, qui ne la Servent Iamais que prosternées. Elle recoit les Reuenus des Prouinces que le Roy lui a donnees.

Thai merchant ships sailed to **Malacca,** the harbours of India, China, and Java. China was considered a sort of 'big brother'. Ayutthayan delegations were sent to Peking to pay their tribute to the Chinese emperor every three years.

The contacts Ayutthaya had with the European powers were also significant. Ever since Malacca had been conquered by **Portugal** in 1511, Portuguese merchants, missionaries, and diplomats frequently visited Ayutthaya. There were even Portuguese mercenaries fighting in the Ayutthayan army. The Dutch and British, who founded commercial centres near the capital and in the harbours of the south of the country, arrived on the scene in the 17th century. In 1664 the Dutch threatened to conquer the country if they were not granted a commercial monopoly in the most important branches of business. In order to check this Dutch threat, Ayutthaya formed a diplomatic alliance with France. In 1687 a French legation arrived with 600 well-armed soldiers. **King Narai,** heavily influenced by the Greek adventurer **Constantine Phaulkon,** became increasingly enamoured with the western way of life. A successful palace revolt took place in 1668. Phaulkon was beheaded, the French soldiers driven out of the country. This marked the beginning of a new era of anti-western politics which was to last for 150 years.

Bangkok

After Ayutthaya was completely destroyed and burnt to the ground by the Burmese arch-enemies in 1767, Thailand experienced a brief period of chaos. As was the custom in those days, those members of the royal family still alive were abducted, as were were a further 106,000 Thais. The provincial governor **Taksin** organized those soldiers who had survived the war and tried to re-unite the country, which had basically fallen apart after the Burmese invasion. In 1768 he was declared King of Thailand in Thonburi, the new capital. In only 14 years and after several wars, Taksin managed to re-unite the shattered nation. His most important military leader was **General Chakri,** who later overthrew the King and was subsequently crowned as King Rama I himself. Thus he became the first king of the dynasty still ruling in Thailand today.

Up until the mid-19th century the Chakri kings were mainly concerned with restoring their country to its former greatness. The glory of Ayutthaya was to be rebuilt in Bangkok, and many of the Ayutthayan ruins were completely dismantled. The bricks were brought to Bangkok, where they were used for the construction of new temples. Social and economic changes came about due to extended economic relationships with China as well as the European powers' new interest in the East Asian countries. Many Chinese immigrants, most of them merchants and business men, began settling in Thailand, mainly in Bangkok. In the mid-19th century over half of the 400,000 inhabitants of the capital were Chinese.

Reforms under Mongkut and Chulalongkorn

Today **King Mongkut** (1851-1868) is considered one of the most important reformers and modernizers of the country. His foreign policy, which was based on the realization that certain western powers were so mighty that it would be foolish to stand in their way, resulted in the United States, France, and other countries being granted special business privileges. Certain territories were even conveyed to these foreign powers. The fate of Burma, which had been completely incorporated into the British Empire by that point, served as a deterring example for Thailand.

His son, **Chulalongkorn** (1868-1910), continued this policy and was also responsible for reforms within the country. Further territorial concessions were made to England and France. All of the vassal states in Laos and large areas of Cambodia were conveyed to the French. French gun-ships on the Menam Chao Phya left Chulalongkorn with no choice. In addition to this appeasement policy, internal reforms were carried out. These reforms were met with opposition, as the royal family and the nobility were asked to give up many of their major privileges. With the European system acting as a model, a centralized administration with different ministries was created. The hierarchic taxation system of Ayutthaya was replaced with a western oriented tax system. The infra-structure was improved considerably under Chulalongkorn's reign. The railway tracks to Malaya and Chiang Mai were built. The whole education service was re-organized and universities were founded. The abolition of slavery was also introduced under his reign (though not completely carried through). It was decreed that no person should ever be born as a slave again. The king opened up the country to various European states and had British, Belgian, and Italian people working for his civil and military administrations. German engineers were responsible for projecting the railway lines to the north.

The King of Siam with the Crown Prince.

The goal of all these reforms was to strengthen Thailand internally, so that it would be able to stand up to the challenge presented by the progressive western nations. Chulalongkorn changed the basic order of Thai society but kept many of the old traditions. Today he is considered the founder of modern Siam.

Constitutional monarchy

In 1932 Siam, as the country was officially called before this date, became a constitutional monarchy by way of an unviolent coup d'état. Intellectuals educated in the western world and a large part of the middle classes felt unsatisfied with **King Prajadhipoks,** who, in contrast to his father Chulalongkorn, showed hardly any interest at all in modernizing the country. Corruption spread rapidly under his regency. **Pridi Phanomyong,** a lawyer educated in France, was the political leader of the radical democratic movement that carried out the coup d'état with the more conservative militia. **Pibul Songgram,** leader of the conservative wing, soon became the most powerful man in the country, which was now called Thailand. In 1940 the country became an ally of Japan, Italy, and Nazi Germany. With Japanese support the Thai army managed to annexe parts of Laos, Cambodia, and Malaya. Pibul Songgram was overthrown in 1944, and Thailand became an ally of its former enemies. Pridi Phanomyong, leader of the anti-Japanese movement during the war, started work on a new constitution with friends. He was overthrown in 1947 in a military putsch led by Songgram, however, and went into exile. Later on he became the leader of the Free Thailand Movement in the People's Republic of China.

Dictatorship

The country became rigorously anti-communist under Songgram and joined the **SEATO** (South East Asia Treaty Organization), the Asian version of NATO. In doing this, Songgram broke the old Thai tradition of a policy of neutrality yet again. This one-man dictatorship was overthrown in 1957 in a military putsch led by **Marshal Sarit,** one of the most controversial figures of recent Thai history. Sarit was actually quite popular among the common people, but in retrospect experts consider him the most corrupt of all Thai leaders.

Field Marshal **Thanom Kittikachorn** became the new Prime Minister. He was responsible for strengthening the country's relationship to the USA. During the Vietnam war Thailand became a network of US military bases. Many B52s on bombing missions to Vietnam or Laos set off from Thailand.

A parliament was formed as a result of the general elections of 1969. Kittikachorn and his generals remained pretty much in control, though. The continuous conflicts between the parliament and the military led to the nullification of the constitution and the National Assembly, as well as to martial law being declared in November 1971. Kittikachorn tried to make this out as a period of transition during which a new constitution was to be formulated. In reality, however, martial law reigned for two years.

At this point, try to imagine the typical Third World dictatorship - usually one does not even attempt to make it seem as if there were any sort of constitutional order in the country; assemblies, demonstrations, political parties, and free unions are forbidden, the basic human rights are blatantly ignored. The independent body of jurisdiction is replaced with military courts. Leaving the country is strictly prohibited. In addition to these measures, it is not at all unusual for inflation to rise drastically while regular wages are no longer even paid. The real power lies in the hands of police and army officers. In Thailand this resulted in massive corruption. Field Marshal Prapas and Kittikachorn's son, Colonel Narong, turned out to be especially adept at this, both managing to hoard away millions.

Recent democratic developments

Several student leaders who were considered among the most active critics of the system were arrested in October of 1973. Hundreds of thousands began protesting against these arrests on October 13th. The police and the militia started shooting into the crowd with heavy machine guns from helicopters and roof-tops. 71 protesters were killed, several hundred were injured - full scale riots developed. When Kittikachorn, Prapas, and Narong fled from the country, the years of unjust military rule were finally over. **King Phumibol** (Rama IX) officially announced the dismissal of the military regime over all radio and television stations of the country. Sanya Dharmasakti, then principal of the Thammasat university, became the new Prime Minister. The university had always been an intellectual centre of resistance, and declaring the principal Prime Minister was universally interpreted as a moral victory for the student movement. Sanya, however, was faced with the thankless task of trying to bring a country back together that was slowly but surely going to ruin. General strikes, rising criminality, an inflation rate of more than 15%, increasingly violent conflicts with the communist guerillas of the north and northeast, and the militant movement of the Muslim minority in the south of the country - these were just some of the problems Sanya had to deal with. The King proclaimed a new constitution one year after the bloody October massacre.

The first free general elections were held in the spring of 1975. No party received the majority of votes necessary to rule, however. For this reason the slightly leftist Democratic Party led by **Seni Pramoi** formed a minority government. The party resigned only a short while later, upon having lost a vote in parliament. Seni's half-brother Kukrit, chairman of the Social Action Party, formed a new government which tended more towards the right. During the next few years one party followed the next in forming new governments. In October of 1976 the militia once again gained control. **General Kriangsak** became new Prime Minister in 1977. He differed from his predecessors in that he carried out reforms within the country while at the same time applying a sensible and realistic foreign policy, especially towards Vietnam. He was overthrown in the spring of 1980. The parliament chose **General Prem** as his successor. He has been ruling the country with various coalition governments ever since.

The only constant, stable force in all these political conflicts and problems is the **royal family,** which still has a considerable amount of influence and political power. Thailand's problems have basically been the same for centuries - nothing ever becomes of reforms within the country, a fact also lamented by several young officers in April 1981. While the Communist Party's guerilla front is gradually falling apart in the north, the Muslim separatist movement in the south remains active. Since Kriangsak Thailand has once again become strictly anti-communist. The conflicts along the border with Kampuchea have led to new arms shipments from, and joint field manoeuvres, with the US Army.

THE SIAMESE TWINS

In as far as their physical 'oneness' permitted, the two brothers Eng and Chang actually led a completely normal life. They lived in a fishing village in the province of Samut Songkran from 1811 to 1829, before being discovered by the British businessman Robert Hunter. This industrious gentleman took them to Europe and the USA, where they were the sensation at many freak shows. The two brothers decided to become their own managers, and after they had made enough money bought themselves a piece of land in North Carolina and each married an American woman. As they were literally inseparable, they had to share each other's love-life, spending joint nights with each other's wives. Under these unusual circumstances Eng and Sara had 12 children, while Chang and Adelaide had ten. When Chang died of a fever in 1847, his brother Eng died only 2 hours later.

BURMA

Early history

The **Mon** were the earliest settlers in Burma of whose existence scientists have found evidence. By the 3rd century B.C. the Mon had already settled in the Menam Chao Phya area (today's Thailand) and had crossed the mountain ranges in the west and reached the Sittang valley. Business relationships with India were formed reasonably early on. Buddhist monks entered into the world of the Mon by way of the harbour in Thaton. It did not take long for the Mon Empire to become one of the most progressive and important states of the entire region. The Mon were responsible for introducing Buddhism to both the Thai people and the Burmese tribes that were arriving from the Tibetan highlands. The **Burmese** had already settled in the upper Irrawaddy valley during the lifetime of the great Buddha himself. At the beginning of the Christian era the **Pyu,** a people belonging to the Tibeto-Burmese ethnic group, founded the town Sri Ksetra, near the present town of Prome. This gave them access to the economically important overland passage to India and China. Ancient Chinese records tell of the high culture of the Pyu, who, in contrast to the Mon, did not have a hereditary crown. They remained a loose confederation of the various tribes.The Pyu gave up Sri Ksetra in the 6th century due to internal conflicts and the fact that they were being heavily attacked by the Mon. Gradually, the Burmese became the dominant force in the country. They settled in upper Burma and founded Pagan in 849 A.D.

Pagan

This was the capital of the empire of the same name up until 1287. Pagan experienced a period of bloom under **King Anawratha.** The country he ruled corresponded geographically to the present national territory of Burma. Buddhism was declared the official state religion, and the Mon alphabet (which came from Sanskrit) was adapted and formed into a new, standardized Burmese alphabet. The gradual fall of Pagan began in the 13th century, when the Mongolian armies as well as the Thai people coming from the northeast (Shan) started attacking the kingdom. The city was almost completely destroyed by the armies of Kublai Khan in 1287.

Several rival kingdoms and Shan principalities were founded on the former national territory of Pagan during the next 200 years. Only Ava gained true political significance. Not until the advent of the **Toungoo Dynasty** (1531 - 1752) did the Burmese finally manage to re-unite parts of their old kingdom and overthrow the Mon and the Shan. Pegu became the new capital. From here, King Tabinshwehti tried to unite the Shan, Mon, and Burmese people into one nation. This second Burmese Empire expanded significantly under his successor. The arch-rival Siam was beaten completely in 1767, its capital Ayutthaya burnt to the ground.

Colonization

The Portuguese were granted special business privileges as early as 1519. The colonial power that has left its mark on the country, however, is of course

England. During the course of three wars (1824/26, 1852, 1886) Burma was gradually integrated into the British Empire. The British were mainly interested in 'getting there' before their French rivals did, and in having an uninterrupted overland passage from British-India to Singapore. The third Anglo-Burmese war, however, was in part due to the British wanting access to the overland passage to China. In order to avoid international protests, the British tried to make out the last independent Burmese leader, *Thibaw,* as a bloodthirsty tyrant. The Burmese army was taken by surprise and hardly had a chance against the well trained Indian troops fighting for the British. Riots arose after the occupation, as well as a guerilla war which lasted for a number of years. The British proved themselves particularly brutal during this war.

Up until this point Burmese society and government had been marked by traditions reaching back to the original Tibeto-Burmese tribes. Every king had to be appointed and confirmed by a council of elders. The king was only allowed to issue decrees, which lost their validity with his death. The high court was the main body of the government, consisting of three parts - the treasury, the executive forces, and the highest court. All proclamations and nominations of the king had to be confirmed by the executive. There were no hereditary titles or social positions in the old Burmese society. Even the king's officers were chosen according to their abilities, at least in theory. There were a few kings, of course, who were powerful enough to have the final say themselves. One of the most fundamental principles of Burmese society is the fact that men and women are born free and equal.

Independence

A nationalistic movement was created in Burma after World War I, just as in most other Asian countries that were being governed by colonial powers. There was a university strike in Rangoon in 1920. The British administration had numerous Indian workers brought to the country to work in Rangoon's harbour and on the still-under-construction railway lines, especially during the 20s and 30s. Before World War II Rangoon was an almost entirely Indian city. In 1930 the Indian dockers went on strike. Burmese dockers were introduced, but these did not share the advantage of the experience their Indian colleagues had. Soon conflicts arose between the two nationalities. A huge peasant's revolt under **Saya San** also arose in the Tharrawaddy region north of Rangoon during the same year. The colonial government took three years to crush the uprising. 10,000 followers of Saya San were killed, 9000 were taken captive, and 128 - among them Saya San himself - were hung. Several student clubs and movements were founded after the mid-30s. **U Nu, U Thant,** and **Ne Win,** all of whom became important politicians later on, were active members of these movements. A little group of nationalistically-minded students who called themselves *Thakin* became especially important. They hoped to bring about Burma's independence with the aid of the Japanese. Several Thakin went to Japan and were trained for combat, among them Ne Win and **Aung San.** In the spring of 1942 Japanese troops invaded the country, among them whole units of the Burmese Independence Army, led by Aung San. The British troops almost immediately withdrew to India.

By 1943 the clever politics of Burma had forced Japan to grant the country its independence. The relationship between the Burmese people and the Japanese Army was becoming increasingly difficult to handle. The **AFPFL** (Anti Fascist People's Freedom League) was founded in 1944. Units of the **Burmese National Army** started preparing the revolt against the Japanese occupants and occupied Rangoon on April 30th, 1945. The British Army arrived on the scene one day later.

After long and complicated negotiations with the old colonial power, elections for a National Assembly which was to work out a constitution were held. The AFPFL won the elections with a staggering majority. Aung San was murdered along with six of his political friends and advisers on July 19th, 1947. U Nu declared Burma a republic on January 4th, 1948. In March of 1962 a military putsch led by General Ne Win overthrew the government which was still being led by U Nu. A socialist minded military dictatorship took control of the country.

Ne Win was President of the Socialist Republic of the Union of Burma from 1974 to 1981. Since 1983 he has been the chairman of the **Burmese Socialist Programme Party.** Ne Win justified the coup d'état of 1962 by saying that he was worried about a gradual disintegration of the Burmese Union. It is true that the conflicts that arose between the different nationalities during that time had assumed war-like dimensions. On the other hand nothing much has changed for the Burmese people since Ne Win has been in power. Riots of ethnic minorities were as frequent then as they are now.

GOVERNMENT & POLITICS

THAILAND

Thailand's first constitution came into force shortly after the revolution of 1932. According to this constitution, the supreme authority lay in the hands of the people. The monarch, the National Assembly, and the council of state act out governmental authority in the name of the people. This guaranteed the sovereignty of the people, as well as equality before the law, and the basic human rights. Several new constitutions have been formulated since, but all of them are based upon these general ideas. Even though the revolution of 1932 put an end to absolute monarchy in Thailand, there has been little change in the people's attitude towards the royal family. Today the royal family can be seen as the central, unifying element of the Thai nation. The intense adoration of the royal family in Thailand surpasses that of British subjects towards their Queen by far.

According to the Constitution, the *king* is the head of the state and the commander of the Thai army. His portrait and that of the queen can be found everywhere, in every house, every shop, in the simple huts of impoverished farmers, in the offices of civil servants, and in restaurants and coffee shops. As in England, the *royal family* is above politics, and *King Phumibol* has witnessed 17 military putsches and violent changes of government since his inauguration in 1946. With the possible exception of the great Chulalongkorn, he is the first Chakri king to show a sincere interest in the common people. He frequently visits remote provinces and is especially concerned with problems of agriculture, both in cultivated and wild areas. An experimental dairy farm, where cattle adapted to the tropical climate are bred for milk production, has been erected in the grounds of the Chitralada Palace, the Bangkok residence of the royal family. His widely acclaimed fish-breeding project is also well known. Tilapia fish, which multiply rapidly and live off weeds and insect larvae, are set free in the paddies of the country. Less chemicals and pesticides have to be used as a result, and in addition the farming population has a constant supply of protein-rich nourishment.

The King has shown particular concern for the problems of the hilltribes in the north of the country. One example would be the Meo village on Doi Inthanon, where the traditional poppy cultivation has been replaced with so-called 'cash-crops' (flowers, peaches, apples, coffee, or strawberries). Crossing the border to Thailand is a definite step towards security and freedom for many ethnic minorities who live on the Burmese side and are constantly exposed to the bloody conflicts between the government and various rebel armies. The Thai King has personally been responsible for allowing numerous village communities to cross the border. As an example, take the villages near Ban Napapak, Mae Hongson province, directly at the border, where the King has also had a summer residence erected for himself.

The intense *patriotism* of the Thai people can also be seen whenever the national anthem is played. The whole nation freezes when the anthem is played over the royal loudspeakers every morning at eight and every evening at six. Traffic in the palace area comes to a complete standstill. In the cinemas the anthem is played after the programme has finished, to a picture of the flag and the King. The whole audience will rise as one. Always.

The country has been ruled by a democratically elected coalition of several parties under Prime Minister Prem Tinsulanond since 1980. Prem introduced his fifth cabinet on July 27th, 1986. The conservative coalition of Democrats, Chart Thai, Social Action Party, and the People's Party has 232 of the 347 seats of the House of Commons. In the 70s, Prem used to be commander of the northeast regions bordering onto Laos. He managed to curb the influence of the pro-communist guerillas through military superiority and financial and social aid for the impoverished farmers of the region. Today these guerillas have lost all military and political significance. After these early successes, Prem was able to make a fast career for himself in politics. Starting in 1977, Prem was declared Prime Minister in March 1980 after General Kriangsak had voluntarily resigned. Still, even in 1988 the army, led by General Chaovalit, has great influence on the country's politics. One frequently speculates whether Chaovalit will be Prem's successor.

Internally, the government has to deal with difficult problems. It is true that the population growth has been reduced to an average of 1.9% between 1977 and 1984 (1986: 1.7%). This compares favourably with other Asian countries. The fact remains, however, that too many impoverished farmers are moving in desperation to the big cities, mainly to Bangkok. There is hardly any work for them, though, and new jobs are not being created. In the economy development plan (1982-86) the problems of the country have been clearly defined. The government has admitted that the development of the past decade has quite definitely been focused on industry. The profits have only been directed into certain channels, agriculture has been shamefully neglected. The improvement of the rural infrastructure, the changes made in the ownership of land suitable for cultivation, and the introduction of a state-run farm price policy are definite steps in the right direction.

Thailand has taken a rigorous anti-communist course in its *foreign policy* since the end of World War II. The country is a military ally of the USA. Thai soldiers fought in Korea and Vietnam. Prem's predecessor, Kriangsak, tried to establish friendly diplomatic relationships with Thailand's neighbours in the east, Laos, Vietnam, and Kampuchea. This step definitely contributed to the traditional goal of Thailand's foreign policy, which was to keep the country's independence by fostering realistic relationships with all three of the world's most important powers, not only the USA, but also China and the USSR. Since Prem has taken over, however, one can note a return to the old, US fixation. These days, the two countries are once again organizing joint military manoeuvres. All the same, problems of economy with 'big brother' have become quite acute since 1984 - importing Thai goods into the US has become extremely difficult due to protectionist measures taken by the US government. In addition, Thailand's rice now has to compete against subsidized American products on the world market.

BURMA

The **Socialist Republic of the Union of Burma,** as the country is officially called, gained its independence in 1948. A new constitution was introduced in 1974, 12 years after General Ne Win came to power. In it, Burma was divided into seven Divisions (Irrawaddy, Magwe, Mandalay, Pegu, Rangoon, Sagaing, and Tenasserim), as well as the autonomous states of Arakan, Chin, Kachin, Karen, Kayah, Mon, and Shan. Autonomy in this case is defined as 'local autonomy under central guidance', a rather ambiguous definition.

A feeling of discontent, in part due to the national chauvinism of the Burmese people, soon resulted in massive uprisings in many of the states. Most of the country has been closed to tourists ever since. Whole areas of the Kachin, Shan, and Karen states are controlled by the various rebel armies. In 1985/86 a renewed attempt was made to unite the different armed rebel forces under one supreme political and military command. The non-communist **NDF** (National Democratic Front) comprises nine of the most important rebel groups, among them the Shan, Karen, Kachin, Karenni, Wa, Pa-O, Palaung, Mon, and the Arakanese. A closer co-operation with the forces of the **BCP** (Burmese Communist Party) has also been agreed on.

The **Burmese Army** comprises 186,000 men. The country has a total population of 37.6 million. Approx. one quarter of the yearly government budget

CITY HALL, RANGOON

goes towards the army. This puts Burma at the top of the list of Asian countries, along with Taiwan, South Korea, and Pakistan. In opposition to the army, there are 40,000 armed rebels, of whom the most important groups are:

BCP (approx. 10,000), Karen National Liberation Army (7500), Kachin Independence Army (8000), Shan United Army (4000), Shan State Army (3500), and the Shan United Revolutionary Army (1000).

One cannot hope to solve Burma's rebel problem through military force, but the chance of finding a solution under the rule of the State Party seems equally remote. The only information available about cities in areas now closed to tourists can be gleaned from old travel guides that were published before 1962. The town of Bhamo would be a perfect example. In theory it can be reached in four days by boat from Mandalay. The capital of the Kachin State, Myitkyina, would be another example. Mogok with its many gem mines lies in

"an extremely beautiful and secluded valley, fronting a large lake. Rubies, sapphires and other stones can be seen being bargained for in eating shops." *"Kentung town, with its old walls, ancient scarlet-painted monasteries, the lake fringed with palms and a white pagoda, is one of the most picturesque towns in the Union."*

These and other such descriptions can be found in the 1961 edition of the *Golden Guide to South and East Asia.* Since that time, western travellers have only very rarely been able to visit the closed areas. Every now and then adventurous tourists cross the border illegally from Thailand to join one of the rebel armies for a while. These are exceptions, though, and people acting in this way take a great personal risk. Two Germans were arrested in Loikaw, the capital of Kayah state, in 1984. They had reached the city by hitch-hiking.

According to the constitution, the highest authority lies in the hands of the 489 members of the **Pyithu Hlutdaw** (People's Council or Assembly). The Hlutdaw was first introduced by the Burmese kings. Pyithu means 'the people'. The fact that this institution still exists under the socialist government demonstrates the unbroken tradition of Burmese history. There are councils on all levels, even on the lowest ones (State, Division, town, village). The Burmese Socialist Programme Party nominates the candidates, of whom the council members are elected from a single list every four years. Organs of the National People's Assembly are the State Council, the council of ministers, the council of the highest judges, the council of the people's lawyers, and the council of the people's inspectors. The 67 year old San Yu is the chairman of the state council. During World War II he fought against the Japanese occupation forces with the Burmese National Army. He is generally considered the successor of Ne Win.

The political life of the country is controlled by the Burmese Socialist Programme Party, the only official party of the country according to the constitution. The Central Committee, consisting of 280 people, includes nearly all of the leading members of the People's Council. Ne Win, now 76 years of age, is the secretary-general of the party.

ECONOMY

THAILAND

Of Thailand's approx. 53.5 million inhabitants (1986) 65% still 'live off the land'. Only about 11% of the population is employed by industry. All the same, 28% of the gross domestic product in 1986 came from industry, while only 20% came from agriculture. In Thailand the term *agriculture* mainly refers to cultivation. There is only a very small market for slaughter cattle, although commercial animal farms have been on the rise throughout the last decade. Rice was Thailand's main agricultural crop until well into the 50s. Since then diversification has taken place - corn, tapioca, and sugar cane are now also cultivated to a large extent. Fruit and vegetable production has also experienced a considerable boom during the last couple of years.

Over half of the farmers living in central Thailand's fertile regions are only leaseholders. Most of them are heavily in debt. During hard times many farmers are forced to mortgage their land to middlemen, big landowners, and money lenders at exorbitant interest rates. Frequently farmers are even forced to pawn their coming crops in order to be able to survive. The agricultural reforms of 1975 have not been able to improve the situation - they have been boycotted by influential landowners and have thus been rendered ineffective. The average farm in Thailand is no larger than 2 1/2 hectares. While the country produces enough rice for its own use and for export, the profits and earnings per hectare have sunk or stagnated, especially in the northeast, where the land is deteriorating into steppe due to the low rainfall. This has led to an expansion of the areas used for cultivation. Unfortunately, rain- and mountain forests have had to be cut down in order to create more room. The following story is a classic example of how farmers are often swindled by mediators or money lenders:

"For decades, Boon and his family owned and tilled a small plot of land. While not being strangers to debt, a certain emergency last year forced him to make his way once again to the nearest money lender. In return for a paltry sum of money, he was obliged to mortgage his paddy fields. Boon intended to repay the loan in full once the harvest came. But when he wanted to sell his paddy, the buyer - who also happened to be the money lender - handed out a rather one-sided settlement. He blamed poor international markets for the abysmal price. He blamed the government in Bangkok for not providing much-needed relief. Then, he charged Boon's interest which effectively worked out to a rate of 40% per annum. Finally, he conveniently failed to locate the title deeds and, therefore, promised to return them in due course. "Among us, long-term relationships matter more", said the money lender. "What use is a minor piece of paper?", he asked. Today, the money lender (or rice merchant, or the biggest landowner in the district) has moved the courts to take possession of Boon's lands. The reason: apparent non-payment of an overdue debt. The proof: title deeds accompanied by the necessary sales confirmation. Up in those parts nobody doubts that, come next year, Boon will be just another of the millions of landless, tenant farmers.". (Bangkok Post, Economic Review 1986)

Over half of the country's *industry* is in and around the Greater Bangkok area, which is growing increasingly attractive and drawing more and more people from the rural areas. The problems created by this growing tendency of moving to the towns can only be solved if the situation in the rural areas is improved - a utopian fantasy? 57% of the country's industrial output comes from Bangkok and its neighbouring provinces. The busy textile industry and the industries processing foods and other agricultural products are the most important branches. The cement industry, which produces significantly more than the much larger cement industry of Indonesia, the automobile industry, which mainly assembles car parts produced abroad, as well as the electrical appliances industry, are reasonably new and on the rise.

Ever since a large reservoir of *natural gas* was discovered in the Gulf of Siam, the country has been able to meet half of its required energy supply itself. While the total industrial output has grown tremendously during the last decade, it has also become clear that this does not automatically entail a proportional growth in jobs. Many of the new industries require expensive technology, not labourers. Those Thais looking for work, therefore, will have to concentrate mainly on the agricultural areas or start rendering services.

Rice and semi luxury foods make up almost 50% of the goods exported from Thailand, which is the world's largest rice-exporting country. All the same, it is suffering greatly from the competition of US-subsidized rice producers. In addition, international prices for other foods exported from Thailand, such as pineapple, cassava, and sugar cane, are sinking year by year. The income of Thai farmers is sinking accordingly, and the very existence of many a Thai business is being threatened. Even though the *export* of raw materials has been reduced in favour of industrial production and finished goods, the country has a foreign trade deficit. By 1986 this had sunk to half the figure of 1985, however. This was mainly due to the import of expensive foreign hi-tech products. A considerable surplus was achieved in dealings made with West Germany, Thailand's most important foreign trade partner in Europe.

Over 2.6 million tourists visit the country per year. Only a small part of the approx. US$1 billion earned by way of tourism actually remains within the country as a foreign exchange cushion, though; most of the money goes to foreign organizers. Another considerable sum of money goes towards importing those goods that no tourist wants to have to do without.

BURMA

65% of the gainfully employed are engaged in *agriculture,* making it the most important branch of Burma's economy. Only 45% of the gross domestic product is achieved in agriculture, though (tillage, forestry, and fish processing industry). In contrast, the 9.5% employed by industry, construction, and mining produce 12.7% of the gross domestic product.

During the period of British colonialism, Burma was the most important rice-exporting country of the South East Asian region. Rice is grown all over the country, especially in the Irrawaddy delta area. Almost two thirds of the entire areas suitable for cultivation in Burma are planted with rice. During World War II production sank drastically, however, as it has continued doing ever since. In the last few years there has been a slight rise. This can be noticed when taking a look at the export figures of the country (1975: 74 million US$, 1977: 117 million US$, 1983: 437 million US$). The entire mountain areas of Burma (approx. 2/3 of the total national territory) are of lesser importance for agriculture. Burning down mountain forests in order to gain new areas suitable for tillage *(slash and burn agriculture)* is a common custom here - the population mainly produces rice for its own use. Fine woods are the second most important goods exported from Burma. One estimates that Burma has the largest teak forests in the world.

According to the 1974 constitution, the state owns all the land in Burma. Land can only be used for agriculture with the state's approval and permission. Local councils can revoke this permission if farmers do not comply with the state's general rules of selling their products to state-run organizations at set prices etc. These days, many farmers have become organized in co-operative associations. During the last few years the contributions farmers have to make to the state have been reduced. For this reason a much larger variety of agricultural products can be found on the free markets than seven or eight years ago.

In 1985 *industrial production* increased by nearly 11%. It still lies beneath the goal of the country's economic plan, though. The oil industry has grown considerably during the last couple of years. This is in part due to foreign investment, a symptom of the gradual economic reforms that are being introduced in the country. All in all there are only 500-600 state-run industrial businesses that employ more than 50 people. They were mainly founded as a means of reducing imports, and as the market for which they produce is reasonably closed, they are in no position to compete with either the quality or the price of foreign products on an international level.

After General Ne Win came to power in 1962, Burma's entire economy was nationalized rather rashly. This upset production in all branches of the economy. One of the results of this policy has been the development of a flourishing black market where products - especially from India, Thailand, and China - can be bought for high prices. Experts estimate that US$1/2 million worth of goods are smuggled over daily from Thailand alone.

Approx. 30,000 tourists visit Burma yearly, too few by far to make up for the country's perpetual shortage of foreign currencies. Even tourists, who, after all, only stay in the country for a week, come into contact with the black market. Here they can get several times the official rate for the US$.

RELIGIONS

Shortly after sunrise, monks dressed in saffron-yellow robes start off on their daily round of alms through towns and villages, some in groups, some alone. At home the women have already cooked the first rice of the day, and part of it has been set aside for the monks. The families are thankful for this chance of proving their worthiness, for it is meant to guarantee good luck and happiness in future life-cycles. The whole ceremony is held in awed silence. If a house has been newly built or a shop opened, a group of monks is always invited. Their presence is said to bring good luck. The population is willing to make great financial sacrifices for the interior decoration of the temples. Most Thai men - including the king - and some Thai women will voluntarily go to live in a monastery or a cloister for at least a few months during the course of their lifetimes. Life in the monasteries is simple and frugal. Buddhism has left its mark outside the monastery walls, too.

Thailand and Burma belong to the **Theravada** Buddhist countries, along with Sri Lanka, Kampuchea and Laos. They ascribe to the Hinayana teachings of the 'small vehicle'. While the Mahayana Buddhism (the 'large vehicle') of the more northerly countries (China, Japan, Korea, and Vietnam) accepts many paths that may lead to redemption, **Hinayana** Buddhism sticks rigorously to the old Pali teachings.

Even though religious freedom is guaranteed in Thailand and Burma, Buddhism is something of a state religion in both countries. The Burmese road to socialism, as the state ideology is officially called, does not stand in contradiction to this. Approx. 85% of the Burmese population professes the Hinayana school of the Buddhist faith (Burmese, Shan, Mon). There are also Hindus and Muslims (Arakanese), and even quite a few Christians, especially among the Karen. In Thailand 95% of the population professes Buddhism, among them a Chinese, Confucian minority. Muslims can be found in the south (approx. 4%), while Christians and animists have mainly settled among the mountain tribes in the north.

563 B.C. The Prince **Siddhartha Gautama** is born in Lumbini (today's southern Nepal), at the foot of the Himalaya mountains. Mahamaya, his mother, dies seven days after his birth. During her pregnancy she had a dream in which an elephant penetrated into her body from the side. Hindu priests interpret this dream as a prophetic sign signifying the birth of a great leader or even Buddha himself. The prince is brought up by his father as successor to the throne. He lives in the lap of luxury. At 16 he marries his cousin, a beautiful princess, who bears him a son. The prince is not blind to the sufferings of mankind, though; legend tells of how, on his 29th birthday, the sight of three men, one old, one sick, one dead, inspire the prince to forego the material pleasures of life and lead a life of self-denial by becoming a beggar-monk in north India. After six years of meditation and chastity he reaches Enlightenment one night at full moon whilst meditating intensely beneath a Bodhi-tree (Ficus religiosa) in today's Bodh Gaya. It is in the deer park of Isipatana near Varanasi that he begins teaching his first five disciples the Four Noble Truths -

misery, the cause of misery, the elimination of misery, and the path that has to be followed in order to eliminate misery. This elimination can neither be achieved by chastity alone, nor by leading a riotous life; one has to find the 'happy medium' and lead a life of moderation in order to eliminate misery. This can only be achieved by following the Eightfold Path.

The **Buddhist concept of the world** is that it is in a constant stage of transition. Nothing can ever be permanent. Thus nothing is unalterable - new things are born of old, while the old things are still able to influence the shape of those things still to come. Human reality starts off as a painful experience from birth - misery and suffering mark every human being's future life and ultimate death. Even in 'happy' situations one is tortured by feelings of the possible impending loss of one's happiness. After death there is the possibility of reincarnation, meaning the beginning of another cycle of misery.

Realizing what the **sources of misery** are and that they must be eradicated leads to patterns of behaviour that can, in turn, lead to an ultimate redemption after a number of life cycles. The source of all misery lies in the human craving for pleasure and the inability to recognize human shortcomings such as egotism and pride. Only those striving for material well-being will come into contact with the destructive powers of hate, greed, fear, misery, and dissatisfaction.

All people are characterized by their personal experiences and life and are a product of the world around them. Buddhism expects individuals to become

THAI BUDDHISTS IN A TEMPLE

the masters of their own fate, not to leave their fate to coincidence. Nirvana, a state in which one is totally free of all prejudices, is the goal of this mental maturing process.

By breaking away from material pleasures and egotism and becoming patient, loving, generous, and compassionate towards others, one reaches satisfaction and a positive emotional state. In this way every person can influence their own *karma* and gain insight into the state of the world.

One can reach this state by practising the eight rules of the *Eightfold Path*.
❑ The right mode of seeing things - one should use one's mental powers to gain insight into the true problems of existence.
❑ The right thinking - without hate, scorn, greed, pride, or cruelty.
❑ The right speech, in which lies and vain self-portrayal should be avoided.
❑ The right action - monks should act according to the strict rules of their faith.
❑ The right mode of living - one should earn one's living without harming others.
❑ The right effort in every mode of being, with which one can mentally overcome an unhealthy state of mind.
❑ The right mindfulness, with which one can gain insights into one's soul and acquire knowledge of one's limitations by way of meditation.
❑ The right concentration and meditation, through which one can learn to concentrate on one thing only, without digressing in thought.

This is the only way to approach *Nirvana* - the state of complete peace and happiness in a mental void, beyond the temporal and spatial reality one is usually bound to. Legend tells us that Buddha himself needed 500 life cycles before he reached Nirvana, the final reality. The enlightened Buddha passed this realization of the ultimate truth (dharma) on to his disciples. Together, they spread his teachings in wide areas of the Ganges valley, until he died at the age of 80. 256 years after his death the mighty emperor of India, *Ashoka*, adopted the Buddhist belief. He is largely responsible for having spread Buddha's teachings beyond the limits of India, and for having had scores of temples and monasteries built in his country. Buddha's teachings were always transmitted orally by his disciples. Not until 400 years after his death were they first inscribed onto palm leaves in Pali. These records are known as 'Tripitaka', literally 'three baskets', because they were kept in three baskets. 300 years after Buddha's teachings were first spread, Buddhism was divided into the so-called 18 schools. Theravada Buddhism is generally considered the school that sticks closest to the original teachings of Buddha.

Early Buddhist monks were able to reach and influence the *Mon*, whose empire stretched from southern Burma all the way to the Nakhon Pathom area. The Buddhist Mon kingdom of Haripoonchai was founded in the 8th century. During this period Thaton and Pegu were the centres of the Mahayana-Buddhistic Mon in Burma. Ancient Chinese chronicles tell us that the Pyu had adopted the Buddhist faith by this time, too. The Burmese, who came from the north, still worshipped natural spirits and so-called Nats (incarnations of the souls of the dead). When *King Anawratha* (1044 - 1077), first of the Pagan dynasty, converted to Theravada Buddhism many of his subjects did, too. The capital, Pagan, already known as the city of the four million pagodas during the Marco Polo period, became an important religious centre. Scores of temple ruins can still be seen there to this day.

Buddhism did not become important in **Thailand** until the 13th century, when the Thais coming from the north founded the Sukhothai empire under King Rama Khamhaeng. The King had monks come from Ceylon to spread the pure Buddhist teachings of the Hinayana school, which belongs to the 'small vehicle'. During the following centuries the kings of Thailand and Burma became important patrons of Buddhism. A close relationship between the state and the sangha, the Buddhist clergy, exists to this day in Thailand. The Thai king appoints the religious leader of the country, but not before this leader has been elected by the Mahanikaya and the Dhammayuttika-Nikaya, the two Buddhist sects of the country.

By the time **Burma** gained its independence, the sangha had become so powerful and important that in 1961 Buddhism was declared the state religion. The sangha has lost much of its political power since. The belief is still firmly imprinted upon the minds of the people, though. The many new temples and pagodas that are built in the hope of acquiring good fortune in future lives are proof of this. These days, modern architectural design and even total kitsch is not at all rare. Tiny blinking coloured lightbulbs are set up around Buddha figures, murals disappear behind loud mosaics of tiny mirrors. These and other measures lend the Buddha figures a 'modern' image, much to the disdain of many archeologists.

Next to the Buddhist teachings, which are strictly bound to the old Pali tradition, the Burmese and Thai believe in **spirits**, mystical influences, and ancestral tales and legends from pre-Buddhistic times. This becomes particularly apparent when one takes a look at Burmese religious art and literature. Depictions of Nats, incarnations of the mischievous and sometimes evil souls of the dead, can be seen in many Burmese temples. Small 'spirit-houses', which house friendly spirits that ward off bad ghosts, can be seen next to almost every Thai house. People selling lucky amulets and fortune-tellers can be found in virtually all Buddhist temples.

The **community of monks (sangha)** are still considered the embodiment of the pure, Buddhistic teachings, regardless of any trivialization their religion may be suffering from. All Thai and many Burmese men enter a monastery at least once during their lifetime. Come the beginning of the rainy season, and many young men, usually of the age of 21, will start making mental preparations for monastery life. For them the three month period that starts with their ordination as monks is a symbolic 'coming of age'. More than 200,000 monks and 100,000 novices (young monks who are under the age of 21) lead a life that strictly corresponds to the rules of Buddhism behind Thailand's monastery walls. They are allowed no personal possessions during their time as monks, nor may they sleep in comfortable beds, use perfume, or sing and dance. They lead a strict life of celibacy and are not allowed to injure people or animals. They receive their meals, which are only allowed to be eaten before twelve noon and after sundown, in the form of alms from the faithful, who, in turn, thus receive merits for their future life cycles. Monks are meant to disengage themselves from all material temptations. Originally, they were not even allowed to speak to women.

What are those monks in their orange robes actually all about? Have you ever asked yourself this question? If yes, you're probably still waiting for a satisfactory answer. This is not surprising, as it is often difficult to understand Buddhism. One reason for this is most surely the way in which the cultural background and experience of, say, a European differs from that of a Thai. The order of Buddhist monks, the sangha, comes from a completely different cultural background and has to be seen before this background in order to be understood. Those not ready to see the problem on these terms will quickly reach premature conclusions, such as: here a hoard of parasites is quite obviously feeding on a backward, unenlightened people.

The fact that there are several different styles of Buddhism practised within the country may also confuse visitors. Take the simple village monasteries that can be found in the traditional rice tillage cultures that make up the basis of Thai and Burmese society, and that are usually maintained by the farmers themselves. Within rural areas such monasteries are considered independent and respectable Buddhistic institutions. This can hardly compare to the Buddhism practised in Bangkok, though. In the town, people's attitude towards monasteries and Buddhism has changed. To a certain extent they have become commercialized. Wealthy citizens and businessmen 'hire' hosts of monks who perform extravagant ceremonies true to the Buddhistic tradition whenever special events are celebrated, e.g. the beginning of construction on a newly-built foundation or marriages within the family. On another level Buddhism has also been politicized to a degree. The King, royal patron of Buddhism, has used the Buddhist faith to bring about progressive developments in the country, but also to quiet the people in times of national unrest. Some say that the biggest dangers of all to the Buddhist faith are western ideas and modern changes in economy, which have forced people to think and act on a profit and greed oriented basis.

The village monastery, possibly the place where Buddhism can still be found in its purest form, is not only a religious centre but also a haven for travellers, the old, and the wise. All men (though unfortunately women only extremely rarely) are welcome to spend a few nights. In these rural areas the monasteries are also an alternative to the public education system. Many farmer's sons remain monks after their official three month period is over. Here they can conclude a 4-6 year basic education, and if they are lucky and particularly gifted they may even have the chance of going to one of the major towns in order to pursue some form of higher education.

There has been a general development towards a more school-like structure in the sangha, particularly during the course of this century, ever since one of King Mongkut's sons, then religious leader, became tired of the constant folklore and mythical elements that were being added to the faith. He decided to reform Buddhism in order to purge, demythologize, and standardize it. An introduction to the basic Buddhist philosophy is now taught in beginners' courses. These courses end with final exams. Amateurs can take part in them too, if they so desire. The next courses concentrate on Pali, the language of Theravada Buddhism. Those who have successfully finished these introductory courses will often be favoured when it comes to getting jobs in the lower orders of public service. This is due to the fact that it is generally assumed that former monks have better character traits and a larger general knowledge than other people.

The sangha runs two Buddhistic universities in Bangkok. Secular courses, in as far as they are somehow related to the lives of the monks, are also offered. There is one course, for example, dealing with the social problems that have developed due to the changes in rural society.

Every Thai becomes a respected and honoured person once he has gone through the ordination, regardless of wealth, power, or education, the usual status symbols in Thailand. Honour and respect play a much larger role in Asian society than they do in the western world. Even the king himself is not above showing a deep respect for any farmer's son who has become a monk. This is doubly remarkable if one considers the way in which the king, in turn, is respected and honoured by the people. The intense respect that is shown towards all monks in the whole of Thailand is due to the fact that a monk is not seen as an individual, but as a representative of the Buddhist ideals. It is for just this reason, losing one's individuality by becoming a representative of the whole, that monks will sometimes cover their faces with fan-like shields during certain ceremonies, e.g. whilst giving the 5 Buddhistic rules of moral conduct.

There are several reasons for the way in which monks are venerated in Thailand. For one, they lead the most honourable and pious life conceivable to a Buddhistic Thai. For another they lead a life totally independent of worldly influences and society. They are the essence of spirituality. Women are of course - unfortunately - largely excluded from an active, Buddhist life. There are nuns who live in cloisters, true, but they are not part of any order, nor do they have any reason to expect the rights and privileges enjoyed by monks. Originally, there was no such sex division in the Buddhist teachings, but, quite typically, male dominance has been integrated into the faith in retrospect.

Buddhism has developed its own form and adapted to the different social conditions in Asia, from Afghanistan all the way to Japan. Usually, local beliefs are incorporated into Buddhism, resulting in a rather folklorish religion. Thus many animistic aspects can be found in Thai Buddhism. There is room for many perceptions of life in Buddhism, different forms of authority, and different perspectives of space and time which may lead to differing moral codes, as well as a simultaneous acceptance of wisdom and magic.

Much of Thai Buddhism is based on local customs and conceptions, particularly the aspect of royal and state Buddhism. The Indian king Ashoka (273-232 B.C.), founder of various Buddhistic cultures in India, tried to rule according to the Buddhist teachings. This has been the model for the Thai kings, where the sovereign is protector, patron, and almost final authority in questions of religion, even though there was never any mention of this kind of connection between faith and sovereign in the original teachings of Buddha.

The influence the royal family has upon the sangha has increased since the 19th century. King Rama VI (1910 - 1925) added a further note of nationalism when he returned to his country after having been educated at a British military academy. He was disappointed in the lack of national pride and discipline in Thailand, which, he felt, stood in marked contrast to the neighbouring countries of Indochina and Burma. His idea of 'Nation, Religion, and Country' is probably based upon the British concept of 'God, King, and Country'. The state and the religion of Thailand have become almost inseparable; prayers are held everywhere in public life, from schools to army barracks. The millitary force has also become increasingly important. This entire development marks the Thai nation to this day. The close relationship between state and sangha has led to religious matters being conducted by the Ministry of Education.

In contrast, the Burmese sangha has become increasingly politicized in connection with the independence movement. Not all of the clergy agrees with the state ideology. This has led to a division within the sangha.

-taken from a text by Helmut Eilert

We cannot go into the Buddhist faith any further than this. If you want more information, there are many good books on the subject that go into great detail. At this point we would like to give you some advice on how to behave in Buddhist countries.

❑ Generally, one should always respect the religion of the country one is visiting, regardless of what one personally thinks of it.

❑ Buddha is always a holy person. Putting a Buddha statue in an unsuitable place (e.g. in a bathroom) is considered almost blasphemous. Never climb onto a statue to have your picture taken!

❑ Monks are venerated. They are greeted with a particularly polite and deep 'wai'. They always have precedence over others. One does not walk next to them; one always remains one step behind.

❑ Women are to be reserved towards monks, are not meant to hand them anything, touch them, sit next to them, or be photographed with them.

❑ One should never disturb monks on their daily round of alms.

❑ If one makes a donation to a monastery or a monk one should always do so with both hands, not half-heartedly (=with only one hand). Do not expect thanks - usually those giving the donations are thankful for the privilege of being able to do such a good deed.

❑ The head is the holiest part of the human body, quite in contrast to the foot, which is considered the least worthy. For this reason you should never touch a Thai's head nor point your feet at one.

The following Thai monasteries will accept foreigners as novices. Accommodation, variety of foods, and restrictions in daily life vary from place to place. All of these monasteries have a meditation centre:

Wat Bovonives (Wat Bovorn)	*Bangkok (Banglampoo)*
Wat Mahathat	*Bangkok (Sanam Luang)*
Wat Dharma Mongkol	*Bangkok Sukhumvit Soi 101)*
Wat Vajira Dharma Sathit	*Bangkok (Sukhumvit Soi 101)*
Wat Paknan Phasi Charoen	*Thonburi (Therdai Road)*
Wat Pleng Vipassana	*Thonburi (Charoen Sahitwong Road)*
Wat Muang Mang	*Chiang Mai*
Wat Umong	*Chiang Mai*
Wat Pah Ban Tart	*Ban Tart near Udon Thani*
Wat Nong Pah Nong	*Warin near Ubon*
Wat Suan Moke	*near Chaiya*
Wat Sukontawas	*Nasan, near Suratthani*

LANGUAGE

Various languages are spoken in Thailand and Burma. This is due to the great variety of ethnic groups that can be found in both countries. According to a population census taken by the British in 1931, there were 136 different languages in Burma at the time. The British seem to have failed to categorize these according to those which constitute independent, fully developed languages, and those that are creoles or dialects. All the same, the figure is staggering. Most of the languages spoken in Thailand and Burma, including the official state languages, belong to the Sino-Tibetan family. Arakan, Shan, Karen, Chin, and Kachin constitute other important varieties. The languages spoken by the Mon, Wa, Palaung, and others in contrast, belong to the Mon-Khmer languages, which are particularly important in a historical context. The term *Austro-Asian* languages is frequently used to refer to both the Mon-Khmer and the Sino-Tibetan groups. Like Chinese, Thai and Burmese are monosyllabic tone-languages. This model, utterly different than that of most western languages, is what constitutes the biggest problem for foreigners.

In Thai the same word can theoretically have five different meanings, depending on the *intonation* of the speaker. In conventional Thai one speaks of five different pitches - rising, falling, high, low, and middle. In north Thailand there are even seven pitches. There are three major different forms of intonation in Burmese. While modern Burmese has gone through major changes and has been standardized, some dialects - especially Arakan - are still spoken in their original form. In addition, words taken from the ancient Mon, Khmer, and Pyu languages have also been incorporated into modern Burmese, as have words taken from Sanskrit and Pali, the religious languages.

Pronunciation is not the only thing foreigners have difficulties with, though; *script* constitutes a further problem. Most nations, including the Thai, Burmese, Mon, and Shan, did not develop their own script until modern times. The Thais adopted the Dewanagari transcription, taken from the Mon who, in turn, developed it out of the Pali-script of south India in the 13th century. In contrast to the flowing Thai characters, the Burmese script seems to consist of a series of more or less complete circles. Their first alphabet, which was also adopted from the Mon script, was developed in the 11th century under King Anawratha. The Rajakumar stone inscriptions from central Burma are considered the country's earliest written record. Thai and Burmese people write from the left to the right, leaving no space between individual words.

English was Burma's official state language during the period of colonial rule. Many old Burmese still speak English exceptionally well. Even though English was the language used in administration, Burmese remained important as a second language in schools as well as a language used in business and literature. Today, English is still seen as an important professional language, though it is of course not as widely spread as it was during the period of colonialism. You will have little difficulty communicating in English in Burma. Other European languages are hardly spoken at all.

SMALL DICTIONARY

THAI

Even with a dictionary you will have many problems with the Thai pronunciation. In addition to the various pitches there are also 44 consonants and 32 vowels, most of which simply do not exist in western languages. The basic vocabulary offered here can only be seen as a small help. We would suggest having a Thai pronounce the words for you. Then try to imitate the sing-song way in which they speak. There is one bright side to the problem - Thai grammar is extremely simple, there are few rules, and absolutely no exceptions to the rules.

There is no English equivalent to many sounds in the Thai language. For this reason we will try to give you a rough idea of how certain, difficult vowels and consonants have been transcribed in Latin letters in the dictionary below.

Vowels:

i	as in tip
ii	as in creep
e	as in pen
ai	as in buy
aa	as in father
a	as in Dad
u	as in loot
uu	as in pool
ue	as in prune
eu	as in French deux
ee	as in Paul Klee, or French Cartier
ae	as in where

ao	as in "how now, brown cow", better yet as in 'ciao'
aw	as in awe
o	as in knock

Consonants:

p	as in put, but closer to a 'b'
ng	as in wrong, frequently used as an initial consonant
t	as in tea, but closer to a 'd'
kh	as in contact
k	closer to a g
ph	as in Peter
th	as in Thai

All other vowels and consonants used below basically correspond to the English pronunciation. Keep this key in mind at all times when pronouncing the words given in the dictionary.

NUMBERS:

NEUNG	1	หนึ่ง	KAU	9	เก้า
SAWNGH	2	สอง	SIP	10	สิบ
SAAM	3	สาม	SIP ET	11	สิบเอ็ด
SII	4	สี่	SIP SAWNGH	12	สิบสอง
HAA	5	ห้า	YII SIP	20	ยี่สิบ
HOK	6	หก	SAAM SIP	30	สามสิบ
CHAET	7	เจ็ด	NOING ROI	100	หนึ่งร้อย
BET	8	แปด	NOING PHAN	1000	หนึ่งพัน

QUESTIONS:

KRAI	who, whom	ใคร
ARAI	what	อะไร
MEU ARAI	when	เมื่อไหร่
THIINAI	where, where to	ที่ไหน
THAORAI	how much/many	เท่าไหร่
TAMMAI	why	ทำไม

PERSONS:

DIICHAN (f) PHOM (m)	I	ดิฉัน . ผม
KHUUN	You (sing. + pl.)	คุณ
KHAO	he, she, it	เขา
RAO	we	เรา

TIME:

CHAO	morning	เช้า
TIANG	noon	เที่ยง
YEN	evening	เย็น
KHUEN	night	คืน
WAN NII	today	วันนี้
PRUNG NII	tomorrow	พรุ่งนี้
MUEA WAAN NII	yesterday	เมื่อวานนี้
DAEO NII	now	เดี๋ยวนี้
TII LANG	later	ที่หลัง
YANG	not yet	ยัง...(ไม่)
LAEU	already/ready	....แล้ว
CHUA MAWNG	hour	ชั่วโมง
NATII	minute	นาที
WELLA	time	เวลา
WAN	day	วัน
ATHIT	week	อาทิตย์
DUEAN	month	เดือน
BII	year	ปี

ADDRESSING OTHERS:

When addressing others one only uses the Christian names, sometimes adding the prefix KHUUN

KHUUN	you (formal and informal), or Mr., Mrs. etc.	คุณ
NUU/KHUUN NUU	young/unmarried woman	หนู / คุณหนู
MAE NAI/KHUN NAI	elder/married woman.	แหม่นาย / คุณนาย

SHOPPING:

SUEH	buy	ซื้อ
KHAI	sell	ขาย
RAKA TAO RAI	how much is it?	ราคาเท่าไหร่
PAENG	expensive	แพง
MAI PAENG	cheap	ไมแพง
MII	there are	มี

DISEASE:

MAI SABAI	ill	ไม่สะบาย
SABAI	healthy	สะบาย
JEP	(it) hurts...	เจ็บ
YAA	medicine	ยา
MAO	drunk	เม้า
RONG PAYABAAN	hospital	โรงพยาบาล
ROT PAI BAAN	ambulance	รถพยาบาล

ACCOMMODATION:

RONG RAEM TIINAI	where is the hotel?	โรงแรมที่ไหน?
RONG RAEM	hotel	โรงแรม
HONG	room	ห้อง
HONG NAAM	bathroom	ห้องน้ำ
HONG SUAM	toilet	ห้องส่วม
GUN CHAE	key	เตียง
YUNG	mosquito	ยุง
MUNG	mosquito net	มุง
NGUANG NAW	tired	งวงนอน
KON DIYO	alone	คนเดียว

TRAVELLING:

THANON NII ARAI?	which street is this (or that)?	ถนนนี้อะไร?
MUEANG NII ARAI?	which town is this (or that)?	เมืองนี้อะไร?
SAI	left	ซ้าย
KHWA	right	ขวา
THRONG PAI	straight ahead	ครงไป
PAI...	I am going to...	ไป....

TRANSPORT:

ROT MEE	bus	รถเมล์
SATHAANIROTMEE	bus station	สถานีรถเมล์
ROT FAI	train	รถไฟ
SATHAANI ROT FAI	railway station	สถานีรถไฟ
RUEHA	boat	เรือ
TAA	harbour	ท่า
RUEHA BIN	aeroplane	เรือบิน
SAANAM BIN	airport	สนามบิน
TEKSI	taxi	แท็กซี่
YUUT	to stop	หยุด
ROT YON	car	รถยนต์
MAWTOESAI	motorbike	มอร์เตอร์ไซ
CHOW	rent	ยืม
BENSIIN	petrol	เบ็นซิน

DESCRIBING YOUR SURROUNDINGS:

MUEANG	town	เมือง
NAKHON	city	นคร
BAAN	village	บ้าน
DOY	mountain	ดอย
KAU	hill	เขา
MAE NAAM	river	แม่น้ำ
KO	island	เกาะ
HAAT	beach	หาด
AO	bay	อ่าว
NAAM TOK	waterfall	น้ำตก
THANOM	road	ถนน
SOI	lane	ซอย

FOOD & DRINK

GIN	eat	กิน
DUEM	drink	ดื่ม
HIYU	hungry/thirsty	หิว
A-HAAN A-RO-I	the food is good!	อาหารอร่อย
GAEP DANG	I would like to pay!	เก็บตังค์
RAANAHAAN	restaurant	ร้านอาหาร
RAWN	hot	ร้อน
YEN	cold	เย็น
WAAN	sweet	หวาน
PRIOWAAN	sweet & sour	เปรี้ยวหวาน
PET	sharp, spicy	เผ็ด
TAWT	roasted/baked	ทอด
TOM	cooked	ตุ๋ม
YANG	grilled	ย่าง
PING	toasted	ปิ้ง
PLAA	fish	ปลา
KUNG	lobster	กุ้ง
PUU	crab	ปู
PLAAMUEK	octopus	ปลาหมึก
MUU	pork	หมู
NUEA	beef	เนื้อ
GAI	chicken	ไก่
PED	duck	เป็ด
BAMII	yellow noodles	บะหมี่
GU-AE TIAO	white noodles	ก๋วยเตี๋ยว
KHAO	rice	ข้าว
KAO PAT	fried rice	ข้าวผัด
KHAI	egg	ไข่
KHAI JIAO	omelette	ไข่เจียว

SAPAROT	pineapple	สับปะรค
GLUAI	banana	กล้วย
MAPRAO	coconut	มะพร้าว
MAMUANG	mango	มะม่วง
MALAKAW	papaya	มะละกอ
SOM	orange	ส้ม
NAM	water	น้ำ
NAM KAENG	ice	น้ำแข็ง
CHA	tea	ชา
GAFAE	coffee	กาแฟ
LAO	alcohol, brandy	เหล้า
BURII	cigarette	บุหรี่

CONVERSATION:

Female speakers add the formal particle KHA to their sentences, male speakers KHRAP. These particles are also used in the sense of 'yes' and as linking particles between sentences.

SABADII	How are you?	สะบายดี (หรือ ?)
YUU RAEM TIINAI?	Where do you come from?	อยู่แรมที่ไหน?
MAI/MAI PEN RA	no/that doesn't matter	ไม่ / ไม่เป็นไร
THAI RUUPDAI MAI?	may I take a picture?	ถ่ายรูปได้ไหม?
PHUUT THAI DAAI MAI?	Do you speak Thai?	พูดไทยได้ไหม?
PHUUT THAI NITNOI	I speak a little Thai.	พูดไทยนิดหน่อย
(MAI) KAOJAI	I (do not) understand.	(ไม่) เข้าใจ ,
KOP KHUN KHRAP/KHA	thank you (m/f)	ขอบคุณครับ / ค่ะ
PRAWT	please (as a request)	โปรด
CHUUN	please (as an invitation)	เชิญ
JUEARAI	What is your name?	ชื่ออะไร?
DJUEA...	my name is...	ชื่อ...
ARUN SAWAT	good morning	อรุณสวัสดิ์
RADI SAWAT	good night	ราตรีสวัสดิ์
FARANG	foreigner	ฝรั่ง
DJOK DII	luck	โชคดี
SUAEY	pretty	สวย
SOKAPOK	dirty	สกปรก
SANUK	to feel good	สนุก
DEK PHUDJAI	boy	เด็กผู้ชาย
DEK PUYING	girl	เด็กผู้หญิง
THONG	to have to	ต้อง...
...DAI	to be able	...ได้
DONGKA	to need	ต้องการ
BANGTI	maybe	บางที่
NITNOI	a little	นิดหน่อย

BURMESE

It is extremely difficult to acquire a basic vocabulary in Burmese during the measly seven days one is allowed to stay. There are only very few good books out. The Burmese alphabet consists of 11 vowels and 32 consonants. The key to the words given below is the same as the one for Thai, with the one difference that in Burmese 'th' is pronounced as in English 'the', 'there' etc. We would suggest learning the Burmese numbers by heart, seeing as they are not too difficult but very important when it comes to catching the right bus or finding the right house.

NUMBERS:

TI	1	၁	KO	9	၉
HNI	2	၂	TAA SAE	10	၁၀
THAWNG	3	၃	SE TI	11	၁၁
LAEI	4	၄	SE HNI	12	၁၂
NGAA	5	၅	HNI SE	20	၂၀
CHAU	6	၆	THAWNG SE	30	၃၀
KUU NII	7	၇	DE YA	100	၁၀၀
SHI	8	၈	DE TAUNG	1000	၁၀၀၀

QUESTIONS:

BAE MA LAE...?	where is...?	ဘယ် မှာ လဲ
BAA LAE...?	what is?	ဘာ လဲ
BETHU LAE...?	who is?	ဘယ် သူ လဲ
BAEDO LAE...?	when...?	ဘယ် တော့ လဲ
BAI LAU LAE...?	how much/many	ဘယ် လောက် လဲ

ADDRESSING OTHERS:

UU	male adults	ဦး
MAUNG	young men	မောင်
DAW	female adults	ဒေါ်
MAEIN MA	young women	မိန်း မ
MAEIN GA LEE	girl	မိန်း ခ လေး

TIME:

YA NAEI/DII NAEI	today	ယ နေ့ / ဒီ နေ့
NE PJIN KE	tomorrow	နက် ဖန် ခါ
MA NE	mornings	မ နက်
NAEI LE	noon	နေ့ လည်
NJA NAEI	evenings	ည နေ
NJA	nights	ည
LA	month	လ
HNEE	year	နှစ်

CONVERSATION:

HOKE	yes	ဟုတ် ကဲ့
HAEIN	no	ဟင့် အင်း
NAI KAUNG LAA	how are you? also: hello,	နေ ကောင်း လား
NAI KAUNG DAI-LAA	goodnight, general greeting	နေ ကောင်း သ လား
THWAA LAIT BA AWNG MAE/	I will leave now	သွား လိုက် ပါ အုံး မယ်/
HKWIN PYU BA AWN	please excuse my leaving	ခွင့် ပြု ပါ အုံး
CHAEI TSU TIIN BA DAE (SHEEN)	thank you (females)	ကျေး ဇူး တင် ပါ တယ် (ရှင်)
NA LEE DE NAW	do you understand?	နား လည် တယ် နော်
NA ME EE BA BUU	I cannot understand anything	နား မ လည် ပါ ဘူး

ACCOMMODATION:

HO TAE	hotel	ဟော်တယ်
A KAAN	room	အ ခန်း
GE DEN	bed	ကု တင်
YAEI CHAW-GAN	bathroom	ရေ ချိုး ခန်း
CHING DAUNG	mosquito net	ခြင် ထောင်
YEECHOUMAE	to bathe	ရေ ချိုး မယ်
HSAT PIAR	soap	ဆပ် ပြာ

PHOTOGRAPHS: *top:* Shwedagon Pagoda, Rangoon; *bottom:* Reclining Buddha in Wat Lokayasutha, Ayutthaya

TRAVELLING:

LAA MAE	to come	လာ မယ်
THWA BAR	to go	သွား ပါ
ENAMAA	near to, close	အနား မှာ
A WAEIMAA	far (away)	အဝေး မှာ
LEN	road	လမ်း
MJUU	town	မြို့
PEYA	pagoda	ဘုရား
HLAEI	boat	လှေ
THIN BAA	ship	သင်္ဘော
MIIYETA	train	မီး ရ ထား
BUDAAJAW	railway station	ဘူတာ ရုံ
BAS KHA HMA THAING	bus stop	ဘစ် ကား မှတ်တိုင်

FOOD & DRINK

SAR THAU SAING	restaurant	စား သောက် ဆိုင်
...SAR MEE	I'm eating...	.... စား မယ်
A SAR	to eat	အ စာ
TAU MEE	to drink	သောက် မယ်
PA GAN BIAA	plate	ပုဂံ ပြား
KHWEO	cup	ခွက်
PUU DAE	hot	ပူ တယ်
E DAE	cold	အေး တယ်
KOFI	coffee	ကော် ဖီ
NWA NAW	milk	နွား နို့
YEE	water	ရေ
LEMONAD	lemonade	လင် မွန် နိတ်
HSAA	salt	ဆား
THAE JAR	sugar	သကြား
THAE MIN	rice	ထ မင်း
KAU HSWAE	noodles	ခေါက် ဆွဲ
NGHA	fish	ငါး
CHE THAA	chicken	ကြက် သား
HSAEI THAA	lamb	ဆိတ် သား
A MAE THAA	beef	အ မဲ သား
WET THAA	pork	ဝက် သား
HIN	curry	ဟင်း
A THI	fruit	အ သီး
HE JUE-E	vegetables	ဟင်း ရွက်

PHOTOGRAPHS: Spirit belief. *top:* In the Erawan National Park; *bottom left:* In the mountains of northern Thailand; *bottom right:* In Bangkok

MEDIA

With the transportation and communication systems becoming increasingly better, media has now found its way even into the most secluded of mountain areas. Radios and televisions are major status symbols in Thailand, and you will find them in every well-to-do household. In addition, the number of *literate people* in Thailand has risen to 84% of the population (literate people above the age of 14). Thus the circle of potential readers has increased considerably. The economy's concentration on the Greater Bangkok area finds its equivalent in the media; almost all daily papers are published in the capital.

Most *newspapers* are published in Thai. There is also a Chinese evening paper and a morning paper, both with a circulation of 60,000 copies. In addition there are two English language dailies, **The Nation** and the **Bangkok Post**, which have a joint circulation of 30,000 copies. These two papers are particularly interesting because of their critical approach to modern Thai society. They have never been reluctant to draw the reader's attention to the shortcomings of the government, and this makes them quite unique among newspapers in the general South East Asian region. Not only the many foreigners living in Bangkok read them; they are also the chosen papers of many Thais who have been educated in western countries, intellectuals, and business people.

Thai Rath and the **Daily News** are Thailand's main representatives of the gutter press. Social happenings, crime, and other extraordinary events are their main themes, always illustrated with large photographs. Thai Rath has a circulation of 500,000 copies, the Daily News a little less. **Siam Rath** and **Phim Thai** are critical papers read by an educated circle of readers.

There are six daily newspapers in Burma, with a total circulation of 350,000 copies. Two of the six papers are written in the English language, the **Working People's Daily** and **The Guardian**. All six papers correspond to the socialist ideology of the country. Why not buy a copy for 25 pyas - you may gain considerable insight into the country's politics.

In addition to the daily newspapers, there are also numerous national (some in English) and international magazines that can be bought in Thailand. The most important supraregional weeklies are the **Far Eastern Economic Review** and **Asiaweek**. These two magazines report on the newest developments in politics, economy, and culture. Regard them as important sources of current information during the course of your travels.

Thailand was the first Asian country to introduce *television* in 1955. Today there are four companies broadcasting nationwide. They are modelled on American commercial TV, with many ads in between the shows. Strictly speaking, the companies are private, though they are financed by state or semi-state offices.

All foreign films and series are dubbed in Thai. One can still receive the original sound over FM radio, though:

Channel 3:	105.5 FM
Channel 7:	103.75 FM
Channel 9:	107 FM

The *radio* stations are organized similarly. Radio Thailand is the most important of the 200 stations that broadcast nationwide - its local and international news has to be adopted by all other stations. With the exception of the Ministry of Education station and Radio Thailand, all of the country's radio stations are commercial. There are three English speaking stations in Bangkok: FM 107, daily from 6:00-2:00 hours, Pop, Disco, Jazz. Radio Thailand broadcasts for 5 1/2 hours daily, FM 97.0.

The Chulalongkorn University station (classical music) broadcasts from 9:00-23:00 hours daily.

Burma has had a TV channel since 1984. It can only be received in the Greater Rangoon area, however. It is estimated that there must be approx. 20,000 TV sets in the country. The Burma Broadcasting Service broadcasts in Burmese and the languages of the national minorities, as well as 2 1/2 hours of English daily. A 1/2 hour news programme can be received at 8:30 (42.14 and 314 m) and 13:30 hours daily (30.85 and 314 m). A general English language programme is broadcast daily between 21:00 and 22:30 hours (59.52 and 314 m).

Video is the 'in' thing in Thailand these days, just as it is in most other Asian countries. Video tapes of American B-movies, Chinese action thrillers, and local melodramas are shown in all of the large, overland ac-buses. Restaurants in the tourist centres (e.g. Chaweng Beach on Ko Samui) announce the nightly video well in advance. The variety ranges from films like 'Apocalypse Now' to 'French Connection'. All age groups are into videos, and there is no law for the protection of young people and children to stop youngsters from watching ultra-violent movies.

Bangkok Post
Established in 1946

THE GUARDIAN

TOURISM

Tourism is one of the most important branches of Thai economy. More foreign currency is brought into Thailand by tourists than by any article of export, more even than by the many Thai migratory workers employed in the Middle East, who will usually send a substantial part of their earnings back home to their families.

International tourism on a grand scale started during the Vietnam war, when many members of the US Army spent their R&R (rest and recuperation) in Thailand. In addition, many US Air Force members would come down to Bangkok and the central region from Air Force bases in the northeast of the country. The tourism industry managed to adapt to the new circumstances very quickly after the war had ended. While the number of European tourists rose, the number of tourists coming from Asia (particularly Malaysia and Singapore) and the Pacific area increased by an even larger degree. Ever since the end of the 70s tourists from the Near and Middle East have also become quite common.

Approx. 3.5 million tourists visited Thailand in 1987, 23% more than in the preceding year. A high proportion of them came from East Asia and the Pacific area (Malaysia over 1/2 million, Japan 300,000, Taiwan and Singapore each 200,000). Approx. 700,000 Europeans visited the country. The average tourist spends 5.5 days in Thailand. Tourists from the Middle East stay longest on average (9.1 days), with European tourists coming in a close second with 8.6 days.

Almost 2/3 of the tourists travel alone (individual tourists). Most Malaysian visitors to Hat Yai also fall into this category. A short visit to this, the largest town in southern Thailand, will suffice should you wish to know why the city seems so attractive to male tourists from neighbouring Malaysia. Generally, this is the explanation for approx 75% of all single male tourists that come to Thailand yearly. Next to Kenia and the Philippines, Thailand is the most important destination in the international sex-tourism industry. The number of Malaysian tourists fell drastically in 1985, when the Thai government became more selective in handing out the border passes necessary to cross the border to Thailand.

A look at how much the average tourist spends per day in Thailand will also prove quite interesting. Tourists from the Middle East: 155 US$, USA: 126 US$, European countries 50 US $. Let us take a closer look at those 50 $ spent by the average, male European tourist. He spends 1357 Baht daily, 350 of which he spends on souvenirs. 400 Baht are spent on accommodation, 250-280 Baht on food and drink. 160 Baht are spent on 'entertainment', while 106 Baht are spent on transportation. A rich Arabian oil sheik will spend 1100 Baht just on a hotel room.

Prostitution in Bangkok

Bangkok's biggest - and saddest - claim to fame are its thousands of 'girls of easy virtue'. It is estimated that there are between 100,000 and 200,000 prostitutes in Bangkok. Only a small number of them specialize exclusively in 'farang' visitors.

There are many reasons why so many young girls from the provinces end up working in this profession. Few of them actually come to Bangkok hoping to make a career as a prostitute, for they know that it will mean that they will never be able to marry a Thai and that they will be ostracized from their village community. Many come hoping to find a job in industry or as a secretary in an office. Frequently they will be paid extremely low wages. Thus they are often forced to find some source of extra income. From a 'dancing girl' it is only a small step to the 'Girlie Bar' or a massage parlour. Others are lured to the city and find themselves in a brothel before they know it. The boyfriends who lured them here in the first place, promising eternal love, will have vanished into thin air by then, taking a fat commission with them.

Articles in The Bangkok Post, telling of poor parents in the provinces who were forced to sell their daughters, can be read again and again. Frequently this is the only way the parents can survive. Sex tourism is definitely a symptom of the late 20th century.

'Bang-bombers' have been bringing scores of male tourists to the 'city of angels' ever since the Vietnam war ended in 1973. Most tourists return home on the infamous 'clap-clippers', for few of them are spared the various venereal diseases that can be found in Bangkok. The WHO estimates that at least 25% of the girls working in this profession carry some sort of venereal disease.

We do not wish to damn prostitution from a moral point of view - the point we are trying to make is that modern sex tourism is yet another form of Third World exploitation. Services that are expensive at home cost very little indeed in Bangkok. Most tourists are not at all interested in anything else this beautiful country may have to offer.

Tragi-comic situations are common in any 'Girlie Bar'. Just spend a night at one of the many coffee-shops and count the number of feeble-minded farang geriatrics having the time of their life with a sixteen year old Thai girl on their knee. Hotel and bar owners make a good deal of money out of prostitution, as do those offering accommodation in so-called 'bachelor hotels'. The girls are reduced to a commodity; they lose their worth after a couple of years of prostitution and are quickly forgotten by pimps and clients alike. Even if their dream of marrying a 'farang' comes true, they will often be disappointed when returning 'home' with hubby. It is then that the generous playboy they met in Thailand turns out to be just another nobody who has to work five days a week and becomes increasingly bad-tempered as time goes by. For most Thai girls living abroad under such circumstances, far from their home, friends, and family, life is very lonely.

ART & CULTURE

ART PERIODS

First and foremost, the cultures of Burma and Thailand are marked by Buddhism. Animistic and Hindu traditions of times gone by have also influenced the development of the two countries' artists, as have the ancient Indian and Chinese cultures. The earliest **prehistoric discoveries**, which are said to be up to 1 million years old, were made in the province of Kanchanaburi. 7000-year old pieces of clay, weapons, jewelry and other things indicating intelligent life were found in what must have been one of Thailand's earliest settlements near the present-day village of Ban Chiang in the northeast of the country. Weapons and tools made of bronze were being fabricated here 4500 years ago, significantly earlier than in China or India.

Various culturally highly developed states existed in the Thailand-Burma area as early as in the first millennium of the Christian era. In the 6th century the south of Thailand was mainly influenced by the **Srivijaya** kingdom of Palembang (southern Sumatra), one of the earliest Buddhist kingdoms, whose art was heavily marked by Indian influences. At the same time various **Mon** principalities had united to form a loose federation in central Thailand (Nakhon Pathom, Lopburi), the Irrawaddy delta, and the Tenasserim mountains. Sculptures and buildings of this period are marked by clear lines and symmetrical, highly stylized patterns. The Buddha figures of the time, most of them standing up, appear large and heavy. Their spiral-shaped, large curls are typical for the period, as are their swung eyebrows that meet above the bridge of the nose.

There were also **Pyu** living in north and central Burma, of whom early writings dating back to the 7th century were discovered near Prome and Shwebo. The Pyu had close contacts to the northeast of India. The highly developed Buddhistic cultures of these two peoples, the Mon and the Pyu, were later adopted by the immigrating Burmese people. These were not at all disinclined to resort to violence to persuade architects, artisans, artists and monks to bring their talents and Buddhist writings to **Pagan**, the newly founded cultural centre of their empire. Many temples of the 11th and 12th centuries were still built in the style of the Mon and the Pyu. The brick and stucco 'cetiya', a combination of a stupa and a shrine with the bell-shaped tower rising from a round or eight-sided plinth, can be seen as a typical example of the period. Later on the Burmese developed their own, independent style; the plinths became larger and larger, finally assuming the shape of terrace-like constructions, with connecting staircases going up all eight sides. The Burmese added front sections to these pyramid-like buildings. These were used for religious ceremonies and were decorated with statues and murals. In contrast to the imposing royal tombs of other cultures, the temples were erected for the people and were open to all levels of society. The Buddha figures with their bent heads crowned with lotus buds resemble those found in northern India.

The **Khmer** of Cambodia were becoming increasingly powerful, and in the 9th century they began securing their territory and expanding towards the west. They managed to drive the Mon out of the Menam Chao Phya area and ruled there until they were themselves driven out by Thai in the 13th century. Examples of Khmer architecture, which was heavily influenced by Mahayana Buddhism, can still be seen in Phimai, Lopburi, Sukhothai, and other towns. The richly decorated temple towers, the prangs, are typical examples of their style. A phallus shaped tower with many Buddha figures adorning its niches stands upon a large, rectangular base. Doors and windows are also heavily decorated with various figures. Depictions of Buddha and other gods of this period seem less standardized than is usually the case. They appear quite individual, with bracelets and necklaces and sometimes cone-shaped head ornaments, whose lower rim runs parallel to the almost completely straight eyebrows. The large, pouting lips and the flat, broad noses give the rectangular faces a rather stern expression.

The impetus for the development of an independent Thai culture was given when the Thai King Rama Khamhaeng founded **Sukhothai** in 1228. The lotus bud tower is a typical example for the temple-architecture of the Sukhothai period. The Buddha figures went through a visible change during this period, too; the Khmer style was almost completely reversed. The faces received an almost female appearance with a serene expression in their eyes. The spiral-shaped curls on the oval heads tower upwards in the shape of a stupa and

MURALS, WAT PHRA KEO, BANGKOK

end as a stylized flame. The swung eyebrows meet over the long, pointed nose, the lips are curled upwards in a strange, knowing smile, and the eyelids are half closed. The harmonious, flowing lines connecting the head to the body are accentuated by the long, protruding earlobes.

When Pagan was destroyed in 1287, large parts of Burma fell under the influence of the Shan principalities. Little money was left for the construction of temples, due to the many wars between the small states. The significant Mon kingdom of *Pegu* near Rangoon gained wealth in the 15th century by trading with India and the European countries. The Pegu incorporated ideas from both these cultures into their own. The kingdom of *Ava* near Mandalay, originally founded by the Shan, became the northern centre of the Burmese Empire after Pagan was destroyed. At its height, this second Burmese Empire reached well into Thailand; at times Chiang Mai and even Ayutthaya lay within its limits. In the arts, the Pagan tradition survived. Palaces and cloisters were mainly built of wood. Thus few of them have survived to this day. Unfortunately, those pagodas built of brick and decorated with stucco were also heavily damaged during an earthquake in 1838.

From the 13th to the 18th century, after the fall of Sukhothai, *Ayutthaya* became the leading force of central and south Thailand. Here, the direction the arts were to take was influenced, too, with elements of the Sukhothai and the Khmer period being merged. In addition, European influences became increasingly important. The royal court had a particularly large influence on Buddhistic art. A rather pompous style was developed. Huge murals decorated temple walls while ornaments, gold, and gems adorned the statues, which were even clothed in royal robes during the 18th century. The expressions on the faces of the Buddha figures changed from the religious ecstasy of the Sukhothai period to one of majestic, exalted distance. Art was produced in massive quantities during this period, thus losing much of its artistic quality.

Not only precious works of art were robbed when the Burmese destroyed Ayutthaya in 1767 - artisans and artists were also abducted, and these contributed significantly to the revival of Burmese culture. Meanwhile the Thai Chakri dynasty had begun to recapture some of the lost splendour of their former royal city in *Bangkok*, the new capital. Construction on the royal temple, the Wat Phra Keo, began in 1785. Since the mid-19th century Chinese and European influences have been adopted and integrated into the arts without a second thought. The Royal Palace in Bangkok can be seen as a typical example - the building is in a neo-classical style with an echelon roof typical of the *Ratanakosin style*, which has been the dominant style in Bangkok during the past 200 years.

Artists in Burma and Thailand were traditionally responsible for decorating the temples. Accordingly, you will mainly find religious objects in Thai and Burmese museums. Much has fallen victim to the tropical climate, fires, and war. This is particularly the case for wood carvings, clothing, and wooden buildings. Stone buildings and Buddha figures made of metal, in contrast, have for the most part survived. Many of the old buildings and sculptures were re-modelled according to the respective taste and style of the following periods. Faded murals were often covered with new ones. New chedis were frequently erected on top of old ones, as artists gained more recognition by creating new works of art than by restoring old ones. Nevertheless, there are still several sculptures and temple ruins which give modern-day travellers a pretty good idea of the aesthetic conceptions of the peoples of past centuries. Even today their artistic quality and expression seem very impressive.

THE TEMPLE

Traditionally, the Buddhist temple has many functions. It is the site of religious ceremonies, festivities, and prayers, the place where believers meditate, where monks live and study, where the village community meets, and where travellers can rest or even spend the night should they so desire. The institutions are open to men and women, believers and unbelievers alike, as long as they show ample respect for the religious sites. Due to these many functions, different buildings can usually be found on one temple-ground, known as a Wat in Thailand. A high wall usually surrounds a wat. One can recognize a temple from afar by its bell-shaped, pointed tower, the *chedi* (Thailand) or the *pagoda* (Burma). According to the region and the cultural epoch during which they were constructed, these towers can also be called *dagobas* (Sri Lanka), *stupas* (India, Nepal), or *prangs* (Khmer). Culturally, these towers are of Indian origin, many holding relics of Buddha. One always walks around a chedi or a pagoda in an anti-clockwise direction. One can even climb some of the towers, though women are often not permitted to do so. The prayer hall, known as the *bot* in Thailand, is the religious centre of every Buddhist temple. The large interior is decorated with many statues, while the walls are often covered with murals or ornaments. A large Buddha statue can invariably be seen making up the centre of attention in any bot. Religious ceremonies are carried out here. Believers sit on the floor, their feet respectfully pointing behind them. The bot is sometimes deemed so sacred in northern Thailand that women are frequently not allowed to enter. You will also find numerous side chapels, the *viharn*, where monks meet and believers pray. A small library, the mondhop, can often be found built upon a large base to protect it from floods during the rainy period. There are also open pavilions, the *sala*, where visitors can rest or seek refuge from rain. The monastery, home of the monks, usually stands slightly apart from the other buildings. While one is expected to take one's shoes off before even entering the temple grounds in Burma, one does not have to do this until one actually enters a temple building in Thailand.

SCULPTURE

Buddha statues have been sculpted out of stone, carved out of wood, built with bricks and then covered with plaster, or cast out of bronze, copper, or gold for centuries. The depiction of Hindu gods and animistic spirits in sculpture or relief, though not uncommon, has always been of secondary importance. Although the artistic styles and the technical possibilities have changed during the course of the centuries, the depiction of Buddha, the Enlightened, is bound to strict principles set by the traditions of ancient Indian art. A depiction of Buddha, according to the Hinayana teachings, is meant to represent the teachings rather than the actual person.

Asana, the body pose, and *mudra*, the position of the hands, are significant in as much as they symbolize certain events and situations in the life of Buddha. There are four traditional poses - sitting, lying, standing, and walking. The first of these is most widely spread and can be seen in many different variations. The symbolic positions of the hands have various meanings.

Dhyana mudra for instance, with Buddha's hands joined palm upwards in his lap, symbolizes the meditating Buddha.

The right hand, raised to shoulder height with the palm pointing away from the body symbolizes *abhaya*, the fearless Buddha who gives protection, reassurance, and blessings to those in need.

The open hand hanging down can have two meanings - if the palm is turned towards the body this symbolizes *bhumisparsa*, Buddha's calling of the Earth to witness his Enlightenment.

With the palm turned away from the body the same pose symbolizes *vara*, the forgiving Buddha who bestows gifts.

One also frequently comes across the explanatory, arguing hand, where the palm of the hand is turned away from the body. This position is called *vitarka*. The fingers are slightly bent, and thumb and index finger touch, forming a circle.

If both hands are held in this position in front of the chest with the palms turned towards the body, this symbolizes *dharmacakra* - Buddha turning the wheel of law, the wheel of the endless cosmic cycle, which calls to mind his first public speech in the deer park of Isipatana.

In some statues the meditating Buddha is also depicted sitting on a seven-headed serpent, whose fan-like arrangement of heads protect the Enlightened from a thunderstorm. Here the Buddhist teachings have merged with Indian mythology. *Naga*, the female servants of Buddha, are semi-divine serpent-beings who live in a rich, underground kingdom. They are able to take the form of human beings and bear strong and powerful children, should they be impregnated by a man. Snakes and sometimes crocodiles (the Naga symbol of the Mon) can often be seen adorning temple staircases and roofs in Thailand and Burma.

Sometimes the Naga are also depicted in the claws of their arch-enemy, *Garuda*, king of the birds. Garuda, with the wings, claws, and head of a bird of prey and the body of a human being, can be found all over the South East Asian area and India. The god Vishnu rides upon him, and he is also the heraldic beast of the Thai coat of arms, seeing as the Thai kings are said to be incarnations of Vishnu. You will also find Garuda on money bills.

Erawan, the three headed elephant, is another royal animal. The god Indra rides upon him, and in the Hindu tradition he is the god of science and art. White elephants used to be kept at the Siamese court as a symbol of the might of the Thai kings. Small elephants carved out of teak wood are often offered as sacrificial gifts in temples or shrines.

Further popular mythological creatures have the function of temple guards, e.g. **Yaksha**, gigantic figures with sombre looking faces, **Kinnara** and **Kinnari**, heavenly beings who are half-bird, half-human, and **Singha**, the fierce Burmese lions with their bared teeth, who can be found guarding temple entrances in central Burma and northern Thailand.

Depictions of **Nats**, spirits of water, mountains, trees, and of ancestors and former heroes can be found in many Burmese temples. Their origin can be traced back to the ancient animistic beliefs of the Burmese people. When Buddhism was introduced under King Anawratha, the king found that he could not possibly eradicate the common people's belief in natural gods and spirits. Instead of doing away with them, he reduced them to 22 Nats who were subordinate to Buddhism in general and to Thagyarmin, god of the Nats, in particular. Sometimes he is regarded as the equivalent to Buddha, and he is definitely considered the keeper and guardian of Buddhism among the Nats, who have by now increased in number to 37. Tragic legends closely related to Burmese history surround the Nats, 'evil' and 'good' ones alike. They are still called upon for help to this day; one contacts them by way of a medium, acknowledges their power, then asks them questions concerning the future. In addition there is a Nat spirit house in every Burmese village, where the mighty Nats are kept at bay by having sacrificial gifts offered to them constantly.

The Thai people also worship protective spirits outside of the Buddhistic temples. Each town has its own temple, the **Lak Muang**, which houses the patron spirit of the area. Every house has a **Chao Thi**, a small house for the domestic spirit. It is always built according to certain traditions. An example of this

SPIRIT HOUSES IN NORTH THAILAND

would be the fact that it may never stand in the shadow of the house which is meant to be protected. Sacrificial gifts are offered regularly. These spirit houses can acquire considerable dimensions, depending on the wealth of the respective house owners and their need for protection. The house temple of the Erawan Hotel in Bangkok, for instance, has become a place of pilgrimage for the entire population.

PERFORMING ARTS

There have always been plenty of reasons to entertain people with dance and music - musical accompaniment is equally appropriate for religious festivities as it is for state ceremonies, and village or family feasts. The earliest instruments of the area were probably bronze gongs, which have been discovered not only in Thailand and Burma, but also in Vietnam and Indonesia. Bronze gongs should be counted the most important of Thai and Burmese musical instruments, along with drums, cymbals, oboes, bamboo flutes, and bamboo xylophones.

In Burma one may also come across *kye-waing* or *saing-waing*, circles consisting of either 18 gongs or 21 drums, with one musician playing them with both hands and a stick from the centre of the circle. These days, female accompaniment on the 'soung', a 13-string harp said to be modelled on an ancient Egyptian instrument and to be over 4000 years old, has become very rare.

There are three types of orchestras in Thailand. Ceremonies and theatre performances at the Royal Court are accompanied by a *pi phat* orchestra consisting of gongs, xylophones, metallophones, and an oboe or a flute. Lutes, zithers, and other string instruments are added to the *mahori orchestra*, which accompanies choirs and sometimes solo-singers. The *krung sai*, the rural orchestra, uses only string and wind instruments.

Indian, Indonesian, and Chinese influences have played a great role in the development of the musical traditions of Thailand and Burma. While many instruments and melodies can be traced back to Chinese origin, the two great Sanskrit epics Ramayana and Mahabharata came from India, first to Siam, later on to Burma.

These two heroic epics form the basis for scores of classical dances and plays. The Thai mask-dance of gods and demons, *Khon*, is based upon the Thai version of the Ramayana. The colourfully masked and clothed actors only ever re-enact certain, single episodes in their regular performances of the dramatic love story of the brave Prince Rama, his beautiful wife Sita, and their eternal battle against the evil Ravana. Theatre, dance, and music are connected in a particularly intricate way in the Khon, seeing as the classical models require a perfect co-operation of orchestra, dancers, and those reciting.

Dances in South East Asia are generally slow, with the exception of a few battle scenes. The dancers move about the stage with small steps and restrained and controlled movements. The gestures they make with their arms and hands are all the more impressive, especially when the fingers are bent as far back as possible, as is often the case.

While the mask dance used to be performed only at the Royal Court, whole village communities were being entertained by **lakon nok** performances, which are less stylized, more humorous, and more realistic. The **lakon nai**, a courtly dance performance, was developed out of the lakon nok in the 18th Century. Here, the king's wives dance gracefully to the accompaniment of an orchestra, singers, and reciters. Inao, a two thousand verse epic created by Rama II, is the most popular theme. The dramatic love story of Prince Inao and Princess Busba is taken from an ancient fairy-tale of Java.

After the destruction of Ayutthaya, these sort of dance performances were also introduced in Burma, where they gained instant popularity. At certain points in history dancers were prohibited from performing the epic classics. String puppets took over for them. These days, string puppet players still travel from town to town with their mobile stages.

The popular Burmese **zat pwe** is based on Buddhistic themes. Performances usually take all night. Clowns and dancers perform during the intermissions to give some relief from the dramatic story. While the dancers here may still improvise if they like, dancers performing religious or courtly dances are bound to strict, set rules of movement.

ARTS & CRAFTS

Many artistic techniques were passed on from generation to generation. While few of the ancient lacquer wares, silk materials, or Celadon ceramics have survived to this day, the method of making them is still clearly remembered and often used. These hand-crafted pieces are not only sold as souvenirs in Thailand and Burma - they are also put to use at feasts and in everyday life.

SILK WEAVING

The women in the villages - particularly the poorer ones - spend lots of time weaving silk on simple looms. This silk is used to manufacture robes or given away as a particularly precious gift. The silk worms are fed with mulberry leaves until they spin themselves into a cocoon. After the rice has been harvested the silk weaving 'season' begins, and the monotonous clatter of the weaving looms can be heard in all villages. The women sit in the shade of their houses weaving fine silk threads which are subsequently dyed many different colours. Indigo plants are used for the colour blue, an insect secretion for red, and a root for yellow. Burmese 'Acheik' silk, with its intricate, wavy, echelon pattern is considered especially precious, as is the Thai 'Mut-Mee' silk, where the threads have to be dyed several times before they are woven.

SILVERWORK

Burmese artisans, who have been working with silver since the 13th century, were responsible for bringing this art form to northern Thailand, where jewelry, objects for everyday life, and the traditional bowls and vessels used for religious ceremonies are still fashioned to this day. The silver is melted down together with old coins, mainly of Indian origin. The cooled, thin sheets of silver are subsequently worked on with chisels of various sizes until they have assumed the form and density the artist requires. The fine ornaments and reliefs that can be seen on silver vessels are then achieved by weeks of fine chiseling on a wooden mould.

WOOD CARVINGS

The facades and interiors of temples and houses in Thailand and Burma have been adorned with wood carvings for millenniums. Particularly beautiful carvings can often be seen on temple doors, windows, and gables. A carving is usually made from a single piece of wood, and it often takes months before the material begins to assume its three dimensional shape. Wood carvings most often depict scenes out of the life of Buddha or from the heroic epics. Precious decorations as well as statues of famous elephants and pieces of furniture are often carved of teak, which has to be stored for a couple of years before one can even begin working on it.

CELADON

This technique of baking earthenware at extremely high temperatures has been known in China for at least 2000 years. When King Rama Kamhaeng of Sukhothai returned from a visit to China in 1294, he brought 300 Chinese potters with him. These started producing Celadon in the baking kilns of Sukhothai and Sawankhalok. Their products were exported to all Asian countries, even reaching the Arab states. With the fall of Sukhothai the Celadon production also experienced a drastic recession. After a war between Ayutthaya and Lanna, all artists from Sukhothai - including the potters - were abducted to Chiang Mai, which remains the centre of Celadon production to this day. Only earthenware materials and such found in the jungle are used for the fabrication of these ceramics with their green, shimmering glaze. No chemical additives are used.

LACQUERWARE

The Yun or the Kern of the northern mountains are said to have introduced this form of art to Burma (Prome, Pagan) as well as Thailand (Chiang Mai), where it is still practised today. It is a long, wearisome process of work to manufacture bowls, cups, and other objects. First one makes a rough form, either of wood or - for objects of higher quality - of plaited bamboo. These are covered with a fine coat of lacquer, made of ashes, limestone, and the juice of the so-called Black-Lacquer-Tree (Melanorrhoea usitatissima). After this first coat has dried and been polished, further coats are added. This process may be repeated up to fifteen times. Once finished, some objects are decorated with gold, others with various colours, whereby the patterns are made by adding coats of coloured lacquer which are subsequently smoothed down again.

LACQUERWARE PRODUCTION IN PAGAN

ENTRY FORMALITIES

THAILAND

VISAS

Entering Thailand is usually no problem. You can enter the country any time without a visa. In this case a *15-day visa* will be stamped into your passport. Customs officials can refuse to let you enter if you don't have at least US$250 and a return ticket, though. Badly dressed individuals are also often turned down.

If you wish to stay longer than 15 days, however, you should definitely apply for a *60-day visa* at the nearest Thai Consulate well in advance. We have heard that the Penang Thai consulate has even issued 90-day visas to tourists. The visa costs US$5 for tourists and US$15 for visitors with non-immigration status. From the date of issue the visa has a validity of 90 days, meaning that you have to enter the country within this period. For the visa you'll need 2 passport pictures, a valid passport, and - in Europe - travel confirmation (= airline ticket or voucher) . On entering the country customs expect you to have at least US$500, but this is rarely checked.

Extending your tourist visa - (15-day visas can sometimes be extended, too) You can have your 60-day tourist visa extended twice for an additional 30 days each time. In Bangkok this will cost you 300 Baht. You can, alternatively, leave the country, pay a short visit to Burma or Malaysia, and then apply for a new visa from there. If you want to have it extended in Thailand, though - go to Immigration, dress well, and look your best. Address:

Immigration Department, Thai Police, Soi Suanplu, Sathon Tai Road, tel 2869176, 2869230. For the extension of your visa you will be expected to show a hefty US$1000.

EMBASSIES

THAI EMBASSIES OVERSEAS

AUSTRALIA: 111 Empire Circuit, Yarralumla, Canberra, ACT 2600. Consulates in Melbourne and Sydney.
CANADA: 85 Range Road, Suite 704, Ottawa, Ontario K1N 8J6, tel 2371517. Consulates in Toronto, Montreal, and Vancouver.
NEW ZEALAND: 2 Burnel Ave, PO Box 2530, Wellington 1, tel 735538.
UNITED KINGDOM: 29/30 Queen's Gate, London SW7 5JB, tel 5890173.
UNITED STATES: 2300 Kalorama Road, NW, Washington DC 20008, tel 6671446. Consulates in Boston, Chicago, Philadelphia, and Honolulu.

THAI EMBASSIES IN NEIGHBOURING COUNTRIES

BURMA, 81 Prome Road, Rangoon, tel 12471/16555.
INDONESIA, Jl.Imam Bonjol 74, Jakarta, tel 343762.
MALAYSIA, 206 Jl.Ampang, Kuala Lumpur, tel 488222.
SINGAPORE, 370 Orchard Road, tel 7372158.

FOREIGN EMBASSIES IN BANGKOK

BURMA, 132 Sathon Nua Road, tel 2344698, open Mon-Fri 9:00-12:00 h.
INDIA, 46 Soi Prasarnmitr Sukhumvit 23, tel 2580300 open Mon-Fri 8:30-11:30 h.
INDONESIA, 600-602 Petchburi Road, tel 2523135, open Mon-Fri 8:30-12:30, 14:00-16:30 h.
MALAYSIA, 35 Sathon Tai Road, tel 2861390-2, open Mon-Fri 8:30-12:30 h.
PHILIPPINES, 760 Sukhumvit Rd:, tel 2590139, open Mon-Fri 8:00-12:00, 13:00-17:00 h.
AUSTRALIA, 37 Sathon Tai Road, tel 2860411, open Mon-Fri 8:00-12:30 h.
CANADA, Bommitr Bldg., 138 Silom Road, tel 2341561, open Mon-Fri 8:00-16:30 h.
NEW ZEALAND, 106 Wireless Road, tel 2518166, open Mon-Fri 7:30-16:30 h.
UNITED KINGDOM, 1031 Wireless Road, tel 2530191, open Mon-Fri 8:00-16:30 h.
UNITED STATES, 95 Wireless Road, tel 2525040, open Mon-Fri 8:00-12:00 h, 13:00-17:00 h.

CUSTOMS

200 cigarettes (or 250 g of tobacco), 1 litre of wine, 1 litre of spirits, 1 camera, and 5 films are **duty free.** All additional gifts have to go through customs. Bringing weapons, pornography, or drugs into the country is prohibited. Nor may Buddha-statues or antiques be taken out. Up to US$10,000 worth of foreign currency may be taken in or out of the country. Thai currency is limited to 2000 Baht when coming in and 500 going out.

Under no circumstances let yourself be tempted to try your hand at drug-smuggling; too many European tourists have ended up spending much more time in Thailand than was originally planned....

All foreigners who spend more than 90 days of one calendar year in Thailand are required to fill out a so-called **tax clearance certificate.** There are offices in Bangkok and all other towns with an Immigration Office. This may cost you between 175 and 1800 Baht; the regulations are rather ambiguous. You should definitely have dealt with this matter before your departure. If not, it may become even more expensive. There is no harm in saving the bank receipts which you received when officially exchanging money. These prove that you have had no need for employment. Officials in the countryside are much more lenient when it comes to this sort of thing, and their offices won't be as crowded as those In Bangkok.

BURMA

A **seven day tourist visa** can be obtained at Burmese consulates and embassies abroad. You'll need a valid passport, a confirmed airline-ticket showing dates of arrival in and exit from Rangoon, as well as three completed application forms and three passport pictures. Forms are available at the consulates. Normally one applies for a visa in India or Thailand.

You can also apply for the visa in Colombo, Jakarta, Kuala Lumpur, or Singapore. The Burmese Consulate in Calcutta no longer issues visas. In Asia the visa will cost you about US$5 (100 Baht in Bangkok). If you get up early enough you might even get your stamped passport back on the same day in Bangkok. In Europe, it usually takes 1 - 2 weeks. The visa is valid for three months starting from the date of issue.

There are a number of wild rumours concerning the possibilities of *extending visas.* Forget them - there is no way you can spend more than seven days in Burma, unless you should fall seriously ill. There is no point in faking, though; you will be thoroughly examined by a Burmese doctor who will confirm your inability to travel. Should this happen, immediately contact the officials. In Rangoon: Ministry of Foreign Affairs (Immigration Department, Phayre Street, between Merchant- and Mahabandoola Street). You will find yourself in deep trouble if you stay in the country without the necessary stamp. A couple of people have had little choice, however, because their flight was over-booked. These unfortunates had to spend their last days scurrying in and out of various offices.

For this reason: Have your return-ticket confirmed as soon as you arrive in Rangoon!

EMBASSIES

BURMESE EMBASSIES OVERSEAS
AUSTRALIA, 85 Mugga Way, Red Hill, Canberra, ACT 2603.
UNITED KINGDOM, 19A Charles Street, Berkeley Square, London W1X 8ER, tel 4998841.
UNITED STATES, 1717 Massachusetts Ave, NW, Washington DC 20036, tel 2323134.

BURMESE EMBASSIES IN NEIGHBOURING COUNTRIES
BANGLADESH, Plot 38 Rd.No.11, Banani Town, Dhaka, tel 301915.
INDIA, 3/50F Shantipath, Chanakyapuri, New Delhi, tel 70251.
INDONESIA, Jl.Agus Salim 109, Jakarta, tel 320440.
MALAYSIA, 7 Jl.Taman U Thant, KL, tel 423863.
NEPAL, Thapathali Rd., Kathmandu, tel 13146.
SINGAPORE, 15 St. Martin Drive, tel 2358704.
THAILAND, 132 North Sathorn Rd., Bangkok, tel 2344698.

FOREIGN EMBASSIES IN RANGOON
BANGLADESH, 340 Prome Road, Rangoon, tel 23818.
INDIA, 545 Merchant Street, Rangoon, tel 82932.
INDONESIA, 100 Pyidaungsu Yeiktha Road, Rangoon, tel 11714.
MALAYSIA, 65 Windsor Road, Rangoon, tel 31031.
NEPAL, 16 Natmauk Yeiktha Road. Rangoon, tel 50633.
THAILAND, 91 Prome Road, Rangoon, tel 12471.
AUSTRALIA, 88 Strand Road, Rangoon, tel 81711.
UNITED KINGDOM, 80 Strand Road, Rangoon, tel 81700.
UNITED STATES, 581 Merchant Street, Rangoon, tel 82055.

CUSTOMS

Burma has thorough customs officials, and on arrival you will have to fill out a number of lengthy and time-consuming forms.

All valuables (cameras, lenses, cine-cameras, jewelry, binoculars, walkmen, transistor radios, wrist-watches) have to be entered on a *customs form,* sometimes even with the serial numbers. This way customs officials can rest assured that you will take the valuables back out of the country when you leave.

The import of 200 cigarettes and one bottle of alcohol is *duty free.* The happy days during which one could pay for one's whole week in Burma by selling a carton of 555 (Triple Five) and a bottle of Red Label Whisky have unfortunately passed. One can still get up to 300-400 Kyat (US$40-50) for them in Rangoon, though (top prices!). The price depends on the supply and demand as well as your adeptness at driving a bargain. It can therefore fluctuate. The price for these items in Bangkok's Airport duty-free shop is US$13. Whether or not you should become involved is your own decision.

There is also a great demand for other "western ware", i.e. T-shirts, jeans, cassette tapes, cosmetics, watches, pens, pocket calculators, medicine etc. (Only sell items that you have not declared!) On the other hand you shouldn't have too many Kyat left over, either, as many expenses (e.g. hotels and transportation) will be documented on your Money Declaration Form and checked up on when you leave. Take care!

CURRENCIES

Any amount of any foreign currency may be imported. This goes for cash as well as travellers cheques. Everything has to be entered in the *Money Declaration Form* on arrival, however. Importing Kyat or undeclared foreign currency is prohibited.

The amount of money you declare on the form has to correspond with the actual amount you have along. Every exchange of currency, as well as all the hotels, train, and plane tickets booked through Tourist Burma will be entered on the form. This way officials make sure that you've exchanged enough money to actually cover the expenses of your trip. Tourist Burma will refuse to sell you an inland flight ticket if you are unable to prove that you have officially exchanged the money.

The *official rate* for Burmese currency is about 7 Kyat for US$1. The free markets of Singapore and Hong Kong sold Kyat at about 60 for one US$ in November of 1987. In Burma, shady black-market characters may offer up to 30 Kyat for a dollar. Often, however, tourists end up buying the old - now worthless - Kyat notes. Beware! Many of these characters turn out to be working for the police. It isn't worth it.

A further tricky way to get Kyat is by shopping at the *Diplomatic Store* in Rangoon. Imported goods that can hardly be found anywhere else in Burma can be bought here. For US$, of course, and for two different sets of prices - one for tourists and one much more reasonable one for diplomats. Here you can buy Burmese export-cigarettes and re-sell them on the black market for Kyat. This way you will be able to get about 20 Kyat per dollar.

Exporting Kyat is forbidden. Excess Kyat can be changed back to US$ when leaving the country. Of course, appropriate amounts of money should have been exchanged beforehand. Always check the rate when changing currency and count your money!

CLIMATE & TRAVEL SEASONS

Sunny, tropical beaches, Buddhist temples whose golden stupas tower high up into the deep blue sky - pictures and brochures often hold the promise of these and other visual delights, but reality can sometimes look quite different. One frequently meets travellers complaining because their planned bathing-trip to Phuket in mid-August was rained on, and others who found themselves slithering through northern Thailand's mudbanks from one Meo-village to the next, their shoulder bags still full of unexposed film because they dreaded nothing more than the idea of bringing home pictures of overcast skies. Others, who found themselves sweltering away at 41°C in the shade in Mandalay and suddenly had no desire to continue their travels are no rarity, either.

Nobody would plan a day-trip to Bournemouth in mid-December, and only people who are not aware of the fact that the summer months are the worst would plan to spend June in San Francisco. All the same, travellers in South East Asia frequently forget that there are rainy and dry periods here, too.

Temperatures at the coast are normally high, and vary between 22°C and 32°C during the course of the day. They may even climb a little higher during dry periods, while they usually drop after it has rained. The closer you get to the equator, the less the degree of temperature variation. In the more continental climates of northern Thailand and Burma, however, the thermometer climbs to 38°C shortly before the monsoon-period, thus bringing an end to all planned activities.

The *rainfalls* are less predictable. Islands have their own system of winds as well as individual periods of rain, which vary from coast to coast. Those who are familiar with the different rain periods can therefore keep following the sun, avoiding the downpours. Those who are not, will find themselves literally flooded. During the course of a single day more rain will fall here than in several months of dismal, English weather. Wild winds upset the usually peaceful oceans, roads are reduced to impassable moats of mud, and whole city districts are flooded with water.

Winds coming from the open sea bring rain - those coming from inland are dry. From May to October the whole South East Asian area comes under the influence of the southwest monsoon, with high precipitation in both Thailand and Burma. From November to February the northeast monsoon causes havoc, bringing rain to Thailand's eastern coast, all the way from Prachuap Khiri Khan down to Malaysia.

All of Thailand - with the exception of the south - is influenced by the monsoon. This leads to three different seasons, which vary from region to region.

THE RAINY SEASON - May to October: the southwest monsoon brings humid air and rain from the Indian Ocean, especially to the west coast (Akyab, Irrawady-Delta, Rangoon, Phuket). There is less rain in the interior, though the amount continuously increases up until September/October. The yearly rates of the coast, however, (3000 mm upwards) are never reached (Korat: 1220 mm). All the same, there have been floods in Bangkok as early as May. The rate of precipitation in Burma is highest during July and August (Rangoon 582 mm; Mandalay 433 mm). There is always the chance, however, of hardly any rain falling in central Burma at all during the monsoon periods, as, say, in 1975. May to August are good months for travelling in north, northeast, central Thailand, and around the south coast on the side of the Gulf of Siam (e.g. Ko Samui). This period is not suitable for travelling around the Indian Ocean, however. From September to October there is a high rate of precipitation everywhere. The only half-way tolerable region during this phase is the northeast of Thailand.

THE COOL SEASON - November to February: relatively cool weather by Thai standards - but this still means temperatures varying between 20°C in the mornings and 30-33°C in the early afternoon. In Mandalay the temperature may fall as low as 16°C and it can get pretty cold at nights, especially in the mountains. There is always the possibility, however, of it still raining so heavily in mid-November (as we ourselves experienced in 1985) that many planned activities are simply not on. The dates we have given here are of course only the standard mean. Beginning and duration of the rainy periods vary from year to year.

THE HOT SEASON - March and April: starting February, the temperatures rise. People moan about the heat, and the ensuing water shortage constitutes a further inconvenience. This is especially noticeable in northeast Thailand and upper Burma, where clouds of dust gather above the dried-out fields. Temperatures of 40°C in the shade and more are not seldom here. The only pleasant place to be during this season is at the coast, where the bathing resorts are usually bustling with activity. The north, which lies higher, is in general cooler, but you should refrain from going trekking at this time of year nonetheless, as the clear cut mountains offer hardly any protection from the burning sun.

The best thing to do during this season is to hit the beaches - anything else would just end in a puddle of sweat.

Always consider the holiday times before planning your trip; obviously, the country is swarming with tourists during the European summer and Christmas holidays. The Thai holidays shouldn't be forgotten either, though. Universities: mid-March - June; schools: mid-May - mid-July. During these times Thais like travelling, sometimes in large groups. You will find that busses and trains are frequently booked out . The same goes for hotels.

PLANNING YOUR TRIP

❑ If you plan to take a bathing holiday, go trekking, or simply want to travel up and down the coast, the **best time** to do this is the dry period between December and March. Phuket rainy season: July-October. Ko Samui: September-December. If you really want to make sure, start your trip a month after the rainy season should have ended.

❏ *Avoid* April and May if you plan to go touring through upper Burma, north- or northeastern Thailand; the heat can become unbearable.

❏ *Avoid* holiday resorts during the school holidays. Chiang Mai, Khao Yai, Hua Hin, Phuket, Pattaya, Ko Samet, and beaches further east are nearly always booked out. The same goes for ferries and busses. Thai holidays - see above.

❏ *Sundays and holidays* are unsuitable for long bus or train rides. The same goes for the Chinese New Year, during which Bangkok's Chinatown seems to be deserted. Christmas/western New Year are frantic times to be travelling about, too.

CLIMATE CHART OF THAILAND AND BURMA

station	Jan	Feb	Mar	Apr	May	Jun	Jul	Aug	Sep	Oct	Nov	Dec
Bangkok					30°C				306mm			
Chiang Mai					29°C			289mm				
Phitsanulok					31°C			275mm				
Udon Thani					30°C		313mm					
Nakhon Sawan					31°C			274mm				
Aranyaprathet					30°C			270mm				
Korat				30°C					244mm			
Chantaburi				28°C	557mm			558mm				
Prachuap Khiri Khan					29°C				253mm			
Chumphon				28°C					327mm			
Ranong				29°C	731mm							
Phuket			29°C					328mm				
Songkhla					29°C					439mm		
Rangoon				30°C	580mm							
Lashio			25°C	305mm								
Mandalay				32°C	151mm							
Akyab			29°C	1400mm								

Average temperature of the warmest month in °C

▨ months with high precipitation; highest precipitation in mm

PLANE TICKETS

For those unfamiliar with the international flightmarket, it may appear bewildering and complicated. The IATA is an important organization. It unites most of the world's major airlines and no matter which IATA airline flies a certain route, the price always remains the same. IATA's world monopoly is no longer unchallenged, however; hardly anyone pays the official one-way IATA rate for Frankfurt-Bangkok these days (a staggering 2600 DM). A cheap one-way ticket in Bangkok costs about US$300.

Luckily, there is the so-called "grey market". Many airlines - including some of the ones belonging to IATA - sell their tickets through cheap travel agencies at "Bangkok rates".

Generally, we would recommend the following:

You have already planned most of your trip: Buy a return ticket to Bangkok or Singapore in Europe or the States. Once there, organize your connecting flights within Asia yourself. Some of the cheap travel agencies offer good package deals, in which your entire route will be put together for you. In such cases the connecting flight from, say, Bangkok to Phuket is almost free of charge.

You haven't planned anything definite yet: In this case a one-way ticket to your destination will be perfectly sufficient (except for Burma and Indonesia; here, you might be required to have a return ticket when applying for a visa). Even if you plan to end your holiday somewhere completely different from where you started off, you will always be able to get the connecting ticket in Bangkok.

You plan to spend a long time travelling around: Usually, an airline ticket has a validity of one year. Many cheap tickets, however, have a more limited validity. This becomes an important factor when planning your return flight; most student-travel tickets are only valid for six months and are non endorsable as well as non refundable. Sometimes one is not quite so strict, though, and if you're lucky you might get your money back upon cancelling your return flight.

You are a student and/or have the International Student Identity Card (ISIC): This card enables you to get airline tickets at reduced prices all over the world. Next to the usual student travel agencies you can also inquire about reduced rates at Thai Airways International, Cathay Pacific, and Malaysian Airlines offices. Whether they will be able to make you a good offer, however, cannot be guaranteed. If you are officially enrolled at a university, getting the ISIC is no problem. In South East Asia the cards are also easily available for non-students. In Bangkok, for example, forgeries can be bought any time at the Atlanta and Malaysia Hotel. Employees of student offices are always able to spot these fakes, however, so if you really want to go ahead and do it, compare the forgery with the real thing beforehand. Otherwise you might end up regretting the wasted 300 Baht.

STUDENT TRAVEL AGENCIES IN ASIA:
JAKARTA: Indo Shangrila Travel, Jl.Gajah Mada 219 G, tel 6392831, 6392376.
BALI: STA, Kuta Beach Club, Kuta Beach, tel 5051 ext.80.
BANGKOK: STA Travel, Thai Hotel, 78 Prajathipatai Road, tel 2815314-5.
KUALA LUMPUR: MSL Travel, South East Asia Hotel, 69 Jl.Haji Hussein, tel 984132.
PENANG: MSL Travel, 340 Chulia Street and Ming Court Hotel, Macalister Road, tel 616112, 616154.
SINGAPORE: Holiday Tours & Travel, 12 Mezzanine Fl., Ming Court Hotel, tel 7347091.
NEW DELHI: STIC Travels, Hotel Imperial, Janpath, tel 344789.
HONGKONG: KKFS-STB, 8/Fl., 130-132 Des Voeux Rd., Central Hong Kong, tel 5-414841.
MANILA: YSTAPHIL, Room 104, Marietta Apartments, 1200 Jorge Bocabo Street, Ermita, tel 5210361.

HEALTH

Being fit and in good health are two of the most important prerequisites for travelling to tropical countries. The climatic change constitutes quite a burden for the body, and because of the additional factors of the unusual foods and the *jet-lag* - you will be missing six to eight hours if you arrive from Europe - tourists should take it easy during the first few days of their holiday.

The same can be said of your last couple of days at home - your body needs to be well prepared. If you work overtime to the last minute, eat badly, and sleep little, don't be surprised if you end up in bed with a cold or other infectious diseases during your first week abroad.

The *climatic change* becomes an especially heavy burden for travellers leaving their homeland during the European winter. The hot, tropical climate can really be a problem then. Try to sleep a lot during your first couple of days and allow your body to adjust itself slowly to the new rhythm.

Start getting your *inoculations* two - three months in advance. Try to consult a doctor who knows about the tropics. Better yet, go to a national inoculation centre, where there is often a tropical medicine section, or a university hospital, where you will also get the prescriptions for the various medications needed. Find out about new inoculation regulations!

All inoculations have to be registered in your *Inoculation Certificate,* with an official health office seal as well as the place and date of immunization and the signature of the doctor.

SMALLPOX: According to the World Health Organization (WHO), this lethal disease was eradicated in 1979. The vaccination is only necessary for people travelling to Chad or Kampuchea.

CHOLERA: Officially, one only needs cholera shots when visiting Niger. On the other hand the disease has certainly not been wiped off the face of the earth. It becomes a special hazard during the rainy season. As long as you stay within the limits of hygiene and are in a general state of good health, you needn't worry too much. Therefore it should be left up to you whether or not you want to have the rather painful shots. It should be said that reactions occur frequently. If you want to have them anyway, you need to have two injections within 14 days. This immunizes your body for a period of six months. After that one injection every six months will be sufficient.

TYPHOID / PARATYPHOID: Symptoms: More than seven days of fever. We would recommend either the oral vaccination *TYPHORAL L* or the Swiss vaccine *VIVOTIF*. This needs to be taken over a period of six days and lasts for three years.

TETANUS: There is always the unfortunate possibility of injuring oneself somewhere along the way. If you have never had a tetanus injection now is the time! You need to have two shots four weeks apart, then a further shot one year later. After that shots every seven-ten years will be sufficient.

POLIO: If you haven't had an oral vaccination within the last ten years, check with your doctor. Full vaccination is essential! Take care of this problem well in advance.

HEPATITIS: Recently, a new vaccine has been developed for this serious disease of the liver. It is called *H-B-VAX* and you will need three shots, one month and then five months apart. A booster is not necessary until five years have passed. The American vaccine *HEPATVAX* is similar, both in effect and dosage. You can also have the *GAMMA-GLOBULIN* shot which, until recently, was the only shot given. This passive immunization is also said to fight many other infectious diseases. Whether you need it or not can be ascertained by taking a simple anti-body test. Avoiding shellfish and oysters will help prevent the infection.

MALARIA: According to a survey by WHO, malaria is once again turning into a serious problem. All of Thailand and Burma - including the cities - is malaria infested. Special care should be taken in the provinces of Rayong (Ko Samet!), Chanthaburi, Khao Yai, and Kanchanaburi. A high level of chloroquine in the blood certainly helps prevent infection, but is, however, no guarantee. Usually one takes *RESOCHIN (or NIVAQUINE, ARALEN, CHLOROQUINE)* tablets, 2-3 per week. Unfortunately, many malaria-carriers have become immune to chloroquin. All the same, one should be wary of using *FANSIDAR*, especially pregnant women. Try combining Resochin with *DARAPRIM* instead (one tablet per week; try Sundays). Start medication one week before leaving home and continue at least four weeks after returning.

If you find yourself suffering from spells of unusually high fever and painfully aching joints - even if this shouldn't occur until after you've returned home - go to a hospital immediately. Tell the doctors that you have visited malaria-infested regions. Early symptoms of the disease are head- and backaches, as well as aching limbs. Frequently doctors misjudge these as being the symptoms of a simple flu and prescribe the wrong treatment. This has led to several unnecessary deaths in Europe over the last few years.

The malaria carrying mosquito, Anopheles, generally only bites between sunset and sunrise. Therefore a mosquito-net or a coil can already help prevent infection. Coils are green, incense-like spirals that take about eight hours to burn down. The smell is rather unpleasant, but one gets used to it quickly and it does keep the mosquitoes away. There are also various insect repellents which can be applied to the skin (e.g. *AUTAN),* but these don't last very long. If you're using a mosquito-net always make sure that none of the insects have managed to get inside; there is nothing worse than spending the night with a mosquito. Always check your net for holes, and - if necessary - seal it with sticking tape.

WORM INFESTATIONS: There is always the slight risk of worms - large or tiny ones - finding their way on and into your body. Often, one does not become aware of their presence for weeks after one has returned home. Most varieties are completely harmless and one can rid oneself of them simply by undergoing a short and painless treatment. Others, the infamous hook-worms for example, are rather dangerous. These enter the human body through the bare soles of the feet. For this reason always wear shoes or sandals when walking through wet or even moist areas. We would recommend having your faeces examined at an institute for tropical diseases upon your return. You should definitely do this if you find yourself suffering from long periods from even only very slight diarrhoea.

INFECTED WOUNDS: Even mosquito bites that have been scratched open can turn into extremely unpleasant infections if not given the proper attention. It is of utmost importance that you treat even the smallest of cuts with iodine. It is sometimes a good idea to apply spray-on-bandage.

SKIN DISEASES: Even sweating can cause the development of unpleasant, itching fungus on the skin. Other problems can easily result after contact with fleas, lice, mites, and bed-bugs. The best precaution is watching out for your personal hygiene. In the tropics it is perfectly okay to shower twice a day - if possible - and to change your underwear daily. Cotton underwear is best. *JACUTIN* smells pretty bad, but it is good for getting rid of parasites. The American shampoo *QUELLADA* is most effective against lice.

SNAKE AND SCORPION BITES: The general paranoia concerning these unpleasant creatures is for the most part unfounded. Lethally poisonous snakes are extremely rare in South East Asia. Those that do exist will only attack humans if threatened. The most dangerous times are shortly after sunset between 18:00 and 20:00 h and during the rainy seasons. Some snakes kill with a blood poison. In this case you will need a serum as soon as possible. Others kill with a nerve poison, and in this case artificial respiration is most important. For further information see *Flora and Fauna*. Scorpions in South East Asia may be poisonous but are generally not considered lethal.

VENEREAL DISEASES: Here, the general paranoia is by no means unfounded; gonorrhea and the more dangerous syphilis are widely spread in South East Asia, especially among prostitutes. The Bangkok and Manila varieties of gonorrhea are penicillin resistant. We would not recommend going to Asian doctors to have this treated; they will only use you as human guinea pigs for their newest antibiotic. If symptoms occur (discharge or sores) go to a good hospital for a blood check and have them find out which treatment will effectively fight your variety. It is important to continue treatment until well after the symptoms have stopped. Ignoring a venereal disease is completely irresponsible. The dreaded AIDS virus has now started spreading in Thailand, too, although there is no mention of this in any of the country's statistics. Beware!

FUNGAL INFECTIONS: In tropical climates women suffer more frequently from fungal infections than usual. Before leaving for Asia have a talk to your gynaecologist and take the necessary precautions. We would recommend the use of ointments rather than suppositories, as the latter tend to melt in the heat.

SCHISTOSOMIASIS (BILHARZIA): When bathing in rivers and lakes in Thailand you always run the risk of being infested by tiny schistosoma worms. This causes an unpleasant infection, early symptoms being diarrhoea, cramps, fever, and coughing fits. If the disease - which can be detected by way of a microscopic scanning of the intestines - remains untreated, it will cause serious shrinking of the liver.

DIARRHOEA: Anyone travelling around Asia will be fighting a losing battle against diarrhoea during the first couple of weeks. It has become such an institution that travellers have come up with a number of amusing names for it; Bali-Belly, Rangoon-Runs, Hong Kong-Dog, Ho-Chi-Minhs, Tokyo-Trots, and even Montezuma's Revenge - in Mexico, that is. A coal-sulfamide compound *(FORMO CIBAZOL or FORBINA)* will usually do the trick. If not, try combining it with *IMODIUM,*which relaxes the bowel movement. This should only be used in very small doses, however. In Thailand the medication *OLETRON* (produced by Bayer) is available. You can also try some of the many "globetrotter-tips", e.g. nutmeg mixed with egg-yolk or days on which you eat nothing except for rice and drink nothing except for tea. Never forget that your body needs sufficient amounts of fluids and salt (we would recommend Coke or lemonade with a pinch of salt).

Don't resort to stronger medications if none of the above mentioned work - see a doctor instead! You might have a form of bacteriological or amoebic dysentery.

Harmless forms of diarrhoea may be caused by infections, spoilt food, unpeeled fruits, or ice-cream. Micro-organisms in your drinking water could also be the cause, though. Drinking water in Asia is always a bit tricky, and you should decide yourself whether you want to risk it or not. Mineral water is not sold everywhere. One of the simplest preventive measures you can take is doing without ice-cubes. Do not drink tap-water! Instead, drink tea. You needn't worry about brushing your teeth with tap-water, though.

Constipation is even more common than diarrhoea. This can be prevented by eating peeled fruits - pineapple is especially effective.

RABIES: Thailand is the country with the world's highest rate of deaths caused by rabies. Stray dogs carry the disease. Dead ones, too. If you are bitten, you need to be treated immediately!

WHAT TO DO IF THERE IS NO CLEAN WATER AVAILABLE

BOILING: This is definitely the safest method for obtaining germ-free water. It is tedious and time-consuming, of course, seeing as the water needs to boil for a good five minutes and then has to cool off again. All the same; even strongly polluted water can be rendered free of germs in this way.

FILTERING: This method of cleansing water is by now practiced all over the world. The water runs through a ceramic filter whose pores are so tiny that only water can get through. Even bacteria and many types of viruses are filtered out. The obtained water is germ-free and can be drunk immediately. These days one can buy handy travel-filters, weighing no more than 700 grammes.

There are drawbacks, however; filters are pretty pricey, and it takes a long time for the water to run through the actual filter. In addition, the filter needs to be cleaned every now and then with a scrubbing brush, causing wear. For this reason filters have to be exchanged every couple of months.

ARGENTIC SALT: Available as tablets or in the form of powder. Add the so-called "silver salt" to clear water and it will be cleansed of all germs. This only works for clear water though, i.e. tap water or water that has been previously boiled or filtered. Allow at least an hour for the chemical substance to take effect. With the aid of argentic salt you can also keep boiled or filtered water free of germs over a longer period of time.

IODINE ADDITIVE: We would not recommend the use of iodine tablets. Nor are we in favour of adding two drops of iodine to every litre of water - allergic reactions are frequent. The quality of the water could be compared to that of water which has been treated with chlorine.

SUGGESTED FIRST AID KIT: (for more developed regions)

FIRST AID: Bandages (elastic bandage, adhesive tape, spray-on plaster) disinfectant (Savlon cream).

PAINS & FEVER: thermometer - aspirin - Buprenorphine (Temgesic) - Nystatin (Nystan) against fungal infections - antibiotics (Bactrim or similar against bacterial infections)

MOTION SICKNESS: Transderm - Dramamine - Marzine.

DIARRHOEA: Imodium - Lomotil - use powders such as Dioralyte, Infalyte or Sodium Chloride against dehydration.

MALARIA: Paludrine - Nivaquine - Aralen - Resochin - Fansidar only for treatment.

OTHER: vitamin pills - insect spray or repellent (Off, Baygon, Autan) - chlorination or iodination tablets (Micropur) for water disinfection - suntan lotion (SPF 12 - 15) - calamine lotion - Indocin for strong sunburn.

Medications for which no prescription is necessary are often cheaper in Thailand than at home, but not in Burma. Vaccinations are also cheaper. The pill is not the most suitable form of birth control for travellers (time difference, diarrhoea). Consider switching to condoms or a diaphragm.

For further information, check Richard Dawood's **TRAVELLERS' HEALTH,** *Oxford University Press 1986.*

If your insurance company back home won't pay for some of these health supplies, remember that they and inoculations are often cheaper in South East Asia.

HEALTH INSURANCE

If you already have health insurance, an additional policy is for the most part unnecessary. You should definitely inform yourself about what your insurance does not cover, though (e.g. transportation back home in case of an accident), and then compare prices and validity of various insurance companies and choose the best one. If your insurance covers the cost of treatment abroad, you will usually be expected to pay yourself at first. The complete sum will then be reimbursed to you upon returning home and filing a claim. To do this, you have to deliver all doctor, hospital, and pharmacy bills to your insurance company once you're back home. Pay attention to the following details:

The bill should specifically name the PLACE and DATE OF TREATMENT, your FULL NAME and DATE OF BIRTH, the complete DIAGNOSIS, SERVICES RENDERED by doctor (medications, laboratory examination, injections, hospitalization), DOCTOR'S SIGNATURE.

The whole thing should look as official as possible, with a letter-head and the doctor's stamp. Have the doctor write in English (if possible) or you will have to have the bill translated once you return home. The cost has to be given in the currency of the country in which you were treated. To avoid loss of money because of fluctuation, however, you should also have the doctor put down the amount in US$ at the current rate of exchange.

If you have very high costs (due to hospitalization, for example), get in touch with your embassy. Explain your situation and ask for financial aid.

Examples of prices (Samrong General Hospital, Bangkok): chest X-ray 130 Baht; porcelain crown 3000 Baht; private bed in a single or double room 450 Baht plus 150 Baht for food.

HEALTH CARE

THAILAND: In many hospitals you will find yourself confronted with Asian apathy. All the same, there are many well equipped hospitals in the country, especially in Bangkok. There are also quite a few good private doctors who speak English. For these, you will have to cover the cost yourself. They are not too high, though. Addresses see Bangkok.

BURMA: Should you get ill, don't go to a private doctor. The hospitals are free, and from here problems concerning the visa-extension are more easily taken care of. Outside of hospitals medication is almost unavailable. Better yet - leave the country!

EQUIPMENT

You can purchase just about anything you might have forgotten in Bangkok's department stores, shopping malls, and supermarkets (not in Burma, though). Local products are usually even cheaper when bought at a market or from a street vendor.

We would even recommend buying certain things in Thailand instead of back home. A complete set of snorkel equipment for instance is much cheaper in Thailand than in western countries. The same goes for jungle boots. Be careful though; if your feet are especially large or your legs unusually long, you might have trouble finding suitable clothes in Thailand. (Max.: jeans length 32, shoe size 43 / 9 1/2) You might be able to find something in the department stores, but it will most probably be more expensive than usual. If you feel that you'll be needing a down sleeping-bag, you'd be better off bringing one with you from home, as this sort of equipment is still of inferior quality in Thailand. Those items marked with an * are cheaper in the big cities than they would be at home.

CLOTHING

❑ *SHOES: GYM SHOES, SANDALS, FLIP-FLOPS** (You should definitely have a pair of rubber flip-flops along, especially if you'll be spending nights in hotels with community showers, toilets, or mandis, which are Indonesian-type bathrooms in which one pours water over one's head out of large stone vessels. As the majority of Asia's population wears flip-flops, they are usually available in all sizes, even XL.)

❑ *TROUSERS / SKIRTS / JEANS or LONG COTTON TROUSERS* (not too tight because of the heat), *SHORTS* (only suitable for the beach or total tourist-resorts)

❑ *JACKET* made of cotton material (the less it creases and crinkles, the better)

❑ *SWEATERS* two thin ones which you should be able to wear on top of each other should it get chilly.

❑ *SHIRT* / BLOUSE* / T-SHIRTS**

❑ *SUN PROTECTION HAT / SUNGLASSES* / LOTION* (in an unbreakable container)

❑ *RAIN PROTECTION PONCHO** (which can also be used as an additional protection for tents etc.) or an *UMBRELLA** (definitely no windbreakers made of rubber of plastic, seeing as the heat finds its way inside, causing profuse perspiration)

❑ *UNDERWEAR / SOCKS / BRIEFS* (even disposable briefs) / for women: sanitary towels, bra (most important!)

❑ *BATHING TRUNKS / BIKINI:* In conservative areas we would recommend a one-piece bathing suit for women. In remoter areas try a

❑ *SARONG** (Longyi, Phasin, Phakama), the local wrap-around skirt made out of a simple piece of patterned material. We consider this the most important item of clothing of all. Apart from bathing, you can also use it as a skirt or a blanket. The sarong is not suitable for wearing in urban centres, however, as it is typical of the countryside and of low social status. In addition you will find yourself ridiculed by the city-dwellers, who are terribly western-oriented as far as clothing is concerned.

OTHER ITEMS

❑ *TOWELS**, possibly two - one for everyday use, the other for bathing.

❑ *WASHBAGS** *SOAP** in an unbreakable container / *TOOTHBRUSH** / *TOOTHPASTE** / *SHAMPOO** / *NAIL SCISSORS** or *CLIPPERS** / *SHAVING KIT* (we would not recommend electric razors; you are bound to have trouble with the plugs and voltage)

❑ *TAMPONS* (available in large drug stores, international hotels, and supermarkets. Not available in rural areas. Tampons are preferable to sanitary towels in the tropical heat.)

❑ *TOILET PAPER* (often unavailable in public lavatories, can also be used as handkerchiefs.)

❑ *SEWING KIT* strong thread, needles, safety pins, ball of string, adhesive tape, miscellaneous items for repairing things and sending away packages.

❑ *PLASTIC SCRUBBING BRUSH* (for doing laundry) / detergent* / plastic bags, good for dirty laundry, are available free when shopping)

❑ *TORCH** / *POCKET KNIFE*

❑ *WATER FLASK* / *CUTLERY*

❑ *TRAVEL ALARM CLOCK* (even better - a wrist-watch with a built-in alarm clock)

❑ *SMALL LOCK** / *MOSQUITO NET**

❑ *FIRST-AID KIT* (see *Health*)

❑ *NOTEBOOK* / *PENS* / *GIFTS*

❑ *DOCUMENTS and MONEY PASSPORT / INTERNATIONAL CERTIFICATE OF VACCINATION / INTERNATIONAL STUDENT CARD / PHOTOCOPIES OF THESE DOCUMENTS / CASH / TRAVELLER'S CHEQUES / RECEIPTS FOR CHEQUES / FLIGHT TICKETS / MONEY BELT / TRAVEL GUIDES / MAPS / BOOKS*

If you plan to do extensive jungle-tours or go mountain climbing, the above mentioned equipment will of course not suffice. You'll certainly need good shoes in the jungle. Thai Army surplus *jungle boots* are just the thing, but again they are only available in Thai-sizes. They can be bought in shops and at the markets of Bangkok and Chiang Mai.

During the course of your travels through Asia you may find yourself being invited to local festivities. If it is a wedding or some other kind of family celebration you will be expected you to dress well. For this reason you should have at least one piece of *"good" clothing* along that can survive a long journey. Do not wear white, blue or black to Chinese festivities unless it is a funeral.

When selecting the clothes you wish to take along, you should try and find a compromise between casual leisure wear and "good" clothing. Judging people by the way they dress is much more prevalent in Thailand than it is in Europe or America. Therefore, wearing Californian-style "beach bum" clothes is not considered proper, especially as even poor people in Thailand do their best to appear well cared for and "decently" clothed. You can have your laundry washed and ironed almost anywhere within 24 hours very cheaply. When staying at the beach or at traveller-hotels you also have the possibility of doing your laundry yourself and saving a couple of Baht.

Whether or not you should take a *tent* or a *sleeping bag* along depends on your planned activities. We would definitely recommend a small tent if you plan to do extensive jungle-touring, especially in the National Parks. As long as you're not planning on sleeping in the mountains somewhere, a simple duvet cover or youth-hostel sleeping bag will do for the warm, tropical nights. We would not recommend a down sleeping bag because of the high humidity.

If you have *electrical devices* along, you need to be aware of the various types of plugs used in Asia. The most suitable devices are those that can run over the electrical current as well as on batteries. You should also be able to change them from 110 to 220 V. The different kinds of plugs you'll need can be bought cheap at Asian markets.

There are numerous TRAVELLER-SHOPS all over the world. Here, you can get expert opinions on what you'll need to take along. Everything - from a pocket knife to a backpack, from a tent to a Landrover - can be bought at these type of shops.

WHERE TO PUT IT

Backpacks are the best thing to carry all your stuff around in. These days there are so many that making a choice can be rather difficult. Your decision should depend on the kind of trip you're planning to make. If you plan to spend most of the time hiking make sure that your backpack is suitable for this. If you plan to spend most of your time travelling in buses, cars, and trains, this factor is not of such importance. The people at your traveller-shop will be able to give you good advice. Unfortunately, backpack-travellers have a rather negative image, especially in tourist resorts and with the officials. If you wish to avoid this problem, you can always have a folding suitcase along (don't laugh; this sort of thing has been seen before) with which to camouflage your backpack when crossing borders etc. This has the additional advantage of extra space for gifts and other items when you return home.

For short trips and people who can get by with very little luggage, a shoulder bag should be perfectly sufficient. These have the advantage of being more easily stored in buses, trains etc., as well as a more positive general image than backpacks.

VALUABLES

Nothing is worse than losing your valuables whilst abroad. Burma is generally considered a reasonably "safe" country, which cannot be said of Thailand. All the same, there is no guarantee for either of the two; time and time again travellers tell of muggings in broad daylight, hotel rooms broken into, or a seemingly friendly fellow-traveller who took off with their camera.

Even before you leave, you should be aware of the fact that you will have to carry all of your valuables around with you while in Asia. This, of course, makes you a tasty target for thieves. In addition, you will be carrying a couple of months' wages around with you by Thai standards, and you will be easily recognized as a foreigner.

It is impossible to do away with all risks, but by taking a few precautionary steps you can at least avoid some of them:

Obviously, cash is of more value to thieves than cheques. For this reason only ever cash as many cheques as necessary. Expensive jewellery should not be taken along! Upon checking in at a hotel, deposit your valuables in the hotel-safe or leave them with the clerk and ask for a receipt.

Whether travel documents should be hung around one's neck, put into a money belt, or sewn into one's jacket is an eternal topic of discussion. We would recommend a money belt. As long as you're wearing trousers you can always discreetly wear it underneath. You can even make money belts yourself. Make sure that you use cotton, so that all perspiration will be soaked up by the material. Other details you should pay attention to are that your belt is not too tight and that it has different compartments of various sizes, of which at least one should be big enough to hold your passport. In addition, all documents should be protected by plastic jackets; sweat destroys, and illegible bank receipts and airline tickets may cause trouble.

Do not keep money in handbags or wallets. The best place for your change and a couple of bills is your front pocket or some other safe compartment close to your body.

You will need a shoulder bag for cameras, though. Make sure that the bag doesn't give away its contents all too obviously, is made of sturdy material (otherwise it might be cut open from behind), and can be closed properly.

If you're going to be on the road for days on end there is no way you can keep your eye on your luggage at all times. Those travelling with friends can always ask their fellow travellers to look out for their stuff for a while. This is especially helpful when frantically searching for a hotel room once you've arrived; one party can go in search of accommodation, the other can stay with the luggage. Always be wary of people you've just met, though; it wouldn't be the first time that someone you considered so "nice" turned out to be a thief.

A good padlock is an absolute must. Many hotel doors can be opened with the simplest of tools. In these cases a padlock is a welcome thing, indeed. Sometimes cheap hotel rooms or beach huts can only be locked with a padlock, and while the locks furnished are usually of reasonable quality, you can never be quite sure who has the second key. When staying in dormitories with no individual lockers you should always lock your backpack. Not all travellers are honest!

While on ships, trains, or buses, it is always rather difficult to keep an eye on your luggage. Do not leave your valuables in your backpack, and make sure you lock it at all times! You should always carry your shoulder bag around with you. Try and choose a friendly neighbour. Local, elder women are often the most trustworthy.

WHAT TO DO IF SOMETHING HAPPENS DESPITE ALL PRECAUTIONS:

Hotel room broken into: You should definitely notify the police. If your luggage is insured against theft, the insurance won't pay unless you have a police protocol. Make sure it is in English. If not, have it translated and attested by a public notary as soon as possible.

Your cheques are stolen: You should always keep the receipts and the cheques themselves separately. You won't receive new cheques unless you have the original receipts. Only AMEXCO (American Express) will give you an immediate compensation. Generally, these are the best cheques to have along.

Your passport disappears: All important documents should be photocopied before you leave. Immediately contact your closest embassy or consulate!

LUGGAGE INSURANCE

Having your luggage insured is always a good idea. Often, however, insurance companies will only cover loss or theft under certain circumstances. Make sure that the policy is adequate and that valuables such as camera equipment etc. are also covered. Under certain circumstances an additional policy covering the total worth of your luggage is advisable. Better yet, put all uninsured items into your hand luggage. The policy should be valid all over the world and should cover the entire time you plan to spend abroad. Make sure your luggage is insured for an adequate amount of money. A check-list of all items with the worth of each one can sometimes come in handy, especially if an airline-company loses your entire luggage.

MONEY

You will receive a good rate of exchange for *traveller's cheques* in US$ and certain European currencies (especially £, DM and sfr). Most banks only exchange traveller's cheques, but money changers will often exchange cash, too. Compare the frequently different rates of exchange and always remember that you will have to pay a commission or "stamp duty", too.

The form of money you should take along depends largely upon where you expect to go. If you plan to go to secluded areas without visiting Bangkok or other large cities, for instance, you should definitely have a generous helping of US$ along. Even if you do plan to spend some time in large cities, US$ are always a good idea. You can pay a taxi ride or take care of the airport tax with them. Dollar bills ("greenbacks") are known all over Thailand, but you might run into problems with British pounds, Australian, or New Zealand dollars. Having cash along is always a certain risk, of course, seeing as you'll be broke if mugged. Still, this risk is sometimes unavoidable.

Traveller's cheques are safest. Generally, they can be bought at any bank for a charge of 1%. Do not buy cheques from small banks, but stick to the large, well-known ones. (In England: Barclays, NatWest etc.)

AMEXCO Traveller's cheques (American Express) are best of all. You can buy them in a number of currencies, but US$ are usually the least problematic. It is most important to keep the receipts separately from the cheques. Your receipts - on which you should always detail when and where which cheque was cashed - are your only proof of ownership if the cheques should be lost or stolen.

If you are reasonably well-off you might want to consider getting yourself an **American Express Card.** For approx. US$70 you can become a member of the American Express Company. You can pay for many things without cash when in possession of the credit card, e.g. airline tickets, hotel bills, and meals. An even greater advantage is the fact that as a member you are eligible to cash a personal cheque of up to US$800 every three weeks. You will be paid partially in the local currency, partially in American Express cheques.

Eurocheques have become slightly problematic ever since Europeans have started trying to deceive with them. They are now no longer accepted everywhere. If they are, you will only be able to cash a certain amount of money for each one (approx. £180).Still, having a couple along by way of reserve is never a bad idea.

MONEY TRANSFERS
If you are planning an extensive journey it is an unnecessary risk to have your entire funds along. Open up an account at a large bank back home, and then have your money transferred to you in adequate quantities. Large banks often have branches or banks with which they correspond in major Asian cities. You can have your money transferred to these banks from your bank back home. This is how it works:

Go to the bank from which you wish to pick up your money. If you need it urgently, they will send a telex (take a note of the telex no. of your bank back home). Otherwise they will do it with a letter. In it, they will ask for the desired amount of money from your account. You can also ask for a transfer by telephone. This goes faster, as you can ask them to telegraph your money over for you (cost: approx. £15. If friends of yours have a full authorization for your bank account, you can also have them take care of the transfer for you. The

Bangkok Bank (Head Office: 333 Silom Road, tel. 2358885) is a good bank for having your money transferred to, as it corresponds with various major European banks. The money transferred will be given to you in local currency or cheques, whichever you prefer.

FREE MARKET
If you want information concerning the official and unofficial rates of exchange, buy the current edition of the Far Eastern Economic Review or Asiaweek. Here, you will find the rates of exchange of the Hong Kong "free market", where money is still exchanged according to the old capitalist tradition of supply and demand. The same principle is used in Singapore. Weak currencies, as, say, the Burmese Kyat, are exchanged at rates comparable to those of the black markets of the countries in question.

MONEY FROM CONSULATES
In many cases, such as theft, you will have to rely on your local consulate to tide you over until you're back home. This, incidentally, is every consulate's duty - to ensure their people's safety and well-being when abroad. Seeing as many travellers have taken advantage of this, however, consulates are not as generous as they used to be.

CURRENCIES

EXCHANGE RATES
1 US $ = 25.90 Baht   1 £ = 45.51 Baht (figures: Spring 1988)
1 US $ = 6.30 Kyat   1 £ = 11.17 Kyat (figures: Spring 1988)
INFLATION RATE: (yearly increase of consumer prices:)
Thailand: 2.6 %
Burma: 6.0 %

THAILAND
Thailand's monetary unit is the **Baht** with 100 **Satang.** The following banknotes are in circulation: 500, 100, 50, 20, and 10 Baht, as well as coins worth 5, 2, and 1 Baht and 50 and 25 Satang.

The worth of the Thai Baht fluctuates little in comparison to the US$. There is no black market rate of exchange. The Baht is subject to fluctuation in comparison to the £, however, and this, in turn, depends on the £ - US$ rate of exchange.

Up to US$10,000 worth of Baht, foreign currency, and cheques may be imported into the country without having to be declared. This is hardly ever checked, though. If you have a great deal of money along and wish to play it safe, you should declare the complete sum of money upon entering the country.

When exchanging large sums of money, you should always check the rates offered by money-changers in the areas around Silom/Suriwong/New Road as well as those offered by the banks. You might be able to save a couple of Baht. Generally speaking, you will receive a better rate of exchange for cheques than for cash. Some banks in Bangkok and Chiang Mai are opened 24 hours a day. Here, you will have no problem cashing cheques. In the countryside, however, cashing a cheque can turn into quite an adventure, with all of the bank's employees becoming involved.

If you plan to spend most of your time in Bangkok and Chiang Mai, US$, £ or A$ traveller's cheques will do. Even taxi-drivers accept US$ by way of payment.

BURMA

The Burmese monetary unit is the *Kyat* (say: Chut) with 100 *Pyas.* The following banknotes are in circulation: 1, 5 and 10 Kyat. In September of 1987 all 25, 35, and 75 Kyat bills were declared invalid overnight. The planned distribution of new 45 and 90 Kyat bills was announced. In 1985 all 20, 50, and 100 Kyat bills had already been declared invalid.There are also coins at 1, 5, 10, 20, 50 Pyas as well as 1 Kyat. Coins are marked with Burmese numerals, bills have both the Burmese and Arabic version. *Watch out when exchanging money - you may be offered old, invalid bills.* Further details see *Entry Formalities - Currencies.*

INCOME AND COST OF LIVING

THAILAND

The minimum wage in Bangkok is 73 Baht a day (April 1987) - this boggles the mind, especially if you consider the fact that officially one is meant to work 48 - 54 hours per week! The minimum wage is 67 Baht in the provinces of Chiang Mai, Korat, and Chonburi, 61 Baht in all other provinces. And these figures are not even binding - they only go for commercial workers, and industrial workers frequently receive even less. The same goes for women and children. Farmers, who usually only have a very limited area of land to cultivate, make less still. A realistic estimate of the yearly (!) income of an inhabitant of the northeast region would lie at around 2000 Baht. An average German tourist spends about 1357 Baht a day, a Swiss about 1968 Baht, and a US citizen almost 3500 Baht!

BURMA

According to the ASIA YEARBOOK 1986, the average yearly income in Burma is US$181. Monthly wages exceeding 200 Kyat are rare. If employed in industry, workers make approx. 1 Kyat per hour. Even here, in this socialist republic, women earn about 20% less than men. The statistics only cover Central Burma, but one can safely assume that people living in remoter states of the country earn even less.

The price for basic foods in the state-run shops are reasonably low. Sudden inflation of up to 100% is not unheard of, however, and people on a low income level are frequently heavily burdened. Most wares are sold at free markets, though, and who knows who controls them.

TRAVEL EXPENSES

When planning your travel budget for Thailand, be aware of the fact that Bangkok is much more expensive than the provinces. Reckon with at least 150-250 Baht a day for accommodation and meals, then add the cost for transportation. One can easily get by on 150 Baht a day in Chiang Mai, Chiang Rai, Phuket, or Ko Samui if one's standards are not too high. This, however, does not include souvenirs, trekking-tours, rents for motorbikes, or trips to the most popular restaurants. All the same, there is no reason to spend 3500 Baht a day!

If you live cheaply, you'll be able to get by on about 40 Kyat a day in Burma. This could make the country cheap to travel around in, even if you exchange money at the official rate. However, by the end of the trip you have to have officially exchanged US$100, otherwise you will end up having trouble. This means a total of 650 Kyat or about 80 Kyat a day.Your trip will be more expensive if you plan to fly, of course. Diethelm Travel in Bangkok offers a Burma package deal for a staggering US$300-400! According to Tourist Burma, approx. 30,000 tourists visit the country every year. Even though each one is only allowed to stay a week, the average visitor manages to spend the yearly income of a Burmese inhabitant per visit!

UNITS OF MEASUREMENT & WEIGHT

Even though the metric system has been introduced in Burma, you will often find distances and units of measurement given in miles, pounds, or pints, a remnant of British Colonialism. Thailand always used the metric system.

inches	0.39	1	2.54	centimetre	1 cm = 0.39 inches
feet	3.28	1	0.30	metre	1 inch = 2.54 cm
miles	0.62	1	1.61	kilometre	
miles/h	6.2	10	16.1	kilometre/h	
pints	1,76	1	0.57	litre	
gallons	0.22	1	4.55	litre	
ounces	0.035	1	28.3	grammes	
pounds	2.2	1	0.45	kilogrammes	

Some old Burmese units of measurement and weights:

1	Viss	=	1.633	grammes
1	Tical	=	16.330	grammes
1	Cubit	=	0.474	metre
1	Span	=	0.230	metre

Some old Thai units of measurement and weights:

1	Baht	=	15	grammes
4	Baht	=	1	Tamlung (= 60 grammes)
20	Tamlung	=	1	Chang (= 1.2 kg)
50	Chang	=	1	Picul (= 60 kg)
1	Rai	=	1600	metre²

POSTAL SERVICES

According to our general experience, letters and parcels sent to or from Thailand usually arrive at their destination.

RECEIVING POST FROM HOME

There are several possibilities. Leaving an approximate timetable of when you will be where, with your friends back home, is a good idea. It ensures that letters addressed to you actually arrive on time. Tell your friends to address their letters to you c/o General Post Office, Poste Restante. If you don't have a definite timetable, you can always write home in advance and tell your friends which will be the next large city you will be visiting. This always works quite well. While airmail letters usually only take about 3-4 days to arrive in Bangkok, it takes longer if they are addressed to towns in the provinces (approx. one week). As one can only spend a week in Burma under normal circumstances, we would not recommend having letters sent there at all. Airmail postcards sent to Europe take ages to arrive.

A letter to you should be addressed as follows:

```
FIRST NAME  LAST NAME
CITY  COUNTRY
GENERAL POST OFFICE
POSTE RESTANTE
```

You will receive your letters upon showing your passport at the poste restante counter. Insist that the clerk look up your Christian name, too, in case of mistakes. The same goes for double names. Usually, a post office will keep letters for three months. If no claim is made for them by then, they will be returned to the sender. Telegrams are often sent back after four weeks. These sometimes have to be claimed at a separate counter (e.g. Bangkok). If you have to leave a town but are still expecting post you can ask to have it sent on to the next town. Careful, though; this is not always successful. Either they will forget to have the letter sent to the next town, or your post will follow you around Asia without ever actually reaching you.

Thailand is in the process of introducing a five-digit postal code system. This has not yet quite become a nationally accepted concept, though.

There is an alternative - you can also have your letter sent to you c/o your local consulate or embassy. In this case a c/o EMBASSY OF...... should be added after your full name.

If you have an American Express Card or even cheques, you can have your post addressed to their offices, too. In this case add c/o AMERICAN EXPRESS.

SENDING LETTERS HOME

Airmail is more expensive than an aerogramme when it comes to sending long letters home. Postcards should always be sent by airmail. Otherwise they might end up arriving home after you do! Important letters should always be sent as registered mail - we would recommend the same when sending back exposed films. There is little point in sending a letter "Express" if you want it to get home quickly; it won't be treated as anything special until it has reached the country of destination. If you do want a letter to arrive quickly, send it from Bangkok or another large city.

SMALL PARCELS & PACKAGES
During long journeys you might find that you have bought too many souvenirs and now wish to get rid of some. We often send parcels back home. Be aware of the following:

Seamail (10 kg 415 Baht) takes 6 - 10 weeks to arrive. It is much cheaper than airmail, though. Airmail is only worth it for light or valuable things, such as slides. Send parcels and small parcels from towns that have a reasonably safe postal system (e.g. Bangkok or Chiang Mai).

AEROGRAMMES	8.50	Baht	1.-	Kyat
AIRMAIL LETTERS (up to 10 gr.)	15.-	Baht	2.15	Kyat
POSTCARDS - airmail	8.-	Baht	1.30	Kyat

FORWARDING
If you have bought large items, you will have to have them forwarded by a for-warding company. This is quite pricey. Sometimes the shop you've bought the item from will take care of the formalities. Should this be the case, always ask for a detailed receipt. The price is determined by the seafreight cost (to the closest harbour) plus the cost of overland-transportation (to the final destina-tion), whereby the latter can sometimes be much more expensive than seafreight.

EXCESS WEIGHT
If you have overweight baggage when returning home, it might be cheaper to have some of your things sent on by seamail than paying the excess baggage fine. You can also have it sent as "unaccompanied luggage" with the airline you fly. In this case your airline company will send it with the next aeroplane that is not fully booked out. This is still cheaper than sending it by airmail.

CUSTOMS
Everything you wish to go through customs has to be registered on a customs declaration, in which you have to specify weight and value of each item and much more. The forms have to be filled out in Thai (or Burmese) and French, which is the official postal language.

TELEPHONES

Local calls from public telephone booths cost approx. 1 Baht for three minutes. Depending on the distance, calls within the country cost between 4 and 15 Baht.

AREA CODES

Phetchburi 032, Kanchanaburi 034, Ayutthaya 035, Lopburi 036, Rayong 038, Chanthaburi 039, Udon 042, Loei 042, Khon Kaen 043, Korat 044, Surin 045, Chiang Mai 053, Chiang Rai 054, Phitsanulok 055, Songkhla 074, Phuket 076, Surat Thani 077, Malaysia 09

IMPORTANT TELEPHONE NUMBERS (valid in Bangkok)

Police 191; Fire Dept. 199; Ambulance 2460199; Long distance phonecalls within Thailand 101; Long distance calls (international) 100; Information (regional) 183; Information (international) 100; International Self-Dial-Service (ISD) 001; Time 181

INTERNATIONAL PHONECALLS

One can make international calls from most telephones in Bangkok. Six seconds count as one unit. For most countries one unit costs 7 Baht.

Codes for international calls: 001 plus country code, plus area code (without the initial 0), plus the number you wish to reach.

Usually, however, you would make international calls from a central telephone office (for addresses, see Regional Section). The minimum chargeable length for one call is three minutes. Even if you don't take that long you will be charged this price. A station-to-station call to the UK costs 210 Baht for 3 minutes, a person-to-person call 320 Baht. A person-to-person ISD-call only costs 55 Baht per minute between 23:00 h and 6:00 h, making it extremely cheap.

You'll have to find out for yourself whether or not it is possible to make reverse-charge calls to a certain country. It is not always possible.

TIME DIFFERENCES FROM G.M.T. (Greenwich Mean Time):

+ 6 1/2 hours: BURMA

+ 7 hours: THAILAND

The American Continent is 13 - 16 hours behind the time zones of South East Asia (with the same differences within the region).

Australia lies in the same time zones as South East Asia.

New Zealand is 5 1/2 to 3 hours ahead.

TRANSPORTATION

Traffic- and roadwise, *Thailand* is a well-developed country. As with London in England, Bangkok forms the centre of its country's railway system. There are many highways in the Greater Bangkok area, and the capital itself is criss-crossed by a network of inner-city expressways. The most important highways are no.1 Bangkok-Chiang Rai, no.2 (Friendship Highway) Bangkok-Nong Khai, no.3 (Sukhumvit) Bangkok-Trat, and no.4 Bangkok-Malaysia. Like the railway network, Thailand's roads used to lead exclusively to the capital. These days, there are a number of good connecting roads in the provinces, too. The Thai government has started building all-weather roads near the borders of its unstable neighbours Laos, Burma and Kampuchea for strategic reasons. There is also an all-weather road from Umphang near the Burmese border leading to Mae Seriang via Maesot. Apart from the border to Malaysia, all Thai borders are closed to foreigners (Burma, Laos, Kampuchea).

STATE RAILWAY OF THAILAND: TIMETABLE 1988

BANGKOK.... HAT YAI-SUNGAI KOLOK & BUTTERWORTH

STATIONS		DRC. 171	DRC. 197	DRC. 233	RAP. 45	EXP. 19	RAP. 11	RAP. 43	RAP. 47	RAP. 41	ORD. 113
Bangkok	d.			09 00	12 30	14 00	15 15	15 00	16 00	17 30	18 30
Thon Buri	d	08 00	13 55								
Nakhon Pathom	d.	09 09	14 58	10 29	14 00	15 25		17 21	18 55	19 53	
Kanchanaburi	d	10 24	16 24								
River Khwae Bridge	d	10 30									
Nam Tok	a	12 20	18 35								
Ratchaburi	d			11 30	14 52	16 13		18 18	19 50	20 41	
Petchaburi				12 10		16 53		19 03	20 39	21 25	
Hua Hin	a			13 10	16 16	17 43	18 53	19 58	21 28	22 14	
Prachuap Khiri Khan	d				17 29			21 27	22 45	23 34	
Chumphon	a				20 00	21 37	22 48	00 32	01 40	02 48	
	d				20 10	21 47	23 02	00 42	01 52	02 58	
Surat Thani	a				23 13	00 36	01 52	03 20	04 42	05 59	
	d				23 18	00 39	01 55	03 25	04 53	06 09	
Thong Song Jn.	a.				01 28	02 44	04 00	05 31	07 19	08 32	
Trang	a									10 10	
Nakhon Si Thammarat	a							08 35			
Phatthalung	d				03 04	04 24	05 49	07 04			
Hat Yai Jn.	a				04 15	05 48	07 05	08 50			
	d				04 30	06 03	07 20				
Yala	a				06 17	07 38					
Sungai Kolok	a				08 15	09 35					
Padang Besar	a					08 00					
	d					*10 00				*15 30	
Butterworth (For Penang)	a					*12 10				*19 10	

THON BURI.... RIVER KHWAE BRIDGE-NAM TOK

STATIONS		DRC. 198	DRC. 172	ORD. 112	RAP. 48	RAP. 42	RAP. 46	EXP. 20	EXP. 12	RAP. 44	DRC. 234
Butterworth (For Penang)	d		*07 00						*13 35		
Padang Besar	a		*10 38						*15 45		
Sungai Kolok	d								15 55		
Yala	d					10 30	11 20				
Hat Yai Jn.	a					12 29	13 13				
	d					14 08	14 47	16 40			
Ratchaburi	a					14 73	15 02	16 55	17 15		
	d					15 37	16 21	18 24	18 58		
Phatthalung	d				13 40						
Nakhon Si Thammarat	d					14 00					
Trang	d				15 03	15 47	17 22	18 14	20 04	20 31	
Thung Song Jn.	a				17 38	18 10	19 29	20 22	22 09	22 39	
Surat Thani	a				17 48	18 20	19 32	20 24	22 12	22 42	
	d				20 38	21 26	22 35	23 16	00 53	01 50	
Chumphon	a				20 48	21 39	22 50	23 26	01 03	02 00	
	d				23 54	00 34	01 22			04 40	
Prachuap Khiri Khan	d				01 16	01 56	02 47	03 29	04 47	06 01	14 20
Hua Hin	a				02 12	02 53				06 55	15 30
Petchaburi	d				02 59	03 35	04 16	04 57		07 43	16 14
Ratchaburi	d								*.		
Nam Tok	d	06 05	12 35								
River Khwae Bridge	a	*.	14 20								
Kanchanaburi	d	08 06	14 26								
Nakhon Pathom	a	09 38	15 49		03 50	04 29	05 08	05 48	*.	08 36	17 14
Thon Buri	a	10 45	17 00								
Bangkok	a				05 10	05 50	06 35	07 05	08 35	10 00	18 45

BUTTERWORTH/KUALA LUMPUR/SINGAPORE

STATIONS		ER. 1	ER. 1	XSP. 3	B. 59	XSP. 7	SM. 61	B. 53	XSP. 55	XSP. 5	M. 57
Butterworth	d.	*06.45		*07.45		*14.45		*20.35	*22.00		
Bt Mertajam	a.	*06.59		*07.59		*14.59		*21.06	*22.17		
Ipoh.	a.	*09.45		*10.44		*17.47		*00.45	*01.56		
Tapah Road	a.	*10.36		‖		*18.38		*02.09	*03.24		
Kuala Lumpur	a.	*13.10	*14.10		*21.15		*05.30	*06.40			
Seremban	a.		*13.30		*20 20		*22.00			*07.30	*08.30
Segamat	a.		*14.49	*21.58		*23 25				*08.41	*09.57
	a.		*16.47	*01.16		*02.30				*10.39	*11.30
Johor Baharu	a.		*19.32	*04.57		*05.40				*13.23	*14.56
Singapore	a		*20.15	*06.55		*06.40				*14.05	*17.50

STATIONS		ER. 2	ER. 2	XSP. 6	M. 58	B. 54	SM. 56	B. 60	SM. 62	XSP. 4	M. 52
Singapore	d.	*06 45		*07.45	*08.30				*20 25	*22.00	
Johor Baharu	d	*07 13		*08.13	*09.03				*20 57	*22.33	
Segamat	a	*09 44		*10.55	*12.48				*00.54	*02.17	
Seremban	a	*11.52		*12.58	*15.39				*04.24	*05.21	
Kuala Lumpur	a	*13.15		*14.20	*17.35				*06.15	*06.55	
	d		*13.40			*20.25	*22.00				*07.35	*08.20
Tapah Road	a		*16.14			*23.39	*01.00				*09.47	*11.22
Ipoh	a		*17.10			*00.55	*02.15				*10.47	*12.52
Bt. Mertajam	a		*20.05			*05.02	*06.04				*13.35	*16.52
Butterworth	a			20 25			*05.30	*06.40			*13.55	*17.20

Burmese statistics proudly speak of 3685 km of railway tracks running through the country (676,552 km[2] in area). There are 22,317 km of roads (officially called highways) and 9201 km of navigable rivers. These figures may be correct as such, but generally the Burmese infrastructure is in a pretty bad state. In no way does it equal or can it be compared with that of Thailand. Economically, this creates many problems, which the government plans to tackle in the near future. Modernization on the 664-km connecting road between Rangoon and Mandalay have almost been completed. New diesel locomotive engines and heavy-duty Toyota trucks have been bought. The railway is introducing new passenger carriages. As the railway tracks are ancient and out-of-date, however, a modern train still needs 13 hours to get from Rangoon to Mandalay.

RAILWAY SYSTEM

The **Thai railway** system is a reliable and safe form of transportation. It is the most suitable for travelling long distances within the country. The first (only

FARES

FROM BANGKOK TO		SINGLE		
Stations	kms.	1st	2nd	3rd
Nakhon Pathom	64	54	28	14
Kanchanaburi	133	111	57	28
River Khwae Bridge	136	115	59	29
Nam Tok	210	168	85	41
Ratchaburi	117	99	52	25
Phetchaburi	167	138	71	34
Hua Hin	229	182	92	44
Prachuap Khiri Khan	318	245	122	58
Chumphon	485	356	172	82
Surat Thani	651	470	224	107
Thung Song	773	550	261	124
Trang	845	597	282	135
Nakhon Si Thammarat	832	590	279	133
Phatthalung	862	611	288	137
Hat Yai	945	664	313	149
Yala	1.055	738	346	165
Sungai Kolok	1.159	808	378	180
Padang Besar	990	694	326	156
Butterworth	1.149	927	431	222
Kuala Lumpur	1.531	1432	659	361
Singapore	1.927	1965	899	512

SUPPLEMENTARY CHARGES

International Express, Express train charge		Baht	30.00	per person
Rapid train charge		Baht	20.00	per person
Air-conditioned 2 nd class coach charge		Baht	40.00	per person
Sleeping berth charges				
1 st class berth air-conditioned	single cabin	Baht	320.00	per person
	double cabin	Baht	210.00	per person
1 st class berth non air-conditioned	double cabin	Baht	130.00	per person
2 nd class berth air-conditioned	Upper	Baht	150.00	per person
	Lower	Baht	180.00	per person
2 nd class berth	Upper	Baht	70.00	per person
	Lower	Baht	100.00	per person
Between Butterworth-Kuala Lumpur, Kuala Lumpur-Singapore				
1 st class berth air-conditioned cabin		M $	20.00	per person
1 st class berth non air conditioned	double cabin	M $	10.00	per person
2 nd class berth	Upper	M $	6.00	per person
	Lower	M $	8.00	per person

ALL TRAINS RUN DAILY

NOTES

EXP		Express train
RAP		Rapid train
ORD		Ordinary train
DRC		Diesel Railcar
SM		Night Express
XSP		Day Express
ER		Express Rayat
M		Mail train
B		Ordinary train
🛏		Sleeping car accommodation
Ⓐ		Air-conditioned first class day coach
Ⓒ		Air-conditioned second class day coach
123		Classes
🏛		Frontier station
· · ·		Train on main line
		No stop
✳		Malaysian time

SPECIAL TRIP TO KOH SAMUI

The State Railway of Thailand has arranged a special trip to Koh Samui by train. The ticket will include train, bus and express ferry boats fares.

By rapid train "Bangkok - Trang" leave Bangkok 6.30p.m. arrival Surat Thani 5.59 a.m. the next day, bus transfer to Donsak and by express ferry boats at 8.30 a.m. arrival Koh Samui 10.30 a.m.

Return trip Koh Samui leave 12 noon, arrival Donsak 2.00 p.m. Special bus transfer to Surat Thani railway station. Departure of train to Bangkok 6.20 p.m. arrival Bangkok 5.50 a.m. the next day.

3rd Class fare B 180/person
2nd Class fare B 299/person
Beds are provided: upper bed B 70 and lower bed B 100 extra.

For more informations please contact
Information
within Bangkok Railway Station Tel: 2237010, 2237020

Subject to alteration without notice.
Please check train times
before you travel at the nearest
stationmaster Information.
(in Bangkok Station)
Tels. 2237010, 2237020

found in Express trains) and second classes resemble a mobile hotel. At 20:00 h the beds are folded out, each adorned with fresh, white linen and set off from the others by a curtain. There are plenty of washrooms aboard - all clean - and there are even showers in the lavatories. The food in the dining car is good and reasonably priced. The same goes for drinks. Seeing as there isn't as much room, however (reservations are necessary), they will also serve you a meal in your own compartment. For this, a small, portable table will be brought directly to your seat. If you feel like eating Tom Yam, though, you might be better off having the hot, sloshing soup served to you in the dining car. First-class compartments are air-conditioned, as are some in the first and part of the second class. A simple fan is just as efficient, though. We would recommend booking the slightly more expensive lower second class bunks, as here you will not have a fan rotating directly over your head. In addition, there is more room here. You'll have to sleep on the floor in third class.

Unfortunately, trains are not too fast and pretty expensive by Thai standards.

NORTHEASTERN LINE.....
BANGKOK-UBON RATCHATHANI NONG KHAI

STATIONS		RAP. 31	ORD. 61	ORD. 63	RAP. 39	EXP. 1	ORD. 65	RAP. 33	DRC. 211	RAP. 29	EXP. 3
		2-3	2-3	2-3	2-3	1-2-3	2-3	2-3	3	2-3	1-2-3
Bangkok	d.	06.50	07.15	15.25	18.45	21.00	23.20	06.30	09.05	19.00	20.30
Don Muang	d.	07.32	07.58	16.08	19.22	21.38	24.00	07.11	09.45	19.37	21.08
Ayutthaya	d.	08.14	08.49	16.52	20.03	22.22	00.46	07.51	10.23	20.18	21.52
Ban Phachi	d.	08.34	09.13	17.14	20.25	||	01.09	08.11	10.42	20.40	||
Saraburi	d.	08.58	09.43	17.48	20.49	23.02	01.40	08.33	11.12	21.04	22.31
Kaeng Khoi Jn.	d.	09.14	10.00	18.03	||	||	01.55	08.47	11.30	21.19	||
Muak Lek	d.	09.50	11.03	18.48	||	||	03.15	||	12.08	||	||
Pak Chong	d.	10.23	11.42	19.26	22.11	00.31	04.04	||	12.46	22.30	23.57
Nakhon Ratchasima	d.	11.46	13.41	21.08	23.33	01.51	05.56	||	14.35	23.57	01.21
Thanon Chira Jn.	d.	11.52	13.47	21.19	23.39	||	06.03	||	||	00.04	||
Lam Plai Mat	r.	13.13	15.17	23.12	00.56	||	07.42				
Buri Ram	d.	13.41	15.49	23.43	01.22	03.27	08.15				
Surin	d.	14.29	16.42	00.31	02.06	04.06	09.21				
Sikhoraphum	d.	15.00	17.22	01.09	02.38	||	10.01				
Si Sa Ket	d.	16.00	18.44	02.27	03.40	05.32	11.18				
Ubon Ratchathani	a.	17.00	20.15	03.35	04.40	06.30	12.30				
Bua Yai Jn.	a.								12.43	01.26	02.31
Ban Prai	a.								13.48	02.26	03.24
Khon Kaen	a.								14.26	03.04	04.02
Udon Thani	a.								16.19	04.53	05.45
Nong Khai	a.								17.10	05.45	06.35

STATIONS		ORD. 64	RAP. 40	EXP. 2	ORD. 66	RAP. 32	ORD. 62	RAP. 30	EXP. 4	RAP. 34	DRC. 214
		2-3	2-3	1-2-3	2-3	2-3	2-3	2-3	1-2-3	2-3	3
Nong Khai	d.							18.05	19.10	06.40	
Udon Thani	d.							18.57	20.00	07.31	
Khon Kaen	d.							20.55	21.42	09.29	
Ban Phai	d.							21.34	22.21	10.07	
Bua Yai Jn.	d.							22.34	23.15	11.13	
Ubon Ratchathani	d.	15.20	18.20	19.35	23.20	06.35	07.00				
Si Sa Ket	d.	16.33	19.26	20.36	00.28	07.30	08.12				
Sikhoraphum	d.	17.47	20.29	||	01.32	08.30	09.22				
Surin	d.	18.26	21.08	22.05	02.10	08.59	10.11				
Buri Ram	d.	19.17	21.53	22.43	02.59	09.51	11.01				
Lam Plai Mat	d.	19.51	22.21	||	03.46	10.21	11.35				
Thanon Chira Jn.	d.	21.18	23.40	||	05.17	11.33	13.08	23.49	||		
Nakhon Ratchasima	d.	21.29	23.50	00.26	05.32	11.43	13.18	00.04	00.40		15.25
Pak Chong	d.	23.20	01.16	01.59	07.32	13.05	15.09	01.37	02.15		17.10
Muak Lek	d.	00.19	||	||	08.09	13.36	15.45	||	||		17.45
Kaeng Khoi Jn.	d.	01.03	||	||	08.53	14.11	16.28	||	||		18.28
Saraburi	a.	01.15	02.33	03.16	09.14	14.23	16.40	02.52	03.32	15.30	18.41
Ban Phachi	a.	01.51	02.57	||	09.58	14.46	17.11	03.16	||	15.52	19.11
Ayutthaya	a.	02.14	03.20	03.57	10.26	15.07	17.32	03.47	04.15	16.13	19.13
Don Muang	a.	03.02	04.02	04.38	11.20	15.48	18.16	04.28	04.57	16.58	20.12
Bangkok	a.	03.45	04.40	05.15	12.05	16.30	19.00	05.05	05.35	17.40	20.50

RAILCAR SPECIAL

BANGKOK - PHITSANULOK

DRC. SPC. 901	DRC. SPC. 903	DRC. SPC. 905	STATIONS		DRC. SPC. 906	DRC. SPC. 902	DRC. SPC. 904
11.05	17.05	23.05	d. Bangkok	a.	04.45	13.45	22.10
11.16	17.15	23.16	d. Sam Sen	a.	04.35	13.34	22.00
11.38	17.38	23.38	d. Don Muang	a.	04.12	13.12	21.38
14.22	20.19	02.45	a. Nakhon Sawan	d.	01.06	10.30	18.45
15.34	21.31	04.10	a. Phichit	d.	23.38	09.16	17.29
16.05	22.02	04.45	s. Phitsanulok	d.	23.00	08.45	17.00

BANGKOK - SURIN

DRC. SPC. 931	DRC. SPC. 933	STATIONS		DRC. SPC. 932	DRC. SPC. 934
10.55	21.50	d. Bangkok	a.	04.05	14.30
11.05	22.01	d. Sam Sen	a.	03.54	14.19
11.27	22.24	d. Don Muang	a.	03.29	13.57
14.54	02.28	a. Nakhon Ratchasima	d.	22.58	10.20
16.32	04.08	a. Buri Ram	d.	21.18	08.36
17.10	04.50	a. Surin	d.	20.40	08.00

BANGKOK - UDON THANI

DRC. SPC. 934	DRC. SPC. 945	DRC. SPC. 947	STATIONS		DRC. SPC. 946	DRC. SPC. 948
04.05	08.20	22.30	d. Bangkok	a.	17.00	06.00
03.54	08.30	22.41	d. Sam Sen	a.	16.50	05.50
03.29	08.52	23.03	d. Don Muang	a.	16.29	05.28
22.58	12.25	02.55	a. Nakhon Ratchasima	d.	13.01	02.00
21.18	15.17	05.30	a. Khon Kaen	d.	10.07	23.00

These days, the railway system is fighting a losing battle against private bus companies. An example: Driving from Bangkok to Chiang Mai in an air-conditioned bus will cost you 250 Baht and will take about 9 hours. A second class ticket for the express train costs 255 Baht plus 70-100 Baht extra charge for a sleeping compartment (non ac) and another 20-30 Baht additional charge for express trains. The train journey takes 13 1/2 hours. You often have to book in advance, especially for night trains, as these are frequently fully booked. The main advantage of the railway is the comfort it offers.

Children less than 1.50 m tall and between the age of three and twelve only have to pay half fare. Children below 3 years of age who are shorter than 1 m and do not need a seat of their own ride for free. Tickets can be bought up to 90 days in advance. Return tickets are valid for the same day only for up to 100 km, for 3 days for up to 200 km, 7 days up to 500 km, and 20 days for more than 500 km.

NORTHERN LINE...　　　　　　　　　　　　　　　　　　**BANGKOK-CHIANG MAI**

STATIONS	RAP. 59	ORD. 101	OKD. 91	RAP. 37	EXP. 7	ORD. 93	ORD. 97	RAP. 35
	2-3	2-3	2-3	2-3	1-2-3	2-3	2-3	2-3
Bangkok d.	06.40	07.05	08.30	15.45	18.00	20.00		22.00
Don Muang a.	07.20	07.47	09.09	16.21	18.36	20.42		22.39
Bang Pa-in d.	||	08.20	09.49	||	||	21.18		
Ayutthaya d.	08.02	08.34	10.04	17.03	19.23	21.31		23.21
Ban Phachi d.	08.27	08.55	10.32	17.25	||	21.53		|| -
Lop Buri d.	09.10	09.46	11.33	18.09	20.26	22.42		00.23
Ban Takhli d.	10.14	10.54	12.58	19.08	21.20	23.52		01.16
Nakhon Sawan d.	11.11	11.56	14.02	20.03	22.07	01.08		02.25
Taphan Hin d.	12.20	13.23	15.50	21.31	23.08	03.10		03.31
Phichit d.	12.53	04.02	16.23	21.57	23.37	03.40		03.57
Phitsanulok d.	13.32	14.48	17.15	22.35	00.14	04.23		04.32
	13.34	14.53		22.38	00.19		06.00	04.34
Uttaradit d.	15.09	16.45		00.26	01.45		07.55	06.09
Sila At d.	15.14	16.58		00.42	02.01		08.05	06.18
DenChai d.	16.10	18.12		01.42	02.59		09.19	07.15
				01.46	03.04		09.22	
Mae Mo a.				03.32	||		11.14	
Nakhon Lampang a.				04.14	05.21		12.00	
Khun Tan a.				05.19	06.22			
Lamphun a.				06.12	07.16			
Chiang Mai a.				06.35	07.40			

STATIONS	ORD. 98	ORD. 94	RAP. 60	RAP. 38	EXP. 8	ORD. 92	ORD. 102	RAP. 36
	2-3	2-3	2-3	2-3	1-2-3	2-3	2-3	2-3
Chiang Mai d.				15.20	16.50			
Lamphun d.				15.44	17.15			
Khun Tan d.				16.38	18.09			
Nakhon Lampang d.		12.25		17.38	19.10			
Mae Mo d.		13.14		18.20	||			
Den Chai d.		15.03		19.58	21.28			
		15.05	18.45	20.05	21.32		06.00	09.00
Sila At d.		16.14	19.51	21.13	22.40		07.16	10.06
Uttaradit d.		16.18	19.56	21.19	22.46		07.20	10.11
Phitsanulok a.	18.10						09.11	11.45
		19.35	21.36	23.08	00.15	08.05	09.14	11.47
Phichit d.		20.18	22.31	23.55	00.53	06.53	09.56	12.26
Taphan Hin d.		20.50	23.08	00.23	01.22	07.30	10.26	12.51
Nakhon Sawan d.		22.56	00.16	01.30	02.24	09.01	11.57	14.01
Ban Takhli d.		23.51	01.01	02.26	03.11	10.01	12.59	14.55
Lop Buri d.		01.06	02.05	03.24	04.05	11.35	14.15	15.48
Ban Phachi d.		02.06	02.50	04.05	||	13.13	15.14	16.29
Ayutthaya d.		02.27	03.10	04.26	05.05	13.42	15.40	16.49
Bang Pa-in d.		02.41	||	||	13.58	15.53	||
Don Muang a.		03.13	03.50	05.07	05.48	14.36	16.44	17.33
Bangkok a.		03.55	04.27	05.45	06.25	15.20	17.25	18.10

EASTERN LINE.....
BANGKOK-ARANYAPRATHET

STATIONS	DRC. 109	DRC. 151	DRC. 203	DRC. 183	MIX. 251	DRC. 187	DRC. 185	DRC. 181
	3	3	3	3	3	3	3	3
Bangkok d.	06.00	07.00	08.05	09.40	11.25	13.10	14.55	17.25
Makkasan d.	06.14	07.15	08.17	09.53	11.50	13.25	15.09	17.41
Hua Mak d.	06.26	07.31	08.29	10.10	12.07	13.42	15.22	17.59
Hua Takhe d.	07.02	07.54	08.53	10.36	12.35	14.06	15.45	18.28
Chachoengsao a.	07.46	08.30	09.33	11.16	13.23	14.46	16.20	19.03
Prachin Buri a.	08.53		10.46	12.30	15.05	15.57	17.48	20.15
Prachantakham a.	09.13		11.05		15.37	16.18	18.08	
Kabin Buri a.	09.41		11.30		16.20	16.46	18.35	
Aranyaprathet a.	11.20				18.30			

STATIONS	DRC. 182	MIX. 252	DRC. 186	DRC. 188	DRC. 154	DRC. 204	DRC. 184	DRC. 110
	3	3	3	3	3	3	3	3
Aranyaprathet d.			06.20					13.30
Kabin Buri d.		05.05	07.00	08.11		12.30		15.13
Prachantakham d.		05.41	07.28	08.39		12.54		15.42
Prachin Buri d.	05.15	06.08	07.47	09.02		13.12	14.10	16.05
Chachoengsao a.	06.24	07.42	09.10	10.22	12.40	14.23	15.28	17.17
Hua Takhe d.	07.03	08.55	09.47	10.59	13.20	14.57	16.06	17.54
Hua Mak d.	07.30	09.27	10.08	11.25	13.41	15.23	16.29	18.16
Makkasan d.	07.41	09.45	10.18	11.36	13.52	15.35	16.41	18.27
Bangkok a.	07.55	10.05	10.30	11.50	14.05	15.50	16.55	18.40

A train bound for Malaysia leaves Bangkok daily (additional charge 30 Baht). Some of the trains bound for the northeast and the south and all trains headed for Nam Tok (River Kwai) and Aranyaprathet (east) only have third-class compartments. Always keep an eye on your luggage and hang on to your shoulder bags. Theft is not unheard of on these trains. Sitting in the back row may be a good idea, as this way at least no one will be able to rob you from behind. Be careful when purchasing train tickets from travel agencies; seats have often been reserved which later turned out to be non-existent. For this reason you'd be better off buying your ticket at the railway station.

All trains go from and to the capital.

NORTHERN LINE: Ayutthaya (72 km), Lopburi (133 km), Phitsanulok (389 km), Lampang (642 km), Chiang Mai (751 km).

NORTHEASTERN LINE: Korat (264 km), Surin (420 km), Ubon (575 km), Khon Kaen (450 km), Udon (569 km), Nong Khai (624 km).

NORTHERN LINE....

FROM BANGKOK TO		SINGLE		
Stations	Kms.	1st	2nd	3rd
Don Muang	22	18	10	5
Bang Pa-in	58	49	26	12
Ayutthaya	71	60	31	15
Lop Buri	133	111	57	28
Ban Takhli	193	157	80	39
Nakhon Sawan	246	197	99	48
Taphan Hin	319	245	122	58
Phichit	347	266	131	63
Phitsanulok	389	292	143	69
Uttaradit	485	356	172	82
Sila At	488	359	174	83
Den Chai	534	389	188	90
Mae Mo	609	440	211	100
Nakhon Lampang	642	463	221	106
Khun Tan	683	490	233	111
Lamphun	729	520	247	118
Chang Mai	751	537	255	121

FROM BANGKOK TO		SINGLE
Stations	Kms.	3rd
Hua Takhe	31	7
Chachoengsao	61	13
Prachin Buri	122	26
Kabin Buri	161	33
Aranyaprathet	255	48

FROM BANGKOK TO		SINGLE		
Stations	Kms.	1st	2nd	3rd
Muak Lek	152	126	65	31
Pak Chong	180	146	74	36
Nakhon Ratchasima	264	207	104	50
Surin	420	312	153	73
Si Sa Ket	515	376	182	87
Ubon Ratchathani	575	416	200	95
Bua Yai	346	266	131	63
Ban Phai	408	306	150	71
Khon Kaen	450	333	162	77
Udon Thani	569	413	198	95
Nong Khai	624	450	215	103

Advance booking: Tickets of all classes may be purchased 90 days in advance at principal stations during the time advertised at each station and at the Advance Booking Office (in Bangkok Station) where the tickets To and From any station by all trains are obtainable during 8.30 a.m. to 6.00 p.m. on weekdays and 8.30 a.m. to 12.00 a.m. on Saturdays, Sundays and Official Holidays.

Reservation from abroad may be made by letter enclosing bank draft to cover the amount of fares and charges, allowing ample time for a reply. TELEX 7242 SRTBKK TH

Availability of ticket: Tickets are valid on the date and train as specified on the tickets only.

Change of Journeys: Passengers may change their journey to a later or earlier train or date. This is allowed twice but in case of postponement the total number of days must not exceed seven. Fee of Baht 2, 5, 10, 20 or 40 is payable if tickets is reserved or unreserved.

Refund on tickets: Passengers who have perchased ticket and are unable to use them may apply for refund of the cost of tickets to the stationmaster at the station where the ticket were obtained not later than 3 hrs. after the departure time of the train by which they intended to travel refund fees vary from 10-40% of ticket value but not more than Baht 300- for through ticket to Malaysia and Singapore not more than Baht 320.- (per ticket.) N.B. Fees vary according to the time of notification.

Children's fares: Children of over 3 years to 12 years and whose height do not exceed 150 cms. are accepted at half adult fares. Children of 3 years or under who are less than 100 cms. in height are conveyed free providing separate seats are not required for them.

Break of Journey: Passengers holding tickets for distances of 200 kms. (one way) and over are allowed to break their journey once at any intermediate station for a period of not more than 2 days reckoning from the day after the journey is broken. Tickets must be endorsed by stationmaster and fee of Baht 1.- paid at the alighting station immediately upon arrival of the train. For a return ticket, a break of journey is allowed each way.

Validity of return tickets:
All classes

return on the same day for distance	1 - 100 kms.
3 days for distances	101 - 200 kms.
7 days for distances	201 - 500 kms.
20 days for distances	501 kms. and over.

Supplementary charges: All supplementary charges are good for one unbroken journey and with one passenger ticket only. When using another passenger ticket for the same journey, changing train or breaking journey, such charges are to be paid again.

Luggage allowance: Passenger are allowed to carry personal luggage free of charge as follows: 1st class 50 kgs., 2nd class 40 kgs. 3rd class 30 kgs. Children paying half fares are allowed half the weight allowed for adult according to class of ticket.

EASTERN LINE: Prachinburi (122 km), Aranyaprathet (255 km).

SOUTHERN LINE: Nakhon Pathom (64 km), Kanchanaburi (133 km), Hua Hin (229 km), Surat Thani (651 km), Haad Yai (945 km), Sungai Golok (1159 km).

In **Burma,** trains are still the most important means of transportation. The only line of interest for tourists is the Rangoon-Mandalay line, which runs past Thazi, from where there are lines to Shwenyaung (Taunggyi) and Myingyan. All other railway lines are closed to tourists. Tickets for tourists are sold exclusively by Tourist Burma. We would recommend getting a ticket at least a day in advance.

In January and July 1985 the Rangoon-Mandalay Express was bombed. It is suspected that Karen guerrillas were responsible. 67 people died and 112 were injured. The same happened again in January 1988.

BUSES

Ever since the 60s, **Thailand** has been putting much work into its road network. Financial aid (primarily coming from the United States) enabled them to modernize the big highways in the north and northeast. Strategically, this had a lot to do with the Vietnam war. You can reach just about every Thai city by non-air-conditioned buses. Air-conditioned buses commute between most of the major cities. Food and drink as well as entertainment in the form of videos are available. Whether you will enjoy the movies shown - mostly loud, violent B-movies in Thai - is another question, especially at night. Ignoring them is virtually impossible. Another problem is the air-conditioning, which is always turned on full blast. Take along a sweater or a jacket, especially for the chilly nights. Otherwise you might end up catching a cold in spite of the tropical climate.

Some not-quite-so-pleasant things you should know: Before a bus leaves, the entire crew and passengers are often filmed with a video-camera. This way, the company knows who was on board, should passengers end up being drugged and robbed during the course of the journey. Armed soldiers often accompany buses that are driving through dangerous areas.

Thai busdrivers frequently drive as if their life depended on it. Driving at a speed of 120 km/h is not rare, nor are risky overtaking manoeuvres. Drivers are especially ambitious when it comes to overtaking buses of competing companies, all of which leave the terminals at the same time. All the same, accidents do not occur too frequently. When they do, however, they are usually pretty serious. Here is an incident that made the international press: Three young German tourists were travelling from Chiang Mai to Chiang Rai in an air-conditioned bus. On the way, a totally drunk Thai boarded the bus. A short while later this individual had taken over the wheel. The young Germans tried desperately to get the drunk to stop. He finally did so at a police-station. The sole reaction of the local, English-speaking cop, however, was: "Never mind, don't worry!" Shortly afterwards the bus smashed through the guard rail and hurtled down a slope. Six people died, among them one of the three Germans, a 20-year old girl.

There is only one thing to do if you should find yourself in a bus with a driver who is either too drunk or sleepy to drive - do not try to convince other passengers of the possible danger, they will probably ignore you. GET OUT!

Ancient buses, WW II jeeps, trucks, and rather more up-to-date Japanese pickups are the most common forms of transportation on *Burma's* roads. During the last few years small Mazdas fabricated in Burma have also become popular, especially in the Greater Rangoon area. No matter how new, though, all Burmese vehicles have the following things in common - they are slow, in constant need of repair, and usually overloaded. The roads they travel on are generally in a terrible state. 12 hours for 350 km is not at all unusual.

FLYING
Thai Airways offers many inland flights. In addition, the company flies to Vientiane, Hanoi, Singapore, and Penang. If you have little time but a lot of money, you might want to try them. When flying within the country, passengers have to pay an airport tax of 20 Baht, for international flights the tax is 120 Baht. Inland tickets are valid for 90 days. When flying from the south to the north (or vice versa) via Bangkok, you will receive a discount of 20%. Flying in so-called "Shorts" (small aircraft that seat 30 - 36 passengers) is an incredible experience. These aircraft rarely exceed an altitude of 10,000 feet, and the view on a clear day is truly amazing. They only fly routes covering small distances, though (e.g. Chiang Mai to Mae Hongson, Phrae, Nan, Lampang, or Chiang Rai). Still, it is often worth paying the extra fare. Chiang Mai - Mae Hongson will cost you 300 Baht (35 minutes). The air-conditioned bus only costs 148 Baht, but it takes 9 hours to get there. Decide for yourself which you would prefer. Thai Airways has now a shuttle service at almost every airport in the country. The cost is usually between 30 and 40 Baht. This way you can avoid the expensive taxi fares.

A new, private airline, *Bangkok Airways* (BA), now flies from Bangkok to Korat and Surin. The airline plans to start flying to Ko Samui and Krabi in 1988.

While flying in *Burma* is definitely more expensive than travelling by land, it can save a lot of time. Getting a seat on a *BAC* flight (Burma Airways Corporation) is not easy, though. All tickets have to be booked through Tourist Burma. The airline flies Fokker F27s and F28s.

BOATS
Boat rides are available up and down the entire length of the Irrawaddy and through the whole delta area. A trip from Rangoon to Mandalay would no doubt be a wonderful experience, but it would take weeks. The only connec-

tion of any significance to tourists is the one from Mandalay to Pagan. As long as they don't run aground, the ancient steamboats need between 14 and 24 hours for the journey.

MOTORBIKES & BICYCLES
Sun-bronzed Farangs limping across the road with one arm in a cast are no rare sight in Phuket, Ko Samui, or Chiang Mai; they probably belong to the large group of people involved in some sort of motorcycle accident. These, unfortunately, occur all the time. As most people drive around in shorts and T-shirts because of their sun tan and see no need to wear helmets, gloves or glasses, even minor accidents can be the cause of serious grazes and other unpleasant injuries. The tropical climate is no great help to the healing process.

One can also rent bicycles in most tourist centres. Look up the towns in question for more details.

PLANNING AN 8-DAY TRIP TO BURMA
It is important to have put some thought into your trip to Burma before actually landing in Rangoon. Always draw up a couple of alternative plans, too, as it is sometimes impossible to book flights to where you want to go. Even trains can be a problem. The following suggested route is the usual one, the one that about 80% of tourists visiting Burma take:

1st day:	*Arrival Rangoon, buy a train ticket, go sightseeing.*
2nd day (or night):	*Trainride to Mandalay.*
3rd day:	*Sightseeing in Mandalay or excursions.*
4th day:	*Bus or boat-trip to Pagan.*
5th day:	*Sightseeing in Pagan.*
6th day:	*Return to Rangoon or go sightseeing to Lake Inle.*
7th day:	*Return to Rangoon or sightseeing in Rangoon.*
8th day:	*Departure from Rangoon.*

Usually, a whole group of people will be doing this trip at the same time. This means that you will be seeing the same faces, riding on the same trains, buses and boats for eight days. If you wish to avoid this, you can try reversing the whole trip, starting from the end. You can save a little time if you fly part of the way. We would recommend flying from Rangoon to Pagan (or the other way around). Even if your departure from Rangoon is set for the late afternoon of the eighth day, you should try to be there well in advance, possibly a full day. Delays of several hours are common in Burma, and if you miss your flight back to Thailand you'll find yourself in a lot of trouble.

You don't have to go on our suggested trip, of course. There are endless possibilities. Once, we spent four full days in the Greater Mandalay area. During our next visit we spent four days in the Taunggyi/Lake Inle area, and after that spent the rest of our time in Pagan. If you decide to do this, you'll be able to spend the night in Kalaw or Maymyo, something hardly anyone ever does. Staying in Pagan is another possibility, of course; the fascinating temples of the former metropolis should be of interest to everyone, not just amateur archeologists.

RENTING CARS

It takes a driver experienced in Asian traffic to actually rent a car and venture out onto the Thai roads. True, the country does have the same basic rules of traffic as all other countries, but no one pays even the slightest attention to them. And the chaos of Bangkok is only the beginning! In the countryside, large vehicles such as buses or trucks always have the right of way. Often, water-buffaloes, pigs, chickens and ducks are treated in the same respectful manner. The official speed limit on the highways is 90 km/h. While it is certainly good that many signs have both Roman and Thai script, we would recommend buying a map with both the Thai and Roman versions, all the same. We would recommend *The Latest Thailand Highway Map,* published by DK Book House in cooperation with the Roads Association of Thailand, a 44-page atlas with numerous detailed maps of towns.

Rental cars are reasonably priced and reliable in Bangkok, where competition is stiffest. In Chiang Mai, in contrast, the cars available at the local car-rentals are usually old and sometimes even dangerous. In the tourist centres outside of Bangkok you can rent jeeps (about 500 Baht a day), pickups (suitable for small groups of up to ten people, approx. 500 Baht a day), and of course motorcycles (200 Baht a day). A litre of regular petrol costs approximately 12 Baht at the large petrol stations in the less isolated areas. If you're somewhere up in the mountains or in the middle of nowhere, of course, the price will rise accordingly.

Before renting a car you should always take it for a trial ride. Never pay the full amount in advance; leave a deposit, instead. This way you'll not be left holding the baby, should the car break down on you. Four-seaters are often uninsured, but international companies usually offer a cheap insurance for the duration of time that you will be driving around. Reckon with about 600 Baht rent per day for a regular four-seater (Honda Civic etc.). Always bargain, even with the large companies, especially if you're planning to rent the car for a longer period of time. You'll be surprised how much they may reduce the price.

A few addresses of car-rental companies in Thailand:

*AVIS,*10/1 North Sathorn, tel 2330397. Also in Phuket and Chiang Mai.
HERTZ, 987 Ploenchit Road, tel 2524903 Also in Chiang Mai and Phuket.
*KLONG TOEY CAR RENT,*1921 Rama IV Road, tel 2519856.
*KING CAR RENT,*18/1 North Sathorn, tel 2337907.
*ROYAL CAR RENT,*2-7 Soi 20,Sukhumvit Road, tel 2581411
BANGKOK CAR RENT, 57/13 Wireless Road, tel 2526428
INTER CAR RENT, 45 Sukhumvit Road, Soi 3, tel 2514910.

ACCOMMODATION

THAILAND

You will always be able to find a hotel in the large cities. Everything from cheap dumps to international luxury is available. In small towns hotel signs are frequently only written in Thai. Cheap and mid-price hotels often turn out to be brothels. Sooner or later every male tourist travelling alone will come to realize this. In the countryside, there is often no alternative to these loud, hectic, and somewhat sleazy institutions. Usually, there is enough room for two people in a single room (or four in a double room). The prices in the provinces are very reasonable, and you will usually get more than your money's worth. A room with a private bathroom or shower and a fan will usually cost 100-150 Baht. The rooms are usually quite clean.

There are luxury hotels of international standard in Bangkok, Chiang Mai, Pattaya, and Phuket. The Oriental Hotel in Bangkok, for instance, is considered one of the world's top five hotels. A room here could easily cost you up to £1000, though.

In places where travellers meet, there is always a fair amount of cheap accommodation. The beach huts of Ko Samui and Ko Samet and the guesthouses of Chiang Mai and Bangkok are generally rather sparsely furnished but are cheaper than even the most reasonably priced Thai hotels. Huts are usually furnished with a thin mattress, a lamp, and (most important of all!) a mosquito net. Beach hut colonies usually have a generator as the source of electricity, and for this reason the lights are often turned off at 10 pm. You'll definitely need a torch in order to go to the toilets after dark! While these huts can easily make one feel like a modern-day Robinson Crusoe with a little effort, one has virtually no privacy at all when staying at a guesthouse. All the same, these have their share of advantages, too; employees offer plenty of tea and coffee, and sometimes even breakfast. If no breakfast is served, you will usually find that there is a small restaurant serving tourist food right next door. In addition, the managers of these institutions - usually quite young - are always willing to give you tips or help sort out a problem. There is no way to avoid being taken advantage of every now and then by a poor Thai, but if something is stolen it could just as easily have been one of your fellow travellers. Take special care in the dormitories. Your own padlock and a locked backpack are always a good idea.

When in one of the many National Parks, you can stay at a bungalow or another of the many state-run guest-houses. Sometimes this can turn into quite an adventure, for you as well as the local inhabitants, especially in the more remote areas; here, your food will be cooked and served to you by local families - without a menu or a translator! The rooms are usually comfortable and clean, but unfortunately rather expensive. (Reckon with at least 200 Baht, sometimes as much as 1000 Baht!) The main advantage of these bungalows is that they are big enough for ten people, something which is not at all unusual, seeing as Thais often travel in large groups. Male tourists travelling on their own often have the additional advantage of being able to sleep in a tent or in the Ranger's house for a couple of Baht.

Men can also spend the night at monasteries - but remember, a monastery is not a hotel; do not outstay your welcome! Women are usually not admitted.

When spending the night in one of the hilltribes' villages (or any other village for that matter), you'll find that people there live on the verge of starvation. For this reason you should be content with sleeping in the porch, and only receiving a simple bowl of rice for dinner. If you insist on more, it might be an idea to bring canned foods along, which you can share with your hosts. Take your shoes off before entering Thai houses, and be careful not to point your bare feet at anyone, as this is considered an insult. Do not expect comfortable sanitary installations. When going for a bathe, take along a large cotton cloth, a 'phasin' or a 'phakama', as you will either have to bathe in a river or pour water over yourself out of a large jug. Even if there is a water-supply, you will never be quite safe from prying eyes and it is considered extremely impolite to expose certain parts of the body.

BURMA

Most hotel rooms in Burma have either to be booked for you by Tourist Burma or to be entered onto your Money Declaration Form. With a little finesse you can easily find out which hotels will give you a room without it having to be registered on this infamous document. This will mean, in effect, that the sum you pay for the night will not be entered onto your Money Declaration Form. You will, in other words, be expected to have a certain amount of surplus Kyat when leaving the country. Where and how you get your hands on this money is your own affair.

On arrival in Rangoon, you will frequently find that most hotel rooms are fully booked. There is not much you can do - try to get through Immigration before the others and take a taxi into town as quickly as possible.

We have decided to give you the following four categories of hotels and the prices to expect for double rooms. If you are travelling alone you will only receive a small discount and sometimes even have to pay the full price.

*	up to	30 Kyat	up to	100 Baht
**	up to	50 Kyat	up to	200 Baht
***	up to	100 Kyat	up to	400 Baht
****	over	100 Kyat	over	400 Baht

FOOD & DRINK

At a first glance Thai food may seem to be just another variety of Chinese food. Once one gets to know it, however, one will soon discover similarities to Malay cooking, as the Thais - like the Malays - frequently cook in coconut milk. The influence of Indian curries is also apparent. Those who have been in the habit of eating Thai food for a long period of time will almost always consider it as belonging to the best food in the world. Generally, Thai food is very spicy. It is not only chilies that dominate its flavour, though; fine blends of fresh vegetables, garlic, lemon grass, coriander seed, curry spices, fish sauce, shrimp paste, tamarind, coconut milk, palm sugar and of course fresh fish, shrimp, crab, crawfish, and much more lie in store for you. Rice *(kao)* is the country's main basic food, and it is served with a variety of side dishes and sauces. Kao is also the general term for 'food', which may give you an idea of how important rice is to this country.

HOW TO EAT?

In Thailand one normally eats with a *spoon* (right hand) and a *fork* (left), whereby the fork is used the way Europeans use a knife, to push the food onto the spoon, with which one then eats. In rural areas one often uses one's hand instead of a spoon. Only the right hand is used for eating, just as in India or Malaysia. The left hand is considered unclean, and should never be used to touch food with. Almost all restaurants have sinks where one can wash one's hands before and after meals. Having to eat Chinese food with *chopsticks* may be a bit trickier at first, but you'll soon get the hang of it. The Chinese will nearly always appreciate your trying to eat with chopsticks, and may sometimes even get a kick out of it.

WHERE TO EAT?

Foodstands are cheapest. A vegetable, fish, or meat soup will only cost you a couple of Baht here. Foodstands can be found in nearly all busy streets, market-places and squares. The food is usually prepared for you while you wait. Drinks will be available at some other stand nearby. Having a meal like this shouldn't be any problem, no matter what time of day or night.

Restaurants do not always have menus. For this reason it is always a good idea to acquire a basic 'restaurant' vocabulary before venturing into one. Sometimes, the food will be sitting there in big pots, and all you'll have to do to order is lift off the lid of each one, make a choice, and point. The food is almost always spicy, and the thousands of little chilies with their preserving properties are also the reason why the food doesn't go bad. Restaurants in tourist-centres and large cities may sometimes have a menu in English, but will nearly always be more expensive.

WHAT TO EAT IN THAILAND?

Apart from the north and northeast of the country, Thailand borders on the open sea. Thus *seafood* is both cheap and tasty. The variety of dishes extends from extremely hot fish curries to lobsters or delicately prepared crab at the seafood-restaurants on the beaches. Here you will often find that there is no menu at all, and even if there is one, prices are hardly ever given. Fresh fish and many other foods are often priced according to their weight. Local guests know the prices. If you don't want to be unpleasantly surprised, it might be an idea to inquire about the prices (usually per 100 grams) beforehand. If you are partial to fish, you'll have a wonderful time.

FOOD
Just about every Thai meal is served with a side dish of *naam plaa prik,* a fish sauce with diced green or red chilies. The smaller the chilies, incidentally, the hotter they are.

There are distinct regional differences. A *speciality of the northeast,* for instance, would be

SOM TAM, a salad made with tomatoes, crushed peanuts, red chilies, papayas, honey, and vinegar. As a side dish you will often receive

KHAO NIEO, sticky rice, which is rolled into small balls and dipped into the salad.

KHAO PAT, fried rice, served with small strips of pork and onions and fried in egg is another cheap meal. Also available in its simpler form *KHAO MUU DAENG.* A side dish of cucumbers in a sweet and sour sauce with chilies will be served.

There are two different types of *noodles: GUE AE TIAO,* white rice-noodles, and *BAMII,* yellowish noodles made out of wheat flour. These, too, are served with various different dishes, mainly *fish and meat:*

MUU	pork	GAI	chicken
NUEA	beef	PED	duck
PLAH	fish	GUNG	prawn
PUU	crab	KUNG	lobster.

There are various degrees of spiciness for *Thai curries:*

GAENG GHAREE is a mild Indian curry, of which the local version is called *GAENG MASMAN. GAENG PET* is a little spicier, and *KHIAU WAAN* is very spicy indeed. These curries are served with a variety of meats and white rice, *KHAO PLAO.*

In Thailand one does not eat *soups* as a starter, but at the same time as all other dishes, as part of the main meal.

KHAO TOM is a rice soup served with different kinds of meat, e.g. with chicken = Kao Tom Gai. The sweet and sour soup *TOM YAM* is delicious and spicy. Try Tom Yam Gang.

KHAI is Thai for *eggs,* not to be mistaken for gai; *KHAI TORD* - fried eggs. *KHAI LUAK / TOM* are soft- / hard-boiled eggs. *KHAI YAD SAI* is a tasty omelette with a meat or vegetable filling.

DRINKS
NAAM, **water,** is available as *NAAM YEN,* cold water, *NAAM KAENG,* ice-water, and *NAAM MANAU,* lemon juice or a fruit-juice made out of a combination of several fresh fruits.

CHA is the word for **tea** used throughout the Orient. *NAAM* (water) *CHA* (tea) *RAWN* (hot) = hot, black tea. *CHA RAWN* is served with milk and sugar, *CHA DAM* only with sugar. Cold tea, *CHA YEN,* is particularly good with lemon, *CHA MANAU.*

GAFAE - is the local form of **coffee,** served with condensed milk, *GAFAE DAM RAWN* without milk. Black, sweet ice-coffee, *GAFAE DAM YEN,* is very refreshing.

The most popular drink - even here - is Coca Cola. Singha, Kloster and Amarit **beer,** are rather more expensive. *MEKHONG WHISKY* is the local alcohol - drug no. 1. It is served at every conceivable occasion, and you may often be invited to drink a glass. Should this be the case, we would recommend diluting it with a little water. The drink tastes of cheap brandy and is extremely potent.

FRUITS
Like all tropical countries, Thailand has a wide variety of tropical fruits to choose from. Everyone should have tried a

DURIAN at least once in their lives. This green, spiky fruit is considered the 'Queen of Fruits' and can't be overlooked, even by those who may never have seen one before; the smell is appalling. Have somebody who knows about them choose one for you. Fruits are only available at certain times, the durian for example only from April to June. During this period you'll also be able to buy

SAPAROT - **pineapples,** ready peeled for a couple of Baht, and

MAMUANG - **mango,** eaten either when still green with a spicy sauce, or as a fruit, once it has ripened. The following fruits aren't in season until a short time later:

NGOH - **rambutans,** red, hairy, little fruits,

LAMYAI - **longan,** especially good in Chiang Mai,

MUNG KUT - **mangosteen** (careful - the colour comes off these very easily and is difficult to remove from fabrics), and

KANOON - the **jackfruit.** The following fruits are available all year round:

GLUAI - various kinds of **bananas,** also available as

GLUAI TORD, fried bananas, at markets and train stations.

SOM - is a cross between an orange and a mandarin,

SOM - OH - **pomelos,** giant oranges, and

MALAKAW - **papayas,** which are especially refreshing when eaten with lime for breakfast.

FOOD & DRINK IN BURMA

Burmese cooking is similar to both Indian and Thai cooking. As in Thailand, rice is the basic food, served as the basis for curries and many other dishes.

TYPICAL BURMESE DISHES

SIBYE, **meat curries** which are not quite as spicy as those served in India.

The usual side dish consists of a salad with *THAKUAHDI* **(cucumber),** *KOH BIE JUA* **(cabbage),** and *KHAI JAN CHEDI* **(tomatoes).**

HINCHO, a mild **vegetable soup** based on fish paste. *CHIN HIN* is a **sour soup.** Every eating place serves a side-order of

NGA MPIA JE with it, a **fish sauce** with chilies. They may also serve side dishes of fresh vegetables, such as cucumbers, lettuce, or cabbage.

BALAUCHAUNG is another common side-dish, made with chilies, dried crab, onions, plenty of garlic, and prawn paste. You will frequently also receive bamboo sprouts as a side-dish.

MOHINGA is a **stew** made with noodles, fish, eggs, onions, and fresh corian-der seed. **National noodle dish** no. 1 is

OH NO KHAUKSWE.. One of the many places to get it is at the foodstands around the Mahumuni pagoda in Mandalay.

Small **cafes** at which one can get tea (free of charge if one takes it without sugar) and sweets can be found everywhere. A typical example would be the Shwe Pa Laung in Rangoon's Mahabandoola Road.

There are various **soft-drinks,** usually lemonades, but they are all sweet and lukewarm. If one has once witnessed the way in which ice is made and dis-tributed in Burma one will probably no longer feel any desire for it, though. Western drinks, e.g. chilled Coca Cola, are only available at the Inya Lake Ho-tel. *MANDALAY BEER* is quite expensive but rather good, too.

The favourite local **alcoholic drinks** are palm-wine and rice-liquor. In Ran-goon there are stands that sell nothing but liquor. Beware - the heat will get to even the most hard-boiled of drinkers.

Next to Indian and Chinese food Rangoon's Strand restaurant also serves Eu-ropean food. The only other place where you can expect such a wide variety is Mandalay.

Generally, one should be rather wary of what one eats and drinks in Burma, as the sanitary and hygienic standards of the country aren't all that high. A case of dysentery could easily spoil your entire holiday!

FEASTS & HOLIDAYS

THAILAND

Many Thai holidays are of Buddhist origin and therefore tied to the religious calendar. As the Buddhist era (1987 is the year 2530 after Buddha, 1988 - 2531) is tied to the lunar cycle, the exact dates of the holidays vary by a few days each year. State holidays are set by the western calendar.

NEW YEAR - Actually, New Year is celebrated three times in Bangkok and many other parts of the country: *Occidental New Year* is celebrated on January 1st. The festivities are generally held at international hotels and on the square in front of Bangkok's Royal Palace. The festivities for the *Chinese New Year* (January/February) are for the most part held within the family. You can watch the preparations in busy Chinatown during the last couple of days beforehand. The exact date is fixed according to the first full moon of the year.

Each year is named after one of twelve animals that have been rotating for centuries. 1988, for instance, is the year of the dragon. It is followed by the year of the snake, horse, goat, monkey, cockerel, dog, pig, rat, buffalo, tiger and rabbit. Days before the actual feast, the whole country starts shopping like mad. A week beforehand all houses and apartments are thoroughly cleaned, since the god of the kitchen will file a report on each family in heaven. A particularly sweet and sticky cake made of molasses is baked, so that only sweetness will touch the god's lips. Others say that the cake is so sticky that the god, after having eaten some, will no longer be able to open his mouth in order to report anything negative. The whole family gets together for a huge meal on the evening of the last day of the old year. Children receive small red envelopes with money. Considering the size of the average Chinese family, the New Year festivities can become quite expensive. The 13th, 14th, and sometimes even 15th monthly salary which is paid at this time of year is therefore often more than welcome.

The *Thai New Year,* better known as *SONGKRAN,* is celebrated in mid-April, at a time when the whole country is suffering from the oppressive heat and waiting for the coming of the rains. For the farming population, this marks the beginning of the harvest. During this time you may find yourself being doused with cold water in the middle of the street, even days before the actual festivities begin. This can be a pleasant refreshment as long as one is prepared for it and not in Bangkok. Here, the water poured upon unsuspecting pedestrians is bound to be filthy Klong-water. A procession carries the Buddha-statue out of the National Museum through Thonburi the day before the feast. The population pours perfumed water over the statue on the Sanam Luang. At home, all Buddha statues are cleaned and bathed, too. Homes are cleaned and families pay their respect to their elders by carrying out ceremonial hand-washings and giving them small gifts. Many go on a pilgrimage to

Chiang Mai, where the festivities are especially elaborate.

The Mon of Plakat, 15 km south of Bangkok, begin their celebrations a few days after Songkran. There is a large procession and a local beauty pageant, and young girls bring fish down to the river in order to give them back their freedom.

VISAKHA BUCHA - celebration of the birth and illumination of Buddha, as well as his final entry into nirvana. Lantern parades are held outside all temples in the evening. Believers circle the buildings three times with flowers and candles held between folded hands. Inside the temples, monks preach the teachings of Buddha. A central celebration is held in the Wat Phra Kaeo. The celebration takes place in mid-May.

THE ROYAL PLOUGHING CEREMONY - is held the following month. Astrologers set the exact date. A representative of the King, usually the Minister of Agriculture, carries out a symbolic sowing ceremony on Sanam Luang. Farmers from all over the country come to witness the ceremony, which for them marks the beginning of the sowing season. One grain of rice from the ceremony mixed with one's own seed is said to guarantee a good harvest.

ASANHA BUCHA - celebration in July, held in memory of Buddha's first sermon. Processions with flowers and candles around the Bot.

KHAO PHANSA - the long period of fasting starts the day after Asanha Bucha and lasts for three months, until the rainy season has passed. Monks are not allowed to leave the monasteries at night during this period, and rules generally become stricter. This is the time of year that young men enter into monasteries, and ordination festivities are held everywhere.

THOT KATHIN - the fasting period ends October/November. It is now that people meet in their local temples to bring the monks new robes and offerings.

LOY KRATHONG - the great lantern parade is celebrated in November, after the rainy season has ended. Small boats made of banana peel and adorned with burning candles, incense and flowers are set afloat on the lakes, klongs and rivers, an offering to the goddess of water, Mae Khingkhe.

PHRA BUDDHABAHT - a footprint of Buddha is venerated in the Wat Phra Buddhabaht, between Saraburi and Lopburi. This large temple celebration with dancers and a market is held in February.

MAKHA BUCHA - lantern parade around the temples, held in honour of the speech Buddha made in front of 1250 people.

Further regional temple celebrations are held throughout the year. We would especially recommend the temple celebration in Nakhon Pathom, at Thailand's largest pagoda, and the one at the Golden Mount in Bangkok, both of which are held in November.

STATE HOLIDAYS
April 6th: CHAKRI DAY - enthronement of the first Chakri king and founder of the Royal City of Bangkok, festivities in the Wat Phra Kaeo.

May 5th: CORONATION DAY - Rama IX, the present king, was crowned on May 5th, 1946. Celebration at the Royal Court.

August 12th: THE QUEEN'S BIRTHDAY - Queen Sirikit has been Thailand's First Lady since 1950.

October 23rd: CHULALONGKORN DAY - death of King Chulalongkorn (Rama V statue in front of the Parliament), who is considered to be the sovereign who opened up the country to western influences.

December 5th: THE KING'S BIRTHDAY - national holiday. His 60th birthday was celebrated all year in 1987 (according to Buddhist tradition, 5 x 12 is a sacred number). Parades and celebrations in honour of the King are held all over the country.

BURMA

The Burmese calendar also corresponds to the lunar year. Every full moon marks the beginning of a new month, all of which have alternately 29 or 30 days. One month is extended by a few days every three years. The months are called:

Tagu - March / April; **Kason** - April / May; **Nayon** - May / June; **Waso** - June / July; **Wagaung** - July / August; **Tawthalin** - August / September; **Thadingyut** - September / October; **Tazaungmon** - October / November; **Nadaw** - November / December; **Pyatho** - December / January; **Tabodwe** - January / February; **Tabound** - February / March

---

PWE - is the general term for all Burmese holidays and festivities. All-night performances of classical Burmese plays are typical examples, as are singers and clowns.

The **FULL MOON OF TABAUNG** is celebrated at the Shwedagon pagoda in March.

In March / April you will be able to witness the famous **FIRE-WALKING** ritual acted out by members of Rangoon's Hindu community. Believers walk across a considerable stretch of glowing coals while in a trance.

The **BURMESE NEW YEAR** is celebrated in mid-April. As in Thailand, it is a tradition to pour water over each other.

In May the **FULL MOON OF KASON** is celebrated outside the Shwedagon. Girls water a Bodhi tree in memory of Buddha's enlightenment, which allegedly took place under just such a tree.

The **FASTING PERIOD** begins in mid-July. New monks enter into the monasteries.

In October, towards the end of the fasting period, Burmese cities are lit up by candles and oil lamps which are put into all windows by the common people. Theatre and other forms of entertainment are once again permitted.

You can find out the exact dates of feasts and celebrations from Tourist Burma.

At the same time, the western calendar applies to:

STATE HOLIDAYS

January 4th: INDEPENDENCE DAY - processions and demonstrations are held everywhere. The city of Rangoon is lit up, and boat races are organized on the Royal Lake.

February 12th: UNION DAY - in memory of the founding of the Union of Burma in 1947. Dances of all the country's different nationalities are performed. Notable celebrations in Rangoon take place at the Royal Lake and on the old race-track (Kyaikkasan).

March 2nd: FARMERS' DAY - exhibition and a county fair in Kyaikkasan.

March 27th: RESISTANCE DAY - big military parade in Rangoon.

May 1st: LABOUR DAY - parades and demonstrations. Classical Burmese plays are performed in the evening.

July 19th: MARTYRS' DAY - commemorative of the murder of Aung San and his comrades. State and party leaders meet in the tombs near the Shwedagon pagoda.

December 25th: CHRISTMAS DAY.

TEMPLE FESTIVAL IN NAKHON PATHOM

PHOTOGRAPHY

There are numerous arguments for and against taking photographs during your holiday. The chief disadvantage is that you will always immediately be identified as a tourist with a camera hung around your neck.

While there is certainly no need to run around with 10 kilos of camera equipment, we have nevertheless always found taking pictures worthwhile. 'Proof pictures' showing you in front of famous landmarks can soon become tedious and boring, but personal impressions of landscapes, people and events can easily become photographs you will want to look at over and over again.

If you do decide to take pictures, you should do it right. If all you have is a pocket or instamatic camera, you might as well leave it at home and enjoy the tropics with your own eyes. What you really need is a camera with an automatic or manual exposure indicator (instead of just 'sun' or 'rain') and a focus meter. Your exposure indicator will help you decide on the best length of exposure for the often tricky light-shadow contrasts.

Owing to the multitude of subjects, you may soon feel the need for more than just one lens. You'll need more, too, if you're the kind of person who wants to get 'all' of the temple onto one picture and also to be able to take more detailed shots. For beginners we would recommend buying a basic model from some well-established camera company. Should you want to buy a better camera later on, you will at least be able to keep and re-use the lenses.

Now - what to buy? Whether you will need a fully automatic camera or one with timer, aperture, or programme control depends largely on what kind of pictures you will be taking. A camera with timer control would be most suitable for taking landscape photographs, for instance, as one can control the depth of focus with these models by changing the apertures. An aperture controlled camera, in contrast, is more suitable for taking pictures of people or events, as one can avoid going out of focus with these models by simply programming the time of exposure beforehand. Cameras which can be programmed to always expose for the least possible amount of time are best. Fans of macro-photography will be especially attracted by cameras with a flashlight control, as one can stop down more easily with these.

The next point of argument is invariably the *lenses.* Your basic tool should be a high speed 50 - 55 mm lens, with which you will be able to avoid overusing the often rather indiscreet flashlight when using a photosensitive film. For long distance shots you will need either a zoom or a telephoto. A zoom gives you many possibilities but is rather low speed (aperture 3.5 - 4). You will find that this makes many shots impossible, especially in the tropics, where many subjects (e.g. jungle etc.) are too shady to capture. We would recommend a 135 mm/2.8 or even a 200 mm/2.8. Always consider how much extra weight this will mean, though. A zoom is ideal for wide-angle shots (28-70 mm or 28-50 mm), of course, since buildings and the like stand perfectly still and you will be able to overcome your lens' low speed by switching to a longer exposure.

In our experience, slide *films* are best to capture the colourful splendour of the tropics. You can always have copies made of them later on. A standard film with 64 ASA will nearly always produce satisfactory results. If you're working with low speed lenses you can also try 200 or 400 ASA films, which you can then have developed at 800 or even 1600 ASA. Often, this can even save one from having to use a flashlight. There is not much point in telling travellers that the best place to store film is in the fridge or even the freezer, as refrigerators are often not available. Even if they are, you may find - upon taking the films out of the fridge - that water has condensed, that is the film 'sweats' due to the sudden change of temperature. This is just about the worst thing that can happen. For this reason you should also be wary of storing films too close to air-conditioners. However, films and cameras should never be left lying in the sun or heat. The best thing to do with exposed films is to put them straight back into their original containers and to keep them somewhere in between your clothes. Watch out for X-ray checks at airports! Always keep cameras and lenses in your hand luggage, away from dust and water. Avoid sudden bumps.

Kodak, Fuji and Agfa films can be developed for less in Bangkok than back home. The prices for the films themselves vary very little, however, and for this reason you'll be better off buying your films at home, where you can at least be sure that they haven't been incorrectly stored for a long period of time.

Always remember how you yourself feel when someone is directing a camera at you. Always try to stay in the background and never jostle others out of the way just to get a good snapshot - their celebrations are not ours; we are the guests! Not letting people pray, eat, sleep, or die in peace and quiet is almost another form of mental slavery, and trying to 'buy' pictures with gifts or money is even worse.

INFORMATION

There is no way we can give you the most up-to-date, concise information in this book, no matter how hard we try. For this reason try and get additional information from the tourist offices before leaving.

TOURISM AUTHORITY OF THAILAND (TAT)

AUSTRALIA: Royal Exchange Building, 56 Pitt Street, Sydney 2000, tel 277549.
HONG KONG: Fairmont House, 8 Cotton Tree Drive, Central, Hong Kong, tel 8680732.
SINGAPORE: c/o Thai Embassy, 370 Orchard Road, tel 2357694.
UNITED KINGDOM: 49 Albemarle Street, London WIX 3FE, tel 01-4997670.
UNITED STATES: 5 World Trade Center, New York, NY 10048, tel 4320433; 3440 Wilshire Blvd., Suite 1101, Los Angeles, CA 90010, tel 3822353.

TOURIST BURMA

BURMA: Hotel & Tourist Corporation, 73-75 Sule Pagoda Road, Rangoon, tel 78376.

WOMEN ABROAD

It is not so much the heavy load of your rucksack as the male-dominated world in which you're travelling which may create problems for you if you are a woman traveller in the Far East. South East Asia is a long way from Europe and America, more so for its inhabitants than for us. The only two sources of information open to the average South East Asian as to the 'western' way of life are travellers themselves and - mainly - films and television. Cheap American soaps present them with a world of violence and hate and death, where glamorous women will jump into the hero's bed at a moment's notice.

Showing these types of films to the prudish Muslim population of Malaysia or southern Thailand is not unproblematic. Here, women frequently still wear veils and never leave the house without wearing a bra. Exchanging any type of caress in public is unheard of. If you act like a miniature film-star you will be considered fair game.

'White is beautiful' - at least it is for many South East Asian men. While the white Memsahib of colonial days gone by was unapproachable, the sexually liberated western tourist of today seems not at all so remote. The news that white women sunbathe semi-nude on the beaches of Ko Samui has made it all the way to northern Thailand. The idea that many white women might consider going to bed with a local inhabitant is common among most Asian men.

There are many easy ways to avoid mosquitos and leeches, but there is not a single effective method for remaining unmolested by men. Even if you walk around Thailand hidden behind a bra, a long sleeved blouse and a long dress, sweating and cursing away to yourself, you will still find yourself being stared at, spoken to, and even touched.

You could of course avoid this by staying exclusively at international hotels and always acting like a real 'lady'. The more tourists travelling around a certain area with a high travel-budget, the more exclusive the atmosphere. This reduces the chance of confrontations with local men (exceptions are liftboys, waiters, chauffeurs etc.). Here, of course, you will be exposed to the sexism of western men, which can be even worse. Anyway, the thought of spending one's entire holiday in western colonies and dressed up as something one isn't might not appeal to many young female travellers of today. Outside of these 'sanctuaries' single female travellers will find themselves confronted with problems one way or another, as the strict Asian moral code for women applies to foreign as well as local females.

Few women really travel about alone in South East Asia. Some travel in pairs, but the most common arrangement by far is that of a couple (man/woman). In areas opened up to tourism one will find a fair number of female travellers, but in the more secluded areas men clearly dominate. Women travelling about on their own despite all disadvantages need a generous helping of self-assurance. Those who already have a hard time travelling around on their own in Europe will have a difficult time indeed. If you're planning on travelling to re-

mote areas, it is definitely a good idea to find some fellow travellers.

Constantly being molested can be both tiring and aggravating. Simply being ignored, receiving neither a cup of tea nor a guide, are some of the simpler forms of Asian sexism. How to react if you are seriously molested always depends on the situation. It is important to avoid problems before they even have a chance of developing. For this reason avoid direct eye contact with strange men, wear a bra, try to keep your shoulders, arms and legs covered, claim to be married (wedding ring, picture of 'husband' and 'children'), avoid 'hot' topics of conversation. In addition, a self-assured appearance and a good sense of humour might be of help. If someone eyes you up, go over to him, give him a vivid description of your 'husband' for whom you're waiting, and ask if he hasn't seen him anywhere. This usually does the trick. Of course you will have to be able to communicate with him in order for this to work.

If the worst comes to the worst and you should find yourself being bodily attacked it is always better to be with someone else. If you're not, try to act cool, talk, tell your attacker that you have a serious venereal disease, or even go along with him - anything is better than being killed. Do not live in constant fear of rape - luckily it only occurs very rarely - and do not let these facts deter you, should you already have decided to travel on your own. Many women who have actually travelled around Asia on their own will tell you that while there are certainly very many obstacles to overcome, it was still well worth it.

Half of South East Asia's population consists of women, too, just like the rest of the world. Even though there is more of a language barrier with Asian women than men (due to a lower standard of education) they are all the more willing to get to know Europeans. There are fewer social barriers and hang ups to overcome in a woman's world, and getting to know the inhabitants of the country you are travelling around in is usually a worthwhile experience.

TRAVELLING WITH CHILDREN

Take the kids along to Italy? - Sure, why not - but Asia? Such an idea will be incomprehensible to most of your friends, especially if the child is still young. Just think of all the things that could happen - disease, the long journey, the nappies... There are hundreds of open questions and only very few answers; travel guides rarely even consider the problem, and there are but few parents who have actually had this experience. Even parents who at some stage or other travelled about the Far East without their children will rarely have given the problem of whether Asia is a suitable place for the kids any thought. Still, being an experienced Asian traveller will make the decision of whether you should try taking the family along after all much easier.

Our own son has accompanied us twice to Thailand, Bali, Singapore, and Malaysia. The first time he was 1 1/2, the second time 3 years of age. Ours is not an experience that can easily be generalized, though, since our research

---

PHOTOGRAPHS: Markets in Thailand and Burma: *top:* Surat Thani; *bottom left:* Taunggyi; *bottom right:* Meiktila

trips are in no way comparable to an average holiday. All the same, we would like to give you a couple of tips:

When planning your route, always consider the needs of your children. The long and tiresome flight to Asia is unavoidable. There is hardly any room for the child to move around in, especially for children under two years of age, who don't even get a seat of their own. Baby beds, for instance, are only available right beneath the movie screens in DC 10s or Boeing 747s, making them unsuitable for anything but infants, who might just sleep through it all. Cheap flights are usually completely booked out. Should there be extra room available, though, spread out immediately in order to gain more room - the stewardesses will probably be very sympathetic.

As long as they are not too heat-sensitive, most children manage to cope with the change of climate quite well. The time difference, however, is another story, and it will take a couple of days - and unfortunately a couple of very active nights, too - until your child has become used to the new rhythm. Try to find a hotel that is not too poorly sound-proofed for your first couple of days, so that you will be able to spend as much time with your child as necessary without disturbing the other guests.

Avoid long and exhausting tours. If this is not possible, try at least to choose a comfortable form of transportation. This will mean spending more money if you plan to travel around a lot. As long as children do not require a seat of their own and are under four years of age and less than one metre tall (this goes for the Thai railway system), they are permitted to ride for free on buses and trains. Between the age of four and twelve you only have to pay half-price for them. If you have a choice, stick to trains or ships and avoid local buses. Always plan a day of recreation after a day of extensive travel, so that you and your children will have time to settle down comfortably and get used to the new surroundings.

There are many things about South East Asia that small children really love. Especially those children who have grown up in a city will be fascinated by the incredible natural environment. Beaches and market-places always seem to be of most interest. Here, merchants, fishermen and craftsmen are often more than willing to show your little ones how their job is done. Definitely take the time to watch artists and carpenters at work in their open shops. You will find amusement-parks or zoos in most large cities. The greatest advantage of Asia are the many local children living here, for your tiny fellow travellers will usually enjoy doing the same things they do. This doesn't mean that you should let your kids roll around in the mud or ride on top of water buffaloes - babies should only be allowed to play on clean beaches and swim in the pools of large hotels - even if you yourself aren't living there.

As medical care is for the most part unproblematic in Thailand, you won't need to take all that many extra medications along. What you will need are malaria-prophylactic pills (we would recommend Resochin Junior), some fever suppositories, electrolytic tablets against diarrhoea, a good antiseptic disinfectant, and lots of adhesive plaster. Even the smallest graze should immediately be cleaned and disinfected, as infections can develop very easily. Protect your child against mosquitoes by applying an effective repellent (try Autan or Mentholenium) even before the sun has set. Take along an extra mosquito net for your child. Rashes are common because of the low standards of hygiene, and for this reason we would recommend showering as frequently as possible. Make sure that water is clean, especially at the beach. You should also watch out for the sun - buy a bottle of baby suntan lotion. Just in case, take along something against allergies, too.

If you're travelling with a backpack, you'll have to limit the amount of baggage you wish to take along to the absolute minimum. The smaller children are, the more baggage they seem to need - the bottles and powdered milk, the nappies and clothes, and of course that oh-so-important favourite teddy-bear, take up more room than you might expect. In addition, babies as well as infants have to be carried. Forget about the baby carriage - you won't get too far with it. Child supporters with a hip belt that can be strapped to your back are a much better alternative. You can buy baby bottles and powdered milk in the big cities and tourist centres. Bring your own bottle brush and cleaning liquids, though. Use disposable nappies, which can be bought in all large cities, when travelling, and re-usable ones whilst staying in one place. You will find that you won't actually need all that many, as the toddlers will often be able to run around without any nappies at all.

Should they already have outgrown the nappy-phase, deciding what to take along and what not might be rather difficult. One possibility would be letting your child have its own little backpack for toys, which it can carry and pack on its own. You yourself can take along a few additional toys and books for good-night-stories as a surprise. Toys and children's clothes (rarely made of cotton, though) can also be bought in Thailand.

You will probably stay at hotels and eat in restaurants. There is no real need to stay at expensive hotels, as even traveller hotels offer rooms with two beds in which there is easily enough room for a four-person-family. They are also quite snug, and you will usually be able to have dinner or spend the evening at the bar while still within hearing distance of your room. Eating Chinese food shouldn't pose any problem for your children, but Thai and Indian food might be too spicy. Generally speaking, you will find that they will try to serve a suitable meal for your children in nearly all restaurants, even if this means preparing an extra small dish, which is often free of charge. If you're going to be on the road for a longer period of time, consider picnics, which are a lot of fun, especially if the whole family has done all the shopping together at some exotic market-place. By way of drinks we would recommend the cheap but rather sweet disposable packets of tea, cocoa and juice which can be bought just about everywhere.

You will come to realize that most potential problems solve themselves, especially as Asians are in general very fond of little children. Your little ones will be the constant centre of attention, and people will always try to make them feel as comfortable as possible. They will receive gifts and be fondled, photographed and kissed. Sometimes this goes beyond the limit of toleration, and small children will often show this crying. If this should be the case, help them - a sun hat on top of their little heads will frequently do the trick.

You as parents will be the only constant and reliable factor for small children in the ever-changing environment of Asia. You will find that they demand even more attention than usual. Even bigger children - if they're shy - may feel lonely and isolated. You will have to be with them 24 hours a day, which can become quite a strain. Your child needs to be considered whenever you make a decision. It might be best, therefore, to plan a joint trip with other people who also have children.

We, as well as many other parents who have been to South East Asia with their children, have always found that the positive factors outweigh the negative ones by far. We are looking forward to future trips. Many new experiences will only be possible with your children, for what better way could there be to get to know local families and get a real inside look into their lives. In addition, you owe a little attention to your child, and this is always easier when away from home, work, and other unpleasant factors of daily life.

The only thing we would definitely warn against is taking your child to Burma, as medical care is quite appalling here. If you're planning to go to Indonesia, stick to those regions which are opened up to tourists - a trip to the remote islands would just be too much for everyone involved.

GUESTS IN A FOREIGN COUNTRY

The readiness to get to know an entirely new country with its own people and culture is an important precondition for a successful holiday. Be prepared to watch and listen instead of giving advice. Take your time - much of what you will see will not be easy to digest; the differences from Europe and America are quite staggering.

The extended family plays an important role in Asian society. It offers security and shelter. The family basically makes up the foundation of society. Those who break the traditional rules by trying to break away from the family are ostracized from the community and will find themselves on their own.

Families are extremely close, emotionally as well as spatially. This means that there is virtually no possibility of having peace and quiet or pursuing individual happiness, which stands in marked contrast to western society. Families have a close physical relationship amongst each other, and you will find that they are not disinclined towards physical contact with strangers, either. Expect to be touched, poked, and stared at. It is a sign of great friendship for two men or two women to walk around holding hands. Physical contact between men and women, however, is frowned upon in public.

While children receive lots of attention and care on the one hand, they are brought up strictly and expected to be dutiful and obedient on the other. As there is no universal pension-programme in Asia, they are the only security parents have for the future. Teachers as well as religious and political leaders have the same unquestionable authority parents have. Children coming from poor and often large families are frequently forced to give up school at an early age and start making money to contribute to the family's well-being. Always bear in mind that this - in part - is the reason why many services and wares are so cheap in so-called Third World countries.

The pursuit of harmony and peace is another basic factor of these communities. Conflicts are always avoided if possible. Arguments held in public are considered extremely out-of-place, and those indulging in them lose face. This applies to tourists, too, who frequently lose their temper or criticize their hosts with typical western presumption.

If you ask for something you will rarely get 'no' for an answer, even if your request is next to impossible. Instead of a simple 'no' they will say 'maybe', signifying their inability to comply by acting hesitant and unenthusiastic. The famous and mysterious Asian smile has often helped overcome tricky and problematic situations, as has the key phrase *mai pen rai* - 'that doesn't matter'.

Stress-plagued tourists who've only just recently managed to escape from the hectic western world will find themselves confronted with a whole new concept of time, especially in rural areas. In Indonesia one calls it *jam karet* - 'rubber time'. It makes no difference whether a bus leaves a certain town at the time it is meant to or five hours later. Enjoying the present seems to be more important than anticipating future events, even if the present means hanging around a bus station for five hours. Here, patience really is a virtue.

The white man has been known in Asia - though not necessarily loved - for centuries. Except in the case of Thailand, they first came as foreign conquerors, to exploit the South East Asian countries for their raw materials. In some countries, they were thrown out by force. These days they return as tourists. All the same, foreigners are treated as guests of the country. People will treat you in a friendly and respectful manner if you attempt to adopt local customs, especially in rural areas. If you act arrogantly and intolerantly you may awaken unpleasant memories in your hosts and be treated accordingly.

You may find yourself invited to a meal or a celebration by a local family. Your hosts will expect you to act according to their traditions, just as any other host anywhere in the world would. There is no way you can know how to behave in every situation, of course, and this is not expected of you; your hosts will, however, be very pleased to see you making a sincere effort to understand their traditions.

Foreigners are mainly judged by their clothing. Very casual clothing or even beach-clothing is frowned upon when not at the seaside. This applies to visits to religious sites in particular. Before entering a house you should remove your shoes, just as you should before entering a Buddhist temple.

At religious ceremonies you should take special care not to act in an inappropriate manner. We would recommend asking for permission before taking photographs. It is considered extremely impolite to walk around in front of those praying, even to be higher than the level of their bowed heads, or to touch or climb about on the huge religious statues. The head is considered sacred and should never be touched, not even with friendly, 'western' intent.

The foot is considered the least worthy of all human limbs. For this reason it should never be pointed at anyone when sitting down. This can be quite problematic, for although Asians may have the stamina to sit cross-legged for hours, Europeans usually do not. The left hand is thought of as unclean; only the right hand should be used to eat with, give things to others, or receive something in return. In general, Thais do not greet each other by shaking hands. Instead, they lay the palms of their hands against each other as if praying (wai). A 'wai' is more than a simple form of greeting, however; it is a way to show one's respect for others. Foreigners needn't greet children, servants, waiters etc (i.e. people of a lower social standing) with a wai. There are certain rules dictating how to use the 'wai' (how to place your folded hands):

Monks:	*in front of one's forehead.*
Elders:	*in front of one's nose.*
Those of a higher social standing:	*in front of one's mouth.*
Those of a lower social standing:	*in front of one's chest.*

There is a wealth of manners and customs which seems quite unknowable, owing to the many different ethnic groups, cultural influences, religions, and geographic regions. In most communities religion plays a central role in daily life. Just consider the role of Buddhism for Thais and Burmese and many Chinese, or the role the Muslim belief plays for Malays or the inhabitants of southern Thailand. The hilltribes, in contrast, are believers in ancient natural religions, and even those belonging to the more established religious groups believe in witches, warlocks and demons.

While traditions have merged in the cities and have become 'westernized' to a certain extent, they still exist in their original forms in the countryside. Eastern and western concepts seem to be trying to come to terms in the cities, but the contrast between wealth and poverty is still staggering. Do not be misled by the facade of shopping centres and tourist attractions - reality isn't quite as splendid. Especially when haggling about the price of some cheap souvenir you should be aware of the fact that you are about to spend the average monthly wage of a Thai. All tourists who visit Thailand or Burma are considered wealthy by the locals. How else could they afford the long journey? Nevertheless, one doesn't like to see them distributing their money by the handful - only extensive, carefully planned financial aid can really change these people's lives, not a few coins dropped into an outstretched hand.

Begging is generally disapproved of - it should not be encouraged. People asking for alms in front of a temple, or monks on their daily round of alms, should not be thought of as beggars, though. It is considered a special privilege to be able to contribute something towards their well-being, and people are very thankful for the chance of proving their worthiness.

When shopping, you should always drive a hard bargain - it is customary. Prices are fixed according to the mood of the merchant and the nature of the potential buyer. Obviously, you will be asked to pay more than an average Thai. Don't be insulted - consider this a welcome chance to learn the fine art of haggling. If you pay the first price the merchant asks you will immediately lose face, something which should be avoided at all costs in Thailand.

TRAVELLING CHEAP

OR "A BILL THAT DOESN'T ADD UP"

The food here is as terrible as ever. Oh well, what else can you expect of the cheapest joint in town? - Hey, one more Coke over here, please! - Christ, the amount one needs to drink in this heat. Coke is still cheap, but when it comes to beer... Come evening I really need a beer, but it knocks me out every time. No, not me myself, I can hold my liquor. It's the price that knocks me out, get it? But at least there's that Chink up the road. He sells beer for 2 Baht less than these guys do. That's where I always end up spending my evenings.

I know my way around here pretty well by now. Hell, I should; I've been here for three full days. I was in Ko Samui before this - everything there was half as expensive. What I need now are a couple of days of rest. I'm telling you, the ride up here was just awful! A whole day wasted on a train ride, third class, totally overcrowded, and of course there had to be a three-hour delay in the middle of nowhere. These people are just totally unorganized. Good thing I bought all those cans of food along from Malaysia. The stuff they serve at the stations is completely inedible. Anyway, as soon as they see someone who's white they'll ask for twice the price. And they don't even speak English. I'll take the supermarket any day. At least there you're not swindled. If you know your way around, that is. When I first arrived here I was too exhausted to walk, and I got myself a ricksha to the hotel. The guy actually had the nerve to ask for 30 Baht, can you imagine that? The impudence! Took ages for me to haggle him down to 20, but if I'd have felt up to it I could easily have had him down to 10. Bummer! And then the hotel. My travelguide has it down for 80 Baht per night. By now the damn place costs 90, can you believe it? Whatever you do, don't buy this guide - it's totally unreliable. I moved out the next day. Now I'm staying at a cheaper place across the street that isn't even in the travelguide. No windows or fan, true, but I spend most of my time hanging round this place, anyway. Here at least things happen.

I've already met a bunch of real characters. Take the Aussie from yesterday for instance. That guy is actually living with the fishermen, out on the beach. They even give him a meal every now and then. I guess you'd do anything if you spend enough time out here. But not me - I'm leaving for Phuket tomorrow. They say there's some pretty cheap places out there. You know, beachhuts without electricity, that sort of thing. Really makes you feel like a local.

See that horde of tourists over there? All they do is sit in air-conditioned buses all day, being chauffeured from one sight to the next. No local colour for them. They should try walking, maybe then they'd stop wanting to see every damn temple in the whole country. Well, I guess today's more or less done with. Went to at least five different travel agencies to try to get my trip to Phuket organized. I'm going to go over to the bus station once it cools down a little. Tickets are supposed to be cheapest there.

TRAVELLER 'EGO'

OR "IN SEARCH OF ONE'S SELF"

Why I came to Thailand? Money goes further here. Hotels, restaurants - who could afford this kind of lifestyle for months on end in Europe? You have to settle for less comfort, of course, but that's okay - my standards aren't that high. And anyway, these are the tropics. They're just less comfortable than it is back home. You have to adapt. If there's one thing I can't handle though, it's rice soup for breakfast. I really need two eggs, know what I mean? And all that dreary folk-music is starting to get to me, too. Just recently I bought myself this cheap walkman and a couple of hot tapes. Good for killing time on those endless bus-rides. This way, the locals don't keep chattering away to you, either. I never understand a word they're saying anyway. Most of them don't speak English, and if they do it's always the same stupid phrases.

I mean hey, if I'm looking for someone to talk to I can just stay at my hotel, right? Those guys just sit around waiting for an experienced traveller like me to come and give them some good tips, anyway. Maybe I'll tell them about that horny Swedish girl in room 12. Good thing my girlfriend moved on with that Canadian a couple of weeks ago. The whole thing wasn't working out, anyway. Since then I've been having a real ball. Some of these single women travelling around are really something else. You know - easy, uncomplicated. They split before there's any chance of an argument. Suits me fine. Having fun with the local ladies is out of the question of course, but getting to know people in the hotels is easy.

Nothing much happens in the evenings anyway. All you do is hang out. With a little luck someone with a bit of dope might turn up. Real mellow. The stuff is dirt cheap in Chiang Mai - they practically force you to buy it. Too dangerous for me, but there's always plenty of guys who have some stash on them. The hotel manager keeps his mouth shut. After all, he makes a stack of money out of us travellers. Anyway, he couldn't give a damn one way or another. He doesn't care what goes on as long as the money is right. I sometimes wish he'd show just a little more initiative, though - especially at breakfast. If you sleep all day you don't want to have to waste additional time waiting for the eggs.

I should wash that Bali-shirt one of these days, and hopefully my Phuket t-shirt will have dried by now. It looks pretty good with the hilltribe-rucksack I bought up in the north. Looking at me, anyone could tell that I've been around. Of course you have to keep one's part to keep the suntan going. A day of motorbiking in shorts usually does the trick. Helmets? When asked I've never heard of 'em. And who cares about running around in shorts? These are my holidays and I'm trying to enjoy them. I've got enough regulations at home - here, I want to do as I please.

THAILAND

BANGKOK

Welcome to Bangkok - just 200 years old, five million inhabitants, and problems wherever one looks. Travellers hurry through this town in a frantic rush - get some information, buy a ticket, go on a quick shopping-spree, and then it's off to enjoy the comfort of some tourist ghetto. Sweating and swearing, they stumble from one travel agency to the next, trying in vain to find the cheapest connecting flight. When they're in a hurry to get to the Immigration bureau they get stuck in traffic jams in the middle of rush-hour, and on top of everything else their travel funds have just about run out.

Many travellers have had this sort of experience in Bangkok. In addition, there is the city's negative image; anyone who has been there has some tale of robbery and deceit to tell. The traveller hotels do their part in contributing to this negative image, too. The city is huge. There is no actual centre of town. You have the tourist area here (Sukhumvit Road), the historical centre there (Sanam Luang), and the shopping centres and government offices somewhere completely different. The distances between the respective areas are too great to be covered on foot. As a result all of Bangkok seems to be mobile, driving through the intricate network of streets in taxis, tuk-tuks, on motorcycles and every other conceivable form of transportation. All this adds up to give the Bangkok air its special 'aroma'.

This is Thailand's metropolis, the city from which 90% of the country's foreign trade is controlled. Here one finds a dense concentration of industry, administration, and Thais hoping to find a better life. By now, every tenth Thai lives in the capital. While the city is heavily influenced by the western way of life, the countryside retains its ancient, rural traditions. Here, so-called progress develops slowly, if at all. But you can get to know the traditional way of life in Bangkok, too, for this is also a city of culture and religion. Nowhere will you find as many English-speaking Thais as in the capital, and nowhere will you receive as much information concerning the history and culture of the country. There are four hundred temples in the city, scores of market-places, and a National Museum in which you can easily spend an entire day. Those who spend a longer period of time in town will soon discover that it has much to offer in the way of night-life, too; restaurants in Bangkok are cosmopolitan, and there is enough entertainment for everyone, even those who are not in search of a hostess. Take your time when exploring Bangkok - it's worth it!

Begin your sightseeing tour by paying a visit to the

TOURIST OFFICE, where you will be able to purchase a good city-map with all bus routes (important!) for only 35 Baht. Ask about anything you might be particularly interested in as the employees have an amazing selection of hectographed brochures. They will not volunteer any unless you ask detailed questions, though. You will also find the administration of bungalows in the Khao Yai National Park here. Address: TAT (Tourist Authority of Thailand),

Ratchdamnoen Nok Road, tel 2821143-7, open 8:30-16:00 h. Right next door you'll find the

RATCHDAMNOEN STADIUM. Thai-boxing competitions are held here. In this form of boxing the use of the entire body is allowed, including the feet. Much atmosphere and heavy gambling - typical Thai entertainment. Take the cheapest seats - they are the most fun. Opening hours: Mon, Wed, and Thurs 18:00 hours, Sundays from 17:00 and 20:00 h. The best fights don't start until about 21:00 h. Prices: 140-280 Baht, ringside seat 600 Baht. More Thai-boxing competitions can be seen at

LUMPINI STADIUM, Rama IV Road: Tues, Fri, Sat, starting at 18:00.h. Those with little time can take a bus directly to

SANAM LUANG, the large square in front of the Royal Palace. This is one of the cultural centres of town, and site of many festivals and ceremonies. There is so much to see around the square that you will barely be able to digest it all at once. On all accounts go to the

NATIONAL MUSEUM. Originally, the *second king,* a sort of vice-sovereign of days gone by, had his palace built here. Parts of it still stand today, as does the temple at the entrance of the museum. A thorough tour through this, the largest of all of Thailand's museums, will give you a good idea of the country's history, from prehistoric days all the way to the Bangkok period.

You'll find the prehistoric collection (which includes a neolithic grave found near Kanchanaburi) in the first large building on the left. The Buddhaisawan chapel on the right was built for one of the most venerated Buddha-statues of the country, Phra Buddha Singh. The statue is carried through Bangkok and Thonburi for the Songkran Festival annually.

The connecting central building of the museum is the former palace of the second king. You will find all sorts of fascinating objects from the Bangkok period here; the royal throne of Thailand's second king, elephant saddles, Khon-masks, marionettes, costumes, stamps, weapons, musical instruments, gifts to the royal family etc.

The newer museum halls surround this old building. Start your tour in the south wing, to the left of the entrance. On both floors you will find South East Asian and specifically Thai works of art, many of which stem from the period before the Thai people had even started populating their present-day national territory (Dvaravati / Mon, Lopburi / Khmer, Srivijaya and others). You will find objects of art from the more recent Bangkok period - sculptures, ceramics, textiles, coins etc. - on the ground-floor halls of the northern wing. In the upper floor you will first come across a hall of Hindu art-objects from Sukhothai, then a hall containing art from the north of the country (Chiang Saen and Chiang Mai). You will find sculptures and ceramics from the Sukhothai period in the adjoining room. Art of the Ayutthaya period and U-Thong (Mon) period can be found in the next two rooms. The last room contains furniture of the Bangkok period.

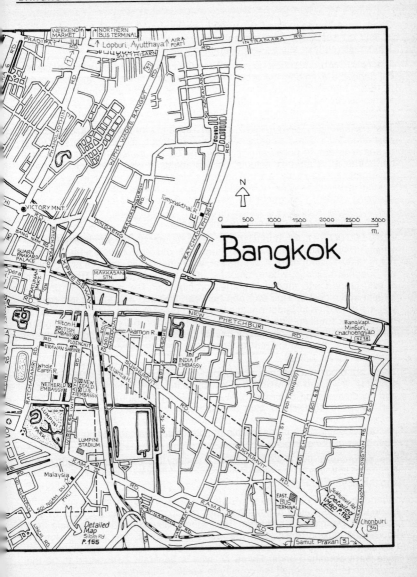

Bangkok

Open: Tues-Thur, Sat/Sun 9:00-16:00 h, admission 30 Baht. A free guided tour is held on Tuesdays (Thai art and culture), Wednesdays (Buddhism) and Thursdays (early or late art-tour alternates weekly).

The *NATIONAL THEATRE* is just around the corner. Demonstrations of classical dances are among the most frequent performances. For information call 2215861 Mon-Fri 8:00-16:30 h. The theatre organizes numerous musical performances from February to April , some of them held at the gallery. Traditional dances are performed on the last Friday of every month. Entrance fee 30 Baht.

The *THAMMASAT UNIVERSITY,* one of Thailand's largest universities, is right next door. Considered a centre of political resistance, this university was taken by force by armed police and militia in 1976. It is generally thought of as a barometer of young intellectuals' political ideas. A coup d'état or change of government, not exactly rare in Thailand's history, is often heralded by general student assemblies. The university is a good place to get to know English-speaking students. Students are instructed in the culture and art of the north and northeast regions (e.g. music played on traditional instruments) in the respective regional departments. You will find the

WAT MAHATHAT, the Buddhist college, in the narrow alley opposite the university. Pali-teachings and old religious traditions are studied here. Opening hours: 9:00-17:00 h daily. A big market within the temple-grounds is organized on Buddhist holidays, where, amongst other things, traditional Thai medicine is sold (import into foreign countries prohibited!). The wat itself is one the largest and oldest in Thailand, and between 300 and 400 monks live here. If you are interested in Buddhism this is a good place to meet monks, as many of them speak English. The meditation centre (section 5) is open to foreigners (even women!!) upon prior appointment. There is a library of English material on Buddhism, open to the public. Good-luck amulets as well as other religious trinkets are sold outside.

There are other meditation-temples open to foreigners in the Greater Bangkok area, too. If you are interested, find out about the conditions, teaching methods and accommodation beforehand. *Wat Pak Nam* (Thonburi), *Wat Pleng* (Thonburi, Bangkok Noi District), *Wat Cholaphratan* (Nonthaburi Province), *Wat Vivekasrom* (Chonburi), *Wat Asokaram* (Samut Prakan). Several monks from western countries live in the marble temple, *Wat Benchamabopitr,* and in *Wat Bovonives* in Banglampoo.

The buildings of the *ROYAL PALACE* occupy the entire area south of the square all the way to the river. An imposing white wall surrounds the palace and the Royal Wat Phra Keo.

When the Royal Palace was moved to Bangkok in 1782, Chinese merchants made up the population of the area. They had to move further south, to what is at present Bangkok's Chinatown. The highest elevation of the city, safe from floods and looking down upon the rest of the capital, was reserved for the Palace. New wings were added over the years, and even western elements of style were permitted under Rama IV, who is generally considered to be the sovereign to have opened the country to western influences.

THE ROYAL PALACE, BANGKOK

Admission to the palace is 100 Baht. Do not be scared off by this exhorbitant price - it's well worth it. A visit to the Vimanmek Teakwood Mansion and a rather confusing brochure containing a ground-plan of the premises and dealing with the interior of the palace and the temple are included in the price. The Royal Palace is open to the public 8:30-11:30 and 13:00-15:30 h. The ticket office is closed at lunchtime. You can still stay inside, though; it is agreeably quiet. People dressed too casually are often not let in by the guards. Shorts are absolutely unacceptable.

Also included in the price of admission is a visit to the temple museum and the royal collection of coins and decorations.

In the first building beyond the entrance you will find the

ROYAL COLLECTION OF COINS AND DECORATIONS - coins from the 11th century to the present day, jeweled medals, flags, coats of arms etc. are exhibited. Open 9:00-15:00 h daily except Sat. Behind this building you will find the

WAT PHRA KEO. The gateway, guarded by gigantic demons called Yaks, leads to the temple-square. The square itself is surrounded by a covered arcade, the walls of which are adorned with beautiful murals depicting scenes out of the Ramayana. The heavily decorated Emerald Buddha stands facing the entrance. The 66 cm statue is probably made of jasper, though experts are not quite certain. The image was first found in 1443 in Chiang Rai, where it was hidden behind a fine coat of plaster. Under no circumstances should you point your feet at it. Photography within the chapel is also strictly prohibited. The beautiful monumental doors are guarded by bronze lions. Various buildings stand on an elevated marble platform opposite the main entrance of the bot. Here, you will see the world-famous royal pantheon, whose echelon roof is crowned by a gilded prang. The library with its pyramid-shaped mondhop roof is next to it, and the golden chedi is situated just beyond. On the north side of the library you will come across a stone model of the Angkor Wat temple. Beyond this, on a lower level, there is the prayer hall, adorned with colourful glass flowers, as well as many other buildings.

You can reach the Royal Palace by walking through the gate southwest of the bot. The first building you will come across is the Amarinda Palace. Originally, Rama I had wanted this to be a courthouse, but it was later used as the setting for coronation ceremonies. The central Chakri Maha Prasad Palace, situated south of the large square, was built no more than 100 years ago. The architectural design seems like an odd mixture of Victorian mansion and Thai temple. The small pavilion, not unlike the one in Bang Pa In, has been considered a typical example of Thai architecture ever since a replica of it was exhibited at the World Fair of 1958. Beyond it, you will find the Dusit Palace, originally intended by Rama I to be a coronation hall . Since the death of this king, however, it has only been used as a site for funerals.

The *TEMPLE MUSEUM* in the west section is well worth a visit. Should you feel like giving your, by now, surely rather sore feet a rest, there is a small restaurant right next door to it. You will find an interesting exhibition on the ground floor of the museum concerning the restoration programme which was started in the early 1980s. Buddha figures and the Manangasila throne are among the things of interest exhibited on the first floor.

The area opposite Wat Phra Keo and the Ministry of Defence (cannons in the front garden) bustles with activity. Birds, turtles and flowers are sold here. The population offers sacrificial gifts to the patron god of the city in the newly erected

LAK MUANG SHRINE. This reaches its climax on the day before the official lottery-draw. Gamblers come in the hope of receiving good luck. In return, they pay for performances of traditional dances, which you can witness for free in an adjoining, open room. The

THORANI WELL is a further shrine in the northeast section of the square. The Indian goddess of the earth causes water to flow by wringing her hair. According to the legend, she once repelled Buddha's enemies by wringing veritable floods out of her hair. If you've had enough of culture and temples for the day, why not walk down Chakraphong Road, which will lead you to

BANGLAMPOO, Bangkok's traditional shopping district. This is also one of the main traveller hang-outs in town, and the shops have adapted accordingly; there were always many shops selling textiles in this area, but now one also sees western-type boutiques, travel agencies, and cassette-shops popping out of the ground almost overnight. Thais usually shop in Tani Road and the small side alleys. A walk through these small sois might be nice. Try the ones west of Chakraphong Road, where cars are a rarity. Here, the streets still belong to the people and animals - you will see street hawkers, children playing, and local women gathered together for a friendly evening gossip while men play music on traditional bamboo instruments. Tiny, weather-beaten houses, almost hidden by palms or mango-trees, lie behind the wooden fences. Banglampoo's most famous temple is

WAT BOVONIVES (Wat Bovorn). It's situated south of the city wall and Klong Banglampoo at the oval square, which is the terminus of many bus routes. The temple was erected under crown prince Mongkut in 1827, as a centre for the traditional sect of Dhammayuti, a sect he founded himself. The prince spent 14 years living here before he became king. The Wat soon became one of the most important temples of Thailand. The prince's successors, King Rama VI and Rama VII, spent some time living here as monks, too, as did the present king. There is a famous four-metre bronze statue of Buddha (Sukhothai period) in the bot. The murals here tell of the shortcomings of the people before Buddhist influences cleansed them, and of the gradual development of a 'good' Buddhist society. It is both interesting and surprising that those European influences depicted - western buildings, horse-races, ship-loads of missionaries, and even church-goers in western clothing - are drawn in a positive, even friendly manner. The two viharn behind the bot are only opened for special occasions. Remains of the former city wall can be seen at the meeting point of Klong Banglampoo and Menam Chao Phya. You will also find the

PHRA SUMEN FORT here. Rama I had the new capital protected by a wall, forts and cannons. Everything was torn down again under Rama V, owing to road construction, with the exception of two forts, this being one of them.

South of the Royal Palace you will reach the

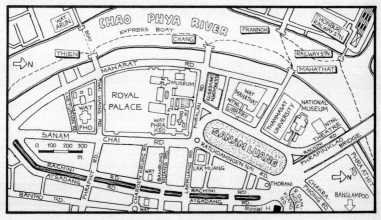

WAT PHO (or Wat Phra Chetuphon) by way of Sanam Chai Road. It is open daily 8:00-17:00 h, entrances can be found on Chetuphon and Thiwong Road. Admission 10 Baht.

Construction of the Wat Pho began as early as 1789, under Rama I. It was erected on the site of an even older wat, said to have been built in the 16th century. Rama III had the wat restored and ordered the general knowledge of his time to be graphically inscribed on the temple walls for the illiterate population. Unfortunately, the murals have for the most part faded. Rama III was also the sovereign under whom the great viharn containing the famous 50 metre reclining Buddha was erected.

Coming through the Chetuphon Road entrance, you will find yourself in the western temple area. Walk north past the numerous souvenir-stands, fortune-tellers, and small buildings, and you will come to the temple of the huge reclining Buddha. The temple was re-gilded in honour of the king's 60th birthday in 1987. East of the temple, you will find four large chedis, each decorated with different-coloured tiles, one green, one orange, one yellow, one blue.

The medical building, founded under Rama III, lies behind the yellow chedi. The first students of medicine were taught here 150 years ago. Traditional eastern medicine is still taught here to this day, and patients are treated in the late afternoons. You can get a good medical massage (80 Baht for 30 minutes, 120 Baht for an hour) in the eastern section of the temple area. Roughly twenty stone statues give you an insight into the method of this form of massage, which was originally taught by Indian *rishis*. The central bot stands in the almost perfectly square eastern courtyard, separated from the rest of the courtyard by four viharns connected by an arcade. There are approximately 400 Buddha figures within the viharn and passageways. Scores of stone figures, brought to Thailand as ballast on Siam-bound ships from China, stand in the inner courtyard. The entrances to the central bot are guarded by bronze lions, the pedestal is decorated with a marble relief depicting scenes out of the Ramayana. Rice-paper reproductions of these scenes can be bought at the souvenir-stands. The doors, decorated with detailed inlays of more scenes out of the Thai-Ramayana, are beautiful, too, as are the carved and gilded window shutters. Scenes out of Buddha's life decorate the inside walls.

Giving shelter to over 300 monks, the monastery bordering onto the sacred buildings south of Chetuphon Road is the largest in the capital.

THONBURI, just west of the river, could actually be considered Bangkok's twin town. It was the first sanctuary for King Taksin's defeated army after the destruction of Ayutthaya. Ever since Rama I had the Royal Court moved to Bangkok in 1782, however, the political, industrial and business life moved with it. Although one could say that today the two huge cities have merged into one densely populated area, there are still marked differences between them. While westernization is on the rise in Bangkok, Thonburi is still very much a traditional Thai town. Although there are plenty of streets and even expressways, the rivers and klongs are the most important connection in town. Speedboats chauffeur well-dressed businessmen and schoolchildren back home in the late afternoons, cement and charcoal are manoeuvred through even the most tricky of canals on wide barges, and the floating supermarket has an extensive stock of all essentials. Life is centred around the waterways; floating petrol-stations are as common as the floating shops that offer their wares at the riverbank. Each house has its own landing-place, which also functions as a bathing and washing-place for the whole family. Toilets, however, are on the mainland. Nevertheless, westerners are shocked again and again by the sight of small children merrily bathing in the murky waters. Sites for new buildings along the big canals near the Menam Chao Phya are just as rare as in any other large town, and as a result the wooden houses stand crowding each other, reaching into the actual rivers. If you drive out into the suburbs you will find that these are not quite as densely populated; trees grow on the riverbanks, and each house has an intensely cared-for garden at the back, giving this part of town an almost rural appearance.

You will only be able to experience this side of Thonburi from a boat (for information on klong-boats, see *Public Transport*). Start your tour shortly after sunrise, when it is still cool and you will be able to watch the families enjoying their morning bathe. If you do not feel like exploring the city on a public boat, we would recommend the informative klong-tour organized by STA Travel, Thai Hotel, 78 Prachathipatei Road. This tour will also take you to a small floating market. The former, large

FLOATING MARKET near Wat Lao has suffered so much from the thousands of tourists that come to look at it daily, that it has been reduced to a cheap tourist attraction. These days the alleged market-women only paddle their vegetable-laden boats up and down the river for the benefit of the tourists' cameras. We would recommend Damnoen Saduak. Thai Wang Road near Wat Pho will lead you to the *Chang landing-place,* and from here you can catch a ferry for 50 Satang to

WAT ARUN, the temple of dawn. Try to be there by sunrise, for then you will see the prangs (chedis built in the Khmer style, each covered with Chinese porcelain) reflect the early rays of sun in many beautiful colours. The various sized towers symbolize the Buddhist universe, with the holy mountain in the middle, surrounded by the world's oceans. You will see stone figures inside, one of them representing a European sea-captain, brought to Thailand from China. You will come across these figures in many other temples, too. A steep stairway leads to the top of the highest prang (86 m), from where you will have a good view of Bangkok. The wat is open daily 8:00-16:30 h. Admission 5 Baht.

You will be able to see the

ROYAL BARGES in a boat shed at the Klong Bangkok Noi. Take an express-boat from one of the landing places to the train station in Thonburi. From here, walk along the road left of the tracks for about 200 metres, then turn right and walk across the bridge to the other side of the klong. You will find a narrow wooden plank-way leading past a number of rather impoverished-looking houses to the boat shed on the northeast side of the bridge. It is easier to get there with one of the boats that travel up the Klong Bangkok Noi. Tickets for these boats cost 5 Baht. The shed is open daily 8:30-16:30 h, admission 10 Baht.

You will see the

WAT KANRAYANIMIT further south, at the point at which the river meets the Klong Bangkok Yai. Thailand's largest bronze bell is in this temple, as well as the highest viharn in the city. In it, you will see a huge sitting Buddha figure. Continue due south and you will circle the

SANTA CRUZ CHURCH, which used to be the heart of the Portuguese district of town as well as the first European business centre. You will find another temple built in the days of Rama III near Memorial Bridge, the

WAT PRAYUN WONG SAWAT. You will be able to see a pool filled with thousands of turtles here, symbolizing long life. The gables and doors are decorated with beautiful mother-of-pearl designs.

Try to climb the *GOLDEN MOUNT* in the late afternoon or early morning, when it is still comparatively cool. This is where the golden chedi of Wat Sraket stands. The chedi contains a highly venerated Buddha-relic, and you will have a fine view from up here. A celebration with a fair and a pilgrimage is held here in November each year. You will find the

WAT SUTHAT southwest of the Golden Mount. This temple was built approximately 150 years ago. Beautiful murals decorate the walls of the huge bot. Much money and effort was invested in having them restored a few years ago. In addition you will be able to admire a large Buddha statue from the Sukhothai period. The temple is open 9:00-17:00 h daily. You will see a gigantic swing in the middle of the busy road in front of the temple. Highly dangerous competitions were held here at a Hindu-Brahman festival of days gone by. These were prohibited under Rama VII.

From here, we would recommend a walk down the Bamrung Muang Road. The shops in this street sell a fascinating variety of temple-accessories. The eternally long road leading east from the Wat Pho,

the *NEW ROAD* or Charoen Krung, was the first road ever to be built in the city on the site of a former elephant-path under Rama IV (1851-1868). Previously, boats were the main form of transportation. European merchants who had their warehouses near the river demanded that the king build them a road to make the transportation of their goods easier. European influences are apparent around the entire area surrounding the Central Post Office.

You will find the

INDIAN MARKET on the west bank of the canal, on Pahurat Road. Here you can buy various textiles, saris, brocade materials for temple-dancers, jewelry etc. Stands selling Indian sweets can be found along Chakrapet Road, where there is also an Indian restaurant opposite the Chinese temple.

The narrow *SAMPENG LANE* can only be traversed on foot. We would recommend starting your walk at the corner of Pahurat Road and crossing the klong in a southeasterly direction. An incredible variety of wares is sold here as well as in the side alleys (Itsaranuphap Lane etc.). The area is always relatively cool, even at noon, as the houses are tall and protected from the harsh sunlight by light-coloured sunblinds. The whole area, from here right up to the railway station, is called Bangkok's

CHINATOWN. Approximately 3 million Chinese live in Thailand. Many of them have been living here for generations. They have been able to establish a role for themselves within Thai society much more easily than in many other South East Asian countries, and this may be due to the common ethnicity shared by the Thai and Chinese people. One can not, however, speak of an unproblematic relationship between the two. Chinatown is especially fascinating when celebrations are held or during the period of preparation for the Chinese New Year.

You can watch Chinese praying and offering sacrificial gifts in *NENG NOI YEE,* a particularly beautiful Chinese temple. The solid gold Buddha in the

WAT TRIMITR weighs almost 6 tons. The figure was made in the 14th century, but wasn't discovered until 1955, when what was thought to be a bronze Buddha was brought from an old ruin to a new wat. It fell to the ground and received a crack in its outer shell, thus revealing the true statue hidden within. The wat is open daily 9:00-17:00 h. Walk down New Road and you will come to one of the oldest banking and business districts in the south of town. You will see the

ORIENTAL HOTEL right next to the river. This old building has lost much of its original charm owing to modernization. Take a look at the old wing ('decent' clothing required), and you will see what it looked like in the days when Joseph Conrad and Somerset Maugham lived here as semi-permanent guests. From the terrace you will have an imposing view of the river and Bangkok's twin town Thonburi. The hotel offers a luxury tour to Ayutthaya and Ancient City. A cold buffet is included in the price. It's rather expensive, though, and we would recommend the much more reasonably priced boat-rental service at the landing-place south of the hotel, instead. From here, boats travel up and down the Chao Phya at regular intervals, a cheap tour, well worth it! A particularly interesting temple, the

SRI MARIAMMAN TEMPLE, can be found in the middle of the busy Silom Road. This is actually a Hindu temple, but next to Brahma, Vishnu, Shiva, Ganesha, and many other Hindu gods you will also see a statue of Buddha here.

If you want to visit any of the following places you'll have to visit them one by one, as they are rather far apart.

Go west down Rama IV Road and you will reach the famous

SNAKE FARM (Pasteur Institute). Poisonous snakes are milked here at 11:00 and 14:30 h Mon-Fri, only at 11:00 h on Sat, Sun, and holidays. The venom is used to produce antivenin serum. The institute was founded in 1922 in order to research and fight the rabies epidemic. A small exhibition about snakes can be looked at. It's open 8:30-16:30 h, Sat, Sun, and holidays till 12:00 h. Admission 40 Baht. This includes a booklet containing interesting facts. Call 2520161-4 for information. Continue east from here; the

LUMPINI PARK, one of the few public gardens in town, is beyond Ratchadamri Road. Many Thais spend their lunch breaks here lying in the shade of its trees. Competitions are held during the kite-flying season. In front of the park you will see the Rama IV memorial.

The very popular ERAWAN SHRINE, a spirit house, stands in front of the large Erawan Hotel (Ratchadamri Road/Ploenchit Road). The four-faced god Brahma is venerated here. His statue is decorated with lotus wreaths and believers ask for blessings. Some even hire musicians and female dancers to circle the shrine clockwise and perform classical dances as a sign of their worthiness.

Walk to the end of Soi Kasemsam (goes off Rama I Road) and you will find the JIM THOMPSON HOUSE. Admission 80 Baht, students 30 Baht. It is well worth the price, seeing that the house is not only beautiful and built in the finest Thai tradition, but contains an extensive collection of South East Asian art objects to boot. These objects were collected by Jim Thompson, the man who managed to re-vitalize the Thai silk-industry after WWII. He disappeared without trace in the jungle of the Cameron Highlands, Malaysia, in 1967. It is open to the public 9:00-17:00 h Mon-Fri.

The SUAN PAKKARD PALACE (Sri Ayutthaya Road) is a small private museum in a traditional Thai setting. The only thing justifying the rather steep price, however (50 Baht, students 30 Baht), is the exotic garden, which is truly beautiful. Open 9:00-16:00 h except for Sundays.

The ZOO, situated near the National Assembly, is not especially exciting. Young Thais roam through the gardens and lovers go rowing on the lake in the late afternoons. This is one of the few quiet and relaxing spots in the hectic city. Admission 8 Baht, open daily 7:30-18:00 h. A tip for ornithologists: there is a nice little aviary with flamingoes, parrots, and other exotic feathered creatures in the Ambassador Hotel, Sukhumvit Road, in between Soi 11 and 13. No admission fee. Opposite the eastern entrance of the zoo you will see the

CHITRALADA PALACE, private residence of the royal family. Nearby you will find

the MARBLE TEMPLE, also known as the Wat Benchamabopitr. It was built mainly out of white Italian marble during the reign of King Chulalongkorn. The palace has a pleasant garden with turtles in the moat. It is open daily 9:00-17:00 h, admission 10 Baht. It's particularly nice in the early mornings when the monks say their prayers. King Chulalongkorn (Rama V) and his father, King Mongkut, were the first Thai kings to be favourably disposed towards western influences. After a visit to Europe the king returned home deeply impressed, and had roads, bridges, and palaces designed and built for him by European architects. As early as 1904 the king had a car - one of the first automobiles in South East Asia - which he proudly drove daily up and down the road in front of the

NATIONAL ASSEMBLY (Parliament). This dome-shaped building built in neo-Venetian style was originally Bangkok's throne room.

The ticket for the Royal Palace and the Wat Phra Keo also gets you into the *VIMANMEK TEAKWOOD MANSION.* This small palace built of teak and in the style of the turn of the century stands behind the General Assembly. King Rama V resided here 1901-1907. Open daily 9:30-16:00 h, admission fee (for those who missed the Royal Palace or lost their ticket) 50 Baht. The entrance is opposite the western entrance of the zoo.

Thailand's biggest chedi, *WAT THAMMAMONGKOL,* measuring almost 100 metres, is the country's newest attraction. The temple is in the east of town, Sukhumvit Road Soi 101. According to the Bangkok Post, the inauguration celebrations (consisting of regular prayers) will continue until August 1993.

HOTELS

You might have a difficult time finding a cheap hotel room if you don't arrive in Bangkok until evening. The first thing you should do in a case like this is start calling the hotels. They are reluctant to name their price on the telephone, however. The many guesthouses are a cheap alternative. You are almost certain to find a room in Khaosan Road, even late at night. If you wish to stay at a 'classy' hotel, there is a way to save money; have a large travel bureau in Bangkok reserve your rooms for you - you will receive a discount of up to 50% (maybe more!) owing to the excessive supply of hotels. Pay attention to the location of your hotel, as distances in Bangkok are great.

In the past few years many new guesthouses have been opened on Khaosan Road in Banglampoo. The area has established itself as a travellers' meeting-point, and accommodation is very cheap. Most guesthouses offer either simple double rooms (80-150 Baht) or dormitories (approx. 40 Baht per person). We would advise bringing your own linen or youth hostel sleeping bag, as well as a padlock for your backpack. The houses are often managed by young people who treat them as private pensions. They sell food and drinks and will help you with any problems you might have. As the walls are very thin, however, guesthouses are rather noisy. In addition, they are likely places to be robbed in. You will find one guesthouse after another on **KHAOSAN ROAD.** You will also find plenty of restaurants, travel bureaus, a launderette (12 Baht per kilo or 25 Baht per machine - self service) and a branch of the Krung Thai Bank, which is open 8:30-20:00 h.

You will find the *BALL BALL** next to the bus stop on Chakraphong Road; the *SIAM** a little further north. There are several guesthouses in the small soi, e.g. *LOTOS*,* or *88 CHAKRA-PHONG*.* You will find the *CHUAN-PIS** (tel 2829948, cheap dormitory) and *J GUESTHOUSE** in no. 86. On Khaosan Road you will find the *V.C.** (with its own restaurant), *P.B.** (with a large billiards-room on the ground floor - 40 Baht an hour), opposite *HELLO*, WALLY*,* and *CHART*.* In a small though rather noisy side-alley *SUNEEPORN** (tel 2819872) near the *LEK** (large with new rooms facing the road, older ones with worse showers behind them, and a restaurant). Further guesthouses can be found opposite the two hotels *NITH CHAROENSUK*** and *NEW SRI PRANATORN***. Rooms with ac: *TOP**, *BONY**, behind these *TUM** (tel 2829954), *V.I.P.** (tel 2825090 - with its own restaurant, popular), *PR 215**, *NUT**, opposite *DIOR**, *ICE**, and *C.H.** (tel 2823276, nice people, pleasant roof-garden, clean, 24-hour restaurant), and *CHADA** (with a pleasant restaurant). In another side alley *VS**, *HARN** and *ET**.

Further east, on Tanao Road, you will find the *NEW PRIVACY** (run by friendly people, quiet courtyard). In the alleys behind it *CENTRAL** (no. 10, tel 2820667 - the modern section is better than the old one). Just around the corner, *S.GH** and *SWEETY** (large rooms). South of Ratchdamnoen you will find *P** and *FRIEND GUESTHOUSE**. There are more guesthouses southwest of the Democracy Monument, e.g. the *T.I.C.** (105 Bunsiri Road - delicious ice-cream is made across the street from here). Another guesthouse, the *V.S.** (6/14 Soi Suphakon, Lan Luang Road) is further east. North of Khaosan Road *BANGLAMPHU** and *TV** (7 Samsen Road, tel 2827451).

On Phra Athit Road, opposite the UNICEF building: *PEACHY**, *BEER**, and *NEW HAWAII**. Mama manages *APPLE 1** (10 Phra Athit Road, tel 2810128), her daughter runs the rather noisy *APPLE 2** (tel. 2816838). In a small alley in between Apple and Khaosan Road you will find the *ROOFGARDEN**, *NGAMPIT**, and *CHUSRI** (100 metres behind the temple).

It is a little more quiet further north, in

TEVES. The *BANGKOK YOUTH HOSTEL*** (with IYHF-card**, dormitory*) can be found at 25/2 Phitsanulok Rd., tel 2820950 (large, clean rooms with showers and wc). In a quiet side-street near the National Library, 71 Samsen Road, Tarat Tawarach Soi 3, you will find the *SAWATDEE GUESTHOUSE** (tel 2825349, family atmosphere, small garden, communal showers and lavatories). Right next door the *SHANTI LODGE**, run by the brother and quite similar (restaurant serving traveller-food). Also *YOON'S***, 241 Ratchavithi Road, near Chitralada Palace (tel 2432420, clean and pleasant but rather noisy).

If you are looking for a little more comfort in Banglampoo, try looking up one of the following hotels: *PHATHANA***, 233 Samsen Rd., tel 2811455. Behind the Mercedes show-room in Ratchdamnoen Road you will find the *RATCHDAMNOEN 90***, tel 2241843 (mainly Thai guests, good, clean rooms). The *ROYAL HOTEL***** is one of the more expensive hotels in the area, tel 2229111, at the corner of Sanam Luang (student discount). You'll receive a discount when booking via a travel agency for the *VIENGTAI HOTEL*****, Tani Road, tel 2828672. The *MAJESTIC HOTEL***** can be found in 97 Ratchdamnoen Road, tel 2815000.

You can always try getting a better rate by bargaining, even in the more expensive hotels. There are several hotels in the centre of the tourist area in **SUKHUMVIT ROAD.** The *ATLANTA****, Sukhumvit Road Soi 2, tel 2526068, is reasonable (many travellers, simple restaurant, large rooms with private bathrooms, swimming-pool). Or try the *GOLDEN PALACE*

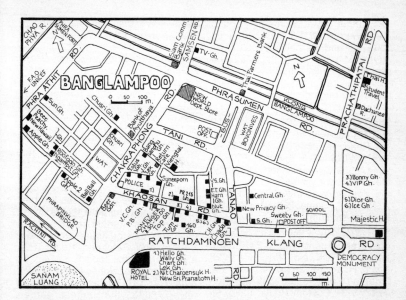

HOTEL*** in Soi 1 (swimming-pool). On Sukhumvit Road itself you will find the *REX HOTEL*****, no. 762, tel 3910100. In the side roads you'll come across the *CROWN HOTEL****, Soi 29, tel 3910511, *STARLIGHT**, Soi 22, tel 3913644 (said to be very sleazy), *FORTUNA*****, Soi 5, tel 2515121 (bargaining possible). The *HOLIDAY***, Soi 6, is new. Many Arabs stay at the rather run down *MI-AMI****, Soi 13, tel 2525140 (private bathrooms, partially air-conditioned, pool). The *OPERA**** is pretty comfortable, Phetchburi Road, Soi Somprasong behind the First Hotel, tel 2524032.

The district around the **RAILWAY STATION** near Chinatown is the best area for finding a cheap room. Try the *SRI HUALAMPONG HOTEL**, 445 Rong Muang Road, tel 2142610 (not too clean), or the *STATION HO-*

TEL** which is directly at the station and not too bad, apart from the fact that it is run by unfriendly people. Cheapest of all is the *PEPSI HOTEL** (Chinese Meng Chen) next to the pharmacy. Do not look for the Pepsi trademark; there is only a hotel sign. You will find the *TT*(*)*, tel 2363053, a good guesthouse hidden in 138 Soi Watmahaphruttharam, Siphraya Mahanakorn Road, approximately 1.5 km from the station (follow the signs). It is clean and has its own little restaurant.

There are more traveller hotels in the **EMBASSY AREA,** near Rama IV Road. The *MALAYSIA***-*****, 54 Soi Ngamduplee, tel 2863582, has acquired a bad reputation these days. There are plenty of bad stories concerning the place, but is nearly always fully booked all the same. There is a notice board in the reception. A little further down the road you'll find *FREDDY'S GUESTHOUSE***, tel 2866722, and the new *LEE GUESTHOUSE***. Opposite the Malaysia (Soi Sri Bamphen), try the *BOSTON INN*** (up to four people can share one of the large double rooms, pool), or the *PRIVACY**** (Mahamek).

The *YMCA **** (no. 27) and *YWCA**** (no. 13) can both be found on Sathon Tai Road, tel 2865134 or 2861936. The *SWISS GUESTHOUSE****, tel 2343729, 3 Convent Road, is nearby. Male travellers can spend the night in the dormitory of the *BOY SCOUT HOSTEL**, Rama I Road, near the National stadium.

There are only a few cheap hotels in the area around the **CENTRAL POST OFFICE**, e.g. *NIAGARA***, 26 Silom Road, tel 2335784. Near the Oriental Hotel is the *SWAN HOTEL****, 31 Custom House Lane, tel 2348594, swimming pool, fully ac, good. The *RAMADA*****, 1169 New Road, tel 2348971 and the *VICTORY*****, 322 Silom Road, tel 2339060 are a little more expensive.

FOOD

As far as eating is concerned, Bangkok is a truly cosmopolitan town. In the old part of town you will be served Thai and Chinese food almost exclusively, though. You can get exquisite **THAI FOOD** at the posh and very expensive *BUSSARACUM*, 35 Soi Phiphat off Convent Road (Silom Road), the *D'JIT POCHANA ORIENTAL*, directly opposite the Oriental Hotel in Thonburi (regular boat service from the Oriental and Royal Orchid Hotels, free of charge), the *KAOLANG*, a floating restaurant on Menam Chao Phya at the very end of Ayutthaya Road, and the *KANABNAM* in Thonburi. From here, restaurant-

boats leave their landing-places at 20:00 h daily. If you are prepared to pay a higher price for a good meal in a beautiful setting, try the *D'JIT POCHANA*, 60 Soi 20 Sukhumvit Road. Among the hundreds of Thai restaurants there are a few that offer entertainment in the form of music and classical dances. These are usually pretty touristy and expensive, though (over 200 Baht!). Try the *BAAN THAI*, Soi 32. One of the few exceptions: *RUEN THEP*, Silom Village in Silom Road, 30-60 Baht for a meal, good choice, large helpings. Classical music and dances are performed free of charge in the garden in the evenings. Further restaurants of this type can be found near Siam Square and Petchburi Road. Thai and international food is served by waiters on roller skates in the *TUMPNAKTHAI*, 131 Ratchadaphisek Road, tel 2778833, the largest garden restaurant in town, with room for 3000 guests, Thai dancing, and fast service. If you wish to have a table near the stage, call and reserve in advance! A meal with several courses will cost you between 100 and 150 Baht and is quite an experience.

While a meal in any of the above mentioned restaurants will cost you at least 60 Baht, there is always the possibility of eating cheap at the many **FOODSTALLS**. A rice or noodle dish, often of surprising quality, will cost you 10-20 Baht. Cheap meals and snacks (e.g. grilled corn on the cob for 3 Baht) are available just about everywhere in the old part of town, as well as at all markets and in the markethalls, e.g. *BAMRUNG MUANG ROAD* on the north side of the road, west of the bridge. No one here speaks English, so do not be too timid to take a peek into the various pots. If you are, why not ask for the delicious-looking meal someone at the next table is eating. Fresh sweet cakes and spicy snacks are available all over the city's streets, e.g. in the streets north of Khaosan Road.

The seafood restaurant in the *PRATUNAM MARKET* is highly recommendable. There is a *FOOD CENTRE* with about 30 foodstalls at the beginning of Sukhumvit Road, underneath the large bridges.

The *YONG LEE* on Sukhumvit/corner of Soi 15 is very popular. Good Tom Yam with giant shrimps and mushrooms is served. You will find a large Thai chicken restaurant near the Malaysia Hotel, on the corner of Rama IV and Soi Ngam Duphli. They have an English menu - try the special, *Chicken in basket.*

Most restaurants in Khaosan Road serve **TRAVELLER FOOD** and are pretty cheap. The Thai meals served are usually rather flavourless, though. The *VIP* and *HELLO RESTAURANT* are popular - saté is served. Good food is also served at the *CHUANPIS.* You can also eat well in the various department stores, especially if you have a craving for European food. The *NEW WORLD DEPARTMENT STORE* in Banglampoo has a food centre on the eighth floor. Here you can enjoy cheap Asian and European meals, as well as a fantastic view of the city.

You will find many **INDIAN RES-TAURANTS** in the area around the GPO. Good curries are served at the *MOTI MAHAL,* 18-20 Old Chartered Bank Lane, opposite the Oriental Plaza. The late Lord Mountbatten's former cook is responsible for the best Indian food in town at the *HI-MALA CHA CHA,* 1229 / 11 Charoen Krung Road (between Surawong and

Silom Road). Equally high prices are charged at the *OMAR KHAYAM* and the *AKBAR,* Soi 3 Sukhumvit Road. Real Indian food is served at the *ROYAL INDIA,* 392/1 Chakraphet Road (restaurant in the back part of the house).

Friends of **JAPANESE COOKERY** will love Bangkok. Fresh ingredients from the nearby sea make sashimis and tempuras particularly tasty, and the prices are reasonable. The excellent *AKAMON* serves delicious food in a distinguished Japanese setting, 233 Sukhumvit Road Soi 21 (Asoke) towards New Phetchburi Road. Good Japanese food is also served at the *AMBASSADOR HOTEL,* 171 Sukhumvit Road, in between Soi 11 and 13. Try the excellent buffet for 90 Baht (+ tax and service) at lunchtime. There is also a food centre with many stalls beyond the large restaurant in the ground floor. There are many good *SUSHI RESTAURANTS* in the small side-roads going off Silom Road.

There are several restaurants serving continental European food in Sukhumvit Road. German restaurants: *HAUS MÜNCHEN,* Soi 15, *GERMAN BIERGARDEN,* Soi 3, and the *GERMAN RESTAURANT,* Soi 4. Nearby, you will also find a Spanish and an Italian restaurant. The average price for a meal is about 80 Baht. The *VILLA NORDEN RESTAURANT,* Sukhumvit Soi 20, near the Windsor Hotel, serves a good Scandinavian smorgasbord.

VEGETARIANS who do not eat fish will have a difficult time in Bangkok. As well as the Indian restaurants already mentioned, we would recommend the *CAFETERIA* on the 4th floor of the Adventist Hospital, 430 Phitsanulok Road and the *WHOLE*

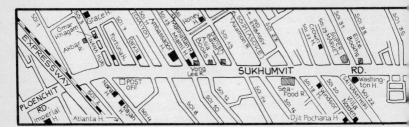

EARTH CAFE, 93/3 Soi Langsuan, Ploenchit Road. A further vegetarian restaurant can be found in Khaosan Road near Tanao Road.

There is a *DANISH BAKERY* in Sukhumvit Road near the Miami Hotel. A French confectionery, *KANIT,* can be found in Thong Road. The Cathay Department Store, Mangkon Road (Chinatown), also has a good bakery. You can get good ice-cream at the *AMARINTR* in Samsen Road, near Luk Luang Road (no sign!).

Something for hungry people: Many of the big hotels offer all-you-can-eat buffet lunches for 80-100 Baht. European, Chinese, and Japanese specialities are frequently served, too.

SHOPPING

If you plan to go shopping in Bangkok, get a copy of Nancy Chandler's *Market Map* (50 Baht) and the monthly *Official Shopping Guide,* which can be obtained free from the Tourist Office (TAT).

ALWAYS BARGAIN! Take your time. Try to learn the Thai numbers by heart and never pay more than a piece is worth, no matter how much you want it. Remember - the average inhabitant of Bangkok lives on 2000 Baht a month.

Do not buy *BUDDHA STATUES!*

Ever since Thais travelling abroad discovered that Europeans use the holy figures as - amongst other things - lamp-stands, it has been forbidden to take them out of the country. Exceptions are only made if you are able to prove convincingly that you are a Buddhist yourself.

Not only merchandise is cheap in Thailand; *SERVICES* are, too. Have your own travelling-bag crafted by local artisans, have your personal shirts or dresses sewn by tailors (who will even copy European models from catalogues), or have a set of letter-paper printed at one of the small printing shops. When in Chinatown or Banglampoo, keep an eye open for workshops. The tailors in Sukhumvit are more expensive, but they speak fluent English for the most part.

There seems to be an inexhaustible supply of *ANTIQUES* in Thailand. Many of them are fakes. A whole section of the working population lives off their production. If you want to take real antiques out of the country you will need the permission of the *Fine Arts Department* in Na Phrathat Road. This takes about three weeks. On the first Saturday of every month 30 antique shops get together to organize an auction in the *Art & Antique Centre,* River City Shopping Complex, 4th floor (near the Royal Orchid Hotel).

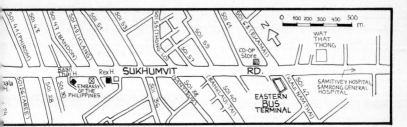

Bangkok is the place to buy **GEMS.** Sapphires and rubies can be bought almost everywhere. Small stones with little flaws are sold for only a couple of Baht. If you do decide to buy, always insist on a certificate of authenticity and a receipt - you wouldn't believe how many foreigners have been swindled. Always remember that all gems can be produced synthetically. You can watch the gems being cut for free on the 5th floor of the Japan Airlines Building, Patpong 1, at *Associated Lapidaries Co. Ltd.* Ban Mo is considered the centre of the gem-business, Pahurat Road, north of Memorial Bridge.

SILK is available in different colours and degrees of purity all over town. You can buy pillows, ties, dresses etc. or simply silk by the yard (= 90 cm). The width is usually 1.20 m. Average quality costs between 100 and 200 Baht. Jim Thompson House quality costs more, of course (see *Jim Thompson House).*

HILLTRIBE ARTS & CRAFTS should be bought in northern Thailand, where the choice is bigger. If you are interested in objects from different regions, take a look around the *State Handicraft Centre* (Narayanaphand) on Lan Luang Road, near the R.S.Hotel, west of the klong - no bargaining! Silverware and niello work, dolls and masks, wood-carv-

ings, rice paper, temple-rubbings, bronze objects, fans, sun umbrellas and much more are available cheaply all over Bangkok.

Longing for wine, bread and cheese? **WESTERN FOOD** can be bought in *Foodland* (the Ploenchit and Patpong Road branches have a particularly central location) and in department stores.

Good **DEPARTMENT STORES:** *SOGO,* Amarin Plaza, near the Erawan Hotel in Ploenchit Road, *NEW WORLD* in Banglampoo, which has its own amusement-centre and a little zoo, Phrasumen Road/Chakraphong Road, and the *CENTRAL DEPARTMENT STORE,* Silom Road, near New Road, with an additional branch on Rama I Road. There are also several shopping-malls in town, e.g. *RIVER CITY* near the Royal Orchid Hotel and *PENINSULA PLAZA,* Charn Issara Tower on Rama IV Road. These are good places to get a general idea of the prices.

FILMS were hardly more expensive than in Europe in 1987. One is officially only allowed to import five rolls, though this is rarely checked. There is a Kodak branch on Sap Road. They do a good job developing Ektachrome, but not, however, Kodachrome films. You will have to pay roughly 130 Baht for 36 prints (10x15 cm) at one of the many Photo-Service shops. This usually includes a voucher for an A4 enlargement.

BOOKS and **MAPS** can be bought at the Asia Bookshop, Sukhumvit Road near Soi 15 (the most extensive stock of books in Bangkok), as well as in the large bookshop on Patpong Road. Further bookshops: Chalermnit Bookshop, Erawan Arcade, Ploenchit Road; DD Books, Soi Asoke; Book Chest, Soi 2, Siam Square (small but with a large supply of good maps). Other bookshops near Siam Square: Robinson (scientific books), Bangkok Books (not too exciting), D.K.Books etc. Second-hand paperbacks can be bought at the Elite Book House, 593 / 5 Sukhumvit Road, tel 2580221. You will also be able to exchange your old paperbacks for new second-hand ones here (2 for 1).

DESIGNER WARE replicas such as Lacoste shirts and socks, Rolex, Cartier, Gucci, Ebel, and Omega watches, as well as Jourdan leather accessories are among the most popular souvenirs tourists take back home. Before buying a watch, have it opened and make sure that the drive mechanism is made exclusively of high-grade steel. Should you find any blue or red plastic parts, do not buy it. Generally, the imitations are of a reasonably high quality and very cheap. Polo-shirts 40-50 Baht (try Patpong, or near the Indra Hotel, especially between 19:00 and 23:00 h). Textiles, shoes, tapes etc. are extremely cheap. Try Tanao Road (Khaosan Road).

You may find that the **PRICE** of identical objects varies from shop to shop. This is particularly the case with clothing. The shopping-arcades of the large hotels are most expensive; after these you get the air-conditioned shops on the main business roads, the shopping malls, and the department stores. Your best bet is to shop at the markets, where you can always bargain.

BANGKOK'S MOST IMPORTANT MARKETS

Weekend Market (Chuan Chatuchak, opposite the Northern Bus Terminal) A very big and colourful market is held here on Saturdays and Sundays 7:00-18:00 h. Clothes, household goods, food, live animals, tapes, souvenirs, electric appliances, and plants are among the things offered. Only plants are sold during the rest of the week. There are many gardening shops on the roads nearby.

Bangrak Market (south of the GPO, near the river) Exotic fruits (early mornings are best), clothing, and flowers for the house-temples are sold here daily.

Teves (north end of Luk Luang Road) Daily flower market selling flowers, plants, orchids, and palmtrees in all shapes, colours, and sizes. On the other side of the klong you'll see a large vegetable and fruit market reaching all the way down Samsen Road. Clothing and foodstalls on the other side of the road.

Pratunam Market (Ratchdamri/ Phetchburi Road junction at the lock) Traditional and western goods sold daily, many craftsmen.

Pak Klong Talaat (near Memorial Bridge at the river) Daily, though mainly in the early mornings - vegetables, fruit, fish, and meat. Come early and watch the sampans (boats) being unloaded!

GENERAL INFORMATION
TOURIST INFORMATION

- the tourist office on Ratchdamnoen Road -TAT is open 8:30-16:00 h. This is the place to get your city map (35 Baht), informative literature (*Official Shopping Guide, Bangkok This Week, Pattaya,* and *Where),* as well as hectographed leaflets.

TOURIST POLICE - an
English-speaking branch of the police has been opened at 509 Vorachak Road, behind the Golden Mount, because of the many 'tourist' problems (mainly robbery). Open daily 8:00-24:00 h, tel 2216206-9.

Here is a well-known example:

"Most travellers will already have heard of the so-called 'friendly Thais' who approach foreigners, offer their services as guides, claim to have cousins in their country, to be going there themselves someday, and even exchange 'addresses' in order to gain their trust. Many fall for them all the same; you get a pleasant guided tour, are invited to a meal, and take a trip down the klongs. At the end it suddenly turns out that your guide is out of money. This is when things get expensive. It might be quite late and dark by this time, and many tourists will think twice before trying to bargain." - taken out of a letter from one of our readers.

Still, don't go about expecting deceit to be lurking around every corner. Many sincere Thais want to get to know foreigners, too, and you will count shared experiences as some of your most pleasant ones later on. Be just a little on the wary side, all the same. If a Thai invites you to a meal it is common decency to return the favour. Where you go and how much you spend, however, should be your own decision.

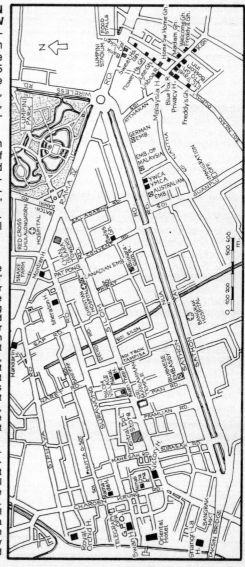

IMMIGRATION - go to Soi Suan-phlu, Sathon Tai Road, tel 2869176 or 2869230. Officially, you can only have your 60-day visa extended (2x2 weeks, 300 Baht each). 14-day visas are sometimes extended for another 7 days, too (300 Baht). Dress well and look your best!

FINE ARTS DEPARTMENT - Na-Phrathat Road (near the National Museum), tel 2214817. Those planning to export antiques will need the permission of this department.

POST OFFICE - the GPO is on New Road, open Mo-Fri 8:00-20:00 h, till 13:00 h at the weekend. Picking up a letter at the poste restante counter will cost you 1 Baht. Telegrams can be picked up in the next room. An airmail letter to Europe costs 15 Baht, an aerogramme 8.50 Baht, and a postcard 8 Baht. Parcels cost approximately 470 Baht for 10 kg and take 8-16 weeks by seamail. Parcels can usually weigh up to 20 kg, sometimes only 10 kg - find out beforehand, the maximum weight can vary from country to country. 1 kg sent by airmail will cost you 250 Baht, 3 kilos 550 Baht. The packing service is open 8:30-16:30 h Mo-Fri, 8:30-12:00 h on Saturdays. You can get a big parcel, complete with plastic string and styrofoam pads, for 40-50 Baht.

TELEPHONES - reaching foreign countries is no problem from the Telecommunication Centre, which is on the right, behind the GPO. It is open around the clock. You can also try calling from any of the large hotels. Collect calls are only possible to France, Italy, Spain, GB, and a couple of countries outside of Europe. A three minute call to the UK will cost you 240 Baht, a person-to-person call 320 Baht, 80 Baht for each additional minute. Calls to Singapore 105 / 140 / 35 Baht, to Burma 90 / 120 / 30 Baht. An inner-city call from a public phone-booth (try to find a quiet one!) will cost you 1 Baht. Old coins are not always accepted. The red telephones and booths are only good for inner-city calls, the blue ones are good for calls within the entire country. Important numbers: Emergency 191, Tourist Police 2216206 (daily 8:00-24:00 h), Ambulance 2811544.

BANKS - large branches of the *THAI FARMERS BANK* will change up to three Eurocheques per person in one month without asking questions. Central branch: 142 Silom Road. The *EUROPEAN ASIAN BANK,* 28 Surasak Road, tel 2338660 accepts international traveller's-cheques. The *BANGKOK BANK* is best suited for having international money orders transferred to. A transfer will take approx. 1 week. You will also receive a good exchange rate here, as at the airport and at the *THAI MILITARY BANK.* All banks are open Mon-Fri 8:30-15:30 h, those that have branches in the tourist-centres are sometimes open 24 hours.

AMERICAN EXPRESS - S.E.A. Tours in the Siam Centre, Rama I Road represent the company in Bangkok. Because stolen cheques are allegedly often used for black-market dealings, you may find that your cheques will not be replaced until you are back home. Do not have letters sent to you poste restante at the office, as many letters have been lost and the employees are rather unfriendly. Should you buy traveller's cheques with your AMEX card here,

be sure to count them upon receipt. You will also be able to get traveller's cheques at the Bangkok Bank with an AMEX card.

MEDICAL AID - the biggest hospitals in town are the *BANGKOK CHRISTIAN HOSPITAL,* 124 Silom Road, tel 2336981, the *RED CROSS HOSPITAL,* Rama IV Road, tel 2526930, and the *ADVENTIST HOSPITAL,* 430 Phitsanulok Road, tel 2811422. The *SAMITIVEJ HOSPITAL,* 137 Sukhumvit Road Soi 49, tel 3920011, *BANGKOK NURSING HOME,* 9 Convent Road, tel 2332610, and the *DENTAL POLYCLINIC,* 211/3 New Phetchburi Road, tel 3145070, are accustomed to treating European patients. The *SAMRONG GENERAL HOSPITAL,* Sukhumvit Road Soi 78, tel 3932131-5, 3931050-4, is a good private clinic. Consultation hours are 8:00-16:30 h, Mon-Fri. The 45 bus stops right in front of the door. 60 doctors work here, many of them educated in Europe or the United States. A private bed costs about 500 Baht plus 150-200 Baht for food daily. Root-canal treatment will cost you 1200 Baht, a chest X-ray 130 Baht. *Sex tourism* has left its mark, even in the medical field. The Grace Hotel, for instance, has its own VD clinic. You will receive better and cheaper treatment at the *BANGRAK HOSPITAL,* Sathon Tai Rd., tel 2860431. This hospital specializes in the treatment of VD and works in cooperation with the WHO. Hundreds of patients are treated daily according to the newest medical methods. The atmosphere is rather unpleasant. The *SEVENTH-DAY ADVENTIST HOSPITAL* is run by missionaries and quite good,

though rather expensive - 430 Phitsanulok Road, tel 2811422. Cholera shots cost 20 Baht at the Pasteur Institute (Snake Farm). Here you will also find a bulletin for tourists concerning the newest medical developments. Thailand is the country with the highest death-rate due to rabies. If you are bitten by a dog or any other stray animal get the necessary shots as soon as possible, i.e. within 5 days. The new HDC vaccine against rabies is now available in the Bangkok Nursing Home Hospital, among others.

NEWSPAPERS - There are two daily English-language newspapers in Bangkok, the *BANGKOK POST* and *THE NATION.* Both cost 8 Baht. You can also get the Asian magazines *ASIA WEEK* and *FAR EASTERN ECONOMIC REVIEW,* as well as *TIME* and *NEWSWEEK.*

CINEMAS - a popular source of entertainment at the weekends. Ancient, second-rate American B-movies, Chinese action films made in Hong Kong, and local productions are shown. A programme can be found in the Bangkok Post. Cinemas are entered on your city-map.

PUBS - most pubs are on Sukhumvit and Patpong Road. Men of all nations have their respective headquarters here. Here they can almost feel as if they were back home, reading their Sunday papers and discussing the newest results of the first division, with a Thai girl on their lap. These strange Thai-European 'alliances' can be seen all over Soi 3, especially in the German Beergarden. What - and if - the girls think about what they have to do for their living is of no import - the main thing is that a good time is had by one and all. But is it?

NIGHTCLUBS - Bangkok's nightlife is notorious. It offers hundreds of ways of spending money. In spite of the male domination, women can have a good time here, too. We would not recommend going out alone, though. The expensive hotels have classy clubs featuring live music or discotheques. Patpong offers shady dance bars with or without gogo dancers, and there are loads of sleazy Thai nightclubs where men can choose one of the many girls sitting behind a large sheet of glass. There is something for everyone here -massage parlours, transvestite bars..

HORSERACING - is worth it, if only to enjoy the setting and the multitudes of visitors. Saturdays from 12.15 h in the *ROYAL BANGKOK SPORTS CLUB,* Henri Dunant Road, Sundays from 12.15 h at the *ROYAL TURF CLUB,* Phitsanulok Road.

THAI-BOXING - can be seen at the Ratchdamnoen Stadium, Mon, Wed, and Thurs, at 18:00 h, Sundays at 17:00 and 20:00 h, also at the Lumpini Stadium, Tue, Fri, Sat, at 18:00 h. The best fights do not begin until 21:00 h. Price of admission: 120-500 Baht.

MASSAGES - have a traditional Thai massage for 120 Baht an hour at the Wat Pho. You can also sign up for massage courses here, lasting 2-3 weeks and costing between 2000 and 3000 Baht. Medical massages are available at Chiropractic Massage on New Road/Soi 44, near the Shangri-La Hotel, open Mon-Sat, 8:30-19:00 h. Most of the city's so-called massage parlours are little more than brothels - be warned!

CLASSICAL THAI DANCING - can be seen daily in various restaurants with dinner (expensive), as well as at the *Kodak Show,* held just for snap-happy tourists every Thursday and Sunday at 11:00 h in the garden of the Oriental. Admission 80 Baht. At weekends during the dry season you can watch classical dances and music being performed free of charge in the garden of the National Museum. Other free performances can be seen. They are held in honour of the patron god of the Lak Muang Shrine and the Erawan Shrine (see *A Walk Through Town & Food*).

THE ROYAL FAMILY - although Thailand has been a constitutional monarchy since 1932, the King is still one of the country's most respected representatives. He is also the spiritual Buddhist leader of his country. The common people are very proud and fond of their king. You will see pictures of the Royal Family everywhere. Thais that happen to be in the area will nearly always proudly turn to face the Royal Palace when the National Anthem is played in the mornings. Even the traffic comes to a complete standstill.

PUBLIC TRANSPORT IN BANGKOK

Everybody knows that rush hour in Bangkok is hell on wheels. Avoid being caught in the traffic between 7:00 and 9:00 h, 16:00 and 17:30 h. German city planners have tried in vain to eradicate the problem by designing modern bridges. You will see for yourself that these are no help. During the past few years the capital has been introducing an extensive one-way street system. Buses now have their own lane and are still allowed to drive in both directions. This has been the cause of numerous tricky situations, but seems to help in the long run nevertheless. These days, travelling by bus in Bangkok is much faster than travelling by car.

TAXIS - approximately 90% of the country's vehicles are registered in Bangkok; these include over 1 million cars. A great number of these are taxis, scores of which can be seen fighting their way through the chaotic traffic at any time of day. The fare always has to be agreed on before you actually set off. Some drivers will try to get an exceptionally high price from you, especially those at the airport or standing in front of the large hotels. Don't get taken for a ride! Send them away, there are plenty of empty cabs around. Always remember that most taxi-drivers have to pay for gas or petrol themselves, as well as the rent for the car (200 Baht daily). Here are some fair prices: short distances 30 Baht (sam sip), medium-length distances outside of rush hour 40 Baht (sih sip), longer distances 50 Baht (hah sip). Taxis with green registration-stickers are more expensive. These can usually be found standing outside of the big hotels. All new cars have air conditioning, but there are plenty of old cars - veritable rubbish-heaps - that don't. And if they have black plastic seats and you get caught in the rush hour....

BUSES - the cheapest form of transportation, though not the least problematic. Beware - pickpockets favour the routes predominantly used by tourists (especially city-airport buses). They have developed a special talent for slicing handbags and back pockets from behind. Ever since buses have been granted their own lane, rush hour has become much less of

an ordeal, particularly because buses are allowed to drive in both directions on one-way streets. The final destinations of the buses are only provided in Thai letters, you'll have to go by the numbers. Be careful not to get into the wrong buses or go in the wrong direction. This can easily happen; ac-buses (with a red sign) and non ac-buses (with a blue sign) have the same numbers but go to completely different destinations. The ac-buses are very comfortable.

A map of Bangkok with all bus routes *(The Latest Tour Guide to Bangkok and Thailand* - 35 Baht) can be bought at the Tourist Office in the airport, the Tourist Office in town, and at most hotels and bookshops. It is a reliable map that will help you get almost anywhere. Tickets for the non ac-buses cost 2 Baht. A ride in one of the ac-buses will cost you 5-15 Baht, depending on the distance. The most important lines:

No. **26** (blue sign): Northern Bus Terminal - Southern Bus Terminal.

No. **29** (blue sign): Airport - Northern Bus Terminal - Train Station.

No. **38** (blue sign): Northern Bus Terminal - Eastern Bus Terminal.

No. **40** (blue sign): Eastern Bus Terminal - Station - Southern Bus Terminal.

No. **59** (blue sign): Airport - Sanam Luang (Khaosan Road).

The above-mentioned non ac-buses for 2 Baht usually run until 22:30 h. The following ac-buses cost 15 Baht for a ride downtown from the airport:

(ac) No. **4**: Airport - Silom Road - Charoen Krung Road (runs till 19:00 hours).

(ac) No. **10**: Airport - Victory Monument - Southern Bus Terminal (runs till 20:00 h).

(ac) No. **13:** Airport - Sukhumvit Road - Eastern Bus Terminal (till 20:00 h).

(ac) No. **29** - Airport - Siam Square - Station (till 19:00 h).

TUK-TUKS - are small, converted scooters (Vespa), also known as Samlors. They are usually a little cheaper than taxis. If you have luggage or are more than two, you might find them a little tight. The drivers rarely go long distances (to the airport, for instance), and we suggest you don't ask them, as you always end up inhaling the exhaust fumes of every car in the radius of a hundred metres. Always make sure that the driver has understood where you want to go - most of them do not speak English. The government tried banning the 8000 tuk-tuks a few years ago, but found that this was met with violent opposition from both the drivers and the general population, an indication of how important these vehicles are to the city.

SONGTHAEW - these are small trucks that have been converted to mini buses. Passengers sit facing each other on low benches. These privately operated buses take care of a large part of commuter travel. They drive set routes and cost 2 Baht, like buses. It's rather difficult for non-Thai speaking 'farangs' to ascertain where they are going, though. Songthaew frequently take over from the buses when it comes to bringing people downtown from the airport in the evenings.

BOATS
Ferries - You can cross the Menam Chao Phya from various landing-

places for a fee of 0.5 Baht. The ferries are relatively tall and have a roof. Most passengers stand.

Klong Boats - these are long, narrow boats with an outboard motor. They can often be rented for about 100 Baht an hour. You will find their landing-places behind Wat Pho, near the Thammasat University, and at the Oriental Hotel (many tourists). Boats for rides down Saen Sae Klong can be rented at the Pratunam Market, boats for rides down the Phra Kanong Klong at the Rung-A-Roon Market behind Soi 71. Boats leave for Klong Mon every half hour from Tha Tien Pier behind Wat Pho between 6:30 and 18:00 h. The price is 4 Baht. Boats going up the Klong Bang Waek leave Samphan Phut Pier (Memorial Bridge every fifteen minutes, 4 Baht, from 6:00 to 17:00 h. Klong boats down the Klong Bang Khoo Wiang and the Klong Bang Yai leave from the Tha Chang Pier. The boats leaving Wat Dao Khanong (Krung Thep) go down the Klong Dao Khanong.

Express Boats - these travel regularly between Nonthaburi (North) and Krung Thep Bridge (South) 6:00-18:00 h daily. They leave every ten minutes 7:00-8:00 h, every quarter of an hour 6:00-7:00 h, 8:00-9:00 h, and 15:00-18:00 h, every 1/2 hour between 9:00 and 15:00 h. These long boats with their many seats are a pleasant, open-air alternative to the hot, crowded buses. Prices:

Zone 1: (3 Baht, approx. 20 minutes). Nonthaburi - Payab or Kiak Kai - Ratchawong or Rachini - Wat Ratchsingkorn

Zone 2: (5 Baht, approx. 50 minutes). Nonthaburi - Ratchawong or Kiak Kai - Wat Ratchsingkorn

Zone 3 (7 Baht, approx. 70 minutes).

Nonthaburi - Wat Ratchsingkorn

Zone 4 (2 Baht, approx. 7 minutes)

Wat Vorachanyawat - Krung Thep Bridge.

You will find plans showing all stops mounted on hoardings at some of the landing-places. The boats do not always call at every stop, however (e.g. No. 11-13) The most important stops from north to south, (B) = Bangkok side, (T) = Thonburi side:

❑ 1 Nonthaburi (B) - final stop on buses 30-33, 64, 90 from Sanam Luang

❑ 2 Pibul Songkhram 2 (B)

❑ 3 Wat Khian (T)

❑ 4 Wat Khema (B)

❑ 5 Pibul Songkhram 1 (B)

* Rama IV Bridge

❑ 6 Bang Pho (B)

❑ 7 Kiak Kai (B) Khieo Khaika Road, buses 30-33, 64, 65, 90

❑ 8 Payab (B), Nakhon Chaisri Rd., final stop on buses 9 and 14

* Krung Thon Bridge

❑ 10 Teves (B), Krung Kasem Road, buses 3, 9, 30-33, 64, 65, 90

❑ 11 Visutkasat (B), Visutkasat Rd., final stop on bus 6

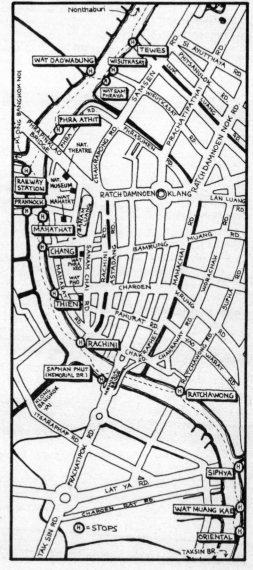

❑ 12 Wat Samphraya (B), Sam
   phraya Road,

❑ 13 Wat Daowadung (T)

❑ 14 Wat Dusit (T) or Phra Athit (B)

   * Phra Pin Klao Bridge

❑ 15 Railway Station (T), Klong Yai,
   Royal Barges, buses 58, 83, 91

❑ 16 Prannock (T), Prannock Road,
   bus 81

❑ 17 Mahathat (B), Wat Mahathat,
   Thammasat University. Between
   this landing-place and number

❑ 18 Chang (B), Na Phra Lan Rd.,
   behind Wat Phra Keo, you will
   find various landing-places from
   which klong boats set out.

❑ 19 Thien, at Ta Thien Market behind Wat Pho. Ferries going to
   Wat Arun can be caught from
   here as well as

❑ 20 Rachini (B), at the end of Ra
   chini Road

❑ 21 Saphan Phut (B), many klong
   boats leave for Thonburi from
   here.

   * Memorial Bridge

❑ 22 Ratchawong (B), Ratchawong
   Rd., Chinatown

❑ 23 Siphya (B), at the Royal Orchid
   Hotel

❑ 24 Wat Muang Kae (B), at the
   General Post Office

❑ 25 Oriental (B), klong boats are
   for hire here

   * Bangrak Market & Taksin Bridge

❑ 26 Wat Yannawa at the end of
   Sathon Tai Road

❑ 27 Wat Sawetchat (T), buses 6,
   86 (Sanam Luang), 88

   * Krung Thep Bridge

❑ 28 Krung Thep (T), the stop is
   close to Wat Dao Khanong

❑ 29 Thanon Tok (B) at the end of
   Charoen Krung Road, final stop
   on buses 1 and 22.

LEAVING BANGKOK
BY PLANE

Don Muang Airport lies 28 km south
of town. The new National Airport is
just 500 m away from the International Airport. A minibus commutes
between the two regularly (20-40
Baht). Banks offering reasonable
rates of exchange can be found in
both airports, e.g. the Thai Military
Bank (open 6:30-24:00 h, sometimes
around the clock). There is also a
post office (in both departure halls,
open 24 hrs. daily), a left luggage office (in both, open 6:00-22:00 h, 20
Baht per day and per item of luggage), a hotel booking agency
(international arrivals; for cheap as
well as expensive hotels), a tourist
office (international arrivals), and the
Airport Transport Service. You have
the following ways of getting into
town:

A *minibus service* will take you to
any major hotel for a fee of 100 Baht.
The bus doesn't leave until it's half
full, but this usually doesn't take too
long.

The *shuttle service,* which leaves
for the Asia Hotel (Phya Thai Road
near Petchburi Road) every 30 minutes, costs 60 Baht. There is also an
expensive limousine service.

In front of the airport you'll see *ac-
taxis* as well as private cars who will
offer a ride into town for 300 Baht.
The taxis just around the corner, on
the main road, will only cost you 150
Baht if you bargain well. A ride to the

airport from town will usually only cost you about 120 Baht.

The cheapest (and slowest) alternative are the *local buses.* Careful, though; pickpockets love these lines. A ride into town from the bus stop, 50 metres from the arrival hall, costs 2 Baht and takes approx. 1 1/2 hours. Buses stop running at around 22:30 h. Bus 59 goes to Khaosan Road, bus 29 goes to the railway station via the Northern Bus Terminal. If you want to get to Rama IV Road (Malaysia Hotel etc.) stay on the bus until you reach Rama IV Road, then change to bus 4, 46, or 47. Ac-bus 10 will take you to Samsen Road for 15 Baht until 20:00 h. If you want to get to Silom Road take ac-bus 4, which runs until 19:00 h. If You want to get to Sukhumvit Road or the Eastern Bus Terminal, your best bet is taking ac-bus 13, which runs until 20:00 h. (see also *Public Transport in Bangkok).*

Once the public buses have stopped running, *private songthaew and minibuses* take over their routes. To play it safe, always ask the conductor if the bus is actually heading for the place you want to go to.

A *train* will take you into town from the suburban station opposite the airport. We would only recommend doing this between 6:30 and 9:00 or 16:30 and 18:00 h, as it is only then that trains leave every 20 minutes.

Airport tax is 150 Baht for international flights, 20 Baht for domestic flights.

Examples of prices (in US$) offered for one-way flights to neighbouring countries at cheap travel bureaus:

CALCUTTA 141, COLOMBO 173, DHAKA 141, DELHI 197, DENPASAR 270, HONG KONG 135, JAKARTA 190, KATHMANDU 175, SINGAPORE 119, MANILA 160, RANGOON 101.

You will hardly ever have to pay the much higher IATA rates if you go to the right places. The following travel agencies offer flights at prices considerably below those of the IATA. This doesn't mean that you will always be able to get a cheap flight from Bangkok; flights to Burma, for instance, cost 4000 Baht return with Thai and 3600 Baht with UBA these days. A flight from Calcutta to Rangoon costs US$132.

Compare the prices of the following *agencies:*

STA TRAVEL, Thai Hotel, 78 Pratchathipatai Road, tel 2815314-5.

TRAD TOURS, Viengtai Hotel, 42 Tani Road, tel 2815788.

TTS TRAVEL SERVICE 2/9 Sri Bamphen Road, off Rama IV, tel 2826095.

These three travel bureaus sell tickets at reduced rates to students with a valid ISIC identification card.

TRU TRAVEL, Dusit Thani Bldg., Silom Road, in between the Indian temple and Pramuan Road, tel 2353813-7.

TAA TRAVEL, 84 Sukhumvit Road, opposite Fiat, tel 2518843.

K TRAVEL, 6 Sukhumvit Road, next to the railway station, tel 2523337.

TTS TRAVEL, Soi Nana Tai, Sukhumvit Road, near Rajah Hotel.

ETC, 2/12 Sri Bamphen Road, 100 metres from the Malaysia Hotel, tel 2871477 and 203 Khaosan Road, tel 2822958.

These travel agencies also sell tickets to Europe at reduced rates. You can get a plane to Athens, Amsterdam,

Rome, Paris, or London via Dhaka with BANGLADESH BIMAN for US$400. AEROFLOT flights to Copenhagen and London cost a little more.

DIETHELM TRAVEL, 544 Ploenchit Road, tel 2524041-9, organizes group-tours to Burma and Vietnam. Getting a visa for Vietnam takes at least three weeks; the cost from Bangkok for a group of at least two people lies between US$1000 and 1400 for a 7-9 day stay.

THAI AIRWAYS offers the following inland-flights: CHIANG MAI 1275 or 1020 (nightflight), CHIANG RAI 1575, HAT YAI 1760 or 1410 (nightflight), MAE HONG SON 1585, PHITSANU-LOK 730 PHRAE 860.-, NAN 900.-, SURAT THANI 1380, PHUKET 1545 or 1240 (nightflight), UBON 1080, UDON 1010 Baht.

Flights can be reserved weeks in advance in the Thai Airways office (by telephone if you like) and can be paid for later in any travel agency. If you have booked a flight with any airline be sure to check up on your reservation, as some agencies sell confirmed tickets for flights that are already fully booked.

The private airline BANGKOK AIR-WAYS allegedly flies to KORAT (380), SURIN (700), KRABI, and KO SAMUI. Nothing much has come of this yet...

ADDRESSES OF IMPORTANT AIRLINES

AEROFLOT, 7 Silom Road, tel 2336965-7

AIR INDIA, Amarin Tower, 500 Ploenchit Road, tel 2569614

AIR LANKA, 1 Patpong Road, tel 2369293

ALIA, 56 Silom Road, tel 2360030-9

BANGKOK AIRWAYS, Don Muang, National Airport, tel 5237116

BANGLADESH BIMAN, 56 Surawong Road, tel 2336178

BURMA AIRWAYS, 208/1 Surawong Road, tel 2349692

CAAC, 134/1-2 Silom Road, tel 2351880-2

CATHAY PACIFIC, 109 Surawong Road, tel 2331331

CHINA AIRLINES, Siam Centre, 965 Rama I Road, tel 2519656-9

EGYPT AIR, 120 Silom Road, tel 2337601-3

GARUDA, 944/19 Rama IV Road, tel 2330981-2

KOREAN AIRLINES, 946 Rama IV Rd., Dusit Thani Bldg., tel 2349283

LOT, 485 Silom Road, tel 2352223-7

LUFTHANSA, 331/1-3 Silom Road, tel 2341350

MALAYSIAN AIRLINE SYSTEM, 98-102 Surawong Road, tel 2349795

PAKISTAN INTERNATIONAL, 52 Surawong Road, tel 2342961-5

PHILIPPINE AIRLINES, 56 Surawong Road, tel 2332350-2

QANTAS AIRWAYS, Charn Issara Bldg., 942/51 Rama IV Road, tel 2360102

ROYAL NEPAL AIRLINES, 1/4 Convent Road, tel 2333921-4

SIA (Singapore Airlines), Silom Centre, 1 Silom Road corner of Rama IV Road, tel 2360303

* THAI AIRWAYS, 6 Larn Luang Road, tel 2800090

* THAI INTERNATIONAL, 89 Vibha-vadi Rangsit Road, tel 5130121,

* for reservations call 2333810

(* there may be changes here, as the two companies are about to merge)

BY BUS

Bangkok has three main bus stations. With the exception of a few ac-buses most buses leave town from one of these stations.

To the east coast: **Eastern Bus Terminal**, Sukhumvit Road, opposite Soi Ekamai, tel 3913301. You can reach the terminal by taking bus 38 from the airport (via Northern Bus Terminal), ac-bus 13 via Sukhumvit Road, or bus 40 from the Southern Bus Terminal via the train station. From the Eastern Bus Terminal you can catch buses to:

BAN PHE (Ko Samet) (70, return 120), ac-buses need approx. 3 hrs., CHANTHABURI (309 km) 56 (105), CHONBURI (80 km) 18 (35), PAT-TAYA (138 km) 29 (50), RAYONG (236 km) 38 (69), TRAT (387 km) 70 (128) Baht. The figures given in parenthesis are for ac-buses.

To the north and northeast: **Northern Bus Terminal**, Phaholyothin Road (road leading to the airport), tel 2794484. This terminal can be reached by taking bus 29 from the railway station, ac-bus 10 from the Southern Bus Terminal, ac-bus 13 from Sukhumvit Road. All three of these buses also run from and to the airport. From the Northern Bus Terminal you can catch buses to:

AYUTTHAYA (75 km)17, BANG PA IN (63 km) 13, CHIANG MAI (713 km; ac-buses need approx. 9 hrs.) 133 (242), CHIANG RAI (844 km) 157 (283), KORAT (Nakhon Rachasima, 256 km) 51 (92), LAMPANG (610 km) 115 (207), LAMPHUN (689 km) 131 (227),

LOPBURI (153 km) 32 (60), LOEI (560 km) 106 (191), NAKHON PANOM (727 km) 136 (245), NONG KHAI (614 km) 115 (209), PHITSA-NULOK (498 km) 78 (171), SUKHOTHAI (544 km) 84 (153), SURIN (452 km) 86 (155), TAK (524 km) 80 (146), UBON (675 km) 126 (229), UDON (561 km) 106 (191) Baht. The figures given in parenthesis are for ac-buses.

To the south and west: **Southern Bus Terminal,** Charan Sanit Wong Rd., Thonburi, tel 4113270. This terminal can be reached by taking bus 28 from the Northern Bus Terminal, bus 40 from the Eastern Bus Terminal via the train station, and ac-bus 10 from the airport. From the Southern Bus Terminal you can catch buses to:

CHUMPHON (499 km) 95 (160), DAMNOEN SADUAK (109 km) 35, HAT YAI (1022 km) 187 (339), HUA HIN (220 km) 47 (74), KANCHANA-BURI (129 km) 23 (53), KRABI (867 km) 161 (290), NAKHON PATHOM (56 km) 13 (24), NAKHON SI THAM-MARAT (814 km) 150 (270), PHETCHBURI (150 km) 35 (54), PRACHUAP KHIRI KHAN (323 km) 63 (105), PHUKET (922 km) 165 (299), RANONG (614 km) 110 (198), SAMUT SONGKHRAM (78 km) 18 (33), SURAT THANI - ferry harbour to Ko Samui (668 km, 10-12 hrs. with ac / non ac-buses) 125 (225) TRANG (1133 km) 174 (314) Baht. The figures in parenthesis are for ac-buses.

Although they are almost twice as expensive as regular buses, we would nevertheless recommend taking ac-buses for long journeys, e.g. to Chiang Mai (9 hours), Surat Thani (10 hours), or Phuket (14 hours). In spite of the rather unnerving videos which are shown for the entire length of the ride, we consider them much more comfortable. Food and drink (though nothing exciting) is included in the price, and sometimes you will even be picked up from your hotel. Nightbuses are cheaper. It is worth paying the extra fare just for the view, though. The drivers are often a bit over-eager, and racing against the buses of competing companies is frequently one of their favourite pastimes. Thieves are often along for the ride, too, so take care! Also do not forget to bring warm clothing; an air-conditioner turned on full blast all night long can get quite chilly. The non ac-buses get cold at nights, too.

The ac-buses either leave from their company offices or from the bus terminals.

Ac-buses to **Chiang Mai** (250-300 Baht):

Indra Tour, Ratchaprarop Road, tel 2516197; Transportation Co., Phanom Yothin Road, tel 2794484-7; Piman Tour, 60 Ratchprasong Road, tel 2516428; Grand Tour, 566 Ploenchit Road, tel 2520335-7.

Ac-buses to **Phuket** (250-300 Baht):

Transportation Co., (see above), departure Southern Bus Terminal; Grand Tour (see above); Prince Travel Service, 295 Bangkok Bazaar Road, tel 2516298; Thai Transport Co., Ratchdamnoen Klang Road, tel 2228147; Phuket Travel Service, 77 / 7 Visutkasat Road, tel 2829837.

Ac-buses to **Ko Samui** (225 Baht):

Thai Transport Co., (see above), Sophon Tour, Majestic Hotel Ratchdamnoen Klang Road, tel 2816172, Pak Thai Tour, Phra Sumane Road, tel 2812283, and Udomrat Tour, Ratchdamnoen Klang Road, tel 2212617.

BY TRAIN

Trains leave Bangkok in five directions - to the north, the northeast, east, south, and northwest. Generally, trains are slower and more expensive than buses. They are much more comfortable, though. You can sleep wonderfully in the second class. Air conditioned trains tend to get a bit chilly at nights. Tourists have been drugged and robbed - not frequently, but a couple of times - so be wary of strangers offering food.

We would suggest buying the tickets yourself up to 90 days in advance at the Advance Booking Office in the Main Railway Station, open Mon-Fri 8:30-18:00 h, Sat and Sun till 12:00 h noon. Reservations from abroad by bank draft are also possible. If you're planning to take the train to Butterworth, definitely book in advance (seats can only be reserved up to the Malaysian border). There is an information office at the railway station, tel 2237010 + 2237020. This is the place to get the newest schedule (if it's available).

Many north- and northeastbound trains also stop at the Samsen station (north of Chitralada Palace) and at Don Muang Airport.

Examples for prices in the 2nd class - figures in parenthesis for 3rd class - without extra charges (for detailed information concerning additional charges see *Transport* in General Information, pp. 103-107):

Northbound

Departures: Den Chai (near Phrae) - 6:40, 7:05, 22:00 h; Phitsanulok - 8:30 and 20:00 h; Chiang Mai - 15:45, 18:00, and 19:40 h; trains to Phitsanulok need only 5 hrs. if you take one of the Railcar Specials, 11:05, 17:05,

23:05 h. AYUTTHAYA 31 (15), LOP-
BURI 57 (28), PHITSANULOK 143
(69), LAMPANG 221 (106), LAM-
PHUN 247 (118), CHIANG MAI 255
(121) Baht.

Northeastbound

Departures: 6:50, 7:15, 15:25, 18:45,
21:00, and 23:20 h to Ubon; 6:30,
19:00, and 20:30 h to Nong Khai;
9:05 h to Korat. Daily Railcar Specials
to Khon Khaen at 8:20 and 22:30 h,
taking 7 hrs., and to Surin at 10:55
and 21:50 h, taking 6-7 hrs.

Eastbound

Departures: Aranyapraphet - 6:00
and 13:10 h; Chachoengsao - 7:00 h;
Prachinburi - 9:40 and 17:25 h; Krabin Buri - 8:05, 11:25, and 14:55 h.

CHACHOENGSAO (13), ARANYA-
PRATHET (48), KRABIN BURI (33)
Baht.

Northwestbound

Departures: Kanchanaburi / River
Kwae - 8:00 and 13:55 h, from the
Thonburi station. The Thai railway
offers a special day-return ticket to
this area at the weekends and on
holidays (75 Baht). The train leaves
from the main station at 6:35 h (!),
stops at Nakhon Pathom (45 minutes), and at the bridge, which can be
crossed on foot. The train stops at the
final station, Nam Tok, for 2 1/2 hours.
There is a further stop at Kanchanaburi on the ride back. Arrival in
Bangkok 19:35 h.

NAKHON PATHOM (14), KANCHA-
NABURI (28), NAM TOK (49) Baht.

Southbound

Departures: Hua Hin - 9:00 h; Sungai
Golok (Malaysian border) - 12:30 and
14:00 h; Butterworth / Penang

(Malaysia) - 15:15 h; Hat Yai - 16:00
h; Nakhon Si Thammarat - 17:30 h;
Trang - 18:30 h.

RATCHBURI 54 (25), PHETCHBURI
73 (34), HUA HIN 94 (45),
PRACHUAP KHIRI KHAN 125 (59),
CHUMPHON 177 (83), SURAT THA-
NI 229 (109), NAKHON SI THAM-
MARAT 285 (136), HAT YAI 319
(152), SUNGAI GOLOK (border) 385
(184), BUTTERWORTH 448, KUALA
LUMPUR 689, SINGAPORE 952
Baht. You will need approximately 2
days for the 1927 km journey from
Bangkok to Singapore.

Combined train-bus-ferry tickets to Ko
Samui cost 229 Baht (2nd Class) or
180 Baht (3rd Class), departure 18:30
h, arrival in Ko Samui the next morning at 10:30 h. Beds cost an additional 70 or 100 Baht, ac 80 Baht.

CAR HIRE

Driving through Bangkok's traffic is
not much fun. All the same, this is the
place to find a good, cheap hire car if
you plan to travel extensively through
Thailand. It is especially worth it if you
intend to go to the National Parks. For
addresses see *Transportation* in
General Information.

MOTORCYCLES

Used motorcycles can be bought
cheaply in Bangkok. A thirteen month
old 125 cc Kawasaki, for instance, will
cost you only 29,000 Baht. Honda
motorcycles are even cheaper. In addition, they need less petrol and are
more suitable for the mountains. The
bikes can be re-sold at the end of
your holiday for only a very slight
overall loss.

THE AREA AROUND BANGKOK

Stuck in Bangkok because of that letter, that plane, or that visa you still have to wait for? Many travellers find themselves in this situation at some stage of their journeys, and it is at this point that they start longing to get out of the city, to enjoy the magnificent tropical countryside just one more time before returning home. You can reach all of the places listed in this chapter in a day, although it might not always be possible to get there and back in this time. If you have plenty of time, stay longer - it's worth it! Avoid the week-ends, however, as this is when the entire city decides to go on a one- or two-day field-trip.

TO THE WEST

A ride to the floating market and to Nakhon Pathom afterwards makes a good day-trip. On Sundays, why not take a day-trip to the River Kwae (see *Leaving Bangkok - Trains).* Kanchanaburi and the River Kwae would definitely also be worth a longer visit. If you're feeling adventurous, sign up for the 2-3 day rafting tour on the river.

DAMNOEN SADUAK

This small town is best known for its floating markets, especially since the markets in Thonburi have become so commercial. We would recommend disembarking before the boat actually starts going through the market; the bridges and riverbanks are the best places from which to watch the tumultuous activity. This way one does not disturb those at work. Unfortunately, large and loud groups of tourists in motor-boats are becoming more and more common these days. Market women have to watch out for the waves caused by these boats, lest their wares get wet. On top of everything else the tourists are only - if at all - interested in buying gaudy souvenirs from the riverbank merchants, not the actual wares offered at the market itself. It is a tragic but safe assumption, therefore, that these markets will soon become thoroughly commercial, too, like those in Thonburi. Bridges and footpaths have been built to protect the market, but these are just a further contribution to the gradual loss of authenticity of these beautiful floating bazaars.

The region southwest of Thonburi, which is criss-crossed by a number of klongs, is considered the 'Garden of Thailand'. From here, the large cities are supplied with fresh fruit and vegetables. One can find truly idyllic places along the klongs of this area. If you are travelling by paddle-boat - as does the majority of the population - you will be able to experience the perfect peace and quiet of the green, palm-studded gardens and the cool, gently flowing klongs.

Fishermen cast out their nets from the riverbanks, sun-tanned children frolic in the refreshing water, and women carefully manoeuvre their fully-laden boats through the current. Most of these women traders still wear the traditional high straw hat and navy blue jackets to protect themselves from the intense rays

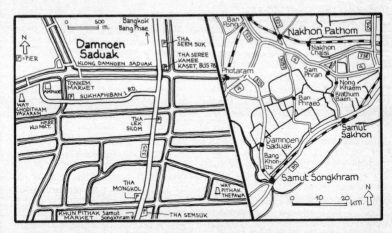

of the sun. In addition, many open large yellow sunshades over their wares. In order to get the fruit and vegetables to the markets as soon as possible, many of these hard-working women leave their homes at night, so as to be at the market before dawn - except for the few that have an outboard motor, that is.

HOW TO GET THERE

Get up early and take the 78 bus from the Southern Bus Terminal in THON-BURI to DAMNOEN SADUAK, 110 km west of Bangkok. The first buses leave at about 7:00 h, after that every 1/2 hour. The ride will cost you 30 Baht. Small motor boats leave for the TONKEM floating market every 15-20 minutes for 5 Baht directly from the bus-stop. If you want to see the other markets nearby, KHUN PITHAK and HERE KUE, you'll have to pay more (approx. 300-400 Baht for a 1 1/2 hour tour - bargain!). You will also find a minibus terminal next to the bus-stop. From here you can catch a ride to the market for 1 Baht, or you can walk along the canal - approx. 1.5 km.

ROSEGARDEN

30 km west of town, on the road leading to Nakhon Pathom, this tourist-park offers the sort of package deal that visitors hoping for an 'instant-Thailand experience' are looking for. The so-called 'Thai village', surrounded by artificial lakes, restaurants, a hotel etc., is the park's main attraction. The show commences at 15:00 h: 5 minutes of cock-fighting, 5 minutes of Thai boxing, a 5-minute traditional wedding, five minutes for the ordination of a monk... For a fee of 140 Baht you can also watch elephants pushing tree-logs back and forth. Bicycles are for hire in the park itself.

NAKHON PATHOM

This is one of Thailand's oldest towns. You will find the country's largest pagoda here, which was the point from which Buddhism spread into this part of the country. A smaller chedi, probably built by the Mon, stood on the site of today's huge *PHRA PATHOM CHEDI* as early as the 4th century. Even in those days the chedi was said to have had a height of 39 metres. In the 11th century the Khmer added a prang. Today it is one of the highest chedis in the whole world (over 120 metres). Because of the imposing design and construction of the temple one speculates that this is where monks from Ceylon must have founded the first Theravada-Buddhism Centre in Thailand.

When he was still prince, King Mongkut set out for numerous pilgrimages to this temple ruin in the middle of the jungle. Once king, he decided to have a gigantic chedi built on top of the ruins. Construction began in 1853 and was completed in 1870. The small settlement Nakhon Chaisri, 20 km south of the chedi, was 'transplanted' to the temple. Four viharn pointing to the north, east, south, and west were erected on top of a platform surrounding the central chedi. In each you will find various works of art as well as a different Buddha statue (N: standing Buddha, S: Buddha being supported by a serpent E: Buddha beneath a Bodhi tree, W: resting Buddha).

A stairway leads up to the second platform from the main entrance in the north. Here you will find beautiful plants, benches, Chinese temple figures and a large, impressive Buddha statue.

During construction, King Mongkut lived in a small palace east of the chedi. The palace no longer stands today. His successor, King Rama VI, often stayed here, too, and also had a small palace built, this one in a thoroughly western style, just two km west of the pagoda. This palace - *SANAM CHAN* - lies in the middle of a beautiful park and is used as an administrative office today. After the Lay Krathong festivities in November, a ten-day temple-celebration is held outside the pagoda. Musical competitions are held each evening and open air films are shown. There is also a fair as well as a very nice market in front of the big chedi every evening.

HOTELS

Spend the night at the *MITPAISAN***, near the station, tel 242422, or near the chedi at the *SUTHATHIP***,44/1 Ratchdamnoen Road, tel 241940.

A little further out of town (more peaceful) you'll find the *SUNYA** and the *CHUANDEE***, 103 Petchkasem Rd., tel 242003-6 - bungalows are also available to rent here.

The *WHALE**-***** and *NAKHON INDRA***** in Ratchavithi Road are expensive but good.

HOW TO GET THERE

You can combine your trip to NAKHON PATHOM with your trip to the floating market. Catch a regular bus leaving the Bangkok Southern Bus Terminal for 13 Baht (ac 24 Baht) or catch a bus from DAMNOEN SADUAK for 15 Baht. The last Bangkok-bound buses leave town at about 16:00 h. If you're planning to go to Damnoen Saduak from Nakhon Pathom, get up early and catch bus 78, which leaves from the big chedi.

Diesel-railcars from Thonburi (Bangkok) and Kanchanaburi (only 3rd class, 14 Baht on both routes) will also bring you to the huge chedi. Trains coming from the south (Phetchburi, Hua Hin, Surat Thani) also stop at Nakhon Pathom. Nakhon Pathom is also the station to change at if you are coming from the south and heading for Kanchanaburi.

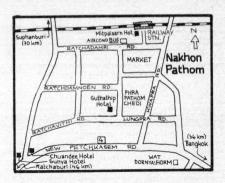

KANCHANABURI

If the only thing of interest here were the famous Bridge of the River Kwae (better known as the River Kwai), which inspired Pierre Boulles' novel as well as the subsequent motion picture, a trip to Kanchanaburi wouldn't really be worth it. But there is more, so plan to stay a couple of days if you have the time.

After arriving, go to the *TOURIST OFFICE*, tel 511200, open daily 8:30-16:30 h. A trishaw from the station costs 10 Baht, shorter distances only 5 Baht. You will receive good information here.

The town itself is sadly lacking in character - just one of many provincial towns. You will find a small *MUSEUM* with a partial reconstruction of the infamous P.O.W. camp that used to be here (admission fee 20 Baht) in the wat at the river. You can get a good idea of what life must have been like for the 60,000 prisoners of war who had to build the railway tracks to Burma during the war. 16,000 of them died due to accidents, malnutrition and diseases, mainly malaria. Many of the dead were buried in one of the two *CEMETERIES*. One of these can be found near the station (20 Baht with a chartered songthaew), the other lies at the Kwae Noi, 3 km south of town, surrounded by beautiful countryside. Small groups would do well to hire a Songthaew, which will give you a 3-4 hour tour of the museum, the temples, and the bridge for 300 Baht. Bicycles can be rented opposite the Aree Bakery for 10 Baht a day - these can be taken aboard any of the ferries for free.

HOTELS

By now, there are several guesthouses in Kanchanaburi, e.g. *THIP VAREE**, 211 1-4 Saeng Chuto Road, tel 511063 (none too clean, but with private bathrooms and lavatories), *P.G.**, 297-303 Pak Phraek Road, tel 5115114, (new and clean with a nice terrace leading out into the garden), or *U.T.**, 25/5 Menam Kwae Road, towards the bridge. *NITA GUEST-HOUSE**, 03 Visudhirangsi Road, tel 511130, quiet, no private bathrooms, with a dormitory. Nitaya and Changkrit are friendly and able to give you good information (approx. 200 metres from the TAT office, towards the museum). If you feel like spending the night at the river in the *NITAYA RAFT HOUSE**, a simple floating bamboo house, bring your mosquito-net. There are a number of hotels along the main road (Saeng Chuto Road), e.g. the *THAI SERI HOTEL***, no. 142, tel 511128, the *PRASOPSUK HOTEL***, ac***, no. 277, tel 511777, and the two *RIVER KWAI HOTELS* (next door to each other), the first* (ac**), tel 511565, the second****, tel 511269, modern, luxurious, with a discotheque. You can rent one of the bungalows offered by *KASEM ISLAND RESORTS*****, tel 511603, south of town, near Chukadon Pier.

FOOD

Foodstalls are opened up in the evening on the road along the river leading to the bridge. You can get good food here (approx. 50 Baht per person) - the atmosphere is best just before the sun sets. The *SOR POONPOL,* opposite the old cinema, is a good restaurant. No menu or sign, though. You'll find the *AREE BAKERY* just around the corner. If you walk down the road from the River Kwai Hotels you'll come to the *SUNYA RESTAURANT*, where good, cheap food is served. Boat tours and floating overnight-accommodation (60 Baht per person) can be organized from here.

HOW TO GET THERE

A ride to NAM TOK (49 Baht) via

NAKHON PATHOM (14 Baht) and KANCHANABURI (28 Baht) from the Thonburi station is an absolute must. The diesel railcar leaves twice daily.

You will have to pay 17 Baht to get to Nam Tok from Kanchanaburi, 1 Baht to get to the bridge. If you take the 8 o' clock train you will be in Kanchanaburi at 10:34 h and in Nam Tok at 12:20 h. This train stops at the bridge at 10:38 h. The second train leaves Thonburi at 13:55 h, arrives in Kanchanaburi at 16:24 h, and in Nam Tok at 18:35 h. The first train from Nam Tok leaves at 6:05 h, from Kanchanaburi at 8:06 h. The train that stops at the bridge leaves Nam Tok at 12:35 h (reaches the bridge at 14:20 h), and arrives in Thonburi at 17:00 h.

Thai railways offers a special Nam Tok package deal at the weekend and on public holidays. Departure 6:35 h, Thonburi, stops in Nakhon Pathom (45 minutes) and at the bridge, which can be crossed on foot. The train stops at Nam Tok, the final station, for 2 1/2 hours before returning to Thonburi. The train also stops at Kanchanaburi on the way back. Arrival in Bangkok 19:35 h - check these figures and book well in advance (tel Bangkok 2237010, Kanchanaburi tel 511285); the schedule changes frequently.

Buses leaving from the Southern Bus Terminal in BANGKOK need 3 hours and cost 28 Baht / ac 53 Baht. NAKHON PATHOM 16 Baht.

EXCURSIONS FROM KANCHANABURI
BOAT RIDES ON THE RIVER KWAE

Hire a boat (up to six people) at the merging point of the Kwae Yai and the Kwae Noi. It will cost you 600 Baht for half a day and is well worth it. There are various tours to choose from.

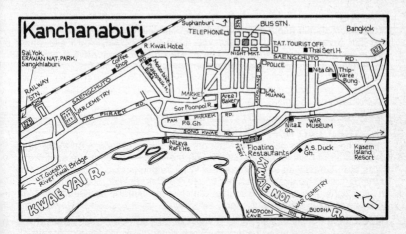

Go up the KWAE NOI and you will come to a cemetery. A little further up you will see a huge Buddha statue looking down upon the river and the mountains beyond. There are no roads in this area and tigers are said to live here. If you head down the MAEKLONG you will pass small islands that are surrounded by lotus blossoms. There is a Chinese cemetery at the riverbank. A grave here may cost up to 10 million Baht. You will also have access to the museum from here. If you go up the KWAE YAI you will pass a number of raft-houses with TV-antennas (!) before reaching the famous bridge.

THE BRIDGE AT THE RIVER KWAE

Another way of getting to the BRIDGE AT THE KWAE, which lies 4 km north-west of town, is to hire a songthaew for 40 Baht per vehicle. Railcars also go up the mountains to what is today the final train station twice daily.

During the war, the Japanese planned a 419-km connecting line between the Burmese and the Thai railway systems. This was to ensure the transportation of future supplies. In only one year, from October 1942 to October 1943, the 60,000 P.O.W.s had completed the line, which went straight through the jungle. It went along the River Kwae, over the Three Pagoda Pass (Chedi Sam Ong), all the way to Thanbyuzayat in Burma. The prisoners, Indians, Thais, Burmese, Chinese, Indonesians, Malays, and members of the Allied Forces, were forced to live a life in the jungle unfit for human beings. Part of the bridge was destroyed during the war. The British had segments of the line dismantled in Burma and at the border.

The rest of the line was later closed down by the Thai government. Today the border to Burma is closed; the line for which thousands died is lost in the jungle.

BOPHLOI

Those interested in gems can visit sapphire mines in the BOPHLOI DISTRICT. Bus 325 (every 1/2 hour) will take you there for 12 Baht. You'll see whole families working on old prospects just outside the village, particularly during the dry season. The gems are dug out and washed in the old-fashioned, traditional way. You can then watch the stones being cut in the village itself. While this is all very fascinating, we would not recommend buying as the quality of the stones is not too high.

WAT THAM KAO NOI / WAT THAM SUA

A road leading to a village (Tha Muang - 2 km away) branches off to the right 11 km south of Kanchanaburi. Go through the village and continue southwest. Cross the river by way of the large new Wachiralongkon Dam after 2 km. Stick to the right once you've crossed the bridge, head northwest, and keep the river on your right. The two new Buddhist temples can already be seen from afar. Separate stairways lead up to them.

The southern temple is built in the typical Chinese style and it may remind you of the Kek Lok Si temple in Penang. Stone lions guard massive doors which have Chinese characters inscribed upon them. The beautiful red-tiled roof is colourfully adorned. Various staircases lead all the way through the temple grounds, to the very top of the seven-floor tower. Unfortunately, there is no way to get over to the neighbouring temple from here; you'll have to go back down and then start climbing anew.

This time you will be entering the completely different world of a Thai temple. A steep stairway leads straight up from the small temples at the foot of the mountain. You will be able to see the golden and red echelon roofs reflecting the sunlight from afar. There is also a huge statue of Buddha gazing down upon the landscape. From the top you'll be able to enjoy a wonderful view of the verdant river landscape.

BAN KAO

Several roads branch off to the Kwae Noi (south) from the road leading to the Three Pagoda Pass. Few of these are paved, though. Traffic is sparse. You will find one road, however, that leads to BAN KAO, 15 km away. Continue southeast past the village and take the road branching off to the right.after 5 km. After a further 1 km you will have reached the RIVER KWAE FARM***. Rafts and simple bamboo huts, suitable only - if indeed at all - for large groups, are available. Very isolated, 32 km from Kanchanaburi. Most of the food served comes straight from the farm.

You will find a small archeological museum 2 km west of BAN KAO (continue for another km after having reached the sign saying *Welcome to Tao*) . A Dutch archeologist made some significant discoveries here while being held prisoner in the P.O.W. camp during WW II. He managed to keep them secret until the war had finished. Later excavations were rewarded with human skeletons, clay pieces, and other objects that are conclusive proof of there having been

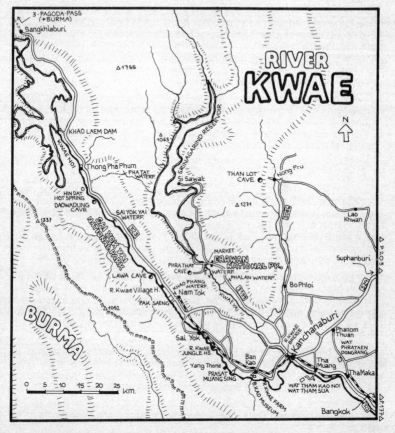

human life in this area over 10,000 years ago. Open Wed-Sun (not public holidays) 9:00-16:00 h, free of charge.

Continue northwest for another 8 km (bad road) and you will reach the weather-beaten ruins of the former *City of Lions* (MUANG SING), which was built in the style of the Khmer (PRASAT). They built a rectangular fort on this bend of the river around the 12th and 13th centuries, hoping to be able to protect their border from here. The moat and the original outer walls can still easily be made out. Paths paved with huge laterite blocks will lead you through the main entrance to the central prang, also built out of laterite stone. Several works of art in the Lopburi style were discovered while the ruins were being restored. These can now be seen in the museums of U Thong and Bangkok.

There is a junction 5 km northwest of the ruins. Turn off to the right and you will reach the main road after a further 5 km. If you turn left instead, you will reach a dead end at the river after 7 km. You will be able to cross over on a ferry for 25 Baht. Go downstream and you will reach the YANG THONE RIVER KWAI bungalow village****, including three meals a day. If you feel like spending the night here you can also charter a songthaew from the Kanchanaburi tourist office or the River Kwai Hotel for 300 Baht.

You can also spend the night at the RIVER KWAE JUNGLE HOUSE**** (including meals), 5 km northwest of the above mentioned junction. It can be reached from the Lum Sum train station. Apart from these, there are other bungalows and rafts where you can also spend the night; information can be obtained at the Kanchanaburi tourist office.

NAM TOK

You can take an adventurous 77-km train-ride past mountains, cliffs, and rivers from Kanchanaburi. It will take 2 hours to reach NAM TOK, the final station on the line, and it will cost you 17 Baht. You can also take the 8203 bus, which costs 15 Baht and gets you there in an hour. The bus leaves every 1/2 hour. To get to the BUNGALOWS SAI YOK NOI**-****, cross the wooden bridge 300 metres north of the station. The bungalows are only 200 metres from the main road, from where the Kanchanaburi-Thong Pha Phum bus can be caught.

Make an excursion to the KHAO PHANG WATERFALL, 1 km north of the big junction (west of Nam Tok). Many picnickers come here at the week-ends - it is only worth it during the rainy season, though (June-August). Organized travel groups will also arrive by train. After the frantic ride with the *Death Railway* they will almost always immediately retire to the rather quiet RIVER KWAI VILLAGE HOTEL****, tel Bangkok 2517552.

Boats can be rented from the PAK SAENG PIER, 3 km west of the station, on the other side of the main road. Up to 12 people will fit into one of the boats leaving for the Sai Yok Nai National Park. The boats will cost at least 800 Baht. A 4-hour tour to the park and back will cost you 1000-1200 Baht.

You can also rent a boat that will take you to LAWA CAVES and back for 500 Baht (approx. 2 hours). The Lawa Caves are the largest stalactite caves in the area.

SAI YOK YAI NATIONAL PARK

You can get to the Sai Yok Yai National Park (108 km from Kanchanaburi) as well as any other place along road 323 by taking bus 8203 headed for Thong Pha Phum (35 Baht). The bus leaves Kanchanaburi every 1/2 hour. If you only want to go as far as the National Park you will have to pay 25 Baht. The road branching off to the park is signposted on the left side of the road. Sometimes motor-cyclists will offer to take you down the 3 remaining km of road for 10 Baht. If not, you will have to walk.

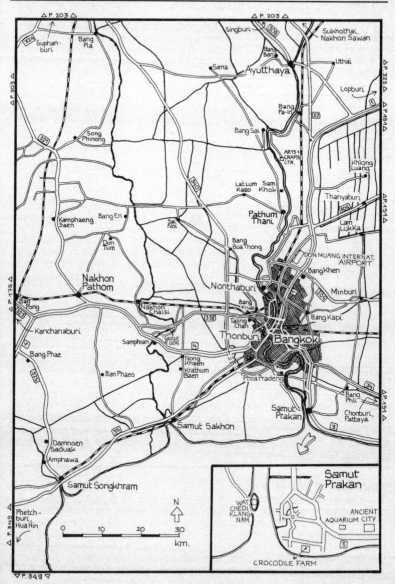

△ P. 203 △
△ P. 203 △
Singburi
Sukhothai,
Nakhon Sawan
Suphan-
buri
Bang
Pia
Sena
Bang
Ban
Ayutthaya
Uthai
Lopburi
Bang
Pa-in
Song
Phinong
Bang Sai
ARTS +
CRAFTS
CTR.
Khlong
Luang
Lat Lum
Kaeo
Sam
Khok
Thanyaburi
Kamphaeng
Saen
Bang En
Sai
Noi
Pathum
Thani
Lam
Luk Ka
Don
Tum
Bang
Bua Thong
DON MUANG INTERNAT.
AIRPORT
Nakhon
Pathom
Bang Khen
Nonthaburi
Minburi
Ban
Pong
Nakhon
Chaisi
Bang
Kruai
Bang Kapi
Kanchanaburi
Taling
Chan
Thonburi
Bangkok
Samphran
ROSE
GDN
Bang Phae
Nong
Khaem
Krathum
Baen
Phra Pradeng
Ban Phaeo
Bang
Phli
Chonburi,
Pattaya
Samut
Prakan
Damnoen
Saduak
Samut Sakhon
Amphawa
Samut Songkhram
Phetch-
buri
Hua Hin
△ P. 349 △

N

0   10   20   30
km.

△ P. 203 △
△ P. 325 △
△ P. 494 △
△ P. 491 △
△ P. 175 △
△ P. 491 △

▽ P. 349 ▽

Samut Prakan

WAT
CHEDI
KLANG
NAM
ANCIENT
AQUARIUM CITY
CROCODILE FARM

Archeological discoveries made in the park include a woman's skeleton from the neolithic period. A former Japanese military camp can be found in the totally overgrown area near the waterfall. WWII veterans often set out in search of it. With a little luck you may even come across some of the original railway tracks. Cross the suspension bridge to the west side of the river. The National park reaches all the way to the Burmese border and most parts of it are almost inaccessible and totally uninhabited. Tigers and wild elephants still live in the Tenasserim mountain area, part of the park. The park's main attraction is the waterfall, which is most beautiful during the dry period, when the water level of the Kwae Noi is lowest.

You can spend the night at expensive bungalows*** run by the park administration (if you bargain, **), as well as at cheap raft houses** floating on the Kwae Noi.

THREE PAGODA PASS
You will reach the Three Pagoda Pass, the border to Burma, if you continue north on road 323. The countryside here has only just recently been opened up to tourism. You will see work-elephants and huge road building machines. The fine wood of the visibly diminishing tropical rainforest is cut in sawmills at the sides of the road, and the gradual degeneration to Alang Alang-grass steppe seems inexorable.

THONG PHA PHUM, where the paved road ends, is the final stop of all buses coming from Kanchanaburi. There is not much to see here, apart from a huge and imposing Buddha set before the most bizarre cliff-formations at the end of the village. You can spend the night at the SOR BOONYONG BUNGALOWS**.

Trucks and songthaew go up to the border but you might have to change in SANGKLABURI. Expect to pay around 200 Baht.

RAFTING
Groups of up to 20 people can rent a large raft with which they can then float down the Kwae Noi for 2-3 days. At night, you will have to camp at the river bank. Cost per raft approx. 5000 Baht, route: from the Sai Yok National Park to the Pak Seng Pier, or from the pier towards Kanchanaburi. Groups of at least 4 people can have 4-day tours organized from Bangkok by Asian Overland Services, Thai Hotel, and others.

ERAWAN NATIONAL PARK
The Erawan National Park is 70 km from Kanchanaburi, at the upper course of the Kwae Yai. It is situated in a narrow, wooded valley encompassing the river. There are a number of beautiful waterfalls along the river, and you can walk past most of these while exploring the valley. We would recommend getting an early start. Do not go at the weekend, as many people come here during their free time. Take the blue 8170 bus from Kanchanaburi (every 45 minutes) to the market-place for 20 Baht. The last Kanchanaburi-bound bus leaves between 15:30 and 16:00 h. You can spend the night on the wooden benches of the

Boy Scout Camp near the bamboo bridge for 20-30 Baht (only with permission, though) or in one of the bungalows*.

You will be able to hire someone to take you to the huge dam of the SRINA-GARIND RESERVOIR for approx. 100 Baht at the market. There is a small exhibition on the west side of the dam with pictures of what life used to be like here, as well as other items of interest. The PHRA THAT cave can only be reached by way of a bad road. Only chartered buses (at least 200 Baht) will do the trip.

TO THE NORTH

When travelling north on Highway 1 you will pass the fertile Menam plain. Here you can see for yourself how important rice tillage is to the country. You will see dams and canals everywhere you look. Depending on the time of year, the whole plain will either be a rich green (July/August) or a barren brown (March /April). Thais from the northern areas first started settling here between the 10th and 13th centuries. The Mon and the Khmer had lived here beforehand. For this reason the towns are very interesting, especially for those interested in 'mixed' cultures. There are several possibilities for going on day-trips to Ayutthaya or Bang Pa In from Bangkok, one of them being by boat. We would suggest spending a night in Lopburi, since it takes so long.

AYUTTHAYA

Ayutthaya was the capital of the Siamese Empire for 417 years. 33 kings ruled the country from here, until the city was destroyed by Burmese troops in 1767. The huge area in which you can visit the ruins of former temples and palaces will give you an idea of how big this city must once have been. In the 17th century, the period marking the peak of Thailand's power, the city could easily have been compared with any large European town of the time. Europeans, Chinese and Japanese lived in some of the city's districts. The imposing temples symbolized the might of the Thai leaders, who paid for all this profusion by collecting taxes.

Rent some form of transport in Ayutthaya - this way you'll be able to see as much as possible. If you are good at bargaining you might be able to hire a tuk tuk for half a day for only 200 Baht. The drivers aren't too keen on acting as tourist guides, though. To really see all there is to see, you will need at least an entire day. Take a ride from the bus station to the centre of the ancient town (approx. 20 Baht). While the restoration scheme of the Thai government has certainly restored some of the buildings to their former appearance, it has also resulted in a sad loss of character. The central grounds, for instance ('English' lawn, paved parking lots), seem quite sterile.

WAT YAI CHAI MONGKOL - can be found southeast of the railway tracks, outside the actual historical city. King U-Thong founded the city's first temple here as early as 1357. It was built for monks who had just returned to Siam from their studies in Ceylon. Later, the First Patriarch resided here. King Naresuan is responsible for the temple's present form; he had the 62-metre Chedi and the reclining Buddha statue added in honour of his great victory over his Burmese adversary in 1592. Naresuan had beaten the Burmese leader in a duel fought from elephants' backs near Nong Sarai (Saraburi province). Continue southwest down this road and you will reach

WAT PHANAN CHOENG - This temple may have stood here before the actual city was founded. Archeologists have found out that the 20 metre sitting Buddha is 26 years older than the town itself. King Mongkut had the statue completely restored. You can hire a boat for a sightseeing tour around the town for 200 Baht from the landing-place behind the monastery. If you have a car or a tuk tuk, start your tour on the island at the

NATIONAL MUSEUM (Chao Sam Phya, admission 20 Baht, open Wed-Sun 9:00-12:00 h and 13:00-16:00 h) - golden amulets, statues and other excavated objects of interest are exhibited here, among them bronze Buddha statues that are over 1000 years old. North of the museum you will find

RAMA PARK - a small park where you can stretch out and relax next to a pleasant little lake . A big fair with musicians and dancers is held here on the Chinese New Year's Day, admission 5 Baht. West of the park you will find

WAT PHRA RAM - which was in built in 1369 during the reign of the second king, Ramesuan, as a burial place for his father, U-Thong, the founder of Ayutthaya. A large Khmer-style prang stands in the centre of the temple grounds. East of the park you will be able to visit the ruins of

WAT MAHATHAT - (admission 20 Baht), the biggest of all of Ayutthaya's temples. It was founded in 1384. Many new parts were added over the centuries. Only the walls of the original building remain. The ruin of the formerly huge central prang will give you an idea of how large it must have once been. Many precious Buddha statues were found hidden beneath the burnt-out temple. They were concealed here to foil Burmese pillagers. Opposite you will find the

WAT RATBURANA - (admission 20 Baht). The seventh king of Ayutthaya had this temple with its Khmer-style prang built in 1424 as a burial-place for his two elder brothers, who had lost the fight to succeed to the throne. One of the city's major treasures - now exhibited on the top floor of the museum - was found in the crypts beneath the prang. You will be able to see beautiful murals on the crypt walls if the crypts are open.

CHANDRA KASEM PALACE - There is a second museum in this reconstructed palace of the Crown Prince. King Mongkut later had a tower built here, from which he observed the stars. There is a further landing for boats nearby. Return down Naresuan Road, past the statue of King U-Thong, and you will reach

WAT PHRA SI SAN PHET - (admission 20 Baht) Construction on the impressive royal temple buildings began in 1448. Several modernizations and alterations were made before the temples were burnt to the ground by the Burmese conquerors in 1767. The viharn used to contain a 16-metre standing bronze Buddha statue known as *Phra Sri Sanphet.* If you enter the enclosed grounds by way of the south entrance you will see three restored viharn containing the ashes of former kings. To the right, the lonely pillars are all that remain of the former viharn. Continue west along the wall and you will reach

VIHARN PHRA MONGKOL BOPHIT - a restored temple with one of the biggest bronze Buddha statues in all of Thailand. It dates back to the 15th century. The viharn was reconstructed with minute attention to detail in 1956. There's a lot going on here, especially at the week-ends - fortune-tellers etc. Drinks and souvenirs can be bought just opposite - try the sticky rice cooked in a bamboo stick! Northwest of here you will find the remnants of the walls of the former

ROYAL PALACE, which was built in 1350 during the reign of the first king. The eighth king decided to have his palace moved a little further north, nearer the river, no more than 100 years later. Here you will find the ruins of the *SURYAT AMARIN HALL,* King Narai's former residence. The neighbouring *SAN PHET PRASAT HALL* (to the south) was built in 1448 as a reception hall for foreign dignitaries. The ceremonial hall *VIHARN SOMDET* was erected during the reign of the 24th king of Ayutthaya at the beginning of the 17th century, as were the next building and the *CHAKRAVAT PHAICHAYON HALL* at the eastern side of the palace. The king used to salute parades and pageants from here. The open-air wooden *TRIMUK* pavilion west of the San Phet Prasat Hall wasn't built until 1907 under King Chulalongkorn. In the west of the town you will find the rather secluded

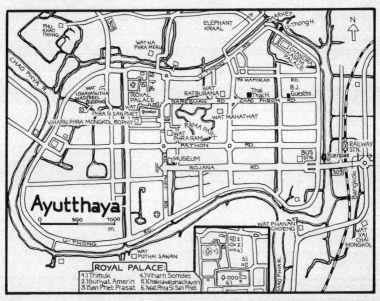

WAT LOKAYASUTHA. One of the biggest-ever reclining Buddhas, made of stucco, can be seen here. Now that the monastery has burnt to the ground, the statue lies beneath open skies. North of the historic town, quite a long way off, you'll find the

ELEPHANT KRAAL (PANIAD). The white royal elephants used to be tamed within this restored enclosure (note the teak posts!). A walk to the

CHEDI PHU KHAO THONG, northwest of town, is also worthwhile. In contrast to all other buildings in Ayutthaya, the 80-metre chedi is built in the Burmese (Mon) style. The Burmese had this temple built to commemorate their victory over the city in 1569. The chedi was re-modeled in the Thai style when the conquerors were repelled fifteen years later. A 2.5-kg gold ball was placed on the tip of the pagoda in honour of 2500 years existence of Buddhism.

HOTELS
If you plan on staying in Ayutthaya for a while, stay at the *B.J. GUEST-HOUSE**, Ng. 16/7 Naresuan Road, tel 251512 (small garden, nice people, bicycles for hire), or at *VAN'S GUESTHOUSE**, 51 Horatanachai Road, tel 241187, near the minibus station (gets rather loud at night). *HOTEL U-THONG*** can be found near the Chandra Kasem Palace, tel 251136 (stuffy, dark, and expensive). *HOTEL THAI THAI*** is at 13 Naresuan Road, tel 251505, east of Wat Ratburana. If you have some surplus money for a good meal try *RUNPAE,* the floating restaurant near the bridge - excellent Thai food!

HOW TO GET THERE
The easiest way of getting to Ayutthaya is by catching a bus from the Northern Bus Terminal or from the Victory Monument (buses for AYUTTHAYA leave every 10 minutes, cost 17 Baht, and take 1-1 1/2 hours). The bus drivers will let you get off at the place from where songthaew can be hired for tours.

You can also catch a train for 31 Baht (15 Baht) in 2nd (3rd) class. It will cost you 11 Baht from Don Muang station. Two trains leave the historic city for Chiang Mai daily, one at 17:03 h, the other at 19:23 h. You can catch a songthaew to the ruins from the station, too. It is impossible to reach Ayutthaya by small boat from Bangkok at the present time unless you charter a boat for a day-tour (cost approx. 1500 Baht).

The *Oriental Queen,* a luxury liner sponsored by the hotel of the same name, leaves the hotel pier daily at 8:00 h. You will reach Ayutthaya at 12:30 h, after an extensive buffet brunch. You will then travel to Bang Pa In by bus, with a guide. The cost for the entire trip is 700 Baht.

BANG PA IN
This former summer palace of the Ayutthayan kings was built in the 17th century. It was forgotten when Bangkok became the new royal city. It was not extended or put to a new use until steam boats started travelling up the river at the end of the 19th century. This is when the curious mixture of Thai, Chinese and European styles came into being.

The actual palace, *AISAWAN THIPPA-AT,* lies surrounded by a small body of water in one of the river bends. The small Thai-style pavilion in the middle of the lake is particularly beautiful. The *WEHAT CHAMRUN* residence was established by wealthy Chinese and built in a thoroughly Chinese style - beautiful furniture with mother-of-pearl inlays and wood carvings. The *WAT NIVET THAMAPRAWAT* was built in the style of a Gothic church under King Chulalongkorn. It seems strangely out of place. You will have to cross over in a sampan (a small, non-motorized boat) to reach it, as it is on the other side of the river. Except on Mondays and Fridays, Bang Pa In is open to the public 8:00 - 15:00 h, admission 10 Baht.

HOW TO GET THERE

Buses for BANG PA IN leave Bangkok's Northern Bus Terminal every 30 minutes, cost 13 Baht, and take approx. 2 hours to get there. There is also a regular bus service between Ayutthaya and Bang Pa In, or you can charter a boat for 300 Baht. The 'Chao Phya Express Boat', tel 2225330, offers a boat ride to Bang Pa In and Wat Phai Lom on Sundays for 120 Baht. The boat leaves Wat Mahathat Pier at 8:30 h and returns at 17:30 h. You will stop at the FOLK ARTS AND CRAFT CENTRE in Bang Sai. Here you will be able to buy traditional hand-crafted objects.

PRANG SAM YOD, LOPBURI

LOPBURI

From the 10th century, large parts of the Menam area came under the influence of the eastern Khmer Empire. Their peculiar culture with its severe bronze Buddha statues and vaguely phallic prangs (a sort of stupa) was adopted by the Thais, who penetrated the area from the north in the 13th century. Lopburi was an important religious and political centre of the independent Mon Empire as early as the 7th century. During the Khmer period it was the seat of the second king. After that, the city lost much of its significance until King Narai of Ayutthaya had it declared second capital of Thailand in the 17th century.

Today the city has about 40,000 inhabitants.When approaching Lopburi from Bangkok, you will already see King Narai looking down upon you 3 km before the actual centre of town, from the middle of a roundabout.

The historic town lies west of the railway tracks. A less impressive, new shrine, the *SARN PRA KARN SHRINE* which stands on the site of a former Hindu shrine, can be seen at the level crossing. The monkeys sitting in the Banyan trees demand food in a most aggressive manner. A little further north you will see the three laterite prangs of the *PRANG SAM YOD* (11th century), distinctive mark of the city. Southwest of the station you will find the partially restored and frequently extended *WAT MAHATHAT,* a large Buddhist temple with a typical Lopburi-style prang. King Narai had the *NARAI RAJA NIWET PALACE* built at the river, southwest of town. Inside you will find a National Museum. Here you will be able to look at Lopburi art objects, all heavily influenced by the Khmer style (open Wed-Sun, 9:00-16:00 h). The buildings were constructed in the Thai as well as the European style. A Greek adventurer, Constans Phaulkon, influenced King Narai when it came to designing the palace.

North of the palace you will find the *WAT THONG THONG,* built during the Ayutthaya period. It was built in the western style and was to be a church for foreign envoys who lived in the city. You cannot go into the Catholic church, the former residence of Phaulkon (to the left of the church), or the former residence of the first French envoy (to the right of the church), northeast of the wat. One of the first European descriptions of the town was given by the representative of Louis XIV. According to this description, Lopburi must have been an impressive city indeed. Today, this is difficult to imagine, as the ruins are barely visible in the typically provincial town. *PRANG KHAEK,* another small Hindu shrine built in Khmer style, can be seen standing north of the palace, in the middle of the chaotic traffic.

HOTELS

There are two large hotels in town, the *HOTEL ASIA**,* 1/7-8 Surasak Road, tel 411892 (ugly new building opposite the palace), and the *TAIPEI HOTEL**,* Surasongkram Road, tel 411524 (which is actually mainly a brothel for Thai men). If these two don't take your fancy, try the cheaper *GOLDEN TOWN*,* opposite the three large stupas. It is rather loud and dirty here, but you'll have a good view of the Prang Sam Yod from the roof. The *TRAVELERS DROP IN CENTRE*,* 34 Wichayen Road, Soi 3, run by New Zealanders, might be an alternative.

FOOD

You can buy good, cheap food at the night market near the cinema or at the railway embankment (watch out for those monkeys!). You will find a restaurant / nightclub with live music behind Wat Mahathat. The girls wear pastel-coloured lace and nurses' caps. Otherwise the place is okay.

HOW TO GET THERE

Five trains stop in Lopburi daily, some from the north (PHITSANULOK), some from the south (BANGKOK - cost 28 / 57 Baht for 3rd / 2nd class). The main advantage of coming by train is that the station is directly in the centre of town. A bus from or to Bang-

kok's Northern Bus Terminal will take about 4 hrs. (50 Baht ac, 36 Baht non-ac). Buses from Lopburi to SINGBURI cost 8 Baht, to SARABURI, the place to change buses if you're heading for the Khao Yai National Park, 12 Baht. The Lopburi bus terminal is south of the second roundabout, approx. 1.5 km away from the town centre.

If you are travelling in your own car or are willing to get out of the bus and catch another one later on, why not take a look at the famous and highly venerated footprint of Buddha in the WAT BUDDHABAT, 30 km beyond Saraburi, 17 km before Lopburi, 1 km south of Highway 1, on a little hill.

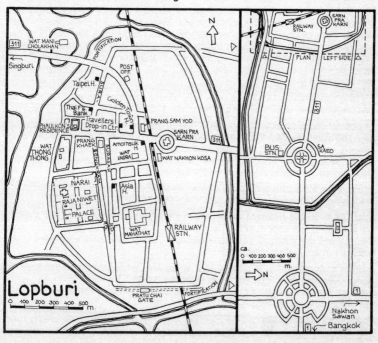

TO THE EAST

The region east of Bangkok has jungle and beaches to offer. You should definitely plan at least 2-3 days for the National Park. If you want to stay in one of the bungalows during the holiday season or at the weekend, book well in advance. The beaches up to Pattaya may not be too exciting, but they are very easy to reach. Pattaya itself has many other 'attractions' apart from its beaches, which make it THE tourist hang-out in Thailand.

KHAO YAI NATIONAL PARK

This second largest of Thailand's National Parks (2000 km²) was the first ever to have been founded in the country (1962). It is situated in the hilly region of the Dongrak mountain range. The park is not at all difficult to reach, and approx. 500,000 people visit it yearly, especially at the weekends, when the Thai railway system offers special cheap package deals.

You can go on several short tours on 11 marked trails of varying degrees of difficulty on your own in the park. If you're interested in one of the longer tours, maybe even climbing a mountain, you will need a guide, a tent, and the necessary equipment. The different trails are marked with their different colours every 25 metres. Always take enough water and plenty of food along. Do not leave the marked trails if you are on your own; even an experienced trekker can break a leg.

A rather unreliable map of the park with all paths, waterfalls etc. included can be bought at the *TOURIST OFFICE* and the *VISITOR'S CENTRE* of Khao Yai.

These offices also organize guides. If you wish to hire one, you will have to pay 100 Baht daily to the Park Headquarters on top of the fee for the guide himself, which you have to agree on beforehand. Animal-observation tours for a minimum of eight, costing 15 Baht per person, are organized every evening. Do not expect to meet a herd of wild elephants, though.

Informative films and slides are shown every Saturday evening at 19:00 h in the Visitor's Centre.

Excursions to the different waterfalls are fun. A short walk from the Visitor's Centre (cross the bridge) will get you to the KONG KAEO WATERFALL - many tourists and very noisy. You can continue up the river-bed from here if you want to get away from the crowd.

A 6-km path marked in red leads east to the *HAEW SUWAT* waterfall from the Kong Kaeo waterfall. You will need between 3 and 4 hours for the walk, which ends at the northwestern dead-end road. Getting back is rather wearisome - few vehicles drive along the road.

The following waterfalls can be reached from the northeastern dead-end road. The footpath that starts at the parking lot at the end of the northeastern road (where snacks and drinks can be bought) leads to two waterfalls. Only a couple of metres from the road you will also find the *HAEW SUWAT* path, clearly marked by the litter of many previous visitors. It gets a little better 1 km further on. The two waterfalls you will find here are a good place for a refreshing bathe and a fantastic shower. The last path leading to the *HAEW PRATHUN* is a little difficult to follow, as paths continuously branch off to the left and right.

A path marked in red leads 3 km from the back end of the parking lot along the stream to the *PHA KAEY MAI CAMP.* Halfway there you will reach the *PHA KAEY MAI WATERFALL,* also known as the orchid waterfall. The name is due to the beautiful, orchid-laden tree you will see next to the waterfall. The path leading here is very beautiful, but the waterfall itself is a bit of a disappointment.

There are several hiking paths leading through the forest west of the Visitor's Centre. A 4.5-km path marked in red begins south of the administration building opposite the restaurant and leads through the forest up the mountain. It crosses many other paths on its way. The first branch, leading south and marked in blue, will take you through a savanna-like landscape to the *MOR SING TO* reservoir, 1.5 km away. After 1 1/2 hours you will reach the road branching off to the golf-course. The second branch, also marked in red, will take you to the Tat restaurant after a 5.5-km hike south. If you continue up the original red trail north you will reach a yellow trail branching off to the right. After about 2 hours (2.5 km) it will lead you back to the Visitor's Centre. A blue path branches off to the right from the original red path at a clearing. The 3.5-km path will take you to the main road (kilometre-stone 36) after a 2 1/2 hour hike, 1 km away from the Visitor's Centre. The original red path ends at the *NONG PUG CHE* observation tower in a wide, grassy area. A 1-km dirt road will take you back to the main road, 2 km north of the Visitor's Centre.

There are other, more extensive jungle-tours you can go on, too. Find out about the condition of the paths beforehand. Various visitors have lost their way on the longer trails and have thus been forced to spend a night in the jungle. This is not much fun unless you come well prepared. Most jungle-paths are old elephant-paths, and fallen tree-trunks as well as animal paths may confuse your sense of direction. In addition, large animals are continuallly making new paths - do not go on long trails without a guide! The hundreds of leeches constitute a further problem, especially during the rainy season.

The rainy season in the park begins in March, and it's worst from July to October. November and December are the best times to visit the park. It is at this time that the elephants come out at night.

LEECHES
Generally speaking, these little creatures are quite harmless. They spend their time sitting on jungle-paths and in trees, waiting for warm-blooded creatures to come by. Once they do, the leeches either drop from the trees or crawl into their boots from the ground. Sometimes they will even crawl up your trouser-leg. Once in, they will attach themselves to the surface of your skin and start sucking your blood. While doing this they excrete an enzyme which temporarily stops the blood from clotting. Once they are full (and amazingly fat!) they will drop off by themselves. If they have found their way to your bare skin, however, they will usually be too swollen to get back out. Do not be surprised, therefore, if your socks are full of blood and your feet full of leeches in the evenings.
Precautions: Tuck your trousers into your boots and spray your boots generously with insect repellent (e.g. Johnson 'OFF' or Baygon).
You can get rid of the leeches in the evenings or while taking a break en route. Do not try to tear them off your skin - this can be painful and the cause of serious infections. Apply a little salt or oil, or touch them briefly with a burning cigarette - they will drop off by themselves. Disinfect the bleeding cuts and dress them with bandages.

KHAO YAI NATIONAL PARK

If you want to observe animals, go to the Visitor's Centre for information. You will also find a small exhibition here. With a little luck and a good eye you will be able to observe wild boars, porcupines, wild oxen, mongooses and civet cats, even during the day-time. The salt-spots at night are better, though. Normally, all noisy humans get to see during the day-time are birds, harmless small animals, and a large variety of creepy-crawlies. Tigers, bears and elephants are very rarely seen, although there are several herds of wild elephant that live around the headquarters, in all a total of approx. 150 animals. Thus Khao Yai has the largest continuous population of wild elephants in Thailand. All big animals prefer the central part of the park because of the many big game poachers causing havoc on its outskirts. One will frequently even hear shots on the road between the TAT bungalows and the headquarters at night - the slain animals are quickly loaded into waiting vehicles and are gone before anyone knows what's happened. The landscape is a mixture of real jungle and grassy steppe, with small artificial lakes and even a golf course.

ACCOMMODATION

The Tourist Office runs the *KHAO YAI MOTOR LODGE***-*****, which is in the centre of the park. Bungalows of various sizes big enough to accommodate up to ten people (with bathroom and kitchen) cost between 600 and 2000 Baht. Contact TAT in Bangkok, tel 2825209, for information and advance booking.

The huge tents on the camping grounds are a cheaper place to spend the night; you will have to pay 10 Baht for a camp-bed, another 10 for a blanket. We would suggest bringing your own sleeping bag, as it can get pretty cool. Male travellers can (sometimes) also spend the night with the Rangers or near the food stalls at the Visitor's Centre, where most people - including the Rangers - eat.

Here you will also find the *WUNG GONG GHEOW RESTAURANT,* where wild deer sometimes come to see if there's anything edible in the litter baskets. It's 3 km from the Visitor's Centre to the Motor Lodge.

HOW TO GET THERE
To get to the National Park from Bangkok, either take a bus or catch a train to PAK CHONG. Buses leave the Northern Bus Terminal at 7:00 and 9:00 h for 74 Baht (ac). It will take you approx. 3 hours to get to the park. Return buses to Bangkok leave at 15:00 h.

Trains do not go as frequently and need a little longer. The special weekend deal (160 Baht) is especially favoured by tourists. The 'Friendship Highway' branches off to the East from the Bangkok-Chiang Mai Road no. 1 shortly before Saraburi. This highway leads straight through the land, past cattle, fruit and vegetable farms. The road leading to the park branches off to the right shortly after the kilometre-stone 165. The minibus in PAK CHONG will take you the rest of the way (leaves 17:00 h Mon-Fri, 10:30 and 17:00 h Sat and Sun, cost 20 Baht, takes approx. 4 hours for 40 km). The yellow TAT-buses drive directly to the bungalows. You could also hire one of the blue songthaew, which stop just about everywhere and will take you as far as the checkpoint. From here it is still another 10 km to the Tourist Office, though. You can catch one of the yellow buses back to Pak Chong for 15 Baht at 7:00 h Mon-Fri, 8:00 and 15:00 h on Saturday and Sunday. Entrance fee for the park is 5 Baht per person, 10 Baht per motorcycle, 30 Baht per car.

SAMUT PRAKAN
The Mon lived at the river-mouth long before Thais ever came here. Samut Prakan used to be of great strategic importance in the days when it was directly at the coast (1600), but it now lies far inland owing to the gradual southward shift of the Menam Chao Phya river mouth area. The kings of Ayutthaya started having the Menam Chao Phya river-traffic monitored by a number of forts controlled by the city in the early 17th century. In 1767 the town was destroyed by the Burmese.

When Bangkok became the capital of the country the Chakri kings had the river mouth itself protected by a number of forts. These became redundant and gradually fell apart during the course of this century, as the country was opened up for foreigners and new forms of transportation were introduced.

The Songkran celebrations in April constitute a big happening in the small town of PHRA PRA DAENG (also known as PAK LAT) - many things to see! There are also two temples here, *WAT SONG THAM* and *WAT PRODKET CHATTARAM,* which has beautiful murals.

The famous *WAT CHEDI KLANG* temple celebration is held in November/December with boat-races, processions, and a big fair. This temple containing a highly venerated relic of Buddha was originally built on an island in the middle of the river during the reign of King Rama II. It was meant to signify the importance of Buddhism in Siam to the incoming ships. These days, you can reach it by way of a road from the Thonburi side. You can also get there by means of ferries, many of which leave from the landing-place at the market in Samut Prakan. The temple is not too exciting when no celebrations are being held, though.

HOTELS
You can spend a night in Phra Pra Daeng at the NEW SRI SAWAT**, 128/14 Soi Suksawat, tel 4627717 or at the BANTHOM THIP**, 401 Soi Aphichat, tel 3942708.

HOW TO GET THERE
Take ac-bus 3 or bus 25 from Siam Square or Sukhumvit Road to SAMUT PRAKAN, approx. 25 km south of town. Nearby PHRA PRA DAENG can be reached from Thonburi. Take a bus down from Suk Sawat Road until you see a road leading off to the left, to a little settlement in the river-bend.

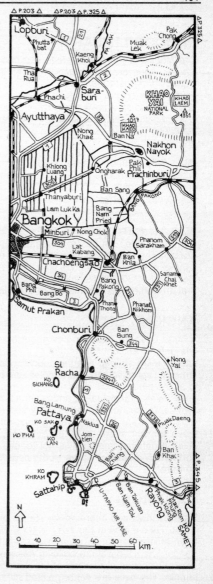

CROCODILE FARM

The local and imported beasts you can see here are actually bred for their leather. They are worth quite a bit live too, though, as you can tell from the masses of tourists. Apart from crocodiles, a number of other creatures are also held captive on the large farm grounds. There is a big self-service restaurant. You can also try a bowl of crocodile-soup at the foodstand opposite. This soup is especially popular among the Chinese, who claim that it has aphrodisiac qualities.

Open daily 8:00-18:00 h, tel 3950477, admission 80 Baht. The animals are fed in the late afternoons 16:30-17:30 h, show Mon-Fri on the hour between 9:00 and 11:00 h, also at 12:00 and 17:00 h at week-ends. Half an hour later there is also an elephant show.

HOW TO GET THERE

Continue due south from Samut Prakan. The road branching off to the right at kilometre-stone 28 leads to the 'Farm of 30,000 Reptiles'. Samut Prakan is the final destination of the ac-buses 11 and 8. You can also get there by regular buses 25, 45, 119, and 102.
A minibus shuttle-service runs regularly from the final stop to the farm (5 Baht). A taxi will cost you 10 Baht.

ANCIENT CITY

A huge open-air museum lies about 6 km further south. The first impression one gets of Ancient City is that of a miniature model of Thailand. The 80-acre park is even shaped like the country. Detailed miniature replicas of about 80 famous Thai buildings and temples can be seen here. This way you can walk to all the places you'll miss during the rest of your trip. There is much greenery here, lovely artificial lakes and waterfalls. Most visitors come by bus or by their own car (prices for parking will vary according to the size of your car). A bicycle would be ideal for discovering this 'shrunken Thailand', but unfortunately these are not allowed. At the entrance, the 'Thai-Malay border', you will be given a detailed 'map' so as not to lose your way when in the 'mountains of northern Thailand' or at the 'south coast'. Open daily 8:30-18:00 h, admission 50 Baht.

CHONBURI

Harbour-town and intermediate station on the way to the beaches of the east coast. Take a look at the *WAT YAI INTRARAM* in the city centre, said to have been built under King Taksin, whose statue can be seen near the temple entrance. The inside of the building has many beautiful murals. The annual bull-racing festivities at the end of the fasting period (end of October) start at this temple. The bulls are either painted different bright colours, or decorated with coloured scarves. To this day the *jockeys* drink incredible amounts of Mekhong before going onto the 150-m track. TAT Bangkok will give you the exact dates.

ANG SILA

You will find the road branching off to ANG SILA beyond the town, at kilometre-stone 100. This small fishing village is also the centre of Thailand's cotton weaving industry. The calm ocean here offers ideal conditions for oyster and mussel breeding. You can watch stone-cutters chiseling pestles and mortars along the road leading to the harbour. These are used for grinding the chillies that are such an important part of Thai cooking.

BANG SAEN

The coastal road 3134 south will bring you to BANG SAEN after 6 km (beautiful view, many oyster-farms). Bangkok families with the necessary cash tend to spend the weekends here, either at the beach or at the golf-course, 10 km inland. If you want to get out of Bangkok to do a little sun-bathing, this is the place to go! The largest *AQUARIUM* in all of South East Asia can be visited in the Scientific Marine Centre on the campus of the university. Except for Mondays it can be viewed 8:30-16:00 h for 40 Baht, as can the adjoining *NATURAL SCIENCE MUSEUM. OCEAN WORLD*, open daily 11:00-19:00 h, from 10:00 at the weekends, offers swimming pools, artificial wave-pools, and huge water-slides.

HOTELS

In Bang Saen you will find some reasonable *BUNGALOWS**** at the unfortunately rather dirty beach.

The rooms of the *BANG SAEN BEACH HOTEL*****, run by TAT (reservations tel Bangkok 2514862) are of extremely high standards.

HOW TO GET THERE

Buses from Bangkok to CHONBURI every 10 minutes (18 Baht). From here take a local bus to ANG SILA or BANG SAEN. You can also get out of the bus at the Bang Saen road which branches off Highway no. 3 (10 km beyond Chonburi), then walk the remaining 3 km to the ocean.

PATTAYA

It's a man's world, and Pattaya might have been created just to prove this to all those still unconvinced. 800,000 tourists come here yearly, making Pattaya Thailand's largest tourist centre apart from Bangkok itself. Here on a cheap package deal, expecting exotic love beneath tropical palms (...in 'bachelor hotels', more likely), the average Pattaya visitor (young, male and single - though not for long) spends more than 4 days cooped up in one of Pattaya's 12,000 hotel rooms. (At least that's what the statistics say - but what they do there in all that time is never mentioned...) Thus Pattaya could be viewed as a wonderful (or rather miserable) example of the problems tourism can create in a Third World country.

Many really do find the holiday in the sun they've always dreamt of, though - tropical sun (even though the beaches are nothing special), wicked motorcycles (in the true sense of the word - sometimes they break down after only 2 km, leaving the tourist to pay the bill), young girls (who have to prostitute themselves in order to survive), an exciting night-life (with exciting prices), many sporting possibilities such as deep-water diving (equipment, boat, and a guide will cost you 500 Baht per person), sailing (300 Baht an hour), motor boats (250 Baht an hour), water-skiing (approx. 1000 Baht an hour), parachute skiing (250 Baht per ascent), windsurfing (approx. 200 Baht an hour), bowling etc. Pattaya also has many European restaurants serving pizza, paella, fish & chips, sauerkraut, and gallons and gallons of beer.

If you feel like cultivating your suntan instead of taking part in the expensive activities, we would suggest moving to the hotels near the YMCA-beach, *JOMTIEN BEACH,* which lies south of Pattaya. The hotels in *NAKLUA,* the northern district of town, are also pleasant. Thai families sometimes stay here, the atmosphere in many of the sois seems more rural than anything else, and you will be woken by the sound of cockerels crowing, not disco-music.

HOTELS
You will be able to get a room anywhere and anytime if you're willing to pay 1200 Baht per night. If not, you might end up getting a sleazy, noisy, and generally totally unacceptable room. There are signs posted at the sides of the roads and in the bars of south Pattaya, telling you where rooms costing 150 Baht and more are still available. If you like peaceful nights, however, don't stay in the Village - the disco music continues till dawn every night of the year.

Most of the cheap hotels can be found on Pattaya 2 Rd., a noisy connecting road. The rooms are usually pretty sleazy. You will find a list of Pattayan guesthouses in the Tourist Office. They are not exactly cheap, but you might have luck bargaining if there isn't too much business. Mosquitoes can be a real pest here at certain times of the year - watch out

for simple bungalows or hotels surrounded by greenery and water.

The *PATTAYA YOUTH HOSTEL**,* Summer Place, Central Pattaya Rd., corner of Pattaya 2 Road, tel 428139, offers rooms starting at 100 Baht, some of them with ac. We found *THE COUNTRY LODGE**-***** (northern Pattaya 2 Road, beyond the Alcazar, tel 418484) quite acceptable - simple and comfortable bungalows with or without ac, two pools, reasonably quiet. Owing to the fact that the hotel has a contract with a big German travel company you will meet many Germans here. In the evenings these get together in the bar on the other side of the street. The *BEACH PLAZA***,* Beach Road near Soi 4, tel 418916, offers ac rooms and a discotheque. There's always a lot of activity in the *PALM LODGE***,* tel 418779. You will find *BOONPRASERT*,* tel 419144 and *CAESAR**(*)*

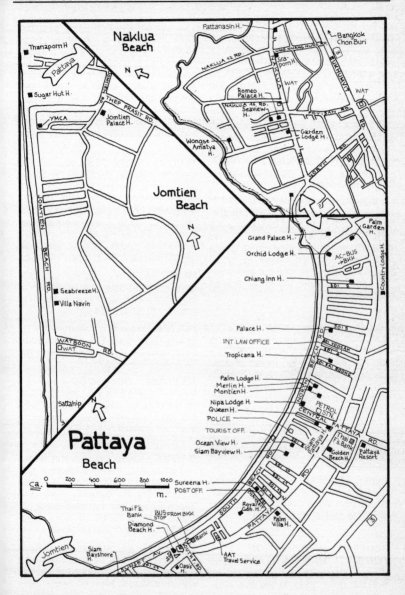

in Soi 10. The *B.R. INN***, tel 419449 and the *DROP INN***, tel 419803, are on Soi 12. The *THIP**(*), SUN & SAND****, tel 419829, *SAREENA****, tel 419526, and *YOUR PLACE***, tel 419917, are on Soi Chaiyasit (near the post office).

In Naklua, try the *GARDEN LODGE *****; tel 419109, pretty and peaceful, with a pool, a private beach, and a beautiful tropical garden. You'll find *J.M.**(*)*, Naklua Road, tel 419727, further out of town - quiet bungalows with large rooms.

In the south, try the *YMCA CAMP***** at the northern end of Jomtien Beach. After a further 2 km of beach you will reach the *SEA BREEZE*****, tel 418475, which has nice rooms and a small pool. All you have to do to reach the beach is step out of the hotel and cross onto the other side of the road.

FOOD
No other South East Asian bathing resort offers such a variety of food - you can eat Chinese, Indian or Japanese meals, enjoy German, French, Italian, Belgian (potato fritters & sausages), Lebanese and Mexican food. You have the choice of being served by well-dressed waiters in high-class restaurants or simply grabbing a quick bite to eat in one of the many fast-food chains. Stroll through the streets in the evenings and study the menus. Breakfast is usually served quite late - a good, English breakfast of bacon, eggs and sausages is available almost everywhere.

GENERAL INFORMATION
TOURIST INFORMATION - TAT office: Pattaya, 382/1 Beach Road, tel 418750, quite close to the bus stop.

The amount of information available here is amazing. Another good source of information is the 'Village'. An evening spent staggering from one bar to the next is all it takes to find out what goes on where. All languages are spoken, and it usually doesn't take long for some 'permanent traveller' to latch onto you and bombard you with all the latest hot infos.

POSTAL SERVICES - you will find the post office in the Chaiyasit Shopping Centre, tel 419340, 183/18 - 20 Soi Chaiyasit. Send and receive telegrams from here. You can make telephone calls (inc. international) from the *TELEPHONE EXCHANGE SERVICE*, South Pattaya Road corner of Pattaya 2 Road, open 24 hours.

IMMIGRATION - you will pay 300 Baht for a 30-day visa extension at the Chonburi District Immigration Office, Soi 8, tel 419374.

POLICE - there is a police station on Beach Road, near Soi 7. The Tourist Police can be found next door to the TAT-office, tel 419371.

MEDICAL SERVICES - you can reach the *PATTAYA MEMORIAL HOSPITAL* by calling 419422 There are also several private clinics in town, all specializing in the treatment of venereal diseases.

BANKS - there are several banks that have a currency exchange service, usually open until the late evening. Try the Bangkok Bank, 545 Beach Road, Thai Farmers Bank, 22 South Pattaya Road, or Siam Commercial Bank, 277 Beach Road.

CABARET - the staggering variety of entertainment may deceive; most of it is aimed at hooking up male tourists with prostitutes. Nevertheless, there are some shows that are really worth it, even in the eyes of traditional, conservative-minded Thais; whole families go and see the drag show put on at the *ALCAZAR,* 78/14 Pattaya 2 Road, tel 418746. The 200 Baht admission fee is pretty steep, but the show is of international standards. You can hardly expect to see a better one in Paris or Berlin. The *TIFFANY SHOW,* Pattaya Sport Bazaar Bldg., tel 429642, is of a similar high standard.

CAR RACES - car races are held at the weekends on a new track near Highway 36, 15 km east of town. Admission is 80-150 Baht, for information call Bangkok 2533970.

ELEPHANTS - working elephants can be watched daily 14:30-17:00 h at the elephant kraal for 160 Baht. Those planning to travel north will be able to see this more cheaply and in a more authentic setting.

TRANSPORT IN PATTAYA - minibuses inside Pattaya cost 5 Baht. The set price to Jomtien Beach (south) is 20 Baht, to Naklua (north) 10 Baht.

Catch a minibus heading in your direction, state your destination, and pay when you get off - bargaining in advance signifies that you wish to charter the bus. If you wish to be taken to a remote place or even outside of the city limits, you should always definitely agree upon a price with the driver before you leave. Charter for 2 people - 30 Baht, 5 Baht for each additional person.

Motorcycles (100-200 Baht an hour or 150-500 Baht a day), jeeps (300-500 Baht), and cars (from 800 Baht) are for hire along Beach Road, as are

sailing boats, surf-boards, water skis and parachutes (for prices see above). Bicycles can be rented, too, for 20 Baht an hour or 80-100 Baht a day. If you are planning to hire a vehicle for a longer period of time you will always be able to bring the price down by bargaining.

EXCURSIONS TO THE OFFSHORE ISLANDS - you can join any of the daily excursions to Ko Larn, Ko Pai, and Ko Sak. Ferries costing 40 Baht (return ticket) leave for KO LARN (Coral Island) from the fishing pier quite regularly. The hydrofoil does the same trip from Siren Bar for 150 Baht. If you want to charter a boat you will have to pay between 700 and 1500 Baht for boats holding up to 12 people. You can also go on one of the frequent daily coral reef tours (280 Baht, 9:30-16:00 h) in glass-bottomed boats.

HOW TO GET THERE

Buses to Pattaya leave Bangkok's Eastern Bus Terminal every half hour. The ride takes 2 1/2 hours, cost 29 Baht, ac 50 Baht, return ticket 90 Baht. Buses also leave the Northern Bus Terminal on the hour, cost 53 / 96 Baht. Ac-buses costing 110 Baht leave from the major hotels. The weekend flight and limousine service from Don Muang Airport (1500 Baht) is only recommended for wealthy travellers. Thai Airways minibuses leave the airport three times daily for Pattaya, cost 190 Baht. There is also a large bus that leaves from the airport on the hour between 7:00 and 19:00 h, cost 100 Baht. Buses from RAYONG cost 20 Baht, from SATTAHIP 11 Baht.

TO THE SOUTH

Phetchburi, 135 km south of Bangkok, is an interesting, though rarely visited town. If you feel that you are able to survive without an English speaking guide, European food and guesthouses, and are interested in Thai culture to boot, then you should definitely spend a couple of days here.

PHETCHBURI

Whilst driving to the city centre from the railway station you will see the Royal Summer Palace, *KHAO WANG,* on a small hill to the right (west). There is a little museum with objects taken from the estate of King Rama IV in the main rooms of the palace. The observation platform, from where the king liked to gaze at the stars, offers a splendid view of the town and countryside. North of the palace you will find the *WAT MAHA SAMANARAM,* also built in the late 19th century. A narrow footpath leads up to it from the end of Rachavithi Road. The walk will take you approx. 30 minutes.

If you have developed a passion for temples by this stage you've come to the right place; there are 30 of them in town. You will be able to admire beautiful wooden houses on the temple grounds of *WAT YAI SUWANNARAM* (Ayutthaya period). Have the central bot opened for you; the murals inside depict mystical creatures amongst other things. The monastery has been named after its most celebrated monk, 'Suwan', teacher of a former king. The windowless viharn has a particularly beautiful entrance, adorned with gilded wood-carvings of flowers.

The five Khmer-style prangs of the *WAT KAMPHAENG LAENG* are the oldest buildings in town. They were built during the period of Khmer rule but have, unfortunately, been severely neglected.

WAT MAHATHAT with its five more recent prangs is in the centre of town. There are 198 Buddha statues inside the passages.

WAT KHAO BANDAI IT, 3 km west of town, is particularly beautiful. You will find the temple at the end of a cul-de-sac, on the right-hand side. A footpath leads up the mountain from here. Halfway up you will reach the entrance to a labyrinth of stalactite caves. Monks used to meditate here. There is a pagoda on the mountain peak. A bot stands on its left, a viharn on its right. The story goes that a rich Thai had the bot built here in memory of his wife, the viharn in memory of his mistress. The pagoda, which definitely leans towards the viharn of the mistress, was built in memory of himself.

There are many grottos with Buddha statues in the area. You will find a further sacred stalactite cave, *KHAO LUANG,* 2 km north of town, open 9:00-15:00 h. After having climbed the steep stairs you will first find yourself in the large central cave. There are several Buddha statues and chedis here. More statues can be found in the numerous neighbouring caves. There is a Sun- and a Mooncave. Both receive their daylight through a hole in the ceiling, one shaped like the moon, the other like the sun. Take a good, strong torch along if you want to explore the passageways connecting the different caves.

When enough people are in town a local English teacher with a pickup sometimes organizes very interesting tours for 60 Baht per person.

HOTELS

Spend the night at the *KHAO WANG**, 174/1-3 Ratchavithi Road, tel 425167, just below the summer palace. It is rather noisy, true, but still the best place in town. Try to get rooms on the upper floors - here it is not quite as noisy and you will have a huge terrace to yourself. Good food is served in the restaurant (menu in Thai), and singers sometimes even perform in the late hours of the evening.

HOW TO GET THERE

Phetchburi lies on Highway 4 as well as on the Southern Line of the Railway. Three local trains leave daily from Thonburi, 5 express trains leave daily from Bangkok. The ride takes approx. 3 hours and costs 73 or 34 Baht (2nd or 3rd class). Buses leave from Bangkok's Southern Bus Terminal every 15 minutes, cost 35 Baht, ac-buses 54 Baht. Buses from HUA HIN cost 15 Baht.

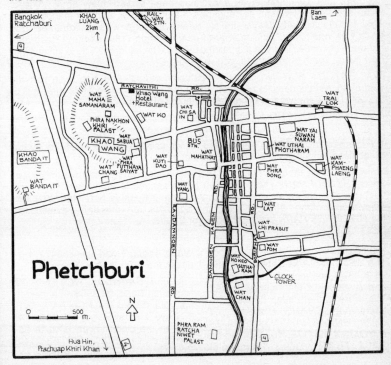

CENTRAL THAILAND

PHITSANULOK

76,000 people live in this town, which lies on the banks of the Nan river and is a significant business-centre of central Thailand. A training camp for soldiers used to be here during the days of the Ayutthayan kings. The king himself even resided here at times. Most of the historical and predominantly wooden houses of the town were destroyed during a huge fire in the fifties. Due to this the town seems rather monotonous in appearance.

The *WAT PHRA SI RATANA MAHATHAT* with its golden, shining prang survived the fire. A particularly beautiful, gilded bronze Buddha figure dating back to the 14th century can be seen in the main temple, which is decorated with elaborate murals. The statue's perfect form is considered a fine example of the matured, late Sukhothai style, and it has been copied many times. One of these copies can be seen in Bangkok's marble temple. Another stands in the Thai temple in Bodh Gaya (India), where Buddha was enlightened and Buddhism originated. Fine mother-of-pearl intarsia (18th century) decorates the main entrance. There is a small museum to the left of the wat. A little further downtown, south of the bridge, you will find

WAT RATCHA BURANA, whose Ayutthayan period chedi has been partially destroyed. Murals depicting scenes out of the Ramayana decorate the walls of the bot. There are two more temples northeast of town.

WAT CHEDI YOT THONG, its brick chedi sporting the typical lotus bud peak (15th century), has been fully restored. The road ends at the

WAT ARANYIK, the forest monastery, which used to have a moat. Today the Singhalese temple is almost a complete ruin.

Many people on the Nan river and in the surrounding swamps live on houseboats *(REON PHAE)*. The population has managed to adapt perfectly to the variations in the water level. There are floating markets here, too. You can enjoy a view of the houseboats and the lazy river from one of the gondolas of the *RIVERSIDE PARK* aerial cableway for 2 Baht.

HOTELS

The *ASIA**, 176 Eka-Thotsarot Road, tel 258378, has a small orchid garden and is close to the railway station. There are further cheap hotels in the same road: *CHANG PHUAK***, no. 63/28, *UNHACHAK*-***, and *SAMAI NIYOM*-***, no. 175. You will find the *SALA THAI***, 999/1 Phitsanulok Wang Thong Road, tel 259471, opposite the bus terminal.

The *PHITSANULOK HOTEL***, 82 Naresuan Road, tel 258425, is next to the train station. The *HOH FA***, 73/1-5, Phya Linthai Road, tel 258484, next to the clock tower, is quite acceptable. The *SIAM HOTEL*-***, 4/8 Athit Wong Road, and the more ex-

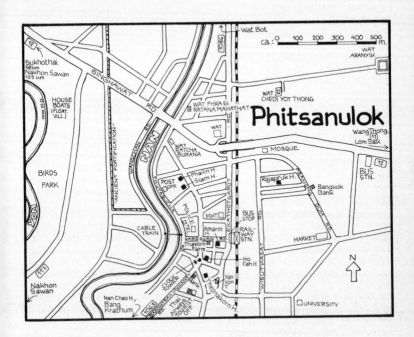

pensive *PHAILIN HOTEL*****, just around the corner, 38 Baromtrail Lokkanat Road, tel 252411-4, are family-type hotels; no girls and no nightly disturbances.

There are more expensive hotels next to the Phailin: *AMARIN HOTEL*****, 3/1 Chao Phya Phitsanulok Road, tel 258588, *THEPNAKORN*****, 43/1 Srithamatraipidok Rd., tel 258507, and *RAJAPRUK*****, 99/9 Phra-Ong Dum Road, tel 258788. All of the above hotels have their own pool.

You'll find the *RESTAURANT BUTTERHOME* and the *PASTIME COFFEE SHOP* 150 metres south of the railway station. Delicious pastries and cakes!

GENERAL INFORMATION

TOURIST INFORMATION - Tourist Office, 209/7-8 Baromtrail Lokkanat Road, tel 252742-3, run by highly competent people, open from 8:00-16:30 hours daily.

POST - you can make international phonecalls from the telephone office at the embankment road north of the park. The main post office is a little further north, on the same road.

BANKS - A branch of the *THAI FARMERS BANK* can be found south of the clock-tower, in Baromtrail Lokkanat Road. The *BANGKOK BANK* is on Pranong Dum Road, southeast of the Rajapruk Hotel.

LEAVING PHITSANULOK
BY PLANE
There are two aeroplanes from BANGKOK to PHITSANULOK daily (730 Baht). The plane from CHIANG MAI (505 Baht) either flies via NAN (480 Baht) and PHRAE (290 Baht), or via MAE SOT (370 Baht) and TAK (216 Baht). There are also flights from LAMPANG (430 Baht) on Tue and Thur, and from LOEI (340 Baht) on Mon, Wed, and Fri. Thai Airways Office: 209/27-28 Baromtrail Lokkanat Road, tel 258020.

BY BUS
The town lies half-way between Bangkok and Chiang Mai. Buses leave BANGKOK'S Northern Bus Terminal all day, cost: 72 Baht, ac-buses 171 Baht (5 hrs.). They mainly drive at night, departure time usually around 22:00 h. From SUKHOTHAI you'll have to pay 14 Baht, CHIANG MAI 67/82, ac 117 Baht. The Phitsanulok bus station is in the northwest of town. Many buses also stop at the railway station square, which is the town's main bus-stop. Some of the ac buses to Bangkok, Chiang Mai,

and Chiang Rai depart from the company offices, e.g. Yan Yon Tour, south of the railway station, and Thavorn Farm, near the central bus-stop.

BY TRAIN
You can also make a transit-visit to this town while heading north, seeing as it lies on the Bangkok-Chiang Mai railway line. The two express trains arrive at a rather unfortunate time, however, between 22:30 and 0:15 hours. There are seven daily trains from BANGKOK to PHITSANULOK. Express trains take approx. 6 hrs., regular trains may take up to 9 hrs. The best connection from Bangkok: 6:40 h, arrival 13:22 h. The price is 69/143 Baht for 3rd/2nd class (not including possible extra charge). There are also three Special-Diesel-Railcars that travel back and forth between Bangkok and Phitsanulok for 115 Baht (fan) and 195 Baht (ac). There are two daily trains to CHIANG MAI (8 hrs.). The railway station, tel 258005, is one of the few buildings that survived the fire of 1959 with little damage.

SUKHOTHAI

When the Thais first came from the north, they managed to conquer this former Khmer-controlled area in 1238 A.D. They gained control over large parts of the country due to a strong army and clever politics. The king had Ceylonese monks come to the country in order to spread the pure teachings of Buddhism (Theravada Buddhism) and to displace the influence of the unpopular Khmer. Many of the former typically Khmer-style religious buildings were re-built according to the taste of the era. King Khamhaeng (1275-1317), the 'Father of Thailand', derived the first Thai alphabet from the Mon script. He managed to unite the country in spite of the many different ethnic groups living there. Sukhothai lost much of its might during the reign of his successors, however, and in the 14th century it became part of the Ayutthayan Empire.

Don't miss the ruins of Sukhothai if you're interested in Thai history and have plenty of time. There are far less tourists here than in Ayutthaya, although these ruins are by no means less fascinating . You will find the ruins 11 km

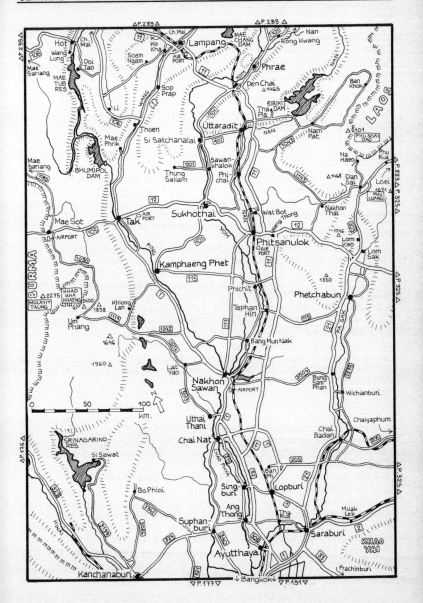

outside of present-day Sukhothai, at road no. 12 leading to Tak. Ancient Sukhothai, former Royal City of Thailand, lies west of its modern version. One kilometre before the old town, to the right, you will pass the

SUKHOTHAI CULTURE CENTRE, which consists of a hotel, a huge restaurant for bus-loads of tourists, and a few shops selling arts and crafts at 'tourist prices'. The hotel grounds (see *Hotels)* are separated from the ruins by a river. You will come across the first temple ruin outside the actual town fortification. Start your tour at the National Museum. The old

TOWN FORTIFICATION and its moat make up a 1810 x 1400 metre rectangle, which used to surround the former city area. The remains of 16 temples and 4 Hindu shrines stand within. In addition, there are 70 further ruins outside the town fortification. The

RAMA KHAMHAENG NATIONAL MUSEUM (4) is closed on Mon, Tue, and on holidays. Otherwise it is open from 9:00-12:00 h and from 13:00-16:00 h. Admission 10 Baht. The exhibits are unfortunately not presented as well as they could be. All the same, the museum is worth a visit; the exhibits on the ground floor will give you a good idea of the art of the Sukhothai period (see *Art & Culture).* A walking Buddha figure, typical of the Sukhothai period, is exhibited in the centre of the main building. Works of art from different cultural periods, also discovered in Sukhothai, can be viewed on the first floor. Even today, excavations still reveal old statues and other artistic treasures. Beware - don't let the merchants convince you that the figurines and bowls they sell were found while ploughing their fields. The genuinely old-looking and rather pretty objects are manufactured in a number of workshops around Sukhothai. Plan your tour through the ancient city at the model of the town.

WAT MAHATHAT (3), the Royal Temple, is in the centre. It was Siam's most significant religious gathering place during the Sukhothai period. Since 1953 the central chedi, the substructure of the ordination hall, the viharn, as well as 209 smaller chedis and several other buildings have been dug up on the 240 x 280 metre temple grounds. The central chedi stands upon a square plinth in the centre of the grounds, surrounded by entrance halls and four stupas. While these smaller buildings are still marked by the style of the Khmer, the main chedi can be seen as a typical example of the Sukhothai style. The circular, lower part of the chedi is crowned with lotus-bud spikes. The plinth is adorned with reliefs. The devout looking figures depicted walking represent the disciples of Buddha. The rows of pillars to the east used to support the wooden roof of the large, adjoining bot. Various Buddha figures have been restored and returned to where they originally stood. The three laterite prasat of the

WAT SI SAWAI (5), a formerly Brahman temple built in the Khmer style in the 13th century, are further south. The Hindu temple was later re-modelled as a Buddhist temple. Shiva statues as well as Buddha figures were discovered here. Unfortunately the recent restoration work on the stucco decorations has only been partially successful. The Ceylonese style stupa and the bot ruins of

WAT SRA SI (2), north of the Royal Temple, are on a small island in a lake. The Loy Kratong celebrations are held here every November. The nearby

MEMORIAL (1) depicts King Rama Khamhaeng.

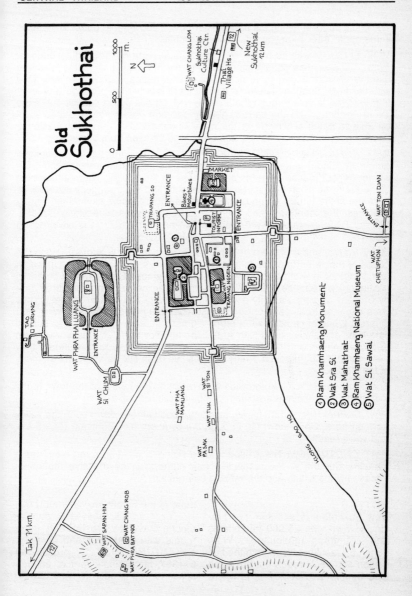

Old Sukhothai

N

1000 m.

500

0

WAT CHANGLOM

Sukhothai Culture Ctr.

Thai Village Hs.

New Sukhothai 12 km

12

MARKET

Buses + Motorbikes

ENTRANCE

TRAPANG SO

ENTRANCE

TOURIST INFORM.

ENTRANCE

WAT TON DUAN

ENTRANCE

TRAPANG NGOEN

WAT CHETUPHON

ENTRANCE

WAT PHRA PHAI LUANG

ENTRANCE

TAO TURIANG

WAT SI CHUM

WAT PHA MAMUANG

WAT SI TON

WAT TUK

WAT PA SAK

KLONG SAO HO

Tak 71 km.

12

WAT SAPAN HIN

WAT CHANG ROB

WAT PHRA BAT NOI

① Ram Khamhaeng Monument
② Wat Sra Si
③ Wat Mahathat
④ Ram Khamhaeng National Museum
⑤ Wat Si Sawai

We would suggest taking the northwestern exit if you want to go on to the ruins in the north. After 1 km you will reach the roof-less

WAT SI CHUM with its highly venerated, huge, 14th century sitting Buddha, *Phra Atchana*. The square mondhop (30 metres long and 15 metres high) used to be surrounded by a moat. The interior space is almost entirely filled with the huge Buddha statue. To the left there is a narrow passage-way leading up to the temple through the 3 metre wall. Murals depict scenes out of the life of Buddha inside the narrow, gloomy passage. Every now and then you'll be able to catch a glimpse of the huge Buddha statue through occasional, small windows. The impressive statue can also be seen from above.

WAT PHRA PHAI LUANG is 700 metres further to the right. This temple (originally Hindu) is said to have been the most important temple during the Khmer period, maybe even the actual centre of the capital. The northernmost of the the three Khmer prasat remains standing and has been fully restored, as have the entire temple grounds, including the square stupa, several monastery buildings, the mondhop, and a chapel which encloses a reclining Buddha. Several Buddha statues were found in bricked up niches in the walls during the period of restoration.

Many *KILNS,* some of them in ruins, some restored, lie scattered among the heaps of rubble north of the temple. These kilns are usually 6 metres in length and 3 metres in width and made of brick. The famous Sawankhalok ceramics (=celadon) were made in these. These fine ceramics were manufactured here by Chinese artisans as early as in the 13th century (see 'Art & Culture'). They were exported to all parts of South East Asia from here. In the beginning, four different types of celadon were produced here - cream coloured, unpatterned ceramics, and similar ones with sun-, fish-, and flower motifs. Many fragments of broken plates and bowls lie about. They were usually broken before they even came out of the oven. Pretty pictures can often still be made out on many of the pieces.

There are further ruins in the wide area reaching from west of the town to the foot of the mountains. We would recommend climbing up to

WAT SAPAN HIN. A 12.5 metre, standing Buddha looks down upon the valley from up here. Good view! Go through the southern exit, continue for 2.5 km, and you'll reach

WAT CHETUPHON. There used to be a sitting, a walking, a reclining, and a standing Buddha at the respective four corners of the massive mondhop. Today only the sitting and the walking one remain.

HOTELS

New Sukhothai is a rather sad provincial town with 23,000 inhabitants and countless mosquitoes. Walk north up Tree Chot Road from the bus station and you'll reach the busy and loud Singhawat Road. This is where most of the hotels are. *SUKHOTHAI HOTEL**,* no. 15, tel 611133, popular among travellers, restaurant, large rooms with a shower and lavatory. *SWASDIPHONG*-**,* no. 56, tel 611567, large single rooms, enough space for two people. *KITMONGKOL*

HOTEL**, opposite in no. 43, tel 611193, large and clean rooms, modern building, peaceful upper floors. *CHINAWAT HOTEL**, 1-3 Nakhon Kasem Road, tel 611385, not far from the bus station, friendly and relaxed atmosphere. *RIVER VIEW HOTEL***, 92/6 Nakhon Kasem Road, tel 611652, south of the bus station, large rooms with showers and lavatories. *RAJTHANEE HOTEL***-*****, 299 Charoen Vithi Road, tel 611031. This modern, five-storey building lies at the city limits towards the old town. It is the top hotel around and well worth its price. The *YUPA** is a guesthouse that was opened on the upper floors of a private home in 1987. Large, well lighted, and with a big terrace. The turn-off is signposted. The *THAI VILLAGE HOUSE*-***** in the Sukhothai Culture Centre, is 1 km in front of the old town, to the right. The wooden bungalows are built in the traditional Thai style and nicely furnished. Some of them have a fan, others ac and even a bathtub.There is also a dormitory for 30 Baht per person.

FOOD

If you're the kind of person who likes a cozy atmosphere and restaurants decorated with many precious small objects, go to the *DREAMCAFE* (ac) next to Swasdiphong Hotel, opened from 8:00-23:30 h. Good Thai food is served cheap here, as well as European breakfast and ice cream. You get to choose from several books and magazines and many cassette tapes. Most of the hotels have their own restaurant. Many travellers go to the *SUKHOTHAI RESTAURANT*. The *INDHIRA RESTAURANT* is downstairs in the Swasdiphong Hotel. Opposite the cinema you'll find the *NIGHT MARKET* beneath a large roof. Good, cheap food. Speciality of the market - sweet crab bread for 1 Baht.

GENERAL INFORMATION
BANKS

There are several banks on Singhawat Road, e.g. the *BANGKOK BANK* behind the Kitmongkol Hotel. The *THAI FARMERS BANK* is on Charoen Vithi Road, directly behind the bridge, and opens from 8:30-15:30 h.

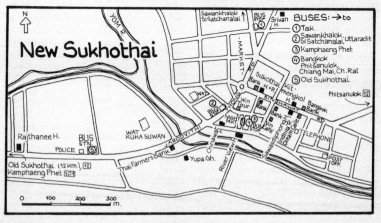

ADMISSION FEES

The admission fee to the Old Sukhothai Historical Park is 20 Baht for foreigners, 5 Baht for Thais. You will have to pay extra to visit the northern, western, eastern, and southern temples. Bicycles (20 Baht for foreigners, 5 Baht for Thais) and other vehicles cost extra, too. All this money goes towards paying for the restoration of the historical park, which sometimes seems to have not quite come off (flower-beds and paved roads, looking rather out of place among the many ancient ruins). Approx. £3.5 million were spent on the project, sponsored in part by Unesco and other international organizations.

TRANSPORTATION TO AND FROM OLD SUKHOTHAI

A *bus* will take you to the ancient city for 5 Baht from the bus-stop at the road to Tak, 300 metres behind the bridge, on the right. Don't get talked into hiring a tuk-tuk for 100 Baht or a taxi for 200 Baht!

Bicycles are for rent for 20 Baht at the restaurants on the road opposite the museum. They're an ideal form of transportation as long as you're not travelling on an extremely hot day. This is also the place to go for a map of the ruins.

K. Vitoon also offers *motorcycles* for 45 Baht an hour. These are more suitable for trips to the temples outside the old town fortification.

Half-day *tuk-tuk* tours (150 Baht) are offered in New Sukhothai, e.g. at the Chinawat Hotel. The Swasdiphong Hotel offers tours with an ac minibus to Old Sukhothai (120 Baht) and Si Satchanalai (150 Baht). Food and drink is included in the price, but not the admission fees to the ruins. You can also rent bicycles from the hotel for 30 Baht. Cars can be rented for 2000 Baht / 4 hours, tuk-tuks for 150 Baht / 4 hours, motorcycles for 100 Baht / 4 hours, bicycles for 30 Baht / day, and bicycle rickshaws for 160 Baht / 6 hours across the road from the state-run bus company.

HOW TO GET THERE

Buses from BANGKOK (440 km, 6-7 hours) leave from the Northern Bus Terminal. Ac buses cost 154 Baht (departure from Sukhothai at 9:00, 11:00, and 22:00 h), non-ac buses are more frequent and cost 84 Baht. Combined bus-train tickets costing 130 Baht (fan) or 210 Baht (ac) are offered by Khaen Inn Tour & Travel in Bangkok, tel 2230341 ext. 4281. Information is available at railway stations and at Sompol Pochana, 16 Prapan Bamrung Road, Sukhothai.

You can catch a bus from AYUT-THAYA for 85 Baht, from CHIANG MAI (300 km, 5 hrs.) for 72 Baht and 100 Baht (ac-buses, departures from Sukhothai: 8:30 h, 9:30 h, 11:00 h, 13:40 h and more), CHIANG RAI 83 Baht (ac-buses leave Sukhothai at 10:30 and 12:00 h and cost 110 Baht), TAK (80 km) 19 Baht, SAWAN-KHALOK (37 km) 10 Baht, PHITSA-NULOK (58 km) 14 Baht, KAM-PHAENG PHET (77 km) 19 Baht, KHON KHAEN (365 km, 6 1/2 hours), 155 Baht (ac), PHRAE (5 hours) 72 Baht, and UTTARADIT (95 km) 20 Baht. The overland buses stop directly in the city centre, local buses from Tak etc. stop north of Singhawat Road. Thanjit Tour buses stop close to the bus station, Win-Tours buses stop at the Chinawat Hotel, where Win-Tours tickets are also sold.

WAT SRA SI, SUKHOTHAI

SAWANKHALOK

Sawankhalok is approx. half-way between Sukhothai and Si Satchanalai. Walk down Kasemrat Road for 800 metres from the Muang Inn and turn right at the end of the road. After a further 700 metres you will reach the

SAWANWARANAYOK NATIONAL MUSEUM, which is in a most peculiar building in a large garden. It is closed on Mon, Tue, and holidays, otherwise it's opened from 9:00-12:00 h and 13:00-16:00 h, admission 5 Baht.

Cotton and silk materials of all patterns and qualities are woven on hand looms in the village of HAT SIEO.

HOTELS
Spend the night at the *MUANG INN**,* 21 Kasemrat Road, tel 642722, 600 metres south of the railway station, near the entrance of town, at highway 101. It is in a reasonably new, two-storey, concrete building in which you will also find a restaurant and the *VIVA CAFE.* You could also try the *SRI SAWAN*, ac**,* 2 Thesaban Damri Road, tel 642259.

HOW TO GET THERE
Buses from SUKHOTHAI to SAWAN-KHALOK cost 10 Baht.

Two daily trains travel back and forth between Bangkok and SAWANKHA-LOK on a dead end line. (departure from Sawankhalok 14:45 and 21:00 h). Buses from SI SATCHANALAI cost 5 Baht.

SI SATCHANALAI

Sukhothai is the place to set off from for a visit to another beautifully situated, former town, Si Satchanalai, approx. 55 km further north.The town was a sort of twin-city of Sukhothai from the 14th - 16th century. The king himself even lived here at times. Si Satchanalai - then called Sawankhalok, lost much of its significance when Ayutthaya became the country's new capital. The town was so severely damaged during the Burmese wars that Rama I ordered its inhabitants to move further south, to present-day Sawankhalok.

Start your tour south of the ruins, at the road branching off to Chaliang. If you're coming from the main road (see *How to get there),* it's 600 metres to the junction. Bicycles are for rent to the right (20 Baht a day). Drive left for 1 km. You will find

WAT MAHATHAT (Wat Phra Si Ratana Mahathat Chaliang) in a river-bend of the Yom river, east of the old village of Chaliang. This is said originally to have been the site of a Khmer temple. Rama Khamhaeng had a wall of gigantic laterite-blocks erected around the temple grounds. The first thing you'll see when entering through the rather unusually conceived eastern entrance are the pillars of the former viharn. A large Sukhothai-style Buddha figure can be seen sitting in front of the 15th century, central prang. You'll find the original 'walking Buddha', a copy of which is also exhibited in the Sukhothai museum, by the southern wall. There are a number of other statues in the temple grounds. A further possibility of reaching the main road is by way of the pedestrian suspension bridge. Cross the bridge from the village of *CHALIANG* and walk down the path until you reach the main road.

You will reach the ruins of Old Satchanalai after a 1/2 hour walk through cotton fields (approx. 2 km). A good map is in front of a restaurant. There is an admission fee for entering the old town fortification: 20 Baht for foreigners, 5 Baht for Thais, 30 Baht per car, 20 Baht for a bicycle or a motorcycle.

This town, dating back to the 13th century, was formerly protected by the Yom river in the northeast and a laterite stone wall measuring 7 metres in height and 1.5 metres in width. In addition, numerous mounds and moats offered extra protection. Of these, little remains. 39 monuments were found within the fortification during excavations, 75 were discovered outside. To the left, you'll see the

ROYAL PALACE. Only the temple ruins are still standing. The restored, central temples are behind them.

WAT CHANG LOM - four entrance-ways lead through the wall surrounding the temple and its high, round central chedi. King Rama Khamhaeng himself is said to have ordered the construction of the chedi, which took 6 years to complete and now encloses a relic of Buddha. The round, Singhalese-style chedi rises upon a high, cubic plinth, whose niches are adorned with Buddha figures at the top and predominantly head-less elephants at the bottom. The viharn used to stand in front of the plinth. Today only its stone pillars remain.

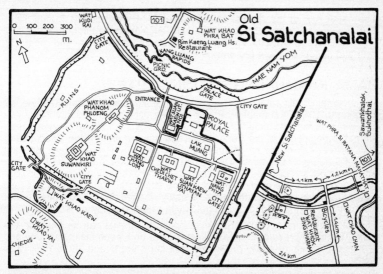

WAT CHEDI CHET THAEW, the main chedi with its Sukhothai-style lotus bud peak, used to be the burial grounds of the Sukhothai princes who ruled from Satchanalai. There are also several smaller chedis of various styles on the temple grounds. The remains of the former ordination hall can be seen in the western area. You will have a good view from the two hills in the north. Climb the wide staircase to

WAT KHAO PHANOM PHLOENG and its large stupa, which already shows elements of the northern Lanna-style. Walk along the ridge and you'll reach the ruins of *WAT KHAO SUWANKIRI.* There are 48 restored *KILNS* 5 km north of town.

HOTELS

The *KRUCHANG HOTEL*,* rooms with fan, shower, and lavatory, is in the new town, 300 metres north of the BANGKOK BANK, 3 houses behind no. 152/2 on the western side of the main road. There's no sign - not even in Thai - so keep your eyes open! The new *SONG SA LAN HOUSE* at the rapids near the old town was still under construction in 1987. Only its restaurant, *RIM KAENG,* was open to the public. The expensive *KANG SAK* restaurant is beautifully set at the river, exactly opposite *WAT KOK SINGKA RAM,* 1 km before the entrance to the ruins.

HOW TO GET THERE

If you can't get a direct bus from SUKHOTHAI, take one to SAWAN-KHALOK (10 Baht), then change to one to SI SATCHANALAI (5 Baht). To get to the old town, disembark 11 km before reaching the present-day city of Si Satchanalai, at km stone 55 (signpost directing you to the archeological project, 2 km). You could also catch one of the regular buses that travel back and forth between UTTARADIT and SUKHOTHAI every hour and get out en route (20 Baht).

The LAMPANG-bound buses from UTTARADIT drive through a beautiful mountain landscape and cost 30 Baht.

RAMA KHAMHAENG NATIONAL PARK

The mountain chain south of the ruins of Old Sukhothai, between Road no. 12 to Tak and 101 to Kamphaeng Phet has been declared a National Park. You can climb its highest mountain, the *KHAO LUANG* (1185 m). Several steep footpaths beginning at the Park HQ on the eastern side of the Khao Luang lead to the peak of the mountain through the ever-green rainforest. You will need 4-5 hours for the climb. The paths aren't marked too well. The first 2 km are extremely steep. Once you've done them the exhausting part is over - the remaining 2.5 km are enjoyable and not too strenuous. You'll have a fantastic view of the Sukhothai plain from the sparsely wooded peak. You'll need a tent if you plan to spend the night, as it gets quite cold and windy.

The pangolin, a rare, unusual looking, nocturnal animal can be found in the park. This scaly creature is an excellent climber and feeds mainly on ants and termites. The skin of a fully grown pangolin is pinned to one of the Park HQ's walls.

The *SAI RUNG WATERFALL* on the western side is another of the park's attractions.

HOW TO GET THERE

You will need your own vehicle to get to the park. There used to be a road leading directly to the park from the Sukhothai ruins. These days all that remains is a dusty path, only paved at the turn-off from Road no. 12 (approx. half-way between the turn-off from Road no. 101 and the ruins). We would suggest taking the 101 towards Kamphaeng Phet. You will reach a signpost directing you to the KHAO LUANG on the right hand side of the road after 19 km. At a Thai signpost after 6 km - turn right. Turn left after another 4 km. From here it's another 6 km to the HQ, where you can spend the night. The Rangers here speak no English. The Sai Rung waterfall at the western side of the mountain can only be reached from a turn-off approx. 40 km beyond Sukhothai.

KAMPHAENG PHET

Another former capital of the Sukhothai Empire lies at the Ping river, 82 km south of Sukhothai. The town, which was founded in 1347, was a garrison town for the kings of Sukhothai and Ayutthaya for centuries. If you're coming down 101 from the north, you'll be able to see the first ruins 2 km before reaching town, to the left and right of the road. There were monasteries in the peaceful forests in front of the town during the 15th and 16th centuries.

In order to get to the archeological park (admission 20 Baht per 'farang' and per 'farang vehicle', Thais 5 Baht), take the road branching off to the right in front of the *WAT AWAT YAI* ruins. Follow the unpaved roads through the overgrown area and you'll reach

WAT CHANG ROP. Little remains of this temple apart from the substructure of the former chedi. This is still an imposing sight, however; a circle of 1 1/2 metre elephant statues surround it. Most of the statues, which were built of brick and decorated with stucco, are unfortunately incomplete. A steep staircase leads up to the chedi. Follow the path, which now heads south, and you'll reach

WAT PRA SI IRYABOT. The laterite stone substructure used to make up the base of a large viharn. Four Buddha statues in different positions used to adorn the square structure in the background. Walk around the temple grounds and you'll come across the well preserved standing Buddha. A large reclining Buddha can be seen in the next temple,

WAT PHRA NON. The statue's remains are still clearly visible. A lonely, weather-beaten Buddha statue can be seen in

WAT PA MEUT. The real cultural attraction of the town, however, is the large, fully restored

WAT PHRA KEO, which lies enclosed by the clearly discernible former town wall and moat (admission: 20 Baht). You will be able to see one of the large Buddha statues from the road. The imposing chedi in the background is built upon a substructure adorned with lion statues. There used to be small Buddha

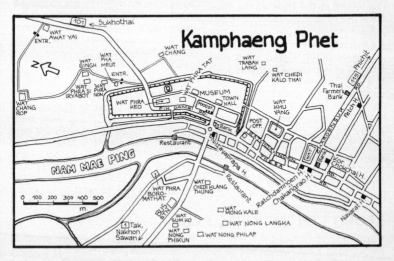

statues in the now empty niches. The emerald Buddha that is now kept at the Royal Temple of Bangkok used to stand here, in this wat. Pass the *WAT PHRA TAT* and you'll reach the

MUSEUM (closed on Mon, Tue, and on holidays, admission 5 Baht). Many of the discoveries made in Kamphaeng Phet are exhibited on the first floor. The bronze statues and ceramics are particularly beautiful. Works of art from different eras, especially the Mon period, are exhibited on the ground floor.

A central roundabout dominates the small town southwest of the ruins. You will find restaurants and several shops here. A large bridge crosses the Ping river in the west. There used to be a different settlement, long before Kamphaeng Phet was even founded, around the

WAT PHRA BOROMATHAT. The new town is south of the roundabout. There are several hotels.

HOTELS

NITTAYAPRAPA*, 2 Thesa 1 Rd., tel 711381, no English sign, rooms with fan, shower, and lavatory, no mosquito nets. The hotel is popular with travellers due to its location at the southwestern corner of the roundabout, not too far from the ruins. Take the rooms at the back of the hotel; these are quieter.

KOR CHOKCHAI** (also called *KACHOKCHAI),* 7-31 Soi 6 Ratchdamnoen Road, is the most comfortable of the cheap hotels in town. The *RATCHDAMNOEN**,* 114 Ratchdamnoen Road, tel 711029, has similar rates. The following hotels are much more expensive:

NAVARAT***-****, 2 Soi Prapan, Tesa Road, tel 711211, no English sign, five-storey, square building, reasonably quiet. *PHET****,* the town's largest hotel, a little out of town, 99 Bamrungrat Rd., tel 711283-

5. *CHAKANGRAO***-****,* 1213 Tesa Road, tel 711315, by the main road in the shopping quarter, English sign.

FOOD

You can dine in the floating restaurants on the river. If you're only going to be here for a short while to see the ruins, try the cheap restaurants at the roundabout. There are several foodstalls here as well as within the old town fortification.

HOW TO GET THERE

The town is rarely visited, although it is only a few kilometres from Road 1, which leads to Chiang Mai from Bangkok. Buses from BANGKOK cost 69 Baht, from CHIANG MAI 70 Baht, from NAKHON SAWAN 27 Baht, from TAK 14 Baht, PHICHIT 22 Baht, and SUKHOTHAI 19 Baht. The bus station is out of town, to the west.

KLONG LAN NATIONAL PARK

Road 1117 branches off to the west from Highway no. 1, 12 km south of Kamphaeng Phet. Minibuses to Klong Lan market-place from Kamphaeng Phet cost 20 Baht (approx. 58 km). It's another 4 km to the imposing, 95 metre *KLONG LAN* waterfall from here. Several footpaths lead up the steep cliff and along the bed of the brook - enjoy the magnificent view! You can spend the night at the Rangers, where you can also stock up on food and drink. There are numerous Meo, Yao, and Lisu villages in the area. *PANG KWAI,* a reservoir with another waterfall, is nearby.

TAK

Most people only ever visit Tak briefly en route to Bangkok or Chiang Mai. The town lies in a valley at the Menam Ping, and is ideally located as a starting point for excursions into the area. The town used to border onto the formerly Burmese-controlled, northern state of Lanna Thai at the peak of the Ayutthayan period. Taksin was born here in 1734. He was responsible for founding the new capital in Thonburi after the Ayutthayan Empire was destroyed by the Burmese, and he became King in 1768. His hometown, proud of its most prominent inhabitant, has built a memorial, the *SALA TAKSIN MAHARAT.*

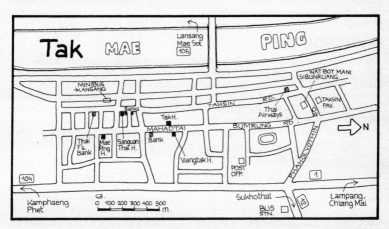

HOTELS

TAK HOTEL*-**, 18/11 Mahat Thai Bamrung Road, tel 511234, clean hotel on an unfortunately rather noisy road. *WUANGTAK***,* 25/3 Mahat Thai Bamrung Road, tel 511910, ac rooms are available in this large hotel. *MAE PING HOTEL*-**,* 231 Mahat Thai Bamrung Road, tel 511807, opposite the fruit market, large and cheap rooms. *SANGUAN THAI HO-*

TEL*-**, 619 Taksin Road, tel 511265, central location, restaurant.

HOW TO GET THERE

You can get into town by minibus for 10 Baht from the overland bus station, which is out of town, by the road to Sukhothai. Buses to the surrounding area leave from town. Buses to MAE SOT cost 20 Baht (taxis 30 Baht, minibuses 25 Baht per person), SUK-

HOTHAI 19 Baht, KAMPHAENG PHET 14 Baht, LAMPANG 40 Baht, CHIANG MAI 56 Baht, and BANGKOK 80 Baht, ac-buses 145 Baht. The ac buses from Bangkok to Chiang Mai stop in Tak. A taxi to Lansang Park will cost you 150 Baht. There is also a minibus which goes to the park entrance via the small villages along the way (10 Baht).

BAN TAK

The settlement of Ban Tak lies on both banks of the Ping river, 23 km north of Tak. You can cross the river on a 300 metre wooden bridge. Careful drivers sometimes even manage to get their car across to the other side. A second, parallel wooden bridge was still under construction in 1987. Many of the traditional houses, built on stilts, can be seen on the river's banks. Small children frolic about in the river while women wash laundry. *WAT PHRA BOROMATHAT,* 4 km west of the settlement, is worth a visit. Drive upstream along the righthand-bank to Sam Ngao and on to the Bhumipol dam if you have your own car.

BHUMIPOL DAM

This dam north of Tak is mainly visited by Thai holiday-makers. It was constructed between 1961 and 1964 and is among South East Asia's largest dams. Its walls, 154 metres high and 486 metres wide, keep the Menam Ping, which stretches back 207 km all the way to Hot, in check. The dam produces 535 megawatts of energy, most of it for the Greater Bangkok area. The dam also contributes to the water regulation in the area, keeping the water levels of the Menam Ping and the Chao Phya as well under control as possible during the rainy period.

Only a small part of the water's surface can be seen from the dam. Boats can be rented for 150 Baht per 1/2 hour. There are many foodstalls and souvenir stands along the banks. The speciality of the area is dried meat, which is dried on the corrugated iron roofs of the foodstalls. There is a small photo documentation of the construction of the dam, the Thai Electrical Company, and the fish living in the artificial lake by the entrance. Apart from this there is not much to see.

HOTELS
We were unable to discover any cheap hotels. The *BHUMIPOL GUESTHOUSE****-**** is beautifully set on the river in between Sam Ngao and the dam. The King himself sometimes comes to stay here.

HOW TO GET THERE
Get out at the road branching off to SAM NGAO from Highway no. 1. Several buses drive to the settlement from here (17 km, 5 Baht). Charter a songthaew for the 3 km to the dam for 5 Baht per person. There are more cars around at weekends.

LANSANG NATIONAL PARK

As soon as you leave the main road to Mae Sot you'll find yourselves in a small valley of bamboo forests which merge with a tropical monsoon jungle further up, in the mountain regions. The park guards have told us that bears and leopards are occasionally seen here - you will probably have to be content with a couple of gibbons and macaques, and even these are usually heard more often than they are seen. A footpath from the HQ leads to three magnificent waterfalls. Look closely and you'll see the small river-bed where the water has managed to dig into the cliff walls over the years. A well-tended trail leads to the Hilltribe Centre in the west of the park, parts of which are set along the banks of the Lansang river. The park is mainly inhabited by hilltribes, especially Lahu and Lisu.

ACCOMMODATION

You can spend the night at the new 2-room*** and 3-room**** bungalows at the end of the dirt road. All rooms have bathing facilities, should the waterfalls not suffice. You can get a big bonfire going in front of your house in the evenings. The women selling snacks and drinks at the small shop will also cook simple meals for you. Nobody here speaks English, however.

HOW TO GET THERE

The park is only 19 km from Tak, 3 km to the left of the road leading to Mae Sot (turn-off at km-stone 19). You can get here by taxi from TAK (150 Baht per vehicle) or by minibus (10 Baht). You can also catch the Tak-Mae Sot bus, disembark at km stone 19, and then walk down the dirt road to the HQ (1.2 km to the barrier, after that it's another 1.6 km to the HQ). Admission fee: 3 Baht, vehicles 20 Baht.

MAE SOT

The town of Mae Sot lies in the frontier area of Thailand and Burma. The Menam Moei, 5 km from town, marks the border. The main source of income of this small, up-and-coming town seems to be smuggling to and from Burma - there are many shops in town that will buy gems. The few customs officials present will allow you to pass through the checkpoint. You can watch the wares being brought over to Burma by foot and boat from the river's bank. One can even walk across during the dry period. The Thai observers sitting at the riverbank (by the flag) will let you cross over without making a fuss. There are numerous stands on the Thai side of the river, selling simple arts and crafts (basketry and leather goods) and other Burmese goods (i.e. gems).

This small town sometimes makes international headlines when the Burmese Army drives guerilla troops of the *KAREN NATIONAL UNION* over the border. This is the point at which the *PAN ASIAN HIGHWAY* (Istanbul-Singapore) is meant to cross the border into Burma. Chances of this happening in the near future are rather slim. Moulmein is 100 km from here. The 86 km road from

Mae Sot to Tak is the only thing that could really be called a highway up to now.

HOTELS
There are three reasonably priced hotels in town, the *FIRST HOTEL*** at the bus station, the *MAE MOEI*,* and the Chinese hotel *SIAM***. The *MAE SOT HILL HOTEL***** is on the by-pass road. There is a bungalow resort east of Mae Sot, on the road leading to Tak; pretty bungalows set in a large park behind a gateway resembling that of a castle.

HOW TO GET THERE
Mae Sot is in the mountains. A bus from TAK will cost you 20 Baht, a minibus 25 Baht, and a taxi 30 Baht per person. You will have to stop at several military check-points along the way. Catch a pick-up for the last 5 km to the border from the stop near Mae Sot's shopping centre (5 Baht). You will pass the airstrip 1 km out of town. There is a daily flight to CHIANG MAI (430 Baht), and to PHITSANULOK (370 Baht) via TAK (155 Baht). A road to MAE SARIANG has already been built. There is no public transportation along this route, however. Getting along by truck is quite wearisome. You can drive as far as UMPHANG in the south, from where you will be able to get to KAMPHAENG PHET.

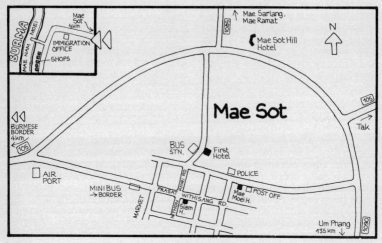

NORTH THAILAND

The northern provinces are among the most fascinating regions in all of Thailand. The landscape here varies, the mountains are the highest in the entire country (Doi Inthanon, 2595 metres), and the valleys are wide and fertile. Most fascinating of all, however, are the many different peoples you will find here, some of whom have only been living in this region for a few decades.

The situation in the territories bordering onto Burma and Laos is unstable - whole smuggling caravans still cross the border to Burma regularly. While shoot-outs at the Mekong and the border have grown less common than in former times, they do still occur. Some of the hilltribes are still cultivating opium, and opium still means money, something which has never failed to lure bandits and the Thai army into the north during the harvest period. Thus there are many reasons for people to carry guns up here, be it an ancient flintlock rifle or a modern M 16.

Chiang Mai, Thailand's second largest city, is the main tourist hang-out of the region and an important centre of traffic and trade. In recent years travellers have also discovered Chiang Rai in the 'high north' and Mae Hong Son in the 'wild west'. The first resort hotels and guesthouses have already been opened in the rural areas. Trekking tourism has expanded considerably; more and more 'new' areas are discovered for organized trekking tours by the season. Now that the area has become safer, many travellers are also starting to explore the region on their own, on foot, by bus, pick-up, or rented motorcycle. A place that may have been unknown just a couple of years ago may now be the place to be. Nobody knows why.

The hilltribes are becoming increasingly commercialized, though this now takes a more subtle form than just a few years back. Do not suffer from pangs of guilt whilst trekking, though; organized trekking tours are certainly not the only thing responsible for the irreversible changes the hilltribe villages are undergoing. These changes are mainly due to the systematic 'Thaization' of the mountain farmers and the destruction of their basis of economy. Take your time and enjoy the still-beautiful landscape with open eyes; you may gain considerable insight into the lives of the various hilltribes as well as a deeper understanding of the problems the rural population of a third world country has to deal with.

Always bear in mind that a trip to the Burmese border can be dangerous. Unaware trekkers are frequently robbed. Some tourists have even been killed. While it is true that armed bus robberies and assaults on boats travelling along the Kok river have become less common during the past few years, one should always remain aware of the fact that the increasing impoverishment of the hilltribes is making desperate; crime is on the rise in those areas particularly affected.

HILLTRIBES

Chao khao (literally mountain people) is the official term of the Thai government for the six minority groups living in northern Thailand at the present time, the *Meo, Yao, Lahu, Lisu, Akha,* and *Karen.* In the vernacular they are referred to as 'hilltribes'. This is a rather inadequate term, however, seeing as most of the hilltribes didn't live in the mountains originally, but in wide fertile valleys from which they were driven away by other, stronger peoples. Tribal hierarchy and a tribal leader are unknown to the hilltribes. All that matters to them is the village community and the village headman.

Linguistically, all of the hilltribes belong to the sino-tibetan group of languages, as do the Thai. Among the main characteristics of the languages of this group are the predominantly monosyllabic words, whose meanings are determined by the pitch and their location in the complete sentence. Although the languages of the hilltribes come from the same group, however, the languages of two tribes may be as different from one another as English is from Russian.

Most of the hilltribes employ so-called slash-and-burn agriculture, just as many Thai farmers do, too. A section of jungle - these days usually secondary forest - is roughly cut down, the remains are burnt to the ground. Whole regions are enshrouded by smoke between February and April. Many bare mountain slopes in northern Thailand are sad reminders of this rather wasteful form of agriculture. The new fields thus gained are cultivated only until they will yield no more, for the process of fertilizing fields is unknown to the hilltribes. Some of the hilltribes only leave a field uncultivated for a couple of years, in order to let it 'regenerate' for a while. These days, however, many of the fallow fields are being confiscated for the government's afforestation schemes.

Most of the hilltribes first came to Thailand as refugees. While 70-80% were actually born in Thailand, less than 20% have the Thai citizenship. The others are considered illegal immigrants. To this day whole village communities seeking refuge from the brutal, murderous, and violent Shan United Army (SUA) cross the border to northern Thailand from Shan State in Burma.

The Thai government has been striving to aid the hilltribes since 1953. The tribes are permitted to settle in the mountains, and the government is busy developing health, agriculture, and education programmes for them. The hilltribes are granted the right to their own languages and cultures. In practice, however, the government has to consider national and international interests first - there is simply no way the government can let the hilltribes burn down the last remains of the Thai mountain forests, regardless of the fact that slash-and-burn agriculture is a substantial part of their culture. The government has also had to prohibit the cultivation of poppy due to international pressure. The object of the aid programmes, therefore, is to get the hilltribes to give up their traditional forms of agriculture and replace them with other, more 'up-to-date' ones. Various foreign organizations, among them the Worldbank, as well as Dutch, German, and Canadian groups, are more or less supporting the Thai government in its efforts. Their alleged goal, next to afforestation, is to offer the

PHOTOGRAPHS: *top:* River landscape in Central Thailand; *bottom left:* Buddha statue in Sukhothai; *bottom right:* Waterfall in the Lansang National Park

hilltribes an alternative to poppy cultivation. Coffee, rubber, nuts, fruits, and vegetables are among the *cash crops* that are being offered. None of these can compete with opium, however; poppy grows more or less on its own, even small amounts of raw opium go for a reasonably large sum of money, merchants come directly to the hilltribes, and transportation is free of charge. The hilltribes have experienced nothing but difficulties with all newly introduced cash crops. As soon as a project has been closed by the government, the hilltribes are left to their own devices; transportation no longer works out, the middle-men are only willing to pay ridiculously low prices, and on top of everything else the farmers of the lowlands start producing the same crop and selling it cheaper.

Thus many hilltribes feel their very existence is being threatened. They are not at all grateful for the government's development programmes. Their mountain-rice fields, which yielded just enough for them to survive, are being drastically reduced due to afforestation schemes and new laws. Their supply of cash is rapidly diminishing. Their basis of economy has thus been almost completely destroyed, and malnutrition is spreading dramatically.

To us tourists, the hilltribes are quite an attraction. Travel agents and trekking companies describe them rather exaggeratedly as fascinating, picturesque, colourful, untouched by civilization, genuine, unspoilt, difficult to reach, almost unknown, newly discovered, and even semi-primitive. We should avoid thinking of them as primitive, though, and think twice before smiling at their spirit-belief, or feeling superior; the fact is that these peoples do have highly developed cultures, though they are very different from ours and in part totally unexplored. One gets the feeling that they are vastly superior to us in some areas. They see their fears as spirits, for instance, and know just how to handle them. We, in contrast, are quite helpless when it comes to tackling our own fears, such as Aids, cancer, and atomic holocaust, nor can our society help the individual overcome his anxieties.

Meeting the hilltribes; if you are interested in the hilltribes, we would recommend that you first learn to tell the respective tribes apart from one another. The easiest way of doing this is by buying a couple of post-cards in Chiang Mai and trying to commit the different clothing, headgear, and jewelry of the hilltribe women to memory. Though the women do not walk around the villages wearing their most festive clothes - as on the pictures - you will find that even their everyday clothes are marked by the same characteristics. Telling the men of the various tribes apart from one another is much more difficult. Most of them wear spacious, black trousers and a western-type jacket or a shirt bought at the market.

In many villages you will see the women's clothing drying outside in the sun. Although you may not actually see any people at first, you will always immediately be able to tell what kind of hilltribe village this is because of the clothes. If you are then able to greet the people in their own tongue, the basis for a friendly relationship will already have been created.

Whilst describing the respective tribes we have tried hard to focus on things that you, as sporadic visitors, will be able to observe, too. Thus we have had to neglect the fascinating themes of birth, death, marriage, and the healing of the diseased. For those interested in these finer points, however, there are a number of good books on the subject listed in our bibliography.

MEO

The Meo (from the Chinese: "barbarians") call themselves Hmong ("free people"). One assumes that they originally came from Tibet and moved to China via Siberia and Mongolia several milleniums ago. Most Meo still live in southern China today, many have also settled in Vietnam, Laos, and Burma. Their first Thai settlements were not founded until the end of the 19th century. These days the approx. 65,000 tribe members make up the second-largest group of hilltribes in the country (second only to the Karen). Their villages are scattered far apart from one another in at least 13 provinces of northern and central Thailand. They are divided into sub-groups of Blue and White Meo according to the clothes worn by the women. They became infamous in the 60s and 70s, when they joined forces with the communists against the Thai Army (Red Meo). 50,000 White Meo also live in refugee camps along the border to Laos. They were on the 'wrong' side during the Vietnam war, when they lived in Laos but sympathized with the Americans.

Clothing and jewelry
The Blue Meo women usually wear short, indigo-coloured, batik, pleated, cross-stitched skirts, and a black blouse, usually also embroidered with stitches. Their hair is held together in a big bun on the top of their heads. The heavy silver jewelry and the beautifully embroidered aprons are only sometimes a part of their everyday costume. The White Meo women wear a blue-black turban and embroidered trousers.

Family, home, and village
The extended Meo families live in ground level houses that have a large common room and several separate sleeping partitions. Only members of one clan live in the same village. Women are integrated into their husbands' clans. The Meo prefer settling at an altitude of 1000 - 1200 metres, usually in an area surrounded by protective mountains. They cultivate rice and corn for their own use, opium for cash. The Meo keep pigs, chicken, and ponies in separate stables set apart from the houses.

Religion
The religion of the Meo is a combination of shamanism and pantheism, with the main emphasis on ancestral worship. The Chinese influence on their religious practices cannot be denied.

Every house has at least one altar opposite the entrance. Sacrifices are offered here, e.g. a chicken on New Year's Day. The garland 'spirit money' plays an important part in every ceremony. It is laid out in a certain way on the floor and later burned in the corners of the house. The most important Meo feast is the celebration of the New Year, which is held in either December or January.

Confronting the present
The Meo were always able to speak the languages of their neighbours and their business associates. It is therefore not surprising that many speak some English.

Many Meo are giving in to the pressure of the government - they are moving into the valleys and doing their best to cultivate rice. The former opium farmers are adopting coffee, soy beans, and fruits as their new cash crops. Quite a few quickly manage to adapt to western technology - the women use sewing-machines to make their clothes, and some of the men are now running flourishing transportation companies using their own pick-ups. It is important to the Meo that their children are educated at Thai schools. All the same, they have always managed to remain true to their own culture - the Meo are proud of being Hmong to this very day.

Tourists in Meo villages
The Meo are usually totally uninfluenced by strangers. They will take a short look at them, then continue with their work. They are most hospitable, but they are not money-hungry. It is against the rules of etiquette to simply walk into a house - if you wish to enter into a Meo building, stand around outside until you are noticed and invited in by a male member of the family. You may enter without being invited if only the women are at home.

YAO

The Yao call themselves Mien. Many of the words in their language come from Chinese. They probably originated in southern China. The first Yao came from Laos in the mid-19th century. Today, the Yao have settled in southern China, Vietnam, Laos, Burma, and northern Thailand (approx. 33,000). Here they have settled mainly in the provinces of Chiang Rai, Phayao, and Nan. A further 10,000 Yao live in refugee camps along the border with Laos. The Yao are the only hilltribe that have an alphabet - they have adopted the Chinese one. With it, they have put their songs, legends, history, and the names of their ancestors down on paper. Sometimes fathers teach their sons how to read, sometimes a Chinese teacher is hired for the whole village. As well as the script, many Chinese customs have also been adopted by the Yao.

The legend of the origin of the Yao
The long history of the Yao is steeped in legends. A Chinese Emperor had promised his daughter's hand in marriage to anyone who would defeat his worst enemy. A dog named Pan Kou was the one to deliver the Emperor's enemy's head to the throne. The Emperor, being a man of honour, stuck to his word, and Pan Kou and the Princess were married. The first Yao were the result of this successful union. The complete legend is told in a Yao epic.

Clothing and jewelry
The traditional costume of the Yao women consists of a black turban, loose and heavily embroidered trousers, and a blue-black coat. Most conspicuous of all, however, are their dark red, woollen scarves, which peek out of the necks

of their blouses like fur collars. Small, heavy silver earrings and silver brace-lets belong to their everyday jewelry.

Family

The Yao live in large, extended families. Polygamy is permitted though not all that common. A young Yao has to find his bride outside his own clan. The couple moves to the groom's parents after the marriage ceremony, which plays a central role in the life of the Yao. Any children the bride might have from earlier affairs are automatically adopted. If the groom is poor or the bride the only daughter of her family, it is the man's decision whether he wishes to move to his wife's family temporarily or possibly even for good.

Religion

The Yao are considered pantheists and ancestral worshippers. They are strongly influenced by Taoism, the ancient Chinese religion of Lao-tze. Their New Year's celebrations are held on the same day as the Chinese New Year, i.e. in January/February.

Confronting the present

The Yao are trying hard to comply with the demands of the government and to co-exist peacefully with their neighbours. The politeness with which they are brought up may make them seem rather distant towards tourists. The old men are worried about the survival of their culture, as the younger generation speaks more Thai than Chinese.

LAHU

The Thais and the Shan call this tribal group Musur or Musoe. One believes that the Lahu originally came from southwestern China, possibly even Tibet, from where they gradually moved south to Burma, Laos, and Thailand over the centuries. The first Lahu settlements in Thailand were reported in 1891. Ap-prox. 39,000 Lahu live in Thailand at the present time, most of them in the province of Chiang Rai as well as in the northern parts of the Chiang Mai and Mae Hong Son provinces. The Lahu are divided into various groups, four of whom have settled in Thailand: Lahu Nyi (red), Lahu Na (black), as well as Lahu She Leh and Lahu Shi (yellow).

Clothing and jewelry

Many Lahu dress like normal Thai farmers - only some of the Lahu Nyi and many Lahu She Leh still wear the traditional Lahu costume on a daily basis. The others only ever dress traditionally for feasts and celebrations. All Lahu put borders on their garments. The Lahu She Leh, for instance, wear black coats with white edges and colourful appliquéd sleeves made of strips of ma-terial. Shorts and colourful knee-socks complete the costume. The everyday jewelry of the Lahu consists of crude silver bangles and braided bracelets made of 8 blades of grass.

Family, home, and village

The Lahu live in small families. The son-in-law only lives at his bride's parents' home until he has 'worked off' the price of his wife.

Most of the relatively small Lahu buildings are built upon stilts. Guests are received on the partially roofed terrace, where most of the housework is also carried out. In order to reach the terrace one has to climb a tree trunk which has had notches carved into it. The floors and walls of the buildings consist of bamboo, as they do with nearly all the hilltribe houses. One can spit through the wide gaps in the floor. This is important, as the Lahu are perpetual betel chewers. The pigs are kept underneath the buildings and put the daily heaps of rubbish to immediate use by eating them. Ponies and chickens have their own stables. Water is channelled into the villages from nearby sources by way of bamboo aqueducts.

Formerly, the Lahu used to prefer living at an altitude of 1000 metres. These days, however, all except for the Lahu She Leh have moved to lower areas. The Lahu grow rice and corn for their own use, as well as melons, chilies, millet, beans, and other vegetables which they sell. Opium is a significant source of income in many Lahu villages.

Religion
The religion of the Lahu is called theistic animism. They worship "Guisha" as their highest god, yet simultaneously believe in good and evil spirits as well as the transmigration of souls.

The Lahu Nyi carry out a bi-weekly ceremony in the village temple, which is characterized by high bamboo canes sporting faded flags. You will find a fenced-in area reserved for ritual dances at the upper end of Lahu She Leh villages. Many of the Lahu Shi and Lahu Na have been converted to Christianity.

The New Year's Feast is the most important event for the traditional Lahu. The moveable feast is held between January and March and is not celebrated at the same time in all villages.

Some Lahu words

hello	*abudadsha*	to	*kai leu*
thanks	*dailo daviiyo*	goodbye	*atsha*
don't want	*maehe-i*	good	*luup*
tired	*zztga*	eat	*odsha*
house	*luu*	sleep	*zzmkyo*
bus	*lu*	tea	*chah*
where (to)?	*hok kai leh?*	I don't know	*naa maa seu*

Confronting the present
The Lahu have many good contacts with the Thais populating the valleys. They do flourishing business, and some of the villages even have a leader who is chosen by the Thai government to act as a mediator between the Lahu and the district administration. Buddhist monasteries have been founded in some of the Lahu settlements, and young Lahu men now have the chance of

entering as novices and receiving a free education. The younger generation is greedily lapping up anything to do with the Thai culture.

LISU

The Thais call the Lisu Lisaw. Linguistically, they belong to the tibeto-burmese branch of the sino-tibetan group of languages. Many words (up to 30%) have been adopted from Yunnanese.

It is thought that the Lisu originally came from southern China. The first Lisu to come to Thailand via Burma (which is the route all Lisu took) arrived in 1921. Approx. 21,000 Lisu live in Thailand at the present time. Their villages can be found in nine different provinces, most of them in the provinces of Chiang Rai and Chiang Mai as well as in the vicinity of Pai.

Clothing and jewelry

The Lisu like dressing colourfully and adorning their garments with many 'fashionable' accessories. These days, bright green and blue nylon materials are especially popular. They are made into jackets that reach the knees in the front and almost the ankles in the back. The sides are slashed all the way up to the hips. Many borders are applied to the shoulders, upper sleeves, and neck. A black sash is wound tightly about the waist. Two bundles of cords dangle down to the hollow of the knee from the hips, their tips adorned with little cotton balls. The turbans, which are worn on special occasions, cannot be described. Young girls adorn them with artificial flowers and lace; anything that glitters will do - there are no restrictions. Lots of the men like wearing loose trousers, also made of blue or green nylon material.

Family, home, village

The father is to be strictly obeyed in the patriarchal Lisu family. Conflicts within the family or between two different families are carried out in public and often end in violence. The clans play an immense role in social relationships.

The usually rather large Lisu buildings are either built on ground level or upon stilts. They are always built next to a slope. The ancestral altar is always placed on the side of the slope, directly opposite the door. The Lisu prefer living at an altitude of approx. 1000 metres, in the hilly, almost inaccessible hinterlands. Because they like to have a feeling of security and kinship as well as entertainment, Lisu villages are usually quite close to one another. They are nearly always situated on one side of a mountain crest. Water is channelled to the villages from the brooks on the other side of the crest by way of expertly constructed bamboo aqueducts.

The Lisu employ alternating field agriculture and cultivate rice, corn, and vegetables for their own daily use. They do not do all of their work themselves; Karen and Lahu are often employed as cheap labour. While pigs and cattle are bred and sold, opium remains the major source of income for the Lisu. Chinese merchants, who also like marrying young Lisu girls, are the main buyers. One frequently comes upon Lisu villages where the majority of the male population is made up of Chinese. Lisu villages often move from one place to another due to social and political factors as well as reasons of economy.

Religion
First and foremost the Lisu are animists and ancestral worshippers. They also believe in a 'highest being', however, *Wu Sa.* You will find a shrine for the protective spirit, *Apa Mu,* beneath a deciduous tree above every Lisu village. The New Year's celebration is the most important religious event of the year. It is celebrated at the same time as the Chinese New Year, i.e. in January/February.

Confronting the present
On the one hand the Lisu enthusiastically incorporate anything they deem worthwhile into their everyday life, including such things as nylon materials, cassette tape recorders, and wireless sets. On the other, they obstinately refuse to give in to the demands of the Thai government. Even when it comes to opium cultivation, they always seem able to find a way to make 'arrangements' with the local authorities.

Tourists in Lisu villages
Guests are received in the main room of the building. They are not permitted to enter the sleeping chambers. One is not allowed to sit or stand on the doorstep. The ancestral altar is considered taboo for foreigners; you may not take photographs of it, nor point your feet in its direction. One is not meant to sleep with one's head pointing towards the fire, which is considered sacred. Foreign men and women should not openly display their affection for one another - they have to sleep in separate rooms. The patron spirit shrine is also taboo for foreigners. Some Lisu do not like having their picture taken. Tourists are an unwelcome sight in those villages which still produce a lot of opium; potential undercover government agents are regarded warily and lead a dangerous life.

Some Lisu words

hello	*a keu cha; ho chwa*
thankyou	*a keu bo moo*
goodbye	*ho chwa gii*
where (to)	*a la jia*
Happy New Year	*tin tyan yu ir*

AKHA

The Akha dislike the name the Thai people have given them, Kor or I-gor. It is thought that the Akha originally came from the highlands of Tibet, and that they entered northern Thailand via Yunnan (where most of them still live today), northern Burma, and Laos over the centuries. The first Akha are said to have settled in northern Thailand around 1900 (the Ulo-Akha). Many - predominantly Loimi-Akha - are still crossing the border from Burma on a regular basis today. Approx. 24,000 Akha live in Thailand at the present time, scattered in six provinces. Most of the villages are in the province of Chiang Rai as well as in the northern part of the Chiang Mai province.

Clothing and jewelry

Their fascinating head-dress and jewelry make Akha women quite unmistakable. They always wear their head-dress, though sometimes in a reduced form or covered with a hood. It consists of silver buttons, silver balls, coins, dyed chicken feathers and monkey hairs, coloured pearls, and woollen balls. The head-dress frames the entire face, and parts of it often dangle all the way down to the chest. An approx. 20 cm disc crowns the head-dress of the Loimi, while that of the Ulo is cone-shaped.

The typical, black-blue mini skirts worn by the women only reach from below the the stomach to just above the knees. When seated, their crotches are chastely covered by a sash embroidered with buttons, coins, and pearls. While one still frequently sees the appliquéd ankle cuffs, the traditional shirt has been almost completely replaced by common, western-type T-shirts. The bamboo pipe, with or without tobacco, is popular among the old and young alike. Many Akha women spin their own thread and from it weave materials on old, foot-powered looms.

Family, home, village

Akha houses are usually built upon stilts. Animals are kept underneath the buildings, where wood is also stored. The houses are covered with large roofs made of thatch. They have no windows. Men and women sleep in separate rooms. A recently married man and woman only spend the first few years of their joint life living in a little hut on the property of the groom's father. After this period they, too, come to live in the house.

The Akha prefer settling on airy mountain crests at an altitude of 1000 metres. They grow rice, corn, millet, chilies, garlic, sesame, and various vegetables on alternating fields. The fields often do not yield enough for the whole village. Pigs, water buffalo, cattle, and poultry are sold and kept for feasts and sacrifices.

The water source is invariably below the village. The women carry the water up to their houses in bamboo receptacles on their backs. They wash themselves as well as their children twice daily.

The Akha always have a solid gate made of massive tree trunks at the upper and lower ends of their villages. The gates are open and not connected to any sort of fence. They represent a symbolic barrier against everything bad and destructive, which includes illness, robbers, vampires, and wild animals. Carved birds perch on the vertical bar of the gate. They are meant to stop falcons from catching too many of the village's chicks. Two crude figures carved of wood, a man and a woman with special emphasis on the respective genitals, stand close to each of the two gates. It is not clear whether these figures are symbols of fertility or protective devices against unwanted guests. New gates and figures are erected annually. Tourists are not required to walk through the gates.

A level square makes up the evening meeting-place of the younger generation of every village. The girls sing and dance, the boys watch and gradually join in. They retire later on, under the cover of darkness, often in pairs.

Religion
The belief of the Akha is based on ancient Chinese philosophies. Their religion should be seen in the widest possible sense - it encompasses their entire life and is called *Akhazang,* the way of life of the Akha. The words of the Akhazang are passed on orally from generation to generation. While the Akhazang describes all religious rituals, ceremonies, and feasts, it also determines the relationships between individuals, between the Akha and animals, nature, and its powers. The Akhazang prescribes in what way a house is to be built or a forest cut down. The harmony and balance between the natural universe and the Akha can only be achieved if everything is carried out in the right way, the right place, and at the right time.

The father's ancestors are worshipped, and most Akha are able to recite the names of up to 64 generations of their ancestors. An ancestral altar can be found in every Akha building. The merry swing feast is held between August and September. The date of the New Year's celebrations varies from village to village. It is usually held in December.

Akha courting song
I am worried, me, a poor boy:
As a poor boy, I cannot marry, perhaps.
I sing for a rich girl and think well
before I say 'come!' to a beautiful girl.
A poor hunter boy asks you, 'come!'
But you, beautiful woman, perhaps you do
not want to marry this very poor man?
Perhaps you do not want to cut the stick
during the marriage ceremony?
But when two people love each other,
and work steadily, they can perhaps marry.

(translated by Dr. Alting von Geusau)

Confronting the present
The impoverishment of the Akha is especially apparent in those villages which are situated within the state's sphere of influence, particularly the villages north of the Kok river. The Akhazang offered protection and support during the centuries of migration, when the Akha moved from one place to another only to be repelled by the respective local populations. These days, however, the Akhazang seems to be a restriction more than anything else - if anything, it is

stopping the Akha from solving their problems. An increasing number of Akha are turning to opium for solace, in spite of the fact that the Akha were traditionally a non-opium smoking hilltribe. The Thai officials consider the Akha the most 'primitive' of all the hilltribes, the ones who cling most stubbornly to their traditions, and are most difficult to develop. It is almost impossible for development aid volunteers to comprehend the highly developed culture of the Akhazang and the various interpretations it offers. The Akha are in great danger of ultimately losing their traditions and giving in to the demands of the government.

Tourists in Akha villages

Quite generally, the Akha dislike foreigners. In contrast to other hilltribes they refuse to imitate the 'western' mode of dressing. They do like using tourists as an excuse for their own shortcomings, though, e.g. their opium abuse. It is not only the fault of tourism that one often feels excluded in an Akha village; the anthropologist Bernatzik experienced the same coldness 50 years ago.

If you wish to walk through an Akha village, be prepared to accept the invitation you will be given to enter into one of the buildings (Akha etiquette prescribes this). Once there you should at least accept a glass of the tea or water which will be offered to you. Men should never enter the women's part of the building without having been invited. If you don't have the time or simply don't feel up to it, take the path leading around the village. Never touch the village gates!

Some Akha words

where are you headed, younger brother?	*aga itee a-jeu-o?* (instead of 'hello')
where are you headed, older brother?	*aga itee a-nii-o?*
goodbye	*roi ma-dee*
man	*ali*
father	*ada*
thankyou	*geu-leu-heu*
woman	*abu*
mother	*ama*

KAREN

The Karen are called Kariang or Yang by the Thai people. Their 240,000 tribe members make them the biggest hilltribe in Thailand (51% of all hilltribes). Their origin is unclear. They lived in Burma for many centuries, and they first came to Thailand during the 18th century. Mainly White Karen live in Thailand at the present time, most of them concentrated along the Burmese border from Mae Hong Son to Kanchanaburi, others scattered in several of the northern and central provinces. The Karen have been waging a bloody guerilla war against the central Burmese government for decades on the other side of the border. The conflict becomes particularly harsh during the dry season of every year. The white Karen are divided into Skaw Karen and Pwo Karen, the latter sometimes falsely labelled Red Karen.

Clothing

The Karen women are well known for their superior weaving, which they carry out sitting on the floor. Narrow strips of material are woven on simple looms and later sewn together to make robes. Young and unmarried women wear a long, white robe which gradually turns grey as the years go by. Apart from this, each of the sub-groups has its own, individual style of dressing.

Family, home, village

The Karen are the only Thai hilltribe with a matriarchal society. They live in small families, and the family is the most important economical unit for all domestic affairs. The Karen have settled in the mountains as well as on the plains. They prefer living at the relatively low altitude of approx. 500 metres, even in the mountains. If a village becomes too large, a satellite village is founded nearby. The relationship to the 'mother' village always remains close, though.

The traditional Karen buildings are built upon stilts. The large interior is not divided into separate rooms. Sometimes a small separate corner is reserved for those daughters reaching puberty. Most of the daytime activity takes place on the spacious, roofed veranda. This is also where guests are invited to spend the night. The Karen are very industrious - you can tell by taking a look at their jackfruit-, citrus-, and mango-tree studded gardens. Their villages are fenced in and very clean. An intricate system of alternating field cultivation used to guarantee a good crop each year and help prevent the fallow fields from eroding. These days, the Karen are no longer permitted to use this method of agricultural cultivation. They grow rice, vegetables, and, very rarely, opium. The Karen breed chicken, pigs, water buffalo, cattle, and elephants. They sell their surplus ware and earn additional money through labour and by renting out their elephants. Those Karen living in the plains have more or less adapted to their Thai neighbours and the Thai way of life.

Religion

The Karen worship a *master of earth and water* as well as numerous spirits. They do not have a house altar, nor do they have a certain place where village ceremonies are carried out. Some Karen have been converted to Christianity, others - especially those living in the lowlands - to Buddhism. The traditional New Year's celebrations are held in February.

Confronting the present

The Karen economy as well as the social structure is suffering great damage under the pressures of the Thai population and the Thai government, which has prohibited alternating field agriculture as well as the foundation of satellite villages. The Karen are gradually giving up their traditional values and adopting the Thai way of life. Wealthy, educated Karen who have settled in the large cities influence the entire tribe in its values and hopes for the future.

Tourists in Karen villages

Foreigners are only ever received on the veranda. This is also the only place where you will be able to spend the night. At night, foreign men and women have to sleep on separate verandas.

LAWA

Called Lua by the population of northern Thailand, the Lawa are not considered a hilltribe by the government. They were amongst the first inhabitants of Thailand and had settled in the river valley of the Ping river as early as in the 8th century, considerably earlier than the Thai people. They are of austroasian origin and belong to the Mon-Khmer group. Most of them have been fully absorbed into Thai society. The approx. 13,500 who have retained their tribal identity have settled on the Bo Luang plateau between Hot and Mae Sariang as well as in the mountains southeast of Mae Hong Son. They are responsible for only very little of the destruction of the mountain forests. This is due to their intricate rotation system of cultivating rice-terraces. The rotation enables them to use the same fields over and over again. The Lawa are animists and ancestral worshippers. They have combined their traditional belief with Buddhism, as have the Thais.

TREKKING TO THE HILLTRIBES

Most of the travellers who come to northern Thailand want to visit the hilltribe villages and experience the adventure that must surround them. Others simply want to get out of the cities and into nature.

When to go trekking: *November - February;* the days are pleasantly warm during this period, the nights cool, the mountains cold, and there is virtually no rain at all - this is the best of all times to go trekking. *March - April;* this is when it gets hot (noontime temperatures 32^0C - 35^0C), the temperatures fall below 12^0C at nights, though, and it is generally very dry and dusty - you won't have much fun trekking at this time. *May - October;* it may rain for 15 or even 25 days of a month during this, the rainy period. It often only rains in the evenings and at nights, though. Still, trekking tours during this period usually end up as mud fights.

How to go trekking: Trekking tourism has expanded considerably during the last couple of years. Dozens of travel agents and tour promoters are willing to furnish you with a tailor-made trekking experience. Increasing numbers of guesthouses are being opened in the very heart of the mountains. Individual trekking (alone; without a guide) is also on the rise, regardless of the many dangers involved.

Visitors

Please do not give money or candy to children: They skip school to beg.
The Donation Box is for benefit of all village children.

Thank you - The parents

SIGHTSEEING TOUR (half or full day)

Tourists are driven to villages which have adapted perfectly to sightseeing-tourism. In most cases this form of tourism is even the major source of the village's income. The women are always dressed festively. They sell arts and crafts and are used to having their picture taken. They have a perfect right to expect you to either buy something off them or give them money, should you wish to take their picture. If you're keen on portrait pictures take them here - the inhabitants of the more 'unspoilt' villages might feel too insecure to pose in front of a camera.

Doi Pui, a Meo settlement close to Chiang Mai, is a perfect example of one of these "tourist villages", as are Phadua (Yao) and Sam Yaek (Akha), both of which are situated north of Chiang Rai.

EXCURSIONS (2-3 days)

On these tours you will walk from one village to the next, along standard routes. Several groups do these tours every day. This type of excursion is also included in most Thailand package deals. Don't go expecting to find any "untouched hilltribes", for you will be disappointed. Usually one doesn't have to hike for more than a maximum of 2-3 hours daily. A boat-ride and an elephant-ride ("safari"!) are nearly always included in the price.

A frequently offered, 3-day excursion from Chiang Mai looks like this: 4 hour bus-ride (to Thaton), 3 1/2 hour boat-trip (on the Mae Kok) to a Karen village (Ruam Mitr), where the entire group spends the night. Next day: 2 1/2 hour elephant-ride to a Yao village (Huay Mae Sai), 1 hour hike to the waterfall, and another 1 1/2 hours to the Akha village (Aboo), where the second night is spent. Next day: 1 1/2 hour hike to a Shan village (Huay Comb), 4 hour return-trip to Chiang Mai. The whole trip (including seven meals) will cost you approx. 1300 Baht per person. The same trip can also be done for a considerably cheaper price from Chiang Rai (two days).

TREKKING TOUR (4-5 days)

Trekking tours for 4 - 10 travellers can be booked at over 40 trekking tour organizers and guesthouses in Chiang Mai. During the main season you will be able to hike to even the most remote places on the day of your choice. Most travellers enjoy their trip, but whether or not it turns out to be the mind-boggling experience that brochures promise depends largely on the guide. There is no point listing the organizations with the best guides at this point, seeing as the guides change frequently. Try to get information from other travellers, and if any of them had a particularly good trip, try to find out the name of their guide. It is always a bonus if your guide is a hilltribe member himself and/or speaks the languages of those hilltribes which you will be visiting. Try to estimate the amount of time you will spend hiking in advance, and bear in mind that the trip often goes steeply up and downhill, and that there is virtually no shade (seeing as the surrounding jungle has been burnt down). Have your guide explain the trip to you in detail before leaving; which villages you will be visiting, how you will be getting there, how long it will take, how long will you have to hike, what will the terrain and the weather be like, how many people can be accommodated, maximum number of people taking part in the tour, meals, how much of the necessary equipment is furnished, how much weight will one have to carry, etc.. Attention: sometimes several groups are put together along the way, contrary to what your guides might have originally told you.

The trekking organizations usually furnish a small, often miserable backpack as well as one blanket per person (which will certainly not suffice during the winter). One hikes 2 - 8 hours per day and spends the night at a hilltribe village, often in the house of the village elder, which is frequently cleared for the trekking tours. The guide usually cooks meals from the supplies brought along, sometimes rice is obtained at the villages. You will usually have to sleep on mats on the ground. Do not expect a toilet and don't be embarrassed to use the garden instead; the pigs will take care of the waste, usually much quicker than you would want them to.

Equipment: good shoes as well as sandals, at least one change of clothing, sun-hat, water flask, argentic salt tablets to cleanse water, sun lotion and insect (mosquito) repellent, toilet paper, torch, matches, personal wash kit, and medicine.

November to February: warm sleeping-bag and an insulation mat to sleep on. If you don't have one along, insist that the tour organizers furnish you with a second blanket. It can get extremely cold at nights (close to freezing point). May to mid-November: rain gear, high shoes.

Valuables: Deposit cheques, cash, travel documents in the safe of your hotel / guesthouse. Have them give you an exact receipt and take a photocopy of your passport along. (Be careful with cheque- and credit cards; they are frequently misused, and you won't notice that you've been taken advantage of until weeks later!!) The safest place to leave your valuables is in one of the safe deposit boxes of the Krung Thai Bank, Charoen Muang Road, Chiang Mai (cost: approx. 30 Baht per week).

Smoking opium: Hilltribe members know very well that many tourists come just to try opium, and they will frequently offer it. Take care; if you want to try some, start off carefully - you never know how a new drug will affect you. Remember that opium is a seriously addictive drug; heavy withdrawal symptoms have been known to occur after only one week of regular consumption. Never take opium when drunk, and above all do not mix it with any other drugs. Do not attempt to bring drugs back to Chiang Mai, let alone Europe, from the mountains - the risk is much too high. Smoking opium is illegal in Thailand. If caught, you may have to go to prison for 1 - 10 years!

Cost: 5-day/4-night tours with ten participants usually cost approx. 800 - 900 Baht per person. Add another couple of hundred Baht if a safari (elephant-ride) is included.

Longer trekking tours: 6 to 10-day tours are rarely offered. If you can afford to wait a couple of days and have already formed a group, however, every trekking organization should be able to arrange a tour for you. Chances of penetrating into the more remote areas and getting to see some 'genuine' villages are much higher here than on any of the shorter tours.

Trekking from different places: Good trekking tours are also organized from Chiang Rai and Mae Hong Son. Guesthouses here either organize tours themselves or will be able to tell you where to go. Tours are also organized by the guesthouses in Mae Sariang, Pai, Thaton, Mae Salong, and Mae Sai.

TREKKING WITH A PRIVATE GUIDE

You can hire a guide who speaks the hilltribe languages and will organize a tour according to your personal interests any time. This is probably the best way of getting to know the hilltribes and gaining insight into their lives. You will also not have to worry about making social blunders or getting lost. This will mean paying a little more than for a group-tour, however, approx. 500 Baht per day from Chiang Mai. You will be able to hire a private guide for less than half of this sum in the smaller towns.

INDIVIDUAL TREKKING

The Thai Tourist Organization (TAT) does not recommend going trekking alone in the hilltribe territories. The region is large and quite rough, and there is no way one can guarantee tourists' safety. Still, an increasing number of adventurous travellers are starting to explore the mountains on their own. Be aware of the fact that you will not be able to communicate in Thai or English with the Akha or the Lisu.

The standard routes (see above, *Excursions)* are pretty safe; one can hardly lose ones way and will not run into many unexpected difficulties, especially if one brings one's own food along. It is easy to find accommodation, the hilltribes here are used to tourists and have adopted certain codes of behaviour. Whether or not you will feel at ease in these villages and be able to handle the perpetually begging children etc. is of course another question.

If you plan to hike to remote areas you should definitely be well equipped, informed, and - if possible - experienced. Ask the English-speaking population in your base (e.g. Chiang Mai) how dangerous the region is at the moment. Take care not to cross the border to Burma by mistake; if you do, you may have an extremely difficult time getting back into Thailand. With a little luck you will encounter some truly wild experiences, at worst you will have spent a couple of days in the mountains without having passed a single village.

You can spend the night at local schools (should you pass any) or in the village elder's hut, though often only on the veranda. Pay for accommodation (approx. 5 - 20 Baht) and food (approx. 5 - 10 Baht). Bring a gift for the head of the family (e.g. tobacco, sugar, tea, or salt), but do not act exaggeratedly magnanimous. Read the hilltribe and trekking section of this book carefully. Pay attention to the non-verbal communication of your hosts - this will increase your awareness as to the limits of how much hospitality to expect. Remember that tourists are by no means a welcome sight in all of the villages! If you act in a friendly and considerate fashion, however, the hilltribes will usually react accordingly. Try to learn a couple of words in the respective languages. Hilltribe members are very patient, and more often than not will gain a great deal of enjoyment out of teaching you some of their language. Avoid wearing khaki materials; you might be mistaken for one of the loathed soldiers, and you will awake painful memories. Black and coloured materials are okay.

Most of the mountain-paths are not signposted. There are no trustworthy maps of the area. A few copies of the by now out-of-date topographical maps (with a scale of 1:250 000) as well as trekking-maps of the areas south of Fang and the Mae Kok river area are available in Chiang Mai.

> *Warning:* Individual trekkers have been shot in the past as well as during the 1987/88 season! Never venture into the mountains on your own!

MOTORCYCLE TREKKING

You will have the chance of covering a large area of beautiful landscape and visiting many hilltribe villages in a relatively short time when travelling by motorcycle. There are many paths suitable for motorcycles off the main roads, but only for those who are experienced in dirt-biking! The paths are frequently washed out or very narrow. They are often unfit for traffic during the rainy season. You can either rent a motorcycle with a driver, or drive yourself and take a guide along on the back. If you plan to go motorcycle-trekking on your own, you will usually receive a hand-drawn map from the rental service. We would strongly recommend you take a good look at the map David has drawn onto his library wall, however (Ratchamanka Road Soi 2, next to the Saitum Guesthouse, Chiang Mai). This is probably the most precise existing map of the area. Avoid those regions marked as dangerous. Motorcycle-trekkers travelling on their own are still frequently shot down from their bikes in the frontier territories. Motorcycles can be rented in Chiang Mai, Chiang Rai, Mae Hong Son, Fang, Mae Sai, and Chiang Saen for 120 - 200 Baht per day.

> *Warning:* Single motorcycle trekkers have been shot down from their bikes in the past! Never venture into the mountains on your own!

HOW TO BEHAVE IN A HILLTRIBE VILLAGE

When visiting the hilltribes Western travellers find themselves confronted with a society and a culture almost incomprehensible to them. Thus a visit to the hilltribes is a challenge to anyone's tolerance and adaptability.

Always remember that you are a guest. Find out about customs and taboos beforehand. Once there, do not forcefully try to find out all there is to know; be satisfied with what the hilltribe members are prepared to show you of their own free will. Observe the people without making a nuisance out of yourself, and only take pictures after previously having asked for permission. You will frequently find that you will enjoy better experiences by leaving your camera in its bag and simply listening and observing. If you do not act in an acceptable way the consequences will be particularly noticeable to those travellers visiting the village after you. The wrong kind of behaviour may even lead to a certain village no longer acting hospitably towards tourists.

Thus the question arises whether we as tourists actually have a negative influence on the hilltribes without even being aware of it. The ethnologist Dr. Alting von Geusau, who has been studying the life of the Akha for the past 10 years, comments as follows:

"The foreign tourists who trek through the hilltribe villages are only responsible for a very small part of the degeneration these villages are experiencing. At most, they could be seen as the cause for approx. 2-5% of the damage which has been caused during the last few years. In contrast to the Thai people, tourists are at least not responsible for taking anything away from the hilltribes, who, over the years, have grown accustomed to surviving in spite of military, pillagers, and robbers. Compared to these, tourists are certainly nice people. They bring a little money and sometimes even entertainment to the villages. True, they do sometimes behave in a rather insensitive manner, by driving through a village with an exposed torso for instance, but while this certainly shocks some of the tribe members and is ridiculed by others, it doesn't actually do them any harm as such. It does harm me, however, seeing as I, as a farang, live and work among the hilltribes and am immediately associated with anyone else of my skin colour. Those tourists who come to the Akha villages in order to smoke opium, however, do pose a serious problem; they set a negative example for the Akha, many of whom are desperate but would usually refuse to smoke opium because it goes against their customs. Seeing farangs indulging in opium abuse, however, will often inspire the Akha to do the same."

CHIANG MAI

Also known as 'the rose of the north', Chiang Mai is slowly but surely developing into a modern city. The town lies in a wide, fertile valley, enclosed on the east and west by mountains 2000 metres in height.

Chiang Mai became the capital of the Lanna Thai kingdom in 1298. The city was founded by King Mengrai, a Thai-Lao prince from Chiang Saen who managed to unite several Thai tribes and extended his sphere of influence over the entire northern region of the country. He founded Chiang Rai in 1262 and made Chiang Mai the capital after having overthrown the Mon kingdom of Haripunchai (present-day Lamphun).

The Lanna Thai kingdom flourished during the 15th century. The 8th Buddhist World Council was held in Chiang Mai in 1478. Relationships with up-and-coming Ayutthaya remained strained, however, marked by competition and conflict. Lampang was conquered by the Ayutthayan forces in 1515. Lanna Thai became a vassal of Burma's mighty King Bayinnaung in 1556. With the exception of a few brief spells of independence, Chiang Mai remained under Burmese regency for the next 220 years. Not until 1775 did General Taksin manage to re-integrate the northern provinces into the new Thai kingdom. A half autonomous prince of the Lampang dynasty ruled the north until 1938, when Chiang Mai became the capital of the province.

There are many places to visit in the town's old quarter. The ground-plan of the actual old city is a perfect square, each side measuring 1500 metres in length. Parts of the former

TOWN FORTIFICATION and *MOAT* (19th century) are still preserved. The city gate on Tapae Road was not built until 1986, however, and it looks more like a cheap facade on a film set than anything else. The rather rural character of the old quarter is quite fascinating; the low, wooden buildings, set in gardens, can only be reached by way of narrow alleys. Of the many typical wats with northern-style architecture you should definitely visit

WAT PHRA SING, religious centre of the western part of the old quarter. There are beautiful murals and wood-carvings inside.

WAT CHIANG MAN, in the northeast of the old town, is even older. Legend has it that King Mengrai resided here while the city was being built. You will find two viharn on the temple grounds. The right hand one enshrines two of Chiang Mai's most famous Buddha statues. One is said to be over 1000 years old and to come from India, the other was made in the 7th century and belonged to a king of the Haripunchai kingdom. The power to bring rain is attributed to the two statues by the local population, and they are carried through town in a procession held annually for the Songkran festivities. The building is usually only opened to the public on Sundays and Buddhist holidays, from 9:00-17:00 h.

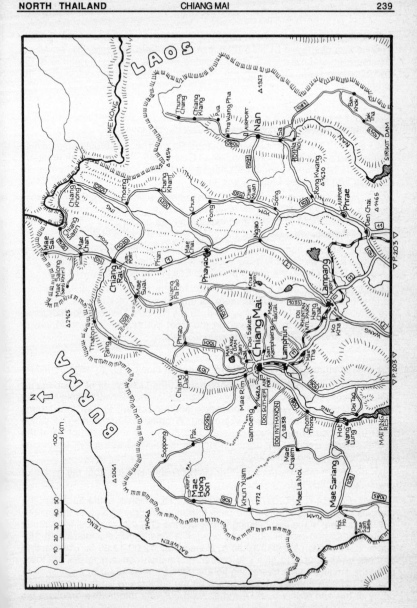

WAT CHEDI LUANG is said to have had a 90 metre chedi from 1454 to 1545, when it was destroyed by an earthquake. A 60 metre ruin remains. An all but disintegrated staircase leads up to a gilded Buddha statue. The shrine of the town's patron spirit, the lak muang, is to the left of the main entrance of the temple.

We would suggest taking a bicycle, a motorcycle, or a bicycle-ricksha to any of the following places, all of which are outside the old town.

WAT SUAN DOK is in the west of Suthep Road. The numerous, small, white chedis are burial sites of former rulers of Chiang Mai. The temple grounds are particularly beautiful at sunset. Continue west down the road for another 3.5 km, then turn left. After 1 km you will reach

WAT UMONG, a forest temple. The monastery, which was founded by King Mengrai, has been pretty much destroyed, however. Tablets sporting inscriptions such as *Today is better than two tomorrows* or *Do good tomorrow, says the fool - the wise man did good yesterday* are fastened to the trees.

WAT JED YOD is north of the old town, by the super-highway, in the middle of a pretty park. It was built in 1455 and modelled on the north Indian Mahabodhi temple in Bodh Gaya, the site of Buddha's Enlightenment. The

NATIONAL MUSEUM is to the west of the temple. Religious works of art from various cultural eras as well as more recent examples of Thai arts and crafts are exhibited on two floors. Kilns, in which the famous Thai celadon ceramics were once baked, can be viewed in the front courtyard. Opened Mon-Sun 9:00-12:00 and 13:00-16:00 h, admission 2 Baht.

The area south of *CHIANG MAI GATE* is another nice district to walk around in.

You will find a number of artisan workshops in the vicinity, all of which manufacture silver jewelry, wood carvings, ceramics, or lacquerware using the old, traditional methods. Watching the black lacquer bottles, boxes, and tablets being produced is particularly interesting. A bamboo fibre netting to which layer upon layer of black lacquer is applied makes up the basis for all of the above objects. Each of the layers of lacquer is polished with a mixture of clay and ashes (see also *Shopping).*

Take bus no. 3 towards the zoo. The *UNIVERSITY* is 5 km from the centre of town. You will find the

TRIBAL RESEARCH CENTER in building no. 15, which is at the far end of the campus, approx. 1.5 km from the main entrance. (A ground plan of the university is available in the first building to the left, the *Office of the Rector).* A study group working on the hilltribes has opened a small and very interesting museum, opened Mon-Fri 8:30-16:30 h, closed from 12:00-13:00 h. The employees are often unable to give you proper information concerning the hilltribes; go to the small but very interesting library (Mon-Fri 9:00-16:00 h) if you wish to find out more. A number of good books on the subject are listed in the bibliography at the end of this book. A rather short but very informative brochure on

WAT CHIANG MAN, CHIANG MAI

the hilltribes can be bought for 35 Baht. Trekking tours are not organized from here. Continue down the road for another 600 metres and you'll reach the

BOTANICAL GARDENS (Arboretum), opened from 8:30-16:30 hours, and the

ZOO, opened daily from 8:00-17:00 hours, admission 10 Baht. The zoo is located on an unusually large and very pretty area on a hill slope. The open-air bird sanctuary covers an entire valley.

Across the road you'll find a

THAI-GERMAN DAIRY FARM stall. Milk, yoghurt, and cheese (100 g for 10 Baht) is sold from 8:00-17:00 h.

GUESTHOUSES

There are well over 100 hotels and guesthouses of all standards and rates in town. You will be given an up-to-date list of guesthouses (who pay to be entered on the list) in the Tourist Office.

The guesthouses are run by families, young men, or women, most of whom are very kind, friendly, and helpful. Most guesthouses have their own trekking service or will at least be able to tell you how to go about organizing a trekking tour. Some rent out bicycles, a few free of charge. The cheaper places usually do not have hot water. Season December to February, better prices can be obtained out of season by bargaining.

The centre of the traveller-scene is in the eastern part of the old town, within the city walls. Most restaurants can be found along the southern part of Moon Muang Road; guesthouses are in the alleys beyond.

Old quarter, southeastern district

For those arriving at Tapae Gate with a town bus (all four lines stop here), it is not far to the first guesthouse;

GEMINI HOUSE*, 22 Ratchdamnoen Road, tel 236355, directly behind the Montri Hotel. Thai-style house with a garden restaurant, very noisy. You will find

KAMOL GH*, 1 Ratchdamnoen Road Soi 2, in the opposite alley. Wooden Thai-style building and bungalows set in a pleasant, rather uncared for garden. Reasonably peaceful. (You can also reach it from Moon Muang Road - pass the Restaurant Supun House.)

Walk south down Moon Muang Road from Tapae Gate (past the restaurants), and you will find the entrance to the

NEW THAI GERMAN GH*, 33/1 Moon Muang Road, behind the Oasis Bar (on the right). The place has a bad reputation. The new

SAI TUM GH*, 21 Moon Muang Road = Ratchamanka Road, Soi 2, tel 211575, is one alley beyond, to the right - flat wooden buildings built upon stilts, connected by one, long balcony. There is also a dormitory. Quite peaceful in spite of the central location. Right next door you'll find

T. N. GUEST HOUSE*, 13 Ratchamanka Road Soi 2; quiet, no garden. The

SOMWHUNG GH*, 2 Ratchamanka Road Soi 2 is opposite. Narrow, long, brick building reaching all the way to the Thai-Danish Dairy Farm on Moon Muang Road. Cheaper rooms are available in the wooden shack next door.

Cross Ratchamanka Road by the canal and go into the next alley. The

TOY HOUSE*, 45/1 Moon Muang Road Soi 2, is a new building. No garden. Some of the rooms have a balcony, the ones on the upper floors are well lit and pleasant.

K. WIN HOUSING, 25 Moon Muang Road Soi 2, is directly opposite. New, two-storey building with sparsely furnished rooms. To the left you'll find

TOP NORTH GH**-***, 15 Moon Muang Road, Soi 2, tel 213900. Very popular, clean, not too expensive. Nice rooms with bathroom and hot water. Multi-storey, concrete building, pretty little garden, bamboo restaurant, peaceful location - cheap really, if you consider all the advantages. You can already book rooms from the Swan Hotel in Bangkok at slightly reduced rates. Just beyond is

DIOR HOUSE*, 48/4 Moon Muang Road, Soi 2, tel 236106, peacefully located brick building. Restaurant in the driveway. You will reach

KENT G.H.*, 5 Ratchamanka Road, Soi 1, tel 217578, by way of the narrow alleys or directly from Ratchamanka Road. New, peacefully located brick building, small garden and roof terrace, dormitory, run by English people. The

CHIANG MAI YOUTH HOSTEL*, 31 Prapokklao Road Soi 3, tel 212863, is nearby. It can also be reached from Chiang Mai Gate (300 m). Rooms or dormitory available, good place for information, extremely peaceful, reduced rates for people with an International Youth Hostel Card. Nearby you will find

MANIT GH*, 55 Ratchapakinai Road, tel 214352. Wooden house with an adjoining building, large garden. Manit takes care of everything and is very friendly. Bicycles for rent.

Old quarter, northeastern district

There are a number of older guesthouses in this area, some of them with a rather negative image. Of the better ones, we would recommend:

ORCHID GH*, 22 Moon Muang Road, Soi 6, tel 236357 - old wooden building with very nice, large rooms. The

NUMBER ONE GH*, 27 Moon Muang Road, Soi 7, is in the next alley, by the Wat Lam Chang. All rooms have a shower and toilet, said to be very clean. The

SRI PHUM*, 27 Moon Muang Road, Soi 8, is in the last alley, close to the Sawatdee Guest House - small, quiet building, bathroom with hot water, home-made whole wheat bread, bicycles available for 20 Baht a day. You will find the

BAN RAI*, Wiang Kaeo Road, above Ratchapakinai Road, next to Wat Chiang Man. The popular, reasonably priced Ban Rai Steakhouse is in the garden.

Outside the eastern city wall

Walk out of the old town through Tapae Gate, then head north for 300 metres. Turn right at the sign. After 100 metres you will reach

LEK HOUSE*, 22 Chaiyapoom Road. Brick house with a large garden and a barracks-style adjoining building. Unstrained atmosphere, many French

guests. The restaurant is run by Yves (not to be mistaken for the Lek Guest House 400 m further south - mere impostors!) Turn east from Tapae Gate and take the first alley leading north. You will reach

CHANG MOI GH*, 29 Chang Moi Kao Road, after approx. 150 metres. Small, clean rooms, peaceful location. Nearby,

RAMA HOUSE*, clean rooms, warm community showers. The place is run by a friendly married couple.

TIMES SQUARE GH**, 2/10 Tapae Road Soi 6, tel 232448, is directly at Tapae Gate, between Tapae Rd. and Kotchasan Road. New, hotel-style building, rooftop restaurant, bathrooms with warm water, run by French people. Continue down Kotchasan Road and you will pass

LEK GUEST HOUSE*, 53 Kotchasan Road. No relation to the Lek House run by Yves. Turn down the alley at the Aroon Rai Restaurant and you'll come to the

GARDEN HOUSE*, 2 Kotchasan Rd. Old Thai-style building, rural atmosphere, whole wheat bread.

On the west bank of the river

There are three well known guesthouses between Charoen Prathet Road - a large, noisy road with much traffic - and the river. You can walk to the night market from here in just a few minutes. There are a few good restaurants and many foodstalls. Walk south down the wide road from the Tourist Office and you'll pass the driveway of the

GALARE GH***, 7-7/1 Charoen Prathet Road, tel 233885, after 150 metres on the left hand side. New Thai-style building, very comfortable, some of the rooms ac - the place is universally praised. Continue on for approx. 300 metres (past the hotels and restaurants) and you'll reach

CHUMPOL GH*-**, 89 Charoen Prathet Road, tel 234526. Rather noisy, boring looking building, reasonably cheap. The garden of the

CHIENGMAI GH** (ac ***), 91 Charoen Prathet Road, tel 236501, is right next door. This is one of the first guesthouses ever to have been opened in the city. The new adjoining buildings make it look pretty silly. There is no view of the river from the garden restaurant, and although the place makes a pretty dignified impression on the whole, much of its original atmosphere is gone.

On the east bank of the river

Start on the eastern side of Nawarat Bridge (buses 1 and 4). Head south for 500 metres, then turn left into a signposted alley. You will find the

RACHA GH* 4/11 Lamphun Road Soi 2, tel 244103, on the right hand side. Two-storey, brick building, burglar proof, hot showers; lounge and restaurant look out on the public alley, pleasant, secluded atmosphere. Motorcycles cost 120 Baht a day, bicycles 20 Baht a day. Go north from Nawarat Bridge, pass the two good restaurants, and you'll reach

RIVERSIDE GH*, 63 Charoenrat Road, tel 241896. Multi-storey, brick building, small terrace, snack-bar down by the river.

Charoenrat Road continues north from Nakhon Ping Bridge (buses 1 and 3). This narrow, twisty road can be quite dangerous for pedestrians and cyclists. There are a couple of guesthouses here, right by the river. There are hardly any traveller-restaurants in the vicinity with the exception

of those in the guesthouses themselves. Head north and you will reach

MEE'S GH*, 193/1 Charoenrat Road, tel 243534 solid building, very peaceful. A little further on you'll find the

JE T'AIME GH*, 247/9 Charoenrat Road, tel 241912. Do not be misled by the name. This is a prim and proper guesthouse, but the woman in charge sometimes has terrible temper tantrums.

PUN PUN GH*, 321 Charoenrat Road, tel 243362; old, two-storey building, gloomy rooms, simple bungalows down by the river. Beds with mosquito nets, restaurant serving health food. Bicycles are free. You will find the famous Khao Soi Lam Doun Noodle Shop just beyond, near the

HOLLANDA MONTRI GH**, 365 Charoenrat Road, tel 242450; clean rooms with bathroom and hot water, motorcycles and bikes for rent. The place is run by Dutch people, You can use the pool of the Rincome Hotel for 20 Baht .

GOLD RIVERSIDE*, 381 Charoenrat Road, tel 244550; brick bungalows with good beds in a large, wonderfully uncared-for garden with many trees. Friendly family, very peaceful. Bicycles cost 10 Baht a day, motorcycles are also for rent. Transportation to and from your train is free of charge.

Towards Doi Suthep

There are many hotels but hardly any guesthouses on Huay Kaeo Road (towards Doi Suthep). Just outside the northeastern corner (buses 1 and 3), you will find the

YMCA INTERNATIONAL HOSTEL** (ac***), 24 Mengrai Rasmi Road, tel

221819; modern building in a quiet alley, more a hotel than anything else, but a good place to get to know young Thais; cafeteria, small shop, and library.

HOTELS

Next to the guesthouses, there are also over 50 hotels in town charging various rates. You will definitely get your money's worth at the

A&P HOTEL**, (ac***), 41 Moon Muang Road, tel 212309; five-storey concrete building, well away from the main road, much greenery, nice rooms, and a good view from the top. Hot water available in the mornings and evenings. Very comfortable for the price.

ANODARD HOTEL*** (ac****), 57 Ratchamanka Road, tel 211055; concrete block with nice rooms and a public pool (18 Baht admission, opened 9:00-21:00 h).

PRINCE****, 3 Tai Wang Road, tel 236744; modern, clean, with a pub and pool.

ROYAL PARK****, 471 Charoen Muang Road, tel 242755, opposite the railway station in a large park. New, five-storey building with modern interior architecture, bungalows, pool, and a baby-sitting service.

MONTRI** (ac***) corner of Ratchdamnoen / Moon Muang Road, tel 211070; clean, all rooms include a hot shower, good food (including Thai) is served downstairs at the Peacock Pizzeria.

NEW CHIANG MAI** (ac***), 22 Chaiyapoon Road, tel 236561; clean, large rooms, central location.

RIVER VIEW LODGE****, 25 Soi 2, Charoen Prathet Road, tel 251110; you will have a wonderful view of the river from the antique-studded hotel, which also has a restored teakhouse, garden, and restaurant. South of Nawarat Bridge.

Now for a couple of the luxury hotels that package deal tourists usually get sent to. (Double rooms cost between 1000 and 5000 Baht, much more than ****).

CHIANG MAI ORCHID, tel 222099, first class hotel of international standards, comfortable ac-rooms, pool. *RINCOME*, pool, tel 221044; both on Huay Kaew Road.

The following three can be found on Chang Klan Road, near the night market:

SURIWONGSE, tel 236789,

CHIANG INN, tel 235655, and

DUSIT INN, tel 251033.

FOOD

"Steak with baked potatoes and veggies" (about 50 Baht) has been the traveller-hit for the last couple of seasons. If this is your scene, go to the *BAN RAI STEAK HOUSE*, Wiang Kaeo Road, west of Phra Pokklao Road, or to the *LEK HOUSE*, 22 Chaiyapoom Rd. This is also a good place for a nice breakfast with whole wheat bread, as is the *GARDEN HOUSE*, Kotchasan Road, Soi 2.

The *PEACOCK*, Moon Muang Road by Tapae Gate, serves the best, indeed the only good pizza in town (35 Baht for a big helping).

The best fruit juices and shakes are served at *DARET'S*, Moon Muang Road, an ancient, and very noisy traveller hang-out. The food here is not too good, though, nor can we vouch for the food which is served at the new branch on Chaiyapoom Rd.

Chiang Mai

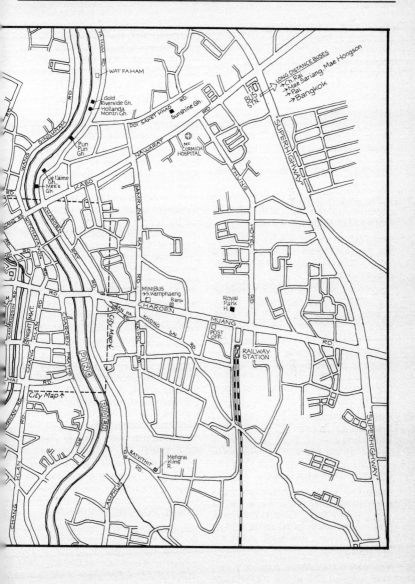

If you wish to eat cheaply, go to the market or to the foodstalls on Chaiyapoom Road, north of Lek House (good noodles). There are also many foodstalls at the *ANUSARN MARKET,* in a side-alley southeast of the night market.

WANGKUNG RENA, an excellent, cheap seafood-restaurant, is nearby. The many restaurants on Chang Klan Road (southern end of the night market) are particularly well-visited in the evenings. Thai, Chinese, and seafood is served.

Indian and Pakistani food is served opposite, at the *AL SHIRAZ,* 123 Chang Klan Road.

The *THAI-DANISH DAIRY FARM* on the southern part of Moon Muang Road offers dairy products and homemade cakes.

Good northern Thai food is served at the *AROON RAI,* Kotchasan Road, approx. 500 metres south of Tapae Gate.

Good Philipino food is served at the *MABUHAY,* which is in a nice, old house in the old quarter, northeast of Wat Phra Singh, on the road next to the District Office. Only open from 7:30 to 15:00 h.

Good northeastern Thai food and fine, cheap chicken (grilled chicken with honey - 34 Baht a piece) is served at the *HONEY BARBEQUE CHICKEN* next to the Porn Ping Hotel, Charoen Prathet Road.

Good Thai food is also served across the road at the *RUENTHAI,* as well as at the *RIVERSIDE,* Charoenrat Road, 200 metres north of Nawarat Bridge, above the river - live music in the bar in the evening.

You can put together your very own Thai meal at any of the markets be-

tween 16:00 and 17:00 h (e.g. Chiang Mai Gate). Buy the different dishes at the different stands. Beware of red dishes, though - they are usually very hot. Just ask: "Prik mai?", then wait for an answer. "Mai prik!" = "Not hot!"

You will find more restaurants and bars along the road leading to the university, e.g. *PIM,* where good, middle-sized steaks cost 35 Baht.

Excellent Indian and Thai vegetarian food is served at the *WHOLE EARTH RESTAURANT,* Sri Dornchai Road near Chang Klan Road, open from 11:00 - 14:00 h and from 18:00 h. The restaurant is set in a nice garden and run by people who are into transcendental meditation - good atmosphere, classical Thai and guitar music is performed live in the evenings, drinks are expensive. There is another vegetarian restaurant, the *MANGSAV IRAT,* approx. 800 metres outside of the Suan Dok Gate (the western gate). Good Lassi is served, about 8 Baht per meal.

There are a number of German restaurants in town - *ALT HEIDELBERG* on Huay Kaeo Road by the Chiang Mai Orchid Hotel, closed on Sundays; *HAUS MÜNCHEN,* 115/3 Loi Krao Road, near the night market, and the *KAFFEEHAUS* which serves traditional German dishes. The German boss has been living in Thailand for 30 years!

You will find several more expensive restaurants along the circular road near the National Museum. We would especially recommend the *SUANG CHANG PUAK RESTAURANT.*

You can consume a traditional northern Thai Khantoke dinner and enjoy a hilltribe dance performance at the touristy and commercial *CHIANG MAI CULTURAL CENTRE* - a place we would definitely not recommend! The food is bad and usually cold, the dances have little to do with anything remotely related to the hilltribes. If you want to go nevertheless - performances are held between 19:00 and 22:00 h, admission 200 Baht. You can also check out the *KHUM KEOW PALACE* on the northern part of Phra Pokklao Road, tel 214315, if you're into this sort of thing.

SHOPPING

Chiang Mai is a veritable shopping paradise for those in love with northern Thai arts and crafts as well as antiques. (Watch out for the export-rules!) When buying opium pipes from the Meo, make sure that they haven't been used - you may have big trouble with the customs officials back home if they have.

A large *NIGHT MARKET* is held daily between 18:00 and 22:00 h (sometimes during the daytime, too) on several floors of a large building (as well as in the cellar and on the surrounding pavements of Chang Klan Road). The building was built just for this purpose. While there isn't much of an oriental atmosphere, the shopping is good, especially for clothing, jewelry, hilltribe arts and crafts, genuine as well as 'new' antiques, imitation designer ware (Lacoste etc.), and cassette tapes. Lacquerware, silk, and umbrellas are also pretty cheap. Next to the many hilltribe stands there are also stands run by business-people who have shops offering a larger variety of wares in town. Definitely try to bargain!!

Most of the shops selling *ARTS & CRAFTS* and *ANTIQUES* can be found on Tapae Road. As at the night market, bargaining is an absolute

must. As the town isn't all that large, you can spend a couple of days trying to get a better price; simply drop in every now and then and see if it's gone down - you're almost certain to get what you want in the end.

Nice, cheap, genuine hilltribe wicker-work can be bought at COOP HANDICRAFT, two doors next to the Thai Farmers Bank on Tapae Road (shop-signs in Thai only). The hill-tribes receive a share of the profits.

Many merchants sell silverware on Wulai Road. You can also buy nice silver in a couple of shops along the road leading to San Kamphaeng. Wood-carvings are manufactured, exhibited, and sold in the wooden building complex of Banyen, 500 metres south of the entrance of town.

MENGRAI KILNS, 31/1 Ratuthit Road, 2 km south of Nawarat Bridge, sells excellent *THAI CELADON.* The shop is run by a New Zealander and has a range of pieces superior to that of the SIAM CELADON in San Kamphaeng.

You will find the *WAROROT MARKET* north of Tapae Road, by Wichayanon Road. Clothing, food, and household goods are sold at this market, which is mainly patronized by the local population.

Fish, meat, fruit, and vegetables are sold at the *SOMPHET MARKET* along the northern end of Moon Muang Road. The market is also known as the 'civil servant's market', seeing as it doesn't open until the early afternoon.

The TANTRAPHAN *SUPERMARKET*, in the cellar of the building on the corner of Tapae / Chang Klan Road, sells good whole wheat bread and buns, as does the KASEM STORE on Ratchawong Road. This is where the guesthouses buy their 'home-made-bread' and their cheese.

Good **MAPS AND BOOKS** are sold at the D.K. BOOKSTORE, 234 Tapae Road. If you plan to go trekking in the mountains, this is the place to come for good trekking maps (so far maps of the area south of Fang as well as the Mae Kok River area have been published). Topographical maps with a scale of 1 : 250 000 (which are now out of print and becoming pretty rare) can also be bought. We would definitely recommend buying *Nancy Chandler's Chiang Mai Map,* which includes the entire city area as well as all bus routes and excursions out of town. All good maps are also available at the TRAVELLER LIBRARY (see below). If you can't find what you're looking for at D.K.'s , try the SURIWONG BOOK CENTRE, Si Dornchai Road (the employees speak very little English, though). There is another bookshop on Chang Klan Road.

Old army surplus **JUNGLE BOOTS** as well as backpacks etc. can be bought at MITHAI'S, Mani Noparat Road, east of Fang Road.

GENERAL INFORMATION
TOURIST INFORMATION - you will find the TAT Office on Praisani Road, corner of Tapae Road, tel 235334. Lists of the departure times of all public transportation as well as the prices of all the official tour companies, hotels, and guesthouses are sometimes available. You will also find the Tourist Police here, tel 232508 and 222977, daily from 6:00-24:00 hours.

TRAVELLER LIBRARY - David's library service can be found on 21/1 Ratchamanka Road Soi 2, 15 metres

from Moon Muang Road, right next to the entrance of the Sai Tum Guest House. David has a gigantic map of northern Thailand drawn onto the wall, which he researched on his own. Maybe the map is even being published and sold by now. He will be able to explain even the most unusual routes to you with the aid of photographs - an absolute MUST for dirt bikers planning to go off the road. You can also read books about Thailand here, borrow novels, buy maps, and drink soft-drinks. Open Mon-Sat 8:00-17:00 h.

THE MOUNTAIN PEOPLE CULTURE & DEVELOPMENT EDUCATIONAL PROJECT - is still under construction, but may be a good future source of information. Address: 137/2 Nantharam Road, tel 236194.

POST OFFICE - The General Post office is on Charoen Muang Road, just before the railway station. All poste restante mail addressed to here is entered in a book. You will find another post office on Praisani Road, 100 metres beyond the TAT Office. The post offices are open from 8:30-12:00 and 13:00-16:30 h Mon-Fri, from 9:00-12:00 h on Sat, Sun, and holidays. The telegram counter is open from 7.00 - 23.00 h, tel 241056.

LONG DISTANCE CALLS - The counter at the GPO offers a 24 hour service. You can also call home from the INTERNATIONAL TELEPHONE SERVICE, 44 Sri Dornchai Road, between 9:00 and 22:30 h. The post office at the airport offers telegram and international telephone services between 8:30 and 16.30 h.

IMMIGRATION - on the road leading to the airport, tel 213510.

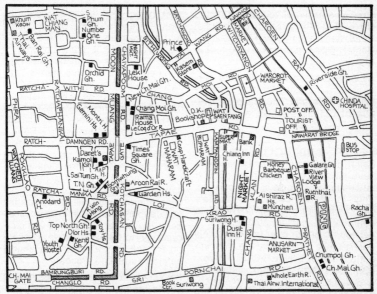

BANKS - There are several banks on Tapae Road. The Exchange Service of the Krung Thai Bank, north of the night market, is open from 8:00-20:00 h daily. The Charoen Muang Road branch also offers safe deposit boxes for tourists for 30 Baht a week.

MEDICAL AID - McCORMICK HOSPITAL, Kaeo Nawarat Road, tel 241107, bus no. 3. The outpatient department's consultation hours are from 13:00-20:00 h, Mon-Fri. Call before going (241311). CHINDA HOSPITAL, Charoenrat Road, shortly behind Nawarat Bridge. LANNA HOSPITAL, by the super-highway, tel 211037-42 (private hospital).

Up-to-date information concerning MALARIA is available at the Malaria Center, 18 Boonruangrit, tel 221529 (beyond the western gate, 300 metres to the right, then turn left).

You may consult the CRISIS CENTER, tel 2778811 and 2777699, free of charge if your problem is a psychological one. Mon-Fri 8:30-20:00 h, Sat and Sun 9:00-18:00 h.

LAUNDRIES - Those returning from a trekking tour always bear a heavy load of dirty laundry. You can do the 'dirty work' for just a few Baht at various laundries in town (10 pieces approx. 25 Baht). Simply ask for the nearest one at your guesthouse. A load will cost you 20 Baht at JI-ARANAI LAUNDRY, 178 Chang Moi Road, a dryer costs 15 Baht - open daily from 8:00-20:00 h.

SWIMMING - there is a clean, public swimming pool in the old section of town, at the ANODARD HOTEL, 57 Ratchamanka Road, tel 211055 (18 Baht, 9:00-21:00 h).

TRADITIONAL MASSAGE - in WAT SUAN DOK on Suthep Road, 1200 metres outside of the western gate, and at the chiropractic oriented RINKAEW PHOVECH on Wualai Road, behind the Chiang Mai Cultural Center. Open from 8:00-20:00 h, 200 Baht per hour.

CLASSICAL DANCES - are performed rather irregularly at the Fine Arts College and The National Theatre of Chiang Mai, Suriwong Road Soi 5, tel 235966.

FEASTS AND HOLIDAYS
Fairs, parades, and beauty pageants have always been extremely popular in Thailand, especially in the north. This is of course not everyone's weakness, but it is IMPORTANT to note that it becomes rather difficult to get rooms at the over-booked hotels during these times. Here the most important dates: WINTER FAIR (approx. from Dec 30th-Jan 8th; especially crowded towards the end of the year); FLOWER FESTIVAL (3 days at the beginning of February), SONGKRAN FESTIVAL (April 13th-15th); Yi Peng - LOY KRATHONG (held at full moon in October or November).

TRANSPORT IN CHIANG MAI
There are four different *BUS LINES* that run through town. A ride on any of the lines costs 2 Baht (some tourists get taken for a ride for 5 Baht). *SONGTHAEW* (motor-samlor) cost 5 Baht per person, *TUK-TUKS* are at least 10 Baht per vehicle. *RICK-SHA* drivers usually ask for outrageous sums of money, the standard rate for a medium-length ride is 10 Baht.

MOTORCYCLES are a wonderful way of getting about in the north - good roads, safe forest and country lanes, little traffic outside of the towns, and a pleasant climate. You will be

able to rent them at the shops on the southern end of Moon Muang Road, at the guesthouses, and in the vicinity of the night market (many Enduros for hire). The bikes are usually in pretty good condition, but give them a thorough check anyway, and make sure that the license plate is well fastened. The kilometre indicator should be in working condition, too. They usually cost between 100 and 200 Baht a day, if you want to rent one for a longer period of time you might get away with 80 Baht a day. One is usually not asked to show a driving license. Unfortunately, insurance is not even offered - you will always be the one responsible in case of an accident! If you feel like buying a motorcycle, go to the *Motorcycle Market* - on the left of the main road shortly before you reach Lamphun.

If you plan to rent motorcycles and go off the road, definitely go to the Traveller Library (see above) for information.

BICYCLES: The shops on the southern end of Moon Muang Road rent out bikes for approx. 20 Baht a day, as do some of the guesthouses. They are ideal for getting around the old section of town and the country roads that surround the city (little traffic here). Beware of the main roads in town, however, as well as the arterial roads leading south, east, and west, which are crowded and dangerous.

RENTING CARS - if you're travelling in a group of four, it would definitely be worth renting a car. The standard rates are 450 to 550 Baht per day. Make sure that the car is in good, working condition before renting it - many of the smaller firms try to rent out absolute wrecks. Once

PHOTOGRAPHS: *top:* Akha village; *bottom left:* Karen women; *bottom right:* Akha woman

you've made sure that the car is ok, start bargaining (even if you're at AVIS or HERTZ). Unfortunately it is not yet possible to rent cars in one town and return them in another (Chiang Mai - Bangkok, for instance). If you do do this, you will have to pay the cost of the transfer, usually between 2000 and 3000 Baht.

HERTZ, Chiang Inn Hotel, 100 Chang Klan Road, tel 235655. AVIS, Huay Kaeo Road (opposite the Chiang Mai Orchid), tel 222013. CHIANG MAI MUL TOUR, 271 Moon Muang Road, tel 233809. JONG JAROEN TOUR, 52/2 Sri Dornchai Road, tel 236588. PHAYATEWAN TOUR, 175/12 Pra Pokklao Road, tel 222086.

LEAVING CHIANG MAI
BY PLANE
The airport is in the southwest of town and can be reached by songthaew for 30 - 40 Baht. THAI INTERNATIONAL: Chang Klan Road, tel 234150. THAI AIRWAYS: 240 Phra Pokklao Road, near Ban Rai, tel 211044-6, opened from 7:30-17:00 h daily, flies to the following places: BANGKOK daily 1275 Baht, CHIANG RAI daily 300 Baht, NAN and PHRAE 5 times weekly for 380 Baht and 280 Baht, PHITSANULOK daily 505 Baht, MAE HONG SON 2-3 times daily 310 Baht, MAE SOT and TAK 4 times weekly for 430 Baht and 415 Baht, KHON KAEN Fri and Sun 1780 Baht, SURAT THANI via Bangkok daily 2260 Baht, PHUKET 2400 Baht, and HAT YAI 2580 Baht.

BY TRAIN
The railway station is east of town on Charoen Muang Road. Buses 1 and 4 stop here, bus no. 3 ends here.

There are three direct daily trains to BANGKOK. Two express trains at 16:50 h (arrival 6:25 h) and 18:30 h (arrival 7:35 h) and one Rapid Train at 15:20 h (only 2nd class), arrival 5:45 h. Trains from Bangkok arrive in town at 6:35, 7:40, and 8:40 h.
SAMPLE PRICES: 537 Baht (1st class), 255 Baht (2nd class), 121 Baht (3rd class). Several extra charges are added to the price - express train 30 Baht, Rapid Train 20 Baht, 2nd class sleeper 70-100 Baht, ac 80 Baht.

BY BUS
The central bus station for all destinations outside of the province as well as CHIANG RAI, MAE HONG SON, MAE SARIANG, PAI, LAMPANG, and NAN is at the super highway by Kaeo Nawarat Road, tel 242664 (buses 3 and 4; tuk-tuk from the old quarter approx. 20 Baht).

If you want to go to THATON, FANG, LAMPHUN, or HOT, you need to go to the Chang Puak bus station on Chotana Road, 211586 (500 metres beyond the north gate). Buses to PA SANG, LAMPHUN, and some of the ones to CHIANG RAI and LAMPANG also stop at Nawarat Bridge (Charoen Muang Road/Lampoon Road). Buses to CHOM THONG and HOT stop at the Chiang Mai Gate (south gate).

To BANGKOK: ac bus no. 18 (orange) approx. every hour between 6:00 and 21:00 h for 133 Baht, 10 hours; Super ac bus no. 18 (blue) at 9:30 and 10:00 h as well as 7 times between 19:15 and 21:30 h for 242 Baht, 8 hrs.), the ac bus also stops in TAK (42 Baht, 4 hrs.) and in KAMPHAENG PHET (70 Baht, 5 hrs.). The large, private ac buses to BANGKOK leave from the respective company offices and from the Anusarn Shopping Centre near the night market (cost: 150-280 Baht). Some guesthouses sell tickets with no extra charge - sometimes the buses will even come and pick you up for free.

To CHIANG RAI: direct with bus no. 166 (green) every half hour between 6:00 and 17:30 h for 47 Baht, 3 1/2 hrs. (ac 66 Baht, 3 hrs., departures at 8:00, 12:00, and 16:45 h; super-ac buses cost 85 Baht, 3 hrs.). To CHIANG RAI via LAMPANG (25 Baht, 1 1/2 hrs.): bus no. 148 (green) every half hour between 5:30 and 16:00 h for 66 Baht, 5 hrs.

To MAE HONG SON via MAE SARIANG (50 Baht, 4 hrs.): bus no. 170 (orange) at 6:30, 8:00, and 11:00 h. There is also a night bus at 20:00 and 21:00 h for 97 Baht, 9 hrs. (the buses departing at 13:00 and 15:00 h only go as far as MAE SARIANG).

To PAI: 7:00, 8:30, 11:00, and 14:00 h for 50 Baht, 4 hrs. Once there catch a pick-up to MAE HONG SON at 14:00 h or at 7:30 or 10:30 h the next day (50 Baht, 4 hrs. - dusty!); ac buses to MAE HONG SON cost 148 Baht.

To SUKHOTHAI: bus no. 155 (orange) at 7:00 and 15:00 h for 72 Baht, 5 hrs. (ac buses at 10:00 and 12:00 h for 100 Baht, 5 hrs.). On to PHITSANULOK from SUKHOTHAI: 6 hrs., 82 Baht, ac buses 117 Baht. Buses to PHITSANULOK every 3 hours from 9:00 h, 67 Baht, 5 hrs.

To NAN: bus no. 169 (orange) every three hours from 8:00 h for 80 Baht, 6 hrs. (ac buses 100 Baht, 5 hrs.). The non-ac bus also stops in PHRAE, 49 Baht, 3 hrs.

To THATON: bus no. 1231 at 6:00, 7:20, 9:00, and 11:30 h for 37 Baht, 4 hrs. (you will reach the CHIANG RAI-bound boats on the Kok river in time with the first two buses).

To FANG: bus no. 1231 every half hour between 6:00 and 17:30 h for 32 Baht. From here you can catch a mini-bus to THATON for 7 Baht, 1 hour; to MAE SAI 60 Baht.

To LAMPHUN: bus no. 181 (blue) and 182 (white) every fifteen minutes between 6:00 and 18:00 h for 6 Baht, 30 minutes. From here it's another 45 minutes to PA SANG, 10 Baht.

You have a choice if you're heading to the northeast; to KORAT (NAKHON RATCHASIMA): bus no. 635 (orange) at 4:30, 6:30, 10:00, and 14:30 h for 145 Baht, 11 hrs. (ac buses leave at 8:00, 17:00, 18:30, and 20:00 h for 262 Baht, 12 hrs.). To KHON KAEN: bus no. 175 (orange) 5 times between 5:00 and 11:00 h, 153 Baht, 12 hrs. (ac buses at 8:00 and 18:10 h for 214 Baht, Super ac buses at 19:00 and 20:00 h, 275 Baht). To LOEI: bus no. 636 (orange) at 7:30, 17:30, and 19:00 h for 109 Baht, 9 hrs. (ac bus at 20:30 h for 195 Baht). From here you can continue on to UDON THANI for 135 Baht, 11 hours (ac buses 242 Baht).

EXCURSIONS FROM CHIANG MAI
BOR SANG/ SAN KAMPHAENG
Minibuses to San Kamphaeng, 13 km southeast of town, leave regularly from the corner of Charoen Muang Road / Bamrung Rat Road. They cost 5 Baht. Buses to Bor Sang, 4 km in front of San Kamphaeng, cost 2 Baht. 4 hours in a tuk-tuk shouldn't cost you more than 80 Baht.

Many workshops that make and sell arts and crafts have been opened up along the road leading to BOR SANG during the last couple of years; lacquerware, silver, wood-carvings, silk, and semi-precious stones are for sale. Watching the men and women at their meticulous work can be quite fascinating. Groups are usually offered a glass of tea or even a soft drink - this is of course done in the hope that they will shop generously without trying to bargain. You will usually not even be noticed, let alone be harassed by a salesperson, if you're on your own - this will give you plenty of time to browse and compare. You will be able to count on a large discount if you're shopping without a commission-hungry 'helper', i.e. a taxi driver or a local guide. The smaller, non-ac shops are usually the cheapest of all. Find out about the standard prices at the Chiang Mai night market beforehand.

Hand-made paper and silk umbrellas are manufactured in the workshops of BOR SANG. You can choose the pattern and material you like best from a catalogue, and for a small additional charge your souvenir will be sent directly home (50 Baht additional charge on the standard postal rate - packages to Europe may weigh up to 20 kg).

Cotton and silk materials, in part still woven on the traditional looms, are produced in SAN KAMPHAENG. You can watch the traditional process of work at the touristy but nevertheless interesting Shinawatra workshop, the largest workshop in the area, 73/5 Mae-on Road. A weaver earns approx. 9 Baht per metre and usually manages to weave about 10 metres a day. The silk materials are characterized by typical geometrical designs and bright colours. Silk and cotton materials (over-expensive!) are offered for sale here as well as along the main road.

If you want to find a bargain, make sure that you are not accompanied by a guide or a taxi driver, and find a non-ac shop!

MAE TAKRAI FOREST PARK

You can make a nice excursion to the MAE TAKRAI FOREST PARK, approx. 30 km east of San Kamphaeng, if you are travelling by motorcycle. Take the road branching off to the left from San Kamphaeng (H1229), and simply keep going straight ahead, past the the road branching off to the San Kamphaeng Hot Springs (which are not worth going to), where you will also find a signpost directing you towards the park. After another 4 km you will reach a signpost saying *Mae Takrai Forest Park 13 km.* Turn right onto the unpaved road and drive through the beautiful mountain pass and teak forest. Turn left onto the intersecting road after 10.5 km. Turn right after another 1 km (before reaching the village of MAE TAKRAI). A couple of picnic tables and huts have been set up around a pretty little artificial lake. You can take a walk along the pleasantly laid out paths.

Instead of taking the same road back, why not take H1230, which leads through a wide valley, due south (39 km). You will pass through numerous villages, some of them inhabited by Karen. Be warned, though - the road is extremely dusty. Another 11 km down H11 will bring you to Lamphun, another 26 km will bring you back to Chiang Mai.

WAT DOI SUTHEP

This wat is 16 km northwest of town. You can get there by taking a minibus from Mani Noparat Road by the northern, White Elephant Gate, or by taking bus no. 3 to the final stop (the zoo) and then changing onto a minibus (departures every 15 minutes until 17:00 h - 30 Baht up, 20 Baht down). A taxi will cost you approx. 200 Baht there and back. The temple is closed to the general public after 16:30 h.

You can reach WAT DOI SUTHEP (at an altitude of 1080 metres) by climbing the 290 steps of the staircase. A cable car service allows even the weary and ill to visit the temple (5 Baht).

Legend has it that the temple was built in 1383 under the reign of King Guena. The king had invited the Ceylonese monk Sumana to come to the Lanna kingdom and spread the teachings of (Theravada-) Buddhism among his people. Sumana brought a relic with him as a gift to the king, part of which is today kept in the Wat Haripunchai in Lamphun. The other part was divided in two, and one part was attached to the back of a white elephant. Once set free, this creature marched into the mountains, all the way to the present-day site of the Doi Suthep. It was then decided that the temple should be erected here and nowhere else.

A winter residence of the King, the PHU PING PALACE with its beautiful gardens, is further up the road, 5 km above the wat (minibus from the wat 10-15 Baht). The palace is only opened to the general public from Fri-Sun, and even then only as long as no member of the Royal Family is staying there at the time. Both the wat and the palace are situated on the slopes of the 1690 metre DOI PUI. You can climb this mountain if you wish. You will reach the summit after an exhausting 3-hours hike from Wat Doi Suthep. Start early!

The unpaved forest path left of the palace leads to DOI PUI, a Meo village. Don't feel that going here is an absolute must, however; everything is very touristy, and the village is included in most of the sightseeing tours offered by the Chiang Mai trekking organizations. The clever Meo are mainly interested in your money.

McKEAN REHABILITATION INSTITUTE (for lepers)

Founded in 1897 by the American Presbyterian doctor McKean, this leper colony is located on the small island of Ko Klang on the Ping river. It has an excellent international reputation and visitors are welcome. Mon-Fri 8:00-12:00 h and 13:00-16:00 h, Sat 8:00-12:00 h. A brochure which is available in the Administrative Office of the institute will give you some insight into the work carried out there. You can circle the island on the 3.5 km road.

Ko Klang island is approx. 7 km south of Chiang Mai. Leave from Nawarat Bridge, go south down Lamphun Road for 2.7 km, turn diagonally right onto H1008 behind the petrol station, then continue straight ahead until you reach the end of the road (approx. 4 km).

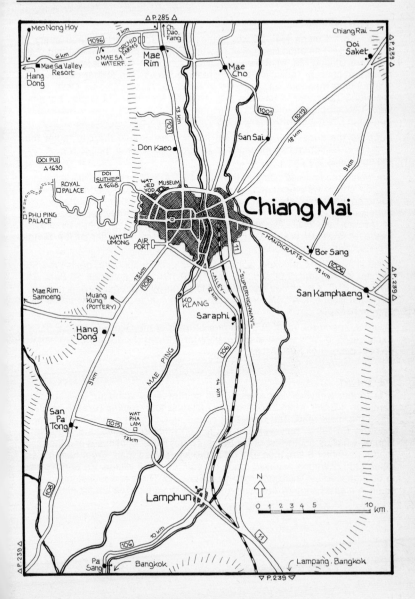

LAMPHUN

Buses from Chiang Mai, 26 km further north, leave for Lamphun every 30 minutes from Lamphun Road near Nawarat Bridge (6 Baht). The first part of the trip from Chiang Mai will take you down a beautiful, rather narrow, tree-lined road. Lamphun is Thailand's oldest preserved town. The former capital of the Haripunchai Kingdom was founded in 660 A.D. Queen Chama Devi, who is still highly honoured to this very day, was the first ruler of the city. Lamphun wasn't incorporated into the Lanna Thai Kingdom until King Mengrai over-threw the Chama Devi dynasty in 1281.

Because the super highway leading south goes around the city rather than through it, Lamphun has managed to retain much of its former charm. A moat still surrounds the entire city today.

We would recommend going to the WAT PHRA THAT HARIPUNCHAI with its golden chedi, which contains a sacred relic. The construction of the chedi commenced in 897, the wat itself was built in 1157. Don't miss the amazing murals in the small building to the right of the entrance. They depict scenes out of Heaven and Hell. The gigantic bronze gong and the rather dilapidated Dvaravati-style SUWANA CHEDI in the northwestern corner of the temple grounds are also noteworthy.

A small MUSEUM definitely worth visiting is directly opposite, open Wed-Sun (except for Fri) from 9:00-12:00 h and 13:00-16:00 h, admission 10 Baht. The WAT KU KUT, sometimes also referred to as the Wat Chama Devi, is approx. 1 km to the west of town. Several Buddha figures can be seen in the niches of its pyramid-shaped chedi.

You can spend the night in the centre of town at the GUEST HOUSE TU'S*. Excellent food is available at the market from 16:00 h - dozens of women set up big pots of their best dishes.

PA SANG

This former weaving village lies 10 km southwest of Lamphun (minibus from Lamphun 4 Baht). Many shops selling materials and clothing can still be found along the main road. The wonderful cotton materials sold here are no longer made in Pa Sang, however, but in the surrounding villages, e.g. Ban Nong Nguak, which is southwest of Pa Sang. To get there, continue along the main road for another 8 km, then turn off at the signposted road. From here it's an-other 2 km down the unpaved road until you reach the village. Pa Sang is said to be inhabited by Thailand's most beautiful girls. There is a tourist information stand in a small shop by the main road. Overpriced bicycles are for rent.

MAE SA VALLEY

The beautiful Mae Sa Valley area has been turned into a weekend resort for Bangkok's upper ten thousand. Everything that is considered oh-so-typically Thai has been laid out, built, and emphasized here; a most pleasant climate, beautiful parks, rare orchids, wonderful roses, gurgling waterfalls, an abundance of fish just waiting to be caught, elephants that can be ridden upon, picturesque hilltribe villages, and expensive restaurants and resorts. All of the respective resorts offer beautifully located, romantic huts in way of accommodation. They are rather simply furnished, however, if you consider the outrageously high prices (400-4000 Baht).

The Mae Rim - Sameung Road (H1096) leading into the Mae Sa Valley turns off Highway 107 (Chiang Mai - Fang) after 12 km (watch out for the signpost!). After a mere 1.4 km you will reach

ADISARA FARM, where you can hunt for shrimps and fish in a tiny artificial lake for a small fee, and then have them prepared for you in the adjoining restaurant. 1 km further on you will pass two

ORCHID FARMS, one on the left and one on the right hand side of the road (admission: 5 Baht). Specially treated, gilded orchid jewelry is available here; you can observe the delicate process at the Mountain Orchid Farm daily at 11:00 h. The road leading to the

MAE SA WATERFALL, which is made up of several small cascades and pools connected by little footpaths, turns off to the left at km stone 7 (admission: 5 Baht). Foodstands have opened up on the parking lot - ideal conditions for a pleasant picnic. The

ELEPHANT CAMP is just 3 km further on, on the left hand side (the signpost is quite difficult to find at first). Admission: 40 Baht. Performances are held daily from 9:00-11:00 h. A 2-3 hour elephant ride through the jungle will cost you 250 Baht. The road branching off to the right at km stone 15 leads to the

ERAWAN RESORT, admission 20 Baht. Beautifully set bungalows and much entertainment available; you can rent boats and go rowing on the small lake, ride through the park on elephants, and buy souvenirs at a mock hilltribe village called "Little Chiang Mai". An expensive and strikingly unauthentic performance of scenes out of the daily life of the hilltribes as well as traditional dances is held daily at 11:00 and 14:00 h. A rather new, but at least authentic Meo village,

BAN HMONG MAE SA MAI, is nearby. Continue past the resort and turn left after just 200 metres. After 1 km you will reach a small bridge. Keep heading slightly to the left. The 7 km stretch is sometimes unfit for traffic after heavy rain. You can spend the night at the

MAE SA MAI BUNGALOWS***, to the right of the village entrance. You'll have a wonderful view from the bungalows of this resort, which is run by the Meo living here. The

CHIANG MAI RESORT, which lies at an altitude of 1050 metres, is the 'highest' of the entire valley's attractions. The nights up here are cool. There is a small zoo that can be visited in the resort.

It is hard to believe that one of northern Thailand's hottest towns, SAMEUNG, is only 15 km from here, at an altitude of 530 metres. Temperatures frequently rise to a staggering 42°C in April. You will be able to make several excursions to hilltribe villages from here. Be warned, however: the villages are extremely difficult to find without a guide or at least the exact village names in Thai writing.

There are several very steep sections to the new circular road - now called H1269 - surrounding Doi Pui. You will reach

SAFARI INN AND RESORT (admission 20 Baht) on the right hand side just beyond KRISDA DOI PASS. The resort is set in beautiful gardens. Nobody here seems to speak English, though. After another 12 km you will once again come to the main road, H108. From here it's another 12 km to Chiang Mai.

HOTELS

There are only resort hotels (with restaurants and bungalows for 4 -20 people) in the Mae Sa Valley area. The spelling of the various resort names varies remarkably.

MAE SA RESORT**** (KM 3); *TONT TONG COUNTRY HOME***-***** (KM 8,5); *RINTR GARDEN**** (KM 9); *MAE SA VALLEY RESORT***** (KM 18,5), camping**; *ERAWAN RESORT*****, (KM 15), *KANGSADAN RESORT*****, camping** (KM 18,5) *CHIANG MAI RESORT***** (KM 20). The *SAFARI INN AND RESORT***** is at KM 14 on H1269, camping**.

HOW TO GET THERE

There are many organized tours that go through the valley. Several trekking tours also start and end here. It is difficult to explore the Mae Sa Valley with public transportation. You could take a bus or a minibus to Mae Rim and walk or hitch-hike from there. With a little luck a passing minibus heading for the waterfall might stop and take you along, though these buses are very rare. You can charter a songthaew in Chiang Mai for a half-day tour for around 150 Baht. The well-built, paved road is also ideally suited for a first venture on a hired motorcycle.

DOI INTHANON

Lying southwest of Chiang Mai, the 2595 metre Doi Inthanon is Thailand's highest mountain. The entire, approx. 1000 km^2 -sized area is a National Park. Many Meo and Karen live in the relatively open, sparsely wooded area. Several waterfalls as well as some dwarfed rhododendron groves and forest in the regions close to the peak make up the park's main attractions. Much of the park's forest has been cut down, and the many big game poachers have also contributed to the gradual disintegration of the natural habitat of the remaining animals living in the area. Elephants and gaur are probably extinct by now, while tigers, clouded leopards, and black bears have become extremely rare.

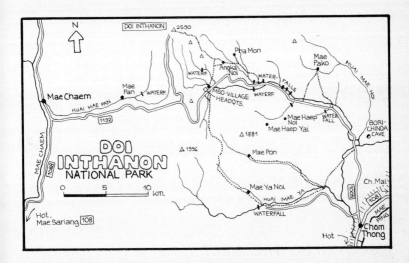

The road leading to Doi Inthanon branches off 1 km in front of Chom Thong. A road leading to the *MAE KLANG WATERFALLS* branches off to the left after 8 km. It's a mere 500 metres to the falls from the turn-off.

Continue along the main road and you'll soon reach the park entrance (road toll: 20 Baht per car, 5 Baht per motorcycle, 30 Baht per pick-up). There are two waterfalls worth a visit along the 47-km uphill road - *WACHIRATHAN* (beyond KM 20, 500 metres off the road) and *SIRIPHUM* (1/2 hour on a foot-path from KM 31). You will pass a Meo village and an experimental farm on your way to the latter. The farm is one of the King's pet projects; the hilltribes are being encouraged to cultivate flowers, vegetables, and strawberries in-stead of opium, and some at least are being taught how, at the farm. You could also pay a visit to the Karen villages of *PAKO* (turn-off at KM 13) and *PHA MON* (KM 25) if you're travelling by motorcycle.

A huge, Air Force *RADAR STATION* was erected on the peak of the mountain, which can be reached by way of a paved road. Don't take any photographs; this is considered a restricted military zone. The *GRAVE* of Chiang Mai's last king, *Inthawichayanon,* is located right next to the parking lot. It was the king's last wish to be buried up here, and thousands come to visit the simple burial site each year. The lowest-ever temperature recorded up here was -8°C. It gets extremely cool every evening and sometimes even at noon. Whilst driving up the road you will pass through the various zones of vegetation on the mountain; the evergreen montane forest begins at 1800 metres and is shrouded in mist for most of the year. The low trees are covered with orchids, moss, and other epiphytes. A Thai signpost west of the road, approx. 50 me-tres below the peak, will direct you to a wildly romantic rhododendron grove and a *HIGH MOOR (BOG)*. Ornithologists have the chance of observing birds extremely rare for Thailand from up here.

HOTELS

The relatively expensive *BUNGA-LOWS**** in the Meo village constitute the only accommodation the park has to offer.

HOW TO GET THERE

First, get to CHOM THONG, 58 km southwest of Chiang Mai (bus 14 Baht, 1 1/2 hrs.). Once there, rent a pick-up for the day (500-600 Baht, pick-ups available next to the temple), and drive up to the peak - there is no regular public transportation on the mountain. You also have the choice of renting a car (500 Baht per day) or a motorcycle in Chiang Mai.

With a car or a motorcycle of your own you will also be able to cruise down the fantastic, paved, mountain road to MAE CHAEM. An unpaved road leading south to the H108 used to branch off shortly before the settlement - very steep at times, unfit for traffic during the rainy season, extremely dusty during the dry season.

DISCOVERING THE WEST

A tour of the northwestern part of Thailand will lead you through some of the country's most impressive landscapes - lonely mountains, untouched jungle, teak and pine forests, savannah, fertile valleys, and lush green rice paddies.

One won't be able to truly appreciate the 600 km stretch unless one has one's own transportation, however; helter skelter all the way to Mae Sariang, 1800 curves just to Mae Hong Son, unpaved dirt road to Pai, and back to Chiang Mai through the breathtaking mountains. If you're looking for the perfect motorcycle route - this may be it, at least during the dry season. Unfortunately, few signposts in the area are inscribed in the Latin script. For this reason we have given very detailed descriptions of the more interesting routes, in the hope that you will be able to find your way with as few problems as possible. You can also get to the various places by bus and set off on hikes from the respective towns - to Karen, Meo, and Lisu villages, to mountain-peak temples, hot springs, and beautiful caves. Raft and boat trips, elephant rides, and jeep tours are also possible.

You can rent motorcycles in Chiang Mai as well as in Mae Hong Son (especially if you only want a bike for a short excursion).

There are five daytime buses to Mae Sariang (the first three continue on to Mae Hong Son). We would not recommend taking a night-bus down this tricky road.

If you don't have much time, why not fly to Mae Hong Son from Chiang Mai (or vice versa.) The small planes used for this route cover the stretch in just 40 minutes.

FROM CHIANG MAI TO MAE SARIANG

Head southwest down H108 (much traffic) from Chiang Mai. You will be travelling through a fertile plain. Stop by at the cattle market (only on Saturday mornings) after 24 km. Soon you will see the rather unimpressive back of the DOI INTHANON mountain looming up in the distance, to the right. The road leading to this, Thailand's highest mountain (2565 metres), branches off at KM 57.

➡ *EXCURSIONS FOR THE ADVENTUROUS*
You can get to MAE CHAEM via the Doi Inthanon (60 km). A dirt road branches off to the right shortly before Mae Chaem. This road (only suitable for motorcycles - on no account cars!) leads through 97 km of unsignposted forest to KHUN YUAM. From here it is another 68 km to Mae Hong Son. If you feel like giving this route a try, definitely go to David's library service for information beforehand (see Chiang Mai section).

When entering CHOM THONG you will be driving directly towards the chedi of the WAT PHRA THAT SI CHOM TONG, which dates back to 1451. A 16th century viharn with a lovely facade enshrines a heavily decorated, altar-like mondop as well as wooden Buddha statues and beautiful ivory carvings. The supports beneath the branches of the Bodhi tree in the courtyard were sponsored by believers hoping to earn merits for future life-cycles.

Chom Thong's only hotel is a brothel, MOTEL PONNIMID*, 500 metres to the right of the road leading to Doi Inthanon.

Many Karen live in the area surrounding HOT (buses from Chiang Mai Gate 22 Baht, 2 1/2 hrs.). Originally, the town used to lie 15 km further south, at the Ping river. It was moved up here after construction on the Bhumipol fill dam was completed. Today, the town is singularly unattractive.

The RUAN COME RESORT**** with bungalows, a camping site (100 Baht for 2 people), and a restaurant is near Hot.

➡ *EXCURSION TO BAN HUAI FANG*
H1012 leads 16 km south, past the ruins of the original Hot, to the small village of WANG LUNG, which was originally meant to become a fishing village by the dam (nice boat-trips are possible after heavy rain). A dirt road continues for 5 km after the main road has ended. It leads to the large Karen village of BAN HUAI FANG, inhabited by approx. 600 people.

➡ *EXCURSION TO MAE PING LAKE*
For those feeling like a raft or boat trip on the MAE PING LAKE, go down H1012 for 1 km, then turn off onto H1103 and continue for 33 km until you reach DOI TAO on the banks of the reservoir. You should be able to organize a roundtrip for 250 Baht, although the boat people are actually used to groups who want to travel the whole 140 km to the Bhumipol dam. Next to the simple floating bungalows on the lake, there are also said to be nicely located bungalows along the banks. Continue down H1103 for another 33 km and you'll reach the H106 which leads back to Lamphun and Chiang Mai.

The H108 takes a sharp turn to the west beyond Hot; the kilometre stones recommence at 0 at this point. You will pass beautiful teak forests on both sides of the rather bumpy road. Many people like coming to the *OB LUANG CANYON* (KM 17) at the weekend; a section of the Chaem river has managed to burrow a 50 metre canal into the cliffs - not exactly breathtaking.

The H1088 (still under construction?) leading to Mae Chaem (45 km) branches off to the right after another 5 km.

The road will gradually start climbing at this point, until it reaches the level of a raised plateau. From here you will have a wonderful view of the mountains. The Karen and the Lawa used to cut down the forests up here in order to make room for their mountain-rice. During the last couple of years, however, the Forestry Dept. has been planting pinetrees in order to protect the thus exposed humus from rain. This has resulted in a obstinate struggle between them and the Karen, who refuse to accept the fact that their fallow fields are being confiscated for afforestation projects. How are they to survive if they are not allowed to create new fields suitable for cultivation?

If you are interested in the dilemma, why not visit the THAI DANISH PINE IMPROVEMENT PROJECT at KM 51, on the right. With a little luck there'll even be an English speaking person present to give you information.

➡ *EXCURSION TO THE PAN HOUSE*
If you are travelling by bus, you can get out at the stop for the village of BAN MAE WAEN (= Pak Tang Ban Mae Waen, 44 Baht from Chiang Mai) at KM 68. From here, walk the 5 km up the mountain (south) - after approx. 75 minutes you will have reached a height of 1800 metres. The English speaking trekking guide Mr. Weerapan Tarasarn (Mr. Pan) has opened his PAN HOUSE* guesthouse up here. You can spend the night for 30 Baht. You will be able to hike to Thai, Karen, and Lawa villages from here, and Mr. Pan can also arrange elephant rides and rafting trips for you.

The road starts taking several hairpin bends down into the valley after having passed KM 73 - many good views. A small road leading to the *TRIBAL DEVELOPMENT AND ASSISTANCE CENTER* on Doi Mae Ho branches off at KM 84. Flowers are cultivated up here.

The H108 turns north at KM 104, below *WAT CHOM THONG* hill. The Viang Mai Road straight ahead will lead you to the centre of Mae Sariang.

MAE SARIANG

This is a small market town with several Burmese-style temples - *WAT UTTHAYAROM* and *WAT SRI BUNRUANG* are in the centre of town, *WAT CHOM CHAENG* is 1 km south of town, on a small hill commanding a fine view.

The town was extremely difficult to reach before 1965, when H108 was finally opened. Even today, Mae Sariang has managed to retain much of its original charm (especially the wooden buildings).

HOTELS

There is a pretty good hotel in the centre of town, the *MITAREE*** - rooms of various standards are available in the main and adjoining building, friendly employees. The *MAE SARIANG GUEST HOUSE**, at the bus station, is not worth the price.

FOOD

There are several good restaurants along the busy Viang Mai Road - the *RENU* has an ac-room, the restaurant opposite even has an English-language menu. You will find the *REUM PRAA* in the alley leading to the wat - rather quiet. The *BLACK AND WHITE CAFE,* opposite the cinema, is said to be the only ac bar between Chiang Mai and Mae Hong Son.

GENERAL INFORMATION

Motorcycle workshops as well as the post office can be found along the main road.

LEAVING MAE SARIANG

4 buses leave for CHIANG MAI daily between 10:30 and 18:00 h (50 Baht, 4 hrs.).

Buses to MAE HONG SON leave at 10:30, 12:00, and 15:00 h (52 Baht, 4 1/2 hrs.). There are also two night-buses for each of the routes (too uncomfortable to be recommended, however!).

EXCURSIONS FROM MAE SARIANG

Information concerning rafting on the YUAM river as well as trekking to the surrounding Karen and Lawa villages is available at the hotel.

TO THE SALWEEN

H1194 will lead you across the bridge in the west of town to BAN MAE SAM LAEP at the Salween river (52 km). Be warned; for the second half of the journey the road is in an extremely bad condition. A pick-up leaves for the river early in the morning and returns in the evening. Men pay 50 Baht, women 100 Baht. As a compensation, women do not have to help push the pick-up up the steep sections of road. You can go on boat rides along the Salween, which marks the border with Burma, but only during the dry period (Dec-April). A 1 1/2 hour boat ride to the river mouth of the Moei river will cost you 500 Baht per person.

TO MAE SOT

Since 1987 it has been possible to drive down the 230 km H1085 to MAE SOT with a car. This will take between 5 and 8 hrs., depending on how far construction on the 90 km unpaved stretch at the beginning of the road has progressed. As yet there is no public transportation along this road.

FROM MAE SARIANG TO MAE HONG SON

Start off by driving along the well built road leading through the MAE NAM YUAM valley. The gigantic lumber depots along the road are proof of the fact that the exploitation of the teak forests has by no means ceased.

You can visit BAN MAE TIA, a well-kept Karen village, at KM 121. These Karen even seem to have understood and accepted the government's method of cultivating rice.

Stop by for a snack at the snack-bar at KM 151.

The road becomes rather narrow after KM 154. Watch out for the oncoming traffic and elephants, especially in the many dangerous curves!

We would recommend making an excursion from KM 173.8; follow the 1300 metre forest path to the *HOT SPRINGS* (a very pleasant 77^{0}C). A wonderful bathing-spot can be found below, at the river (running hot and cold water!).

You can admire a large, sacred Banyan tree in the Shan village of KHUN YUAM (KM 199), directly by the road. Should you wish to stay here for a while, spend the night at the MITTR KHUN YUAM HOTEL** , also directly by the road. The *WAT MOI TO,* just beyond the village, has amazingly beautiful chedis.

➥ *EXCURSIONS FOR NATURE FREAKS*
An unpaved dirt road branches off to the right at KM 201.5. Go down this road for 13 km, then turn left onto an even worse path (watch out for the occasional fords!), which leads to an agricultural development project. Continue for another 19 km and the MAE SURIN WATERFALL will come into sight. The water falls for a total of approx. 200 metres, making this probably the highest and least well known of all of Thailand's waterfalls. Continue along the now slightly better dirt road for 19 km until you reach a TOURIST HOUSE - we were unable to find this, maybe it no longer exists. The dirt road gradually disintegrates beyond the village of Pang Ung. It ends in MAE CHAEM after 97 km (but only for those who don't get lost along the way). We would definitely recommend going to David's library service in Chiang Mai before setting out on this rather difficult trip. The dirt road will soon be transformed into the main connecting road between Chiang Mai and Mae Hong Son.

If you have bought something to eat in Khun Yuam (which might be a good idea), why not stop at the little reservoir at KM 206 - nice place for a picnic. A steep, paved, 10 km uphill road leading to a relay station branches off at KM 234.9. It was too steep for our minibus. There is said to be an absolutely stunning view from the top, however. You can reach a nearby Meo village on foot.

Enjoy the beautiful view of the "scenic area" - the Pai river valley - on the right hand side of the road at KM 243.6. The road starts channeling its way through the Mae Hong Son plain just beyond.

If you like proof of having 'been there', go to the Governor in the Government Office at the town entrance. Here you will be given a document certifying that you have survived the 1864 curves to the so-called *Switzerland of Thailand.*

MAE HONG SON

It is difficult to say just when this provincial town was actually founded. The Prince of Chiang Mai didn't send an expedition to the secluded valley until 1832, and even then the idea was to catch elephants, and not to found the city. Mainly Shan and a few Lawa lived here at the time, although the Meo and Karen must have also passed through the almost inaccessible frontier region during the course of their wanderings. The HQ of the expedition was probably moved further south after first having been set up on the present-day site of Pang Mu. The HQ soon developed into a small village, almost exclusively inhabited by Shan. The ruler of Chiang Mai proclaimed that a settlement should be founded here in 1874, and thus Mae Hong Son was born.

Approx. one half of the province's population is made up of various hilltribes, the other half of Shan. Only in Mae Hong Son itself are 2 % of the population Thai. The town was peaceful and secluded until well into the 50s. Elephant paths constituted the only connection to the outside world, and an elephant-ride to Chiang Mai could easily take several weeks in those days. Many of the city's inhabitants can still remember the good old days, when the stables of every farm were still filled with elephants. Then the airstrip was finished, and in 1968 an all-weather-road was built to the town. These days the northern route (via Pai) is also open to traffic during the dry season.

The town's main attractions are the secluded, unspoilt mountain landscape as well as the closeness to Burma. While there is no official check point, there are several smuggling paths leading across the border. The Burmese army takes the offensive against the Karenni army (which controls the frontier territory on the Burmese side) every year during the dry period, i.e. from Jan-March, when Karen refugees come pouring over the border into Thailand. We would strongly suggest keeping well away from the border.

The area is particularly beautiful when the sunflowers bloom in November/December. Mae Hong Son is also known as "Muang Sam Mok", the town of all-year-round fog. In truth, however, the town is only shrouded in fog for an average of 104 days per year.

The daily *MARKET* in the centre of town (6:00-18:00 h) has little more to offer than any other market in northern Thailand. Few local products are offered for sale. You may occasionally see Meo and Karen shopping in their traditional costumes.

You will be able to see a highly venerated bronze Buddha statue, which was cast in Burma and brought to Thailand by way of mountain paths and rivers, in the rather inconspicuous *WAT HUA WIANG,* in between the bus station and the market. The statue is modelled on a Buddha statue which is in Mandalay at the present time.

Two Burmese-style chedis, *WAT CHONG KAM* and *WAT CHONG KLANG,* are reflected in the little lake in the centre of town. More than 30 interesting wooden statues are kept in a back room on the left side of the right hand temple. The figures depict characters out of the Vessantara Jataka, an epic describing the former lives of the Buddha. They were brought over from Burma 130 years ago. Wat Chong Kam is the final destination of the *POI SANG LONG* procession. 10 - 16-year-old boys are inaugurated as novices all over Thailand at the beginning of March. This traditional Buddhist ordination ceremony is celebrated in a particularly colourful fashion in Mae Hong Son; the shaven boys are carried to the temple gates on the shoulders of a relative. Music accompanies them on their way. Once there, they don the traditional monks' robes and take their first solemn vow.

A walk up to *WAT DOI KONG MU,* whose chedis tower over the entire town, is most pleasant. The temple was built under the reign of the first Governor, Phaya Singnatraja, in 1874. You will have a fine view of the town, the valley, and the green, jungle-overgrown mountains in the west from up here.

GUESTHOUSES

An increasing number of guesthouses are being built now that Mae Hong Son is becoming so popular. They are still pleasant and simply furnished at the present time, but who knows how long it will take until the first luxury hotel is built. Most of the guesthouses advertise their locations with maps, which are pinned onto a wall of the bus station.

Turn right twice, then walk straight ahead for 400 metres and you'll find the

MAE HONG SON GUEST HOUSE*, 18 Khunlum Praphat Rd. Soi 2, north of the runway of the airport. This comfortable, wooden house is built upon stilts and has a pleasant family atmosphere - small rooms with two mattresses, big enough for four people during the height of the season. Simple meals are made to order, but one can also cook oneself if one so desires. Great place for information, several guides available.

GALARE GUEST HOUSE*, Thai house in rural surroundings, about 800 metres out of town, to the north. Rooms are separated from each other by mats and furnished with proper beds. The owners are very helpful and friendly.

If you turn left instead of right once you've reached the level of the Mae Hong Son Guest House, you will have to walk another 200 metres before reaching

GUYSORN GUEST HOUSE*, Praeha Utis Rd., tel 611308 - the new, simple bungalows and restaurant with a campfire site were built by a friendly Bangkok artist, who is usually also willing to act as a jungle guide for visitors.

You will reach other guesthouses by turning left twice from the bus station. Walk to the end of the road and then a couple of metres to the right and you'll reach

PETER'S GUEST HOUSE*, an old wooden building in a shady, uncared-

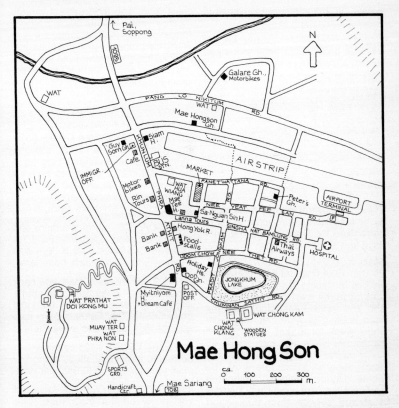

Mae Hong Son

ca.
0   100   200   300
m.

for garden. Two large private rooms, the rest of the building is used as a dormitory. Muesli and fruit yoghurts are served for breakfast.

HOLIDAY HOUSE*, also known as Chong Kham Guest House, is west of the small lake. It is a new, very clean terrace-house commanding a nice view of the lake all the way to the temples.

DON'S GUEST HOUSE*, opposite the Mitniyom Hotel - this is part of Don's Trekking Organization. A cou-

ple of guides privately rent out mattresses. New guesthouses will no doubt develop here soon.

HOTELS

You'll have to go to a hotel if you want more than just basic comfort. You'll find the

SA-NGUAN SIN HOTEL*-**, 35 Singhanat Road, tel 611241, bordering onto the southern part of the market. Old Thai hotel, large rooms, some shower/lav, fan, mosquito net, but no lounge. You will find the following hotels on the main road, Khunlum Praphat (from north to south):

SIAM HOTEL**-***, no. 23, tel 611148; presentable hotel with clean rooms, shower/lav, some ac;

MAE TEE HOTEL**-***, no. 55; clean hotel in the centre of town;

MITNIYOM HOTEL*-***, no. 90; new building, some rooms ac; you'll find the *DREAM CAFE* downstairs; music and dancing from 21:00-2:00 h.

SARM MORK VILLAS***, tel 611478; brand new - huts and rooms with "complete facilities", whatever that may mean.

There are several resorts in the vicinity of Mae Hong Son, most of them patronized by Thais during the holidays and at the weekends.

MAE HONG SON RESORT***-****, 24 Ban Huai Dua, tel 611406 (reservations in Chiang Mai (053) 235344); turn off to the west between KM 265 and 266 (large Pepsi sign) from the road leading to Mae Sariang. Continue west for 6 km; well tended bungalows set in a beautiful park, directly on the Pai river. The best and most expensive restaurant of the whole district; camping**; elephant and boat trips are organized. There is a shuttle service from the airport (Airport Shop).

RIM NAM GLANG DOI RESORT**-***, Ban Huai Dua; 2 km north of the Mae Hong Son Resort; huts of various standards and sizes, beautifully located on the river; fireplaces, camping, dormitory. A new resort is being built six km north of town, between the road and the river.

FOOD
Excellent food is available at the foodstalls of the night market, by the main road. The food here is vintage Thai, in spite of the many English-language menus. The cooks are also wiling to prepare special dishes just for you, though. Try the TOM YAM GAI mushroom soup, but we would recommend saying *mai paeht!* or *mai prik!* - not too spicy!

GENERAL INFORMATION
TOURIST INFORMATION - go to the guesthouses and the trekking agencies for information - very helpful. In spite of the Tourist Police's touching sign, "Tourists we are proud to serve you", nobody here seems to speak any English (main road).

POST OFFICE - at the southern end of the main road, open Mon-Fri 8:30-16:30 h, Sat 9:00-12:00 h. You can also make telephone calls from here.

BANKS - on the main road, you can't miss them - cash and traveller's cheques are also accepted; the local branch of the Thai Farmers Bank also accepts Visa, as it does everywhere.

MOTORCYCLES - 125 cc bikes can be rented at several shops along the main road for 120 - 200 Baht per day.

TREKKING AGENCIES - you will find many on the main road. The guides will make sure that you aren't blown to bits by a mine and don't wander into the crossfire, should you wish to trek to the border. Boat trips, rafting, and elephant rides can also be arranged, motorcycles and jeeps are for rent.

CELEBRATIONS - The POY SANG LONG procession is held at the beginning of March, the Winter Festival in January. Check with the Chiang Mai Tourist Office for the exact dates.

HOW TO GET THERE
If you're coming from CHI-ANG MAI by bus, you can either take the still-under-construction, northern route via PAI (where you will have to change), or the southern route via MAE SARIANG.

Northern route (245 km): From CHIANG MAI to PAI at 7:00, 8:30, 11:00, and 14:00 h (50 Baht, 4 hrs.). Once there, catch the MAE HONG SON-bound pick-up (dusty!) at 14:00 h, or the ones at 7:30 and 10:30 h the next day (50 Baht, 4 1/2 hrs.).

Southern route: From CHIANG MAI: bus 170 (orange) via MAE SARIANG (50 Baht, 4 hrs.), departures: 6:30, 8:00, and 11:00 h; there is also a night-bus at 20:00 and 21:00 h (97 Baht, 9 hrs.). The buses departing at 13:00 and 15:00 h only go as far as MAE SARIANG.

LEAVING MAE HONG SON
BY BUS
The PAI-bound 4-wheel pick-up leaves at 7:30, 10:30, and 14:00 h (50 Baht, 4 1/2 hrs.). Only the first pick-up will get you to PAI in time to catch the 13:30 bus to CHIANG MAI. You will need dust-proof goggles if you wish to see any of the marvelous landscape.

To CHIANG MAI via MAE SARIANG: take the bus at 6:00, 8:00, 10:30, or 14:00 h (97 Baht, 9 hrs.). There are

also two night-buses (which we wouldn't recommend). There is even said to be a BANGKOK-bound ac bus (358 Baht, approx. 16 hrs.).

BY PLANE
Thai Airways Office: 71 Singhanat Bamlung Road (tel 611297). There are 2 - 3 daily flights from and to CHIANG MAI (310 Baht, flights arrive and depart around noon).

EXCURSIONS FROM MAE HONG SON
Many 1 - 2-day excursions are possible from Mae Hong Son. You can either set out on your own, with a guesthouse guide, or on a tour organized by one of the trekking agencies.

You will often return to Mae Hong Son for the night during the course of longer trekking tours, which sometimes include boat trips and elephant rides; no interesting round-trips with visits to several different hilltribe villages are offered at the moment.

PHA SUA WATERFALL / PANG TONG / NAPAPAK
One of the excursions heads northwest, to the Meo village Napapak, at the Burmese border. Drive down the road leading to Pai until just before KM 17, shortly before HUAI PHA (sometimes HEU PA). Turn off at KM 10 or 17; both of the dusty roads branching off lead to HUAI KHAN (7 km).

Continue down the road another 4 km from here, and you'll reach the PHA SUA WATERFALL - ideal for a bathe. The Kuomintang village MAE AW and the Karen village HUAI MAK are both nearby. Beyond the waterfall you will have to drive up extremely steep, unpaved roads.

The road branching off to the left leads to the PANG TONG ROYAL PALACE (21 km). This is where the King stays when he visits the region; pleasant wood- and bamboo garden with a horse husbandry. You will be able to reach a lake enclosed by bamboo forests on foot (to the west, at the Burmese border).

The passable road straight ahead will lead you to Meo, Kuomintang, Shan, and Karen villages, all situated in the unstable frontier area. Avoid this area if you're travelling on your own. You'll arrive in NAPAPAK after 24 km.

We would recommend taking a guide plus pick-up (1000 Baht) for this trip. You will be travelling along a road which was recently built under the army's supervision and has incredibly steep sections to it. MAE AW, a Kuomintang village, is shortly beyond Napapak. When we first visited this village in 1986, it was practically at war with Khun Sa, the Opium King, who had set up his HQ at the Loi Lam mountain on the Burmese side of the border. Only venture this far if accompanied by guides who know their way around and are well informed as to the current political situation. There is said to be a songthaew (minibus) from Mae Hong Son to Mae Aw during times of peace - ask at the guesthouses.

Khun Sa - the Opium King

Khun Sa, 55 years old at the present time and leader of the heavily armed, several thousand strong Shan United Army, is one of the most fascinating personalities to be living in the Burmese Shan State. His HQ is set up on the 2179 metre Loi Lam, close to the Thai border, not too far from Mae Hong Son. All paths leading to his hide-out are mined, and even air raids have no effect - Khun Sa and his followers live in deep caves. The soldiers of the Shan United Army refuse to let anyone near their leader. Half Chinese, half Shan, Khun Sa rules one of the most powerful empires in the world - the opium business in the golden triangle.

In 1982, the Thai Army destroyed the small village of Ban Hin Taek, close to the Burmese border. With it, they destroyed Khun Sa's HQ and several opium refineries. The battle went on for three days. There were numerous casualties on both sides.

After this defeat, Khun Sa retreated to Burmese territory, which was controlled by his army's soldiers. Not until 1984 did he stage a reappearance in the frontier territory, near Mae Hong Son.

Khun Sa has been dealing in opium, cultivated by various hilltribes in the golden triangle area, since 1963. The bulk of the world's opium comes from the Shan State, from where it is brought to refineries near the Thai border and converted into heroin. From Thailand, it is distributed all over the world. In an interview he gave to French journalists, Khun Sa himself said that he needed his earnings from the drug business to pay for his army's fight for freedom against the central Burmese government. He had in fact offered to sell the entire golden triangle opium crop to the US government on several occasions. Washington, however, declined each time.

Who is Khun Sa really, what are his goals, and why is he dealing with opium and heroin? Questions such as these remained unanswered until Khun Sa gave a press conference to a dozen assorted international journalists in the spring of 1987. He answered all questions brilliantly, managing to present himself as a freedom-fighter for the Shan State, and even managing to destroy the image of himself as the Opium King. On top of this, he even claimed to be an enemy of the 'true' opium dealers, the Kuomintang: "If I win the Shan State, 8 million Shan shall be happy, but if I solve the drug problem, the whole world will rejoice."

The Burmese Army took the offensive against Khun Sa in the weeks immediately following this press conference, and allegedly drove him out of the country into Laos. Is he back in Burma today, possibly even on the Loi Lam?

You will quickly realize that many others want to make money with opium upon arriving in the Kuomintang village of Mae Aw. Many have in fact made plenty of money, especially on the Thai side of the border.

NAM PHLANG DIN

Charter a pick-up to the village of HUAI DUA, by the Pai river in the southwest (6 km, 80 Baht per vehicle). After a one-hour boat ride (charter approx. 700-800 Baht) you will arrive in NAM PHLANG DIN, just before the border with Burma. You will have to pay the Karenni Guerilla Army 500 Baht per person (for which you will receive receipts) in order to be let over the border. Two Padaung women who artificially elongate their necks by wearing tight, metal rings were forced to live in a village on the Burmese side as a tourist attraction. Travel agencies in Chiang Mai offer the trip at a high price - it's not worth it! The two women are said to have fled during the heavy fighting in the spring of 1987.

WARNING: *Crossing the border means leaving Thailand. To set an example, the government had several returning tourists arrested for "illegally crossing the border" in 1987. The culprits were later expelled from the country.*

THE HOT SPRINGS OF PHA BONG

Drive south down H108 towards PHA BONG. You will see a fenced-in area with a gate and ticket booth (although no admission is charged up to now) after 10 km, just beyond KM 256, on the right hand side. The fence encloses the BHO NUEM LOON hot springs. The spring water flows from one large pool into a second one, which is lower. The pools don't look too inviting, but there is a good bathing spot in the overflow - shoulder-deep water, temperatures just bearable, no algae. An enjoyable form of relaxation after an exhausting trek. CAREFUL, though - very slippery!!

FROM MAE HONG SON TO PAI

The 111 km H1095 from Mae Hong Son to Pai has been under construction for years. The road becomes unfit for motorcycles after heavy rain - we would suggest putting your bikes aboard a bus, should you get caught in a downpour.

➡ *You can turn off to the left at KM 10 or 17 for an excursion to the PHA SUA WATERFALL and the Kuomintang village of MAE AW. Some extremely steep stretches are in store for you (see previous section).*

The *THAM PLA* cave is in a little park on the left hand side of the road, shortly before KM 18. An underground brook flows into a small pool full of semi-tame fish, just waiting to be fed. Fish food can be bought at the parking lot.

You will reach HUAI PHA, the last village for the next 50 km, just beyond. After this the road only remains paved for a few km - then it becomes extremely tricky. The kilometre stones gradually peter out - did you make a mental note of your odometer in Mae Hong Son? You will pass the last couple of huts and fields, then the road starts climbing to the first pass (769 metres). You will be swallowed by jungle, at times by thick fog. Orchids can be seen growing in gnarled trees, and the vines form curtains behind which one suspects the mountains and valleys rather than seeing them. You will finally have a good, unobstructed view of Burma in the north after 48 km. After a fleeting glance into the deep valley on the right it's back into the jungle. You will reach MAE LANA JUNCTION after 56 km - once here, you're halfway to Pai!

➥ EXCURSION TO THE LAHU GUEST HOUSE

A Thai signpost giving 8 different distances in km will direct you to the Shan- and Lahu villages in the north. You will pass BAN JABO (Black Lahu) after 3 km on H1226. A dirt road branches off to the left after another 1.5 km. This road improves rapidly after the first few hairpin bends. It becomes so wide that one must seriously ask oneself what kind of vehicles are destined to drive down here. You will frequently pass soldiers by the side of the road - which army they belong to, however, remains unknown. The view becomes quite impressive along the way; steep mountains, deep valleys, and many mountain- ranges reaching all the way into Burma. You will reach the Lahu village of HUAY HEA, which you will already have seen on a mountain crest from afar, after a total of 16 km. Once there, you're only 1 km from the border with Burma.

A simple guest house, the LAHU GUEST HOUSE*, has been built in Huay Hea by Mr. Yai, the village teacher, and the friendly Black Lahu. The wind whistles through the building, true, but it's a fair deal for the 20 Baht you will have to pay into the village cash-box. The village patroness will cook meals for you if you order in advance. Only if you are able to communicate with the mini Lahu-English dictionary, however, seeing as nobody here speaks English apart from the teacher (or has this already changed in such a short time?) Like Mr. Tan at the Lisu Lodge, Mr. Yai is doing his best to act as a mediator be- tween tourists and villagers.

You can go on a day's hike to the south, but on no account to the north; the Shan United Army is up there.

WARNING: There is sometimes heavy fighting on the other side of the border. Stay well away! The Soppong police warned tourists not to go trekking in this area in the spring of 1987 - at this time a Danish woman had still not returned to pick up her valuables at the Cave Lodge after 2 months of trekking . You will definitely need a guide in this area!

Drive 12 km back down the road, and you will be able to turn off to the MAE LANA Shan village on the left. A river cuts through a plain of wide rice fields and heads straight for a sheer cliff wall, in which it disappears. Fanatic cave explorers will have a great time exploring the underground cavern with John from the Cave Lodge.

The road becomes very bad beyond Mae Lana - bridges constructed of trees and extremely steep sections of the road will make your nerves tingle. After having mastered them, you will reach YAPANAE, a rather uncomfortable Red

Lahu village. From here it is said to be a mere 11 km to Tham Lot. The road is only suitable for jeeps and dirt bikes, however.

The road beyond MAE LANA JUNCTION goes through a depression measuring 100 metres in length, which sometimes turns into a deep mud-hole after heavy rain - you will only be able to get through here with 4-wheel drive. Sometimes it can take days to get across.

The worst part of the road is still ahead of you, though - it becomes very narrow and rocky whilst leading through the jungle, then starts its steep descent into the Soppong Valley. Construction had progressed to this point and no further in 1987.

A small foot-path leads up to the left into the forest shortly beyond KM 64 (rather difficult to find). If you do a little climbing on the cliff wall you may see strange looking, wooden beams in the various caves. These are ancient coffins, dating back 2000 years! They weren't discovered until last year. Nobody is able to say which people hollowed out these tree trunks and left their dead in them. The same type of coffins can be seen in the Tham Lot. You will pass the Meo village of MAE LANG JAN at KM 65, Soppong is 3 km from here.

SOPPONG

This Shan village has developed into a centre of commerce for the surrounding hilltribe villages. Buses from Pai and Mae Hong Son stop by here for a 15-minute sojourn - just enough for some delicious dumplings and a glass of tea. A meal costs 7 - 15 Baht.

GUESTHOUSES
There are at least three guesthouses here already, all of very simple standards - the *J GUEST HOUSE**, tiny bamboo huts with thin mattresses; *DUM GUEST HOUSE** with 3 rooms, and *SO CHEAP GUEST HOUSE**, with small bungalows behind the restaurant. None of these have a toilet yet, the use of the public lavatory costs 1 Baht!

LEAVING SOPPONG
The 4-wheel drive bus to PAI leaves at 10:00, 13:00, and 16:30 h (20 Baht, 2 hrs.). Buses to MAE HONG SON depart at 9:00, 13:00, and 15:30 h (30 Baht, 2 1/2 hrs.).

EXCURSIONS FROM SOPPONG
Soppong is not (not yet?) a good base for excursions to Meo, Lisu, Lahu, and Karen villages. Pai, the Lisu Lodge, and the Cave Lodge are better places to set off from, however.

WARNING: *Never trek to the Lisu villages south of Soppong without a guide! Some villages suspect tourists of being government opium-spies, and tourists are forbidden to enter many of the village territories.*

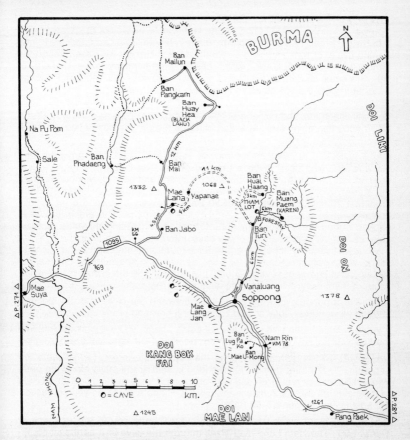

THE GERMAN DEVELOPMENT PROJECT

If you are interested in development programmes, why not stop by at the *Thai-German Highland Development Programme* in the very west of Soppong. With a little luck you'll meet an English-speaking person who'll be able to fill you in. According to our information, the German development programmes are particularly unpopular up here. It seems that they go about everything - including the eradication of poppy cultivation - with the proverbial German thoroughness, without, however, considering the fatal consequences for the hilltribes once the development project stops, as all sooner or later do. Foreign development programmes should, in our opinion, be more willing to make compromises and consider the so-called human factor.

THAM LOT STALACTITE CAVE

You will reach the THAM LOT STALACTITE CAVE by way of the "New Road", a bad forest road measuring approx. 8 km in length. You can either walk, ride a motorcycle, or rent a truck in Soppong. After 2 km you will pass through the Lahu village of VANALUANG, which has adapted perfectly to the Thai way of life. The small fill dam at the Nam Lang river provides the Lahu with enough water to irrigate their fields and successfully cultivate garlic.

You will reach the Shan village of BAN TUM (also known as Tumlord) after 6 km. If you keep going straight ahead at the turn-off in the village you will reach the

CAVE LODGE after another 300 metres. It is run by an Australian, John, and his wife Pio, who used to be a trekking guide. The lodge is a large house, open in the front, with many mattresses for rent and several bamboo-huts on the steeply sloping banks of the Nam Lang river. A mattress costs 30 Baht, breakfast 20, lunch 20, and dinner 30 Baht. The very efficient Pio (especially business-wise) also bakes wonderful cakes and buns. The place is always packed during the season. Helpful information concerning day-trips is available, as is a very precise map of the cave, information concerning the right behaviour in hilltribe villages, a guide for excursions, news from the traveller scene, an excellent guide (ask for Don), as well as a specialist for unusual activities (John knows of several 'secret' passageways in the caves, for instance, some of them several kilometres in length).

A couple of bungalows were being built between the cave and the lodge in 1987. If all went well, they should be standing now and ready for business.

If you turn right in the village instead of going ahead, you will walk straight into the FORESTRY NATIONAL PARK. You can spend the night at the very simple

NATIONAL PARK BUNGALOWS* at the edge of the forest. Lav/showers are separate, 20 Baht per person. Cheap food is sold at the stalls along the path. You will be able to rent large and very bright gas lamps at the office for 50 Baht (a normal torch will not suffice in the cave!!). Hiring a guide - if you so desire - will again cost you approx. 50 Baht.

A nice, 400 metre walk through the forest will bring you to the entrance of THAM LOT. The Nam Lang river flows through the cave in a northeast-southwesterly direction for 400 metres. You will have to wade through the knee-deep water 5 times. Don't miss the side caverns, though; turn right into the BIG COLUMN CAVERN after 50 metres (huge stalactites and stalagmites), turn left into the CRYSTAL CAVE after 100 metres (beautiful stalactites which can be reached by way of 2 ladders), and turn left into the COFFIN CHAMBER 50 metres before reaching the exit (here you will find the remains of old coffins, which weren't discovered until a few years ago, and whose origin baffles all ethnologists - similar long, wooden, lidded coffins can be seen in various caves in the surrounding area). You can hardly miss the dung at the exit; multitudes of black martins have their breeding places here. The fuss they make when they return to the cave in the late afternoons defies description. You will be able to reach the park entrance in 20 minutes by way of a path leading back over the top of the cave. Several nice, downstream hikes are also possible from the cave exit. On these you will again have to wade through the Nam Lang at times.

Continue along the new (by now possibly paved?) route of the H1095 from Soppong. You will be able to see the Lisu village of NAM RIN below, to the right, after 10 km (km stone 78).

Mr. Tan, the Thai village teacher, is married to a Lisu woman. He is trying to offer some future prospects to the impoverished village population. The Lisu Lodge was erected with the most idealistic of motives; the profits enable two young villagers to attend a Thai school. When these return, they are able to help the village community tackle many of its problems. Mr. Tan is convinced of the fact that the basis of the hilltribe villages' economy can only be improved from within. He has experiences which strengthen his attitude: "Foreign development programmes, as well as those sponsored by Thais, only speed up the impoverishment of the respective villages." He puts all of his hopes into the young people of the village - they are to learn as much as possible of the modern world. Travellers who stay at the Lisu Lodge are also incorporated into this learning process. Mr. Tan takes the tourists to various Lisu houses in the evenings. Here, everyone learns from everyone else. An example for an alternative tourism project? Or just another idealistic dream?

You will find the LISU LODGE* beyond the school, at the edge of the village. It is a large hut with several comfortable community rooms and a balcony. There is a lavatory in the house, bathing facilities at the brook. Everyone helps cook. The pretty garden (with roses and a pond) gives Mr. Tan away as a typical Thai. By now a second building should also be standing.

The 4-wheel drive buses will stop in Nam Rin if you ask the drivers (15 Baht from Pai).

➡ *You can also visit the nearby Karen villages of Lug Pa Ko (6 km) and Mae U Mong (a further 3 km).*

From here, the H1095 winds its way up a 1261 metre pass, which you will reach after 8 km. Beautiful view! After another 5 km and several hairpin bends you will be back in the valley of the Pai river, which you left shortly beyond Mae Hong Son. You will reach Pai after a total of 111 km through hills and areas used for agricultural cultivation.

PAI

Surrounded by high mountains and narrow valleys, Pai was isolated from the rest of the country for a long time. The H1095 is responsible for bringing scores of travellers to the clean town, which has managed to retain much of its easygoing atmosphere nevertheless. Apart from its obvious usefulness, the

H1095 is unfortunately also responsible for having brought various waste products of civilization to town.

There are no tourist attractions in Pai. Still, the chedis of *WAT KLANG* (in the centre of town) and the *WAT LUANG* are worth a visit. Pai is ideally located for setting off on hikes or longer excursions to hilltribe villages. "BUFFALO BILL", an unforgettable original, also lives here. Go ahead and buy him a drink if you like - "No money, no honey, no funny!"

It gets so cold up here between November and February that you will often see people wearing thick woollen caps and anoraks.

GUESTHOUSES
All of Pai's guesthouses offer double rooms for 30-80 Baht. They are very simple. You will find that many guesthouse owners share a common hobby - drawing maps.

DUANG GUESTHOUSE* is opposite the bus station. One wooden and one brick building offer a total of 7 double-rooms with proper beds and mattresses, as well as a dormitory. Good protection against mosquitoes, lav/showers are separate. Walk south down the main road and you'll reach

PAI GUESTHOUSE* after 400 metres; a two-storey, wooden building with double rooms and a lounge, 4 bungalows in the garden. There are only 2 lav/showers for a maximum of 20 guests; guides for jungle excursions available. There might be a restaurant by now, too. "Buffalo Bill" will entertain you with his tall tales and comments. His 'information' has repeatedly turned out to be hogwash, but who cares with a character like this?

PAI HOUSE CAFE* is directly opposite. There are small wooden bungalows behind the restaurant. Friendly owner, who is also able to give you some proper information. The

PAI HOTEL* is 50 metres further on. Two large wooden houses and one brick building in the background (for those who want something more solid) offer a total of 17 rooms.

KIM GUESTHOUSE* (=DUANG 2) is approx. 400 metres out of town, to the west, just beyond the hospital. The rooms are separated from each other by plywood, warm showers are available. There is a small shop out front, but the whole complex is not too well thought out. Continue along this road for another 3 km, and you'll reach the

MUSLIM GUESTHOUSE*, Ban Nam Ho, just beyond the wat; large, two-storey country-house. If you want to stay out here, contact the Muslim shop on the main road; the young woman here, a teacher, speaks excellent English.

FOOD
You will have an amazing choice of good places to eat in Pai. The owner of the *PAI HOUSE CAFE* cooks delicious meals; cheap and large helpings. His Suki Yaki (personal recipe) is excellent, the fruit pancake is huge, and tea refills are free of charge! Good local food is available at the corner next to the Duang GH - large variety and big helpings for little money. The restaurants behind the hotel and at the crossroad towards the hospital also offer good meals. "Buffalo Bill" frequently cooks at the Pai GH; a real treat!

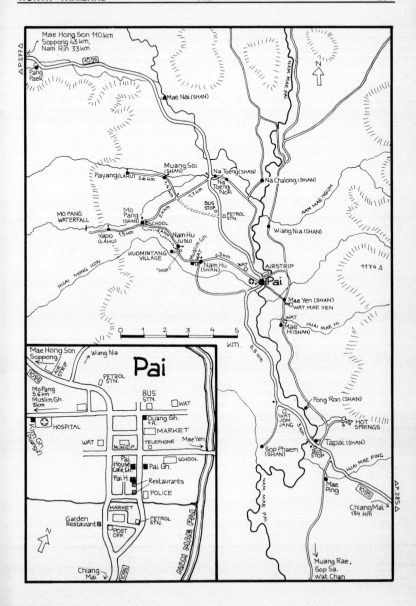

And should all this not suffice, there is a garden restaurant (menue only in Thai) at the southern exit of town, opposite the new market.

GENERAL INFORMATION
INFORMATION concerning excursions and trekking is available at the guesthouses. Young men offer their services as guides.

POST OFFICE - southern end of the main road, by the new market, open Mon - Fri 8:30 - 16:30 h, Sat 9:00 - 12:00 h.

HOSPITAL - Is your appendix acting up? Have it removed in Pai! Clinically clean, barely visible scars, and after 18 hours you'll be as good as new! At least this is the way it was when a fat friend of ours suffered a sudden attack of appendicitis.

REPAIR SHOP - diagonally across from the Pai GH.

PETROL STATION - at the exit leading to Mae Hong Son: Fill 'er up, please!

CELEBRATIONS - The Lisu hold their 3-day New Year's celebrations at the same time as the Chinese. Tarted up with all sorts of fashionable glitter, the young Lisu women dance the traditional circular dance. You will usually be quite welcome in most villages if you come with a guide, especially if you make a financial contribution. Definitely act in the way your guide tells you to, however; otherwise you might break a taboo, which could bring ill fate to the whole village. You can watch traditional dances in the Lisu village of NAM HU, 6 km west of Pai. The Lisu Lodge in NAM RIN is completely booked out at these times. You will have to go on longer trekking tours to reach any of the more distant villages. Ask for a guide and information at the guesthouses.

HOW TO GET THERE
The trip from Chiang Mai through the mountains is one of the most beautiful ones conceivable. Buses from CHIANG MAI (Arcade Bus Station) depart at 7:00, 8:30, 11:00, and 14:00 h (50 Baht, 4 hrs.); 4-wheel drive pick-ups from MAE HONG SON depart at 7:30, 10:30, and 14:00 h (50 Baht, 4 1/2 hrs.).

LEAVING PAI
The route to Mae Hong Son leads through dense jungle. An 88 km stretch of the road was still unpaved in 1987. A real challenge for bikers - especially if it's wet.

Buses to CHIANG MAI depart at 6:30, 8:30, 10:30, and 13:30 h (50 Baht, 4 hrs.); 4-wheel drive pick-ups to MAE HONG SON via NAM RIN (Lisu Lodge 15 Baht) and SOPPONG (20 Baht) depart at 7:00, 11:00, and 13:30 h (50 Baht, 4 1/2 hrs.). You will have to wear dust-proof goggles if you want to see anything of the marvelous landscape.

EXCURSIONS FROM PAI
HIKES
It's fun hiking in the vicinity of Pai, although the places you can go to aren't too spectacular. You can visit Lisu, Shan, Red Lahu, and Kuomintang-Chinese villages in the west without getting lost. Stop by at the WAT NAM HU (3 km, at the fork in the road) and look at the Chiang Saen Buddha, whose hinged hairbun contains sacred water. The waterfalls at the end of the paths are not too exciting.

WAT MAE YEN in the east (3 km) stands upon a hill from which you will have a fine view. The hot springs (11 km) aren't really worth going to; there is hardly a chance of bathing. The last path branching off to the left before you reach the springs will lead you to a female ELEPHANT and her calf after 800 metres; take a ride (sometimes the owner will already be waiting for you at the springs). You can also watch all three, Mummy, calf, and owner, enjoying their morning bathe by the bridge across the Pai river (9 km).

RAFTING TRIPS
You can make a rafting trip to Pai from the Lisu village of HUAY SHANG TAO if the water level is okay (information at the Pai GH). Real nature freaks can also go on a 5-day rafting trip from BAN MUANG PANG (26 km south of Pai) to PANG MU (8 km north of Mae Hong Son). The trip will take you through beautiful, untouched wilderness. You will even have to construct a new raft after having passed one of the particularly violent rapids (information and guides at the Pai GH).

FROM PAI TO CHIANG MAI

A large variety of landscapes await you: Wide valleys, dense jungles, teak- and pine forests, a beautiful mountain pass with many hairpin bends (1300 metres), fantastic views of deep valleys and mountains reaching up to 2005 metres in height, a twisty descent past many rice terraces, and a final level stretch through a plain of wide rice paddies.

There are several excursions you can make, e.g. to the Karen villages of MAE PING NOI (turn right 10 km from Pai) and WAT JAN (turn off onto H1265 11.5 km from Pai), to Royal village development centres, or to the thermal springs of PONG DEUT (turn left 58 km beyond Pai, then continue along the bad road for a further 8 km).

An excursion to the *MOFKA WATERFALL* (turn right 76 km from Pai, then continue along the country lane for 1,5 km) is really worth it. It's a pretty, 600 metre walk along a brook and beneath a roof of bamboo leaves from the parking lot. One arm of the waterfall falls approx. 30 metres into a beautiful pool. Nice place for a picnic.

You will reach the H107 after 98 km. From here it's 34 km to the northern, White Elephant Gate (Chang Puak) of Chiang Mai.

FROM CHIANG MAI TO THATON

You will be able to visit elephant training camps, Buddhist cave-temples, Royal village development centres, and hilltribe villages en route to Thaton. The H107 mainly leads through a flat landscape, but the surroundings become quite spectacular at the point where the road passes two of Thailand's highest mountains. Most travellers take a bus to Thaton from the Chang Puak bus station, then continue with a boat or a raft on the Mae Kok until they reach Chiang Rai. You will also be able to change onto the boat if you're travelling by motorcycle. You will otherwise have to return to Chiang Mai or go down a rarely used road, as the extension of the road beyond Thaton will probably not be completed for a couple of years.

Leave Chiang Mai through the northern Chang Puak gate. You will be surrounded by heavy traffic for the first couple of kilometres. The H1096 leading to the MAE SA VALLEY (see there) branches off after 12 km. The H1095 to PAI and MAE HONG SON (see above) branches off after 36 km. You can turn right to the MAE FAEK RESERVOIR - a good place for a snack - shortly before km stone 41.

➡ *EXCURSION TO THE MAE NGAD RESERVOIR*

A concrete signpost will direct you to the MAE NGAD dam (14 km) and a small harbour (1,3 km further on) shortly beyond km stone 41. A boat will take you to the LAKE VIEW KINGFISHER COTTAGE**** (4 km, 250 Baht return); there are floating bungalows on the lake, right by a peninsula. The comfortable huts are furnished for those bringing their own supplies with them: Laundry facilities, cutlery, plates, a gas stove, refrigerator, and a barbecue grill; lavatories on the peninsula, no restaurant, drinks available. This is a good spot for fishing, windsurfing (200 Baht a day), boat rides, and swimming. You can also go on jungle hikes in the nearby LANNA NATIONAL PARK. An 8-bed bungalow will cost you approx. 1500 Baht, 2 people will have to pay approx. 900 Baht for a smaller, 3-bed bungalow. Travellers can also spend the night outside; in this case you will have to agree on the price with the owners yourselves. Bargain! Advance booking is definitely necessary at the weekends, to a lesser degree during the week. Call 053/214711, or go to the office in Chiang Mai, 12/6 Huay Kaew Road.

The road leaves the fertile plain and starts its twisty descent into the Ping river canyon after 49 km.

The YOUNG ELEPHANTS TRAINING CENTRE is to the right of the river, at km stone 56 (bus from Chiang Mai 13 Baht, 1 1/2 hrs.). Young elephants are trained for jungle work here, except during the hot months (from March - May). Very touristy; whole busloads of tourists come to see the daily show from 9:30-11:00 h (admission 40 Baht). It is interesting and amusing nevertheless, especially if there are any particularly young elephant calves around. You can ride through the jungle on an elephant's back after the show (100 Baht per person if you drive a hard bargain). (Further elephant-shows are held in Mae Sa Valley as well as north of Lampang). You can spend the night at the simple camp-HUTS (with showers!) for 100 Baht per person.

➡ *EXCURSION TO THE MOUNTAINS*

An unpaved road branches off to the left and winds its way up 8 km to the HILLTRIBE DEVELOPMENT AND WELFARE CENTER at KM 61. This centre is responsible for the numerous villages on the slopes of the Doi Chiang Dao and those on the other surrounding mountains. Efforts are being made to introduce new products into agriculture, to improve the medical aid in the area, and to generally raise the standard of living. Experiments are being carried out with tea and coffee in one of the research buildings. There is a Lahu village approx. 1 km from here. There is no public transport to the village. Sometimes motorcycles or trucks will come by, and these might take you along. The best way of getting there, of course, is with a rented motorbike. The road is unsuitable for normal cars.

The large village of CHIANG DAO at the Doi Chiang Dao, Thailand's third-highest mountain (2175 metres), is the starting-point for an excursion to the caves. As yet, there is no accommodation whatsoever. Buses from Chiang Mai cost 17 Baht and take 2 hrs. for the 72 km stretch.

➡ **EXCURSION TO THE CAVES**
A 5-km road, surfaced at this point, leads to the CHIANG DAO CAVES from the northern edge of the village (opposite the petrol-station). You'll reach the cave entrance by way of a roofed staircase (5 Baht admission).
A couple of Buddha statues can be seen right near the entrance. The following 300 metres are lit up, but they are not too impressive to those who have already visited other caves. There are several as yet unexplored cave passages beyond. You will reach the domicile of the Buddhist master Sim after a further 2 km along the narrow road. You will have to climb many steps and walk through jungle, past a chedi, and several monks' huts before reaching the votive-gift-studded entrance of the cave. The highly venerated master lives at the

exit on the opposite side. You might be able to arrange an appointment with him through his secretary, who speaks excellent English.

➤ EXCURSION TO THE BORDER
An unpaved road constructed under the army's supervision and leading to the Burmese border branches off at KM 78, 6 km north of Chiang Dao. You will reach the small village of BAN MUANG NGAI after approx. 5 km. King Naresuan had a large army-camp built here around 1594. From here he organized his military campaign against Burma. A wooden fort measuring 35 x 35 metres has been erected here in honour of the great King.

An unpaved road branching off shortly behind the village (only suitable for trucks and motorcycles) leads through the mountains to the fertile NAM MAE TAENG valley. The small villages here were completely cut off from the rest of the country until this road was built in 1982.

A second road branches off here, too, the H1178 which leads directly to the Burmese border, 30 km north of here. There is no public transportation on either of the two roads, only occasional trucks. Road conditions vary from just acceptable to absolutely miserable, the latter being particularly the case in the mountains and river-fords. Even experienced bikers may have a difficult time. It is not advisable to travel on your own here; the political situation in the frontier territory is rather unstable. We would suggest only going on these kind of trips if you speak Thai well or have someone along who does. We would warn anyone against setting out on treks to even more remote areas from here. We were intercepted by a military patrol and sent back after only 20 km in 1987.

➤ EXCURSIONS FOR THE ADVENTUROUS
The H1150 leads through a bizarre landscape of cliff formations all the way to PHRAO (32 km) from KM 83. The road passes through a fertile valley in a straight line. It later becomes a safe unpaved road leading across a breathtaking, jungle-overgrown mountain range. You will only pass two Meo villages and two signposts directing you to further villages (2-3 km off the road) along the 53 km stretch. The road meets the H1019 (from where it's 91 km to Chiang Mai and Chiang Rai, respectively) south of WIANG PA PAO.

You will be surrounded by picturesque cliffs and hills after having passed kmstone 90. The Meo of HUAY LUK have managed to retain much of their cultural identity, despite the fact that their village is so close to the road.

The CHIANG DAO HILL RESORT**** , a 1/2 km beyond km stone 100, is a perfect example of the new resort hotels of northern Thailand (admission 10 Baht); beautiful, comfortable country-houses (for 2-22 people) are built around a small lake, situated in a beautiful park at the edge of the jungle. There is a restaurant, bar, playground, and jogging path, as well as fishing facilities, a games room, and a video room. The whole resort is intended to host rich Bangkok families looking for a little peace and quiet in a natural surrounding.

An average 400 Baht per bed makes this quite an expensive resort, and even the camping grounds cost 150 Baht (including mattress and sleeping bag).

The road goes uphill until it reaches km stone 109. This is the watershed separating the Mae Nam Chao Phraya and the Mekong river catchment-basins. The pretty SUAN SA KAEO restaurant just past km stone 114 is a nice place to stop for a quick meal; small reservoir, picnic tables, cheap food, and friendly waitresses.

➡ EXCURSION TO THE CAVES AND THE THERMAL SPRINGS
The road leading to the TUBTAO CAVES (3 km) branches off just before km stone 118, after the road has gone downhill and is back on level ground again. Rays of sun fall upon a reclining Buddha statue (1000 years old according to an untrue legend) as well as several other Buddha figures (very folklorish) through the ceiling of the "Light Cave". The "Dark Cave" on the right is rather dilapidated.

You will reach BAN MAI NONG POUR if you continue west for another 8 km along this dirt road, and then turn left at the crossroads. You will feel as if you've just walked into China upon entering this village, which measures 2 km in length. Hua-Chinese, who were driven out of the southwestern Chinese province of Yunnan over 100 years ago, have settled here and managed to retain their cultural identity. The incredibly well-cared for fields are proof of this people's industriousness. Real Chinese noodle soup is served for lunch at a small foodstand.

Why not visit the THERMAL BATHS (=Nam Rae), at the village-exit - you may make use of this public institution for an admission fee of 2 or 3 Baht. A family cabin will cost you 15 Baht, soap and towels are also available. A new Chinese temple featuring a laughing Buddha, the Goddess of Mercy, and the historical Buddha Sakyamuni, all in loud colours, stands upon the hill next to the baths.

A narrow tarmac road winds its way up to a telecommunications tower just before KM 118 - you will have a good view of the Fang plain and the mountains in the south and east. A small path leading to the FOREST LAND RESORT**** (800 metres) branches off to the right 1.5 km further on. This is a nice resort with a bathing lake with slide as well as a lake with pedal boats; 7 huts at 500 Baht each, restaurant.

➡ EXCURSION TO DOI ANGKHAN
The road now runs through the fertile plain of Fang. The H1249 leading to DOI ANGKHANG (28 km) branches off to the west at KM 137. You will first pass through villages and lychee-gardens. Then the road begins climbing. The steepest five km of this stretch are impassable for a car, but by no means for a motorcycle. An agricultural development centre sponsored by the King is in the valley lying 2 km beyond this pass. Fruits and vegetables, mainly those used

to a more moderate climate, are being tested for their suitability for northern Thailand here. There are many flowers and apple, and peach trees in the area. There are some Lahu villages close nearby, and you can also hike to some Lisu- and Meo villages from here. The first village, BAN KHUM, is inhabited by Hua-Chinese and Lahu. Simple BUNGALOWS* on the mountain slope are for rent. Simple meals are served at the old Chinese man's village-shop. Here you will also be able to buy lychee-wine and "Senji", yellowish booze containing hairy roots.

A few old oil pumps along the H107 are a reminder of the short "oil rush" at the end of the 50s. The "main road" branching off to the right, the H109, deteriorates into a country path after a few kilometres. The road is only passable during the dry season. A pick-up drives the Fang-Chiang Mai route along the H109 when road conditions permit.

➥ *EXCURSION TO NAM RON*

A dirt road leading to the agricultural EXPERIMENTAL STATION BO NAM RON (7 km) branches off to the left at the entrance of FANG (KM 151). Various crops from more moderate climatic zones are tested here for their suitability for growth in northern Thailand, especially coffee, peaches, apples, potatoes, and tea.

You will come to the sulphurous HOT SPRINGS of BO NAM RON 2 km further on. The 90^0C of the hottest spring are enough to boil eggs! A geyser throws up columns of water (up to 25 metres in height) every half hour. The sheltered tables in the grounds are a nice place place for a picnic.

You will be able to see a thermal power-station 200 metres further on, to the right. There is a rather squalid Red Lahu village 1 km further on, above a brook. Nobody here wears the traditional clothing any more. A taxi-motorcycle to Fang will cost you 60 Baht.

FANG

Its closeness to Burma and its involvement with opium and arms smuggling have characterized this town. When we first came here in 1973 most of the town's men walked around armed with rifles or colts. Taxi drivers always had a loaded gun along. These days things have quieted down; the Thai Border Police now have everything under control.

HOTELS

At the entrance of town: *ROZA***, modern concrete building, 200 metres from the road, next to the hospital. You'll find the new and huge *CHOK THANI*** (ac***) nearby, on the right hand side. *D.J.** (ac**) is also relatively new, set back slightly from the road.

For fans of hotels built in the old Thai style, there are three to choose from: *METTA WATTANA*, SHRI CHUKIT*,* and *WIANG FANG*,* which is by the bend of the main road; all three organize trekking tours. *NAIFHUN HOTEL** is at the northern town exit, to the left; motel-style, clean rooms with large beds.

HOW TO GET THERE
A bus leaves from CHIANG MAI (Chang Puak Bus Station) every half hour (32 Baht, 3 hrs.)

A minibus leaves THATON every 10 minutes (7 Baht, 40 min.). A pick-up ride along the H109 from CHIANG RAI will cost you 50-60 Baht (only possible if it's dry).

H107 becomes H1089 beyond Fang. The stretch leading to Mae Chan beyond Thaton may be passable by next year.

You will pass the RAI NAKORN BURIN RESORT after 9 1/2 km. A path leading to Thailand's second-highest mountain, DOI PHA NHOM POK (2285 metres), branches off at km stone 12.1 km before Mae Ai. You will reach an agricultural development centre which is said to have BUNGALOWS for rent 14 km further on. A path leads up to the mountain peak.

THATON

The small settlement lies by the Mae Kok river. This is the place to set out from for one of the most beautiful boat rides in Thailand. Rafting trips can be incredibly romantic and adventurous. A monumental, sitting, white Buddha in Chiang Saen style towers over Thaton. *WAT THATON* on the hill slopes, with its pretty monks' houses, lies nestled at the statue's feet. Beautiful bronze Buddhas fashioned in the Sukhothai and Chiang Saen styles can be seen in the new bot. An energetic abbot and many young monks are turning this into one of the north's most splendid temples. You will have a wonderful view over the plain and the river all the way to the mountains from the white Buddha; it is particularly beautiful in the early morning, when the many fog banks gradually rise.

GUESTHOUSES
There are only guesthouses in Thaton up to now, no hotels. Turn left just before the bridge and you'll reach *THIP'S TRAVELLERS HOUSE** after 100 metres. Rather mean little huts are for rent below the temple hill, some with lav/shower and even mosquito nets. The *BEER GARDEN RESTAURANT,* which also belongs to the complex, is nicely located, directly at the river. Beware - the patroness is very business-minded and the food none too good. If you turn right at the bridge you'll reach the *SIAM MAE-KOK GUESTHOUSE** after 100 metres; wooden building with small, simple rooms. The two women who own it have opened a very cozy *COFFEE SHOP* downstairs. *CHANKASEM GUESTHOUSE*,* is on the same road, 20 metres further on, directly at the landing place. Interlocking rooms, large restaurant directly by the river. A second branch, *CHANKASEM No.2 GUESTHOUSE*,*

is on the northern side of the bridge, at the minibus stop. This one is cheaper but less appealing.

HOW TO GET THERE

There is a direct bus from CHIANG MAI (Chang Puak Bus Station) that departs at 6:00, 7:20, 9:00, and 11:30 h (37 Baht, 4 hrs.); a bus to FANG departs every 1/2 hour (23 Baht, 3 hrs.). Once there, a minibus to Thaton will cost you 7 Baht (40 min.).

The river boat from CHIANG RAI departs at 10:00 h (160 Baht, 6 hrs.).

LEAVING THATON

The direct bus to CHIANG MAI costs 37 Baht and takes 4 hrs.; you can also take the minibus to FANG (7 Baht) and then one of the Chiang Mai-bound buses (32 Baht, 3 hrs.) that leave every 1/2 hour until 17:30h.

The river-boat to CHIANG RAI departs at 12:30 h (160 Baht, 4-5 hrs.); taking a motorcycle along will cost you an additional 200 Baht. There are twelve stops before Chiang Rai at which you can also disembark, e.g. BAN MAI (30 Baht), MAE SALAK (40 Baht), and RUAM MITR (Karen village, 140 Baht).

Pick-ups heading for the villages in the west (e.g. to BAN MAI or BAN MUANG NGAM, both for 15 Baht) depart from the stop on the other side of the bridge.

EXCURSIONS FROM THATON

Trekking tours through the area surrounding Thaton are organized by every guesthouse. One of the trips includes a total of 6 hrs. of hiking, as well as short, regular visits to Karen, Lahu, and Akha villages.

TO THE BORDER

You can only walk 2-3 km to the left, beyond the bridge. After that you must STOP; it gets too dangerous. The Burmese border is extremely close nearby. Don't feel as if you're missing anything, though - it's pretty uninteresting.

BAN MAI

You can get to the small village of BAN MAI (full name: BAN MAI MOK JAM) with the river-boat (30 Baht, lovely trip through cultivated countryside, many hairpin bends on the Mae Kok) or by pick-up (15 Baht). An upstream boat from Chiang Rai will cost you 130 Baht.

You can watch paper being made by hand from the wood of the Sa tree (Paper Mulberry) in the village. You will find the BAN MAI GUESTHOUSE*, a two-storey wooden building with a dormitory, mattresses, and blankets, just 100 metres downstream from the landing place. You can spend the night here and have a meal for a total of 30 Baht. Reach an Ulo Akha village after a 1/2 hour walk north along a path leading through the fields. The village seems incredibly dilapidated, in marked contrast to the development project right next to it.

BAN MUANG NGAM

You can get to the Karen village of BAN MUANG NGAM by minibus for 15 Baht (every 30 min. from 7:00-17:30 h), or with a pick-up (5 Baht). You will need 15 minutes to climb the path beyond the village. This leads to the KAREN COFFEE SHOP* guesthouse, also known as PHANGA'S HOUSE; bamboo-huts (30 Baht), and restaurant (dinner 20 Baht, fried rice 15 Baht) on a hill. Nice view of the wide valley, pleasant and relaxed atmosphere. You can set off on walks through the hilly countryside from here, hike to Lisu, Akha, and Lahu villages, or go trekking with a guide (50 Baht per person). You can bathe in the river, build your own raft, or ride upon one of the three elephants (380 Baht per day for 2 people). You can also set out an a 2-day trekking tour to the LAAN TONG LODGE (north of Chiang Rai), on the other side of the hills.

BOAT RIDES ON THE KOK RIVER
SPEEDBOATS
Longtail-boats (no seats!) leave the boathouse at 12:30 h. The trip to Chiang Rai along the MAE KOK RIVER costs 160 Baht and takes 4-5 hrs., if nothing goes wrong. You will not be able to get at your baggage during the ride. Passengers have to spend the trip sitting on the floor, cooped up like chickens. Take a jacket or a blanket along for padding. These boats are unfortunately much too fast and loud for people to enjoy the magnificent river landscape - fertile plains and picturesque settlements, a new view of the immense white Buddha of Thaton with every twist and bend of the river, high mountains covered with dense jungle, occasional hilltribe villages, and exciting rapids. If nobody wishes to disembark or get on along the way, the boat will only stop once, at MAE SALAK, for a quick registration of the passengers (passport or

KAREN WOMAN WITH CHILD

photocopy with visa number necessary). Akha women will model in front of your camera lenses for a small fee. There are also 12 other stops at which you can be let off, should you so desire. You will be able to trek to various hilltribe villages from these, and then catch the next day's boat. (Make sure you catch their attention as they zoom by, otherwise you might have to wait yet another day). You can also walk certain routes along the northern riverbank.

You will have to charter a boat of your own if you want more independence and want to stop wherever you feel like it. This will cost you approx. 1600 Baht.

RAFTING
If you've got time to spare, why not do the trip in a total of three days, on a bamboo raft? All of the guesthouses in Thaton organize these kind of trips; there are always plenty of travellers willing to go along during the season, and the rafts are ready and waiting. A raft can hold up to 6 people, has a cabin and even a primitive 'lavatory'. Two boat-guides and many mats, blankets, mattresses and portable cooking plates are included in the price of 2400 Baht per boat. Food will cost you extra. You can spend the nights sleeping on the raft or the riverbanks, whichever you prefer. The adventurous among you could even buy their own raft and set out alone. Be careful at the rapids on the level of the Forest Development Centre on the second day, should you decide to do this!

> **WARNING:** *Two tourists are said to have been shot dead on the Kok river in the summer of 1987. This has been the first incident after a long and peaceful period. It's best to travel in larger groups!*

FROM CHIANG MAI TO CHIANG RAI

The 182 km stretch between Chiang Mai and Chiang Rai can be covered in 3 1/2 hrs. by car and 4 hrs. by bus, now that the H1019 has been opened to traffic. Pleasant rest areas invite you to come and picnic, while narrow side-roads lead into the jungle along the way. You can spend the night at one of the simple guesthouses in the mountains. Several "better" resort hotels are now also being built along the road.

You will be surrounded by paddies for the first 20 km, after that you will be driving through a hilly, wooded landscape until you reach the other side of the pass at km stone 53. Once there, you will have entered the extremely fertile province of Chiang Rai, Thailand's northernmost province.

➨ *EXCURSION TO THE TREKKER HOUSE*
A signpost halfway between km stones 63 and 64 will direct you to the right. You can have the bus stop here if you like. It's a 7 km, uphill walk from the signpost. Only few pick-ups ever come by. You will have to pass through an unfriendly Lahu Sheh Leh village as well as a Thai village, Ban Muang Noy, before reaching the TREKKER HOUSE* by a slope on the right; two wooden buildings with simple rooms, easy-going atmosphere, campfires in the evenings. Rice and unspiced meat (15 Baht) is served as dinner on some

days, flavourless spaghetti (20 Baht) on others. The leftovers are sometimes served for breakfast. The house is owned by a former trekking guide. Thank God for the noodle stand (delicious soup available) just beyond the house.

There are two Lahu Sheh Leh villages close nearby. You will be able to reach Lisu, KMT (Kuomintang), Meo, Yao, and White Karen villages during the course of 1 - 3-day trekking tours. The guesthouse boys are good guides.

You can buy eggs freshly boiled in the HOT SPRINGS at KM 65. The water at the riverbank has a temperature of 90ºC. From here, continue through the plain of WIANG PA PAO.

➥ EXCURSION FOR THE ADVENTUROUS
A well-built for the most part but rarely used dirt road (H1150) turns off to the left at km stone 91. The road winds its way along a breathtaking, densely wooded mountain range. There are only two Meo villages and a couple of signposts directing you to further villages off the road (2-3 km) along the way. You will reach the fertile PHRAO valley after 53 km. Keep going straight ahead. The now surfaced road winds its way through a fantastic cliff landscape for 32 km before reaching Highway H107. It's another 83 km to Chiang Mai from here.

The road starts its descent into the wide Chiang Rai plain after yet another hilly stretch with many nice rest areas along the road. A hill with a temple towers above the village of MAE SUAI. You will have a wonderful view of the entire area from up here.

➥ EXCURSION FOR THE BRAVE
You can turn left down H109 towards Fang beyond Mae Suai if you're travelling by motorcycle (and only if it's completely dry!). The road becomes noticeably worse and narrower than the maps would have you expect after only a few km. Untouched jungle, no traffic, no villages near the road, only a couple of paths leading to Lisu and Akha villages at the beginning of the road. We would only recommend this for people with strong nerves! A pick-up also drives back and forth between Mae Suai and Fang (50-60 Baht).

The new road meets the old Highway H1 soon after this, and from here it's another 23 km to Chiang Rai.

CHIANG RAI
Almost 1 million people live in this, the northernmost of Thailand's provinces. Chiang Rai produces most rice of all of the Thai provinces, although only 1/3 of its area is used for agricultural cultivation. The capital, Chiang Rai, was founded as early as 1262 by King Mengrai as the centre of his kingdom. Chi-

ang Mai was not founded for another 48 years. The town has a peaceful and relaxed feeling to it, in spite of the many modern buildings that have been erected during the last couple of years. It is nowhere near as hectic as Chiang Mai.

The famous Emerald Buddha was discovered in the chedi of *WAT PHRA KAEO* in 1436. Legend has it that the chedi was once partially destroyed by a flash of lightening, thus revealing the statue. Back then it still had an outer coat of plaster, however, and not until part of the plaster chipped off did one discover the actual, green Buddha beneath. The actual material, incidentally, was jasper. There are few sights in Chiang Rai. No cultural musts!

GUESTHOUSES

It has become fashionable to open up guesthouses in Chiang Rai lately. Some of these institutions disappear as quickly as they pop out of the ground. In contrast to Chiang Mai, most of the guesthouses here offer showers and running hot water. Most run their own trekking agencies. All are able to give you good information. Motorcycles can be rented for 100-200 Baht in most of the houses. Bicycles are also available, sometimes even for free.

Near the river: go towards town from the landing-place. You will reach

CHAT GUEST HOUSE*, 1 Trairat Rd., tel 713459, after 200 metres, on the right; wooden building with a comfortable lounge, dormitory, rooms, and little sheds with tiny sleeping partitions in the back yard; mosquito nets, good laundry facilities, Freak Bros. atmosphere, noisy traffic. Turn left here (east). To your left you will see the

MAEKOK VILLA*-*** (= CHIANG RAI YOUTH HOSTEL), 445 Singhakai Rd., tel 311786; old mansion with gigantic dormitories, as well as beautifully set bungalows and comfortable terraced houses beyond. Walk past the YMCA, turn left into the next road, then right into the alley: the

GOLDEN HOUSE* (=GOLDEN TOUR HOUSE), 246 Soi Pitagrad, Singhakai Rd. is a peacefully located, new building; various sized rooms available, dormitory.

Centre of town: 400 metres east of the bus station, beyond Wat Jet Yod:

BOONBUNDAN GUEST HOUSE*-**, 1005/13 Jet Yod Rd., tel 712914; various huts set in a large garden, restaurant with videos, new terraced house with ac, all very quiet and peaceful; Toyota Corolla (500 Baht/day) and a jeep (400 Baht/day) for rent, an additional 250 Baht for a driver and petrol. Continue southeast for another 400 metres and you'll reach

BOONYOUNG GUEST HOUSE *-** (formerly Ton's House), 1054 Sanambin Rd., tel 712893; large main building with rooms and dormitory, sweet, small huts built in various styles beyond; small garden with an open-air restaurant; very relaxing. Turn right at the bus station and walk up the main road (north) to

PORN HOUSE*, 503 Rattanaket Rd, on the right hand side; two large Thai buildings in a yard, dormitory, large balcony, many lavatories; quiet in spite of its central location. If you turn right at the church, you will find the

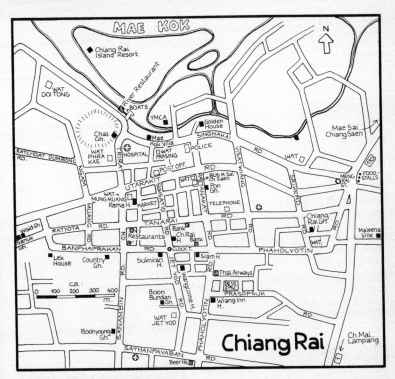

GOLDEN TRIANGLE***, 590 Phaholyotin Rd., tel 711339, on the left hand side (behind the cafe and the travel agency belonging to the same complex); very pretty, flat terraced houses; nicely furnished rooms for those with refined tastes, some ac. Continue left towards the edge of town.

CHIANG RAI GUESTHOUSE*, 717/2 Sriked Rd., is on the right (opposite the Wat); very simple, rather dark rooms in an old house (maybe it has been renovated by now?); very friendly, helpful young owner.

Continue even further east, to beyond the H1:

MALEENA VILLE** (ac***), 863 Wat Pranon Rd., tel 712931; new, solid bungalows on a narrow piece of land; best mattresses in town; a hilarious Thai automobile (with a two-stroke engine) can be rented for 300 Baht a day. The

BAN THAI*, said to be at 330 Soi 18 Mituna, Phaholyotin Road, has been recommended to us; family-run guesthouse.

To the west: Go west from the clock tower, then turn left beyond the Samakee School:

LEK HOUSE*, 163/1 Banphaprakan

Rd.; nice Thai style wooden building with large and small rooms as well as a few bungalows; garden with benches and tables; family atmosphere. A little further on you'll find the

COUNTRY GUEST HOUSE*, Banphaprakan Rd.; newly renovated, lovely mansion with a small park and a garden restaurant; tiled bathrooms and marble sinks; the young owners speak English very well. You'll find the following three guesthouses next to each other, on Ratyota Road (=Ratchayotha Road, much traffic):

WISID GUEST HOUSE*, 21/4 Ratyota Rd.; Thai building and airy bamboo huts on a small piece of land; restaurant serving exotic dishes - birds, lizards, and snakes; car and minibus for rent.

SANUK GUEST HOUSE*, 21/3 Ratyota Rd.; Thai building and bungalow; cozy atmosphere, meals are eaten with the family; the owners are a German man and his Thai wife.

DIARY GUEST HOUSE*, near Ratyota Rd.; not recommendable.

HOTELS
The cheaper hotels in town are not really worth the money. For those demanding quality, how about the *RAMA HOTEL**-****, 331/4 Trirat Rd., tel 311344; clean town hotel. *CHIANG RAI ISLAND RESORT*-*****, tel 311865; spacious bungalow resort on the island in the Kok river. *WIANG INN HOTEL*****, 893 Phaholyotin Rd., tel 711543; average standard hotel. *WANGCOME HOTEL*****, 869 Pemawibhata Rd., tel 711800; luxurious hotel with very reasonable prices.

FOOD
You can eat good meals for a reasonable price at the various night markets in town. The DOH RUNG MARKET is opposite the Wiang Inn Hotel. You will find a further night market on Sanambin Road. Good, cheap Thai and Chinese food is available at the HOR NALIGA by the clock tower. You will find more good Chinese restaurants along the southern side of Tanarai Road, opposite the market. Rather expensive, but excellent Tom Yam is served at the RUEN THONG by the Super Highway, not far from Wat Sriked. Nobody here speaks a word of English.

The two restaurants by the landing-place are wonderfully located as long as there are no noisy longtail boats about (try the early afternoon). The food is none too good, however, and the service is unfriendly.

Karlheinz's *BIERSTUBE* is south of the Wiang Inn Hotel, by Phaholyotin Rd.; draught beer and German food available.

GENERAL INFORMATION
TOURIST INFORMATION - go to the YMCA, easy to find from Singhakai Road (follow the signposts), on the island in the river, tel 311313, open Mon-Sat from 8:30-19:00 h.

TREKKING TOURS - all guesthouses organize trekking tours. Prices for typical tours: 2 days/1 night 350 Baht; 3 days/2 nights 500 Baht; 5 days/4 nights 750 Baht. Raft trips on the Kok river are offered for 1500 Baht. The trip takes 3 days / 2 nights and goes all the way to the Mekong. You will spend one night sleeping on the raft, the other in a hilltribe village.

MEDICAL AID - the Overbrook Hospital is at the landing place, opposite Chat House, tel 311366. There is a provincial hospital on Sanambin Road.

ENTERTAINMENT - the *TAN COF-FEE SHOP* is the place to be at night: live Thai bands and the newest Thai hits. Western type discos can be found in the expensive hotels.

LEAVING CHIANG RAI
BY PLANE
Thai Airways Office: 870 Phaholyotin Rd., tel 711179, right by the bus station. The small "shorts" fly to CHIANG MAI (300 Baht), BANGKOK (1575 Baht), and PHITSANULOK (805 Baht) daily.

BY BUS
The central bus station is on Phaholyotin Rd. All ac buses leave from here, as do most local buses. Buses to Mae Sai and Chiang Saen also stop at Rattanaket Road, in front of the police station.

18 buses leave for BANGKOK (175 Baht, 14 hrs.). 5 ac buses leave between 17:00 and 19:30 h (283 Baht, 12 hrs.).

13 buses leave for CHIANG MAI between 6:00 and 16:00 h (47 Baht, 3 1/2 hrs.). 5 ac buses between 7:00 and 15:30 h (66 Baht, 3 hrs.), super-ac bus at 8:00, 12:00, and 16:45 h (85 Baht, 3 hrs.)

Buses to SUKHOTHAI leave at 7:45, 8:30 and 10:00 h (83 Baht, 6 hrs., ac 110 Baht). There are two daily ac buses to Nan (109 Baht, 5 hrs.).

Buses leave for LAMPANG every 1/2 hour (50 Baht, 3 1/2 hrs.). It's 44 Baht to CHIANG KHONG, 15 Baht respectively to CHIANG SAEN and MAE SAI (every 30 min.). If there's no bus around, you can always resort to the local pick-ups.

Pick-ups travel back and forth on the H109 to Fang (only if it's completely dry, though) for 50-60 Baht.

BY BOAT
River-boats depart for THATON daily at around 10:00 h, (160 Baht, 5-6 hrs.). There is always at least one stop in MAE SALAK for a registration of the passengers (passport or photocopy incl. visa number necessary). The rapids and whirlpools can get quite dangerous during the rainy season (July-October).

> *Warning:* Two tourists are said to have been shot dead on the Kok river during the summer of 1987.

EXCURSIONS FROM CHIANG RAI
Chiang Rai is a good base for excursions to the north, especially outings into the mountains between MAE CHAN and MAE SAI. You can easily get to Mae Salong (67 km), to the top of the Doi Tung (60 km), to Chiang Saen (62 km), or to the Golden Triangle (73 km) with a motorcycle, bus, or pick-up.

All guesthouses organize trips. These are also the best places to go for good information, hand-drawn maps (usually more remarkable for their artistry than their accuracy), guides, and bicycles. Some also have motorcycles, jeeps, and cars for rent.

HUAY MAE SAI WATERFALL
Head down the first dirt road on the left beyond the Mae Kok Bridge, and then turn left after 11 km. You will reach the Yao village of HUAY MAE SAI (final destination of the elephant safari which sets out from Ruam Mitr) after 4 km. You will reach the HUAY MAE SAI WATERFALL after a further 4 km (past an

Akha village) and a final, short hike. The falls are quite nice but nothing special. This is the right place for people into mass outings; dozens of organized groups come by here daily on their search for "unspoilt tribal life". We would recommend avoiding the Lahu village of JA LAA, 30 min. from here - its inhabitants have quite obviously simply had enough of tourists.

HIKING TO THE LAAN TONG LODGE
The pick-up (10 Baht) to BAN HUAY COMB (also known as BAN HUI KOM), starts off on the dirt road mentioned above. Continue going straight on after the final bus stop. Turn right at the fork in the road. Make sure that you're still doing okay by occasionally naming your destination to passers-by, BAN HUAI MA HIN FON (HUAI HIN FON for short). You will pass through three Akha villages, the Lahu village of DJA PUEH, and the Yao village of LAO SHI GUAY along the barely passable road (only recommended for pick-ups); you will reach the main road at Huay Ma Hin Fon after approx. 18 km. Turn right; you will see the LAAN TONG LODGE on the right hand side of the road after 2.5 km.

FROM CHIANG RAI TO MAE SAI

The first 29 km of the H110 to MAE CHAN are as straight as an arrow. You will pass through a fertile area used for growing rice. Stands along the roadside sell expensive strawberries. This is a typical example of how difficult the whole 'alternative cash crop' concept actually is; while the hilltribes had little problem getting rid of their opium at high prices, their strawberry crops are usually totally bruised and squashed after a lorry-trip down the bumpy roads.

The small business town of MAE CHAN is the closest place to go shopping for the many hilltribes in the area, who make up the majority of this district's population. MAE CHAN is also well known for the excellent quality of its lychees.

➥ EXCURSION TO THE LAAN TONG LODGE
A minibus from Mae Chan will cost you 10 Baht (regularly between 9:00 and 17:00 h). The H1089 turns off to the left towards HUAI MA HIN FON exactly 1 km beyond Mae Chan. Pass the HOT SPRINGS (8 km) and a pleasant green valley. You will see the

LAAN TONG LODGE after 13 km, on the left hand side. Many pretty bamboo huts with thatched straw roofs of various hilltribe styles, all set on a large piece of land by the river; solar showers available in a separate house, large restaurant with a menu (excellent TOM YAM for 25 Baht); the whole resort belongs to two women, one from Thailand, the other from Australia. There are several Yao-, Lahu-, Lisu-, and Akha villages in the vicinity, all of which can be easily reached (guides and information available at the lodge). You can also drift along the river on old inner tubes.

The H1089 beyond the lodge is still under construction. It is said that the stretch to Thaton will be finished and opened up to traffic by next year. This could mean the end of peace and quiet in this hitherto relaxing valley.

The paved, 36 km H1130 to MAE SALONG starts 2.3 km north of Mae Chan, in the village of PHA SANG, at km stone 860. Pick-ups start from the fork in the road. The one hour trip will cost you 40 Baht. You'd be better off with a rented motorcycle, of course, as always.

You will reach the HILLTRIBE CENTER after a 12 km drive through a lush, fertile valley. Efforts are being made to support the hilltribes socially as well as economically here. Cash crops such as soy beans, flowers, strawberries, lychees, corn, and coffee are being introduced in the hope that they will be considered a satisfactory alternative to opium, the cultivation of which has been radically eradicated in this area. The actual development work is being carried out by *mobile units* in distant villages, however; this is merely the administrative and research HQ. There is very little to see apart from rusty construction machinery and the pleasant gardens of the employees - oh yes, a band with electric guitars, a keyboard, and huge speakers practises western-type pop music in the evenings, much to the amazement of the on-looking Akha boys.

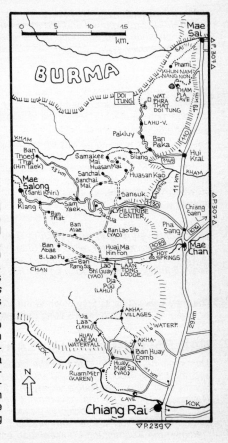

➥ *EXCURSIONS TO AKHA VILLAGES*

The dirt road branching off to the right 100 metres before the centre leads to seven Akha villages of the Ulo and Loimi tribes (road only passable during the dry season). Tourism is the main source of income in the first of these villages, SANSUK; you will meet the first traditionally clothed Akha women selling chains, belts, bags, bracelets, and other souvenirs long before actually reaching the village. Quite a few minibus-loads full of sightseeing tourists venture out this far.

You will be able to form your own opinion as to how successful the Hilltribe Center's development programmes have been in the villages of HUASAN

KAO (6 km) and HUASAN MAI (8 km) as well as SANCHAI MAI (5 km) and SANCHAI (6 km); you will find few Akha who are as impoverished, dilapidated, badly nourished, and apathetic as the ones here, in the close vicinity of the centre. Truthfully now - do you see coffee, flowers, or strawberries growing anywhere?

The Yao village of PHADUA is below H1130, at KM 18. A large part of the population here lives off sightseeing tourism, too; the main village road is studded with souvenir stands. The village inhabitants seem to have retained their formal, polite manner nevertheless.

The road starts winding its way up the mountain, which commands a wonderful view over the entire valley. You will reach the pass after 5 km, at the Akha village of SAM YAEK, which has even opened a tourist park with a dancing stage, ceremonial swing, and village gates. The park immediately becomes crowded with people, all ready for an 'action photo', as soon as groups of tourists are seen approaching.

➡ *The unpaved road to BAN THOED THAI (13 km), which is sometimes very steep, also branches off here. This Shan village made international headlines in 1982, when Opium King Khun Sa was chased away after three days of heavy fighting. There is said to be a GUESTHOUSE here.*

The road now winds its way down to the Mae Salong river, only to start climbing again all the way to Mae Salong (two extremely steep stretches).

MAE SALONG (IN THAI: SANTI KHIRI)

This settlement was founded on the slope of the Doi Mae Salong 27 years ago, by former Kuomintang soldiers of the 93rd Regiment, who had fled to Burma after Mao Tse Tung's victory in 1949 and were later driven away to Thailand in 1961. The Thai government welcomed them with open arms back then, seeing them as an additional protective force which could help guard the border. Not until too late did they realize that the exact opposite was actually the case; the Kuomintang-Chinese soon encouraged and controlled the cultivation and transportation of opium in the entire Golden Triangle area. It was no coincidence that the Opium King Khun Sa settled down in the village of Ban Hin Taek, only a short walk from here. New roads and paths have been constructed in the entire area during the last few years with the express object of making the region easier to supervise and putting an end to the opium business. Today it is most probably (smuggling-) business with Burma (only 7 km away) that is responsible for the village's obvious wealth. Mandarin is still the main language spoken in Mae Salong today. Small Chinese children run about screaming and laughing under the supervision of old, bearded veterans. The houses are built in the Chinese style, with each door guarded by the typical protective gods. Chinese specialities are for sale in the shops along the main road - healing herbs and medicine, tea, tobacco, rice noodles, and 'Senji', a yellowish liquor with Chinese herbs and roots. Many Loimi Akha women, dressed in their traditional, festive costume, come to the markets in the early morning. They bring vegetable-loaded carrier baskets supported by the typical carrier-poles. Many return to their village as early as 9:00 h. Most of them do not want to be photographed (though some may pose for a small fee) - please respect this!

There are several spots in Mae Salong from which you will have a splendid view of the surrounding mountain landscape.

ACCOMMODATION
Take the steep right hand road at the fork. The

MAE SALONG GUESTHOUSE* is on the left hand side, after 100 metres; flat building with clean rooms, some with lav/shower for 40 Baht per person; Chinese food is served if ordered in advance, very friendly owner; treks can be organized, with mules if necessary. The

JIN SAE HOTEL* is around the corner, to the right; wooden building with 10 rooms, the top hotel in town. Continue along the steep road and turn left at the wat. You will reach the

MAE SALONG RESORT**** after 400 metres; well tended resort with bungalows (700 Baht) and terraced houses (500 Baht), a viewpoint, and

several souvenir stands offering Chinese ware.

FOOD
Chinese rice and noodle soup is served for lunch at the foodstands on the main road and all day in the houses to the left, which don't look like restaurants at all. The women here will also gladly prepare their speciality for you.

HOW TO GET THERE
You will reach the road branching off to BAN PHA SANG (2 km north of MAE CHAN) with the MAE SAI-bound bus from CHIANG RAI (8 Baht); once there, catch a pick-up (40 Baht). It's only 30 Baht for the trip back down.

➡ EXCURSIONS TO AKHA VILLAGES
Walk down the footpath leading past the wat; you will reach the Akha village of BAN MAE TOEN after 4 km, the Akha village of BAN MAE CHAN after 5 km. Nobody here wants to have their picture taken, so show some respect.

➡ HIKES TO THE LAAN TONG LODGE
The Laan Tong Lodge is in the Mae Chan Valley, 23 km from Mae Salong. You can hike there on good country lanes or go there with a motorcycle; wide land with good viewpoints, charming forests and intermittent pine groves. You will pass close by 3-4 Akha- and Lisu villages along the way. You will first have to go down the road for 5 km until you reach the Chinese settlement of BAN KLANG (just beyond the steep section). Then turn right at the school, onto the path along the crest. Turn left at the fork in the road 5 km further on (if you take the right hand road you will reach the valley a little earlier). After another 5

*km, take the right hand path (the left one will lead you to the Hilltribe Center).
Once in the valley, turn left and go through BAN HUAI MA HIN FON. It's 3 km to
the lodge from here. Minibuses also travel along this final section of the route
during the daytime.*

You will have to drive back to the H110 over the paved road from Mae Salong.
Continue north through the fertile plain.

➡ EXCURSION TO DOI TUNG

*The signposted H1149 to the huge DOI TUNG (18 km) branches off to the left
after 11 km, in the village of BAN HUI KRAI (19 km before reaching Mae Sai).
A bus to this turn-off from Mae Sai will cost you 5 Baht, a minibus to the peak
another 30 Baht. Although it is paved, the road gets too steep for some cars
after km stones 7 and 17. We would recommend going here just for the fantastic view. You will first pass through a Shan village. After 7 km you'll reach the
Akha village of BAN PAKA. The AKHA GUEST HOUSE* is at the village exit, to
the left; very simple bamboo huts; bad reputation; a minibus to here will cost
you 10 Baht. The first steep section of the road (200 metres) is just beyond the
village. You will see PAKLUY, a pretty Loimi Akha village, below the road at
km-stone 13. All tour groups headed for the Doi Tung stop here along the way,
hence the many business-minded souvenir peddlers. A large sign asks all visitors to refrain from giving the village children sweets or money, as this en-
courages them to skip school. Unfortunately, even travellers are not above a
little bribe when it comes to making new friends. If you really want to do
something for the village, why not put some money into the village donation
box. There is a modern Lahu village 2 km further on, in a bend of the road.
Most inhabitants have been converted to Christianity, and the women go to
mass dressed in the finest of Thai clothes on Sunday morning.*

*You will reach the mountain saddle and a military post shortly before KM 18.
The next 300 metres are extremely steep, after that you've made it - the WAT
PHRA THAT DOI TUNG lies at an altitude of over 1500 metres. You will have a
glorious view of the wide valley and the hills all the way to Burma on a clear
day. Relics of Buddha are said to have been put here by King Achutaraj of
Chiang Saen in 911.*

Warning: *We would not recommend continuing on to the Burmese border
and the Akha village of BAN PHAHE at the present time. The population is
none too friendly. An individual motorcycle-trekker was shot dead here in the
summer of 1986. The Thai police have no power whatsoever up here.*

You will definitely have to return back down the H1149 in order to get to Mae
Sai from here. There is no passable road that will lead you past the Akha village of BAN PHAMI.

You will see a mountain range said to resemble a sleeping woman lying on her back on your way north (approx. 13 km before Mae Sai). Only a hermit of long standing can possibly have drawn this comparison!

MAE SAI

This northernmost of all Thai settlements mainly thrives by doing business with Burma. Shan and Burmese even come all the way from Kengtung (100 km north of here) in order to buy things that are not available in Burma. A bridge crosses the river which marks the border. You can watch the many people scurrying back and forth. Many Thais buy Chinese wares in Tachilek, the Burmese settlement on the other side of the Mae Sai river. After all, China is also only 120 km away.

You will have to buy Burmese souvenirs at the many shops in front of the bridge, seeing as only the Thai are allowed to enter Burma. There is a *JADE FACTORY* on the main road which can be visited (closed on Mon). Mainly kitsch-souvenirs are offered, however. You will have a good view of the area from the *WAT DOI WAO* on the hill to the left, in front of the river.

ACCOMMODATION

You will find one of Thailand's most beautiful guesthouses here, at the northernmost point of the country. Turn left before the bridge and continue towards the river for almost 1 km. The

MAE SAI GUESTHOUSE*-** is directly on the river; many bungalows of various sizes by the river and up the slope, good restaurant, lots of places to relax; friendly owners; information concerning excursions available; motorcycles 150 Baht, bicycles 15 Baht. You might have to stay somewhere else, though, seeing as this bungalow resort is often booked up during the season. The

CHAD GUESTHOUSE*, Soi Wiangpan, is at the entrance of town, in front of the bus station, down the alley leading to the wat; nice, traditional rooms, garden with tables; warm water; very friendly and helpful family; good motorcycles for rent.

Walk down the main road from the bus station. You will see the *MAE SAI HOTEL*** (not too clean) on the right hand side. The

TOP NORTH** is 50 metres further on, on the left hand side. Turn left into the alley beyond and you'll reach the

THAI-BURMESE GUESTHOUSE*.

FOOD
Those spending the night here will probably choose to eat at their guesthouse. Good cake is served at the *JOJO COFFEESHOP,* snacks can be bought at the night market foodstands, just beyond. You can sit out on the terraces of the *RESTAU-RANTS* at the bridge and watch the border traffic.

LEAVING MAE SAI
Regular buses leave for CHIANG RAI (15 Baht) via BAN HUI KRAI (turn-off to Doi Tung, 5 Baht), BAN PHA SANG (turn-off to Mae Salong, 8 Baht), and MAE CHAN (turn-off to Chiang Saen, 8 Baht).

Buses to CHIANG SAEN cost 15 Baht (you will probably have to get off before Mae Chan, at the turn-off, and then wait for the Chiang Saen bus). You will only be able to get to SOB RUAK (Golden Triangle) via Chiang Saen if you want to get there by bus. There are 3 daily ac buses to CHIANG MAI (83 Baht). There is a direct bus to BANGKOK at 16:30 h (169 Baht), as well as 5 ac buses between 8:00 and 17:30 h (305 Baht).

EXCURSIONS FROM MAE SAI
Mae Sai is another good place for setting off on excursions to Mae Salong (68 km), to the Doi Tung (37 km), to Chiang Saen (66 km), and to the Golden Triangle (77 km, 33 km with a motorcycle).

Information concerning nice hikes is available at the guesthouses, e.g. to the Akha village of BAN PHAMI. Find out about the current border situation - sometimes it can be quite dangerous. You may find yourself in a whole lot of trouble, should you cross the border to Burma by mistake.

KHUNNAM NANG NON
This cliff formation, surrounded by a wonderful countryside full of shady trees and crystal clear water, is said to resemble a sleeping woman. The 'Sleeping Lady' lies approx. 2 km west of the main road (H110), almost 13 km from Mae Sai.

THAM PLA CAVES / PHYANAK LAKE
The large THAM PLA CAVE is approx. 1 km south of Khunnam Nang Non. You can reach the cave by way of a well-built staircase. The PHYANAK CAVE and the PHYANAK LAKE (a reservoir) are only a couple of hundred metres from here.

Four newly discovered caves can be explored north of Khunnam Nang Non. You will be able go down the passages of the largest of these stalactite caves, THAM LUANG, for a total of 2 km if you are well equipped.

CHIANG SAEN

It is thought today that Chiang Saen must have been built around 1325, most probably on the site of an even earlier town, which must have been very significant during the period of Thai migration south. Several Thai army commanders had reached the Mekong valley by 750 A.D., and many areas surrounding present-day Luang Prabang and Vientiane had already come under their control. One of them, Chaiyapongse, moved to present-day northern Thailand and was probably responsible for having founded Chiang Saen. The city was destroyed between 1000 and 1100, either by the Khmer or by a particularly serious earthquake. Ancient chronicles dating back to 1328 tell of how Chiang Saen was re-founded in 1325. It was then put under the sovereignty of the Lanna Thai kings, who resided in Chiang Mai.

Chiang Saen is northeast of Chiang Rai. Today it is a quiet, peaceful market town. Neighbouring Laos can be seen on the other side of the Mekong river. The 1000-year history of the town has been subtly integrated into the architecture. Parts of the ancient town wall as well as ruins of former temples can be

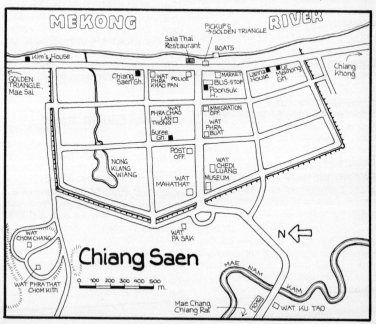

seen standing unobtrusively next to modern-day buildings and gardens. *WAT CHEDI LUANG* with its 58 metre, octagonal chedi is beautifully set in a tree-studded park. The pyramid-shaped *WAT PA SAK* (admission 20 Baht!!) is just outside the western town gate. It looks splendid when seen from the west, too. You will be able to climb the 300 steps to the *WAT PHRA THAT CHOM KITTI* and enjoy the splendid view of the town, the Mekong, and the plain, if you walk north up the path next to the town wall.

You will also find the *MUSEUM* at the western town gate, open daily from 8:30-12:00 and 13:00-16:00 h, closed on Mon and Tues. You will be able to look at a most impressive collection of typically Chiang Saen style Buddha figures here, as well as several other cultural heirlooms.

GUESTHOUSES
Walk straight on towards the river from the bus station, then turn right onto the embankment road. You will reach the *LANNA HOUSE**, 39 Rim Khong Road, on the right hand side after 300 metres; wooden bungalows and a dormitory; hot showers and a restaurant.

LE MEKONG* is just a little further on, also separated from the river by the busy road. If you turn north from the embankment road, in contrast, you will reach the

CHIANG SAEN GUEST HOUSE* behind the Wat Phra Khao Pan; simple rooms, nice restaurant, no view of the river, however. There have been a few complaints concerning the owners in recent times. The pretty

KIM HOUSE* is at the riverbank, approx. 1 km further upstream; simple rooms, dormitory, bungalows, restaurant, information, and bicycles.

You will find the *SUREE GUEST HOUSE** in town, a modern building behind the post office, on the right. The friendly owner is a good cook, bicycles for tours into the surrounding areas are available.

Just follow the signs from the bus station in order to reach *SIAM GUEST HOUSE**. The *POONSUK HOTEL** on the main road is not commendable.

FOOD
The *SALA THAI RESTAURANT* is beautifully located above the Mekong. The food isn't too bad, either, and the prices are okay considering the setting (there are also bicycles for rent here). You can buy cheap, excellently prepared Thai meals in the market hall.

LEAVING CHIANG SAEN
Buses to CHIANG RAI or MAE SAI (you will usually have to change at the turn-off in front of Mae Chan) cost 15 Baht. It is said that the Mekong boat rides to CHIANG KHONG - which had stopped for a long time - are now running again. You can charter a boat of your own for 3000 Baht. Minibuses to Sob Ruak, the Golden Triangle, leave from next to the Sala Thai Restaurant at the Mekong (10 Baht, until 17:00 h).

You can also get there by boat from here (30 Baht return).

EXCURSIONS FROM CHIANG SAEN

You will be able to rent bicycles for around 25 Baht a day at the guesthouses. Motorcycles can be rented by the hour at the Chiang Saen GH. Make sure they are in a good running condition before renting one.

CHIANG SAEN LAKE

Beautiful sunsets at the lake. Good food is served at the YONOK right by the lake; bungalows** with individual bathrooms, boats for rent. The path leading to the lake branches off from the H1016 in BAN KU TAO.

WAT PHRA THAT PHA NGAO

Drive south along the Mekong river for a good 4 km; you will see a modern, 'bunker-style', concrete chedi measuring approx. 30 metres in height upon a hill to the right. The chedi, which has four bastions, was built by an American architect. You can walk through the WAT PHRA THAT PHA NGAO along an uphill, tarred path, past a small chedi artfully built upon a large, round rock. You will have a wonderful view of the Mekong and Laos beyond from the top of the hill. The modern chedi encloses an ancient brick chedi as well as a Chiang Saen Buddha made of bronze.

CHIANG KHONG

Few pick-ups drive along the Mekong to Chiang Khong. Should you be planning to get there by motorcycle via NAM YEN, you might be held up by the Kuomintang soldiers (or were they Thai?) who control all the crossroads. There is a hotel* on Chiang Khong's main road.

It used to be possible to catch a boat over to the village of BAN HOUEI SAI (Laos) before 1975. You can see the village lying on the opposite riverbank.

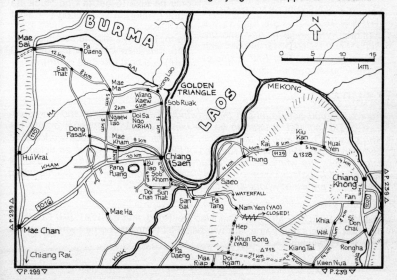

GOLDEN TRIANGLE (SOB RUAK)

The prestige of the notorious Golden Triangle, an area covering several hundred square miles and in which roughly three quarters of the world's opium is produced, has been concentrated into one single point on the map for tourists: the triangle made up of Laos, Burma, and Thailand at the point at which the Mae Sai river (Ruak river) merges with the Mekong. This picturesque, formerly peaceful settlement has recently become almost absurdly popular. Don't come expecting to find poppy growing out of every nook and cranny - you'll find souvenir stands, guesthouses, and restaurants instead. The town quiets down in the late afternoon, and you will be able to spend a relaxing evening on a restaurant terrace with a bottle of Mekong, gazing down upon the river of the same name.

GUESTHOUSES
The guesthouses are all quite close to one another. New ones are being built all the time. We would suggest checking them out one by one and then making your selection. The *GOLDEN HUT**, the first guesthouse, stands alone at the river mouth of the Mae Sai river, just a stone's throw from Burma.

You will find the *GOLDEN TRIANGLE GUEST HOUSE** right next to the memorial. We would recommend the *GOLDEN LODGE*** for people with higher standards. The *KN** is one of the new guesthouses in town.

You will find the *THAM CHAT VILLAGE CENTER** 6 km northwest of the village, at the road leading to Mae Sai, in Wiang Kaew; simple rooms, food made to order; Akha and Yao villages nearby.

HOW TO GET THERE
If you don't have a motorcycle you will only be able to get to Sob Ruak via Chiang Saen. If you spend the night in Chiang Saen you can rent a bicycle for the day's trip the next morning. You can also catch a minibus (10 Baht) or a boat (30 Baht return).

LAMPANG

Approx. 50,000 people inhabit this provincial capital, which is 100 km southeast of Chiang Mai. It used to be the centre of a Mon kingdom before the Khmer and Thai came to this region. Remains of Hindu stucco-works have been excavated here. All that remains of the former town wall is an octagonal brick tower. The white, earthen ceramics from Lampang, which are usually subsequently painted blue or brown, are well known. Pretty, duck-shaped teapots are particularly popular at the present time.

The *WAT SI RONG MUANG*, Tha Krao Noi Road, and the *WAT SRI CHUM* in the road of the same name, are two beautiful temples adorned with Burmese style wood-carvings.

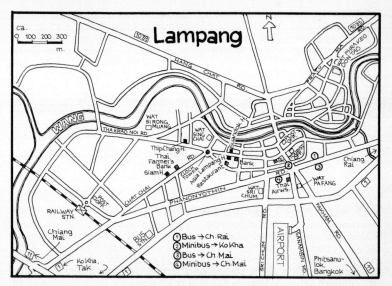

You will find one of the most beautiful temples of northern Thailand just a few km from Lampang. The *WAT PHRA KAEO DON TAO* is on the right hand bank of the Wang river, 1 km northeast of the central Rasada Phisek Bridge. The famous Emerald Buddha of the Royal Temple in Bangkok used to be kept here. You will be able to see a mighty chedi, a splendid Burmese style chapel, and a beautiful Thai style temple. There is also a small museum in the temple grounds. The 'temple of the 20 chedis', *WAT CHEDI SAO,* is 3 km further northeast from here, surrounded by paddies; it is particularly beautiful during the rainy season, when the rice glows a lush green.

You will have to plan a longer outing in order to get to Lampang's most famous temple, the *WAT PHRA THAT LAMPANG LUANG* (see below).

HOTELS

There are several cheap hotels on Boonyawat Road, e.g. the *SRI SA-NGA*,* no. 213, tel 217070; cheap double rooms with lav/shower. You will find the *ASIA LAMPANG*** (ac***), no. 229, tel 217844, by the large roundabout with the clock tower; generally for people with higher standards; restaurant.

THIP CHANG***, 54/22 Thakrao Noi Road, tel 218222, beyond the clock tower, on the extension of Boonyawat Road; this is Lampang's no. 1 place, with ac, pool, coffee shop, and a restaurant. The *LAMPANG**,* 696 Suan Dok Road, tel 217311, is also in the centre of town, while the *SIAM**,* 260 /29 Chat Chai Rd., tel 217472 is a little further out of town, towards the railway station.

LEAVING LAMPANG
BY PLANE
Thai Airways Office: 314 Sanam Bin Road, tel 217078. Flights to PHIT-SANULOK (430 Baht) and PHRAE (140 Baht) depart on Tues and Thur.

BY TRAIN
Bicycle rickshas and horse-drawn carriages (rather unusual for Thailand) are the main forms of public transport in Lampang. Minibuses within the city limits cost 3 - 6 Baht. A train (the station is definitely worth visiting!) to CHIANG MAI costs 25 Baht (3rd class only runs early in the mornings, at 4:14 and 5:21 h, 2nd class directly to Chiang Mai at 6:34 h). A train to PHITSANULOK or directly to BANGKOK will cost 221 Baht 2nd class, 3 trains per evening.

BY BUS
The bus station is far in the southeast of town. Good connections to CHIANG MAI 25 Baht, TAK 40 Baht, CHIANG RAI 50 Baht, PHITSANULOK, and SUKHOTHAI. There are nine daily buses to BANGKOK (115 Baht, ac 207 Baht).

EXCURSIONS FROM LAMPANG
WAT PHRA THAT LAMPANG LUANG
This temple, one of the most beautiful in northern Thailand, is 18 km southwest of town, on the right hand side of the Wang river. Take a minibus from the centre of Lampang to KO KHA (10 Baht). Once there, walk 3 km (turn right beyond the bridge) to the monastery (motorcycle taxi 10 Baht, minibus 2-3 Baht, very rare, though). If you're coming on a motorcycle from Chiang Mai on the H11, you can turn right towards KO KHA at km stone 13. From here it's 12 km south on the H1034. If you're coming up the H1 from the south, turn left between km stones 587 and 588. It's another 5 km to the temple from here.

The WAT PHRA THAT LAMPANG LUANG is at least 1300 years old. It lies slightly elevated, surrounded by a strong wall - the temple used to be used as a fort. You will have to enter left of the main gate, between the two modern Chinese temples. Many posts donated by the faithful support the branches of the Bodhi tree, thus preventing them from breaking off. There is an emerald Buddha said to be of the same material as the much more famous emerald Buddha in Bangkok (i.e. jade) in the museum at the end of the first courtyard; numerous other Buddha statues are exhibited rather unattractively.

The inner courtyard is dominated by a 45 metre chedi. Six viharn and chapels, some with beautifully carved facades, contain Buddha statues and splendid relic-shrines. Most of them are between 500 and 700 years of age.

You will easily be able to spend a couple of hours here, should you be into temples. The brochure entitled "The history of..." (10 Baht) is unfortunately rather lacking. Admission (donation): 5 Baht.

ELEPHANT TRAINING CENTRE
The training centre for young elephants is 54 km northeast of Lampang. You will have to turn off the Chiang Rai-bound H1 to the west between km-stones 655 and 656; walk down the path for 1,5 km. Approx. a dozen young elephants are trained for their future forest-work in a beautiful valley basin, by a brook.

WAT SI RONG MUANG, LAMPANG

The elephant calves are between 3 and 5 years of age when they first come to this centre. What follows is a five-year period of education and training, in which they learn how to walk next to each other as well as behind each other, to roll, pull, and pile up tree trunks, and - overall - to obey their 'mahout'. An elephant is worth 100,000 Baht after it has gone through this training course. The whole thing is organized by the Forestry Industry Organization (FIO). There aren't nearly as many on-looking tourists here as there are in the training centres near Chiang Mai. The performances are very interesting and a lot of fun, especially when very young calves are among the elephants.

The elephants are 'taught' between 9:00 and 11:00 h daily, except for Buddhist holidays, those days on which a half or a full moon will follow, and the dry season from March to May. Buses to the village of BAN PANG LA (we would suggest getting off at the signpost) leave Lampang from 6:15 h (17 Baht, 90 min.). A taxi from Lampang will cost you approx. 300 Baht. Market women sell bananas and sugar cane, with which you can feed the pupils, at the parking lot.

If you've come by motorcycle, why not continue on to the THAM PHA THAI cave. Wonderful light effects dance about on the huge stalagmite in the hall at the end of the 400 metre cave between 10:00 and 13:00 h. Continue along the

H1 until just past km stone 665 and then turn left into the forest path. You will reach the 336 steps leading up to the cave after only 800 metres.

A working elephant's life		
1-2	*years:*	*the calf lives with its mother*
3-5	*years:*	*first training experiences*
6-10	*years:*	*second period of training in a training centre*
11-15	*years:*	*easy forest work*
16-38	*years:*	*hard labour begins*
39-50	*years:*	*extremely hard labour*
51-60	*years:*	*easier work*
61	*years:*	*FIO elephants officially retire, i.e. each elephant gets a personal 'mahout' with whom it spends the rest of its life.*

DOI KHUNTAN NATIONAL PARK

You will only be able to reach the 225 km^2 -sized park by train. We would suggest taking the 5:21 from Lampang or the 15:20 from Chiang Mai, which arrive at the small station of KHUNTAN at 6:22 and 16:38 h respectively. You can spend the night at one of the bamboo park bungalows (for 5-10 people, 200-1200 Baht) or at the railway bungalows, which can be booked in advance at the Thai Railway in Chiang Mai or Bangkok. There are also several camping grounds. You will have to bring your own tents and supplies, though. Many people come at the weekends, we would recommend coming during the week.

The temperature sometimes drops below 5^{0}C from November - February; there are heavy rains from May to October.

A 1.3 km path leads up to the park HQ from the railway station. Once there, it's another steep 2.5 km to the bungalows. By this time you will already have become aware of the peace and quiet of the mountains, the cool, clean air, and the wonderful view of the surrounding hills and valleys. A 1/2 day outing leads through 5 km of evergreen monsoon-rainforest before reaching the bare peak of the Doi Khuntan - marvellous view. Few large, wild animals are ever seen.

EXCURSIONS FOR ADVENTURERS ON MOTORCYCLES (UNVERIFIED!)
JAE SON and WANG KAEW WATERFALLS

Drive approx. 52 km north along the H1035, then turn west beyond MUANG PAN. You will soon reach the WATERFALL and the HOT SPRINGS of JAE SON; the 80^{0}C are enough to boil eggs in. BAN WANG NUA is by km stone 92 on H1035; from here you will be able to reach the WANG KAEW WATERFALLS, considered to be Thailand's most beautiful cascades (110 steps). You will reach the H1019, the new road from Chiang Mai - Chiang Rai, beyond Wang Nua.

INACTIVE VOLCANO CHAMPA DAD
Start off by driving southeast for 10 km along H11, then turn left towards MAE HOH; turn left at the signpost after another 6 km. From here you can hardly miss the crater, which is 200 metres above. You can climb to the edge of the crater and see the thick forest which is now growing inside.

BROWN COAL OPEN-PIT MINE BY MAE MOH
You will find a gigantic pit from which brown coal is extracted a good 10 km towards MAE MOH - very impressive with excavators' shovels holding up to 11m^3, trucks that can carry up to 85 tons, and conveyer belts with a capacity of 1200 tons per hour. 20,000 tons of brown coal are brought to a power plant of 825 megawatt daily. This plant, in turn, supplies the provinces of Lampang, Chiang Mai, Lamphun, and Tak with electricity. Smaller quantities of coal are also brought to a nearby fertilizer factory.

KEW LOM RESERVOIR
One is said to be able to go on boat rides on this reservoir and spend the night at the bungalows*** of a nearby resort. Drive down the H1 towards Chiang Rai and turn west shortly before km stone 624 (14 km).

MAE WANG CAMP
This 'jungle resort' on both banks of the Wang river is approx. 60 km south of Lampang, 1500 metres to the right of the H1. It has been recommended to us on numerous occasions, but we were unfortunately never able to check it out. Floating huts, bungalows, and tents are said to be available. You can go for walks in the bamboo- and teak forests.

PHAYAO

Lying 87 km south of Chiang Rai, this small provincial capital lies on the banks of a reservoir measuring 6 km in length and 4 km in width. The mountain-range beyond rises to an altitude of 1700 metres. There are many fish and water lilies in the shallow lake. The lake's water-level rises so drastically during the rainy season that many of the surrounding fields and even parts of town are flooded. Tourists hardly ever come here.

There are two old temples which are worth a visit. The *WAT LUANG RATCHA SANTHAN* is near the market, opposite the Bangkok Bank. Its two chedis are said to have been built in the 12th century, and the viharn, which is supported by huge teak columns, is also very old.

You will be able to see a 13 metre Buddha, more than 400 years old, in the *WAT SI KHO KHAM*. A garden of statues is just beyond; you will find representations of hell, Buddha, two dinosaurs, and even E.T. here.

HOTELS
There are three hotels in town, the largest of which is *THAN THONG** (ac***), 57 Donsanam Road. The *WATTANA*-** is right next door. You will find the *CHALERMSAK** directly by the minibus terminal. There are many prostitutes at all of the hotels. Several restaurants on the banks of the lake.

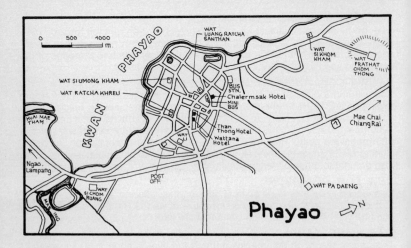

Phayao

HOW TO GET THERE

Phayao is on the Lampang - Chiang Rai road. Buses from CHIANG MAI via Lampang take 5 hrs. and cost 50 Baht.

Buses to BANGKOK depart at 8:00 and 20:00 h (140 Baht). There is an ac bus at 20:15 h (254 Baht).

NAN

The small kingdom of Nan was founded in the 13th century, the town itself in 1368. The kingdom managed to remain semi-autonomous up until 1931 due to the clever policy exercised towards its mighty neighbours by the ruling dynasty.

The present-day provincial capital of Nan is on the right hand bank of the Nan river. Small bridges lead across floating islands. Ox-drawn carts are loaded with water plants at the river's banks.

Nan is actually only of interest to temple freaks. The famous *WAT PHUMIN* was built in 1596 and completely restored in the late 19th century. It is in the centre of town. You will easily recognize it by the four orange lions upon its main entrance. The cross-shaped temple seems to be supported only by the unusually beautiful snakes and the staircases leading up to it. It contains a central relic-shrine with four Buddha statues. The old, partially faded murals depict interesting scenes out of everyday life. The doors are made of beautifully carved wood. Everything seems just right in this temple; no kitsch has been added. A 40 metre, white prang towers above the *WAT SUAN TAN* at the northern end of town. The temple enshrines an impressive Sukhothai style Buddha statue.

You will find the *WAT PHRA THAT CHAE HAENG* 2 km beyond the bridge, hidden behind tall trees on top of a hill. The elegant *CHEDI* in the inner courtyard is covered with fine sheets of copper. There is a a wonderful view of the area from the mountain of the *WAT PHRA THAT KHAO NOI,* 2 km west of the centre. You will pass *WAT PHAYAWAT* with its small, pyramid shaped chedi along the way.

You can get a good idea of the town and its history at the *MUSEUM,* which is in the centre of town, in a palace that was erected in 1903 (captions given in English, too).

Thousands of swallows settling down for their night's rest on the power lines in front of the Dhevaraj Hotel present a dizzying spectacle every evening, just before dusk.

HOTELS
The *DHEVARAJ* ** (ac***), 466 Sumondhevaraj Road, is the best hotel in town; singposted in English; slightly shabby rooms; good restaurant. The *NAN FA* * is right next door, no 438-440; very simple, in a restaurant. Go left around the corner, then turn right at the next crossroads:

AMORN SRI *, 97 Mahayot Road. Continue on a little further. The

SUK KASEM ** on the unpronounceably named street is right next to the cinema, diagonally across from the market; large lounge and bus schedules.

FOOD
There are many restaurants on the modern roads in the centre of town. The restaurant in the *DHEVARAJ* is open from 18:00 h. The 'green restaurant' by the crossroads in front of the Amorn Sri Hotel is also commendable. Many foodstands open for business opposite the Suk Kasem Hotel in the evening.

GENERAL INFORMATION
INFORMATION - Hardly anyone speaks English in Nan. An employee at the Dhevaraj was able to give us some information concerning outings.

FESTIVAL - Many teams from the surrounding villages enter their long, narrow boats in the annual LANNA BOAT RACES; they will be held from Oct. 5-11 in 1988.

HOW TO GET THERE
It's worth going to Nan by motorcycle. There's the beautiful countryside for one, the many possible excursions for another, all of which can be quite adventurous for those who do not speak Thai.

Drive the beautiful, hilly route to NGAO via LAMPANG from CHIANG MAI (with a motorcycle). Once there, turn off onto the lonely dirt road H1154; many small bridges, teak forests, piles of elephant dung, tobacco fields, and a nice river. Turn off onto the uninteresting H 1120 after having driven north for 46 km. Turn right onto the nice H1091 (unfortunately, the view is obliterated by the high elephant grass along the sides of the road) 4 km before reaching CHIANG MUAN.

There are 9 daily buses from CHIANG MAI between 8:00 and 17:00 h (80 Baht, 6 hrs.), as well as ac buses (100 Baht, 5 hrs). Most buses drive via PHRAE.

From CHIANG RAI: The province of Nan, which starts before THA WANG PHA can be reached via THOENG and CHIANG KHOM. The wild mountain route will lead you through teak forests and jungle. There are several hilltribe villages along the way, predominantly Yao. The costumes worn in the village of Ban Hua Feang are particularly beautiful. Local minibuses only drive along this route before noon (and very irregularly at that). There are two daily direct buses from CHIANG RAI (109 Baht, 6 hrs.).

LEAVING NAN
BY BUS
To CHIANG MAI via PHRAE: 8:00, 9:00, 10:00, 15:00, and 22:00 h (100 Baht, 6-7 hrs.). To CHIANG RAI: 9:00 h (100 Baht, 6 hrs.).

To SUKHOTHAI: 10 daily buses between 8:30 and 20:30 h. 7 non-ac buses leave town for BANGKOK between 7:00 and 20:30 h (140 Baht). Ac buses leave at 18:00 and 18:30 h (252 Baht).

Minibuses to SA and NA NOI as well as CHIANG KHOM and THOENG (from where you will be able to get to CHIANG RAI) leave from the local bus station in the east of town.

BY PLANE
Thai Airways Office: 34 Mahaprom Road, tel 710377. Daily flights (except for Tues and Thurs) to PHITSANU-LOK (480 Baht) and CHIANG MAI (380 Baht), both via PHRAE (190 Baht).

EXCURSIONS FROM NAN
SILA PHET WATERFALL
Head north to PUA along the H1080 (60 km). From here it's only 15 km to a beautiful cataract.

PHA THAM FOREST PARK
By H1080, approx. 12 km north. There are numerous caves in the park.

SAO DIN
Drive south down the H101 to SA (a minibus from the local bus station will cost you 6 Baht, 23 km), then turn off onto the H1026 to NA NOI (i.e. change buses - you are in for a beautiful, 36 km stretch). From here you can cover the remaining 5.6 km to SAO DIN on foot; take the path leading west beyond the police-station, turn left again after approx. 300 metres and keep going until you reach a village (1.6 km). Once there, turn left to the next village (800 metres) and then turn right at the fork in the road (you will also see a signpost here: "2.9 km"). Sao Din is a small, but very beautiful eroded valley. The washed-out, rather small cliff formations are reminiscent of the Bryce Canyon in Utah - many Thai films are filmed here. Similar valleys can be found all over the area. The largest - though not the nicest - is known as 'ghost-town' (PHAE MUANG PI). You will pass it on your way south from here, shortly before Phrae.

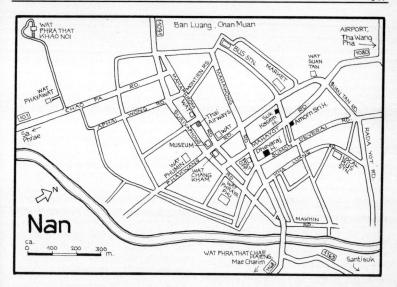

Nan

INTO THE SOUTH ALONG THE LAOTIAN BORDER

You'll be able to drive around the eastern end of the Sirikit reservoir along a dirt road from the SAO DIN valley near NA NOI with a car or motorcycle. Once you've passed the eastern end of the lake you'll be able to drive all the way south to UTTARADIT. Reckon with at least 5 hrs. of driving for this 162 km stretch.

The steep, uphill H1083 east will take you through a beautiful, lonely landscape to the first pass (16 km), over the Nan Bridge (km stone 30), through teak forests, and over two further passes. You will be able to make an outing to the Laotian border on the left (21 km from here) after 68 km. Continue to the right on the original road after this, and you will pass through a wide valley with many villages and fields. Another road turns off 11 km from here. Head down it and you will reach BAN KHOK at the border (23 km, you will probably even be able to drive all the way to LOEI in the northeast along H1268 and H2113). Head southwest along the incredibly dusty H1047 until it finally turns into a surfaced road again. From here it's 25 km to FAK THA. Keep going straight on for 46 km until you reach the point at which H1146 branches off.

At this point an excursion to the SAK YAI NATIONAL PARK with the thickest teak tree in the world might be worth considering. To get there, continue along the H1047 for another 6.7 km, then turn right onto a forest path (1.3 km) at the Thai signpost. The gigantic tree is said to be over 1000 years old. A storm blew off its crown 10 years ago, leaving the tree looking a little worse for wear, but it still continues to grow. The tree had a circumference of 987 cm in 1987.

You will reach the SIRIKIT DAM (in Thai: "Khoen Sirikit") by turning west onto H1146. You will reach the dam after 12 km of beautiful, hilly countryside. You will receive your permit for the dam at the first check-point. The next check-point is just 2,6 km further on, and from here it's just a short, uphill stretch to the top of the dam. The Sirikit dam, which is named after the Thai Queen, measures 800 metres in length and 113 metres in height. This makes it the largest earth bank in all of Thailand. Next to the production of electricity and irrigation, the dam is also used for fishing; several fishing villages on stilts lie on its wooded banks.

ACCOMMODATION

A 900 metre, uphill road (turn right twice) beyond the first check-point leads to the four bungalows of

LANG NO KA JOG**. Good double rooms with fan or ac, nicely set, restaurant nearby (should you not be able to handle the two boys here, you may have to continue for another 2 km to the Tourist Office on the other side of the river: "pai song thii pachaa samphan" - "I would like to get to the Tourist Office"). The rooms just below, in the

LANG NO KA JAB** terraced house, are a little cheaper, but you will probably not find them satisfactory after the long and tiring journey. You will be able to spend the night at the nice

THONG THA LA RESORT* on a 2-room raft for 30 Baht per person; fresh fish from the lake is served for dinner, and you can go fishing and swimming, too. To get here, take one of the 3 boats that leave from the dam (200 Baht, approx. 2 hrs). You can only make advance reservations at the Tourist Office by the river, which is also the place to go for information concerning two rather more expensive resorts**** at the lake.

The *SAMOSOON* restaurant is 1.2 km downstream from the Tourist Office.

HOW TO GET THERE

Buses travel back and forth between UTTARADIT and the SIRIKIT DAM from 6:00 to 17:00 h (10 Baht, approx. 1 hr.) - minibuses 30 Baht.

Continue along the H1045 and you will reach the north-south highway H11 after 41 km. From here it's approx. 215 km to CHIANG MAI, 110 km to PHITSANULOK.

You will reach UTTARADIT if you continue going straight on. The centre of town was completely destroyed by a fire in 1967. There are several places of interest in the vicinity, particularly for archeologists and temple-freaks, some of them only partially excavated. Ask how to get to Wat Phra Boromathat Thung Yang, Wat Phra Yun Phutthabat Yukhon, Wat Phra Thaen Sila-At (to the west), or Wat Don Sak (to the east).

There are buses from UTTARADIT to CHIANG MAI 49 Baht, 3 hrs., to SUKHOTHAI 20 Baht, 2 hrs. (via SI SATCHANALAI, 10 Baht), as well as buses to PHITSANULOK and BANGKOK.

NORTHEAST THAILAND

Ever since the border to Laos has been closed, few tourists travel to the north-east of the country, which is also known as Isan. A tour to Korat and Phimai might be the furthest the average traveller will venture; the wide highlands that stretch all the way to the border belong to the least visited areas of Thailand. The rather monotonous landscape has few sights as such to offer. The people living in the densely populated area are poor. The land regularly dries out during the dry period, only to be flooded again during the rainy period. Many forests that formerly helped regulate the area's water supply have now been cut down. These days an effort is being made to prevent further damage by building dams and initiating other water-regulation projects.

The inhabitants of Isan speak a Thai dialect very similar to the language spo-ken in Laos. The Khmer culture, which influenced this region for centuries, has left its mark - many statues and memorials are reminders of this period. Isan was the area with the most Communist guerilla activity in all of Thailand during the 60s and 70s. General Prem, the present Prime Minister, was the first to be able to check the communist activity through military and social action. When whole, armed units of the Communist Party gave themselves up to government troops in the early 80s, this made international headlines. Today the guerillas are no longer influential in the northeast.

Many inhabitants of Bangkok come from this, the poorest area of Thailand. Should you meet someone in the capital who speaks English and is prepared to take you home to the family, we would certainly recommend doing so; this may be a unique chance to gain some insight into the traditional, rural life of this region.

The US government helped pay for and construct the Friendship Highway No. 2, which leads to the northeast, and was built mainly for strategic reasons. The area bordering onto Laos was of great political significance during the Viet-nam war . Up until 1973, numerous American bases in this region helped con-siderably to boost the economy of the surrounding provincial towns. Many bomb attacks on Laos and Vietnam were launched from here.

The best time to travel to the northeast is after the rainy period has ended, in November/December. In all, there is less precipitation here than in the low-lands. Midday temperatures have been known to rise to 40ºC in the shade at the end of the dry period. Beware!

KORAT

Korat, officially called Nakhon Ratchasima, is the northeastern region's second largest town with 205,000 inhabitants. It constitutes an important centre of trade and traffic, connecting the northeastern highlands to Bangkok. This is where many US airbases were stationed. The numerous nightclubs and bars in the town remind one of this era. It was from here that General Prem orga-

nized the resistance against the officers who tried to overthrow the Thai government in April of 1981. The town is the first settlement found on the highlands when travelling north from Bangkok, and a good point from which to set off on various excursions.

In the centre of the old town one can still see the remains of the former *TOWN FORTIFICATION*. The former, rectangular town wall (its long sides 1700 metres in length, the adjacent sides 1500 metres), the moat, and several ruins within the fortification are relics of a period in the 8th-10th centuries when this was an important and influential town .

In front of the town gate, in between Ratchdamnoen and Chumphon Road, you will be able to see the

KHUNYING MO MEMORIAL (Thao Suranari). This woman led the forces responsible for repelling the Laotian invaders when most of the men of the region were at war against Burma. The bronze monument, which was erected in 1934, contains her ashes. The local inhabitants constantly decorate the memorial with wreaths of flowers and other sacrificial gifts. Khunying Mo remains a regional heroine to this day. The

MAHA WIRAWONG MUSEUM in the courtyard of the Wat Suthachinda has an interesting collection of Khmer art and objects of former eras. Open Wed - Sun 9:00-12:00 h and 13:00-16:00 h, admission fee 5 Baht.

HOTELS
There are some cheap hotels in the old town, e.g. *LUK MUENG***, 1925 Chumphon Road, tel 242837, *CHUMPHON***, 701 Pho Klang Road, tel 242453, *SRI SUA***, 809 Suranari Road, tel 243321, or the *MUANG THONG**, 1302 Chumphon Road, tel 242090, a wooden building. The largest hotel in the area lies a little out of town, *SRI PATTANA****, 346 Suranari Road.; tel 242833, ac, restaurant, nightclub.

FOOD
The extremely popular *VIETNAM VETERANS CLUB* is downstairs in the Siri Hotel, Phoklang Road - you will find excellent western food and a real pub atmosphere.

GENERAL INFORMATION
The **TOURIST OFFICE** can be found at the highway, shortly before the road leading to the centre of town branches off. Address: 53/1 - 4 Mukmontri Road, tel 243427 and 423751. A giant swimming pool is right next door. There is also a smaller information office at the station in town, where a map with all bus lines and hotels can be bought. If you want more general information concerning the northeast, however, we would definitely recommend going to the official, main office, even though it may be a little out of the way. (Take bus no. 2.)

BUSES - there are four main lines in town. In addition, bicycle rickshas are a popular form of transport.

LEAVING KORAT
BY BUS
Local buses leave the bus terminal in the northwest of town. Buses to PAK CHONG (Khao Yai National Park - 2

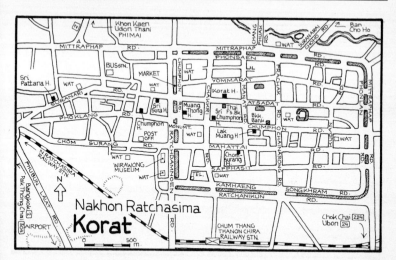

hour ride) leave every 20 minutes, cost: 20 Baht. The last bus leaves at 16:00 h. Buses to CHOKCHAI every 20 minutes for 6 Baht, last bus: 19:30 h. Buses to PHIMAI (14 Baht) leave every half hour, as do buses to Surin (3 hrs.; 33 Baht) and several buses that travel along the Highway no. 2: to KHON KAEN (2 1/2 hours; 39 Baht), UDON THANI (3 1/2 hours; 43 Baht), NONG KHAI at the border to Laos (4 hours; 60 Baht), YASOTHON (54 Baht), and CHAIYAPHUM (27 Baht). Regular buses to Bangkok (256 km) cost 51 Baht, ac buses usually leave from the company offices (for the most part in Chumphon Road), cost: 92 Baht, 3 hours. There are also buses headed for the east coast, e.g. RAYONG (4 hours; 50 Baht).

BY TRAIN
The northeastern railway line from BANGKOK to NONG KHAI also passes Korat (104/50 Baht - 2nd/3rd class). The Thanom Chira station is more central than the Korat station. Long distance trains rarely stop here, however. The railway offers good connections to KHON KAEN, UDON, and NONG KHAI, though buses are faster and better. The other train line running through Korat leads east. As the roads here are not too good, we would recommend taking a train if you're heading for SURIN or UBON.

EXCURSIONS FROM KORAT
BAN DAN KWIEN
Rust-coloured, red clay earth which is used for pottery can be found at the river near this village. The beautiful objects made from it are exhibited at the sides of the road and are for sale. You can hardly miss the village. You will find an exhibition of 100 Asian carts and a collection of wood turning to the right of the village entrance.

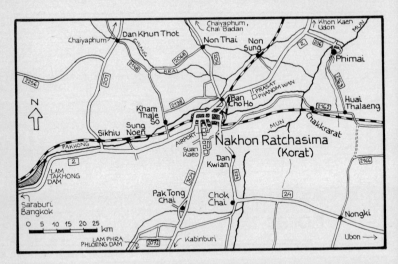

Take one of the buses that leave for CHOKCHAI every 15 minutes. You'll be able to watch the potters at work 15 km behind Korat, at Road no. 24. Beautiful vases, stools, tiles, and lamp shades are made here with the simplest of tools before being baked in kilns. Most of the objects are too heavy and large to be taken home as souvenirs, though.

PAK THONG CHAI

Buses headed to this silk-weaving village leave Korat every 30 minutes till 20:00 h, cost: 9 Baht. It takes approx. 1 hour to cover the 35 km stretch. You will find most of the silk weavers in the following street: take the second road left after the telephone station, then turn left again. Here you will find women weaving the hand-spun and -coloured silk to colourful materials on their old weaving looms. It takes them a long time to finish one metre of silk material patterned with the traditional rhombic design, and the price of 150 Baht per metre is definitely fair. In many cases you will find that the small family businesses only manufacture materials intended for special, festive clothing, which have to be ordered weeks in advance. If you want to buy some silk yourself, you'd be better off shopping at the larger businesses, to the right of the main road. Here modern weaving looms are used. There are also two hotels (*) in the village.

PHIMAI

Several Khmer ruins dating back to the 11th - 13th centuries were discovered in and around this small town, among them the large
PRASAT HIN PHIMAI, one of the most beautiful Khmer temple grounds in the country, which has been restored to its former splendour. At the time when it

was built, the Khmer had extended their sphere of influence well into the west. The Buddhist-Hindu temple grounds are proof of the fact that Phimai must have once been an important Khmer centre. The monumental Angkor Wat in present-day Kampuchea was probably modelled on this temple. The central prang, which symbolizes the sacred mountain and the seat of gods, can be reached from all four cardinal points by way of four paths. These in turn can be reached by way of four entrances in the rectangular wall which surrounds the sacred grounds. The temple is open from 7:30-17:00 h, admission 20 Baht.

Some of the discoveries made here as well as some beautiful pieces of stone masonry are exhibited in the small

MUSEUM opposite the temple grounds at the main road. It is open daily from 8:30-16:30 h, admission 20 Baht. One of the country's most beautiful

BANYAN TREES (ficus benjamini) can be found near the town. Its incredible amount of foliage, branches, and aerial roots make an impressive sight. Take the road towards Korat and turn right 400 metres after the bridge. After a further kilometre and a narrow bridge across a storage lake you will already be able to see the huge tree from afar. A small temple stands beneath its enormous roof of leaves. You will find several foodstalls under a corrugated iron roof opposite.

Rellevos: 1. Dancing Lopburi Buddha; 2. Rama and monkeys fighting with Rawana (Ramayana); 3. Paying tribute to Budha; 4. Rama and Laksamana bound (Ramayana); 5. Buddha on lotus lake; 6. Buddha with many heads and arms dancing on top of an elephant, many Buddhas, women, and priests (tantric Mahayana Buddhism); 7. Chariot; 8. Buddha with many heads and arms, further Budhas, women dancers; 9. Cart, dancing Buddha; 10. Buddha receiving gifts; 11. Chariot, battle scene.

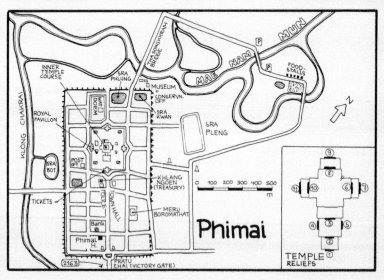

Phimai

HOTEL
You can spend a night at the *PHIMAI HOTEL***, 305 Nakhon Ratchasima Road, tel 471689.

HOW TO GET THERE
Take a bus from KORAT for 14 Baht. Buses leave every half hour and take 60-90 min. for the 55 km stretch.

PRASAT HIN KHAO PANOM RUNG

Various temple ruins dating back to the Khmer period can be viewed between Korat and Surin. The temple grounds near Road 24 between Prakhon Chai and Nang Rong are the most well-known. Nang Rong itself has nothing to offer apart from a pretty temple and three hotels. Noodle soup and the local speciality - pig's trotters - are served in the restaurants. The two temple grounds are 26 and 34 km out of town.

PRASAT HIN KHAO PANOM RUNG, which can be found on the mountain of the same name, is another well-preserved reminder of the Khmer period. Admission: 20 Baht. There are several stalls selling food and drink at the entrance. A monumental staircase framed by two huge Naga snakes leads up to the sacred grounds. The fine relievo ornaments on the windows, doors, and ledges of the viharn as well as one large and one smaller prang are still extremely well preserved. Most of the themes depicted are taken from Hindu mythology. While one reckons that the temple grounds were built in the 12th century, the remains of a Hindu shrine probably dating back even further were discovered here during archeological excavations. It was most probably built during the Baphuan period (1010-1080). A further Khmer temple,

PRASAT HIN MUANG TAM (20 Baht admission), lies a little further east of Panom Rung.

HOTELS
You can spend a night in Nang Rong at any of the following hotels: *KA-SEMSUK**, tel 631039, *SANGUAN MID**, tel 631045, and *NANG RONG**, tel 631014, all three with showers and lavatories.

HOW TO GET THERE
Take a minibus for 5 Baht from NANG RONG to BAN TAPEK at the foot of the mountain. As minibuses only rare-

ly drive the remaining 7 km to the PRASAT HIN KHAO PANOM RUNG, we would suggest either renting a motorcycle (50 Baht) or walking.

In order to get to the PRASAT HIN MUANG TAM, head southwest down the narrow Road 2075 from Prakhon Chai. A road branching off (signposts!) will lead you to the ruins after a further 8 km. There is no public transport along this route.

SURIN

The 40,000 inhabitants of this provincial town, 450 km from Bangkok, experience an annual tourist invasion during the third weekend of November for the splendid

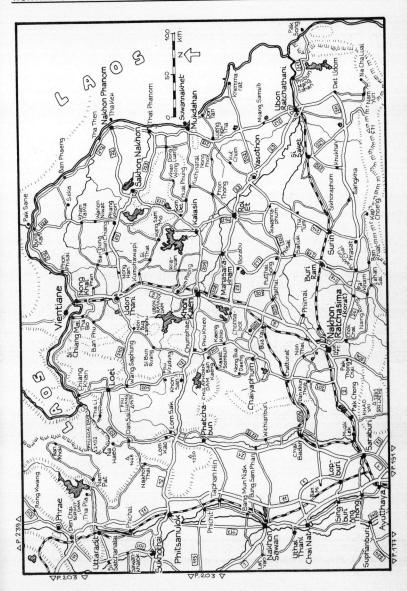

ELEPHANT ROUND-UP. Approx. 200 elephants are organized for this spectacle. They show off their strength and agility in parades and competitions. Few of these creatures are still used for carrying tree trunks out of the jungle. Most of them still have to work in the Surin area, though.

You will be able to observe some of these trained creatures at work in THATUM, 48 km north of Surin on the road to Roi-et. Over the last few years machines have been taking over the elephants, however, as the animals are unable to work during the dry period, when the heat becomes too intense. The best time to come here is between June and October.

HOTELS

Predictably, the entire town is booked up for the elephant round-up. You will have little hope of finding a room unless you're taking part in an organized tour . (A second round-up is said to be held in CHAYAPHUM in April - try to get information at the Bangkok Tourist Office!) During the rest of the year accommodation poses no problem in Surin. There are two ac hotels on Thanasarn Road, the *NEW HOTEL**** (no. 22), tel 511341 and the *SAENG THONG**** (no. 155-161), tel 512099. Two further hotels can be found on Krung Sri Road, the *KRUNG SRI**, no. 15/14, tel 511037 and the *ERAWAN**, no. 37, tel 511328, both non-ac.

HOW TO GET THERE

Many travel agencies offer organized tours for those wishing to witness the elephant spectacle in late November. During the rest of the year trains from BANGKOK to KORAT are best. A one way, 2nd class (3rd class) ticket costs 153 Baht (73 Baht). Two special diesel-trains headed for Surin leave BANGKOK at 10:55 h and 21:50 h daily. The ride takes 6-7 hours.

Buses from BANGKOK's Northern Bus Terminal drive directly to Surin (451 km) for 86 Baht (ac 155 Baht), departures: 11:00, 21:00, 21:30, and 22:00 h, from KORAT for 33 Baht.

CHAIYAPHUM

This provincial town, 342 km from Bangkok and north of Korat has little to offer apart from the daily

FRUIT AND VEGETABLE MARKET. 2 km north of town you'll find

PRANG KU, a Khmer ruin containing an old Buddha statue which is highly venerated by the local population. The asphalt road leading north ends after 21 km at

TAD TON, a small village which can be reached by minibus from Chaiyaphum for 5 Baht. From here you can also enter the National Park of the same name, no admission fee. There are several waterfalls 4 km from the park entrance. The largest is 40 metres wide and falls down a cliff. There are stalls selling drinks in the park, as well as three bungalows**-**** at which one can spend the night. Elephants can be observed at work.

HOTELS

The *PHAIBOON**, 227/40-4 Yutti-Dham Road, tel 811261 is an old Chinese hotel. If you would prefer an ac room, go to the *CHAROEN*** or the *SI RI CHA***, Nonmuang Road, tel 811543, in town. The rather expensive looking *LOERD NIMIT**-***** is opposite the bus station, 447 Nivesrak Road, tel 811523 (two-storey bungalows * with bathroom and fan).

HOW TO GET THERE

Buses from BANGKOK (332 km) cost 65 Baht, ac 117 Baht, from KORAT 27 Baht, BUA YAI (at the highway) 13 Baht, CHAT (nearest railway station) 8 Baht, CHUM PHAE 23 Baht, and from KHON KAEN 28 Baht.

KHON KAEN

This town is the capital of the province of the same name, frequently also called Isan. Because it lies near the point at which the Friendship Highway meets the National Road no. 12 from Tak / Phitsanulok (444 km from Bangkok), and has its own airport to boot, the city has become one of the most important centres of traffic in northeastern Thailand.

A number of prehistoric discoveries are exhibited in a

MUSEUM in Kasikorn Tungsang Road, a little out of town. They were found by archeologists excavating near Ban Chiang and in other areas of the Kalasin and Mahasarakham provinces. More recent pieces of art found in these areas are also exhibited here. Open Tue-Thu and Sat/Sun 9:00-17:00 h, closed across noon, admission 3 Baht.

4 km out of town you'll find the

UNIVERSITY with its large campus. Apart from these two buildings, the town has little to offer. The

SILK FEAST and the *FEAST OF FRIENDS* are celebrated at the end of November / beginning of December. Dances and processions are held, and the best local silk-weavings are exhibited.

Silk materials and other pieces of handicraft are offered for sale on the large square near the town hall. 10,000 Baht is the price for a piece of Mut Mee silk, which requires months of tedious work before it is finished. It is the favoured weaving technique of the women of CHONNABOT, 60 km

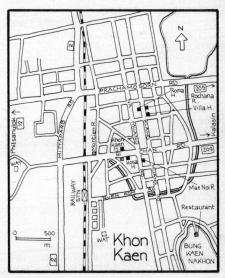

south of the town (see also *Art and Culture*). To get to this town, drive down the highway for 46 km until you reach Ban Phai, then continue west for a further 12 km. Women and children can be observed weaving silk here after the harvesting season has ended. You'll be able to reach the

UBON RATANA DAM, 26 km southwest of town. The 800 m long and 32 m high dam walls can hold up to 2550 million cubic metres of water in an area of more than 400 square kilometres. The power plant nearby supplies many provinces of the northeastern region with energy.

HOTELS

The *KHON KAEN*****, 43/2 Pimpasut Road, tel 237766 and the *KOSA****, 250 Srichan Road, tel 236014 are the top hotels in town. If you want something cheaper try *KHON KAEN BUNGALOW** (ac**), 75-81 Srichan Road, the *ROMA****, 50/2 Klang Muang Road, tel 236276, or the *SAWASDI***, 177-9 Na Muang Road, tel 236600. Simple, cheap rooms are available at the *GRAND**, ac**, 39 Soi Samaki Utid, Lan Muang Road, tel 236690.

HOW TO GET THERE

Various *buses* leave Bangkok daily for 153 Baht ac, 85 Baht non-ac (444 km). Buses from KORAT cost 39

Baht. The overland bus from SUK-HOTHAI takes 6 1/2 hrs. to cover the 365 km, cost 86 Baht, ac buses 155 Baht. Buses from NONG KHAI 35 Baht, LOEI 29 Baht.

There are also three daily *trains* from BANGKOK via KORAT, taking 9 hours and costing 162 Baht / 77 Baht for 2nd/3rd class.

You can get a seat on the daily *plane* from BANGKOK for 670 Baht. A plane to UBON costs 560 Baht from KHON KAEN, while non-stop flights to CHIANG MAI cost 1030 Baht (special flights twice weekly). The regular price is 1680 Baht. For information: Thai Airways office, 183/6 Maliwan Road, tel 236523.

UDON THANI

This town, lying close to the border to Laos, is an important centre of commerce in the northeast of the country. Many American soldiers were stationed here during the Vietnam war. Peace and quiet returned to the area when they were withdrawn by the US government in 1973 - many of the bars and night-clubs have since been closed down. Most of the night-club owners, by then rich, moved south to Bangkok, where, 15 years later, they are probably making even more.

HOTELS

There is a great supply of empty hotel rooms in Udon, a remnant of the American days gone by. The *KING***, 57 Pho Sri Road, has nice rooms, as does the *VICTORY*** in no. 60, ac, tel 221462. The *CHAIYAPORN***, 209-211 Mak Khaeng Road and the *SRI UDON***, 79-91 Amphoe Road, tel 221816, are similar. You will find the cheap *PARADISE*** near the bus station, 44/29 Pho Sri Road, tel 221956. The *CHAROEN***-*****, 549 Pho Sri Road, tel 211331, is the best hotel.

HOW TO GET THERE
Buses from BANGKOK (561 km, 7 hrs.) cost 106 Baht, ac 191 Baht. We would recommend stopping somewhere for the night, however, e.g. in KORAT. From here buses cost 43 Baht. There are also buses from NONG KHAI (12 Baht) or MUKDAHAN (38 Baht).

The three daily **trains** from BANGKOK take approx. 10 hours. A ride via KORAT and KHON KAEN costs 198 / 95 Baht, 2nd/3rd class.

While **planes** are fastest, they are also most expensive - 820 Baht via Khon Kaen. The plane continues to Ubon from Udon, cost: 700 Baht. Thai Airways, 60 Mak Khaeng Road, tel 221004.

There are two possibilities of getting to the north of Thailand from the northeast: Take a bus to UDON - LOEI (3 1/2 hours - 31 Baht). From here take a bus down the newly built road to LOM SAK (3 1/2 hours - 50 Baht), then catch one to PHITSANULOK (2 1/2 hours, 37 Baht). You can also take a bus directly to SUKHOTHAI.

EXCURSIONS FROM UDON THANI
BAN PHUE
You will reach a rocky landscape characterized by bizarre sandstone formations just beyond BAN PHUE, 65 km northwest of Udon, near the border to Laos. Buddha statues can be seen standing in and on some of the cliffs. Paintings dating back to prehistoric times are proof of the fact that this area was populated thousands of years ago.

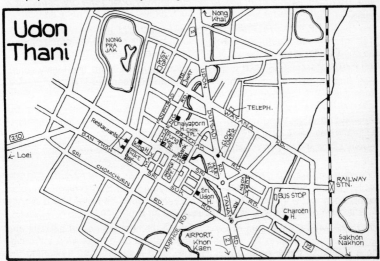

Several caves, among them THAM KON, surround the 30 m chedi of WAT PHRATHAT BUABOK on the mountain slope 8 km beyond BAN PHUE. Take a minibus from Ban Phue. A footpath will bring you to HOA NANG USA, grotesque looking eroded cliff formations, after a 30 minute walk. Even though a map has been posted up at the park entrance, the different footpaths are difficult to find. The monks of the monastery live far apart from each other in little cottages at various springs in the bamboo groves.

BAN CHIANG

The discoveries dating back furthest of all were made in the village of BAN CHIANG, 47 km east of Udon. The human bones that were discovered here by the local inhabitants were considered magical until an American decided to take a closer look at them in 1966. It was then realized that these bones were almost 7000 years old. Further excavations, carried out on a grand scale in the 70s, revealed fragments of clay, weapons, and other items of daily use. Many of the discoveries are exhibited in a small museum near the excavation sites. Buses from Udon to Ban Chiang cost 25 Baht.

NONG KHAI

Nong Khai lies 54 km north of Udon and used to lie en route to Vientiane, the capital of Laos, which is just 24 km away. These days the border to Laos is closed to foreigners, and tourists rarely visit this small town by the Mekong river. French and Laotian influences can be seen everywhere. You will have to walk down a massive staircase to reach the river during the dry period. It is incredible that the water should rise to such a level during the rainy season.

The chedi of *WAT PHRATHAT NONGKHAI*, which slid into the river in 1847, is proof of this fact. If you look carefully you'll be able to spot the stone spire of the chedi peeking out of the water in the middle of the river.

WAT PHO CHAI is the most well known temple in the area. The highly venerated Buddha statue Luang Pho Phra Sai can be seen here. An annual fireworks festival is held every April for the full moon.

WAT NERNPA NAO NARAM lies in a forest near the city limits, next to the highway. 60 monks and nuns live in this meditation centre. A large variety of fruits and vegetables are offered for sale at the

CHAIYAPORN MARKET. Silk and other materials of good quality are sold at the

NORTHEAST HANDICRAFT CENTER, also known as the *VILLAGE WEAVER.* Many Laotian girls work in this Catholic oriented self-help project. You can watch them weaving and tailoring in the back rooms. You can hire a bicycle ricksha for 3 or 5 Baht. We would recommend an excursion to

WAT GUGAEW, 4 km east of town. Strange, cement statues of animals and humans, reaching up to 20 metres in height, stand on a huge area surrounding a small fish pond. Among them you will see a serpent-god devouring the planet earth, ten-armed warriors with the heads of their enemies dangling from

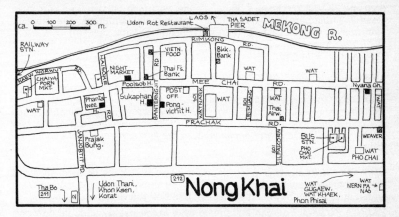

their hands, and a mob of dogs attacking an elephant - the dogs are strangest of all; there are hundreds of them, many looking strangely human, driving cars or motorboats, dressed as market women, wearing glasses, reading, smoking, drinking, carrying machine-guns, and proudly sporting erect penises.

HOTELS

The *NIYANA GUESTHOUSE**, 239 Meechai Road, tel 411919, offers the cheapest accommodation in town. It was extremely clean when it opened in 1987, but these things change rapidly... They will organize trips up and down the river and through the area for you. There is also a bicycle and moped rental service. The friendly people at the *SUKAPHAN**, Banterngjit Road, also rent bicycles. The *POOLSOB**, 843 Meechai Road, tel 411031, can be found near the river. The *PRAJAK BUNGALOWS*** (some of them ac), 1187 Prachak Road, tel 411116, near the bus station, are better. Walk down Hai Sok Road from here and you'll reach the *PHAN-TAWEE****, 1241 Haisoke Road, the best hotel in town. Vietnamese sate and fruit juices are sold at the corner of Banterngjit Road / Rimkhong Road.

HOW TO GET THERE

Nong Khai lies at the end of the Friendship Highway and the northeastern railway line, 616 km from Bangkok. Ac *buses* from BANGKOK cost 209 Baht and leave at 9:00, 21:00, and 21:30 h. Non-ac buses leave more often and cost 115 Baht. There are regular buses from UDON THANI for 12 Baht, from CHIANG KHAN for 20 Baht, from LOEI in the west for 65 and 70 Baht, from KORAT 60 Baht, PAK CHOM 50 Baht, NAKHON PHANOM 70 Baht, BAN PHU 30 Baht, BUNG KAN 30 Baht, and KHON KAEN 35 Baht.

The BANGKOK - SARABURI - KORAT - KHON KAEN - UDON - NONG KHAI express takes 11 hours and leaves Bangkok three times daily. Cost: 450 / 215 / 103 Baht for the 1st / 2nd / 3rd class (not including extra charge). A special diesel train leaves Bangkok at

8:20 and 22:30 h and takes 7 hrs. Road 212 runs parallel to the Mekong river until it reaches Chiang Khan in the west (see below), then continues far into the southeast via Nakhon Phanom (approx. 300 km).

CHIANG KHAN

This is a picturesque, peaceful border town on the banks of the Mekong river. You can enjoy a beautiful view of the river islands and Laos from the steep riverbanks. These days fishermen only rarely catch Pla Buk, a table-sized river fish which may weigh up to 220 kg. With a little luck you might be able to see the passenger ship chugging by on one of its infrequent trips to the new Laotian capital Viangchan (Vientiane) from the former royal city of Luang Prabang.

WAT SRI KHUN MUANG, a temple with a viharn built in the northern style and murals that were painted 80 years ago, can be found north of the market. 6 km further up the river, beyond the village of Ban Noi, you will reach the rapids,

KAENG KUDKU. You can eat shrimp cake in the nearby park, lie down on mats, and enjoy the beautiful view of Laos, its sandy banks, cliffs, and mountains. The fishermen cast out their nets from bamboo boats in the bend of the Mekong and will frequently let themselves drift along, dragging their nets behind them. Best time to be travelling here: February to March.

FROM CHIANG KHAN TO NONG KHAI

PAK CHOM
Buses to Nong Khai in the east cost 20 Baht and drive along the road running parallel to the Mekong - enjoy the interesting river landscape. Islands, sandbanks, and rapids develop during the dry period, when the water level sinks by 8 - 14 metres. Spend a night at the CHUMPEE GUESTHOUSE in PAM CHOK - a bus from Chiang Khan costs 15 Baht. The refugee camp BAN VINAI is nearby.

TAAN TIP
Continue east towards SANG KHOM and stop at the TAAN TIP waterfall after 14 km. The waterfall can be found 3 km from the road.

TAAN THONG
Halfway between SANG KHOM and SI CHIANG MAI you'll find a second waterfall, the TAAN THONG, which is 30 metres high and falls straight into the Mekong. The WAT HIN MAAK BENG can be found just beyond, in a bamboo forest on the steep, cliff riverbank.

SI CHIANG MAI
You can enjoy the best view of Laos from SI CHIANG MAI, approx. 40 km west of NONG KHAI. Hire a songthaew from town for 25 Baht.

WAT SIKHOM PHRA ONG DUE

This temple can be visited shortly before reaching THA BO. The wat contains a highly venerated 4 m Buddha statue dating back to the 17th century. Many pilgrims come here to see it. You can observe fishermen fishing with nets attached to 8 metre poles in the various small rivers of the area. Old water-wheels can be seen here, too.

WAT PHRA THAT BANGPUAN

Continue along the main road from here and you will reach WAT PHRA THAT BANGPUAN in the village of the same name, 10 km before the road meets Highway no. 2. The ruins of several chedis dating back to the 15th - 17th centuries can be seen in a small area just off the road. You will also find restored Buddha statues and the remains of a stupa here. There is a tiny museum inside the temple grounds. Many of the exhibits are even labelled in English. Minibuses to / from NONG KHAI via NONG SONG cost 8 Baht.

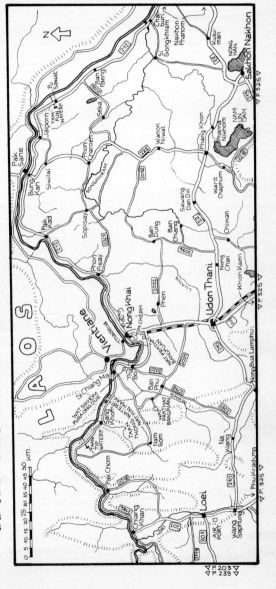

CHOM CHERM

The CHOM CHERM rapids are 10 km west of NONG KHAI. You can wade all the way to the middle of the river during the dry period - a good place for a swim.

LOEI

This small provincial capital with its 20,000 inhabitants lies in a mountainous area at the very edge of the northeastern region. The area generally resembles the north more than it does the northeast. A road from Udon Thani leads up to Loei. Small buses drive through the beautiful landscape from Loei (48 km) to CHIANG KHAN by the Mekong river for 16 Baht.

HOTELS

Spend a night at the *SRISAWAT** or the *SARAI THONG*-***, 25/5 Ruamchit Road, tel 811582. More ac hotels can be found in Charoen Rat Road, e.g. *THAI WANIT***, also known as *PHU LUANG,* no. 55, tel 811532 or the *THAI UDOM***, no. 122, tel 811763.

HOW TO GET THERE

A bus from UDON THANI costs 31 Baht, from NONG KHAI 65-70 Baht, KHON KAEN 29 Baht, from BANGKOK (560 km) 106 or 141 Baht (ac), departures: 9:00, 20:00, 21:00, 21:30, and 22:00 h. From SUK-HOTHAI, take a bus to LOM SAK, then change onto a bus to LOEI for 45 Baht. If you're coming from central Thailand and wish to go directly to the PHU KRADUNG NATIONAL PARK, the biggest attraction of the entire province, we would recommend taking a bus to CHUM PHAE for 72 Baht (5 hours). From here it's another 74 km to the park, 17 Baht for a bus. The park is 82 km from Loei.

Road no. 203 via Lom Sak and Dan Sai runs through breathtaking landscape.

EXCURSIONS FROM LOEI
THAM ERAWAN

Charter a songthaew to WANG SAPUNG, 23 km south of town. From here you can get to the stalactite cave THAM ERAWAN, 31 km further east - bizarre stalactites of all shapes and sizes, among them one resembling a life-size elephant. The natural cliff labyrinth SEMA HINSAY can be found near the villages of BAGBENG and NALANG, near the Loei river.

THA LI

You will be able to receive a good general impression of the mountainous border region whilst visiting THA LI. Buses from Loei cost 15 Baht. The road leading to Chiang Khan from here has been closed. The border to Laos runs 8 km further north, and Laotian influences can be noted everywhere. The trade channels between the two countries have by no means been closed; apart from the legally imported rice spirits, there are also quite a few illegal wares for sale in the back rooms of the shops. The 33 metre pagoda of the WAT PRATHAT SATDJA can be found 2 km out of the village. 7 km further on, in

AAHIE, you'll find the 900 year old MUANG DUHM, a totally secluded statue of Buddha with a Naga serpent.

PHU LUANG
This National Park was founded on top of a wooded plateau rising to a height of 1500 metres. Public transport rarely comes out this far, 47 km southwest of Loei. If you wish to visit the park, be sure to make arrangements beforehand, either in Bangkok or in the village of PHU LUANG, where you will find the administrative office of the park, tel 042 / 811776. You can spend some nights in small huts or tents. The PAPUANG cave, TONG TARN waterfall, and the many beautiful flowers found here make the park a place well worth a visit.

PHU RUA
This is another National Park, 30 km west of Loei, 95 km north of Lom Sak, and 4 km south of the connecting Road 203. Cotton fields and pine woods thrive on the red laterite ground - there are several vantage points from which to enjoy the view. One can either spend the night in a bungalow*** or on a camping ground*.

LOM SAK
You can spend a night at the HOTEL SAWANG* in Lom Sak. The well-built Highway no. 12 to Phitsanulok in the west runs over mountains that look rather barren due to the slash-and-burn agriculture favoured by local farmers. You'll reach the TUNG SALAENG NATIONAL PARK 64 km before Phitsanulok at kilometre stone 80. The park offers bungalows**** and a camping ground* by way of accommodation. Visit the KAENG SOPHA waterfalls in the forest. There is another national park, the NAM NAO NATIONAL PARK, 50 km east of Lom Sak near Highway 12. Here you can either stay at one of the 9 bungalows**** or pitch a tent for the night.

PHU KRADUNG

The mountains surrounding Loei are considered the coolest region in all of Thailand. Temperatures sometimes fall to below the freezing point in the cool months (November - January). During the hot season (March - May) temperatures in the lowlands have been known to rise above 40°C. An incredible variation of flora has developed in the 60 km² sized park - which stretches from the foot of a mountain to the very top of a raised plateau - due to this temperature fluctuation. The landscape often reminds one of Europe. While dry, deciduous monsoon forests dominate the lowlands, the plateau itself is characterized by pine, oak, and maple trees, whose leaves become a flaming red in March and April. At the same time the splendid foliage of rhododendron groves and azalea bushes (in the Suan Sawan), both of which thrive on the cliff walls, add a further note of colour to the beautiful park. Rare birds live here (hornbills, peacocks), as well as wild boars, sambar-deer, various monkeys, langurs, bears, and even a couple of wild elephants.

The steppe-like landscape of the 1500 m plateau is ideally suited for hiking. One of the most popular treks leads to various waterfalls - the vegetation in the river valleys is particularly beautiful. Other paths lead along the precariously steep cliff walls. There are several vantage points offering a breathtaking view of the valley below.

Dial 5790529 for the National Park Division of the Forestry Department for the Phu Kradung National Park.

ACCOMMODATION

You can spend the night in a tent for 40 Baht per person. Unless you have your own sleeping bag along, you will probably have to rent a blanket for the night. The park also offers 16 expensive bungalows****.

HOW TO GET THERE

Minibuses leave from LOEI and KHON KAEN in the early morning. Coming from LOEI or CHUM PHAE, you can also get off the bus at the point where the road leading to the park branches off. From here catch a share taxi to the park entrance, BAN SI THAN STATION (5 Baht - 8 km),

where you will find an information centre offering maps showing all hiking treks in the park. The park is closed during the rainy period, from June to September. During the rest of the year it is well visited, though; even people from Bangkok (444 km away) often come up here for the weekend. Getting to the Park HQ is no piece of cake - you will have to hike uphill for three hours. Leave your superfluous luggage at the information centre or hire a carrier for 5 Baht per kilo. After a 5.5 km hike - much of it up ladders and staircases - you will finally have reached the edge of the plateau. From here it is another 3 km to the HQ.

BUNG KAN

This small settlement by the Mekong river lies opposite the Laotian town of Pak Xan, which lies at the river mouth of the Nam Xan. The sandy riverbanks are put to agricultural use during the dry season, when vegetables are grown on them. The youths of the village meet here in the evenings for a drink. The settlement has little to offer in way of sights apart from the clock-less clock tower at the roundabout. Many fishermen can be watched fishing from the cliffs at the *AHONG* rapids, 19 km west of here - Bus 5 Baht. The 3000 hectare sized

CHETIYA KIRI VIHARN forest temple, which can be found on top of the isolated sandstone hills of Phu Toak, is also very interesting. To get here, catch a bus from Bung Kan to Siwilai or Jaiporn for 10 Baht. For a further 10 Baht you can catch one of the early-morning minibuses headed for the temple from either of these two settlements. The only public transport going back from the temple leaves at 6:30 h in the morning. For this reason be prepared to spend a night. The path leading to the mountain peak will take you over bridges, through tunnels, and up staircases, all of them chiselled into the rock. The path leads around the mountain seven times before finally reaching the top. After having passed grottoes and overhanging cliffs you will reach the fourth level, from where you will have a fine view of the east. The nuns of the monastery live here, the monks live further up. You will pass more caves on the way to the peak.

HOTELS
All hotel rooms have a fan, some
even a bathroom. Try *NERAMID**,
SANTISUP*, or *SOMANMID**.

HOW TO GET THERE
Buses from NONG KHAI 30 Baht,
from NAKHON PHANOM 45 Baht,
from BANGKOK 252 Baht (ac).

NAKHON PHANOM

The road continues running east, parallel to the Mekong which forms the bor-
der to Laos, until it reaches Nakhon Pathom, a former US military base. 30,000
Vietnamese live in this province. There is a second road, rarely used, on the
Laotian side, which runs along the rugged mountain formations. Halfway to
Nakhon Phanom, approx. 2 km before Phu Sawar, you will reach the

TAM FUN waterfalls. Nakhon Phanom itself has little to offer apart from some
beautiful murals in *WAT SRITHEP*.

HOTELS
There are several hotels in town, e.g.
CHAROENSUK*, 692 Bamrung Muang Rd., tel 511130. The *WINDSOR**
is on the same street, no. 692 /19, tel
511156. The *FIRST** is a pleasant
hotel, 370 Srithep Rd. Also the *SRI-
THEP***, no. 708, tel 511036, the
GRAND*, no. 576/26-27, tel 511526,
and the *RIVER INN*** at the river.

HOW TO GET THERE
Buses from BUNG KAN cost 45 Baht,
from THAT PHANOM 12 Baht, NONG
KHAI 70 Baht, and MUKDAHAN 25
Baht.

THAT PHANOM

This settlement, lying directly at the steep banks of the Mekong, is sometimes
referred to as *Raadu* by the common people. Silk materials and copies from
Laos are offered for sale in many shops and at the big market. You will also
see the 52 m stupa of

WAT PHRA THAT PHANOM near the market. Archeologists estimate that the
temple was built 1500 years ago. This would make it one of the oldest standing buildings of northeastern Thailand. The original tower, built in the Laotian
style, collapsed during heavy rainfalls in 1975 and had to be replaced. The top
of the present tower is studded with 10 kg of gold. The temple is considered
particularly sacred by the population of the northeast, and the annual mid-
February temple feast is correspondingly sumptuous. There is a large park
next to the temple. An arch built in 1926, with two figures guarding its flanks,
stands on the only large road in the settlement, which connects the temple
grounds to the river.

Even though there are no great distances to be covered here, there are 200
rickshas in the village, whose drivers will offer their services for 2-3 Baht.

HOTELS
Both the *SANG THONG** and the
CHAI WON* are pretty houses with
nice rooms. The restaurants serve
very spicy curries, made with game.

HOW TO GET THERE
Non ac buses from Bangkok cost 127 Baht, UBON 50 Baht, MUKDA- HAN 12 Baht, NAKHON PHANOM 12 Baht, SAKHON NAKHON 17 Baht, and RENU NAKHON 10 Baht.

EXCURSIONS FROM THAT PHANOM
RENU NAKHON
Take a minibus from That Phanom for 10 Baht. The clatter of the weaving looms can be heard coming from nearly every house of the village. The women of the village are known for their exceptional beauty and the wonderfully woven Ikat materials. In this technique of weaving, the single threads are reeled and dyed several times before they are finally woven together. Cotton and silk materials, blankets, and other textiles are offered for sale in the village. A conspicuously colourful tower can be seen in the WAT RAADU RENU. Stands offering all kinds of ware surround the temple.

SAKHON NAKHON

In contrast to the usually dry and steppe-like areas of northeastern Thailand, this province is characterized by many small lakes and ponds. There is no water shortage here. The capital, Sakhon Nakhon, formerly called Sakalanagara, lies at the banks of the largest natural lake in all of Thailand, the Nong Han. You can rent boats and row out to the islands in the middle of the lake. There are many large lakes in the area, true, but most of them are artificial, with large dams storing the water of the rainy period to prevent floods and to supply the area with water during the dry period. Large artificial lakes can be found west (Nam Un), as well as south of town (Nam Phung). The Lam Pao dam north of Kalasin is much larger of course, holding 1260 million cubic metres of water.

The *THAT CHOENGCHUM* temple with its 24 metre prang (10th century) and the colourful, shimmering bot with splendid wooden doors and windows adorned with carvings is well worth a visit. You'll find the

MARKET near the bus station. You'll be able to try some rather unusual local delicacies here, e.g. snake, bat, and flying squirrel, all of which are prepared in various different ways. The great number of soldiers in town is slightly disconcerting.

NARAI CHENGWENG (WAT THAT NAWENG), a Khmer ruin of laterite stone dating back to the 11th century, lies 6 km northwest of the highway, minibus 3 Baht. The

PHU PHAN National Park lies in the mountains on the road leading to Kalasin. It is a densely wooded park with many animals, 3 waterfalls, and various caves. You will need your own tent if you wish to spend a night.

HOTELS
The *DUSIT**** is the largest hotel in town. If you're looking for a cheaper room, try one of the following: *SI-* *RIMIT*,* 200 metres from the bus station, *SOMKAIT*,* Gam Djapay Rd., and *SUPON PAKDI*,* right next door, or *KUSUMA*,* Charoen Muang Road.

HOW TO GET THERE
Buses from THAT PHANOM cost 17 Baht, from BANGKOK (633 km) 119 Baht, ac 215 Baht.

The local airport is 6 km out of town. Daily flights to BANGKOK cost 960 Baht, the flight to UDON (4 x weekly) costs 310 Baht.

MUKDAHAN

90,000 people inhabit this border town by the Mekong. The Laotian city of Savannakhet lies on the opposite bank. Passenger boats headed for Viangchan leave once or twice monthly from here. *WAT JOK KEO,* right by the river, has beautiful murals. The second temple, *WAT SRI MONGKARN,* was built in a peculiar mixture of Thai, Chinese, and Vietnamese styles by Vietnamese refugees.

The traditional way of weaving is still favoured by most of the people living in the nearby villages. You can visit several vantage points on the wooded cliff ranges of the surrounding area, e.g. PHU MUU (7 km out of town) or PHU MANORAM (3 km). There are many bizarre cliff formations in the PHU HINTERB National Park. A minibus will take you to GABAO, the rapids, for 4 Baht.

HOTELS
Try the *HUANAM*,* tel 611137, 20 Samut Sakdarn Road, the *BAN-THOM** (same road), or the *HONG-XONG*.*

HOW TO GET THERE
Buses from NAKHON PHANOM cost 25 Baht, from UDON THANI 38 Baht, AMNAT CHAROEN (a large Buddha figure in Wat Phra Mongkol) 13 Baht.

YASOTHON

There is a large Muslim community in this town, as well as many Indians. Hand-woven materials can be bought in the shops. Many tourists come here for the annual firework celebration at the beginning of March,

BUNG BANG FAI. Colourful fireworks are set off in the hope that they will bring about the long awaited rains. Elaborate processions accompany the rockets to the Lak Muang shrine on the second day of the celebration, where the local populace pays its respects to the patron god of the town. After this the rockets are brought to the town hall, where they are let off.

The weaving village of BAN THA TONG lies 7 km out of town, by the road leading to Udon, surrounded by rice-paddies. Prehistoric skeletons and ceramics quite similar to those found in Ban Chiang were discovered here whilst making excavations. The local population annually pours water over the Buddha figure in the square, Laotian-style stupa, *THAT GONG KHAO NOI,* during the fifth Buddhist month of each year (April). This is meant to help bring about the rains.

HOTELS
UDOMPON*, 80 Utairamrit Road is not too clean. Try *YOT NAKORN**,* 169 Utairamrit Road, tel 711122.

HOW TO GET THERE
Buses from KORAT cost 54 Baht, from AMNAT CHAROEN 13 Baht.

THE EAST COAST

The coastal area east of Bangkok has always been an area put to intensively agricultural use - the people living at the ocean fish, those living further inland cultivate sugar cane, cassava, and rubber trees. The area has always been extremely popular among travellers, too; at the weekends many of Bangkok's inhabitants will come here to escape the heat and humidity of the city and to catch a refreshing breath of cool, sea air. The long periods of good weather and the beautiful beaches have now also enticed many tourists and travel firms to come here. Numerous large hotels and restaurants were opened in Pattaya, goal of many package tourists, and the little fishing village soon became one of the world's centres of international sex-tourism. There is still a lot of 'real' atmosphere in the area east of Pattaya, though, and this is a region well worth visiting. All excursions that can be made from Bangkok up to Pattaya are described in the 'Around Bangkok' chapter.

CHONG SAMAESAN

You will come across the road leading to CHONG SAMAESAN on the way to Rayong, shortly after Sattahip. A boat can be rented from the fishermen at the harbour, should you wish to pay a visit to the off-shore islands of KO AIRAET, KO SAMAESAN, KO CHUANG, KO CHAN, and KO KHAM. The village itself lies on the edge of a small peninsula.

BEACH ON KO SAMET

HAT SAI THONG

Only a few kilometres after having passed Sattahip you will reach U-TAPAO, a former US Air Force base. Planes that used to bomb Vietnam now stand rusting away in the gardens of the local inhabitants. A 6 km road leads to TAKUAN from Ban Mae Taphut, 11 km before Rayong. There is a beautiful beach near the village, HAT SAI THONG - the golden beach. You will find the atrociously over-priced SAI THONG BEACH**** bungalows here. The off-shore island of KO SAKET can be reached within 20 minutes by boat.

RAYONG

'Nam pla'- those who have spent a while travelling around in Thailand will probably recognize the strong smell of this fish sauce, which is of equal importance to Thai cooking as HP sauce is to the British. Tiny fishes are used to make this fish sauce in Rayong. It is sold in containers in the shops of the old quarter. A tongue of land has shifted the river mouth out into the open sea. This is where the picturesque fishing boats drop anchor.

HOTELS
Spend a night at the *RAYONG**** or the *OTHANI****, 65 and 69 Sukhumvit Road, at the road leading to the harbour. The *ASIA HOTEL*** is a little further west.

HOW TO GET THERE
BANGKOK and PATTAYA travel to Rayong over Highway 3. From Bangkok: 38 Baht, ac buses 69 Baht. A bus to CHANTABURI leaves Rayong at 10:30 h and takes 2 1/2 hours.

KO SAMET

The Khao Laem Ya Samet island group was declared a nature reserve in 1981. Numerous bungalow villages with cheap restaurants have been opened on the white, sandy beaches of Ko Samet since (5 Baht admission), making the island one of the most important traveller meeting-points on the east coast.

The fresh-water supply as well as the many malaria-carrying mosquitoes constitute quite a problem on the island. Should you notice early symptoms of a possible case of malaria, go to the Ko Samet Health Centre or the Ko Samet Malaria Clinic immediately. The latter can be found in the village, near the Buddhist temple. A free blood test will be administered here.

PARADISE BEACH (Ao Phao)
is the only beach on the west coast of the island. There are beautiful sunsets here. The beach lies in a rather flat bay, surrounded by rocks. The surf is generally low, and the beach can reached by boat or foot. Due to its being so flat the beach becomes very large indeed at low tide, but it is not quite as nice as those on the east coast of the island. There are many stones and corals. You can go fishing from here or do some coral diving. Excursions to the neighbouring islands of Kudee and Talu cost 120 Baht.

The tides on the east coast are much stronger, and the surf, in consequence, much rougher. Sometimes entire beaches are flooded when the tide rises. The northern beaches can be reached from a road starting at the large landing-place in the village. The bungalows here are usually supplied with fresh water regularly.

HAT SAI KAEO
is in the very north of the island. Thai groups like coming here, especially at the weekends or on holidays, when they enjoy seafood beneath the palm-trees of the restaurants at the northern end of the beach. While the grown-ups spend their time fooling around with surfboards, the children are usually allowed to venture into the shallow water with large car tires which are used as life preservers. Some of the bungalow villages here are very well built and quite expensive. Thai groups often pitch their tents beneath the palm trees during the holiday season.

AO PHAI
with its 3 kilometres of coconut palm studded bay has the finest sand of the entire island. Surfboards can be rented here (350 Baht a day; lessons 80 Baht an hour, also available at many other beaches on the island), as well as sailing boats (100 Baht per hour). A trip to the coral reef in the 'glass bottom boat' costs 150 Baht. You will mainly find farang tourists here, and the music and food in the restaurants is correspondingly 'western'. Cliffs start separating the bays from one another towards the south, where the caves become smaller and smaller.

PUDSA
This beach can still be reached by walking. There are many palms on the sandy, white beach.

CHAW (also known as Nuan Beach)
is surrounded by the steep KHOK and TAWON cliffs. Predominantly simple huts have been built on the beautiful beaches. A footpath, which becomes worse and worse as it progresses, leads along the beach, over the cliffs, to the southernmost tip of the long island. Other paths lead through the island's woody thickets to the west coast. A dead end road leading through part of the island will take you to

WONGDUAIN
a large beach with a mixed group of visitors and several restaurants. Further south you will reach

THIAN (Sangtain, Candlelight-Beach)
which has small, rather rocky beaches. Here wells provide the water, i.e. the water - if available at all - will be brackish. You can also buy water in containers (20 Baht for 20 l), which are brought over from the mainland.

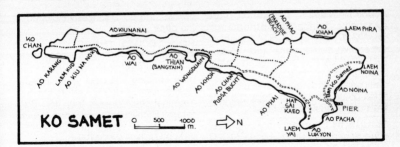

KO SAMET 0 500 1000 m. ⇨N

ACCOMMODATION

Outside of the main season you will be able to get a hut with a fan and shower for 40 Baht. The prices rise dramatically during the season (November - March), sometimes to 100 Baht. Many of the resorts have running water and electricity.

Paradise Beach: The bungalows of *S.K.HUT**, with a view of the peninsula, *DHOM**, and *RATANAS*** are all rather simple.

Ao Phai: *CHARLEE VILLA* offers huts with*** and without showers*. *TAP TONG BUNGALOWS* have their own restaurant and windsurfing school. The huts of *SEABREEZE** are behind the restaurant, not directly on the beach. Pleasant atmosphere. This is where the road to Paradise Beach branches off. *AO PHAI INN**, with its own restaurant, offers huts on cliffs with no protection from the sun whatsoever. Continue north up the blindingly white beach and you'll reach *NUI'S**, *NAGA** (with a traveller-library), both set on cliffs, *SEA SAND**, a large resort at the beach, and *WHITE SAND BUNGALOWS*-****, which has huts of varying standards. The huts of the *SAIKOEW VILLA**** are well built and have showers. The huts of *TOY*** are crowded into a pretty garden. *SAMET KOAW*****, a large and beautiful settlement, can be found further north.

Ao Pudsa: The large *TUBTIM BUNGALOWS** resort has its own restaurant with a TV and a fine view. The huts are rather crowded. The *PUDSA BUNGALOWS** can be found in a palm grove.

Ao Chaw: The *SEA GULL BUNGALOWS*** are comfortable. You can also pitch tent here.

Ao Khok: The cheap *SUNFLOWER BUNGALOWS** can be found north of the landing place. Double huts** are also available with shower and lavatory. Two cheap restaurants lie beyond the bungalow village.

Ao Tawon: The pretty huts of *THARN TAWON**-****, which lies in a charming area, have shower and fan. There is also a pretty good, though rather expensive restaurant commanding a fine view of the bay. People staying in the huts receive food-coupons.

Wongduain: Some of the large bamboo huts of the *SAMET RESORT*** have their own shower. Simple huts* are also available. The huts of the *SUWITT*** (with shower) are smaller. The two restaurants that stand next to each other on the beach are extremely popular among travellers. Here virtually transparent huts can be rented*, as well as well-built wooden houses**. Two rather more expensive bungalow settlements, *WONG DUEN RESORT*** (with an expensive restaurant) and WONG DUEN VILLA*** can be found further south. Although the bungalows have bathrooms and there is a disco, a ticket office, and much more, the huts are outrageously overpriced.

Sangtain: Pleasant atmosphere, good pancakes. The *CANDLELIGHT BEACH*-** settlement offers tiny bungalows on cliffs as well as a restaurant. *DURNGTIEN VILLA** has a simple restaurant and a number of huts on a pretty little beach.

Ao Wai: The *SAMET VILLE**** offers luxurious and comfortable bungalows, three meals a day included in the price.

HOW TO GET THERE
The small fishing village of BAN PHE lies 18 km east of Rayong. A minibus from Rayong will cost you 10 Baht. Buses from BANGKOK's Eastern Bus Terminal cost 70 Baht (ac), 120 Baht return. Small boats will bring you to the off-shore island of KO SAMET from BAN PHE for 20 Baht.

There are several restaurants and hotels in BAN PHE, many shops selling shell and coral jewelry, fruit-stands at which to stock up for the trip over to the island, and an international pay-phone at the landing place for boats to Rayong.

WANG KAEO

There are 15 - 20 smaller bungalow settlements on various nice beaches along the 17 km road between Ban Phe and Laem Ma Phim. We would only recommend these for people who are willing to pay at least 400-500 Baht for accommodation. Most of the beaches are only patronized by local holiday-makers. WANG KAEO****, 7 km east of Ban Phe, is the nicest of all these settlements. Charter a pick-up for 80 Baht. Many 2-6 bed bungalows, costing between 600 and 2900 Baht, are set in a huge, park-like area. Excellent seafood! Reservations from Bangkok: 155/19 Ratchdamri Road, tel 2510836.

KHAO CHAMAO NATIONAL PARK

There is only one wooded area left in the province of Rayong; the granite mountain area of the Khao Chamao National Park. The other forests of the province have been cut down to make room for large-scale agricultural development programmes, arterial roads (Chachoengsao - Klaeng), and newly established villages. One assumes that a vast majority of the remaining wildlife of the province has retreated to the reserve due to this massive destruction of the fauna and flora's natural habitat. There can be no other explanation for the many large mammals living here, e.g. elephants, tigers, banteng, black bears, and various types of monkeys. Many visitors come to the park at the weekends, as is customary in Thailand. Most of them stay in the vicinity of the

KHAO CHAMAO WATERFALL, 200 metres from the Park HQ. A second waterfall, the *CHONG KHAEP,* is 2 km from here. You can also go on a tour to the top of the mountain. Don't go without a guide, though.

Several bungalows*** have been built in the park HQ in NAMSAI.

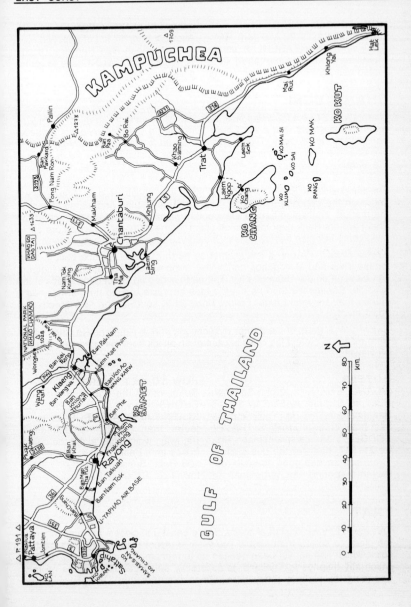

HOW TO GET THERE

BAN NAM SAI is 72 km from RAY-ONG and CHANTABURI. If you're travelling towards Chantaburi in a rented car, turn off 7 km after having passed KLAENG, in BAN KHAO DIN. After a further 17 km of unpaved road you will reach Ban Nam Sai. If you don't have a car you'll have to rent a pick-up in Klaeng.

CHANTABURI

Chantaburi, 342 km from Bangkok, has 38,000 inhabitants, many of them Vietnamese Christians who settled here after having suffered religious persecution in their own country. Their influence can be felt everywhere. Most of them live near the river. The typical, red Vietnamese plaitworks are sold in some of the shops.

The *CATHEDRAL,* built in the French style, was constructed in 1880. You will find it on the opposite river-bank. There are pedestrian bridges southeast of the market, concealed behind the wooden buildings. Change currency at the Thai Farmers Bank near the market-place. Some of the gems which are cut in town come from the nearby mines. Should you wish to visit these, drive to

KHAO PHLOI WAEN, a few kilometres north of town. A stupa built in Ceylonese style and a mondhop containing a reproduction of Buddha's footprint can be seen on the 150 metre hill. The earth is dug up out of deep shafts in the hill-side. Sometimes there is even a blue sapphire among the normally dark stones that are found here. Follow Road 3146 south to the river mouth and you'll reach

LAEM SING. Parts of the former fortifications of Pak Nam and Ka Chai, which were meant to protect the cities in case of an attack from the open sea, can still be viewed.

HOTELS

*MUANG CHANT**,* 257-9 Sri Chan Road, tel 312909, *KAEMSAN 1**,* 98 Benjamarachuthid Rd. You'll find the best hotel in town, *MARK'S TRAVEL LODGE***,* 14 Raksakchamoon Rd., tel 311647, north of the bus station. There are several good seafood restaurants around the large lake in Taksin Park.

HOW TO GET THERE

Going down the shorter road from CHONBURI via BAN BUNG and KLAENG to CHANTABURI is much faster than taking the Sukhumvit Highway, which runs along the coast. Buses from Bangkok cost 56 Baht, ac 103 Baht. Buses to RAYONG leave town from 10:30 (40 Baht ac).

TRAT

This town, furthest east of all towns on the coast and closest to Kampuchea, is the place to set off from should you wish to discover the part of the eastern coast which has not yet been opened up to tourism. The narrow coastal strip, which still belongs to Thailand, is constantly being patrolled by the military. Spending the night is cheap here (bungalows 150 Baht), but you might be

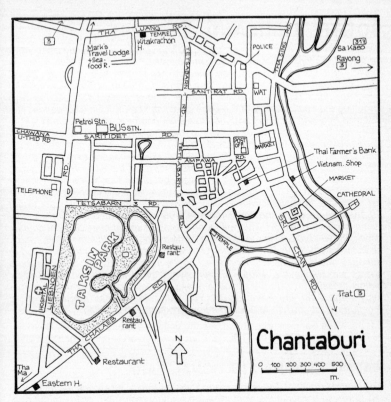

Chantaburi

disturbed by the many shots during the night. The road to KLONG YAI is sometimes closed when diplomatic relations with Kampuchea become strained. Buses are rare, and the paths leading to the beaches from the main road are none too good. Most of the beaches can be found between kilometre stones 41 and 47 - there is no accommodation available here, though. If you want to get to the off-shore islands, leave Trat for LAEM NGOP in the early mornings. As the boats are rather expensive, we would recommend bargaining one day in advance in order to avoid unpleasant surprises. Visiting KO KUT and KO MAK, the islands furthest south, is particularly expensive. You might spend the night on KO KRAAT or KO CHANG. Ask the fishermen.

HOTELS

Try *MUANG TRAT HOTEL***, 4 Sukhumvit Rd., or the *THAI ROON ROJANA****, 98 Benjamarachuthid Road.

HOW TO GET THERE

There are four ac buses that leave BANGKOK daily for Trat (128 Baht).

SOUTH THAILAND

If you're travelling south from Bangkok, down Highway no. 4 or by train, you'll be travelling along the main traffic connections of the region, which reach all the way through the Malaysian peninsula to Singapore. You will never be far from the ocean whilst travelling down this 1600 km stretch - wonderful beaches, coral reefs, and small, tropical islands perfect for relaxing and forgetting the hectic activity of the large cities, can be found in abundance. The distance between Bangkok and the Malaysian border is 1000 km. Don't let the many fast buses and trains tempt you to rush through this area - there is much to see. Excursions to the traditional bathing resorts and the mountains cost time and effort, true, but they offer an almost unique chance of gaining an insight into the life of the people of this area. If you're travelling by train, small excursions are no problem - you can always get off and catch the next train. At most, you may have to spend one night and then catch the next day's train. The big ac buses, in contrast, usually only leave from Bangkok. If you want to get off somewhere along the line, therefore, you will be forced to resort to local forms of public transport. This will mean having to spend more time, of course, especially when crossing the central mountain range. It is this mountain range, stretching from the Indian Ocean on the west coast to the Gulf of Thailand in the east, that is responsible for preventing the monsoon from occurring on both coasts simultaneously. Thus you can always avoid the rains in Thailand by simply crossing over to the opposite coast. The landscape becomes increasingly tropical as you travel south. You will come across more and more mosques in the towns - Malaysian influences cannot be denied.

For the route Bangkok-Phetchburi see the chapter 'Around Bangkok'. Road no. 3175 to the Kaeng Krachan National Park branches off shortly after Tha Yang.

KAENG KRACHAN NATIONAL PARK

This is the largest of Thailand's many National Parks; it reaches all the way to the Burmese border in the west, where a scattering of Karen make up the population of the dense, sub-tropical rainforest along with a few remaining wild elephants, tigers, banteng (wild cattle), and much smaller jungle dwellers such as gibbons, loris, and hornbills.

The La-u reservoir (approx. 25 km in length) is held in check by the 760 m long and 58 m high Kaeng Krachan dam. A well-built road will lead you there. A rather sad and very dry, steppe-like landscape has developed here. This is due to the fact that the jungle has been mercilessly cut down. For this reason be prepared to head west for at least another hour, should you wish to experience some real jungle.

We would recommend organizing a guide at the Park HQ for hikes to waterfalls, caves, and rafting trips. Be prepared for some pretty tough hikes and possibly a couple of nights in the jungle. You will find that the English-speaking representatives of the Forestry Department do not always have the time to act as guides, however. There is a map as well as a luminous bulletin-board with photographs of the highlights of an earlier trekking-tour hanging on a wall in the HQ. Shortly before the rainy period begins the landscape is completely arid (March-May), and the water level of the storage lake sinks considerably.

ACCOMMODATION
The only accommodation available in the park is at the HQ, on a little hill at the western end of the dam. The cheapest bungalows cost 300 Baht, food is served at the restaurant down by the lake. Camping is permitted. You also have the choice of spending the night in one of the floating houses of the much more expensive *KAEN KRACHAN RESORTS****,* situated near the islands of the reservoir. Reservations in Bangkok: tel 5133238.

HOW TO GET THERE
If you're travelling south by bus, disembark in THA YANG, 18 km south of Phetchburi. You can catch a pick-up to the checkpoint from here. If you have your own car, turn down the first signposted road beyond Tha Yang. Be warned: the first 10 km of the 38 km stretch along the canal are in a miserable condition. This road soon meets the well-built main road leading to the dam. The second road branching off from the main road, 3 km further south, is better. Drive via PETCH DAM (6.5 km), and you will also be able to reach the road leading to the dam, which branches off to the right. An approx. 3 km road leads to the dam from the checkpoint. In order to get to the HQ,

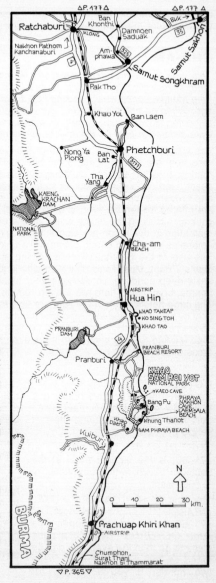

▽ P. 365 ▽

take the road branching off to the left shortly before the dam, pass the em-

ployee's quarters, and head towards the western end of the dam.

CHA-AM

This typically Thai bathing resort lies 40 km south of Phetchburi and 25 km north of Hua Hin. Don't be scared off by the many bloodthirsty mosquitoes, as King Mongkut once was. The king had a summer-palace built here many years ago. When he and his following came to bathe here, however, they were virtually eaten alive by huge swarms of mosquitoes. All of the children of the village were ordered to help kill the insects, but to no avail; the king soon gave up.

The village itself is west (=inland) of the main road and the railway tracks. A road from the station leads to the beach. This road meets a second, narrow road at a rather useless traffic-light. This second road runs parallel to the beach, and you will find several small hotels, private weekend villas, souvenir and grocery shops, foodstands, and restaurants here. Bicycles and tandems are offered for rent all over, should you feel like exploring. You can also have yourself led along the beach sitting on the back of a horse. The main forms of recreation in this resort are picnicking, playing cards, and lazing beneath sunumbrellas on rented beach chairs while loud music blares in the background. The use of the Santisuk Hotel's bathing and shower cubicles costs 5 Baht, toilets 2 Baht. Most Thais do not indulge in any form of water-sports apart from ankle-deep paddling, so do not bother trying to find a place renting out surfboards, boats etc. There are further, remote hotels north of the fishing-village. The large hotels south of the river are also rather isolated. You can reach them only by way of a dead-end road which branches off from the main road approx. 15 km before Hua Hin. You will find the post office and the police station on the road leading to the beach from the station. A bank can be found at the main crossroads.

HOTELS

Several rather expensive hotels and bungalow developments have been built near the beach during the last couple of years.

THE REGENT CHA-AM****, tel 471480, is the biggest hotel at the southern beach, with room-prices up to 5000 Baht.

The new *BEACH GARDEN HOTEL CHA-AM*****, right next door, tel 471350, is not much cheaper. The large *OCTOPUS DISCO,* a good place to go to in the evenings, can be found on the road leading to these two hotels. If you're looking for

cheaper accommodation, try the central beach. Bargaining is possible during the week, when you should be able to get a room with a fan, shower, and lavatory for 250 Baht (ac 500 Baht). The bungalows, which are actually meant to accommodate large Thai families, are usually even more expensive. Most of the hotel rooms have balconies on which you can also spend quiet evenings alone, though - don't forget mosquito coils!

You'll find the *ARUNTIP***, the cheapest place in town, south of the point at which the road from the station meets the beach road.

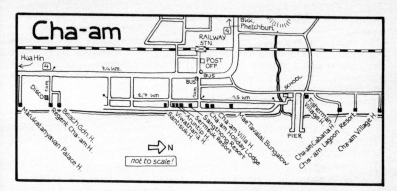

Here you will also find the *SANG-THONG RESORT****, tel 471462, a two-storey hotel with an average restaurant.

The *SERMSUK RESORT****, tel 471118 is a little off the road.

The *VIWATHANA***-*****, tel 471298, 10 bungalows of varying standards.

The *SANTISUK BUNGALOW****, tel 471211, has public toilets and showers, as well as a shady, tree-studded courtyard.

You will find the *MAE TAVALAI BUN-GALOW***-*****, tel 471028, with bungalows set in a well-cared for garden, north of the meeting-point of the two roads.

Here you will also find the *CHA-AM HOLIDAY LODGE***-*****, tel 471595, built in the motel style, with garages on ground level and rooms on the first floor, as well as the *CHA-AM VILLA*

***, 471010, a small place run by friendly people. Rooms with fans get cheaper outside of the season (**). Public telephone downstairs.

FOOD

Simple meals can be bought at any of the many foodstands. We were unable to discover any good restaurants while we were here. This may be due to our having been spoiled by the excellent seafood of Hua Hin. Has anyone else managed to find a noteworthy restaurant here? If yes, write! Excellent dried bananas with wild honey are sold at the shops.

HOW TO GET THERE

All buses stop at the main crossroads. Buses from BANGKOK (178 km) cost 38 Baht, ac 55 Baht. A bus from PHETCHBURI costs 10 Baht, HUA HIN (25 km) 10 Baht.

HUA HIN

The smell of freshly-baked sweets hangs over the night market. People sit about enjoying the cool evening and the food sold at the various cook-houses. Imitation Lacoste shirts and Rolex lie neatly arranged next to the many fruits of the foodstands. Two rather forlorn looking backpack travellers stand in the midst of all this. Though they have only just arrived, they have already decided to go straight on to Ko Samui - 'cause there certainly doesn't seem to be much going on here! This was witnessed in 1987 in Hua Hin. And if you've come expecting to find secluded, palm-studded beaches, you really should move further south. You will have an equally hard and fruitless time trying to find a Pattayan-type night-life, exotic temples, or any other traditional sights. If you are content with a genuine Thai bathing resort atmosphere, family picnics at the beach, shops full of shell souvenirs, and truly delicious seafood, however, then you've come to the right place! You can also set off for various excursions into the beautiful surrounding area from here.

38,000 people live here, in the oldest of all of Thailand's bathing resorts, which lies only 188 km from Bangkok on the southern railway line. When construction on the line was completed in 1921, the royal head of the railway, Prince Purachtra, ordered the

RAILWAY HOTEL to be built. This European-style hotel with tennis courts and a golf course (the first in the country, incidentally) was intended for a rich, distinguished clientele. The high society would meet here during the hot season and enjoy the cool sea breeze. Rama VI was so enchanted by the place that he decided to have a

SUMMER RESIDENCE (Klai Kangwon=without troubles) built just 2 km north of the harbour. The Royal Family still visits frequently to this very day. Unfortunately, the residence is fenced in - no visitors are allowed. The bungalows of other members of the Royal Family can also be found in and around Hua Hin. The

QUEEN'S SUMMER PALACE (Rampaiphani) is a little further inland, approx. 3 km to the south. Don't be daunted by all these celebrities - there are plenty of cheap hotels and restaurants in town, too. You can ride horses along the beach with its many large cliffs, or observe Thai beach life. The fishermen return to the

HARBOUR with their boats in the evenings, when the day's catch is unloaded onto the pier. Fishing is obviously still the main source of income for those people living in the narrow lanes south of the harbour.

HOTELS

You'll find the *RAILWAY HOTEL*****, very stylish with rooms costing over 1000 Baht, directly at the beach, at the end of Damnoen Kasem Road, tel 511012, reservations from Bangkok: 2330256. It has been restored entirely to its original style and is now called *THE CENTRAL HUA HIN RESORT*. It offers bungalows at the beach as well as huge, Victorian-style rooms commanding a fine view over the ocean. It may seem strangely familiar to those who have seen the film 'The Killing Fields'.

Private rooms costing between 50-100 Baht can be rented across the road, behind the tourist market. Good and cheap western breakfast is served here. We would recommend the new

JED PEE NONG HOTEL**-***, 17 Damnoen Kasem Road, tel 512381. All rooms are clean and have a bathroom and lavatory, a fan or ac.

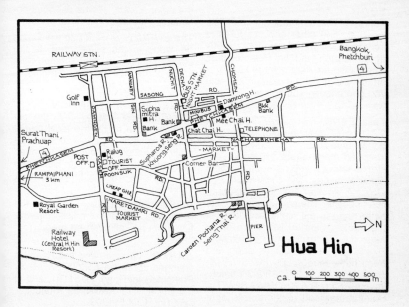

Hua Hin

The *RAMUNG HOTEL***, tel 511940, Damnoen Kasem Road, towards the railway station, offers rooms with a fan, bathroom, and balcony. The following hotels all have similar prices:

SUPHAMITRA HOTEL** (ac***), 19 Amnuaey Sin Road, tel 511208, with showers and fans or ac, new and quite nice, near the market.

HUA HIN GUESTHOUSE***-****, Poonsuk Road, tel 511653, small and pleasant.

MEECHAI*, 57/2 Phetchkasem Road, tel 511035, with its own restaurant, simple and cheap, though rather loud because of the nearby through street.

HUA HIN HIGHLAND RESORT****, tel 511676, can be found north of town on a little hill. Those who have had enough of the beach can relax in bungalows or a country house. South of town you'll find a large international beach hotel, the

ROYAL GARDEN RESORT****, tel 511881-4, turn-off 1 km out of town.

The *SAI-LOM HOTEL****, tel 511890 as well as some cheaper places, e..g. *PHANI VILLA*** and *ST. JOHN'S VILLA*** are even further out of town. Once you've reached Takeap Beach you'll be back on bungalow territory. Most bungalows here are patronized by Thai families and have several rooms and a kitchen.

The main holiday season is between June and October, as well as December/January, at the weekends, and during holidays. For the rest of the year you shouldn't have any problems finding a place to stay.

FOOD

Fantastic Thai seafood with fresh fish, lobsters, and other sea creatures is served at several restaurants directly at the beach and on Phetchkasem Road. Fish are kept in large basins or on ice in front of the restaurants, and you can choose yourself the fish you wish to eat.

The *SEANG THAI SEAFOOD RESTAURANT* near the pier is our personal favourite. The extensive, illustrated menu offers expensive lobster meals as well as equally good, cheaper dishes. The *CHAROEN POCHANA*, another seafood restaurant, lies opposite. The atmosphere here is better than in the restaurants east of the market, most of which are on or near the rather loud Phetchkasem Road. The fish is just as good and fresh here, though. Try the *SUPHAROS RESTAURANT*, 69/2-3 Phetchkasem Road. The *KHOUNG SENG*, a Chinese seafood restaurant, is right next door.

Good and very cheap seafood is also served at the *BAN TAPPIKAEW RESTAURANT*, 7 Naebkhehat Road, north of town and directly on the sea. Friendly service. A bicycle ricksha from town will cost you 20 Baht.

Cheap food is served behind the tourist market, where private rooms are also available. This is also the place to go for a western-style breakfast. The food served at the *NIGHT MARKET* is cheap, too. The market begins as soon as it gets dark, and chairs and tables are set up on the large, central square, so that you can sit comfortably and observe the bustling activity around you whilst eating.

The *KHAOKANG BAANTHAI*, Dechanuchit Road, only a few metres east of the night market, serves delicious coconut ice-cream.

The *CORNER BAR*, a pub which can be found in the same road, is the place to go late at night, opened from 16:00 hours until the early morning.

GENERAL INFORMATION

TOURIST INFORMATION - the last time we were there, the local tourist office (competent people, good information concerning everything, even connections) was in the Damnoen Kasem Road - by now they may have moved.

POST - the post office is across the road from the tourist office. International phone calls can be made from here.

BANKS - cheques and cash can be changed at the BANGKOK BANK, 29 Phetchkasem Road, tel 51171, and at the SIAM CITY BANK, 92 Phetchkasem Road, tel 511203.

SHOPPING - clothing and food is sold at the night market, which is mainly patronized by Thai holidaymakers. A few of the stands have also adapted to Western demands.

A large daytime market is held on several of the streets near the centre of town. There are several stalls selling European sized clothing at the fork in the road.

Next to antiques, the many souvenir shops in town sell shells in all sizes and all conceivable variations - as chains, rings, and other pieces of jewelry. Mother-of-pearl inlays and ornaments are also sold. The stands at the tourist market and at Takeap's and Suan Son's beaches sell similar wares.

TRANSPORTATION IN AND AROUND HUA HIN - bicycle rickshas are a popular form of transportation - 5-10 Baht for short distances, 15 Baht for longer ones, e.g. from the railway station to the beach. Minibuses for 3-4 Baht per person leave Chatchai Hotel for the area surrounding town. Bicycles (80 Baht a day) and motorcycles (150-200 Baht) can be rented opposite the tourist market. A day's sightseeing with a taxi will cost you approx. 300 Baht plus petrol - the set price for a ride to the Khao Sam Roi Yot Park is 600 Baht.

LEAVING HUA HIN
BY TRAIN
The railway station is approx. 1 km from the beach. Most of the trains to BANGKOK (87 / 44 Baht for the 2nd/3rd class) via NAKHON PATHOM (69 / 33 Baht) and PHETCHBURI (27 / 13 Baht) leave at night. We would recommend taking the train that leaves Hua Hin at 6:01 hours and arrives in Bangkok at 10:00 hours. Change to the diesel train in Nakhon Pathom (departure 9:09 hours), if you're headed towards Kanchanaburi. Southbound trains to the border leave at 16:16 and 17:43 hours, the train to Malaysia and SINGAPORE (837 Baht - 2nd class) leaves at 18:53 hours. Trains to HAAD YAI (244 / 116 Baht) leave at 19:58, to NAKHON SI THAMMARAT (209 / 100 Baht) at 21:28, and the train to TRANG (200 / 95 Baht) at 22:14 hours. If you're headed towards SURAT THANI (154 / 74 Baht) we would recommend taking the last train at 22:14, which reaches the ferry-harbour for boats to Ko Samui the next morning at 5:59 hours. The prices listed do not include possible extra charges.

BY BUS
Most buses stop at the downtown bus station, west of the night market. Ac buses to BANGKOK (74 Baht, 3 1/2 hours) leave every hour. The cheaper ones (47 Baht, 4 hours) leave every half hour. Buses to PHETCHBURI cost 15 Baht, 1 hour; CHA-AM 10 Baht, 30 minutes; PRACHUAP KHIRI KHAN 21 Baht, 1 1/2 hours; SURAT THANI 89 Baht, 8 1/2 hours; RA-NONG 74 Baht, 6 1/2 hours. Ac buses from Bangkok to SURAT THANI stop at the overland bus station, 3-4 km north of town at the Suphapchon Restaurant. They are frequently booked up, however. A minibus from Hua Hin to the restaurant will cost you 4 Baht.

EXCURSIONS FROM HUA HIN
KO SINGH TOH
You can cross over to this island with a boat rented from the long jetties. The island lies approx. 10 km off shore.

TAKEAP AND KRILAS CLIFFS
Take a pick-up or hike the 6 km along the beach to the Takeap cliff at the southern end of the bay. There is a temple on this cliff, directly at the sea. Next to the numerous souvenir stands, there are also several reasonably cheap seafood restaurants nearby, most of which do not open until the evening. The high Krilas cliffs, which appear to be completely covered with temples, are a little further inland. You will have a good view from up here if there is no mist.

There are several bungalows along the road to the beach, most of them rather expensive and sadly lacking in character, however.

SUAN SON
This stretch of sandy beach is 8 km south of the two cliffs. There are many pines offering shade here. A small fishing village lies at the southern end of the beach, at the Tao cliff. Shell jewelry and other shell souvenirs can be bought here. Should you manage to communicate with the fishermen, you might be able to rent a boat to the tiny offshore island of Singh Toh. You might also be able to rent a boat from Takeap. The Rung-Arun Guesthouse, 125 Khao Takeap Road, offers half-day tours to the island for 500-800 Baht per boat.

PRANBURI
You will find a signpost directing you to the PRANBURI BEACH RESORT**** 24 km south of Hua Hin (near km-stone 256). The bungalow resort is on a wonderful beach; rather boring huts, all with a terrace commanding a view of the connecting planks.

If you have your own vehicle and camping gear you can camp out in the Pranburi Forest Park. The Pranburi river has been banked up at the foot of the mountain range, approx. 30 km further to the east. Minibuses to the dam leave Pranburi between 6:00 and 15:00 h (6 Baht).

DOLE PLANTATION
The famous canned pineapples that can be bought in just about every western supermarket are grown here, 23 km inland from Hua Hin.

KHAO SAM ROI YOT NATIONAL PARK

The so-called 'mountains of the 300 peaks' that make up the approx. 130 km^2 sized National Park between Hua Hin and Prachuap Khiri Khan lie south of Pranburi. Bizarre limestone formations rise rather abruptly from a wide, green plain of paddies and shrimp ponds, where many white herons and storks can be seen circling the sky in search of food. The mountains, in contrast, make up the natural habitat of the rare serow (Capricornis sumatrensins, Asian mountain-goat). You may come across incredibly cheeky hoards of monkeys in the forests, who love robbing human visitors of their food. Irrawaddy dolphins are sometimes sighted near the coast.

A country lane that starts shortly before the checkpoint, north of Bang Pu, leads to a secluded beach with many shells but little shade. There are (private?) bungalows on the bigger of the two offshore islands and at the beach. There is only one small restaurant in the vicinity, at the end of the road.

The fishing village of BANG PU can be found in the next bay. A 1.5 km, poorly tended path branches off from the road leading to the village after three km. Follow this path through the many shrimp ponds and you'll reach the KAEW CAVE. Only venture into this stalactite cave with a guide; some of the slippery paths within the cave are extremely dangerous.

In the village, fishermen will offer their services for boat trips to the *PHRAYA NAKHON CAVE* and the *LAEM SALA BEACH*. The approx. 25 min. trip there and back costs 150 Baht per boat. Pine trees and coconut palms offer much-needed shade at the beach. A 20-minute hike over the mountain will also bring you to the cave. Simply follow the path leading over the mountain from the wat. A small restaurant can be found close to the beach. Here you will meet guides, who will climb up to the caves with you. You can hardly miss the exhausting, 1/2 hour trail, though, as it leads up a steep, rocky river-bed most of the time. You will not need torches to explore the two large caves; enough light is let in through large holes in the ceiling, and even trees grow here. Several kings have walked along this rocky path - a small Thai-style pavilion was built inside the cave for Rama V, and several of his successors have come here since. We would not recommend climbing up to the caves at noon; apart from the heat, the lighting in the caves is best in the mornings and afternoons.

Another cave, *SAI CAVE*, can be reached by driving through the fishing village of *KHUNG TANOT* and climbing up the steep path leading through the cactus forest at the end of the beach (at the parking lot, the climb will take about 15 min.). Light filters into the large cavern through two old, collapsed shafts. The stalactites and stalagmites here are up to 15 metres in length. The 'dissected pillars', which were formed due to the ground sinking, are especially fascinating. You will not need a guide for this cave. A path branches off to the Phraya Nakhon cave from the path leading to the Sai cave. You will reach this second cave after a 2-hour climb.

You will reach the road leading to *SAM PHRAYA BEACH* by going back to the main road and continuing down it for another 2 km. A friendly park guard has his house (with toilet and drinking water) at the end of the long casuarina and bench-lined beach. You can camp in total isolation here outside of the Thai school holidays.

You can rent boats to explore the islands and beaches of the coast (200-700 Baht, depending on the size of the boat and the length of time you wish to have it) from the fishermen of the *KHAO DAENG* village, which is close to the HQ. Boat rides along the *KHAO DAENG CANAL* in the early mornings and evenings are especially beautiful. Tours are organized by the administration of the park (150 Baht from the Park HQ to Phraya Nakhon Cave).

It takes approx. 1/2 hour to reach the peak of the *KHAO DAENG* from the HQ. You'll have a fantastic view from up here, especially in the mornings and evenings. The peak of the 605 m *KHAO KRACHOM* is rather more difficult to reach.

The rainy period is between August and November, the best time to visit the park between December and February. It becomes increasingly hot after this date, making climbing and even simply lying around on the beaches quite an ordeal.

ACCOMMODATION

Spend the night at the four bunga-lows**** of the HQ (with kitchen) or in the four bungalows on Laem Sala Beach. All of these are meant for groups of 8-25 people - if you're less, try to bargain (approx. 200-250 Baht for two people).

Two-person tents cost 50 Baht per night at the HQ camping grounds as well as the grounds on Laem Sala and Sam Phya Beach. If you pitch a tent of your own, you will have to pay 5 Baht. No food is available at the HQ. There is a small restaurant at the Laem Sala Beach. For information and reservations go to the HQ or contact the Department of Forestry in Bangkok, tel 5790529.

HOW TO GET THERE

The park is definitely worth an excursion from Hua Hin. A taxi there and back will cost you 600 Baht, which is cheaper than renting a motorcycle. Organized tours are also offered. You can also catch a bus up to Pranburi for 7 Baht.

Those coming from the north need to take the first road branching off to the left in Pranburi (km 256,3), and then take the next right. You will reach the checkpost after 18 km. Try getting a pick-up in Pranburi or catching one of the trucks that drive to the villages of BANG PU, PHU NOI (10 Baht each), KHAO DAENG (15 Baht) and some-times straight to the HQ in the morn-ings. You can rent a minibus for a tour of the National Park in Pranburi for 250 Baht. Those coming from the south, take the signposted road lead-ing to the Park HQ, which branches off to the east from H4 at km 286.5 (14 km).

Admission: 20 Baht per vehicle.

PRACHUAP KHIRI KHAN

This provincial town lies at the southern end of a bay. Many fishing boats lie moored in its natural harbour, which has the additional protection of a number of offshore cliff islands. The 'mirror mountain', KHAO CHONGKRACHOK, home of many cheeky monkeys, is quite close to the beach. You will be re-warded with a fine view if you climb the 415 steps of the staircase leading to the small temple on the mountain's peak. Next to the offshore islands and the town, you'll be able to see a mountain range which is actually in Burma. At this point, Thailand is just a couple of kilometres in width. There are large pineap-ple plantations on the rolling hills of the hinterland

You will find a small Tourist Office run by friendly people at the northeastern end of the large square, where the night market is held. Rather difficult to find.

The town isn't really worth an extended stay, though - it has too little to offer. The beaches close to town and along the bay are none too clean and the water is murky.

HOTELS

There are many BUNGALOWS**-*** with fan, showers, and lavatories along the embankment road at the northern bay, close to the beach. Most of these are patronized by Thai holiday-makers.

The people running the SUK SAN BUNGALOWS, tel 6111145, are not particularly friendly. At the weekends it is very difficult to get a room here, but outside of the season the place is nearly always empty. Loud motorcycles are a nuisance in the evenings, as are the many hungry monkeys roaming about, and the mosquitoes. Bring a mosquito net or coils.

There are more hotels around, e.g. *HOTEL YUTTIICHAI**, 200 metres from the railway station. We would not recommend *KING'S HOTEL**.

FOOD
Don't miss the foodstands at the beach promenade south of the harbour in the evenings. The seafood served here is fantastic! We would definitely recommend trying the Tom Yam prepared by the fat, jolly cook. The young, particularly spicy coconuts sold at the stands along the embankment road are a further culinary delight.

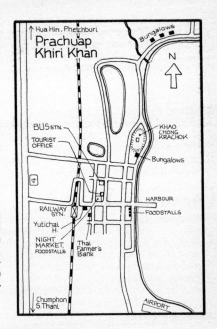

HOW TO GET THERE
BY TRAIN
We would suggest taking the train from BANGKOK at 12:30 h for 142/78 Baht in the 2nd/3rd class (incl. Rapid extra charge), arrival 17:20; the other three trains do not arrive until much later (between 21:27 and 23:34 h).

BY BUS
Buses leave BANGKOK regularly between 4:30 and 17:20 h (63 Baht, 323 km), ac buses leave at 8:00, 12:00, and 16:30 h (105 Baht).

EXCURSIONS FROM PRACHUAP KHIRI KHAN
VANAKORN BEACH
A dirt road leading to VANAKORN BEACH turns off to the east 22 km south of Prachuap (km stone 345.5). You will reach the secluded beach - which is as straight as an arrow - after 3.5 km. You can relax in the shade of the kasuarina-trees. A large-scale holiday resort is apparently being planned here by the government.

HUAI YANG WATERFALL
To get there, head south for 27 kilometres. The road leading to the waterfall branches off to the west in BAN HUAI YANG. Motorcyclists will take you to the falls (5.5 km) for 10 Baht. Refreshments are available near the parking lot,

where you will find stands selling food and drinks. A walk will lead you through the sparsely wooded forest to the foot of a waterfall. There are many nice bathing-spots here. The path is not all that steep, and you can walk up part of the river-bed during the dry season. The waterfall is most beautiful at the end of the rainy season, however.

The further south you go, the more tropical the surrounding landscape becomes. The mountains in the north have only a few trees, while the ones in the south are covered with thick, almost impenetrable jungle. Coconut trees grow in the coastal regions of the south, as well as rubber trees and oil palms, which are mainly grown on large plantations. While the cities are still mainly populated by Thais and Chinese, the fishing people of the coastal villages are of Malay and Muslim origin.

BANG SAPHAN

Go down H3169, which branches off 76 km south of Prachuap, at km stone 399; you will reach the traditional village of BANG SAPHAN with its narrow alleys and many old wooden buildings after 10 km. Trains stop here, too. Continue on for 3 km and you'll reach a bay which almost forms a full circle. The offshore islands seem to complete the circle. Few tourists come to this extraordinarily picturesque bay with its many fishing villages, because it is not suitable for bathing. People who like fishing will love it here, though, especially if they join the Bang Saphan Game Fishing Group on one of its regular deep-sea fishing expeditions. The club uses special boats for these tours. For information contact Sarikar Fishing Club opposite Sarikar Villa.

BUNGALOWS
VAVEENA BUNGALOW**, tel 611053; clean, nicely furnished rooms with lav/shower and fan in two-storey terraced houses, along the sand road; friendly owner; the restaurant is right next to the houses.

SARIKAR VILLA**-*****, also on the sand road, 400 metres further on; large, cheap rooms in a dilapidated main building, expensive but appealing rooms in the new buildings; opposite Sarikar Fishing Club, restaurant on the beach.

CHUMPHON

The lively capital of the province with the same name is almost 500 km south of Bangkok, at the narrowest point of the Isthmus of Kra. The town may not have many sights as such to offer, but it is ideally located as a starting point for excursions into the fascinating surrounding areas. This is a region which still hasn't been properly opened up to tourism. Nice beaches, offshore islands, virgin forest, spectacular caves, and wonderful waterfalls make this an area particularly worthwhile for nature lovers.

HOTELS

There are several hotels offering cheap overnight accommodation on Chumphon's main road, Saladaeng Road.

SURIYA*, the smallest hotel in town.

SRI CHUMPHON**, tel 511280, some rooms ac.

THAI PRASERT*, the cheapest place in town.

If you want to live more comfortably, try *THA TAPHAO HOTEL*** (ac***), Tha Taphao Road, tel 511479, next to a cinema.

PHARADON INN***-****, Pharadon Road, tel 511500, modern, fully ac hotel in the centre of town; high standards.

HOW TO GET THERE

There are 6 daily trains from BANG-KOK for 192/102 Baht in the 2nd/3rd class (incl. Rapid extra charge); the trains that leave at 12:30 and 14:00 h arrive at 20:00 and 21:37 h respectively, all others do not arrive until late at night.

The trains from HAT YAI arrive at midnight, the first two trains from SURAT THANI at 20:38 and 21:28 h.

There are four daily ac buses from BANGKOK between 21:30 and 22:00 h (160 Baht); non ac buses leave at 4:00 and 6:05 h (95 Baht).

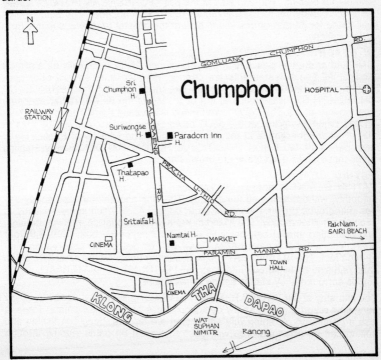

BEACHES
THUNG BUA LAEN BEACH
This beautiful beach is 16 km north of Chumphon. The sand is white and fine and the water clear at high as well as low tide. The surf stays moderate all year round, even during the rainy season; ideal bathing conditions. Accommodation is available at CHUMPHON CABANA BEACH RESORT**-***, tel 511680, 30% discount during the week (but not during the holidays). Nice resort with bungalows distributed among the young kasuarina-trees on the beach. Good restaurant and beach bar. A diving base from Phuket is stationed here during the season (June-October). Boat trips to the offshore islands can be organized. You will reach the resort by way of a bumpy but well-signposted road from Chumphon. A songthaew will cost you 15 Baht from town. Beware: taxi drivers here like to ask for ridiculous fares. A motorcycle-taxi costs 50 Baht (you will recognize one by the driver's orange vest and the number which is printed on it).

PARADONPAP BEACH
17 km south of Chumphon, near a river mouth. There are very nice seafood restaurants as well as a fishing village on the beach, which is unfortunately not suitable for bathing. You can stay at the posh PORNSAWAN HOTEL****, Pak-nam, Chumphon, tel 521031, luxurious rooms with ac; pool. The resort is in a well-cared for garden on the inland side of the coastal road. Not suitable for a beach holiday.

RI BEACH
5 km further on, this beach is a favourite among Thais, especially as a site for picnics. All beach restaurants are open at the weekend, and all offer deck chairs, sun umbrellas, and large, old inner tubes. The PRINCE OF CHUMPHON SHRINE stands at the beginning of the beach, rather exposed. The founder of the Thai Navy is venerated like a saint here. The torpedo boat "HTMS Chumphon" lies at the dock, down by the beach. You will be able to visit a small tiger temple at the end of the bay. The Ministry of Public Health has opened the MO PHON TRADITIONAL HERBAL GARDEN nearby. Healing herbs that are still used today are grown here.

PATHIU BEACH
PATHIU BEACH is approx. 30 km north of Chumphon. The beach ends smoothly, without falling off too sharply. The long and palm-fringed sandy bay has mangroves growing along its outer edges. As a result some sections of beach are rather muddy. The island of KO KHAI (good for snorkelling, bathing, and collecting shells) can be reached in 20 minutes by boat (400 Baht per boat). You will reach cape LAEM THAN with its overgrown observation platform on foot. The BO MAO BAY (many kasuarina-trees) on the other side of the cape can also be explored on foot, as can the THUNG YO WATERFALL, which stands surrounded by stands selling refreshments.

You can stay at the PATHIU RESORT**, 74 Moo 1, Pathiu, tel 5132078; pretty bungalow resort beneath shady deciduous trees and coconut palms. There is also a dormitory*. A motorcycle and a boat are for hire, deep-sea fishing and trolling can be arranged. You will reach the resort on paths leading through coconut-plantations from Chumphon Cabanas or by way of the H4; turn off to Pathiu at km-stone 476 (17 km). Once there, continue on to the beach for another 8 km (the trip measures a total of 57 km in length). You can also take a train to the Pathiu station and catch a taxi from there.

TO THE OFFSHORE ISLANDS

The busy fishing harbour PAKNAM CHUMPHON is 13 km southeast of town, by the Klong Tha Tapho river mouth. Boats with which you can reach the beautiful offshore islands are for hire. You will only receive a good price, however, if you're in a larger group and drive a hard bargain.

KO LANG KA CHIU

(45 min.), south of the harbour; thousands of swallows (salangan) live here. They build their nests in the caves and cliffs of the island. The nests are gathered together during the mating season (March-August) only to end up in Chinese stomachs as the famous swallow nest soup. The sight of the men climbing around the precarious cliffs is breathtaking. The right to collect nests has to be bought, and once someone has acquired it they will try to keep it as long as possible. Snipers have even been hired to protect the area. Should you wish to visit the island, go to the Concession Holders Office in Chumphon for a permit.

KO THANG LANG

(40 min.), close to the swallow island; nice beaches and places to camp.

KO RAT

(30 min.), further to the north, vaguely shaped like a rhinoceros. Excellent diving; long, perfectly preserved coral reefs and scores of colourful fish and sea creatures.

KO MATTRA

(30 min.), called TANG KUAY by the local inhabitants. This island, which is a little larger than the others, is north of Ko Rat; suitable for fishing and camping. Beautiful coral reefs surround the island; perfect snorkelling conditions.

Further islands that are worth exploring:

KO THALU, KO CHARAKHE, KO NGAM LEK, KO NGAM YAI, and *KO NGAM NOI* can be reached most quickly directly from Chumphon Cabanas; birds' nests are gathered on the last three of the islands.

KO SAMET can be reached most easily from Paknam Chumphon, *KO KHAI* from Pathiu Beach.

CHAIYA

This small town is on the road leading to Surat Thani. It was a centre of the Sri Vijaya Empire approx. 1000 years ago. This empire stretched all the way from Java to the Isthmus of Kra, where the Khmer Empire began. *WAT PHRA BOROMATHAT,* a highly venerated temple west of town, may remind you of the temple grounds and candis that are found in central Java. There are more Sri Vijaya-style temples in the area, e.g. *WAT WIENG, WAT LONG,* and *WAT KAEO* with a formerly imposing stupa. Don't come expecting to find great monuments of the past, however; you will only be disappointed. You will have to be content with rather unspectacular remains. Maybe the fact that you are walking upon the ground of a once-great empire will make up for this.

You will find replicas of statues now standing in Bangkok's National Museum in the small, efficiently run museum. Many works of art discovered in the Chaiya area are also exhibited here. Open 9:00-12:00 and 13:00-16:00 h except for Mon and Tues. There is a simple hotel* in town.

HOW TO GET THERE

You can reach Chaiya by train from SURAT THANI (8 Baht 3rd class). All trains coming from the north (BANG-KOK, HUA HIN, CHUMPHON) arrive in the middle of the night.

Buses leave regularly from SURAT THANI.

WAT SUAN MOKE

You will come across the modern *WAT SUAN MOKE* in a forest, 4 km out of town. Pilgrims from all over the world come here in order to meet one of Thailand's most famous monks, Achaan Buddhadasa, who speaks excellent English. Achaan doesn't see himself as an instructor in meditation, but rather as a 'good friend' who is able to give sound advice and answer questions.

The architecture and the decorations of the monastery buildings are quite amazing. The bot, for instance, is built in the shape of a boat, which symbolizes the entrance into Nirvana. The outside of the central building is adorned with low reliefs which depict scenes out of Buddha's life and have been copied from Indian originals. The interior seems like a marvellous collection of paintings, only the artists painted their pictures straight onto the walls instead of on canvas. All of the paintings deal with reaching a state of perfect nirvana, even though each artist seems to have approached the problem from a different angle. The murals and verses of Emanuel Schermann, a slightly surrealistic travelling Zen Buddhist, have contributed to the temple's special image. There are still several bare spots of wall on the second floor, just waiting for talented visitors.

10 days of *DHAMMA MEDITATION COURSES* are held free of charge at the beginning of every month. You will only have to pay 40 Baht a day for food.

Many foodstalls have been opened around the monastery, most of them specializing in the local delicacy, boiled and salted duck eggs.

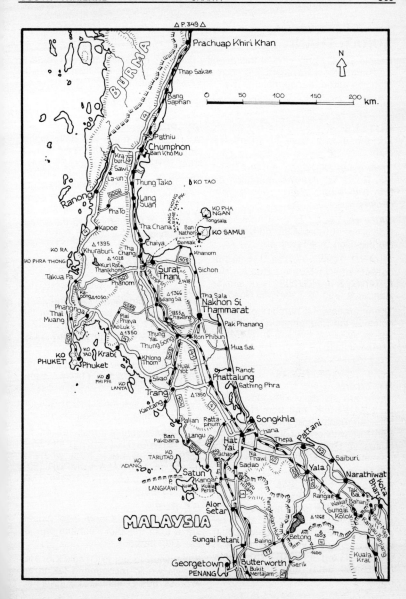

△ P.349 △

Prachuap Khiri Khan

N

Thap Sakae

Bang Saphan

0   50   100   150   200 km.

BURMA

Pathiu
Chumphon
Ban Kho Mu

Kra buri
Sawi
La-un

Thung Tako

KO TAO

Ranong

Lang Suan

Pha To

Kapoe

Tha Chana

Ban Nathon

KO PHA NGAN
Tongsala

KO SAMUI

Chaiya

Donsak

KO RA

△1395
Khuraburi

Tha Chang

△1028
Kuri Rat
Thanikhom

Khanom

KO PHRA THONG

Takua Pa

Phanom

Surat Thani

Sichon

△1438

Ka-pong △1050

△1366
Wiang Sa

Tha Sala

Nakhon Si Thammarat

Phang-nga
Thai Muang

Plai Phaya
Ao Luk
△1350

Thung Yai
Thung Song

△1855
Chawang

Pak Phanang

KO PHUKET

KO YAO

Krabi

Phuket

Khlong Thom

Huai Yot

Ron Phibun

Hua Sai

Ranot

KO PHI PHI

KO LANTA

Sikao

Phattalung

Sathing Phra

Trang

Kantang

△1350

Palian

Ratta phum

Songkhla

Chana

Thepa

Pattani

Ban Paikbara

Langu

Hat Yai

Prachan

Saiburi

KO TARUTAO

Na Thawi

Sadao

Yala

KO ADANG

Satun

Kangar

Kuala Perlis

Pengkalan Kubu

△1268

Narathiwat

Kota Bharu

Tak Bai

Rangae

Wakaf Bharu

LANGKAWI

Alor Setar

Sungai Kolok

MALAYSIA

Sungai Petani

Baling

Betong △1203

Kuala Krai

Georgetown
PENANG

Butterworth

Gerik

1400

Bukit Mertajam

SURAT THANI

People usually only stop at this actually rather uninteresting town en route to Ko Samui. Most travellers see no reason to stay here longer than it takes to organize further transportation. The

TOURIST OFFICE is in the west of town, on Na Muang Road.

HOTELS

For those who have to spend the night:

THAI TANI HOTEL**, 306-308 Talat Mai Road, tel 272977, reception on the 3rd floor, clean rooms with shower.

TAPI HOTEL*** is on Chonkasem Road, no. 100, near the harbour and the Ban Don Bus Terminal.

MUANG TONG HOTEL** is on the corner of Na-Muang Road. The *MUANG TAI HOTEL*** is of similar standards, 390-92 Talad Mai Road.

There are also a number of cheap hotels at the Phunpin train station, 13 km away *(QUEEN*, SRI RAMIE*, THAI FAH** etc.).

HOW TO GET THERE
BY TRAIN

There are six daily afternoon trains from BANGKOK, four from HAT YAI. You can reach Surat Thani by taxi (10 Baht) or with one of the orange-red buses (7 Baht) from the PHUNPIN train station, 13 km from town.

BY BUS

All non-ac buses stop at the Bus Terminal, east of Ban Don harbour. Ac buses either stop here or in the road parallel to the harbour, at the respective company offices. Local buses arrive from virtually all towns in the south, e.g. PHUKET (61 Baht), KRABI (50 Baht), and HAT YAI (67 Baht).

BY PLANE

Around noon there are daily flights from BANGKOK (1380 Baht, 1 hr.), from PHUKET (315 Baht, 35 min. - wonderful flight in a small aircraft), and from NAKHON SI THAMMARAT (230 Baht). Continue on to Surat Thani with the Thai Airways Bus (35 Baht) or to Ko Samui with the limousine service (150 Baht incl. ferry).

LEAVING SURAT THANI
BY TRAIN

There are six daily trains to BANGKOK between 17:48 and 22:42 h. Seats can only be reserved for the trains at 17:48, 18:20, and 20:42 h (224/107 Baht for the 2nd/3rd class, approx. 11 hrs.).

Four daily trains to HAT YAI between 23:18 h and 3:25 h (144/57 Baht, 2nd/3rd class).

Two trains leave for SUNGAI GOLOK around midnight (216 Baht).

An international express leaves for BUTTERWORTH (Penang) at 1:55 h (279 Baht, 9 hrs.), from where it heads on to KUALA LUMPUR (507 Baht, 18 hrs.), and SINGAPORE (747 Baht, 28 hrs.)

BY BUS

All non-ac buses and local buses leave from the Bus Terminal east of Ban Don harbour.

If you want to get to Bangkok or Hat Yai we would recommend taking an express bus. These leave from the

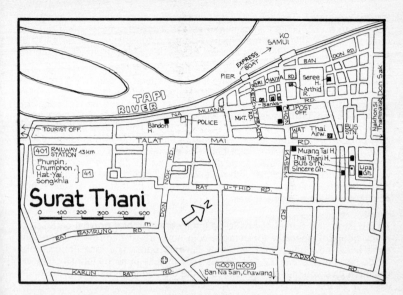

respective company offices. You will find several offices on the road running parallel to the river. Ac buses to BANGKOK leave 11:15 and 20:00 h (225 Baht, 9 hrs.) many non-ac buses leave between 7:00 and 21:00 h (125 Baht, 10 hrs.). Ac buses to HAT YAI leave at 5:30 h (this one will get you there in time to catch the connecting bus to KUALA LUMPUR and SINGAPORE) and at 16:00 h (150 Baht, 5 hrs.), several non-ac buses leave for Hat Yai before noon (67 Baht).

The Surat Thani-PHUKET route leads through one of the most beautiful stretches of countryside in Thailand; many non-ac buses leave between 5:30 and 13:00 h (61 Baht, 6 hrs.).

BY PLANE
Thai Airways Office, 3/27-28 Karun Rat Road, tel 272610 (1 km south of the Bus Terminal). Daily flights to BANGKOK, to PHUKET, and to NAKHON SI THAMMARAT.

BY BOAT
Speed boats, express boats, and night boats leave Ban Don, Don Sak, and Khanom for KO SAMUI and KO PHA NGAN all day and night, as do (car-) ferries (see *How to get there: Ko Samui* and *Ko Pha Ngan*).

KO SAMUI

Ko Samui, the country's third-largest island, lies in the southwestern part of the Gulf of Thailand. The island measures a total of 247 km² in size, 14 km in width, and 20 km in length. 25 % of the island consists of plains, mainly used for raising coconut-palms. An alleged 2 million coconuts are shipped to

Bangkok monthly. The central, jungle-overgrown highlands of the island are only put to a very limited agricultural use; the local inhabitants plant durians, rambutans, langsats, and mangosteen on the outer slopes, in their gardens, which the unpractised tourist's eye will barely be able to distinguish from the jungle.

The days when Ko Samui was still a well-kept secret among travellers, when the island could only be reached by fishing boat and could only be travelled around on foot, have long since passed. Car ferries and speedboats now travel back and forth regularly, a 50 km, concrete road circles the island, and a few smaller roads branch off to the highlands within. An airstrip has even been built on the northeastern tip of the island. Scores of tourist bungalow resorts have been founded on the most beautiful of the beaches, and it didn't take long for large, modern hotels to be erected. Ko Samui, in other words, is on its way to becoming yet another international tourist ghetto. The only thing which has stopped this from happening yet is the fact that the water supply constitutes quite a problem which the owners of the large hotels have been trying to solve for years.

All the same, Ko Samui seems to be the incarnation of a tropical paradise to many people, especially to all those who have never been here before and don't know how beautiful it was only 5 years back. The local inhabitants, incidentally, are as friendly and nice as ever, in spite of all the tourism; they will still often give you the feeling that you're the first foreigner to have come to the island in years.

NATHON

The island's main town generates a laid back atmosphere of laissez-faire. It has adapted perfectly to the needs of western travellers, without, however, competing for their business. The speed boats and night boats arrive here. Obstinate Thais may try to talk you into renting a bungalow at their resort if you arrive outside of the main season, but this will be the last annoyance you will have to deal with once there. Nathon seems swept clean of tourists soon after the boats have left, especially in the evening; a mysterious magnetic force seems to immediately attract all travellers to the nearest beaches. Don't worry if you should arrive too late to find a bungalow on your first night there; there are plenty of places in town that can offer perfectly acceptable temporary accommodation.

HOTELS
There are a few hotels on Beach Rd., e.g. *CHOKHANA*** and *CHINTA***.

SAMUI BUNGALOWS**, next to the post office; with fan and bathroom.

CHAO KAO***-****, tel 2528150, is a little further on; comfortable bungalows.

FOOD
There are many restaurants (mainly serving European food) along the pier and the northern intersecting road. If you've been longing for pizza, a hamburger, or a steak, you've come to the right place. Chinese restaurants and restaurants serving the typical Thai curries can be found on the side roads. Those wishing to cook

for themselves can stock up at the supermarket in the first parallel road. If you're looking for specifically western-type foods, e.g. ham, salami, fresh cheese, or bread rolls, go to the shop run by the Spaniard on the northern intersecting road. The market (in the morning) is the best place to go for fruit, vegetables, and fish.

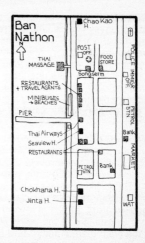

GENERAL INFORMATION

WHEN TO GO - Ko Samui has its own micro-climate; you can theoretically spend the entire year on the island if you are in the right districts at the right time. You had better stay in the north, west, or south of the island during the northeast monsoon from mid-December to mid-February. The wind seems to stop blowing between April and June, when it sometimes becomes unbearably hot. The short cloud-bursts in the evenings hardly bring any refreshment at all. The local inhabitants will assure you that the weather is always good for the full moon. Chaweng and Lamai are both totally booked up in July/August as well as over Christmas/New Year. The height of the season is between mid-December and March.

TRAVEL AGENCIES - there are many small travel agencies along the pier offering bus, train, boat, and plane tickets. You can also have a flight confirmed from here (for a small fee), and book international flights. This will cost you approx. 1000 Baht more than it would in Bangkok. You will be able to buy train tickets without having to pay any extra charge at the Thai Airways Office. Generally, all travel agencies will give you friendly and helpful information concerning the various possible ways of leaving the island.

POST OFFICE - at the northern end of the pier, with an international telephone and poste restante service, very helpful employees. The packing service is in front of the post office. Seamail packages need 4 months to reach Europe from here. Open Mon-Fri 8:30-16:30 h, Sat till 12:00 h.

IMMIGRATION OFFICE - on the main road, right next to the police station. You can have your 2 month tourist visa extended by 30 days here; bring 2 passport pictures and a photocopy of your passport.

TOURIST POLICE - 3 km south of town, tel 421245.

BANKS - You will find the Krung Thai Bank and the Thai Farmers Bank on the main road. The Krung Thai Bank is open daily from 8:30-20:00 h. Having a money order wired here is no problem. There are also safe deposit boxes and a poste restante service.

DOCTORS - practise in their private clinics from 7:00-8:00 h and from

17:00-19:00 h except for Sundays and holidays. They spend the rest of their time working at the hospital, 2 km south of Nathon. Medical aid is cheaper here; consult the doctor in charge if you're suffering from anything serious. The doctors also sell those medications which are difficult to get at the poorly stocked drugstores.

MOTORCYCLES / JEEPS - are cheaper in Nathon than they are at the beaches. Motorcycle 150-250 Baht, moped 120-200 Baht, jeep 400-500 Baht. You will be able to tell which places rent out vehicles by the signs in front of the shops. Petrol costs 9 Baht/litre at the petrol station on the main road, a hefty 11-12 Baht / litre at the mini-petrol stations along the circular road.

CLOTHES SHOPS - there are more than enough in town. Should you not be able to find anything in your size, why not have something tailored? Tailors will make excellent and cheap copies if you bring a pattern or - better yet - an article of clothing in your size.

PUBLIC TRANSPORT ON THE ISLAND
Pick-ups with bench seats (songthaew) are the most common form of public transport on the island. They come to all of the island's beaches at least twice daily. Their final destinations are usually written on the front of the car. They are standing waiting whenever a boat arrives at the pier or the ferry jetty, and the drivers will announce their destinations as the passengers disembark. You will see them waiting at the market in the morning. You can stop them (or have them let you out) anywhere along the

line. A ride will cost you between 10 and 20 Baht, depending on the distance. Those longing for more independence will have to rent a motorcycle, moped, or a jeep.

HOW TO GET THERE
BY TRAIN / BUS
From BANGKOK: A particularly pleasant trip for those who buy the combined train - bus - boat - ticket, which leaves Bangkok at 18:30 h (arrival Ko Samui 10:30 h), 180 Baht for 3rd class, 299 Baht for 2nd class (seat), 369 Baht (sleeper - upper bunk), 399 Baht (lower bunk), 449 Baht (ac-sleeper - upper bunk), 479 Baht (lower bunk); these are the prices for those buying their tickets at the train station. You will have to pay an extra 40 Baht at travel agents. You can buy your tickets up to 90 days in advance at the Advance Booking Office in Bangkok's main train station. Make sure that you are not put on the wrong bus once you've arrived at 5:59 h. You will have to pay again, should this happen. 5 further trains arrive between 23:13 and 4:42 h; we would not recommend taking any of these as you'll have to hang around for ages upon arriving.

A direct ac bus leaves for Ko Samui at 20:00 h (288 Baht, incl. ferry, 15 hrs.). A non-ac bus leaves at 19:00 h (143 Baht, 16 hrs.).

From PHUKET: Several ac minibuses leave for Ko Samui before noon (150 Baht, 4 hrs. + ferry). 8 local buses to SURAT THANI leave before noon (61 Baht, 6 hrs.). You can also take a hired car (Peugeot 504) from the Pansea Hotel on Surin Beach to the Pansea on Chaweng Beach (approx. 350 km). This will cost you 2200 Baht if you make the trip in one day, 3300

Baht for 2 days. The same trip with a driver will cost you 2700 or 4300 Baht; unlimited mileage, insurance, detailed description of the route. Petrol and the cost of the ferry are not included in the price.

From KRABI: Direct ac minibuses leave every morning (100 Baht, approx. 7 hrs.). The local bus to SURAT THANI leaves every hour between 6:00 and 14:30 h (50 Baht, 3 hrs.).

From HAT YAI: Direct ac minibuses cost 150 Baht. Three local buses to SURAT THANI leave in the morning (67 Baht, 5 hrs.).

From PENANG: Daily ac minibuses at 4:30 h for 40 M$ (400 Baht, 12-14 hrs.). There is also a daily train at 13:35 h (arrival in SURAT THANI 22:09 h; you might just make it in time to catch the night boat) - 2nd class seats 279 Baht.

BY BOAT
New boats and companies are constantly offering their services to KO SAMUI from SURAT THANI or vice versa.

A Nathon-bound speedboat leaves Ban Don daily at 9:30, 14:30, and 17:00 h (60 Baht, 2 hrs.).

Express boats leave Don Sak and Khanom 3 times daily (60 Baht, 1 h plus bus 1 h). The ferry to the Ko Samui ferry jetty leaves from Don Sak (from Khanom when the surf is particularly high) 5 times daily between 8:00 and 17:30 h (40 Baht, 1 1/2 hrs.). Motorcycles 30 Baht, cars 175 Baht (incl. driver), minibus 200 Baht. Ko Samui looks its best as you approach the ferry jetty from the sea; pretty bungalows beneath a long, palm-fringed beach. The night boat from Ban Don leaves at 23:00 h (50 Baht, 6 hrs.) - not recommended, seeing as the entire crew sometimes sleeps

through the trip along with the passengers. There have been two collisions with the boat returning from the island during the last two years!

BY PLANE
A flight directly to Ko Samui? We-ell... the airport has been 'almost' ready for years - luckily there are plenty of people putting up enough resistance. Up until now all flights go as far as the airport 30 km west of SURAT THANI and no further (see p. 366).

LEAVING KO SAMUI
BY BUS
Getting information concerning the various possible ways of leaving the island is no problem in Nathon. All travel agencies offer rides with their ac buses and faster ac minibuses to BANGKOK (starting at 275 Baht), PHUKET (150 Baht), KRABI (100 Baht), HAT YAI (150 Baht), PENANG (starting at 400 Baht), KUALA LUMPUR (550 Baht), and SINGAPORE (590 Baht).

BY TRAIN
Six daily trains leave SURAT THANI for BANGKOK, seats can only be reserved on three: ac at 17:48 h (arrival 5:10 h), non ac at 18:20 and 20:24 h (arrival at 5:50 and 7:05 h). All travel agencies are able to book seats for you over their wireless telephones (40 Baht). Thai Airways will do this for no extra charge. A combined boat /bus trip to the train station will cost you 60 Baht (departs from the island at 12:00 noon). All trains to the south leave in the middle of the night.

BY BOAT
The corresponding boat ticket will usually be sold to you along with your bus, train, or plane ticket. Missing the train because of problems with the boat's motor would be a typical thing

to happen on an Asian holiday. Don't
take it too seriously! Daily boats leave
Nathon for Ko Pha Ngan at 10:00 and
15:00 h (30 Baht, 40 min, + 5 Baht for
the small boat), from Bo Phut at 15:30
h (50 Baht).

BY PLANE
Daily flights from SURAT THANI to
BANGKOK, PHUKET, and NAKHON
SI THAMMARAT. You can reach the
airport with the limousine service for
150 Baht (incl. ferry) from Nathon.

BEACHES AND BUNGALOWS

The word that Ko Samui is a traveller's paradise has spread rapidly in the last
couple of years. The more travellers go, the more bungalow resorts are
opened. But there is no cause for panic yet; you will nearly always find what
you're looking for if you consider carefully before deciding which beach and
which bungalow you wish to stay at.

We would recommend the following course of action. Choose a beach from
the descriptions given and have yourself taken there by pick-up. Leave your
luggage at a restaurant and then set out in search of a hut on foot. Take anything for the first night but try to reserve something better for the next couple of
days. If you feel that the beach you've ended up on isn't really the one you had
in mind, simply rent a motorcycle and continue your search on the island's
other beaches the next day. You can always reserve your dream bungalow,
should it be momentarily booked up. Heavy bargaining is possible outside of
the season if there are only a few travellers around. Those with sensitive ears
would be well advised to find a bungalow not too close to the generators and
restaurants.

The most popular beaches (and the ones that are most frequently overcrowded) are in the east of the island. Those in the north are not visited quite as often, and those in the west and south even offer perfect solitude at times. The
simple 'Robinson'-type bungalows are slowly but surely vanishing off the face
of the island. The new ones are much more comfortable. The price you will be
expected to pay depends largely on the facilities offered (size, private bathroom, glass windows, good mattress, easy chair, terrace, fan, or even ac), as
well as the general prices at the rest of the beach. Prices have little to do with
the location or quality of the resort.

Simple bungalows can still be rented for approx. 30 Baht a night. Expect to
have to pay between 50 and 100 Baht if you want to have a private lavatory or
shower. Those bungalows with chairs, tables, a good mattress, and a fan will
cost between 120 and 180 Baht.

The better resorts raise their prices by 25-100% during the high season (June
16th-August 31st and December 20th-January 10th).

All bungalow resorts have their own restaurants. The food served at many of
them is both cheap and good. Plan on staying for at least a couple of months if
you want to try them all.

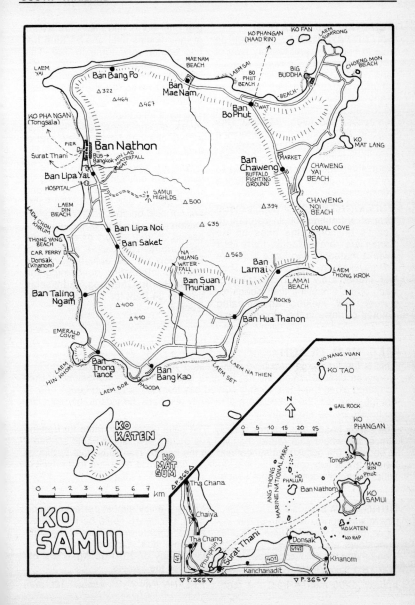

GENERAL INFORMATION

ENTERTAINMENT - You will be able to find the usual touristy type of entertainment at Chaweng Beach (and to a lesser degree also at Lamai Beach); regular, western videos in many of the restaurants, discos, beach parties, bars with and without hostesses, and even classical Thai dancing with dinner. If you're looking for 'girly' entertainment, however, bars, nightclubs, and massage parlours, then you'd be well advised to go to Pattaya or Phuket's Patong Beach instead.

BULLFIGHTS - are a popular local form of entertainment. In contrast to Spain's bullfights, the ones on Ko Samui are rarely bloody; there isn't even a matador. Two large bulls are first psyched up, then set loose. They will immediately start charging at each other, smashing their heads together and making an amazing amount of noise in the process. Both use their horns and the entire weight of their bodies until one of them has had enough and turns to flee. This sometimes happens after only a few seconds. The longest bullfight on the island, however, is said to have lasted for two hours.

The local inhabitants like gambling at these competitions, and a lot of money changes hands at the end of each fight.

There are several places on the island where bullfights are held, e.g. in Chaweng, Bo Phut, and Na Meung (southwest of Ban Lamai). The fights are not held on specific days; any occasion will do. We would suggest asking at your resort or one of the restaurants. The people at the First Bungalow will be able to give you detailed information concerning the bullfights in Chaweng. Admission there is 60 Baht for men, 50 Baht for women.

MAE NAM BEACH

This is the first large beach you will pass if you drive around the island in a clockwise direction. You will not be able to see the many bungalow villages scattered along the 4 km, slightly curved bay from the road. The beach here is not too crowded, the atmosphere pleasantly laid back; no videos, no night-life, no hotels. Prices are relatively low.

The sandy beach ends rather steeply. The calm water is suitable for bathing almost the whole year round. You will see quite a few fishing boats scattered in between the occasional sunbathers on the beach. The salas (rest pavilions) belong to the fishermen. The heat seems more intense here due to the lack of wind, especially during the hot season.

BUNGALOWS

There are approx. 20 bungalow villages, most of them *. Some also offer bungalows at **. We would recommend trying the following ones:

PALARN INN 1; this is the first one, approx. 1200 metres from the road.

You will enjoy almost perfect solitude here; the beach could be considered almost private and is framed by cliffs on one side. Camping tours to a lonely bay on Ko Pha Ngan are offered by the owners.

PALARN INN 2-***, approx. 100 me-

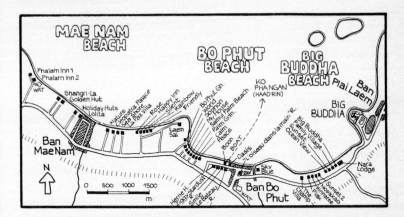

tres from the sea, very quiet and peaceful. Simple bungalows as well as more comfortable ones are available. The
LAEM SAI BUNGALOWS* are situated at the cape on the eastern end of the bay. Spacious 'village' with pretty

bungalows (private bathrooms) in a small inner courtyard. One can choose between two beaches, one in the west and one in the east, one with wind and one without, one with sunshine and one with shade.

BAN MAE NAM

The fishing village of Ban Mae Nam is situated in the centre of the long beach. You will be able to buy all necessary things here. Cheap seafood is sold at the market in the morning. *ALPHA* and *COBRA* offer windsurfing.

BO PHUT BEACH

This rather steep, coarse beach is in a 3 km, curved bay in the north. Suitable for swimming and windsurfing all year round. A couple of windsurfing schools have been opened here during the past few years. The beach is nicest at the northern end of the bay, it merges with the village of Ban Bo Phut in the south. Many French travellers come here. There are even a few French and Belgian restaurants. Prices are a little above average.

BUNGALOWS AND HOTELS
There're 11 bungalow 'villages', most of them*, some of them**-***, e.g.

WORLD BUNGALOW*-***, bungalows of various standards in a nice garden, some of them commanding a

good view. Rowing and motor boats can be rented.

Both the *PALM GARDEN** and the *CALM** offer tidy bungalows in a palm-tree plantation.

The *PEACE*-*** offers larger bungalows, especially suited for families, as well as a nice beach.

The *SAMUI PALM BEACH***** offers well-tended bungalows with parquet floors, ac, and large terraces, 9 of them directly on the sea. Appealing operation at the northern end of the bay.

HEME*** offers two terraced houses at the exit of the village.

BAN BO PHUT

This small Thai village has a typically rural atmosphere. Apart from brooms and rice, the small shops also offer suntan lotion and toilet paper. Tourist accommodation and tourist bars have been integrated into the village, something quite unique for Ko Samui. The French touch is apparent here, too.

A KO PHA NGAN-bound boat departs from the OASIS RESTAURANT daily at 15:30 h (50 Baht, 45 min.). The boat will take you to Haad Rin Beach at the southern tip of the island. It returns to Ko Samui at 9:00 h.

BIG BUDDHA BEACH

This relatively small bay commands a view of two offshore islands and a colossal Buddha statue. Whether or not it is tasteful to expose oneself in front of Buddha's eyes is something everyone will have to decide for themselves.

The white sandy beach is quite beautiful in the summer, when the wind blows from the west. The water becomes rather choppy when the wind gets stronger. The sea retreats a little when the wind blows from the east (in the winter), and it is then that the beach suddenly becomes very wide and rather ugly (mud and slippery stones), especially at low tide. The beach is not suitable for swimming at all during this time of the year.

BUNGALOWS AND HOTELS

Big Buddha Beach has become increasingly popular in recent times, in spite (or maybe just because) of the nearby road. As a result, more and more bungalow villages are squeezing themselves in between those already existing. The newer resorts all offer bungalows of very high standards, some built of brick, with fans, and even tiled bathrooms. The prices are generally rather high. There are 13 bungalow resorts here at the present time, most of them *-**.

Try the *FAMILY VILLAGE BUNGALOW*-*** (ac***), brick huts painted grey, clean and tidy; good restaurant by the road, family atmosphere.

The *SUNSET BUNGALOWS** are right next door; simple huts in the old style.

KINNAREE BUNGALOW*-** and *PIAK BUNGALOW*-*** are among the more recent resorts, both with slightly superior, though rather crowded, bungalows.

NARA LODGE*** (ac****), tel 22774240; a well-cared for hotel with terraced houses, hidden behind a high wall. The new road to the airport branches off from here.

CHOENG MON BEACH

This beautiful, small bay is at the northern tip of the island. The white, sandy beach is lined with coconut-palms and kasuarina-trees. The middle section of the bay has a wonderful beach and is suitable for bathing all year round. It is most suitable for children, too.

The small offshore island to the west is a challenge to any traveller. Exploring its rather rugged terrain can be quite exhausting, though. You can walk over to the island when the tide is low in the summer, you will have to swim across at high tide in the winter.

The seclusion of this lovely bay came to a rather abrupt end in 1987, when the Imperial Group decided to have two hotels built here. Though they did not turn out quite as ugly as everyone feared, they are still a thorn in many a traveller's side.

BUNGALOWS AND HOTELS

There are 6 bungalow villages on the bay at the present time. The cheapest (and simplest) huts are still those closest to the sea, those further back are more comfortable and more expensive. You will find the

OASIS**-*** in the very east, on top of the hill; new bungalows situated in a palm grove. You will be able to reach the secluded and rocky Phung Bay from here.

ISLAND VIEW*, a spacious resort run by a nice family, offering simple bungalows with and without bathrooms. The beach in front of it is not suitable for bathing.

CHATKAEO RESORT* is run by a Chinese woman; new bungalows with glass windows and small terraces, all with a view of the restaurant.

CHOENGMON BUNGALOWS* offers simple as well as more comfortable huts.

T & T BUNGALOWS*** is owned by a German; the large, high, and well furnished huts stand in a circular arrangement, quite far from the actual beach. The exclusive restaurant furnished with chairs made from tree roots at the driveway also belongs to T & T.

P.S. VILLA* offers bungalows of varying standards and has a nice restaurant.

The *TONGSAI BAY HOTEL***** is Ko Samui's most expensive hotel (over 2000 Baht). Its white bungalows on the slope and the 3-storey hotel complex give it a vaguely Mediterranean appearance. All of the bungalows are fully-ac suites with large terraces commanding a wonderful view of the bay. The hotel has a salt-water pool as well as a small stretch of private beach. Drinking water is obtained from a spring which is 5 km away from the hotel. For reservations from Bangkok, call 2540023.

BOAT HOTEL****; the same hotel group has dreamed up a particularly expensive gag; 36 boats from Bangkok's klongs have been hauled ashore and converted into luxury suites. They now lie scattered among the beach's cheaper bungalows.

YAI NOI BAY

This small bay is still quite peaceful. Although it doesn't have a long beach, there are plenty of sandy spots suitable for sunbathing in between the many large rocks.

BUNGALOWS AND HOTELS

I.K.K.**; new, secluded bungalow village beneath palms, small stretch of sandy beach, bathing possible at high tide.

CORAL BAY RESORT****; spacious bungalows with fan or ac in a large, rather wild, garden with palm trees. Most suitable for relaxing; not, however, for bathing.

CHAWENG BAY

This 6 km, slightly curved bay opens up to the east. One bungalow resort stands next to the other, but one still gets the impression of a totally uninhabited, tropical beach when regarding it from the view point in the south. All resorts are between the rarely used laterite path and the wide and beautiful sandy beach. Prices here are higher than at the other beaches, furnishings posher, and the general atmosphere is much more touristy. There are differences between the respective sections of the beach, so we have given separate descriptions.

CHAWENG YAI BEACH, NORTHERN END

This is the section of the bay favoured by real beach freaks; the sea is so shallow that the beach becomes several hundred metres long at low tide - perfect for jogging and frisbee. You will be able to reach the island of Ko Matlang on foot at these times. The reef to the south forms a small lagoon of warm water at low tide, in which you can safely bathe all year round, even in the winter.

BUNGALOWS AND HOTELS

There are around two dozen bungalow resorts on this part of the beach, most of them of rather high standards. Try the following:

MATLANG RESORT**, tidy, rather crowded bungalows in a nice, small, sandy garden with flowers.

THE BLUE LAGOON*, this resort has erected new, simple bungalows of bast mats.

POPPY INN**, pretty bungalows (with fan) beneath palms; large restaurant with open terrace; this resort doesn't seem quite as crowded as many others.

O.P. BUNGALOW*-**, this resort is owned by a Chinese, the bungalows have been erected to the right and left of a nice garden. Chinese restaurant and a wonderful stretch of beach beneath shady, deciduous trees.

SAMUI CABANA***-****, tel 272222 ext. 205; this resort becomes increasingly crowded towards the back, very comfortable bungalows, room service, coffee shop, beach bar, and seafood terrace.

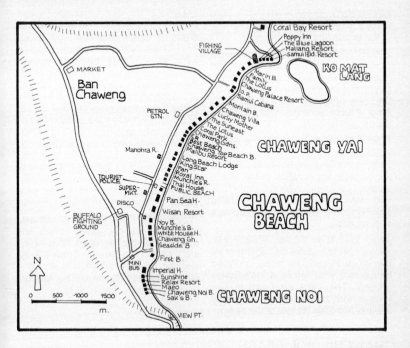

CHAWENG YAI BEACH, CENTRE

This beach looks like the tropical paradise everyone has always spent their lives dreaming of; fine, white sand, palm-trees and blue water, ideal bathing conditions at high as well as low tide. The surf can get quite high in the winter, though, when the beach becomes very narrow. And this beach has more to offer than just stunning natural splendour; there's lots happening here, too. There are beach restaurants featuring regular video performances, discos, a Thai restaurant with classical Thai dancing (the Manohra), windsurfing schools (at the Arabian Restaurant), a diving base (Ko Samui Divers in the Malibu Resort), a supermarket with a travel agency, and a branch of the tourist police. Those travellers who are willing to pay a little extra for entertainment, activities, and accommodation will feel at home here.

BUNGALOWS AND HOTELS

There are approx. two dozen bungalow resorts on this section of the beach. Many of them charge the highest prices on the island. Try the following:

CHAWENG GARDENS**-***, bungalows without fan. The nicest section of the beach starts at this resort.

MALIBU RESORT**, during the height of the season ***. Bungalows without a view of the sea; the only two-storey restaurant on the island is directly on the sea. The KO SAMUI DIVERS have a base here (for information on diving, see p. 387).

FIRST BUNGALOW*-***, the southernmost resort, bustling with activity. Luckily, the large hotels hardly disrupt the general appearance of the beach at all. The rows of beach umbrellas and deck chairs are the only thing signifying the presence of package deal tourists.

THE VILLAGE****, tel 272222 ext. 221, under the same management as the White House; 19 rather crowded bungalows with fan in a lush flower garden. They are arranged in two lines at right angles to the beach; only the first two have a view of the sea.

PANSEA****, for reservations call Phuket 076/216137. The international chain of hotels has had 100 luxury bungalows with all extras erected here, all in a large, beautiful garden. The bungalows are very spacious, all have ac and a large terrace, and all are connected to each other by little paths. Very few have a view of the sea. Many activities are offered free of charge, e.g. catamaran-sailing, windsurfing, bicycles, and badminton. Motorboat outings will cost you 600 Baht per person per day. Cars are available. Those with enough money can hire a teak schooner, a junk, or a yacht.

WHITE HOUSE****, tel 272222 ext. 208; tastefully decorated rooms are available in the terraced houses as well as in the white, three-storey building, all with full service and private terraces. Beware: The lagoon beyond the path smells terrible!

CHAWENG NOI BEACH

Separated from Chaweng Yai Beach by a small cape, this is a picturesque bay with smooth cliffs. The surf gets too high for bathing in the winter.

BUNGALOWS AND HOTELS

Few of the original bungalow resorts have survived; most of them had to make way for the new, large luxury hotel. Of the ones remaining we would recommend:

SUNSHINE*, RELAX RESORT*, or *CHAWENG NOI**, all with very cheap huts, all at the southern, rocky end of the beach.

IMPERIAL SAMUI****, for reservations from Bangkok call 2540023. All rooms of the tastefully arranged buildings command a view of the sea. Terraces, a restaurant, and a salt water pool have been built on various levels of the slope. The pool with its natural cliffs is fascinating. It is unfortunately also rather difficult to keep clean.

CORAL COVE

2 km south of Chaweng Noi, this picturesque little bay of sandy, white beach is situated between two passes of the coastal road and framed by round boul-

ders. There is only one resort on the narrow strip of land between the road and the sea:

BUNGALOWS
CORAL COVE*, bungalows on the beach and scattered beneath the palms on a little hill, simple restaurant, friendly people. Snorkelling through the bizarre cliff channels is fun.

The *GOLDEN CLIFF RESORT* is 1 km further up, on the cliffs.

THONG TA KHIEN BAY
Apart from the THONG TA KIAN restaurant you will also find the KATA GARDEN* resort and a peaceful, idyllic fishing village on this little bay.

LAMAI BAY
This sickle-shaped, 5 km bay attracts travellers from all over the world. Many come in search of an easy life for little money, and indeed, Lamai Bay does seem to offer everything the traveller's heart may desire, including a rich natural splendour and good connections to the rest of the island. As there are marked differences between the respective sections of beach, however, we will give you separate descriptions.

LAMAI BEACH, EASTERN BAY
The sea is very shallow here, only hip-deep at low tide. White, sandy beach alternates with smooth, flat boulders. The heavy breakers in the winter are for the most part held in check by the offshore cape. Thus bathing is possible all year round.

BUNGALOWS
The few resorts on this part of the beach are all situated on the slope, surrounded by coconut plantations which are great places for taking nice walks. This area is still quite peaceful and relatively far from the road. New resorts will no doubt be built here in the not-too-distant future.

We'd recommend *SILVER CLIFF**, all bungalows on the slope, with a view of the sea. You will have a particularly nice view of your section of the bay as well as the whole of Lamai Beach from the restaurant, which is on a projecting cliff ridge.

LAMAI, NORTHERN BEACH
There is an offshore reef right up to the level of the village of BAN LAMAI in front of this section of the beach. Rocks peek out of the water at low tide; unsuitable for bathing.

BUNGALOWS

There are well over a dozen bungalow resorts here. While the first couple can still be reached by way of a side road, the others are all quite close to the main road or the village. Try the

WEEKENDER VILLA*, which is a very nice resort in spite of its closeness to the main road; 3 different types of bungalows, many activities: windsurfing, canoe rides to the reef, snorkelling, dirt biking, boat trips to the islands, and currency exchange.

CENTRAL LAMAI

This nice section of the beach with its intermittent boulders is suitable for bathing at high and low tide. The sand is rather coarse. The waves get very high in the winter, when the beach becomes rather short. This beach still generates an atmosphere of total freedom, in spite of the fact that new bungalow resorts are constantly being opened, some even behind those already existing, others along the driveways. This is one of the favourite haunts of permanent travellers, who float back and forth between Goa, Bali, Kathmandu, and Ko Samui. You will meet romantic hippies for whom time seems to have stood still here, as well as children who have never had to experience a bitter, European winter. Many travellers manufacture jewelry in their bungalows and then sell it; a flea market is held every Sunday. You will find the cheapest restaurants with the best traveller food here, as well as the cheapest huts. Spontaneous beach parties are an everyday occurrence.

There are two things you should know. People have been known to be robbed on this beach, one of the sad side-effects of this kind of 'alternative' tourism. In addition, several of the resorts smell simply terrible due to the fact that the soaking pits, which are used as junk heaps, are filled to the brim (e.g. Paradise Bungalow and Bungalow Bills).

BUNGALOWS

There are two dozen bungalow resorts on the beach at the present time, and more are being built by the season (mainly in the terraced house style and with corrugated-iron roofs).

The WHITE SAND* resort is still built in the old style. Many permanent travellers stay here, and this is where the flea market is held on Sundays.

PALM* offers bungalows at various prices, the cheapest ones directly on the sea.

The NICE RESORT* makes up a mind-boggling sight; A-frame-bungalows standing next to each other like rabbit hutches; only recommended for those travellers who like feeling crowded.

LAMAI, SOUTHERN COAST

The WONDERFUL ROCK makes up the end of Lamai Bay in the south. Those resorts even further south actually belong to BANG NAM CHUET BAY, but they still profit from the well-known name of Lamai.

FISHING BOATS

The Wonderful Rock is an oddly shaped cliff reaching far into the sea and commanding a fine view of the bay. The surf gets rather high and wild in the winter, while bathing in between the rocks in the summertime can be a lot of fun. Wonderful Rock is especially popular among Thai holiday-makers because of its many souvenir-stands and snack-bars.

BUNGALOWS
WONDERFUL ROCK BUNGALOWS* offers very simple huts dotted between the boulders.

There are several cheap resorts on the road along the flat beach (many pebbles), e.g. *NOI BUNGALOW**.

The *SWISS CHALETS*** are situated at a raised altitude and command a spectacular view of the sea; spacious bungalows in a large resort with a very nice restaurant serving Thai and Swiss dishes.

ROCKY BUNGALOW*, the last resort on Lamai, has a private, sandy beach framed by round boulders. The off-shore reef 100 m from the island keeps the surf in check in the winter, making this a pleasant time to stay here. The sea is too shallow for bathing in the summer, however. The bungalows are situated in a palm grove, approx. 100 m from the road.

SOUTH COAST

Though you won't find any endless beaches down here, you will find secluded bays with truly idyllic bungalow resorts. You should definitely have visited this part of the island before claiming that Ko Samui is totally spoilt and over-crowded. If you are more into peace and nature than perfect but crowded beaches, then you've come to the right place. As the bungalow resorts are not as close to one another here as they are on the rest of the island, we have given more detailed descriptions of the main ones. No arterial road runs along this part of the coast up to now (though one is planned); you will only be able to reach the resorts by way of dead ends.

LAEM SET

Turn off H4170 towards the sea at the sign saying "Laem Set". You will reach the rocky bathing resort after 1.3 km.

BUNGALOWS AND HOTELS

CHATALET**** (the name may have changed by now), immediately to the left, at an approx. 200 metre beach with coarse sand. Comfortable ter-raced houses. Bungalows and a two-storey main building frame an ex-tended palm garden with a restau-rant, pool, and pool bar. Cliffs and coral rise out of the sea at low tide. The beach is safe for swimming when the tide is high.

A 200 metre driveway turning off to the right from the dead end road will lead you to NATAIN BUNGALOW*, a small, beautiful resort on a slope, commanding a wonderful view of the coastline. Nice restaurant. You should be able to find a nice se-cluded bathing-spot somewhere in between the many boulders on the otherwise sandy beach. You can also hire motorcycles here.

Continue on down the dead end road for 400 metres to the LAEM SET INN***, tel 077/273130 (wireless telephone), this resort is run by Mr. Parry, an Englishman. The restaurant is good but rather expensive. Many picturesque boulders lie distributed on the white beach. The water level depends on the winds, but it is always safe to go swimming. Mr. Parry orga-nizes boat-trips to lonely islands with secluded beaches. Laem Set Inn may be just the thing for those travellers who do not really wish to spend their holiday among 'cheap' travellers and might need to be reached by tele-phone but still want to experience the romance of a lonely beach hut.

LAEM SOR

You will find a pagoda belonging to a wat inhabited by friendly monks at the southernmost tip of the island. A wide reef rises out of the water just in front of it. When the water level is right, this is said to be an excellent place for snor-kelling.

BUNGALOWS

LAEM SOR ROCK BEACH BUNGA-LOW* is 300 metres to the right, beyond the pagoda, idyllically located on a lonely tip of land. You will be able to enjoy beautiful sunsets and sunrises from here. The bungalows and restaurant are distributed in a large area of exquisite natural splendour. The owner offers bathing trips to a nearby, uninhabited island with nice, sandy beaches. Fishing boats can also be rented.

EMERALD COVE

This secluded bay at the southwestern tip of the island can be reached by way of a 2 km, rather bad, dirt road. There is nothing but a sleepy fishing village down here, as well as two bungalow resorts, one to the left of the village and one to the right. There is quite a distance between the two resorts. You will be able to walk out towards the four strange looking cliffs in the sea for a whole kilometre when the tide is low. Even when the tide is high the water only ever gets chest-deep at the most.

BUNGALOWS

The *EMERALD COVE BUNGA-LOWS** are arranged in two lines, at right angles to the beach. They make a rather dismal impression. The restaurant is not at the beach, but on the other side of the bungalows.

The huts of the *SEAGULL BUNGA-LOW**, about 500 metres further on, have been artfully integrated into the landscape, some on the jungle-overgrown slope, others directly on the beach, in between the mangroves; nice beach restaurant.

WEST COAST

The very flat beaches on the western side of the island are not as exciting as those in the east. Relatively few travellers come here. Those who are into sunsets will simply love it, though. The calm western beaches are ideally suited for swimming, even in the winter, when bathing becomes impossible at the eastern beaches because of the high surf. All of the resorts are pretty close to the ferry jetty, so getting here isn't too much of a problem.

BUNGALOWS

The southern THONG YANG BAY is 1500 metres south of the ferry jetty. You will find the *COCO CABANA BEACH CLUB*** here, a beautiful bungalow resort on a sandy, palm-studded beach measuring several hundred metres in length. This resort already makes a favourable impression as one approaches the island by ferry. The tastefully decorated interiors of the bungalows and the restaurant are proof of the Italian owner's good taste. He likes sharing his hobbies with his guests - snorkeling, water skiing, windsurfing, fishing, sailing, volleyball, and badminton. He even offers a diving course and arranges diving excursions (Samui Divers, see p. 387).

The *SUNFLOWER BUNGALOW** is on the northern end of THONG YANG BAY, 1.3 km north of the jetty. This is a quiet and peaceful resort. You will reach LAEM DIN BAY by continuing straight on at the bend in H4174.

There are two resorts on this bay, the *PHLOEN GUESTHOUSE*-*** and the *LIPA LODGE*-****, the latter has put its cheaper huts farthest from the sea, quite contrary to the usual island custom.

A TOUR OF THE ISLAND

The island has nothing spectacular to offer apart from its beaches. There are no cultural "musts". All the same, a tour of the island is well worth it and very beautiful; the narrow roads leading through the gardens full of palm trees, the wonderful view points, the many beautiful beaches, and the "sights", which constitute a welcome change, are all very nice. The easiest way to do such a tour is by motorcycle or jeep. You can also set out on a bicycle, though you will sometimes have to get off and push. The public pick-ups do not drive around the whole island. You can drive all the way to Chaweng Noi, then get out, walk 4 km, and catch another pick-up to the rest of the island at Lamai Beach. This 4 km stretch between Lamai and Chaweng Noi is one of the most beautiful roads of South East Asia. Don't miss it!

If you start your tour in Nathon and circle the island in a clockwise direction, turn around after you've climbed the first hill and enjoy the magnificent view. You will pass MAE NAM BEACH and BO PHUT BEACH (both of which cannot be seen from the road), as well as BIG BUDDHA BEACH before reaching the first attraction after 25 km; the 12 metre statue of the sitting BIG BUDDHA and the wat that goes with it are located on a small island connected to the mainland by two dams. The statue is not particularly old, nor is it particularly beautiful. Still, set against the blue,sky and the tropical ocean it does seem quite impressive. There are many souvenir- and foodstands, making this a popular place for outings, especially among Thais.

A bumpy dirt road will lead you through palm-tree plantations to the northeastern tip of the island. Don't forget to enjoy the splendid sight of Choeng Mon Beach and Chaweng Beach along the way. You can stop by at the BEVERLY HILLS CAFE on the second pass between Chaweng and Lamai and enjoy the truly unique view whilst having a refreshing drink.

Turn right at the bend of the road in Ban Lamai and you'll reach the CULTURAL HALL. You will mainly find objects brought to the island by Chinese merchants during the last century exhibited here, i.e. weapons, tea services, instruments, clocks, and old, agricultural tools. The WONDERFUL ROCK (also known as GRAND ROCK) is at the end of Lamai Beach. Mainly Thais seem to be attracted to the large, strangely shaped Grand Ma and Grand Pa cliffs. Western travellers might be more interested in the wild surf, which seems particularly savage during the rainy season. There are many stands selling refreshments and souvenirs here.

Continue along the main road of the Muslim fishing village of Ban Hua Thanon until you reach the road branching off to the NA MUANG WATERFALL. A brook forms many pretty cascades here. The pools are good for bathing. Continue back to the settlement of Suan Thurian from here. Once there, go down H4173 towards the sea. Turn right and then left again (at the sign), and you will reach the PAGODA, which makes an impressive sight directly by the sea. You will ultimately return to the main road at Ban Saket by continuing through the dense palm-trees along H4170. An unsignposted, most impressive road built for the Air Force branches off at this small settlement. It leads to a radar station on top of a hill, from where you will have a splendid view. Back on the main road, you will reach the road branching off to the HIN LAT WATERFALL after approx. 1 km. You will have to walk upstream for 30 minutes in order to reach the highest of the cascades. You can combine this outing with a proper little jungle-trek; just stick to the brook and keep going inland.

You will find a signpost directing you to the SAMUI HIGHLANDS, a privately-owned piece of property with many pretty flowers on a hill. You might be able to make it halfway up the hill with a very good motorcycle or a jeep. You will most definitely have to walk the last 30 minutes, however. You will receive a glass of water, a coconut, bananas,a towel, and the magnificent view for a fee of 20 Baht. It is particularly beautiful at sunset. One can even spend the night up here (*).

DIVING OFF THE COAST OF KO SAMUI

Ko Samui's diving season is from mid-February to mid-November. There are numerous nice reefs around the island, but it is rather difficult to predict when the water will be clear where. For this reason the diving-guides will usually drive to the various spots to check them out before taking you there.

One of the many one-day diving-tours includes a trip to the SOUTHERN IS-LANDS, to SAIL ROCK (Ko Hin Bay, 3 hrs. north of Chaweng), and to some of the islands north of the MARINE NATIONAL PARK. 3-day tours are organized to KO TAO, which is the best area for diving in the whole region.

Expect to have to pay around 350 Baht for equipment and one extended dive, 900-1400 Baht for a day's tour with 2 dives, equipment, and a boat, depending on the distance.

Diving bases:

SAMUI DIVERS, at the Malibu Resort, Chaweng Beach, or at the Coco Cabana Beach Club. Cesare Benelli has been gathering experience in Ko Samui's diving areas for ten years now. Ralf Jackewitz is generally considered a particularly reliable and experienced diving instructor (PADI). Lots of good, reasonably new equipment is available.

SCUBA DIVING CLUB, contact Highway Travel Booking, Yai Travel Booking, or Marine Fantasy Club, all in Nathon.

An elderly (rather inexperienced) American also rents out scuba diving equipment. He lives at the path leading to the Lipa Lodge (signposted).

ANG THONG MARINE NATIONAL PARK

There are several places in Nathon that organize boat trips to the Marine National Park. Boats leave daily. Depending on the type of craft, the trip will take between 1 and 2 1/2 hours. It will cost you 150 Baht per person (incl. lunch and soft drinks). Two of the 40 islands of the archipelago are visited during the course of a 1-day tour. You will be able to gaze upon KO MAE'S THALE NOI, a green, crystal clear, salt water lake also known as the BLUE LAGOON. An incredible underwater world awaits you beneath the water's surface. Don't forget to bring your diving-mask and snorkel! You can spend as much time as you like snorkelling about among the corals, shells, and fish. It is strictly prohibited to take any shells or coral away with you.

We would strongly recommend climbing the UTTHAYAN HILL on the island of WU TALAP, regardless of the fact that it is a strenuous, 30 minute climb; the view of the many small, jungle-overgrown islands you will have from up here is definitely worth it. The park HQ is located on this island, which has a constant supply of fresh drinking water. You can spend the night at the PARK BUNGALOWS*** or in TENTS*. There is a restaurant on the island. You should tell your tour organizer your planned date of return when you buy your ticket, should you wish to stay on the island for a couple of days.

SOUTHERN ISLANDS

Seven islands south of Ko Samui make up the KATEN ARCHIPELAGO.

KO TAN - if you love dogs, avoid this island at all costs; there is a curse on the island saying that all dogs have to be killed, and even mere dog owners have run into trouble here.

KO MAT SUM - the beach with many pebbles is good for bathing. There are also several sandy beaches with many pieces of coral and shell (bring flip flops!). The coral reefs are wonderful for snorkelling and are said to be comparable to those of the Maldives.

The islands of **KO MOD DANG, KO RAB,** and **KO MAT KONG** are well known for their snow white beaches.

Samui Holiday Tour organizes a tour to the islands every Saturday from 8:30-17:00 h (150 Baht incl. lunch). Ko Samui Travel Centre goes out to the islands on Tuesdays, from 9:00-15:00 h (100 Baht). 3-day tours costing 350 Baht are also organized. You will be able to rent boats and go out on a tour of your own from several bungalow resorts along the south coast as well as from Lamai Beach. Keep your eyes open for notices pinned to bulletin boards etc.

KO PHA NGAN

This island is only 20 km north of Ko Samui. It covers an area approx. 2/3 the size of that of its 'big sister'. The two islands can't really be compared, though; while Ko Samui is gentle and easy-going, Ko Pha Ngan seems rather wild and savage. Tourists for whom Ko Samui is simply too touristy come here, to Ko Pha Ngan. Quite a few seem to do this, so there are not enough bungalows to go round during the height of the season, when tents are offered by way of temporary accommodation. In the expectation that the island might turn into a gold mine one day, just as Ko Samui did, new bungalow resorts are being built by the season. These resorts are not run by the local inhabitants, though; they are branches of resorts already existing on Ko Samui, usually managed by employees. Don't come expecting a hearty family atmosphere, in other words; you'll be disappointed. Rather more expensive bungalows with lav/shower have been built here, too, in the mean time, but there are no hotels on the island up to now (thank God!).

TONGSALA
The main settlement of the island is a tiny fishing village which has practically nothing to offer. There is a post office and a telegraph service (poste restante possible), a currency exchange booth (15% additional charge), a small travel agency, and a couple of shops.

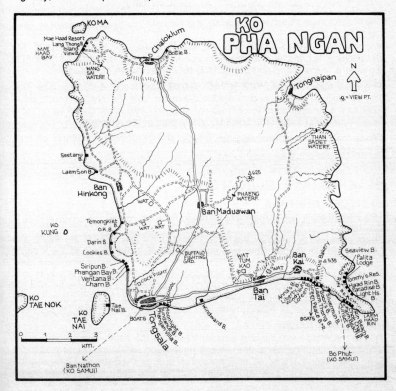

GENERAL INFORMATION
TRANSPORTATION ON THE IS-LAND Pick-ups that will take you to the island's beaches for 5-20 Baht await you as the boat comes into the harbour of Thong Sala. Motorcycle-taxis are also available. You can hire a motorcycle for 200 Baht per day on the island. Longtail boats travel to and from the southern and south-eastern islands from Ban Kai.

HOW TO GET THERE
Catch the speedboat from SURAT THANI / BAN DON via Ko Samui at 12:30 h (75 Baht, arrival 16:15 h). The night boat at 21:00 h will cost you 60 Baht. Speedboats from NATHON (Ko Samui) leave at 10:00 and 15:00 h (30 Baht, 40 min.).

There are no landing-places at the pier, so you will have to change onto a smaller boat once there, which will then bring you to the beach for another 5 Baht. More boats offer their services as the season progresses.

A boat leaves BO PHUT (Ko Samui) for HAAD RIN BEACH at 15:30 h (50 Baht, 45 min.).

EXCURSIONS
You will be able to reach two waterfalls on foot or by motorcycle, the ***PHAENG FALL*** (there is a small footpath to the viewpoint on top of the hill) in the centre of the island and the ***WANG SAI FALL*** in the northwest.

The meditation temple ***WAT KHAO THAM*** is on top of a little hill near Ban Tai. You will be able to reach it within 10 minutes from the village. A footprint of Buddha's is venerated in the mondhop. You will have a wonderful view of the beach and the sea from the small square in front of the temple.

Those feeling adventurous can go on a several-day tour of the island, on foot, of course.

BEACHES AND BUNGALOWS
EAST OF TONGSALA
The first section of the beach is disappointing; we would not recommend to stay here.
There are several bungalow resorts on sandy bays and cliffs all the way to the Laem Haad Rin (cape). The road stops at Ban Kai; from here you will either have to walk or organize a boat. This is the right area for those travellers looking for peace and quiet. Try the following: *LAEM THONG**, simple huts in a beautiful area. *SUNSET BUNGALOW**, cheap huts set on cliffs. *PALM BEACH**, bungalows set in a palm-tree plantation.

HAAD RIN BEACH
This is the most beautiful and popular beach on the southwestern part of the island; fine sand, corals to the left and right, good swimming. More and more bungalow resorts are being built here. The surf gets extremely high (and the swimming a little dangerous) between October and February. You can reach

this beach from Ban Tai by longtail boat (20 Baht) or on foot (2 hrs.). You can also catch a boat from BO PHUT on Ko Samui.

Try the following resorts: *SEAVIEW**, said to serve the best food on the beach. *HAAD RIN BUNGALOW**, directly by the sea. *SEA WIND*, SUN RISE*, PALITA LODGE*, PARADISE**, all at the southern end of the beach, and *LIGHTHOUSE**, on the cape. You will be able to exchange foreign currency at a very bad rate at the *PHUSIRI RESTAURANT*.

MAE HAAD BAY
This bay is in the northwestern part of the island. The beach here ends rather steeply and is made up of coarse sand. You can reach the bay by pick-up from THONG SALA (20 Baht, 1 hour). Try *MAE HAAD RESORT** or *ISLAND VIEW**, bungalows of various standards, good restaurant, directly by the sea. From here you can reach Wang Sai waterfall.

SEETANU BAY (also SRITHANU or SI THANOO)
Long, yellow, sandy beach in a curved bay with many palm-trees and mangroves in the western part of the island. *SRITHANU BUNGALOWS**, very simple huts with an even simpler restaurant.

WOK TUM BAY
This section of the island's coast is characterized by small coves and minibeaches. Many travellers come here in spite of the fact that the swimming is not too good. The beaches can easily be reached by pick-up from Thong Sala (10 Baht). More and more new bungalow resorts are being built here. *CHARN'S BUNGALOW**, with fantastic food, e.g. shark curry, crab soup with coconut milk, Irish Coffee. *SIRIPUN BUNGALOW*-*** serves even bigger helpings and offers even larger bungalows with lav/shower. *PHANGAN*-***, also with lav/shower. *COOKIES**, the name says it all (special cookies available). *SUNSET*, DARIN**, and *OK** are all located on the small beaches, in between the boulders. Mr. Ban of *KIET** offers island tours with a boat as well as snorkelling expeditions. He will sometimes venture as far as Ko Samui and the Marine National Park.

KO TAE NAI
This tiny island opposite Thong Sala offers bungalows** with running water and electricity, but - alas - no beach.

KO TAO
The island of Ko Tao (tortoise island) is 38 km north of Ko Pha Ngan and 58 km from Ko Samui. The island measures 7 km in length and 3.5 km in width. Mountains rise to a modest height of 379 metres.

The village of *BAN AO MAE HAT* is embedded in a picturesque bay framed by fascinating granite cliffs in the southwest of the island. You will find the beautiful *HAT SAI SI BEACH* beyond the cape, north of the village. Bathing is good all year round here, due to the shelter offered by the offshore corals. The small, shady beaches in the east of the island can only be reached by boat.

Particularly beautiful coral reefs surround the offshore island of *NANG YUAN,* northwest of Ko Tao. The local inhabitants call the island *HANG TAO* ('the tortoise's tail'). 3-day diving expeditions to the island are offered by Ko Samui Divers (see p. 387) and by Chumphon Cabanas (see p. 362).

ACCOMMODATION

You can stay at *NIYOM** or *NEPTUN*;* both offer simple bungalows and simple traveller food.

The fresh water supply constitutes quite a problem on the island, especially after a particularly dry period.

HOW TO GET THERE

The island can be reached by fishing boat from KO PHA NGAN (100 Baht, 4-5 hrs.). For information, ask at Cookies or Sunset on Wok Tum Bay. A chartered boat from CHUMPHON takes 6-7 hrs. to make it to the island. This is only worth it for a group of at least 6-8 people.

KHANOM AND SICHON

These two settlements are on the east coast, approx. 75 km east of Surat Thani, not too far from the landing-places for the boats from Ko Samui, on the Gulf of Thailand. The two fishing villages are 30 km apart (H4014 and H401). Several beautiful beaches were made accessible to tourists thanks to a new roadway between the interesting coast and the 814 metre Khao Phra (construction had almost been completed at the end of 1987).

BEACHES AND BUNGALOWS

The beaches here are diverse in nature; those at the northern and southern ends are seemingly endless, while those in between are curved, almost sickle-shaped, and marked off by rocky capes. The bungalows here are much more expensive than those on Ko Samui, due to the fact that there is little business (except for weekends and holidays, when many Thais come). Even so, new resorts are being built by the season.

On **KHANOM BAY**, with its 5 km, white beach:

WATANYOU VILLA*-**, just 1.5 km from Khanom, on Nadan Beach; nice bungalows in a palm garden, slightly set back, imposing restaurant on the white beach.

6 km further on, on the fine sandy beaches of **NAI PLAO BAY:**

FERN BAY RESORT***, 6 tiny bungalows with lav/shower, restaurant.

NAI PLAO BAY RESORT***, 51/3 Khanom tel 075/342237; 20 comfortable, spacious bungalows arranged in two lines running parallel to the beach, large palm garden out front; good restaurant.

The 40 rooms of the *DIAMOND CLIFF**** are at a raised altitude - magnificent view. The film "Devil's Paradise" was filmed here in 1986.

There are two waterfalls you can hike to, the **HINLAD WATERFALL** (1.5 km) and another one further up in the mountains.

Bungalow resorts will soon be opened on the beaches towards Sichon, too, e.g. on **THONG HYEE BAY** (3 km further on) and **TONG YANG BAY** (6 km).

The wide, sandy beach of **HIN NGAM BAY** can be reached from Sichon; just take the road leading to the sea. Young Thais like to camp here at the week-end.

You will find the *PRASARNSOOK VILLA**** here, too (discount given during the week); 30 pretty bamboo bungalows and a big restaurant spread over a large area. You will have a good view from the hill by the access road.

You will come across a signpost proclaiming "Beach 2 km" 3 km south of Si-chon. Don't fall for it - there is nothing but a small Muslim fishing village at the end of the dead end road; not at all suitable for bathing.

GIRLS SELLING FOOD AT THE BUS STATION

NAKHON SI THAMMARAT

This settlement along the eastern coastal road (which runs through the mainland for 10 km at this point) lies distributed along a stretch of several kilometres. It is assumed that an important town of the Sri Vijaya Empire or one ruled by an autonomous king from Palembang used to stand on the site of present-day Nakhon Si Thammarat. Fragments of the old town fortification, which are said to date back as far as 655 A.D., can still be viewed. The earthen walls were renewed under King Ramesuan (1407) and Narai (1677) and were later replaced by brick walls. You will still be able to find remains of the old

TOWN FORTIFICATION and *TOWN WALL* (the long sides measuring 2238 metres, the adjacent sides 456 metres) today. The centre of the new city and its business centre are north of the old settlement, east of the train station. Most hotels and restaurants are here, too. Catch one of the many town buses heading south to

WAT MAHATHAT (all town buses head only north or south, so you needn't worry about ending up somewhere in the east or west of this slender town) The wat is the oldest and most interesting of the many temples in town. According to written records, the temple was built under King Si Thanna Sokarat in the 8th century. Judging from archeological discoveries made here, however, it cannot have been erected until the 12th century. Thailand's second highest stupa, known as Phra Borommathat, was built here during the period of Sri Vijayan rule, when Buddhism was first spreading into the country.

A colonnade containing over 100 Buddha statues surrounds the temple grounds. Further Buddha statues can be viewed in the square sub-structure of the central, Ceylonese style, 77 metre stupa with its golden tip. The stupa is surrounded by smaller chedis. The building bordering onto the northern end of the colonnade contains a large standing Buddha statue surrounded by various mythical creatures. The monastery treasures are exhibited in the

TEMPLE MUSEUM (open from 8:30-12:00 and 13:00-16:30 h). You will find the world's most famous Buddha statue, Buddha Phra Singh, in the bot. This is one of the three statues said to be the originals from Ceylon. The other two can be seen in Bangkok's National Museum and in Chiang Mai's Wat Phra Singh. You can purchase souvenirs at the

HANDICRAFT CENTRE in the southern temple ground area. The many stands offer arts and crafts from the region, e.g. brass, bronze, and silverware, jewelry, shadow-play figures, baskets, shells, and much more. Food and drink are also available. Go south down Tha Chang Road (behind the beautiful *MOSQUE*) and you will come upon more shops selling leather articles, jewelry, and arts and crafts. Traditional shadow-play performances can be seen in town on holidays. This form of entertainment is particularly popular in Malaysia and Indonesia. Continue even further south and you'll reach the large, new

NATIONAL MUSEUM. Discoveries dating back to prehistoric times, Buddhist and Hindu works of art from the Malaysian peninsula, and ancient stone inscriptions are exhibited on the ground floor. Pieces from various regions are exhibited on the upper floors: Sa-wankhalok ceramics, Chinese porce-lain, bronze Hindu statues, and shad-ow-play figures. Open (except for Mon and Tues) from 9:00-16:00 h, closed from 12:00-13:00 h, admission 10 Baht.

The large *HUA IT MARKET* is held daily near the bus station. You will find another large market on Pak Nakhon Road in the northwest of town, a street market in the narrow alleys opposite the station.

HOTELS
There are many hotels in the vicinity of the bus station, e.g. the *MON-TIEN**-****, next to the station, 1509/40 Yommaraj Road, tel 341908, and the *SI THONG**, opposite the sta-tion, 1547/2 Yommaraj Road, tel 356357. On the same road: the *LAEM THONG**, 1213/5-6 Yommaraj Road, tel 356478, and the *NAKORN***, 1477/5 Yommaraj Road, tel 356318. The *SIAM** is on the road running parallel, 1403/17 Chamroen Vithi Road, tel 3563560, the *MUANG THONG** is directly opposite. The *TAK SIN**-*****, Siprat Rd., tel 356788-90 and the *THAI HOTEL**-*****, 1373-1375 Ratchdamnoen Road, tel 356505, are the two best hotels in town. It's worth taking more expensive rooms here!

FOOD
There are many foodstalls and bak-eries in town. The *SINOCHA BAKERY* is opposite the Thai Hotel. A good *CHINESE DUCK RESTAURANT* can be found a little north of the train sta-tion, opposite the cinema. You will find more restaurants on Charoen Vithi Road, the road running parallel.

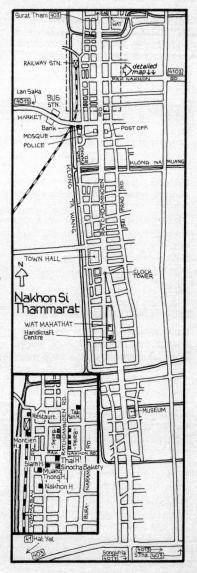

GENERAL INFORMATION

INFORMATION - the Nakhon Si Thammarat Business Association publishes a map and an informative brochure which can be bought at KP BOOKS HOUSE 1478/16-17 Chamroen Vithi Road, tel 341554, as well as many other places in town.

POST - post office on Ratchdamnoen Road, north of the clock tower. International phone calls can be made from the Telephone Office, behind the town hall.

BANKS - there are numerous banks in town, most of them on Ratchdamnoen Rd., north of Pak Nakhon Rd.

TRANSPORTATION IN NAKHON - buses travel up and down the town's long main road. A ride will cost you 2 Baht. There are also song-thaew and bicycle rickshas.

HOW TO GET THERE

A branch of the southern train line ends here. There is only one daily train from BANGKOK, which leaves at 17:30 h (299/153 Baht for the 2nd/3rd class). All other trains stop in Khao Chum Thong, 30 km west of town.

Buses from SURAT THANI cost 230 Baht, PHATTALUNG 22 Baht, BANGKOK 150 Baht (805 km). Ac buses leave Bangkok between 18:30 and 19:50 h (270 Baht). Ac buses from Nakhon can be booked at Muang Tai Tour, tel 342435. The bus station is approx. 1 km southwest of the station on Road 4015 west. SURAT THANI, HAT YAI (70 Baht, 2 1/2 hrs., 189 km) and SONGKHLA can also be reached by overland taxi.

There are daily flights to SURAT THANI (230 Baht) with possible connections to PHUKET (315 Bah.t) and BANGKOK (1380 Baht). The airport is in the north of town, where a large paratroop unit is also stationed. Thai Airways tickets cab be bought at Nakorn Bhan, 1612 Ratchdamnoen Road, tel 342491.

EXCURSIONS FROM NAKHON SI THAMMARAT

KHAO LUANG NATIONAL PARK

The park surrounding the 1800 metre KHAO LUANG was opened to the public in 1984. It can be found 29 km west of town, 2 km north of the road leading to Chawang. Take the road branching off to the right in BAN RON, 8 km before LANSAKA. Minibuses from Nakhon Si Thammarat cost 8 Baht. Several stands selling drinks can be found at the lower end of the footpath leading to the waterfalls. The water masses of the KAROM FALLS (measuring approx. 30 metres in width and surrounded by dense jungle) fall down cliff walls measuring up to 40 metres in height. Take a walk along the path running next to the river and ending at the impressive falls. There is another waterfall 20 km west of town, near Phrorn Kiri - NAM TOK PROMLOK. Continue down the other branch of the main road for 5 km and you'll reach the WAT KHAO KU PHANOM, located at the foot of a mountain. A staircase leads up to a hermit's cave.

BEACHES

SAVANIWAT BEACH, 20 km north of town, is rather dirty, as are the beaches that can be found nearer to Nakhon Si Thammarat. The fishing village of PAK PHANANG, 28 km southeast of town, has nothing particularly interesting to offer either. The road goes to the tip of the narrow LAEM TALUMPUK peninsula. From here you can catch a ferry to PAK NAKHON , a village lying east of Nakhon Si Thammarat.

THE WEST COAST

Up until two years ago, there was only one destination for travellers on Thailand's west coast - the beaches of Phuket Island in the Andaman Sea. Then the word got around that Krabi, too, has plenty of fine, white beaches to offer, and thus a new traveller-centre was born. The offshore islands with their marvellous beaches were 'discovered' for 'Robinson Crusoe-types'. The many flat beaches further south will probably remain Thai territory, with the possible exception of a couple of 'white' beach-joggers and nature freaks. Many of the beaches and islands towards Ranong have been integrated into National Parks in order to protect them from all-too-rapid exploitation. These might be worthwhile places for those travellers who are more into simple beauty and solitude than the loud and hectic traveller scene.

KRABI

This busy provincial capital on the west coast was still completely unknown to travellers in 1986. Nothing much has changed in the town since, but the wonderful surrounding countryside, particularly the beaches and offshore islands, has proved to be a tempting lure for travellers from all over the world. You will now even find the name of Krabi mentioned in the brochures of travel agencies who usually specialize in package deals. The (sad?) results are already clearly visible - Krabi was virtually flooded with tourists in January of 1988. You will find a particularly large number of German tourists fighting their way through the four streets of the small town. As there are only a limited number of rather short beaches, Krabi is not as suitable for accommodating hoards of tourists as, say, Phuket or Ko Samui. Those who have heard of Krabi, however, desperately want to go there - tourists looking for peace and quiet will thus be terribly disappointed.

ACCOMMODATION

A few business-minded Thais have recognized the needs of western travellers and have opened guesthouses in town. Up until now these guesthouses have been restricted to single floors in large apartment buildings, but this will no doubt change soon. Ask for information at the Amata Coffee Shop, in the Tip House, or at Krabi Travel & Tour. One normally only spends a night in town if one is planning to continue on to Phi Phi or one of the other islands the next day.

MAD MAX GUEST HOUSE*, 36 Joafa Road, friendly and clean.

SU GUEST HOUSE*, central location, above Suzuki; rooms with fan and mosquito-nets, community shower.

BLUE BUILDING GUEST HOUSE* (no official name as yet), Soi Ruam Chat, on one of the upper floors of the blue building. We'd suggest avoiding the

NEW HOTEL** with its small, shabby rooms. The

VIENG THONG HOTEL**, 155 Uttarakit Road, tel 611288, very central, opposite the floating restaurant, has acquired a bad reputation due to the many professional girls that work there. Travel agencies selling bus and boat tickets can be found in the lounge. The new

THAI HOTEL** (ac***), Isara Road 3, tel 611122, is in the centre of town. The tastefully decorated interior makes quite a good impression. The

NAOWARAT HOTEL***-****, tel 611581, is approx. 2 km out of town, on the arterial road; all rooms ac.

FOOD

There are many small restaurants and foodstands in town. Travellers like hanging out at the *AMATA COF-FEE SHOP* and the *TIP HOUSE*, both of which serve pancakes, fruit shakes, and ice cream. The *REAN PARE* (the *FLOATING RESTAURANT)* is particularly beautifully located. A gangplank connects the restaurant to the riverbank. Good meals at prices a little above average.

GENERAL INFORMATION

BEST TIME TO COME - between November and April. According to the manageress of the Krabi Resort, however (and she, after all, has been living here for years), the weather is usually nice during the so-called rainy period, too.

INFORMATION - maps, informative brochures, and tips for excursions to Ko Phi Phi are available at the TIP HOUSE, which is run by friendly young men. Breakfast, snacks, and drinks are also served.

BANKS - There are several banks on Uttarakit Road, Mon-Fri 9:00-15:30 h. You will not be able to exchange money at the beaches or on the islands.

POST - the post office on Uttarakit Road has a Poste Restante counter and an international telephone, Mon-Fri 8:30-16:30 h, Sat 9:00-12:00 h, near the pier.

IMMIGRATION OFFICE - on Uttarakit Road, one block beyond the post office. Visa extensions no problem at all. Open Mon-Fri 8:30-16:00 h.

TRAVEL AGENCIES - new travel agencies that can procure bungalows, buses, and boats to the islands are opening up all over Krabi.

MOTORCYCLE RENTALS - you can hire a Honda TX (110 cc) for 150-200 Baht a day. Travel & Tours also rent out motorcycles.

HOW TO GET THERE

From BANGKOK: four daily buses leave from the Southern Bus Terminal between 19:00 and 21:00 h (161 Baht, 13 hrs.), ac buses 290 Baht.

From PHUKET: Several local buses leave daily (38 Baht, 4 hrs.). They drive through beautiful countryside via PHANG NGA (22 Baht).

From KO SAMUI: daily ac minibuses in the morning (100 Baht).

From SURAT THANI: Ac buses leave at 10:00 and 11:00 h (50 Baht, 3 hrs.); local buses leave every hour from 5:30 h (4 1/2 hrs.)

FROM HAT YAI: Local buses for 26 Baht (ac 60 Baht).

FROM PENANG: Ac minibus for 40 M$ (=400 Baht), 9 hrs.

LEAVING KRABI
BY BUS

To the beaches: pick-ups to AO NANG BAY (15 Baht) drive through town and stop at various places, e.g. Pattana Road, in front of Travel & Tour. You will be able to reach further beaches on foot or by boat from the bay.

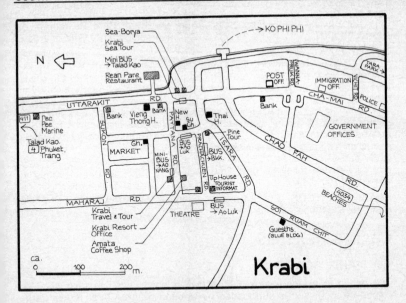

Krabi

Buses to AO LUK leave from two different places in town (see map). Direct ac buses to BANGKOK leave the Krabi Bus Office at 16:00 and 16:30 h (290 Baht, 14 hrs.). Non ac buses leave town at 16:00 and 17:00 h (161 Baht). Local buses to all destinations in the south leave from the bus station at Krabi Junction in Talad Kao, 5 km north of Krabi (catch one of the many minibuses for 3 Baht on Uttarakit Road). Buses to PHUKET leave every hour between 6:00 and 15:00 h (35 Baht, 4 hrs.). Buses to KO SAMUI via SURAT THANI (50 Baht) leave at 9:00 and 11:00 h (100 Baht, approx. 7 hrs.- price includes the ferry to Ko Samui).

Buses to SURAT THANI leave every hour between 6:00 and 14:30 h (50 Baht, 3 hrs). There are 4 buses to HAT YAI via TRANG (30 Baht) and PHATTALUNG (40 Baht) between 10:25 and 13:55 h (60 Baht, 5 hrs.).

You will have to change in TRANG in order to get to SATUN.

You will be able to buy tickets for long distance buses at the Bus Office on Prachuanchuen Road as well as at all travel agencies in town.

There are daily ac minibuses to KO SAMUI (190 Baht) and SURAT THANI (150 Baht) at 11:00 h. Ac minibuses to SINGAPORE (495 Baht), KUALA LUMPUR (440 Baht), PENANG (385 Baht), and HAT YAI (150 Baht) leave at 7:00 h - tickets and information available at Krabi Sea Tour, 256 Uttarakit Road, tel 611110, and others.

BY TRAIN
In order to get to the stations on the southern railway line, you will have to catch the bus to THUNG SONG, which leaves every hour (37 Baht, 3 hrs.). 6 trains to BANGKOK leave from there between 15:00 and 20:30 h

(261/124 Baht in the 2nd/3rd class, approx. 14 hrs.).

BOATS TO KO PHI PHI

PEE PEE MARINE TRAVEL, 201/3-4 Uttarakit Road, tel 611496, Mon-Fri 8:00-16:00 h. A large boat, formerly used for fishing, leaves the pier daily at 9:00 h. The trip to Ko Phi Phi takes approx. 3 hrs. A 3-hour sightseeing and bathing trip around Phi Phi Le and all its natural beauties is included in the price of 200 Baht, as is the return trip on the following day. One way ticket: 150 Baht.

KRABI SEA TOUR, 256 Uttarakit Road, tel 611110; a boat leaves daily from the Rean Pare Restaurant at 9:00 and 13:00 h (100 Baht one way, 2 1/2 hrs.).

The SONGSERM express boat (tickets for sale at the desk of the Vieng Thong Hotel) only heads for Ko Phi Phi on Tuesdays and Thursdays at 13:00 h - 1 1/2 hrs., 200 Baht one way. The boat also leaves for PHUKET from Ko Phi Phi daily (200 Baht).

BY PLANE

Bangkok Air has been promising flights from Bangkok to Krabi; it remains questionable whether anything will ever come of this.

KRABI'S BEACHES

AO NANG BEACH

This beach measures approx. 800 metres in length, has fine sand with little pieces of coral, and is surrounded by wooded cliffs on three sides. Large stones peek through the sand at the northern end of the beach. The view of the picturesque cliffs and the offshore islands is wonderful. Minibuses from Krabi cost 15 Baht.

BUNGALOWS

The KRABI RESORT**** (dormitory*) is at the northern, rocky end of the beach. Office in Krabi: 53-57 Pattana Road, tel 611389. This is the best resort on the beach; 45 very luxurious bungalows (non-ac, 4 beds) built of natural materials, surrounded by lawn, palms, and tropical trees. Good restaurant with a nice bar; good ice cream is served. Windsurfing, fishing, diving, and ping pong also possible. The

CORAL BEACH BUNGALOWS* are right next door; very simple huts, also directly by the rocky beach.

There are several very simple bungalow resorts in a palm grove beyond the dusty road. Prices start at 50 Baht.

AO NANG BEACH BUNGALOWS*, extremely dusty. You can hire surfboards at the nearby MARINE SPORTS CENTRE.

ANDAMAN BUNGALOWS*; you will also find ANDAMAN TRAVELS here. Trips to the offshore islands as well as the Phi Phi islands can be organized (longtail boats costing approx. 130 Baht per person, only recommended when the water is extremely calm!).

COCONUT GARDEN BUNGALOWS*; there is still a vacant spot next to this resort.

PRINCESS GARDEN*-** (with dormitory); this resort lies at a slightly higher altitude than most others, at the feeder road. Although it is not directly on the beach, you will have a wonderful view from the restaurant (western food) and some of the bungalows. Rooms with bathrooms, veranda, and fans. The owner is English. Travel & Tours in Krabi also belongs to him.

AO NANG VILLA*-***, large, pretty resort with simple huts as well as more comfortable ones with fan, lav/shower; very clean. Excellent food is served at the nice open air restaurant. Good information as well as boats and motorcycles available. Excursions are arranged for only a very small fee. The owner is a very friendly doctor from Krabi, who lives here himself with his family and keeps an eye on everything.

PEACE BUNGALOW*; not directly on the beach, a little further inland. Simple huts with mosquito-nets - usually very peaceful.

PAI PONG BEACH

Hidden behind cliffs, beautiful, white Pai Pong Beach forms a pretty bay with clear, blue water. It is truly idyllic, with palm trees and even a little jungle. You can reach the beach by walking over the small hill (15 min.) or by boat.

BUNGALOWS

There is only one resort here, the *PAI PONG BEACH BUNGALOWS*-***; nice huts scattered amongst the palm trees; good, rather expensive restaurant. Go to the Amata Coffee Shop for information and reservations.

RAI LEH BEACH/ PRANANG CAVE (PRINCESS CAVE)

This peninsula, surrounded by steep cliffs, can only be reached by boat. The fantastic limestone formations tower above the beach and reach all the way into the sea. The water has formed several large caves in the cliff walls. There are three beaches with fine white sand here, as well as one rather unexciting, mangrove-overgrown bay. The first bungalows were built on the two most beautiful beaches in 1986. Back then, these four beaches were still a well-kept secret among travellers. It is almost tragic - the most beautiful of them all is soon to become an exclusive playground for Club Mediteranee members! What is even more shameful is the fact that the beaches have become so popular in such a short time, that bungalows have to be built virtually overnight in order to accommodate all the tourists. At first, the young fishermen of the village had quite a difficult time dealing with the loose morals of many of the tourists. This problem was solved for them, however, when the entire village had to re-settle in order to make room for a new bungalow resort. The beautiful PRANANG CAVE, directly on the sea, has been misused for holding parties in. This, too, will probably have lasting effects. You can reach Rai Leh Beach by boat from Ao Nang Beach for 20 Baht per person.

BUNGALOWS

The northern bay is flat and rocky. This makes it rather unsuitable for bathing. The bungalows which had opened when we were there last did not have a name yet. They'll probably have to close down soon, anyway; of all the four beaches, this seems to be the one least suited for tourism. You will be able to reach the second large bay (Rai Leh) on foot from here, but only when the tide is low. Walk past the solidly built bungalows of the apparently privately-owned resort. The PINE* resort, right next to it, has expanded to an incredible 60 bungalows by now. Good restaurant serving excellent seafood. Advance reservations at Pine Tour, 20 Isra Muang, Krabi. Walk inland along the footpath from here, past the mangrove bay, and on to the beach with the many cliffs and the Pranang Cave, which can be seen on the cover of many travel brochures these days.

The CLIFF* and the GIFT* were the first resorts to open bungalows here, but many have since followed, some of them actually building their resorts directly beneath the cliffs. At times, one felt as if one were living in the middle of a construction site. Soon, however, the whole beach will belong to the Club Med; at least that is how it seems.

HAT NOPARAT THARA

Continue along road 4202 beyond the Krabi Resort. You will reach a very flat beach after 1 km. One can walk over to the offshore islands without even getting one's feet wet when the tide is low. Many starfish can be seen lying in the tidal gullies. Single kasuarina-trees grow along the beach, becoming more dense towards the end. There are many open air restaurants here, as well as the HQ of the MU KO PHI PHI National Park. You can spend the night at the PARK BUNGALOWS**.

EXCURSIONS FROM KRABI

Some of the sights can be reached easily with a motorcycle; others can only be reached on foot.

SHELL CEMETERY (SUSAN HOI)
An entire ledge of rock is made of thousands of small, fossilized shells, said to be 75 million years old. Many Thais like coming here. Most travellers, however, remain pretty unmoved by the sight. You can either come here via H4204 or with a chartered boat.

PRANANG CAVE
The Pranang Beach grotto can easily be reached by boat from Ao Nang Beach. The phallic rocks here are venerated as symbols of fertility by the local fishermen, and the beautiful bay is perfect for snorkelling.

WAT THAM SUEA
134 monks and 133 nuns live in this cave-monastery. Their master, PRA ARCHAN JUMNEAN SEELASETTHO, is venerated in a large, extended grotto containing Buddha statues, stands, and meditation pictures. He teaches a highly individual form of meditation which does not, however, contradict the Buddhist teachings; reflecting upon one's inner organs. He distributes photographs of corpses with their innards exposed as a meditation help. Many devout Buddhists who have come here gaze upon these photographs with

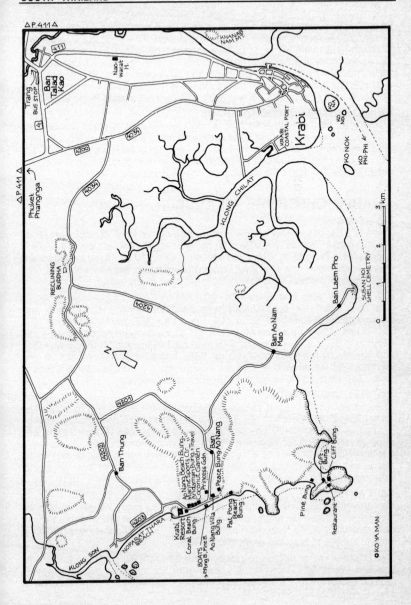

△P.411△

411

Trang
Bus stop

(4)
Ban
Talad
Kao

4200

△P.411△
←Phuket
Phangnga

4034

Nao-
warat H.

4034

KHANAB
NAM MT.

KRABI
COASTAL PORT

Krabi

KLONG CHILAT

KO
NOK

KO NOK

KO
PHI·PHI

RECLINING
BUDDHA

4204

Ban Ao Nam
Mao

Ban Laem Pho

SUSAN HOI
SHELL CEMETERY

0   1   2   3 km.

4201

N

Ban Thung

4202

Ao Nang Beach Bung
Marine Sports Ctr.
Coral Beach Bung.
Andaman Bung.+Travel
Coconut Garden
Princess Gdn

Ban
Ao Nang

◆ Peace Bung

Krabi
Resort
Coral Beach
Bung.

Ao Nang Villa
Bung

BOATS
→Phng B. Pine B.

4203

NOPARAT·THARA
BEACH

KLONG SON

Pat Pong
Beach
Bung

Pine Bung

Gift
Bung.

Cliff Bung.

Restaurant

○ KO YA MAN

barely controllable revulsion. The master himself hardly speaks any English. Several of his monks speak it excellently, though. The staircase approx. 200 metres further to the left leads up to a pass and down into an enclosed valley. Monks live here in small huts and grottoes beneath the rocky ledges of cliff. Walk down the path into the forest with the huge trees. Turn off onto H4 2 km east of Krabi Junction, shortly before km stone 107. You will find several pickups here, ready to drive you down the remaining 2 km of road to the wat.

PHANOM BENJA NATIONAL PARK
A passable, narrow road branching off 500 metres east of Krabi Junction will lead you to this wild, almost inaccessible National Park. You will pass a waterfall with many levels along the way. You will reach the HQ after 20 km. You can climb to the top of KHAO PHANOM on a five-day, guided tour through the dense jungle. Go to the Tip House for further information.

KRABI'S OFFSHORE ISLANDS

KO BA DA
There is a beautiful beach on the eastern side of this 1km² -sized, uninhabited island, which is approx. 8 km from Ao Nang Beach. The west side of the island is perfect for snorkelling. The Krabi Resort opened 20 comfortable bungalows here, which have, however, been closed down again; tourists allegedly start suffering from rashes if they spend too much time on the island.

KO SIBOYA (Also known as SEA BORYA)
This small island has only recently been discovered for tourists. There is only one bungalow resort there up to now, the *ISLANDER HUT**, only open from Dec-March. The huts are located on a flat beach beneath coconut-palms and deciduous trees. There is a village beyond the hill, approx. 30 min. away. Getting here from Krabi will cost you 50 Baht, boats leave between 13:30 and 14:30 h. The trip will last a good two hours. Contact the Sea-Borya Office in Krabi, 246 Uttarakit Road, tel 611108; open round noon.

KO PU (JUM ISLAND)
There is a bungalow resort on this island, too, on the southwestern coast. The *JUM ISLAND RESORT*-*** offers simple as well as more comfortable bamboo bungalows with fans on a nice beach with kasuarina-trees. A small island with another nice beach lies opposite. There is also a large open air restaurant, a garden with palm trees, and a wooden pier. There is a daily boat at 8:00 h, the trip takes 1 1/2 hrs. Boats also leave for excursions to Phi Phi from the island. Information and advance booking at the New Hotel in Krabi, tel 611541.

KO LANTA YAI
Few travellers have visited this large island with its many villages up to now. Bungalows*-** can be rented on the southwestern coast (information and advance booking at the New Hotel in Krabi, tel 611541). The best way of getting around the island is by taxi or motorcycle-taxi.

The island is rather difficult to reach. Drive 44 km towards Trang from Krabi Junction. Turn right onto H4206 shortly after km stone 64 (signpost saying "Ban Khlong Yan 10"). Continue on to the small settlement of BAN HUA HIN at the end of the road for another 25 km. From here you will be able to catch a boat to Ko Lanta Noi. Once there, get a taxi to the other side of the island, from where you can get a boat to Ko Lanta Yai. There is also a second way of getting there; continue on towards Trang until you reach km stone 46, then turn right onto H4042. Drive to BAN BO MUANG (14 km). You will be able to catch a ferry (2 hrs.) to Ko Lanta Yai from here.

KO PHI PHI

The perfect island for living one's tropical dreams - imagine two large and rugged limestone cliff formations, coconut-palms on the one side and jungle on the other. They are connected to each other by a flat land bridge, which forms semi-circular, blindingly white bays of sand on either side. The clear water of the bays shimmers in every conceivable shade of blue, and you will already be able to make out the corals from the boat - wonderful for snorkelling and diving.

Even though there are no cars or roads on the island, peace-loving tourists may find themselves being disturbed by the sound of engines nevertheless; the sound of generators and - in particular - the many boats travelling to and from the island echoes from the steep cliff walls. Fishermen leave for the open sea in the early morning, and the ferries and tourist boats start arriving only a short while later.

Actually, Ko Phi Phi consists of two islands; all resorts can be found on KO PHI PHI DON, while the rather coarse, uninhabited KO PHI PHI LE is only suited for outings. Part of Ko Phi Phi has been declared a National Park. The HQ can be found at the Noparat Thara Beach near Krabi.

BEACHES AND BUNGALOWS

Most of the traveller bungalow resorts are east of the village, in TON SAI BAY. All resorts offer simple bungalows costing between 50 and 100 Baht. There are a few more comfortable ones with lav/shower. For these, the prices rise accordingly (160-200 Baht). The bungalows can only be reached on foot or by boat. You will need half an hour to reach the last resort, on Long Beach. Some of the resorts are located directly on the beaches, others on the cliffs, some stand crowded next to each other, others are spacious. Phi Phi bustles with activity during the season, and we would recommend taking the first

hut available and then setting out in search of a permanent place to stay from there. You can move immediately, should you find something better.

PHI PHI ANDAMAN-**, (*with dormitory) is in between the village and the school. There is often a water shortage during the height of the season.

LAEM INN*; the huts lie at a slightly raised altitude, beneath palm-trees.

TON MA PLAO* has been built on a cape; almost no shade at all.

All other bungalows are located on the long LONG BEACH, which reaches all the way to the Laem Tong Cape (more resorts have been opened in the meantime).

HAD HIN*; the beach is a little rocky here.

BANG MAN* belongs to a Muslim.

LONG BEACH* is located near a fishing village.

This is the best resort from which to go snorkelling to the offshore reef. Regular boats travel back and forth between the small fishing village and the island's main village. You can catch one of these if you want to come here to go snorkelling.

The *PEE PEE ISLANDS CABANA**-***** are located west of the main village, at the lowest point of the bay. Contact Pee Pee Marine Travel, 201 Uttarakit Road, Krabi, tel 075/611496 for advance booking. All the posh day-visitors from Phuket are fed at the restaurant of this high class resort, and the surrounding parks, beaches, and restaurants bustle with as much activity as any Mediterranean package deal resort. The speedboats from Songserm and many day-trip boats drop anchor here.

One can still find peaceful bungalows in this resort nevertheless, as unlikely as it may seem. To find them, cross over to the other side of the narrow land bridge, to YONG GA LEM BAY (also known as BACK BEACH). This bay is very beautiful at high tide, though rather ugly when the tide is low. You will also find the

P. P. CHARLIE BEACH RESORT*** here, in the coconut-palm plantation; spacious bungalows with lav/showers and small terraces commanding a fine view over the bay. Reservations from Phuket at P.P Charlie Beach Resorts, Makham Bay. There is a

daily boat from there to Ko Phi Phi. You will find the

GIFT BUNGALOW NO. 2* at the very edge of the bay; very simple huts (some in the jungle), nice restaurant.

TON SAI VILLAGE**, at the end of Ton Sai Bay, offers bungalows with good mattresses. The first row of bungalows are extremely popular. The community washing facilities consist of an Indonesian type 'shower', which tourists unfortunately seem unable to use properly. The many coral stones on the beach in front of the bungalows make this a rather unsuitable spot for bathing.

LO BA KAO BEACH is located somewhere completely different, on the east coast of the island. You will only find the *PEE PEE ISLAND VILLAGE***** here up to now, tel Krabi 075/612064 (contact Pee Pee Island Resort, 158/20 Yaowaraj Road, Phuket, tel 076/215014 for advance booking). Approx. 80 comfortable bungalows stand upon stilts in a palm tree plantation measuring 9 hectares in size. Sailing, windsurfing, snorkelling, diving, and fishing are possible.

FOOD

All bungalow resorts have their own restaurant. The prices are a little higher than they would be on the mainland. This is due to the fact that everything - with the obvious exception of seafood - has to be brought over by boat. There is sometimes a shortage of vegetables. You will be able to dine most cheaply at the various *FISHERMEN PUBS* in the village. These are always very full. The *MUSLIM RESTAURANT* west of the village serves good grilled fish. You will be able to eat 'à la carte' at the

PEE PEE ISLANDS CABANA for a rather exorbitant price.

HOW TO GET THERE
From KRABI: by boat, either with Pee Pee Marine Travel, Krabi Sea Tour, or on the "Sea King" from Songserm (see Krabi, p. 400, for detailed information). Longtail-boats from AO NANG BEACH cost approx. 130 Baht per person and need 3-4 hrs. - only recommended when the water is extremely calm.

From PHUKET: with day-trip boats or on the "Sea King".

LEAVING KO PHI PHI
To KRABI: Pee Pee Marine Travel, 13:00 h (150 Baht, 3 hrs.); Krabi Sea Tour, 8:30 and 13:00 h, (100 Baht, 2 1/2 hrs.); Songserm only Tues and Thur, 10:30 h (200 Baht 1 1/2 hrs.)

To PHUKET: Songserm daily (except for Tues and Thur) at 10:30 as well as daily at 16:00 h (200 Baht, 1 1/2 hrs.).

There is also said to be a daily boat to PHUKET from the Phi Phi Andaman Bungalows at 13:30 h (150 Baht).

You will be able to get to JUM ISLAND and KO LANTA with the boats of the resorts on these islands. Ask around; you will soon find out on which days the boats normally come.

EXCURSIONS
VIEW POINTS
A climb to one of the VIEW POINTS is an absolute must for those planning to spend a couple of days on Ko Phi Phi. You will only be able to fully appreciate the beauty of this island by looking down upon it. Photographers might enjoy climbing the eastern hill in the morning. The ascent begins behind the village. Ask for LANG HUA. You will be able to see all the way to the northern cape of the island from there. The hill beyond Ton Sai Village is best suited for the afternoon. You will need 15 minutes to climb it, part of the way along safety ropes.

ISLAND TOUR

You can organize a boat-trip around Phi Phi Don yourself. Hire a longtail-boat (1/2 day) at the village or with the aid of the people running your resort. There is enough room for about 8 people in one of these boats. Snorkelling is best in front of LONG BEACH and in front of LO BU DI, the southernmost beach on the island's west coast.

KO PHI PHI LE

Regular boat-trips are offered to the rugged, southern island of Phi Phi Le with its interesting cliff formations (100 Baht). A visit to the island is included in the price for those who have bought a return ticket from Pee Pee Marine in Krabi as well as those who have made an outing arrangement from Phuket.

The following places are visited: VIKING CAVE, with prehistoric cave-paintings and many swallows' nests; you can visit the cave for 20 Baht if the sea is relatively calm and the mating season has passed. The LO SA MAY BAY looks like a deep fjord. One usually drops anchor in the nice MAYA BAY in order to go snorkeling. Beware of the water serpents!

DIVING OUTINGS

1 - 3-day diving outings to Ko Phi Phi are organized from the diving bases of Phuket. The shallow bays and the colourful coral reefs are perfect for beginners and advanced divers alike. Semi-professionals may find it a little boring - at best you might see a couple of miniature leopard sharks.

FROM KRABI TO PHUKET

A wonderful route through a magnificent, rocky landscape leads due north from Krabi. The well built, almost perfectly straight and level road is rarely used and leads through rubber plantations and past ricefields. The many jungle-overgrown, rugged cliffs are good places to stop and go off on small outings. We really feel sorry for anyone travelling along this route by bus. One could easily spend several days here. Take your time and enjoy the incredible countryside - it may be a while before you return to such natural splendour. (Some of the outings suggested are not recommended during the rainy season, June-October, but the landscape can seem even more beautiful during this period - if it stops raining for a while.) You will even be able to organize a round-trip if you're travelling by motorcycle; once in Phuket (185 km), you can simply have the bike loaded onto the Songserm's "Sea King", which will take it back to Krabi via Ko Phi Phi. Organize the whole thing in Krabi with the place you rented the motorcycle from.

Take the western arterial road H4200 from Krabi - terrific cliffs ahead! You will reach the H4 at km stone 110. Turn north. After only 2 km you will be passing through an amazing landscape of cliffs. After this, jungle and rubber plantations seem to alternate for a while.

The H4025 turns off at km stone 137 and leads to the village of BAN BAKAN at a small inlet.

➥ EXCURSION TO THE YUAN TONG CAVE

There is a Thai signpost ("900 m") pointing to the left at km stone 144.5. Walk down the laterite path, through the village. You will reach a lonely cliff after 600 metres. The lake in front of it has just recently been artificially extended and secured. You will reach the THAM YUAN TONG CAVE by way of the right hand side entrance. There is a deep lake with cool, clear water within - the village's main water source and bathing-spot. The cave usually bustles with activity, especially before noon. There are very many stalactites, most of them still growing. A steep uphill passage leads to a large, partially caved-in chamber on the far left. Stay on the left hand side if you wish to climb around. You will have a wonderful view of palm tree gardens, a village, and two cliff ranges from a natural viewing platform.

The H4 passes through another beautiful chain of cliffs at km stone 146. You will reach *AO LUK JUNCTION* after 2 km; many shops, a vegetable market, and a rather unattractive restaurant. The H4035 to Surat Thani turns off to the right (approx. 180 km). It's still 140 km straight on from here to Phuket.

You will reach the entrance of the *THANBOKE KHORANEE NATIONAL PARK* (which is spelt in many different ways) by turning left down the H4039 (1.3 km). A small brook wells up in a grotto, in a pool formed by cliffs. The brook winds its way through the park, forming several beautiful cascades along the way. You will be able to reach the natural pool of the grotto by way of small bridges and narrow paths. Have you got your bathing suit along? If yes, you'll be able to change in the restrooms for a couple of Baht and swim into the grotto. Beautiful stalactites fringe the entrance. Overweight swimmers may scrape their stomachs on a couple of underwater stalagmites - careful! You won't be able to climb about on the grotto walls, they are too smooth. You will reach the end of the grotto after approx. 15 metres. Turn around and check out the truly spectacular view. The only thing marring the idyllic effect are the new bright lamps in the grotto.

There is an INFORMATION CENTRE with many photographs of the caves, mountains, and the surrounding area opposite the many foodstands at the main entrance of the park. Some of the employees, who are as thrilled by the amazing landscape as you yourself will no doubt be, speak a little English. They will tell you which are the most beautiful spots to go to. Do you feel like climbing one of the seemingly insurmountable cliffs? One of the employees can act as an escort to the top of one of the easier ones. It's an hour's tough climbing to the top, but once there you will be rewarded with a splendid view. There are still a few 'virgin peaks' in the vicinity waiting for professionals.

The *WATERFALL INN*** (ac***) is situated at the outlet of the brook, surrounded by imposing cliffs; nice bungalows with bathrooms and fans, terraced houses with ac, restaurant.

Continue along the H1039 for another 1 km and turn right (not suitable for cars). Cross the brook after 500 metres and keep going for another 3 km; you will find the *THAM KOU PRA KOU RANG* cave here.

You will reach a shop on the left hand side of the road after a further 4 km down H1039. Turn right at the Thai signpost just beyond the shop. This road (also suitable for cars) will lead you to a small harbour. Boats can be chartered (150-200 Baht), and the *THAM HUA KALOK* cave can be reached within 15 minutes. The black and ochre cave paintings representing animals and humans are said to be between 2000 and 3000 years old. After you've seen all there is to see continue on to *THAM LOD*, a beautiful, vault-like, stalactite cave. Make sure that you don't leave at low tide, otherwise you will probably not be able to reach the bizarre stalactites. It would definitely be worth extending the boat-ride at this point and chugging past the picturesque cliffs, through the verdant landscape.

Continue along the H1039 for another 2 km from here, and you'll be able to explore the *THAM KHAO KWEI* cave in the cliffs to the right.

The fishing village of LAEM SAK is at the end of H1039, 17 km from the Ao Luk Junction. You can charter a boat for approx. 150 Baht, should you wish to cross over to the *KO MAK NOI* island.

➡ EXCURSION TO THE WA RI RIN CAVE

You can also make an excursion to the WA RI RIN CAVE from the Ao Luk Junction, should you still not have had enough. This cave is said to be very large and beautiful, with many stalactites. To get there, drive down H4035 to beyond km stone 8, then turn right (road also suitable for cars). You will reach the cave after approx. 5 km.

Feel like another? Drive towards Phuket on the H4 from Ao Luk Junction, and stop at the High School after only 800 metres. After a short walk you will reach the *THAM THALU FA* cave in the cliff opposite; a few stalagmites outside, beautiful stalactites within.

The limestone cliffs end after 14 km. The rather uninteresting H4040 to Surat Thani turns off to the right shortly afterwards. A bus drives to the Khao Sok National Park along this road (see p. 432).

The new H4152 turns off to the left in *THAP PUT*, at km stone 169. You will save 9 km by going down this level road if you're headed to Phuket. It's not really worth it, though; the road isn't particularly nice or interesting.

Continue straight ahead on the H4 and you'll reach the *WAT KIRIWONG* hermitage after 9 km, on the right hand side. You will be able to recognize it easily by the folk-art Buddha.

The road starts climbing steeply all the way to the pass just beyond. The higher you drive, the more spectacular the view of the Phang Nga plain and the many surrounding mountains. Once on top, the road winds its way down into the valley with a series of breathtaking, sharp curves. The well-built H4090 branches off north to the right after 6 km. There is a nice restaurant on the right hand side of this road only 500 metres from the turn-off. Continue going straight ahead and you will enter the limestone cliff region of PHANG NGA. A narrow road turns off to the east at a small lake after approx. 4 km. This road will take you to the *SAR NANG MANORA FOREST PARK*. Don't expect anything spectacular; peaceful picnic-tables, pretty waterfalls, and a small patch of jungle, that's all. A tiny road branches off to the right beyond the Phang Nga river, between km stones 42 and 43. Park your motorcycle after 4 km and take a nice walk through the paddies to the *NAM TOK TON PHANG NGA* cascades (approx. 2 hrs.).

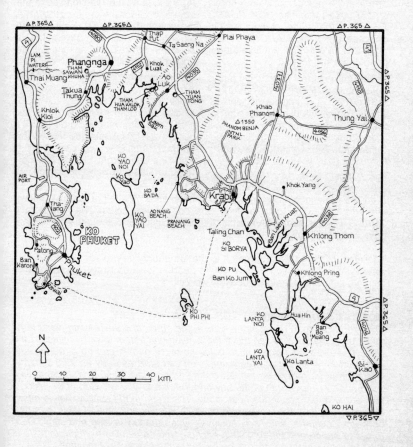

PHANG NGA

The provincial capital Phang Nga is exactly 93 km from Krabi as well as Phuket. The town is famous for its beautiful bay with the steep limestone cliffs towering out of the sea. There is a Tourist Office in the government buildings opposite the striking cliff, 3.3 km out of town, towards Phuket.

HOTELS

There are a number of cheap hotels on the main road. The *RUK PHANG NGA** is in the centre, at the bus-stop, opposite the *RATANAPONG***. The nicer *LAK MUANG*** is a little further out of town; rooms with lav/sink.

There are no hotels of middling prices in town. The *PHANG NGA VALLEY RESORT*****, 4 km out of town towards Phuket, 400 m to the right of the H4, is an expensive Thai-hotel with bungalows and a guesthouse, restaurant, Thai Dance Show, and a fish-pond (admission 10 Baht).

The *PHANG NGA BAY RESORT HO TEL*****, 20 Tha Dan, Panyee, tel 076 /411067, is on the road leading to the bay, 8 km from the centre of town. A large, new building by the river with all modern facilities. Bargaining is possible, but tax and service will be added to the bill one way or another. The boat-trips offered are overpriced.

HOW TO GET THERE

A local bus from KRABI will cost approx. 25 Baht. The bus from PHUKET costs 22 Baht. A minibus ride to the harbour from town will cost 8 Baht. Package deals from PHUKET are offered for 250-500 Baht per person.

A couple of striking limestone cliffs can be seen on the left at the exit of town (km stone 36). The lower sections are riddled with holes. The hermit cave *THAM RUSSI* is somewhere within the cliffs. Concrete paths and a small park have been built around it.

The new H4151 to Krabi turns off to the left shortly before km stone 36. This level road will save you 9 km if you're headed towards Krabi, but it is rather uninteresting and therefore not really worth it.

➡ BOAT RIDE THROUGH THE PHANG NGA BAY

The road leading to the customs-house, the hotel, and the landing-place turns off at km stone 35. You can reach the landing-place from town by minibus for 8 Baht. A slow, roofed boat which holds up to 10 people can be hired for 300-400 Baht for a 4-hour trip (bargain!). You can start as early as 7:00 h, faster boats for larger groups do not leave the harbour until 10:00 h. You can gain a good general impression of the bay and the places you will stop at by taking a look at the large map in the hotel lobby. The water in the shallow bay is nearly always calm, thus the trip can be done at virtually any time of year. It is best between December and April, however, when the sky is blue and clear. Don't forget to bring your sun-hat, suntan lotion, and something to drink; in spite of the sun-roof it is not possible to be seated in the shade all of the time.

Your trip will start with a ride down the wide KHLONG KHAO THALU, past mangrove swamps and striking, overgrown cliff formations, e.g. the 'small dog', KHAO MA CHU. You will then reach the PHANG NGA BAY with its many steep and rugged limestone cliffs rising out of the sea. These seem to be held together only by the intricate root-systems of the tropical plants growing upon them. There are also many dark grottoes and stalactite caves in the area. The James Bond film "The Man with the Golden Gun" made these bizarre cliff formations famous back in the early 70s. You will stop for a short break at the small island opposite the 'James Bond cliff', KHAO TAPU. You will be one of literally hundreds of tourists taking this cliff's photograph if you're not there early enough. The trip gets really exciting when the boat chugs towards a sheer, seemingly solid cliff wall, only to nose its way into a last-minute cave entrance just in time. A Muslim village in which all the houses are built upon stilts is right next to the island of KO PANYI. The village has developed into a veritable mecca of restaurants and souvenir-stands in recent times. All tour groups are spoilt with loads of fresh seafood upon arriving in the village. At the end of the trip you will chug through another mangrove swamp before visiting one last cave, THAM LOT (this cave is sometimes also visited at the beginning of the trip, depending on the tides).

Turn off to the right at km stone 28 in order to reach the *THAM SAWAN KHUHA* grotto. You will see the entrance of the highly venerated grotto in the overgrown cliff wall beyond the wat. There are many Buddha statues inside the cave. The area between the cliff and the river beyond is also very nice.

PHANG NGA BAY

A small road leading to the harbour branches off at the bend in the road in the village of *TAKUA THUNG* (km stone 24). Only large, roofed speedboats set off on tours of the PHANG NGA BAY from here (400 Baht for 3 hrs., 14 people at the most). When we tried to join another small group in order to split the price, this was prevented by the local boat-Mafia. In the end we had to drive on to the harbour of Phang Nga.

H402 to Phuket Island branches off to the left in KHOK KLOI. It's another 53 km to Phuket from here. The road will lead you across the *SARASIN BRIDGE*, past the long Mai Khao Beach with its scattering of foodstands, and through coconut and rubber plantations.

PHUKET

Thailand's largest island lies at the edge of the Andaman Sea, in the Indian Ocean. The island is connected to the mainland by the Sarasin Bridge. Large and smaller bays as well as white, sandy beaches make this an ideal traveller hang-out. The island airport has now also made Phuket accessible for jet-set tourists. The beaches have accordingly been transformed into tourist traps. The island's wealth is based on extensive tin resources, which are found on the island itself as well as in the sea.

Malaysian influences can be seen everywhere - 25 % of Phuket's population (from 'bukit' - Malaysian for 'hill') is Muslim. Buddhist Thais (55 %) and Chinese continue making up the bulk of the population, however. These days, environmentalists have started becoming active in Thailand, too; international headlines were made when 50,000 irate protesters burnt a brand new US-American Tantalum factory to the ground in June of 1986, causing US$44 million damage.

> **Warning:** Phuket is no longer the low-budget travel paradise that it used to be! Those who don't believe us will only have themselves to blame for the wasted time and money later on!

PHUKET TOWN

The centre of the island, PHUKET TOWN, 50,000 inhabitants, is little more than a transit stop en route to the beaches for most travellers. There are a couple of very nice BUILDINGS in town, e.g. the Thai Airways building near the market and the Chinese building on Yaowaraj Road near Talang Road. A shopping spree might be a good idea for those planning to spend a longer time at the beaches; you can buy cheap fruit (at the market), souvenirs (shell necklaces and tin products), and cheap clothes.

HOTELS

You'd be better off spending the night at one of the beaches. For those who have to stay in town, however, we would suggest trying the following hotels: *THAVON HOTEL****, 74 Rasada Road, tel 211333; large ac hotel, not too expensive.

ON ON HOTEL*-**, 19 Phang-Nga Road (one parallel to the one above), tel 211154; impressive facade and interesting staircases. SINTAWEE*-***, no. 81, tel 212153, on the same road.

FOOD
A night market and several noodle restaurants can be found at the *HOLIDAY PLAZA*, on the corner of Phuket and Rasada Road. There are more restaurants on Phang-Nga Road.

GENERAL INFORMATION
WHEN TO COME - The best time to visit Phuket is between November and March. It can get unbearably hot between April and May, when the wind sometimes seems to stop blowing. The southwest winds start in June, bringing damp air and rain with them. The heaviest rainfalls are in September and October.

TOURIST INFORMATION - 73-75 Phuket Road, tel 212213, open daily until 16:30 h; information and maps available. You will also receive a brochure distributed by the local police here, warning against drug abuse and skinny dipping, both of which are heavily fined on the island. There are many plainclothes policemen out to nab tourists with drugs - beware!

TOURIST POLICE - the beaches on Phuket are not safe, in two respects. Tourists (particularly women) are often mugged on the beaches in the evening, while the surf gets dangerously high during the monsoon period (European summer). The savage waves and the unpredictable currents have been the cause of several tourists' deaths in the past. In case of an emergency call the Tourist Police, tel 212213, open till 16:30 h daily, or the police, tel 212046.

IMMIGRATION OFFICE - Phuket Road, shortly before the peninsula, open Mon-Fri from 8:30-16:30 h.

POST - General Post Office, Montri Road, open 8:30-12:00 and 13:00-16:30 h, from 9:00-12:00 h on holidays. The Telephone Centre on Phang-Nga Road, just around the corner, is open 24 hours. If you want to call for less than the minimum of three minutes, we would recommend going to the private telephone office opposite, instead; here you will be timed.

BANKS - there are several banks east of the roundabout, e.g. Bangkok Bank and Thai Farmers Bank on Phang Nga Road. You can also exchange money at the Thai Farmers Bank on Patong Beach, open Mon-Fri 8:00-15:00 h. Moneychangers will exchange money at the weekends, too.

HOSPITALS - the state-run WACHIRA HOSPITAL, tel 211114, is on Yaowaraj Road, a little out of town. You will find the more expensive but definitely superior MISSION HOSPITAL (private) on Thepkasattree Road, tel 212386.

SUPERMARKETS - on Suthat Road north of the post office and on Bangkok Road, near the stop for the Nai Harn and Narai-bound pick-ups.

BOOKS - there is only one bookshop offering a very limited choice of English-language literature in town, next to the Pearl Hotel. You can trade (and buy) second-hand books at the southern end of Karon beach, next to the Marina.

ENTERTAINMENT - there is a boxing stadium south of town, at the end of Phuket Road. Competitions are held every Saturday evening at 19:30 h - seats 60-150 Baht. There is a little recreation park on the small peninsula in the south. The park can also be reached by continuing on down the extension of Phuket Road.

FESTIVALS - the VEGETARIAN FESTIVAL is based on an old religious tradition from China. Those taking part in the 9-day celebrations wear white and only eat vegetarian foods, either at home or at one of the island's five Chinese temples. Boys and men in a trance-like state have spears pushed through their cheeks or hooks fastened to their arms, face, and legs. This is said to have a cleansing effect if the hooks and spears draw no blood (as they usually do not). A large procession into town is held on the eighth day. The festival ends with the symbolic expulsion of all evil on the ninth day. For this, men in trance walk across glowing pieces of coal. Dates: Oct 11th-19th (1988), and Sep 30th-Oct 8th (1989).

TRANSPORTATION ON PHUKET
BUSES, MINIBUSES, TUK-TUKS, PICK-UPS
Upon arriving on the island you will be greeted by pick-ups waiting to take you to the beach of your choice. Be aware of the fact that many drivers receive a commission from the resort owners. It can therefore happen that you end up being taken to a resort which pays a higher commission than the one you actually wanted to go to. In addition, the drivers at the bus station sometimes ask for outrageous prices. If you want to avoid this whole mess, just take a tuk-tuk to the market, where you can change onto a normal bus. This will save you from having to pay the overpriced rates, while your resort owner saves part of the commission he would normally have had to give to the pick-up driver. Resort owners will sometimes show their appreciation by reimbursing your bus fare.

Tuk-tuks and minibuses in town cost 5 Baht within the city limits. Buses to RAWAI and NAI HARN leave from the roundabout (Bangkok Road/Ranong Road), all other local buses leave from Ranong Road (next to the market).

To PHA TU or WAT CHALONG 6 Baht, KO SIRAY or AO PO 8 Baht, LAEM KA, RAWAI, KATA, KARON, SURIN, or PATONG 10 Baht, NAI YANG or KAMALA 15 Baht, NAI HARN 20 Baht. All of the above rates are only valid during the daytime. You will have to drive a hard bargain in the evenings. Don't let yourself be swindled into paying 150 Baht for a ride to the beach, something which happens to newcomers again and again.

TAXIS
Taxi drivers demand outrageously high prices. Try to do without them; resort to local buses if necessary. These may take longer, but it would be foolish to encourage the taxi drivers by giving in to their demands. If you do take a taxi, definitely try to bargain. You will have to pay approx. 250 Baht for a ride to the airport from town, 350 Baht to the beaches.

MOTORCYCLES / JEEPS
These constitute a popular form of transport. Motorcycles can be hired at all of the bungalow resorts for about 150-250 Baht, jeeps cost approx. 500 Baht. You will not be able to rent a car for under 900 Baht per day (in Phuket town).

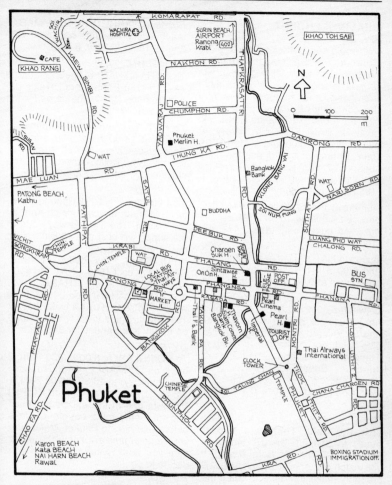

HOW TO GET THERE

There is an ac-night bus from BANGKOK (we would not recommend taking the non ac bus). Local buses from many cities in the south drive to Phuket, e.g. HAT YAI, TRANG, KRABI, SURAT THANI, and RANONG (you will have to change in Trang if you're coming from SATUN). There are direct minibuses from KO SAMUI and PENANG. The "Sea King" does the trip up to Phuket daily from KO PHI PHI, only on Tuesdays and Thursdays from KRABI. There are daily flights from BANGKOK, HAT YAI, and SURAT THANI.

LEAVING PHUKET
BY BUS
We would suggest taking a tuk-tuk (5 Baht) to the bus station, which is southwest of town. All regular buses as well as some of the ac buses leave from here. Other ac buses leave from the company offices, most of which can be found on Phuket Road. Ac buses to BANGKOK leave every 20 min. between 16:00 and 17:40 h (299 Baht, 14 hrs. - longer during the rainy season). 7 non ac buses leave for Bangkok between 6:00 and 18:30 h (165 Baht - not recommended!).

Numerous buses leave for RANONG between 6:00 and 18:30 h (61 Baht, 4 hrs.). Ac buses only take 3 1/2 hrs. (180 Baht).

Buses to HAT YAI leave at 6:20, 7:40, and 9:00 h (91 Baht, 8 hrs.). An ac bus leaves at 9:00 h (200 Baht).

There are numerous buses to TRANG between 5:00 and 12:20 h (62 Baht, 6 hrs.). Buses to KRABI leave at 12:50 and 14:30 h (38 Baht, 4 hrs.). You can also catch one of the buses going to Trang or Hat Yai and get off at Krabi Junction. Buses to PHANG NGA leave approx. every 100 min. between 6:20 and 18:00 h (22 Baht, 2 hrs.).

Non-stop ac minibuses for KO SAMUI cost 150 Baht. There are 6 daily buses to SURAT THANI between 5:30 and 13:50 h (61 Baht, 6 hrs.). If you catch the one at 9:00 h you will probably make it in time to catch the last Ko Samui-bound ferry at 17:30 h.

Buses to NAKHON SI THAMMARAT leave every 50 min. between 4:30 and 19:15 h (75 Baht, 8 hrs.).

BY SHARE TAXI
To SURAT THANI between 7:30 and 14:00 h (150 Baht, 4 hrs.). Taxis depart from the Pearl Cinema on Phang Nga Road.

To HAT YAI and TRANG between 9:30 and 14:00 h for 200 and 150 Baht respectively (6 and 4 hrs. respectively). Taxis depart from the crossroads near the Pearl Cinema.

BY PLANE
Thai Airways Office, 78 Ranong Road, tel 211195, in a nice building right by the market. The Thai Airways bus to the airport will cost you 40 Baht, local buses leave between 9:00 and 11:00 h (10 Baht). The daily flights to BANGKOK cost 1545.-, HAT YAI 510.- and 595.- (for a jet), TRANG 315.-, and SURAT THANI also 315 Baht. 4 weekly flights to KUALA LUMPUR for 1640 Baht, flights to PENANG depart on Friday and Sunday for 990 Baht.

BY BOAT
To KO PHI PHI at 8:00 h (200 Baht, 2 hrs.), on to KRABI (only on Tuesday and Thursday) at 10:30 h (200 Baht, 1 1/2 hrs.). You can also get to KO PHI PHI with one of the excursion boats and then stay for a couple of days before returning to Phuket. Make sure your tour organizers know the exact date you wish to return, should you decide to do this.

BY SHIP
Some yacht owners offer passages to Malaysia, Singapore, and elsewhere.

BEACHES AND BUNGALOWS
Phuket's most beautiful beaches are in the west. The eastern beaches are rather flat and not particularly suitable for bathing. A road leading to LAEM PHAN WA branches off to the left from the road leading south from Phuket

Town. It ends 10 km from town, at the new *AQUARIUM* and *MARINE BIOLOGICAL RESEARCH CENTRE*, both of which are worth visiting (10 Baht).

You will pass a small road branching off to the harbour and *MAKHAM BAY* on the left, before driving past the large tin refinery by the sea. The "Sang Jan" junk drops anchor at the above-mentioned harbour, daily island tours from 7:00 h for 600 Baht. An excursion boat to Ko Phi Phi also leaves from here daily; ask at P.P. Charlie Beach Resorts. 10 m in front of the aquarium a road branches off to the left to *CAPE PANWA*, a small peninsula with sandy beaches and an old lighthouse. There is a new luxury hotel, *CAPE PANWA*****, tel 213563.

CHALONG BAY - LAEM KA BEACH

Shallow Chalong Bay can be reached by way of the H4024 (11 km from Phuket Town). The bay terminates in the south at a small cliff formation called Laem Ka. Chalong Bay is not suitable for bathing. It is a good place to set off on boat rides to the offshore islands, though.

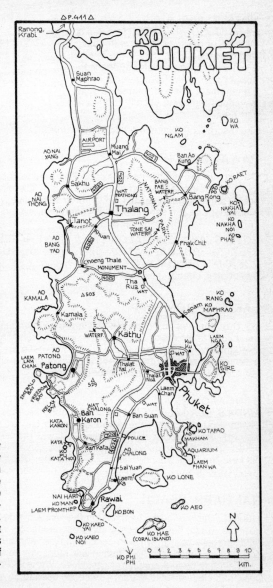

HOTELS AND BUNGALOWS

PHUKET ISLAND RESORT****, on a hill east of the main road, with some rooms costing over 1800 Baht. There is not even a single metre of beach in front of the hotel. For this reason the management offers a shuttle service to various beaches, usually Nai Harn and Kata.

The resorts at the southern end of the bay are of Rawai-type standards, e.g. *ROONGROJ RESORT***, AO CHALONG***, or *LAEM KA BEACH INN***.

Fresh fish and other sea creatures are prepared at the huge *KAN EANG 1* and *KAN EANG 2* restaurants, directly on the beach, beneath the shade of kasuarina-trees (a signpost will direct you there from the main road).

RAWAI BEACH

(17 km). In the south of the island. This area has been fully developed for tourism. The narrow beach sometimes gets a little dirty, though. You can hire boats to the offshore islands, which offer such effective protection against the winds that one can safely bathe all year round, even during the monsoon.

HOTELS AND BUNGALOWS

SALALOI BUNGALOW*-*** and PORNMAE BUNGALOW** are both reasonably cheap. The RAWAI RE-SORT HOTEL***-**** is considerably more expensive.

Good seafood is served at the *RIMLAY*.

LAEM PHROMTHEP

(19 km). There is no beach at the island's southernmost tip. Instead there is a beautiful, rather rocky landscape. A winding road from Rawai Beach leads through coconut-groves to the highest point of the area. Organize a pick-up or a motorcycle and go up in the evening; there are beautiful sunsets sometimes, but it is unfortunately always rather crowded.

BUNGALOWS

LINDA'S BUNGALOWS** on a small beach. You can reach the resort by way of an unpaved road leading north. Once here, you are only one hill from Nai Harn Beach.

PHROMTEP PALACE COUNTRY RESORT****, tel 211599, 600 metres from the cape, very pretty bungalows on a hill, all commanding a view of Rawai Bay. The observation restaurant serves exquisite dishes. Bathing at Nai Harn Beach (800 metres), shuttle service free of charge.

NAI HARN BEACH

(18 km). This wonderful beach is on the western side of the island's southern tip. Fine, white, sandy beach, a picturesque lagoon, rocky hills to the left and right, partially overgrown with coconut-palms, and breathtaking sunsets. The surf gets exceptionally high during the monsoon period, however, and there have already been a number of casualties. We would only recommend staying here from November to March. The beach used to be a veritable El Dorado for

all travellers, but now the cheap resorts and restaurants have had to make room for high society.

BUNGALOWS AND HOTELS

NAI HARN BUNGALOW**, behind the lagoon, 10 min. to the beach on foot, there is also a shuttle service, good restaurant (LUK NOI).

Go through the garage of the Yacht Club. Once on the other side, you will come upon *ON THE ROCKS*,* no direct access to the beach, clean, good food, great tunes.

AO SANE*-** is also nearby, on a small sandy beach with pieces of coral; nice bungalows on a slope and between trees. The swimming is said to be good here, even during the monsoon period.

PHUKET YACHT CLUB****, tel Bangkok 2514707; ostentatious modern building which seems to eat its way up the slope in steps, rooms cost between 2000 and 6000 Baht!

JUNGLE BEACH RESORT****, far beyond the Yacht Club on a slope with ancient trees. Rooms and bungalows with fan or ac cost between 400 and 1000 Baht. There is a small beach good for snorkelling down below. Unsuitable for bathing, though; shuttle service to Nai Harn Beach free of charge. More hotels are being built at the present time.

KATA BEACH

(17 km). On the island's west coast. Beautiful beach, but it can get pretty windy at times. There are two bays here, KATA NOI and KATA YAI, separated from each other by a projecting cliff. There are many corals and fish all around the small island of KO PU; good snorkelling. CLUB MED occupies over half of the Kata Noi Bay area. Video bars with Thai girls have popped out of the remaining ground like magic mushrooms. The centre, with many discos, bars, pizza parlours, restaurants, motorcycle and jeep rentals as well as a couple of cheaper resorts, is in the north of the bay, which is sometimes also called Kata-Karon. The prices at the restaurants are outrageous. Only well versed private detectives might be able to find a cheap restaurant in the area, and even they will have a hard time.

A souvenir stand selling unusually beautiful and clean shells at a very reasonable price can be found at the southern end of Kata Yai.

BUNGALOWS

In Kata Noi: *KATA NOI RESORT**-****, *MABUHAY**, *WESTERN INN**. In Kata Yai: *WEST WIND BUNGALOW** behind Club Med, *FRIENDSHIP*** at the crossroads, and *CHAO KHUAN**** on the southern end of the bay, next to several seafood restaurants (*MIA'S* and *BOUNTY* are excellent).

On Kata-Karon Beach: *KATA GUEST HOUSE***, *KATA VILLA**, *TROPICANA**, *SHANGRI-LA**-**** (many complaints) and others.

The resorts are completely booked up during the height of the season, when the rates are doubled.

KARON BEACH

(20 km) Karon Beach merges with Kata in the north. 3 km in length and with many dunes, this beach isn't really all that special. It is marked off by cliffs and a pretty offshore lagoon in the north. A motorcycle path leading to Patong Beach via Relax Bay starts at this point.

Industrious people have started building hotels on Karon beach like mad. All cheap resorts have had to make room for these new projects. The restaurants here overcharge their customers. Ask your fellow travellers which of them currently has the best reputation. More and more video-bars with Thai girls are opening up here, too, on this hitherto very proper beach. You can trade and buy second hand books next to Marina Cottage.

HOTELS AND BUNGALOWS

At the southern end, crowded in between the hill, the road, and the nice beach:

MARINA COTTAGE****, alpine hut-like bungalows beneath palm-trees, popular restaurant;

KAKATA INN 85**** and *RUAN THEP INN*****, all with bungalows for approx. 600 Baht.

Lying in an open field, separated from the beach by a road, you'll find (among others) *THAVORN PALM BEACH*****, a gigantic, newly-built

hotel for package deal tourists, all rooms ac and with a view of the ocean.

KARON VILLA****, large hotel with 2 pools. *KARON BUNGALOW****, *MY FRIEND*-****, and *DREAM HUT*-*** are beyond. To the north, beyond the lagoon:

PHUKET OCEAN RESORT***, *KAMPONG KARON***** (beautiful wood carvings), *KARON ON SEA***-*****, nice resort on a slope, beneath palm trees.

There are several foodstands and bars around the large tree.

RELAX BAY

(18 km). This beautiful, white, sandy bay with its occasional kasuarina-trees lies in between Karon and Patong Beach. Relax Bay can only be reached on foot (20 min.) or by motorcycle right along the coast. You will also be able to reach the bay by jeep from Patong (3 km).

HOTEL

Almost the entire beach is now occupied by the large *LE MERIDIEN PHUKET*****, a seven-storey luxury hotel with tastefully decorated rooms, all with a balcony and a view of the sea; fantastic pool with a pool bar, fitness centre, and many activities, e.g. tennis, squash, archery, windsurfing, and sailing.

FREEDOM BAY / EMERALD BAY

(19 km). Excursion boats often come to these two pretty, small bays southwest of Patpong. There is good diving and snorkelling here, and the beach is ideal for picnickers. The two bays can also be reached on foot, by motorcycle, or jeep by way of several very steep paths. Emerald Bay can also be reached by walking through the Coral Beach Hotel grounds.

PATONG BEACH

(15 km). This delightful beach with its fine, white sand has been fully developed for tourism. Western package deal tourists as well as individual travellers inhabit the scores of hotel and bungalow resorts (over 50!) along the 3 km beach. Dozens of bars, discos, massage parlours, nightclubs, shops, and restaurants stand crowded on the central sand road as well as on part of Bangla Road. These tourists traps will cater for anyone (even whole families or senior citizens), but they have mainly specialized in single male travellers. Life doesn't really get off the ground until evening.

Active holiday-makers can spend the daytime windsurfing, snorkeling, diving, or driving around with Jeeps and motorcycles. The more unathletic visitors are content with a couple of lengths in the pool, an afternoon tanning session, a few drinks at the pool bar, newspapers from home, and killing time - a beach perfectly suited for a typical bathing holiday, in other words.

Prices here are not much higher than at the resorts further south. Many more activities are offered, though, especially specifically 'western' ones.

HOTELS AND BUNGALOWS

You will find many different types of places offering accommodation here, from fully ac, first class hotels to simple bamboo huts. There is nothing for low budget travellers, though. Most of the resorts are very close to each other; it shouldn't take you all that long to check them out and make your choice. Prices for a room range from 150-3600 Baht, the average seems to lie somewhere between 300 and 600 Baht (cheaper still if you bargain!). The rates are reduced to half of this during the rainy period (May-October).

Most of the hotels are separated from the beach by the road. Some are situated up to 400 metres beyond the road. There are only 6 resorts directly on the beach, of which only the following offer huts for less than 600 Baht:

PATONG BEACH BUNGALOWS***-****, 34 simple bungalows; PATONG BAY GARDEN RESORT****, terraced houses at right angles to the beach, lawns and a restaurant in between the houses, small rooms with refrigerator.

The following places offer rooms with electricity and a shower for under 300 Baht: SALA THAI**, ALOHA**, and ROYAL PALM**-*** at the southern end; BANGLA** and HAPPY HEART *** on the central section of beach.

SUNSHINE GARDEN***, at the northern end of the beach.

The CLUB ANDAMAN**** resort with a hotel and bungalows at the northern end of the beach is particularly appealing.

BAAN SUKHOTHAI**** offers an unusually extensive service; bungalows with fully furnished, modern kitchens (even washing machines!).

Those wishing to get away from this consumer-oriented beach can go to the PATPONG HILL ESTATE****, in the mountains on the way to Karon.

GENERAL INFORMATION

TOURIST POLICE - turn left at the southern end of the beach, behind Holiday Resort. You will find a local police station on the central sand road. Open 8:30-12:00 and 13:00-16:30 h, from 9:00-12:00 on holidays.

POST OFFICE - right in the centre of town diagonally across from the police station. Open daily 8.30-12.00 and 13.00-18.30 h.

BANKS - exchange foreign currency at Thai Farmers Bank, closed over noon.

TRAVEL AGENCIES - there are roughly a dozen travel agents offering all sorts of excursions. These outings are usually cheaper than those offered at the hotel travel counters.

SUPERMARKETS - there are also three supermarkets in the centre. You can buy toiletries, insect repellent, and sweet Thai wine here, as well as western foods and magazines (at very steep prices!)

ENTERTAINMENT - more entertainment is offered than any sane person can possibly handle.

CAR RENTALS - PHUKET RENT A CAR is on the sand road, tel 321292, SEAGULL COTTAGE TOUR is on the road leading to the beach, tel 321238. The petrol sold at the station by the beach is at least 10 % more expensive than it is elsewhere.

DIVING BASES - there are at least five here, with equipment of varying standards (for details see 'Scuba Diving', p. 426).

VILLAGES ON THE EDGES OF PATONG BAY

Very few tourists ever venture into any of the three villages at the foot of the mountains. If you feel like going, we would recommend leaving on foot in the early morning. Go east from Phuket Cabana. You will first reach *BAN SAI NAM YEN*. The next path branching off to the right will lead you to *BAN NAA NAI*. The path leading towards the mountains winds its way past pretty buildings and a waterfall to the village of *BAN MON*, whose inhabitants are said to descend from the Mon.

KAMALA BEACH

(26 km). A partially unpaved road leading north from Patong will take you past a restaurant (good view from here), past NACHA BEACH, up a very steep mountain, and through a beautiful landscape all the way to KAMALA BAY. Pick-ups rarely drive along this 5 km coastal road (10 Baht). You will reach Kamala more easily from Surin; a narrow road leads all the way to long and bare Kamala Beach - many pretty, small coves en route. Only very few rooms of the KRATHOMTHIP** in the fishing village on the southern end of the bay offer lav/fan. Fish will be prepared according to your specific requests at the simple restaurant.

SURIN BEACH

(24 km). The large parking lot and the many food and souvenir stands are a dead giveaway - this beach is mainly patronized by Thais. The village cattle can sometimes be seen grazing on the lawn of the golf course.

HOTELS

*NANGKUAN BUNGALOWS** and its RESTAURANT* are right next to it.

Continue north and you will reach a private bay with what could be considered Phuket's most beautiful bungalow resort,

*PANSEA****,* all bungalows on a slope with a view of the sea, comfortably furnished, ac. The community buildings have been artfully integrated into the surroundings.

*BANG TAO HUTS**** * are behind Pansea, on a cliff.

BANG THAO BAY

(24 km). A secluded section of beach north of Surin. The film "Killing Fields" was made here. Thai families used to enjoy coming here for picnics. Now most of the beach's area is occupied by the large

HOTEL

*DUSIT LAGUNA RESORT HOTEL****,* bounded by lagoons on both sides, nice beach out front. The resort resembles a nice castle set in a large

park. Many activities are offered, including tennis, water sports, and a golf course.

NAI YANG BEACH

(30 km). Located in the northwest of Phuket, this pretty beach is most suitable for bathing. The airport is nearby (but it is still reasonably quiet). Many shady kasuarina-trees directly on the beach. This bay has been declared a National Park, because giant turtles come here in order to lay their eggs in the sand. The friendly employees are able to tell you where hiking is best on this part of the island.

BUNGALOWS AND HOTELS

PARK BUNGALOWS***, pretty huts scattered among kasuarina-trees, 2 rooms, 4 beds, and a bathroom, 4 people can share a hut for 250 Baht. Tents* are also available. The restaurant closes at 20:00 h on the dot.

PEARL VILLAGE****, a new beach resort of slightly raised standards, hidden behind the kasuarina-trees, right next to the National Park. Many activities, including a mini golf course and a diving school.

MAI KHAO

(35 km) The longest beach in the northwest of the island; unfortunately rather difficult to reach.

DIVING FROM PHUKET

We would only recommend diving from the island for absolute beginners or people who haven't been diving for years and want to start off easily. Those places that can be reached by boat in a short period of time (e.g. Shark Point and Ko Doc) are also pretty unspectacular. At best, you might see a couple of leopard sharks. Ko Phi Phi is much more rewarding, especially for underwater-photographers and hobby-divers. The absolutely best place in Thailand bar none is the Similan Island group.

SNORKELLING

Most reefs can be found on the western side of the island. The longest of all the reefs (1,5 km) is located off the coast of Nai Yang Beach, approx. 1 km from the shore, at the level of the Park Office. The water is 10-20 metres deep here. Other good places to go snorkeling: along northern Patong Beach and the Coral Beach Hotel; along Freedom Bay and Emerald Bay; off the Laem Promthep cliffs; off the beach of Laem Son, north of Surin; around the island of Ko Pu at northern Kata Beach from Club Med; and at the western end of Nai Harn Beach, off Ao Sane and the Jungle Beach Resort.

Good islands for snorkeling: Ko Man (off Nai Harn), Ko Kaeo (off the southern tips), Ko Hae (=Coral Island, off Rawai Beach), Ko Mai Thon (12 km southeast), Ko Racha Yai and Ko Racha Noi (far off in the south).

Equipment can be hired at some resorts and in diving shops. Expect to pay about 45 Baht for a mask, 20 Baht for a snorkel, 45 Baht for rubber flippers.

SCUBA DIVING

There are more than a dozen diving bases on Phuket. The first ones were founded by German instructors, the more recent ones by their early students.

Try the following in PATONG: Ocean Divers, Patong Beach Hotel, tel 321166; Phuket International Diving Centre, Coral Beach Hotel, tel 321106; Santana, Dieter Eichler, 86/1 Patong, tel 321360; Fantasea, Martin and Geronimo, 61/12 Mu 3 Thawiwong Road, tel 321309 (these use the diving yacht "Andaman Explorer"); Andaman Divers, 83/8 Thawiwong Road, tel 321155, probably the cheapest base (but the equipment available here is borrowed from elsewhere).

In CHALONG: PEC Diving Centre, 39/4 Chao Fa Road, Mu 9, tel 215527; P.N. Club in the Phuket Island Resort.

In PHUKET TOWN (some of these do not organize tours; they merely rent out equipment): Phuket Aquatic Safaris, 62/9 Ratsada Centre, tel 216562; Phuket Divers, 7/70 Phunphon Road, tel 215738. Before booking, we would definitely recommend having a good talk to the instructor and taking a look at the equipment you will be given. Any special deals need to be written down on paper, e.g. how much money will be reimbursed should you fall ill before the tour gets off the ground etc.

One dive will cost you approx. 400 Baht (including the ride, tank, weights, and backpack), 2 dives 700 Baht. Approximate price for equipment (per day): tank 120 Baht, backpack 45 Baht, regulator with pressure gauge 130 Baht, buoyancy compensator 130 Baht, belt 20 Baht, 1 kg lead 10 Baht, air refill 40-60 Baht. Phuket's diving season is from Dec 1st to May 15th.

FISHING BOATS, PHUKET

DIVING AND SNORKELLING

Thailand's many coral reefs are clearly visible as one flies along the coast. There are scores of them around the offshore islands, on both the east and west coast. The reefs have not formed atolls, however, which would encircle whole islands in a wreath-like fashion. Snorkelling and diving trips can be wonderful experiences if one pays attention to a few important details.

Coral reefs should be considered among the most important natural eco-systems of the sea. Their basis is made up of single corals, tiny, invertebrate sea-organisms that can grow together to 'gardens' measuring several kilometres in length. This is the way most tropical coral reefs are formed. A reef usually starts off with just one stone coral, which settles on an underwater cliff or stone, attaches itself by secreting calcium from the underside of its cylindrical body, and then starts reproducing. Corals reproduce in two ways. Sometimes sperm and eggs are produced by two separate corals and expelled through their mouth-like, upper openings. Eggs and sperm (sometimes) meet in the water, where fertilization ultimately takes place. The new coral thus formed then floats about for a while before settling on a stone of its own and reproducing itself. 'Budding' is a more common form of reproduction. Quite similar to a plant, a coral will 'bud' a new limb by secreting calcium. These calcium buds remain attached to the original coral, but they soon start forming buds of their own. Continuous budding and secretion will ultimately result in the birth of a brand new coral reef. A reef grows by 0.8-2.5 cm per year. It takes centuries for one to develop. In contrast to the dead white skeleton corals, a living coral can assume the most diverse colours. A coral reef makes up the natural habitat of coral fish, molluscs, crabs, jellyfish, sea anemones, and micro-organisms.

The soft or horny corals you will find in tropical areas such as South East Asia live off algae, which doesn't grow in the deeper, darker parts of the ocean. Thus tropical coral reefs are mainly found at a depth of 3-50 metres.

You will be able to go scuba diving from Phuket, Ko Samui, and Chumphon, where you will find many diving bases and diving-tour organizers. Diving courses are also held.

Snorkelling with fins and a mask is becoming increasingly popular. Many reefs are only a few metres from the shore, so this is an excellent way to get to know the mysterious and fascinating underwater world. Pay attention to the following details:

Whatever you do, wear a T-shirt! The rays of sun which penetrate the water are quite merciless, and you might end up with disastrous sunburn if you're not careful. We would also recommend wearing long, thin trousers. This way you will avoid cutting and grazing yourself when accidentally brushing a coral.

There are only two kinds of fish you need seriously worry about. Watch out for stone fish, which have highly poisonous spikes on their backs and can only be told apart from a normal stone with great difficulty. Sting rays, which also have poisonous spikes, are dangerous, too. Moray eels and poisonous sea serpents rarely attack divers. Sea urchins may not be poisonous, but their spikes may cause of serious wounds that heal very slowly when trodden upon. Do not touch jellyfish or fire corals; they may cause a very unpleasant, intensely burning rash.

EXCURSIONS ON THE ISLAND
KHAO RANG
Charter a pick-up or walk to KHAO RANG hill from Phuket town. You will have a wonderful view of the town and the entire island from the TUNG-KA CAFE and the small park nearby.

TIN MINES
You will find quite a few mines in the east, near Phang Nga Bay, as well as along the road leading to the airport, further north. Large areas are excavated in the open-cast mines. Dredgers are now also being used in the bays, seeing as the method of dredging saves quite a bit of money. The refinery was built 8 km south of Phuket Town, directly at the coast, on the road leading to Laem Phan Wa.

WAT CHALONG
This famous temple is 8 km southwest of Phuket Town. There are several venerated statues of monks who were considered particularly worthy under the reign of Rama V here (you may hear a different story concerning the significance of the statues - there are many versions).

KHAO PHRA TAEO WILDLIFE PARK
Go down H402 to Thalang, then turn off to the east and follow the signposts directing you to the TON SAI WATERFALL (turn right at the fork in the road). The administrative offices and BUNGALOWS**** (room for up to 20 visitors) are in the middle of one of Phuket's few remaining patches of unspoilt jungle. Several monkeys and birds live in this wildlife preserve. There are even said to be wild bears. Some of the animals live in large, fenced-in areas (macaques, birds, tortoises and others). There is also a small restaurant down by a lake and a very worthwhile exhibition dealing with the important ecological system 'rainforest'. You will be able to hike along several paths. One of the simple tours leads past the waterfall, which is only pretty during the rainy season.

KO SIRAY (also called SIRE)
An island off the east coast, connected to Phuket by a bridge. A large reclining Buddha was erected on the highest point of the island. The touristy village in the south of the island is home to a few sea gypsies, a group of people who must either have descended from the Andaman/Nikobar people or have originated in Melanesia. They are considered excellent navigators, are animists, and have quite a few customs and traditions. Apart from their very dark skin and slightly reddish hair, they can hardly be told apart from Thais.

On the east coast you find restaurants and picnic grounds along a shallow, sandy beach. MADAM PUYE, well known for her fantastic food from Nai Harn Beach, has opened her new restaurant right on the beach. She rents BUNGALOWS** with private shower and toilet, too. From here you can rent boats to KO KHAI NAI, an island with white beaches and coral reefs. You can reach the island by a 20 minutes boat ride.

EXCURSIONS BY BOAT
You will be able to set out on excursions to the offshore islands and coral reefs from all of Phuket's beaches. It is worth organizing these outings yourself. Try

to get a couple of people organized, so that the boat will be at least half full. Expect to have to pay approx. 600 Baht for an outboard motorboat for the day. Outings to Ko Bon cost 150 Baht per boat from Chalong Beach, 300 Baht to Coral Islands. The latter outing is offered for less from Rawai.

CORAL ISLAND
KO HAE is approx. 6 km off the coast of Rawai, off Phuket's southern tip. Many snorkelling expeditions come here to see the beautiful reefs, and the island has been nicknamed CORAL ISLAND as a result. There are huts** for all those who want just beach, palms, and ocean. The food here is expensive, however.

KO LONE
There is a hotel, the LONE ISLAND RESORT***-****, on this island, which is 3 km off Chalong Beach. You will be brought over free of charge if you contact the town office in advance, 243/7 Ranong Road, Phuket Town, tel 211526.

KO MAI THON
Day outings are also organized to this island, 16 km off Chalong Beach. Many nice beaches and reefs make this a place well worth going to. The fishing is said to be pretty good here, too.

KO PHI PHI (SEE P. 405-408)
A day's trip to Ko Phi Phi (approx. 400 Baht) is definitely worth it - beautiful coral reefs in the crystal clear water off the coastal region of PHI PHI DON. The southern sister island, PHI PHI LE, is circled during the course of the outing. The boat stops in a magnificent bay for a half-hour snorkelling expedition. You might want to spend a couple of nights on Phi Phi Don (we would certainly recommend it wholeheartedly). If so, ask your tour organizer if he can pick you up and take you back to Phuket on his next time round.

PHANG NGA BAY (SEE P. 412-413)
A trip through the bay of Phang Nga can also be very beautiful. Tours from Phuket cost between 250 and 500· Baht per person. If you want to organize the tour on your own, catch a bus to Phang Nga (22 Baht), then a minibus to the harbour (8 Baht). A boat will cost 300-400 Baht (for 3-4 hrs.).

SIMILAN ISLANDS
This archipelago of 9 islands has been declared a National Park. Similan is ideally suited for scuba diving and snorkelling, as the reefs start at a depth of 2 metres. The islands are not suitable for a bathing holiday, however, as there is no drinking water on any of them. Island no. 8 has a beautiful bay with a lovely, sandy beach and fantastically shaped cliffs similar to the ones found on the Seychelles - no palm trees, though. Diving expeditions usually pitch tent here for a couple of days, hence the strong smell of human waste. Great heaps of rubbish surround the camping grounds. There are 4 simple BUNGALOWS**-*** as well as several tents (60 Baht per tent, not including mattresses or blankets), public showers, lavatories, and a restaurant on island no. 4. The latter only receives fresh supplies of food and water twice weekly, however.

The north and east of island no. 4 are most suitable for snorkelling, as is the bay of island no. 8. Scuba divers out to see large fish will not be disappointed;

we were able to spot three different types of large sharks on 5 of 10 dives last February (even a couple of medium-sized white sharks), as well as some huge manta rays, most of them at a depth of 25-30 metres. Vision was limited to a meagre 15-20 metres, but our guide assured us that this was just about the best one could expect. Every dive was out to spot sharks, and we frequently had to swim against strong currents - not recommended for pleasure-divers.

The following diving bases (amongst others) offer trips to Similan (for addresses etc. see p. 427): Santana, Fantasea, and Ocean Divers. A day's diving will cost you approx. 1500 Baht (incl. the trip, diving, accommodation on the boat or in tents, rationed food and drinking water). You will have to pay extra for the equipment, the prices vary according to the base you have chosen. Non-divers will have to pay 700-900 Baht per day. You can organize a tour of your own from Thai Muang (70 km north of Phuket).

Non-diving excursions to Similan (snorkelling!) are offered by Seatran Travel, 65 Phuket Road, tel 212335, from November-March on the 'Seatran Queen' The price for the two-day trip (every second Fri-Sun) is 1370 Baht for a 4-bed cabin.

A Songserm Travel express-boat leaves for day-trips to the islands thrice weekly. If you wish to stay longer than 3 hours, spend the night on island no. 4 and catch the following tour's boat back. Advance booking at Songserm, 64/2 Rasada Shopping Centre, Rasada Road, Phuket, tel 216820.

A boat from Searching Holiday (which is a little faster than the above-mentioned) goes to the Similan Islands daily for the same price. 158/29 Yaowaraj Road, tel 215300.

FROM PHUKET TO RANONG

This route was infamous for the many armed jungle hold-ups just a few years back. Night buses only used to travel along the road in convoys and with at least one heavily armed police escort. Nowadays the danger seems to have passed. The true beauty of this route can only be experienced by those who are travelling with their own means of transportation; jungle paths in National Parks, secluded waterfalls, and beautiful, unspoilt beaches. The lovely off-shore islands are rather difficult to reach, and even in cases when transportation can be arranged, prices for getting there are usually pretty steep.

Leave Phuket by way of the *SARASIN BRIDGE*. The road branching off to the right in KHOK KLOI will lead you to Krabi and Hat Yai. You, however, want to be going straight on, due north, through paddies and rubber plantations. The kilometre stones have become a little erratic due to the extension of the H4, so we would recommend going by the distances given up to Takua Pa.

You will first have to travel through the small town of THAI MUANG, which is heavily influenced by Chinese traditions. The beach here has been declared a National Park *(HAAD THAI MUANG NATIONAL PARK)*, because giant turtles lay their eggs in its sand.

You can hire boats to the *SIMILAN ISLANDS* at the Thai Muang harbour. The trip will take 4-5 hrs.

Those feeling like a freshwater bathe can turn off to the right 57 km before reaching Takua Pa. The *LAM PI WATERFALL*, which has also been integrated into the Hadd Thai Muang National Park, is not too far. Whole families frequently bathe in the large natural pool beneath the threefold falls.

The road will lead you through a jungle-overgrown, hilly landscape. Every now and then you will catch a glimpse of the sea to the west. You will reach the *KHAO LAK NATIONAL PARK* 33 km before Takua Pa, on the left hand side (beautiful beach).

The brand new *KHAO LAK BUNGALOW** resort is 1 km further on, to the left, on the beach. Simple huts and a restaurant in a lovely environment. A bus from Phuket will cost you 25 Baht (102 km).

Casuarina-trees, which ultimately collapse into the ocean because of their closeness to the sea line the long beach of *BANG SAK* (13 km before reaching Takua Pa).

The tin town *TAKUA PA* (134 km north of Phuket) has little to offer. If you turn right onto the H4032 at the entrance of town, however, you will reach *TAKUA PA MARKET* after only 7 km. This is a pleasant small town with a charming Chinese centre. The Takua Pa bus station is 1 km east of the town, at the H4. You can change to Surat Thani or Ranong here.

➡ *EXCURSION TO THE KHAO SOK NATIONAL PARK*

The new H401 to Surat Thani (156 km) turns off to the right 4 km beyond Takua Pa. The road will first lead you along the edge of the wide Takua Pa valley. The good H4090 to Phang Nga and Krabi turns off to the right after 11 km. H401 continues winding its way into the now hilly area in a series of elegant curves. You will soon find yourself surrounded by a wonderful landscape of jungle-overgrown limestone cliffs. A small road leading to the KHAO SOK NATIONAL PARK (1 km) turns off to the left at km stone 109. Dense jungle, nice waterfalls, and beautiful hiking trails await you. Many wild animals live in the park, but the chance of you meeting any is quite remote. Group bungalows can be rented (no set rates for individual tourists - bargain), and simple meals can be ordered at the small shop near the barrier. Nobody here speaks English, but everyone is very helpful. It's not worth coming during the rainy season, which is from May-October.

Buses from SURAT THANI (120 km) and PHUKET (174 km) drive past the park. You can catch a local bus from KRABI to Thap Put, where you will have to change onto a bus to Phanom (48 km on H4040), where you will again have to change onto a bus to Takua Pa (40 km to the park) - each part of the trip will cost you about 15 Baht.

Continue along H401. A path leading to the TREETOPS GUEST HOUSE*** turns off to the left after another 500 metres. This tree-guesthouse is unique in Thailand - you will be able to sleep 6-9 metres above the ground. Dwaila Armstrong, an Australian woman who has been living in this part of the forest for

16 years, built her bungalows at the foot of a jungle-overgrown limestone cliff. Apart from the 5 tree-houses with lav/shower there are also several bungalows, tents (50 Baht per person), a restaurant (expensive food of varying quality), and a bar and lounge in a teak house. You can go rafting, cave-exploring, and jungle-trekking (with or without a guide). This is the right place for people who want to have some 'real' jungle experiences - fishing, building camps for the night, cooking rice in pieces of bamboo cane etc... If you are not into this kind of thing or don't have much money left, skip it. A discount is given during the rainy period, May-October. For reservations call 077/272452.

A narrow road turning off to the right at km stone 756 on H4 (the km stones are okay again now) will lead you to the *SRI PHANG NGA NATIONAL PARK.* You will reach the gate after 5 km. There is a parking lot in the middle of the jungle, 1 km further on. Roofed picnic-tables, salas, and a public toilet standing beneath gigantic trees. A nice, 500 metre path will take you to the *TUNMUNG WATERFALL.* Its beautiful natural pool is ideal for bathing.

The further you progress, the more beautiful the surroundings become - jungle-covered mountains in endless shades of green, and even the normally rather boring looking rubber trees seem full of life and beauty. The valleys here are put to agricultural use, but there are only a few settlements along the road.

➡ *BOAT TRIP TO THE SURIN ISLANDS*

You will find a harbour as well as the *MU KO SURIN NATIONAL PARK OF-FICE* in *KHURA BURI* (km stone 727). The office is in one of the wooden buildings to the left of the town entrance (directly opposite a narrow tarred road, next to a restaurant). The friendly young men who run the office speak no English. The only brochures available are in Thai. There is a sign on one of the office walls from which you will (hopefully) be able to tell when the next tour-boat leaves for the islands. You can join the tours for about 500 Baht per person (return). The trip takes 4 hrs. one way, you can stay as long as you like.

The Surin island group is approx. 60 km off the coastal region surrounding Khura Buri. There are two large main islands, Ko Surin Nua (south) and Ko Surin Tai (north). The latter island is inhabited by sea-gypsies (Chao Ley) who are of Polynesian descent. Fantastic coral reefs, especially in the narrow channel between the islands, make this a good place for snorkelling and diving. Many Thais like coming here at the weekend. The island group was declared a National Park in 1981 (admission 5 Baht).

The Park HQ is on the northern island. It offers four bungalows by way of accommodation (600 Baht for 6 people, you may receive a small discount if you are only 2), as well as a restaurant.

There is a camping ground directly opposite, on the southern island. A small, 2-person tent will cost you 60 Baht per night. There is no fresh water supply on the island. The diving bases on Phuket (very) occasionally offer excursions to Ko Surin. Do not expect too much; seeing as few diving guides know their way

*around the reefs. Rest assured that there are extremely beautiful corals here,
though. You only have to find them.*

PRAPAD BEACH

A dirt road leading to the beach (3 km) turns off to the left at km stone 702. The
road is passable all year round and passes jungle-covered hills and
pineapple plantations before finally reaching Headquarter 2 of the LAEM SON
NATIONAL PARK. The 2 km beach is covered with fine, grey sand. There is
much driftwood lying about - everything seems very natural and pleasantly
uncared-for. Thais like having picnics beneath the shady kasuarina and
deciduous trees. There is a fishing village at a lagoon at the northern end of
the beach.

The road leading to the *THUNG NA KHA NATIONAL PARK* turns off to the right
just after km stone 686. A barrier will stop you from getting any further by car
after 500 metres. We would appreciate letters telling us if there is anything of
interest here. The jungle here is incredibly green, even during the dry season.

BANG BAEN BEACH

This beach has been integrated into the *LAEM SON NATIONAL PARK*, which
stretches along 50 km of coast and consists almost solely of beach, mangrove
forest, ocean, and a couple of islands. Turn west between km stones 657 and
658, at the Thai sign saying "10 km". Disembark here if you're coming by bus
and wait for one of the pick-ups to the village (which is 2 km from the park).

The 10 km causeway leads across several bridges and through mangrove
swamps. It is barely passable during the rainy season.

A thin, park-like mangrove forest measuring 2 km in length and up to 100
metres in width lies beyond the barrier (admission 5 Baht). The fine, light sand
of the wide beach beyond glistens invitingly from afar. An offshore sandbank
breaks the waves, making the marked bathing spots safe all year round. The
water is wonderfully warm.

The islands of *KAM NOI, KAM YAI*, and *LU KAM TOK* can be seen in the
southwest. These islands can be reached in 2 hrs. by longtail boat, in 1 hr. by
speedboat. The National Park Administration, however, does not officially hire
out boats to tourists as yet. Tiny, rather unexciting coral reefs surround the
islands.

You can spend the night at the *PARK BUNGALOWS***** (usually booked up at
the weekend and during the holidays), or in your own tent. Public lavatory, and
a restaurant nearby.

The *KOMAIN VILLA*** with its 10 small bungalows is opposite the park entrance. You will find small shops and foodstands nearby.

The lush hills known as the *GRASSY MOUNTAINS* (km stone 624) constitute
a 'scenic area' for Thai travellers. You will reach the road branching off to RA-
NONG (between km stones 615 and 614) 280 km after having left Phuket.

RANONG

This busy provincial capital was founded approx. 200 years ago by the immigrant Hokkien Chinese, whose influence can still clearly be felt today. The nearby tin mines were the main reason they decided to settle here.

Many Burmese from KAWTHAUNG (Victoria Point), the southernmost point of Burma, come to buy western wares in Ranong. The town does quite well due to this. Remember that crossing the border here is illegal.

Next to the tin industry, fishing is responsible for much of the town's wealth. Now that international prices for tin are going down and the mines are not yielding as much as they used to, however, the town's population is trying to

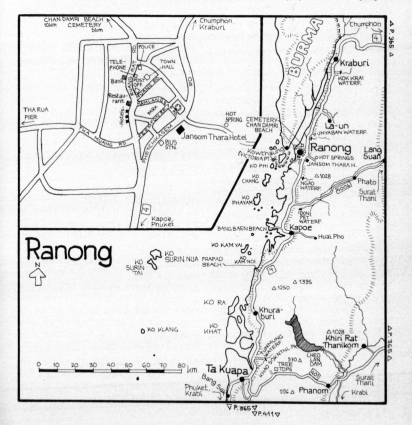

find new sources of income, e.g. coffee and cashew nuts (ka yoo), well known for their excellent quality. In addition, more and more fishing boats are being converted into passenger boats which take tourists to the islands of Ko Surin, Ko Payam, Ko Rayam, or on deep-sea fishing trips.

Up to now only few tourists visit this town at the Phetchkasem Highway, 291 km north of Phuket. Business people, who constitute the bulk of all visitors, come frequently to relax at the local hot springs. A few well-to-do tourists also come to spend a couple of days at the luxurious Thara Hotel.

The natural, 70°C, *THERMAL SPRINGS* are at the foot of a densely forested mountain, in the *WAT TAPOTHARAM*. To get there, follow the road along the river until you've reached a point approx. 2 km northeast of town. The three springs and small brooks are situated in a wooded area. There is a small park beyond the suspension bridge.

Those staying at the *JANSOM THARA HOTEL*, 1 km from here, can also bathe in the hotel pool (cold) and the two jacuzzis (one for men, one for women). The water for the jacuzzis is channelled here by way of pipes, and it cools down to a very pleasant 42°C by the time it reaches the hotel. Those not staying here can make use of the jacuzzis and the pool for a fee of 50 Baht - it's worth it.

Ranong is among the towns with the highest rate of precipitation in all of Thailand. A glance at the lush vegetation will immediately give you an idea of how much it rains here. The rainy season is from mid-April to the beginning of December. It pours non-stop from June to August.

HOTELS

You will find most of the hotels on the main road, Ruangrat Road. The new *SIN SARONG** (ac**), opposite the market, is quite good. The ASIA*, diagonally across, is also acceptable. We would not recommend staying at either the *SURIYANAN** or the *RATTANASIN** (many professional girls at work). The *JANSOM THARA*****, 2/10 Phetchkasem Road, tel 811510, is out of town, at the highway, surrounded by jungle; all rooms ac, TV, bathroom, all conceivable extras. In addition, the hotel has a reasonably priced restaurant, a pool, fitness centre, and jacuzzis.

FOOD

There is a good *SEAFOOD RESTAURANT* near the cinemas, opposite the road junction. You will also find a large *CHINESE RESTAURANT* on the same road.

HOW TO GET THERE

Ac buses from BANGKOK leave at 9:30 h and four times between 20:20 and 21:10 h (198 Baht). Non-ac buses cost 110 Baht, 10 hrs.

Non-ac buses leave PHUKET 7 times daily (61 Baht, 5 1/2 hrs.). Four non ac buses leave PHANG NGA in the afternoon (60 Baht, 4 1/2 hrs.). The local bus station is in the centre of town, near the post office. Minibuses leave for Khura Buri harbour (30 Baht) and Takua Pa.

An airport is planned 12 km out of town. Thai Airways tickets can be bought at the travel agency in the Jansom Thara Hotel.

There are three urban bus lines between 6:00 and 18:00 h (4 Baht for a ride): No. 1 travels back and forth between the market and the bank, no. 2 from the market to the thermal springs, no. 3 from the market to the harbour.

EXCURSIONS FROM RANONG
TO THE NORTH
The Ranong province is one of the most densely forested regions in Thailand. 86% of the province is still covered with jungle. This is mainly due to the fact that the steep mountains here are almost inaccessible. You will soon find yourself crossing the central mountain range when travelling north. The frontier region to Burma can be reached by way of a mountain pass. The government is planning to construct a canal here, at the narrowest point of the Isthmus of Kra. Nothing has come of this up to now, however.

Thai holiday-makers like resting by the PUNYABAN WATERFALL, 15 km north of town, in order to cleanse themselves of the dust from the road.

CHAN DAMRI BEACH
There is a rather muddy beach 12 km northwest of town, at the river mouth by the Burmese border. This beach is to become a holiday resort some day. The small Burmese town of KAWTHAUNG lies on the opposite riverbank. The nearest off-shore island, PULO RU, also belongs to Burma.

SOM BEN
Continue upstream from the hot springs. The village of SOM BEN is at the end of the road (7 km).

BOAT RIDES
Boats to the offshore islands can be hired 2 km southwest of town, at the harbour of THA RUA. A trip to KO PHAYAM will take you 2 1/2 hours. The Japanese helped set up a pearl farm off the island's coast.

The Jansom Hotel's fully ac excursion ship *J.S. Queen of Ranong* sets off for a bathing and swimming tour to KO PHAYAM on one day of each weekend. It goes up the KRA BURI FJORD, which marks the Burmese border, on the other day of each weekend. Both of the day-trips will cost you 300 Baht per person, incl. food.

THE FAR SOUTH

Those heading south from the bathing resorts will soon become aware of the fact that the Thai culture and mentality seems to fade away down here, to be replaced by that of the Malays. Malays dominate in the southernmost towns. Girls and women still wear traditional shawls in rural areas, men and boys sport the typical Muslim cap. The few remaining Buddhist wats and yellow-robed monks seem almost like alien creatures amongst the many mosques.

This part of the country was still considered an underdeveloped region with no infrastructure only a few years back. The discontented population was very much influenced by the "freedom fighters" back then, a group who demanded total autonomy for the southern states.

These days the Thai government is investing much time, effort, and money in the southern states. Efforts are being made to give the population a feeling of equality. The king, who is equally popular down here as in all other provinces, has even started organizing some of his impressive agricultural projects in the south. And even 'farangs' can't help noticing that the roads down here are without a doubt the best in the entire country.

TRANG

A pleasant, lively provincial capital with modern, well-stocked shops and a large market hall. Trang has 50,000 inhabitants, many of whom are Chinese. Trang lay on the coast for almost 2000 years. Back then the city used to be an important port. The town was 'transplanted' further inland in the 19th century due to the constant threat posed by tidal waves. Today the town is an important centre of commerce, especially for rubber, which is grown by many family businesses in the surrounding area. The town makes quite a wealthy overall impression. It is of little significance for travellers, though; you will only have to change buses here if you are driving to Satun from Krabi (or vice versa).

HOTELS
If necessary, spend the night at the *HOTEL PET*, KOH TENG*(ac**), QUEENS** (ac**),* or in the ac *TRANG*** at the clock tower. All hotels have a very central location. There are several Chinese restaurants on the road behind the market hall.

HOW TO GET THERE
A local bus from PHUKET will cost you 62 Baht (6 hrs.), from KRABI 30 Baht (2 hrs., 130 km). A bus from SATUN costs 30 Baht, a taxi 50 Baht (146 km). The train leaving BANG-KOK at 18:30 h arrives at 10:10 h (302/155 Baht for the 2nd/3rd class).

EXCURSIONS FROM TRANG
PAK MENG BEACH
This 5 km sandy beach dotted with casuarinas is almost exclusively patronized by Thais at the weekend and during the holidays. Too shallow for bathing, Pak

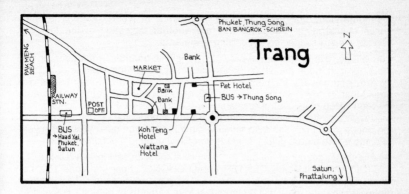

Meng is ideal for walks along the beach and the mud flats at low tide, as well as for collecting shells. You will be served excellent fish at the beach restaurants (with a little luck). The sunsets here are a photographer's dream come true. Charcoal-burners go about their hard, hot work at the northern end of the beach.

You can spend the night at the *PAK MENG 155*** in Mr. Prathin Watanasin's bungalows, next to his restaurant at the junction. 4 large, sparsely furnished rooms are for rent at the two-storey, so-called *BUNGALOW***, 500 metres further south, slightly set back from the road. You can also rent water-scooters here, with which you can then cruise over to the islands.

In order to reach Pak Meng, turn west onto the new H4162 29 km west of Trang (5 km before reaching Sikao) from H4046. Drive down H4162 for 10 km. Those coming from the north can already turn onto the laterite road (Thai sign "9 km") at the southern exit of Sikao. A bus will also take you to Sikao. Once there, catch a pick-up to Ban Klong Meng.

HAT CHAO MAI BEACH
Chao Mai Beach (6 km south of Pak Meng) can be reached by way of the new bridge. The impressive offshore islands of Ko Pring and Ko Chao Mai were one of the reasons this area was declared the official CHAO MAI NATIONAL PARK. Bungalows offer overnight accommodation at the beach (300 Baht for the smaller ones, 500 Baht for the big ones).

YAO BEACH
The so-called "long beach" (which is rather short, actually) is 15 km south of Pak Meng. There is a Muslim village here. You might be able to spend a night at the large house of the solicitor.

KHAO CHONG NATIONAL PARK
This area used to be the hide-out of many bandits just a few years back. Now that it has been declared a National Park, however, it is easier to keep under control. The formerly winding road from Trang to Phattalung has been improved, and the surrounding mountain slope forests have all been cut down. A

gruesome sight, but this is all done for reasons of (your) safety. The many police check-points along the way are another indication of the fact that bandits are still suspected to be living in the area.

You will be able to rest at the brook by the picnic-grounds in the park, or visit the small zoo in the middle of the forest. Of the many local species of animals we were particularly impressed by the binturong and the white-handed gibbon. Most of the animals live in small cages. Only the game has a large fenced-in area of its own. A few tame monkeys are allowed to run around. You will reach a beautiful waterfall after an approx. 2-hour hike on the other side of the bridge. The thick and fascinating virgin forest can be quite tricky; only venture into it with a park guide. There is no official overnight accommodation.

Getting there: get out of the bus (or turn off) at the sign saying "NATURE EDUCATION AND WILDLIFE CENTER KHAO CHONG", near km stone 150, between Trang and Phattalung on the H4. The park entrance is 1.7 km beyond the military camp. There is a restaurant in front of the main gate. It's 500 metres past a couple of small waterfalls to the zoo from here. If you have to ask for directions, say: "Utayan haeng chat Khao Chong yuu tii nay, ha?" - "Where is the Khao Chong National Park, please?"

BAN PAKBARA

This settlement 58 km northwest of Satun is the departure point for trips to the island of Ko Tarutao. You will be able to find out about boats leaving to the island at the National Park Office in the lively fishing harbour ("Ru-ah waa-nii pay mai?" - "Is there a boat leaving today?"). You'll be in trouble if the next boat doesn't leave until the following morning, as the town has no hotels or guesthouses. Some travellers spend the night at the beach. If you, too, decide to do this, we would suggest leaving your baggage at the nice beach-pub at the southern end of the beach. Alternatively, you can return to La-Ngu (10 km) and spend the night at the cheap Chinese hotel on the main road. (The last syllable of the name Ban Pakbara has to be stressed, incidentally, otherwise hardly anyone will be able to understand you).

HOW TO GET THERE

Catch a bus to LA-NGU from TRANG. Once there, catch a pick-up to BAN PAKBARA (7 Baht). A share taxi from SATUN will cost you 20 Baht, a bus to La-Ngu 10 Baht. A direct bus leaves HAT YAI at 7:45 h (returns at 16:30 h), departure from the Hat Yai Plaza.

TARUTAO NATIONAL PARK

Over 1400 km² of the Andaman Sea and 51 islands (most of them uninhabited) belong to this National Park off Thailand's southwestern tip. The islands used to be popular hide-outs for pirates and smugglers, but the park administration has opened a few check-points now, which help keep the situation under control. The different types of islands here, the long, untouched beaches, the jungle-overgrown mountains, the mangrove swamps, and the stalactite caves made us feel as if we had entered a truly magnificent, last tropical paradise. Be warned, however: you will need much time, patience, and money to explore the islands.

GENERAL INFORMATION
BEST TIME TO BE TRAVELLING HERE - the season is from November to February. The huts are closed from May to August because of the monsoon. The islands seem positively lonely except at the weekend and on holidays.

INFORMATION - in Bangkok - National Park Division, tel 5790529, or at Mr. Wichai Lamiwilai's, Chief of Tarutao National Park, Pakbara.

FOOD - plenty of food is available on the two main islands. We would suggest bringing your own fruit and vegetables if possible. Those planning to camp should bring a padded mat and a blanket. Don't forget to bring your torch along.

HOW TO GET THERE
A National Park Office can be found in the harbour in Ban Pakbara. Boat trips to the island of KO TARUTAO can be booked for approx. 100 Baht. The supply ships only travel back and forth sporadically, quite frequently at the weekend or on holidays. We would suggest trying to get to Ban Pakbara on Friday morning, spending a week on the islands, and returning with one of the tours on the following Sunday.

Seeing as there is now a daily direct bus from HAT YAI, it is a pretty safe assumption that there must be daily boats to the island, too.

An occasional supply ship will bring you to KO ADANG and the other more distant islands from Ko Tarutao for 120 Baht. The trip takes 3-9 hrs., depending on the crew's degree of intoxication.

If you don't want to run the risk of missing the boat or being stuck on Tarutao, we would suggest the following: join one of the group tours, most of which are organized in Bangkok: Napha Tour, 120/33-34 Ratprarop Road, tel 2523857, and Tasmana Tour, 45 Phran Nok Rd., tel 4112409; in Hat Yai: Southern Paradise Tours, Rama President Hotel, room 216, tel 24447, day-trips from 9:00-17:00 h for 350 Baht.

KO TARUTAO
The Park HQ is stationed here, on the largest of the islands (admission 5 Baht). The island is 22 km from the mainland and only 8 km from the Malaysian Langkawi island group. Nature lovers will have the time of their lives here; exploring the islands can take weeks. It's a worthwhile trip for those only planning to spend a couple of days, too, though; wonderful bathing beaches, hikes along the shore, up the 50 metre cliff behind the tourist resort (20 min.), and incredible vantage points. Longtail boats to the CROCODILE CAVE, which lies surrounded by mangrove swamps, can be organized (10 Baht, rather complicated for those who do not speak Thai). You can walk along plankways through the water-filled cave - many beautiful stalactites and stalagmites, some of them as white as snow (a torch is an absolute must!). You can also visit a small museum in the visitor's centre and nightly slide shows.

BUNGALOWS

2-room chalets**** for 6-8 people, sometimes 1 room can be rented for ***. Dormitory in a bamboo hut**, mattresses cost 60 Baht. 2-person tent*, no padding furnished.

FOOD

Fried rice costs 15 Baht at the restaurant, other meals cost between 30 and 40 Baht. Hardly any food is sold at the little shop. Loads of Mekong and smelling-bottles against sea-sickness, however.

EXCURSIONS ON KO TARUTAO

How about a hike into the island, to TALU WAO BAY, where you can still view the remains of a former prison? Mainly political prisoners were held captive here between 1939 and 1947. By now birds have once again taken over the small, shady bay - a good place for observing large rhinoceros hornbills. The path leads on to the southern tip of the island (20 km), where you will find another National Park Office at TALU UDANG (crab bay). The guard might let you spend the night at his hut.

KO ADANG

There are many jungle-overgrown mountains and some nice, though almost inaccessible, waterfalls on this island, 40 km west of Ko Tarutao. Wonderful coral reefs surround Ko Adang and the neighbouring islands. Good for snorkelling - many colourful fish and rare micro-organisms, e.g. thousands of tube worms. Scuba diving equipment is not available.

You can spend the night at community bungalows** and tents*, on the beach. There is a restaurant here, too, with a wide variety of dishes available at the weekend.

THE OTHER ISLANDS

You will have a very difficult time indeed reaching any of the other islands on your own. Some travellers manage to join one of the park's employees' patrol boats or one of the weekend excursion boats.

KO LIPE, opposite Ko Adang, with a village inhabited by sea-gypsies. **HIN NGAM** is a small island with granite cliffs that have been washed so smooth by the sea that they look like huge, black pebbles glistening in the sun. Wonderful snorkelling off this pebble beach.

KO RAWI, giant turtles, sometimes lay their eggs in the sand of this island's beaches.

SATUN

Satun, the capital of the southernmost province on Thailand's west coast, is mainly inhabited by Muslims and Chinese. This small, rather out of the way port has little to offer in way of attractions. Some travellers come here in order to catch a boat to KUALA PERLIS in Malaysia. From there, the Langkawi islands can be reached more easily.

HOTELS

SALINDA HOTEL** (ac***), 11 Wiset Mayura Road, tel 711115; information and rather shabby rooms available.

SATULTANEE** (ac***) (also known as SA-TUN THANI), 90 Satun Thani Road, tel 711010, cheaper, in the centre of town.

RIAN THONG HOTEL* (also RAIN TONG), 124 Samunta Pradit Road, tel 711036, a Chinese hotel with large, clean rooms, opposite the landing-place.

WANGMAI HOTEL***-****, 43 Satun Thani Road, tel 711607, modern, ac hotel at the edge of town, mainly accommodates business people and Malaysian tourists.

GENERAL INFORMATION

IMMIGRATION OFFICE - 500 metres from the landing-place, opposite the large mosque. Don't forget to have an entry stamp put into your passport - you will have great difficulties when leaving the country if you do.

HOW TO GET THERE

Buses and taxis from HAT YAI (96 km) and TRANG (bus 30 Baht, taxi 50 Baht - 146 km).

LEAVING SATUN

Buses leave for TRANG every hour between 5:30 and 11:30 h (30 Baht).

From there you can catch buses to KRABI or PHUKET.

A bus to HAT YAI will cost you 20 Baht, a share taxi 35 Baht - these leave from the Salinda Hotel, the ones driving to La-Ngu leave from the Satultanee Hotel. A share taxi to the border check-point WANGPRACHAN (40 km) will cost you 20 Baht. 7 longtail boats leave for KUALA PERLIS in MALAYSIA between 6:30 and 14:00 h (30 Baht or 3 M$). Once there, you will find an Immigration Office directly at the landing-place for the Langkawi ferry. Attention: Banks in Kuala Perlis are closed on Thursday afternoon and Friday.

THALE BAN NATIONAL PARK

This, the southernmost park in Thailand, is directly on the Malaysian border. The Park HQ is just 2 km from the Wangprachan border check-point and 75 km from Alor Setar in Malaysia. You can spend the night in the park bungalows**, which are situated around a pretty lake. Meals can be ordered at the canteen. A 6 km path through the jungle leads to a mountain peak, where you will be able to pitch tent. A path leading to a cave branches off to the left 2 km north of the HQ, at a run-down shack. Many bats gather here in the evening. After another 4 km down the road, turn right and walk the remaining 700 metres to a waterfall. You can hike uphill along the cascades. There is a beautiful natural basin in the middle of untouched jungle, perfect for bathing.

HAT YAI

Southern Thailand's centre of commerce and traffic (130 000 inhabitants), almost 1300 km south of Bangkok, is a modern town sadly lacking in character. Malaysians come here to buy the wares that are cheaper in Thailand than in their own country, and of course to indulge in night-time activities that are forbidden in puritanical, Muslim Malaysia. In contrast to Pattaya and Bangkok, most of Hat Yai's nightlife goes on in the hotels. The city has more to offer than just prostitution, however - there are numerous discos, some of them with live music and laser shows.

The viharn of *WAT HAT YAI NAI* contains a Buddha statue measuring 35 m in length and 15 m in height. The statue, 'Phra Ohut Mahathat Mongkol' is highly venerated by the population of the town as well as the Malaysian Chinese. The votive gifts brought to the statue are exhibited atits foot. The temple is 4 km southwest of town, towards the airport in Ban Hat Yai Nan.

HOTELS

If Hat Yai's entertainment and shops are not your cup of tea and you feel that you would rather be staying in a place with a typically Thai atmosphere, get on a bus and go to Songkhla.

For those who can handle it there are many hotels. The *LAEMTHONG HOTEL***, Thamnoon Vithi Road, tel 244959, ac rooms***, is clean and well worth its price. Central location, 400 metres from the railway station.

KING'S**, tel 243966, ac-rooms*** and the *MANDARIN***, tel 243438, are both on the same road, Niphat-U-Thid 1 Road.

The *HOK CHIN HIN**, tel 243258, is a cheap Chinese hotel. There are further hotels on the parallel street, Niphat-U-Thid 2 Road, e.g. the *CATHAY***, tel 243815, the *METRO***, tel 244422, and the *PACIFIC***, tel 245202 - reckon on a 100-Baht extra

charge for ac rooms in all hotels.

The cheapest hotels on Niphat-U-Thid 3 Road are the *KIM HAU***, tel 243532, the *SEANG FAH****, tel 243833, and the *YOUNG DEE****, tel 244499.

Prostitutes work in just about all of Hat Yai's hotels. All the same - or maybe just because of this - there is no designated red-light district. There are a couple of massage parlours and bars in town. No flair, though.

You will find nightclubs of higher standards in the *SUKHONTHA HOTEL*****, Sanehanusarin Road, tel 243999 (with pool) and *KOSIT*****, Niphat-U-Thid 2 Road, tel 244711.

FOOD

You should have no problem with food in Hat Yai - there are many small restaurants and foodstalls. There is

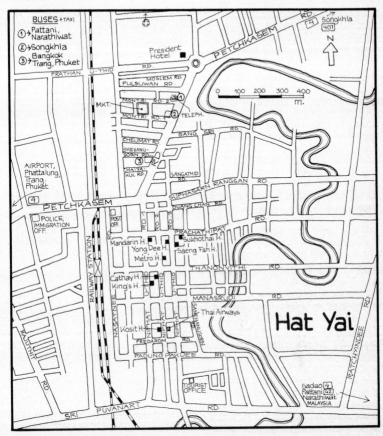

also a small night market near the Savoy Hotel in the evenings.

Cakes and pastries can be bought at the *ROYAL BAKERY*, 41 Thamnoon Vithi Road and 200/11 Niphat-U-Thid 1 Road. You'll find *THE BEST CAFE* (live music) right next door.

There's a large Muslim restaurant near King's Hotel, the *MUSLIM-O-CHA*. Good seafood restaurants can be found all over town. Food will frequently be served to you outside.

GENERAL INFORMATION
TOURIST OFFICE - on 1/1 Soi 2 Niphat-U-Thid 3 Road, tel 243747, 245986 - rather difficult to find in a small side-alley. The entrance is below the sign saying 'Telephone 191'. This is the place to go for up to date

---

PHOTOGRAPHS: *top:* Fisherman, Ko Samui; *bottom:* A beach waiting for tourists, Phuket

information concerning traffic connections and hotels in Hat Yai and Songkhla. Contact the Tourist Police in an emergency, same office, same number.

BANKS - If you're coming from Malaysia and haven't had the chance to exchange any money, go to the THAI FARMERS BANK, 188 Petchkasem Road, or the BANGKOK BANK, 37 Niphat-U-Thid 2 Road. There are more banks in Road 1, some of them open until 19:00 or even 20:00 h. If you arrive late at night or at the weekend you'll have to go to the money changers or to one of the big hotels, e.g. King's Hotel. The rates you will receive at the money changers are none too good, however - they usually exchange M$, only sometimes will they exchange US$.

POST - The General Post Office is near the large bridge. You can make international phone calls at any time of the day or night from the Telephone Centre, Phang-nga Road.

TRANSPORT - tuk-tuks within the city limits cost 4-5 Baht. We would suggest taking a songthaew to the airport (12 km, 30 Baht - the cheapest deal in town). Thai Airways also offers a good transportation service. Taxis are expensive - bargain! Hotels and travel agencies will frequently add the driver's commission to their price if you let yourself be chauffeured about in a bicycle ricksha .

SHOPPING - An extensive variety of ware is offered in Hat Yai, a veritable shopping paradise, especially for Malaysians. Try the areas around Niphat-U-Thid 3 Road and the parallel Roads 1 and 2. Clothing, cassette tapes, leather ware, and arts & crafts are cheap. Fruits and nuts are particularly good - try the cashew nuts. You will find a large market at the Songkhla bus stop.

BULLFIGHTS - are held in Hat Yai's new arena near the Nora Hotel on the first of every month, also at the Hat Yai Nan Arena near the airport, where two bulls are made to fight against each other on the second weekend of every month. Admission: 30 Baht.

THAI BOXING - competitions are held every Saturday from 14:00-17:00 hours in the Television Stadium, admission 5 Baht.

CINEMAS - in order to live up to the image of an 'international' town, some of Hat Yai's cinemas now show films in English, e.g. the COLESIUM, Prachathipat Road, CHALOEM THAI, Suphasarnrangsan Road, and the SIAM, RAMA, and PLAZA on Petchkasem Road.

LEAVING HAT YAI
BY PLANE
In order to get to the airport, 12 km west of town, take the Thai Airways airport bus or a songthaew for 30 Baht. If you're headed towards Malaysia or Singapore, you'll have to pay 150 Baht airport tax, otherwise it's 20 Baht. Prices for daily flights: BANGKOK 1760 Baht, night flight 1340 Baht; PHUKET 510 Baht (595 Baht with a jet); CHIANG MAI via Bangkok 2450 Baht; KUALA LUMPUR 1500 Baht (return fare), PENANG 730 Baht, if you return within 14 days 1110 Baht return, SINGAPORE 3500 Baht, if you return within 14 days 3760 Baht return.

Thai Airways office: 166/4 Niphat-U-Thid Road 2, tel 245851-2. You'll find the MAS office in the Nora Hotel, Thamnoon Vithi Road, tel 243729, 245443.

BY BUS

All non-ac buses leave from the Muncipal Market. The new bus station for all overland buses is out of town.

Buses to SONGKHLA cost 11 Baht and leave every 15 minutes between 6:00 and 19:00 h, 45 minute ride; PADANG BESAR 13 Baht, 1 hour; PATTANI 30 Baht, 2 1/2 hrs.; NARATHIWAT 50 Baht, 3 hrs., SURAT THANI 67 Baht, 5 hrs., departures at 5:30, 8:30 and 11:30 h; PHATTALUNG 22 Baht, 2 hrs.; TRANG 35 Baht, 3 hrs.; SATUN 22 Baht, 2 hrs.; KRABI 60 Baht, 5 hrs.; PHUKET 94 Baht, 8 hrs.; and NAKHON SI THAMMARAT 110 Baht.

Ac buses to SURAT THANI (160 Baht) leave at 14:00 and 17:00 h. There is a daily ac bus to PHUKET (169 Baht, approx. 6 hrs.) at 9:30 h. Direct buses to KO SAMUI including ferry for 150 Baht.

Should you seriously be planning to take a bus all the way to BANGKOK from here, there are several companies offering ac rides (300-339 Baht, approx. 15 hrs., departures between 13:30 and 18:00 h)

Further buses to Malaysia: There is a daily bus to BUTTERWORTH (Penang) at 12:00 and 14:30 h for 200 Baht. There are also buses to KL for 380 Baht (12 hrs.) and SINGAPORE for 450 Baht (19 hrs.).

You'll find the bus company offices in the following hotels: RADO, Sanehanusarin Road (to Bangkok) - LAEM THONG, Thamnoon Vithi Rd. (to Bangkok and Singapore) - PRESIDENT, Petchkasem Rd. (Penang, KL, Singapore) - SOKOL, Sanehanusarin Road (Singapore) - the TRANSPORTATION CO. can be found on Shevanusorn Road, tel 244574.

BY TRAIN

We would suggest buying the tickets for the rest of your journey as soon as you arrive in town. The railway station is in the centre of town.

An 'International Express' leaves daily from Hat Yai to Malaysia. The ride to Butterworth takes 4 hrs. including a one hour stop in Padang Besar. You will arrive at 12:10 h Malaysian time (= Thai time + 1 hour). You can catch the 14:45 express to KUALA LUMPUR from Butterworth, arrival 21:15. A train to SINGAPORE leaves KL at 22:00 h. You will arrive in Singapore at 6:40 h on the following morning. 2nd class prices (not including possible extra charge): BUTTERWORTH (Penang) 118 Baht, from here to KUALA LUMPUR 240 Baht, from here to SINGAPORE 240 Baht.

There are also two trains to SUNGEI GOLOK at the eastern border via YALA, departures at 4:30 and 6:03 h, 42 Baht, 4 hrs.

Trains to the north leave at 14:23, 15:02, 16:55, 17:15 h and many other times. They drive via SURAT THANI (114 / 55 Baht 2nd / 3rd class) and HUA HIN (244 / 116 Baht), and reach BANGKOK (313 / 149 Baht) at 6:35, 7:05, 8:35, and 10:00 h.

Some prices for the 2nd / 3rd class: PADANG BESAR 30 / 11 Baht, SUNGEI GOLOK 87 / 42 Baht, PHATTALUNG 37 / 18 Baht, PRACHUAP KHIRI KHAN 217 / 103 Baht, YALA 48 / 23 Baht.

SHARE TAXIS

Share taxis leave town daily to various places in southern Thailand as well as Malaysia between 7:00 and 17:00 h. They will not leave until they are fully loaded with 6 passengers, however. Prices per person:

SONGKHLA 12 Baht, 30 minutes, 30 km; SATUN 35 Baht, 1 1/2 hrs., 96 km; PADANG BESAR 25 Baht, 1 hour, 67 km, point of departure: near the market and the President Hotel, Prathan-U-Thid Road. Taxis to Songkhla also leave from the railway station and Wat Cheu Chang (see below).

PHATTALUNG 35 Baht, 1 1/2 hrs., 96 km; NAKHON SI THAMMARAT 70 Baht, 2 1/2 hrs., 189 km; SUNGAI GOLOK 120 Baht, 3 hrs., 285 km, point of departure: near the Wat Cheu Chang, Suphasarnrangsan Road.

PHUKET 220 Baht, 6 hrs., 480 km; KRABI 120 Baht, 5 hrs., 311 km, point of departure: Sang Chan Road near the Hat Yai Inter Hotel.

SURAT THANI 150 Baht, 4 hrs., 330 km, point of departure: Niphat-U-Thid 2 Road, in front of the Cathay House.

PATTANI 50 Baht, 1 1/2 hrs., 132 km, point of departure: opposite the Cathay Hotel, Niphat-U-Thid 2 Road.

BETONG 110 Baht, 4 hrs., 276 km, point of departure: Chaiyakul Road.

PENANG 200 Baht, 5 hrs., 220 km, point of departure: various hotels.

SONGKHLA

Mainly Thai holiday-makers come to visit this provincial capital on the Gulf of Thailand. The coastal town has 85 000 inhabitants. Boats and ships can reach the Thale Sap inland lake, which is separated from the sea by an 80 km strip of land, by way of a narrow canal north of town. Putting a harbour here was of course the natural thing to do, and the once important harbour city still has much of its former atmosphere. The harbour is not suitable for today's huge ships, though; the canal is too shallow for them. In consequence, only small fishing boats and Thai Navy ships drop anchor here these days. Songkhla has lost much of its business importance ever since Hat Yai blossomed to its present state. All the same, Songkhla has much more to offer to tourists.

The south of Thailand has always been a particularly restless region. The Ayutthayan King Prasat Thong had protective *FORTS* built around the town - which was founded in the 14th century - as early as in 1642. The idea was to protect the city from rebels. In 1642 it was the city of Songkhla itself, however, that rebelled against the Ayutthayan rulers. Some of the forts are still standing and are in pretty good condition. Try the one on Laem Sai Road.

Several beef-wood trees have been planted along the approx. 5 km

SAMILA BEACH, which stretches all the way from the road leading to the lake to the Muslim fishing village of *KAO SENG*, south of town. Do not come expecting some kind of Hawaiian athmosphere - the city is too close and the water isn't clean enough. Outside of the rainy period (October - December) the beach is always well-visited. Large Thai families like coming here to picnic below the beef-wood trees or to enjoy the fresh fish and other seafood dishes served at the open-air restaurants. The nicest part of the beach is in the south, near the fishing village. Here you can also the see the carved fishing boats painted in many different colours. Use your imagination and the two offshore islands of *KO MEO* and *KO NU* ('cat' and 'mouse') may even start looking a bit like the creatures they have been named after. In the northeast of town, next to the Samila Hotel, you'll see the

MERMAID STATUE, the trademark of the city. The statue was modelled on the one in Copenhagen, Denmark. Many seafood restaurants, a camping site, the Navy's anchorage, and a ferry can be found on the long, narrow, sandy tongue of land beyond. Up until a couple of years ago the ferry was the only connection to Road 4038, which runs north over the tongue of land along the coast. Today there is also a huge bridge further inland, which crosses over the lake via the island of Ya. The

FISHING HARBOUR is in town, at the western bank. Baskets full of shrimps, fish, and other sea creatures are unloaded onto the narrow planks behind the old houses in the evening. Boats leave for

KO YA from here. The island can also be reached by way of a newly constructed bridge, however. You can visit two old temples on the island and watch the 'Pha Ko Yo' - the chequered cotton material that is also sold at the stands by the bridge - being woven in the village. The central

WAT MATCHIMAWAT (Wat Klang), Saiburi Road, is 400 years old and the most important temple in town. It has many nice sculptures and murals, as well as beautiful stone cuttings and stucco decorations, in part influenced by Chinese art. There is a little museum in the northern temple complex. Archeological discoveries made in southern Thailand as well as the population's votive gifts are exhibited here. It is closed on Mon and Tues, as are nearly all Thai museums. A couple of old houses influenced by the Malaysian and Chinese style of architecture are still standing in the quarter west of the temple. You will find another

MUSEUM between Jana and Roimuang Road, near the bus station. The Chinese-style palace was built as a private residence for the influential Phraya Sunthranuraksa family in 1878. Later on it became the town hall, later still the local poor-house. The exhibits - which come from various different historical eras - are mainly ones that were found in southern Thailand. Open from 9:00-12:00 and 13:00-16:00 h except for Mon and Tues. A Ceylonese-style stupa and a small pavilion were erected in honour of King Rama IV. on the

KHAO TONG KUAN, a small hill close to town, in 1888. There is a park on the smaller hill towards the beach.

You can visit an exhibition of the arts and crafts of southern Thailand at the 'Southern Thai Studies' department of the Sinakarinwirot University in the

MUSEUM OF SOUTHERN FOLKARTS, 4 km out of town, by the road leading to Hat Yai. Open Mon-Fri 8:30-16:30 h.

HOTELS

For those with enough money we would recommend the bungalows and rooms of the *SAMILA HOTEL*****, tel 311310, directly at the beach. The rooms are not always in the best condition, however. The hotel has a garden with a pool and tennis-court.

There are some cheaper hotels in town - the *SOOKSOMBOON 1****, tel

311049, Petchkiri Road, is a new hotel, rooms with bathroom and fan or ac available. The old *SOOKSOM-BOON 2***, Saiburi Road, tel 311149, is managed by the brother of the number 1's owner. You'll find the *QUEEN****, tel 311138, right next door. The *NARAI HOTEL**, 1212 Chai Khao Road, tel 311078, is cheap. The *SAN SABAI***, 1 Petchkiri Road corner of Ramviti Road, tel 311106, has new rooms with bathrooms and fans.

FOOD
We would recommend the food served at the *RAM THEA* Chinese restaurant, Nang Ngam Road, in spite of the unfriendly service.There are many good, albeit expensive, seafood restaurants at the beach. Steer clear of the of the first restaurant in front of the Samila Hotel, though ('Harry' or something like that). Truly excellent seafood is served at the ROY HIM, a large, open-air restaurant south of the hospital on Ramviti Road. You may choose from the displays out on the street.

GENERAL INFORMATION
POST - opposite the market on Vichianchom Road. International calls can be made from the nearby Telephone Office.

BANKS - you will find branches of the BANGKOK BANK, THAI FARMERS BANK, and the BANK OF AYUTTHAYA on Vichianchom Road near the market.

TRANSPORTATION IN SONG-KHLA - songthaew within the city limits cost 3 Baht per person.

SHOPPING - as far as shopping is concerned, Songkhla is quite similar to Hat Yai, only a lot less hectic; clothing, cassette tapes, cashew nuts,

Pha Ko Yo cotton materials and other souvenirs can be bought at many small shops in town. A walk through the market and down Petchkiri Road is well worth it. There are also many shops on Nakhon Nawk Road.

TAX CLEARING - the Tax-Clearing Office for South Thailand is near the golf course on Sadao Road - necessary for anyone who spends more than 90 days a year in the country.

MALAYSIAN CONSULATE - on Ratchdamnoen Road, corner of Sukhum Road.

GOLF - a small, 9-hole golf course can be found next to the Samila Hotel. Information and advance booking at the Samila Hotel. Cost: club fees 150 Baht, daily fee 50 Baht, caddy 50 Baht per round.

BOAT TRIPS ON THE LAKE - are organized daily at 9:00 and 14:00 h for 50 Baht per person. A minimum of six passengers have to get together, otherwise the trip is off. Tickets can be bought on Jana Road, west of the museum. The boats leave from the end of the Jana Road extension.

HOW TO GET THERE
Buses and taxis from NAKHON SI THAMMARAT and SURAT THANI come here via the tongue of land and the new bridge. The fastest way of getting here is via Hat Yai, as the latter is better developed traffic-wise. A regular bus commutes between the two towns for 11 Baht. Buses depart from Rong Muang Road in Songkhla. If you're coming from Narathiwat, first take a bus to Pattani (24 Baht), then one to Nathawi (18 Baht), and finally one to Songkhla (13 Baht). Taxis to HAT YAI (12 Baht) and Pattani leave from the Ramviti Road near the former bus station and from the corner of

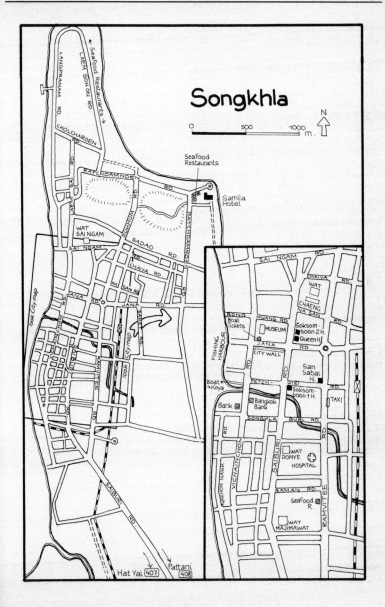

Songkhla

0   500   1000 m.

N

Jana Road and Saiburi Road. Taxis and buses bound for Nakhon Si Thammarat leave from the southern end of Ramviti Road.

EXCURSIONS FROM SONGKHLA
TO THE NORTH
The 140 km coast to PAK PHANANG is one endless beach, occasionally interrupted by mangrove swamps or fishing villages. Many Muslim fishing villages along the way. Cross the bridge or take the ferry north. You will come across the *HAAD KAEW VILLA**** (ac****), tel 24324 ext. 081 (more than 30 bungalows by a small lagoon, boats, fishing; long beach with fine sand) at km stone 6. A little further on, at km stone 11 , you'll be able to watch the artisans who manufacture the WAYANG KULIT (shadow play) figures at work. The road to the KHU KHUT BIRD PARK branches off to the left at km stone 33. Thousands and thousands of birds inhabit the islands and the shallow lake. Boats can be rented at the end of the road. The best time to observe the birds is during the cool hours of the morning or the evening. The WAT PHRA KHO, once run by a highly venerated, now legendary monk, can be found at km stone 48. A footprint of his is venerated in the temple, where you will also be able to admire beautiful murals, a reclining Buddha, and a Sri Vijaya style chedi.

PHATTALUNG

This town lies surrounded by paddies, west of the highway, at the railway line leading north from Hat Yai. Buddhist cave-temples can be found in the two large limestone cliffs that rise out of the plain, e.g. the *WAT KUHA SAWAN* in the west of town. It is thought that these caves were already in use as meditation monasteries during the Sri Vijaya period (8th-13th century), as several votive plates dating back to that period were discovered here. A large reclining Buddha is among the 40 Buddha statues in the nearby stalactite cave. You will have a fine view from the cliff, which is the home of many monkeys.

HOTELS
You will find most of the hotels on Rames Road. The people at the UNIVERSAL* are very friendly. The GING FAH*, tel 611055, and the PHATTALUNG* are also on Rames Road, while the new THAI HOTEL**(*), is in a nearby side alley.

HOW TO GET THERE
A train from HAT YAI costs 37 / 18 Baht in the 2nd / 3rd class (83 km). From NAKHON SI THAMMARAT 22 Baht, SURAT THANI 42 Baht (3rd class). Buses from HAT YAI cost 22 Baht, 2 hrs., 92 km, from NAKHON SI THAMMARAT 28 Baht, and from TRANG 21 Baht.

EXCURSIONS FROM PHATTALUNG
THAM MALAI
Walk along the railway lines to the north for approx. 2 km and you'll reach the cave-monastery of THAM MALAI. You'll need a torch if you want to go in and explore. The central chedi is surrounded by 32 monk and Buddha figures in

various different positions. From the top of the hill you'll be able to see across the rice paddies to the mountains in the west and beyond the limsestone cliffs all the way to the sea and the large THALE SAP inland lake in the east.

THALE NOI
A large bird sanctuary is on and around the shallow THALE NOI fresh-water lake, approx. 30 km northeast of town. Many migratory birds, mainly water birds, can be observed here from January to April, after the monsoon winds have calmed down. We would advise setting off on boat-rides before 7:00 h. Prices for bungalows (built upon stilts - 2, 4, or 8 beds) start at 300 Baht. Loud music blares out of two loudspeakers in the village all night long - bring ear plugs!

PATTANI

This town is the capital of the province of the same name. Pattani, Narathiwat, and Yala are the most Malaysian of all of Thailand's provinces. Many people speak Malay and go to mosques to pray. Children are often educated at Muslim Koran schools. There are frequent conflicts between the Buddhistic Thais and the Muslim population of the region. This is the territory of the Pattani United Liberation Organization, an armed organization fighting for Pattani's independence from the southern provinces. You can watch boats and ships being built almost entirely of wood at the dockyards on the western riverbank in town. There is also a good night market in the settlement.

If you feel like a beach, try *DALOPAGA*, 16 km east of town, near the village of YARING.

HOTELS
Spend a night in the JUNE*, 308 Pattani Road, CHANG ARE*, 190 Prida Road, SUNTISUK**, 1/16 Phipit Road, tel 349209, or at the PALACE***. The TYE ANN* and THAI WA* are two cheap hotels in wooden buildings by the river. You can watch the boats and ships from your balcony.

HOW TO GET THERE
A bus from HAT YAI will cost you 50 Baht, from SONGKHLA via NATHAWI 13 and 18 Baht, from NARATHIWAT 24 Baht. The two weekly flights from HAT YAI cost 150 Baht. Taxis from NARATHIWAT cost 35 Baht, from SONGKHLA 40 Baht.

YALA

This almost Malaysian town is surrounded by ranges of hills. The large, modern *MOSQUE* towers over the city. The shrine of the patron spirit of town, the *LAK MUANG*, belief in whom can be traced back to Brahman influences, is in the park.

The *WAT KUHAPIMOOK*, a cave-temple estimated to be approx. 1200 years old, can be found by the road leading to Hat Yai, 5 km out of town. You can get

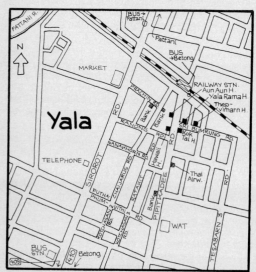

there on bus no. 470 for 2 Baht. A rather grim looking demon guards the main hall with its 25 metre, reclining Buddha, which is among the most highly venerated statues in all of southern Thailand. Some of the stalactite caves in the limestone cliffs towering over the park-like temple grounds (the ones at a height of 25 metres) can be visited. You will find dozens of Buddha figures here. There is also a lake within the temple grounds. Murals dating back to the Sri Vijaya period (8th - 13th centuries) decorate the interior of the second cave-temple, the

THAM SILPA. The paintings are probably the oldest of their kind in all of Thailand. Huge grapefruits are grown in the area surrounding the cave-temples.

HOTELS
Spend the night at one of the hotels opposite the railway station, e.g. AUN AUN*, KOK TAI*, ASIA*, or HAWAII*. The YALA RAMA***-****, 21 Si Bamroong Road, tel 212815, is the best hotel in town. The THEPVIMARN** is on the same road, no. 31-37.

HOW TO GET THERE
You can reach YALA by train from HAT YAI or SUNGAI GOLOK (Malaysia). There is a regular bus service from PATTANI (9 Baht), BETONG (31 Baht, twice daily), and NARATHIWAT.

NARATHIWAT

If you're not planning to visit Malaysia, you can at least catch a glimpse of Malaysian village life at the beaches between Pattani and Narathiwat. The coast here is just as beautiful as it is further south. Colourful fishing boats can be seen all over.

HOTELS
The TANYONG***, 16/1 Sopapisai Road, tel 511477, all rooms ac, with restaurant and nightclub, is the best hotel in town. Both the REX**, 6/1-3 Chamroon Nara Road, tel 511134 and the YAOWARAJ**, 131 Pichit Bamrung Road, 511148 are cheaper

- both only have rooms with fans. The CATHAY*, 275 Phupapakdi Road, tel 511014, is run by friendly people - only a couple of rooms available, however. On the same road: NARATHIWAT*, no. 341, tel 511063, a wooden building at the river, and BANG NARA*, no. 274, tel 511036. Excellent seafood is served at the CHOEANCHIM RESTAURANT, no. 280.

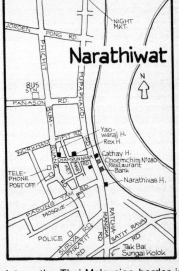

HOW TO GET THERE
Flights leave Hat Yai 4 times weekly for 280 Baht. A bus from Hat Yai will cost you 70 Baht.

FROM THAILAND TO MALAYSIA

WANGPRACHAN

The westernmost land border check-point on the Thai-Malaysian border is 40 km northeast of Satun, in the Thale Ban National Park. A share taxi from Satun will cost you approx. 20 Baht. The closest Malaysian town, Kangar, can only be reached by taxi (20 M$).

Crossing the border between 11:00 and 13:00 h is unfortunately impossible, due to the lunch breaks of the officials in Thailand and Malaysia, which (predictably) are at 11:00 and 12:00 h respectively.

The Thai and Malay custom offices are right next to each other, so that you will be able to carry out the Double-Entry-Visa procedure (out-in-out-in) in approx. 1/2 an hour. With a little luck your share taxi might even still be around upon re-entering Thailand.

PADANG BESAR

Take a bus to PADANG BESAR from Hat Yai for 15 Baht. You will be let out right at the border. Ask for an exit-stamp to be put into your passport, then walk approx. 10 minutes until you reach the Malaysian check point. As a pedestrian you will be checked quite thoroughly, but as long as you are able to produce a reasonably large sum of money (or cheques etc...), you will be given the stamp and permission to enter. Exchange currency at the railway station or in the coffee-shop near the bus station (bad rates!). Buses bound for Butterworth leave from here, the last one at 20:00 h (5.70 M$). The border is closed at 17:30 h Thai time, which is 18:30 h Malaysian time.

SA DAO

This, the most frequently used border check-point, is used by most taxis and Penang-bound buses from Hat Yai and is just a few kilometres south of town. One usually drives through here after a short sojourn at the border.

BETONG

This frontier town is inhabited by 40,000 people and lies at an altitude of 580 metres. It is situated on a narrow strip of land reaching well into the national territory of Malaysia. The town is usually shrouded in fog. A bus ride from Yala (down a lovely 140 km road and through a beautiful limestone formation landscape) will cost you 31 Baht and take 4 1/2 hrs. The Pattani river has been dammed east of the road, approx. 50 km towards Betong, and has thus created the 50 km^2 BANGLANG LAKE. You will be able to visit a SAKAI settlement after having travelled towards Betong for 80 km. The Sakai are the Negroid, first inhabitants of the Malaysian peninsula, and their settlement is just 4 km off the road. There are many palm-oil, coffee, and rubber plantations in the wide valleys of the area. You will be stopped and thoroughly checked at several check points along the way. You will reach the southernmost tip of Thailand and the border to the Malaysian state of Perak shortly beyond Bentong.

SUNGAI GOLOK

There is a further border check-point on the east coast, especially interesting for those who plan to continue straight on to the east coast of Malaysia. Sungai Golok is already strongly influenced by the Malaysian way of life. Generally, it is a rather uninteresting town. The post office is next to the Plaza Hotel.

HOTELS

The rooms of the *ASIA HOTEL***, 44 Charoenket Road, tel 611101, some rooms ac***, are good and well worth the price.

The same can be said of all of the following: *MERRY***, tel 611214, and *THANI***, tel 611046, both on Chuenmaraka Road, *MERLIN****, tel 611003, and the *SAVOY***, tel 611093, both on Charoenket Road.

Cheap and simple rooms are available at the *ERAWAN GUEST HOUSE**, 21 Chuenmaraka Road.

There are many more hotels in town, some of them in the more expensive categories, with discos and massage parlours. The town's largest hotel, the

GRAND HOTEL****, 104 Arifmarka Road, tel 611219, is the only hotel in town that has a pool.

HOW TO GET THERE

A normal train heads for Sungai Golok from Hat Yai at 4:30 h, arrival 8:15 h. The express leaves Hat Yai at 6:03 h, arrival at the border 9:35, 2nd class 87, 3rd class 42 Baht.

FROM SUNGAI GOLOK TO MALAYSIA

Either cross the border on foot, or catch a motorcycle for 5, a ricksha for 10 Baht. Once in Malaysia, take bus 29 to KOTA BHARU (2 M$, taxi 3.30 M$). The border is closed at 17:30 h Thai time (18:30 h Malaysian time).

TAK BAI

You will find this border check point 38 km further east, directly at the coast. A bus from Narathiwat will cost you 10 Baht. The ferry to Kampong Pengkupor (Malaysia) costs 5 Baht or 50 Malaysian cents. From here a bus to KOTA BHARU will cost you 1.40 M$, a taxi 2.30 M$.

IN MALAYSIA

Once there, you will probably be planning to go to PENANG on the west coast or KOTA BHARU on the east coast. You will be able to apply for a new visa to Thailand in both of these towns:

PENANG

This island lies off the west coast. Its largest town is Georgetown, rather Chinese in appearance. Car- and passenger ferries travel back and forth between Penang and Butterworth (mainland) all day, in spite of the connecting bridge. Overland buses and taxis stop at the landing place in Butterworth.

HOTELS - on average, the rates in Malaysia are higher than those in Thailand. Most of the budget-hotels have a central location on or near Leboh Chulia, e.g. TYE ANN HOTEL, no. 282, very noisy. We would recommend the YEE HING, no. 302, tel 63506, as well as the ENG AUN HOTEL, no. 380, tel 612333, with dormitory, spacious, safe-service. There are more hotels in the side roads, e.g. on Love Lane. Slightly more expensive hotels can be found on the loud Penang Road. The CATHAY HOTEL, 15 Leith Street, tel 26271, is better though. The EASTERN & ORIENTAL HOTEL, Farquhar Street, tel 375322, used to be one of Somerset Maugham's favourite haunts. A room with a view of the ocean will cost you 150 M$. The YOUTH HOSTEL is right next door, tel 60553. Here you will have to pay 4 M$ for the first night, 3 M$ for every additional night.

INFORMATION - Penang Tourist Association Information Centre, 10 Jl. Tun Syed Sheikh Barakbah, tel 616663. Open Mon-Thur from 8:30-12:45 and 14:00-16:30 h; Fri 8:30-12:30 and 14:45-16:30 h; Sat 8:30-13:00 h.

BANKS - go to the old district of administration, which surrounds the GPO. Banks are open Mon-Fri 10:00-15:00 h, Sat 9:30-11:30 h. MONEY CHANGERS, usually Indians who can be found in the old bank district and on Leboh Pitt, frequently offer better rates.

CONSULATES - Royal Thai Consulate, 1 Ayer Rajah Road, tel 63377 (bus no. 7), open Mon-Fri 9:00-12:00 h and 14:00-16:00 h. You will need three passport pictures and 15.- M$ for a new visa. Indonesian Consulate, 467 Jl. Burmah, tel 25162/3, open Mon-Fri from 9:00-12:00 h and from 14:00-15:00 h.

LEAVING PENANG - The Bayan Lepas Airport is 18 km south of town, a yellow taxi from Jl.Maxwell will cost you 85c, a coupon-taxi costs 13.50 M$.

Georgetown N ↑

Penang

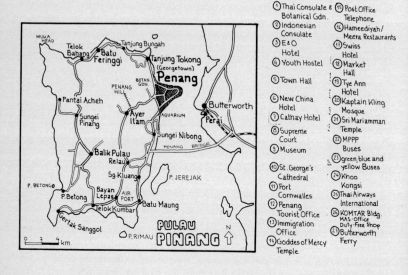

Pulau Pinang N ↑

① Thai Consulate & Botanical Gdn.
② Indonesian Consulate
③ E&O Hotel
④ Youth Hostel
⑤ Town Hall
⑥ New China Hotel
⑦ Cathay Hotel
⑧ Supreme Court
⑨ Museum
⑩ St. George's Cathedral
⑪ Fort Cornwalles
⑫ Penang Tourist Office
⑬ Immigration Office
⑭ Goddes of Mercy Temple
⑮ Post Office Telephone
⑯ Hameediyah / Meera Restaurants
⑰ Swiss Hotel
⑱ Market Hall
⑲ Tye Ann Hotel
⑳ Kaptain Kling Mosque
㉑ Sri Mariamman Temple
㉒ MPPP Buses
㉓ green, blue and yellow Buses
㉔ Khoo Kongsi
㉕ Thai Airways International
㉖ KOMTAR Bldg. MAS-Office Duty-Free Shop
㉗ Butterworth Ferry

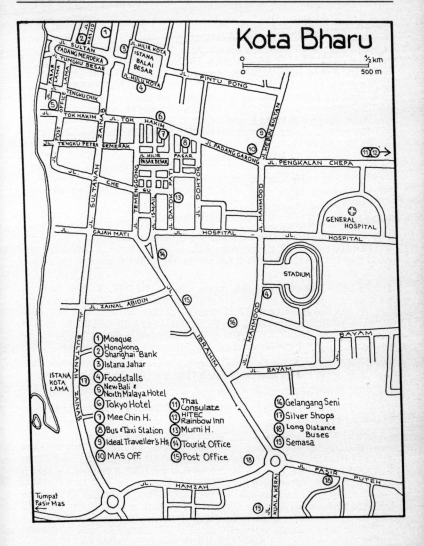

Kota Bharu

½ km
500 m

1 Mosque
2 Hongkong Shanghai Bank
3 Istana Jahar
4 Foodstalls
5 New Bali & North Malaya Hotel
6 Tokyo Hotel
7 Mee Chin H.
8 Bus & Taxi Station
9 Ideal Traveller's Hs
10 MAS OFF.
11 Thai Consulate
12 HITEC Rainbow Inn
13 Murni H.
14 Tourist Office
15 Post Office
16 Gelangang Seni
17 Silver Shops
18 Long Distance Buses
19 Semasa

Airport tax: international flights 15.- M$, Singapore, Brunei 5.- M$, inland flights 3.- M$. SOME PRICES: MEDAN approx. 100.- M$ (there is also a regular ship), Europe and Australia approx. 700 - 900.- M$. MAS flies to IPOH 41.-, KOTA BHARU 72.-, KL 86.-, KUALA TRENGGANU 80.-, and SINGAPORE 150.- M$. Trains leave from the Butterworth Railway Station. There are six daily trains to KUALA LUMPUR, 54.- / 25.- / 17.- M$ for the 1st / 2nd / 3rd class not including possible additional charges. The cheapest way of getting to SINGAPORE is with the Ekspres Rakyat, which leaves Butterworth at 7:00 h, continues from KL at 13:30 h, and arrives in Singapore at 20:15 h. If you want to head north, catch the international express to BANGKOK, departure: 13:35 h for 83.30 / 38.70 M$ for the 1st / 2nd class. There is also a normal train to PADANG BESAR for 9.30 / 5.80 M$, departure 6:45 h. Minibuses to HAT YAI 20.-, PHUKET 36.-, and KO SAMUI 37.- M$. Daily ac buses leave for SINGAPORE for 21.-, KOTA BHARU for 20.- M$. An ac bus leaves twice daily for KL, 15.-M$. Overland taxis to HAT YAI cost 20.-, to KUALA LUMPUR 30.- M$.

KOTA BHARU

This Malaysian town is just a few kilometres south of the Thai border. This is the departure point for a tour of the east coast of Malaysia. There are also good connections to the west coast and to the central regions of the country (newly built roads).

HOTELS - The following are pretty cheap: RAINBOW INN, 4423 Jl. Pengkalan Chepa, next to the Thai Consulate, bus no. 4, 1 1/2 km towards the airport, opposite MUMMY'S HITEC HOSTEL (4398). The REBANA HOUSE is opposite the Istana Kota Lama, the IDEAL TRAVELLERS HOUSE on 5504 Jl. Padang Garong. The TOKYO, 3945 Jl. Tok Hakim, tel 22466, as well as the AH CHEW and the MEE CHIN, both opposite, are slightly more expensive.

INFORMATION - Jl. Sultan Ibrahim (next to Majlis Perbandaran), open Sun-Wed 8:30-16:30 h, Thur and Sat 8:30-13:15 h. Very helpful people!

MONEY CHANGERS - in Jl. Gajah Mati.

THAI CONSULATE - 4426 Jl. Pengkalan Chepa, tel 782545, open Sun-Thur from 9:00-16:00 h.

LEAVING KOTA BHARU - The Sultan Ismail Detra Airport is 10 km out of town. MAS, Jl. Padang Garong (Hotel Kesina Baru), tel 743144. Daily flights to KL 86.- (61.-), IPOH 113.-, PENANG 72.-, JOHORE BHARU 163.-, and ALOR SETAR 59.- M$. The railway lines are west of the river. If you want to take a jungle train south, either leave from PASIR MAS (bus no. 6) or WAKAF BHARU (buses 19 and 27). Local buses and taxis leave from Jl. Pendek. Most of the overland buses leave from the Langgar bus station, Jl Pasir Puteh; buses to Alor Setar, Malacca, and Seremban leave from Jl. Hamzah. SOME PRICES for buses and (taxis): JOHORE BHARU 22.-, ac 27.- (50.-), KUALA TRENGGANU 6.80, (12.-), KUALA DUNGUN 11.-, (17.-), KUANTAN 16.- (23.-), KL 21.-, (45.-), MALACCA 22.-, SINGAPORE 31.-, BUTTERWORTH 20.- (30.-), PASIR MAS 1.50, (5.-), RANTAU PANJANG 2.-, (3.30), and KUALA KRAI 3.-M$.

BURMA

RANGOON

Rangoon has been Burma's capital since 1885. The British were responsible for founding the city. They needed a good harbour and an administrative centre for their colony and thus decided to found the capital here, on the site of the former village of Dagon, best known for its association with the nearby Shwedagon pagoda. The streets in the centre of town (south) are as straight as arrows and arranged in a lattice-like structure, lending this section a very geometric appearance when seen from above. It is rather difficult to lose one's way in town, as the roads always meet at right angles and are consecutively numbered, with the first road being the one furthest west, running from the north to the south. The city, its fascinating inhabitants, and the colonial-style buildings overgrown with moss leave a lasting impression on visitors. Almost 4 million people live in the Burmese metropolis, which used to be inhabited almost exclusively by Indians. These days it is the Burmese that dominate and have left their mark on the town, not the few remaining Chinese and Indians. Rangoon is not as crowded north of the railway lines as it is in the south - there are many parks here, several lakes, and the residential areas of the well-to-do.

The *SHWEDAGON PAGODA*, which is north of town towards the airport, is the trademark of the city. It may not be the highest, but it is certainly the most impressive pagoda in the entire South East Asian area. Take your time whilst visiting!

Legend has it that a pagoda was erected here in 585 B.C. It was extended and enlarged in 1446. By the end of the 18th century it had reached its present height of 107 metres. The entire temple grounds are set on a 60 metre hill. You can hardly miss it - even when approaching Rangoon by air the huge, golden stupa is clearly visible. Religious ceremonies are carried out in a number of smaller temples that are situated on the platform surrounding the pagoda. The Shwedagon itself is decorated with thin plates of gold. The peak consists of a series of umbrella-shaped bands, adorned with diamonds, sapphires, and rubies. A wind vane adorned with approx. 2500 gems is on top of these. The very top is made up of an orb (approx. 25 cm in diameter) decorated with more than 4000 diamonds and other gems.

It is most important that you take off your shoes before climbing up the staircase leading to the platform. Take them with you. We would suggest going up during the late afternoon, before the sun has set. Staircases lead up from all four points of the compass, with the southern staircase making up the main entrance. There are very many souvenir shops along the southern steps, as indeed there are in the entire Shwedagon area. Few visitors choose to climb the rather steep steps on the western side. Once on the platform, be sure to circle the pagoda in a clockwise direction, as is the custom. In order to get to the pagoda, catch bus no. 10 from the YMCA (Theinbyu Road).

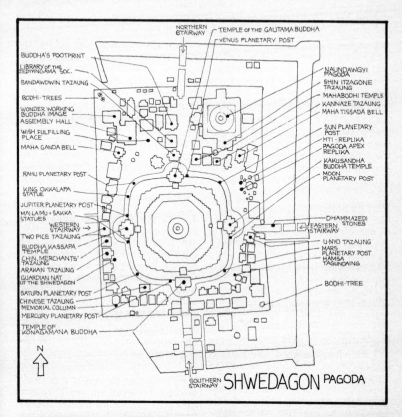

NORTHERN STAIRWAY
TEMPLE OF THE GAUTAMA BUDDHA
VENUS PLANETARY POST

BUDDHA'S FOOTPRINT
LIBRARY OF THE ZEDIYINGAMA SOC.
SANDAWDWIN TAZAUNG
BODHI-TREES
WONDER WORKING BUDDHA IMAGE ASSEMBLY HALL
WISH FULFILLING PLACE
MAHA GANDA BELL
RAHU PLANETARY POST
KING OKKALAPA STATUE
JUPITER PLANETARY POST
MAI LA MU + SAKKA STATUES
WESTERN STAIRWAY →
TWO PICE TAZAUNG
BUDDHA KASSAPA TEMPLE
CHIN MERCHANTS' TAZAUNG
ARAKAN TAZAUNG
GUARDIAN NAT OF THE SHWEDAGON
SATURN PLANETARY POST
CHINESE TAZAUNG MEMORIAL COLUMN
MERCURY PLANETARY POST
TEMPLE OF KONAGAMANA BUDDHA

NAUNDAWGYI PAGODA
SHIN ITZAGONE TAZAUNG
MAHABODHI TEMPLE
KANNAZE TAZAUNG
MAHA TISSADA BELL
SUN PLANETARY POST
HTI-REPLIKA PAGODA APEX REPLIKA
KAKUSANDHA BUDDHA TEMPLE
MOON PLANETARY POST
DHAMMAZEDI STONES
EASTERN STAIRWAY
U-NYO TAZAUNG
MARS PLANETARY POST
HAMSA TAGUNDAING
BODHI-TREE

N

SOUTHERN STAIRWAY SHWEDAGON PAGODA

The *MARTYRS' MAUSOLEUM* is quite close to the Shwedagon. Aung San and seven other national heroes are buried here.

There are two more pagodas well worth a visit in the middle of town - the octagonal, 70 metre

SULE PAGODA was built 2200 years ago, in the year 235 of the Buddhist era. The pagoda enshrines one of Buddha's hairs. The

BOTATAUNG PAGODA, by the Rangoon River, has more relics of Buddha. The pagoda was fully restored to its original splendour after having been destroyed in World War II. The interior is decorated with countless small pieces of mirror. The

KYUAK HTAT GYI PAGODA (Shwegondine Road, northeast of the Shwedagon) has a beautiful, reclining Buddha who gazes down upon visitors with dreamy eyes. The statue's 71 metre length makes it even larger than the one in Pegu. You should also definitely pay a visit to the

NATIONAL MUSEUM, Phayre Street (Pansodan Street), just behind the Strand Hotel (open Sun-Thur 10:00-15:00 h, Sat 12:00-15:00 h, closed on Fri and holidays). King Thibaw's famous lion throne is kept here. The British stole this throne along with a number of other precious things that they took back to England with them after the 3rd Anglo-Burmese war. They were not returned until 1964, when Ne Win paid an official state visit to London. The

STATE SCHOOL OF MUSIC AND DRAMA has settled in the Jubilee Hall, Shwedagon Road. It is open from 8:00-16:30 h daily. Performances for the public are held at the weekends during the rainy period. You can also watch the rehearsals during the week. Tourist Burma will give you information concerning performances given by the music and drama school. The dance performances that Tourist Burma organizes in the Inya Lake Hotel are expensive.

HOTELS

The *YMCA**-****, 263 Mahabandoola Street, tel 72110, double rooms and three-bed rooms, is the main traveller hang-out in the city. You'll receive lots of information here. There is also a left luggage office (open from 7:00-21:30 h), as well as a pretty good cafeteria. Women can also spend the night at the YWCA, 119 Brooking Street, tel 12108, dormitory*.

The *GARDEN GUEST HOUSE***, (ac ***), Sule Pagoda Road, tel 71516, is an alternative. The hotel is located right next to Tourist Burma and Thai Airways. It's quite clean, but the 'rooms' are extremely small and only separated by very thin walls, dormitory*.

The *PYIN OO LWIN GUESTHOUSE ****, 183 Barr Street, is new. Friendly people, constant supply of fresh drinking water.

If you have a little money to spare, why not try the *DAGON**-****, 256 Sule Pagoda Road, tel 71140. The hotel, which was called the 'Oriental' in the days of the British Empire, still has a little of its former atmosphere, though it now seems rather faded.

The rooms include sinks and are reasonably clean. The rooms to the front are quite noisy, as the hotel is on a main road and located right next to a cinema. The price for a bed in one of the cheap board partitions starts at 25 Kyat. The toilet is dirty. The beer-drinking population of the town meets on the first floor at noon.

The *THAMMADA*****, tel 71499, Signal Pagoda Road, is north of the railway lines near the station, rooms with ac.

If you're going to spend that much anyway, however, we would recommend the old, almost classic colonial hotel *STRAND*****, 92 Strand Road, tel 77635. Somerset Maugham and the former viceroy of India, Lord Curzon, are among the more prominent guests to have stayed here.

Package tourists usually stay at the *INYA LAKE HOTEL*****, construction of which was sponsored by the USSR. All rooms of this, the best hotel in town, have ac and a wonderful view of the lake. There are also tennis courts, gardens, and a swimming pool.

SHWEDAGON PAGODA, RANGOON

The *KANDAWGYI HOTEL*****, tel 80412, is in the former English Boat Club building, Lake Road, directly on the lake. Rooms with ac and bathroom.

FOOD

Start off the day with a hearty breakfast - Rangoon's cafés serve Burmese cake (Beik Moke or Htan Thi Moke) and as much tea as you can drink. Try the *SHWE PA LAUNG CAFE,* Mahabandoola Street, opposite Tourist Burma. The *GOLDEN COIN* on the other side of the road is also pretty good.

Burmese Mohinga, a popular fish, egg, and noodle dish, is available on Botaung Pagoda Road. The *DANA-PU,* 29th Street (parallel to Shwebontha Street, to the east, near Anawratha Street) has a genuinely Burmese atmosphere.

You will find an *ARAKANESE RES-TAURANT* on 30th Street, no. 84.

There are many Chinese restaurants in town, quite a few of them on Latha Street, e.g. *SHANGHAI* (no. 159) and *MWEE KOON.* You'll find more on Sule Pagoda Rd., e.g. *CHUNG WAH,* no. 162. The *PALACE RESTAURANT* on 37th Street (parallel to Phayre Street, on the west), no. 84, serves good Sichuan food.

Cheap Indian food is served at the *YANNAN,* at the corner of Sule Pagoda Road and Anawratha Street. Continue down Anawratha Street and you'll come across more Indian restaurants.

NILAR WIN'S, 377 Mahabandoola Street (in between 37th and 38th) serves excellent shakes and yoghurts.

A dinner at the *STRAND* (with cheap, cold beer if it's available) is an experience well worth the money. The lobster is fantastic, as are the typically English menus. The price (which usually comes to approx. US$4 per person) is fair.

Cool Mandalay Beer is available for 18 Kyat in the first floor of the *DAGON HOTEL* at noon and in the evenings until 21:00 h. Good, though rather expensive, Indian food is also served.

Two more expensive restaurants: *BAMBOO HOUSE*, 3 Thapyenyo St. (by Prome Road) and *BURMAH KITCHEN*, 141 West Shwegondine Road.

You're expected you to pay in dollars at the *KARAWEIK* restaurant on Royal Lake, which looks like a huge boat made of concrete. Menus with Kyat prices are also available, though - all you have to do is ask. Traditional dances are performed in the evenings from 20:30 h - admission 50 Kyat.

GENERAL INFORMATION

INFORMATION - Tourist Burma, 77-79 Sule Pagoda Road, tel 78376, 75328, and 80321 is the country's state-run tourist office. This is the place to go for information, coupons, tickets, and Kyat (for US$). You can pay in cash, with traveller's cheques, and with an American Express Card. You may well be reminded of the all-embracing Intourist in the USSR, but the people here are more friendly! The newest hotel and transportation prices are given on a large sign on the wall. Open Mon-Fri 9:30-20:00 h, Sat until 12:00 h.

GENERAL POST OFFICE - on the corner of Strand Road and Aung Kyaw Street. You can also have letters sent poste restante here. Open Mon-Fri 9:30-16:00 h, Sat until 12:30 h.

TELEPHONES - we would suggest only going to the Central Telegraph office, Pansodan / Mahabandoola Street if it's absolutely necessary. Open daily from 8:00-21:00 h. We would not recommend making international calls from here, as the lines are bad and you will be charged approx. 70 Kyat for three minutes.

MEDICAL AID - Generally, foreigners should go to the Diplomatic Hospital by the Royal Lakes, tel 50149. The doctors here will deal with your visa-extension, should it be necessary.

NEWSPAPERS - two English-language dailies are sold in Rangoon: THE WORKING PEOPLE'S DAILY (with a circulation of 20,000) and the GUARDIAN (with a circulation of 17,500). Take a look at them!

ENTERTAINMENT - there is practically no nightlife in Rangoon. The Burmese and western films shown at the cinemas in the evenings are extremely popular and nearly always sold out. Restaurants close at 21:00 and 22:00 h.

PUBLIC TRANSPORT - ancient buses and small Mazdas that are not quite as old cost 1 Kyat. They drive certain routes regularly. A 2 km ride in a trishaw will cost you approx. 5 Kyat. If you wish to charter a small Mazda for a ride around town you will have to pay approx. 5 Kyat.

SHOPPING & MARKETS

Even though there is no large variety of goods, a visit to the various markets of Rangoon may be worthwhile - much atmosphere!

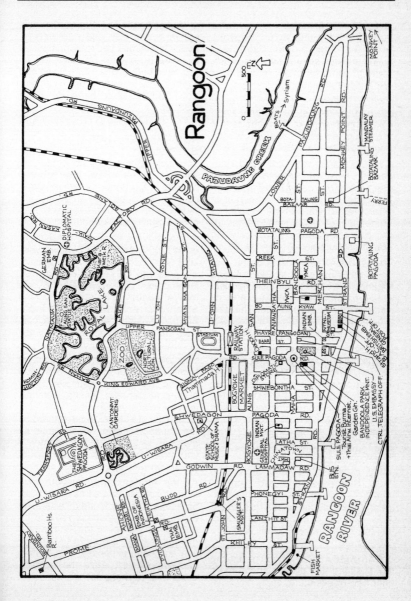

BOGYOKE MARKET - the town's largest market-hall is on Bogyoke Aung San Street. Shan-bags, Burmese lacquer boxes, Longyis (traditional trousers for men), as well as a few antiques are for sale.

SMUGGLER'S MARKET - quite close to the market-hall (Prome Road / St. John Road). All the products that are smuggled over the 'green border' from Thailand are sold here.

CHINATOWN - a walk through Rangoon's Chinatown, which is mainly on Lanmadaw Rd., is interesting. There is a Chinese temple on the corner of Strand Road. You can still experience something of a Chinese market atmosphere on Strand Road, between Mahabandoola and Anawratha St.

INDIAN MARKET - 26th Street. Today this is more a general fruit and vegetable market than anything else. Huge mountains of chilies and all sorts of spices are for sale. The best time to go to any of the above markets is in the late morning, before noon.

BOOKS - there are several bookshops on Muang Talay Street. Many of them trade used paperback novels, e.g. the Theingy Maw Bookstall, no. 355. The Pagan Bookshop, no. 100, 37th Street, is something for lovers of old books.

DIPLOMATIC STORE - tourists and foreigners who live in Burma - i.e. those working for the embassies - can shop at the Diplomatic Store with US$. Souvenirs, postcards, books, cheroots, gems, jade, mother-of-pearl, and lacquerworks are available. A carton of cigarettes - 100 Kyat on the black market - will cost you US$5 here.

THAI EMBASSY - If you're leaving for Thailand and plan to spend more than two weeks there, apply for a visa at the embassy, 81 Prome Road. It will take one day and cost you 35 Kyat. Sometimes you're not permitted to leave Burma for Bangkok unless you have both a visa for Thailand and a ticket back home from Thailand. You should also have at least US$250.

HOW TO GET THERE
BY PLANE
You can come to Burma either by ship or plane. Few international cruisers drop anchor here these days, so you will probably arrive by air. Along with your visa you will also need a confirmed return ticket.

A Thai Airways flight from BANGKOK costs 4000 Baht return nowadays, UBA 3600 Baht. A flight from Calcutta will cost you US$155. You can also incorporate your one week of Burma into a general circuit flight round South East Asia. Many of the India-Burma-Thailand package deals plan less than the officially allowed week in Burma, however.

You will have to fill out a stack of forms in the aeroplane before even arriving; all of your valuables (cameras, cine cameras, lenses, watches, jewelry, transistor radios, walkmen, binoculars etc.) have to be entered on the Customs Form. Video cameras may not be taken into the country. If you have one along it will be kept at the airport until you depart.

All the foreign currency you have along (cheques as well as cash) must be entered on the Money Declaration Form. All your expenses have to be entered on the form, too - nowadays this applies particularly to transportation and hotel expenses. The form is checked as you leave the country, though not all that closely.

> Do not change any declared foreign currency on the black market!

Try to be the first in line when you arrive in Rangoon - checking your passport and all the forms can turn into a long and wearisome procedure, especially when the Thai Airlines Airbus has just arrived.

You'll have to exchange money after you've been through the passport and customs check. A minimum exchange of US$100 was introduced in September 1987. Both cash and traveller's cheques are accepted, cheque cards are not. You will receive a better rate for traveller's cheques.

There is a Tourist Burma counter at the airport. While you cannot buy tickets for the rest of your seven-day stay here, information concerning hotels is available, and taxis to Rangoon can be booked for 60 Kyat + entry on the Money Declaration Form. The taxi drivers will usually show an immediate interest in any duty-free cigarettes or booze you may have along.

> Officially, black market dealers can be sentenced to up to three years' imprisonment.

After you've been to the Tourist Burma counter you should have your return ticket out of Burma confirmed as soon as possible! Do this while still at the airport. Thai Airways opens a desk next to the bank counter when they are expecting incoming flights.

If you don't have your ticket confirmed at the airport, have it done the next day at the town office:

AIR FRANCE, 69 Sule Pagoda Road, tel 70736.
AEROFLOT, 18 Prome Road.

BANGLADESH BIMAN, 106/108 Phayre Road, tel 75882.
BURMA AIRWAYS CORPORATION (BAC), 104 Strand Road, tel 74566.

You may be better off flying with another airline if you want good service; BAC flights are frequently overbooked. This doesn't mean that you will have an enjoyable extended stay, though - you will have to stay in Rangoon for the time it takes to organize another flight, and you will have a frantic time rushing in and out of the BAC office. You will also have to pay for the visa extension - 35 Kyat a day.

CAAC, 67 Prome Road.
INDIAN AIRLINES, 533 Merchant Street, tel 72410.
THAI AIRWAYS INTERNATIONAL, 441-45 Mahabandoola Street, tel 75936.

You can get together with other travellers for the taxi ride into town (maximum of 4 people permitted). You can also get rid of your cigarette and whisky rations during the ride. There's plenty of time to bargain, but be be warned - the rates given by the taxi drivers are not very good. We would not recommend taking Bus 9 which leaves for town 1 km from the airport (1 Kyat) - it is frequently overcrowded.

Once in town, immediately contact Tourist Burma to organize the tickets for the rest of your travels in Burma!

LEAVING RANGOON
BY PLANE
Buy a coupon for a taxi ride to the airport in the hotels or at Tourist Burma, should you not feel like taking the bus and having to walk the 1 km from the bus stop. Taxis can frequently be found waiting in front of the Tourist Burma office. A ride will cost you 60

Kyat, 50 Kyat from the Inya Lake Hotel. As you will already have to have a confirmed return-ticket when applying for your visa to Burma, you will not have to book an international flight from Rangoon.

When leaving the country make sure that you arrive at the airport well in time and that your Customs and Money Declaration Forms are in order.

The weekly flight to Kunming may be interesting for travellers planning to go to China from here (2076 Kyat - approx. 280 US$).

Individual tourists will have a difficult time organizing inland flights. They have to be booked through Tourist Burma. Inland flight tickets bought abroad are not accepted!!! Up until now one-way inland tickets only have been available, i.e. return tickets to Rangoon have to be organized from the towns you choose to fly to.

BAC flights frequently leave early. The airport tax in Rangoon is US$2 (15 Kyat).

Some prices for inland flights: MANDALAY 545 Kyat, HEHO 460 Kyat, PAGAN 495 Kyat.

The plane flies RANGOON (departure: 6.45 h) - PAGAN (8.35 h) - MANDALAY (9.35 h) - HEHO (10.30 h) - RANGOON. In the afternoon there is a flight RANGOON (13.00 h) - HEHO (14.50 h) - MANDALAY (15.50 h) - PAGAN (16.40 h) - RANGOON.

BY TRAIN

You will have to buy tickets to Mandalay, Thazi, and Shwenyaung at Tourist Burma. Get the tickets as soon as you can; the few seats reserved for tourists are quickly booked up.

Always keep an eye on your luggage when travelling by train - thieves are not uncommon in Burma. Try not to stand near a door, as this makes escape all the more easy for thieves. Trains are frequently so full that one can only get in by way of the windows.

A 2nd class ticket to MANDALAY costs 44 Kyat, 1st class 98 Kyat, Upper Class 110 Kyat, Upper Class Sleeper (not on all trains) 138 Kyat.

THAZI 36 Kyat / 88 Kyat / 99 Kyat / 136 Kyat.

You will be seated on wooden benches that can be reserved in advance in the 2nd class. The Upper Class (1st class) offers fans and padded seats - many of the springs have burst through the padding, though. Sleepers can only be booked on a few days of the week.

There are two daily trains from Rangoon to Mandalay (6:00 and 21:00 h). It's 13-14 hrs. to Mandalay, 11 hrs. to Thazi - sometimes trips may take even longer due to the bad condition of the trains and tracks. Food and drinks are available at every station. If you have a water flask along you can always have it re-filled.

BY BUS

All buses must be booked through Tourist Burma. Hardly any buses at all leave from Rangoon these days. Should you be lucky enough to get a ticket for one of the extremely rare rides you'll have to pay 121 Kyat to get to TAUNGGYI, 88 to get to MANDALAY.

SYRIAM

The average visitor to Burma will hardly want to spend any of his limited time making excursions to the area around Rangoon. If this is not your first visit to the country, however, you might find it worthwhile going to these lesser-known places, especially as they are so close.

The town, like many villages in the Irrawaddy delta, is mainly inhabited by Indians. Thousands used to live in Burma during the days of the British Empire, but most of them were deported after the country gained its independence in 1962. When the Portugese made Syriam a base in the beginning of the 16th century, the town became the centre of Burma's foreign trade. Rangoon took over this role when Syriam was destroyed in 1756. Few ruins remain. An excursion to the *KYAUK TAN PAGODA* from here is worth it - the pagoda is on a small island in the middle of the river.

HOW TO GET THERE

From Rangoon, take bus no. 9 or 12 to the ferry. You can cross the Pazungdaung River for 1 Kyat. The ferry leaves every hour from the pier at the end of Mahabandoola Street - sometimes the ferry-people take an extended lunch-break. Once on the other side, take a converted truck (1 Kyat), a jeep, or a pick-up (3 Kyat each) to the KYAUK TAN pagoda. Return trips to the island cost 50 Paise.

PEGU

The former capital of the Mon kingdom was founded in the 8th century. The Mon were the rivals of the Burmese people for almost 1000 years. Originally from the the delta area of the Red river in present-day Vietnam, the Mon settled in the western part of central Thailand and southern Burma. Their culture was strongly influenced by Indian ideas. It was through the Mon that the Burmese first came into contact with Buddhism. After a long period of violent conflict with the Burmese, the Mon lost the war as well as their autonomy in 1752. Pegu, which had gained considerable importance as a port due to to its dealings with Europe, India, China, and other Asian countries, became unimportant because of the gradual silting up of the Irrawaddy river.

You will be able to see the 114 metre stupa of the

SHWEMAWDAW PAGODA from the river-bridge. The main entrance is guarded by two gigantic red stone lions. Legend has it that a small, approx. 30 metre, pagoda was erected over two hairs of Buddha almost 1000 years ago. The pagoda was completely destroyed by an earthquake in 1930 after having been enlarged numerous times. The reconstruction was not completed until 1954. You will also come across a number of shrines with Nats on the upper platform.

We would suggest taking a taxi to the pagoda on the opposite river bank, as the two are far apart and the roads are in a bad condition.

The *KALYANI SIMA* is a 15th century ordination hall. Young monks are still ordained here to this day. You should definitely go and see the huge, reclining Buddha of the nearby

SHWETHALYAUNG PAGODA. The 55 metre figure was made in the 13th century and seems strangely alive. It represents Buddha going into the final stages of Nirvana, and the eyes of the statue have a correspondingly transfigured expression. The soles of the statue's feet (7.80 metres in length) are nicely adorned.

Of the many other pagodas in town we would definitely recommend the mondhop of the

KYAUKPUN PAGODA, 4 km to the south, by the road leading to Rangoon. Four statues stand in front of the four inside walls. One depicts Buddha, while the other three are representations of his earlier incarnations. The four figures gaze north, south, east and west. The 30 metre, sitting figures are made of brick and cement. The pagoda was built in 1476 and partially destroyed by an earthquake in 1930.

HOW TO GET THERE

Trains to PEGU, approx. 80 km north of Rangoon, leave more or less every hour, cost 3.5 Kyat. You can also take the night train from MANDALAY to RANGOON, disembark at Pegu, and continue on to Rangoon with a local train after you have explored. Buses from Rangoon leave from 18th Street for 5 Kyat. You can also hire a taxi for an entire day in Rangoon (approx. 120 Kyat). This way you will not have to organize any further transportation once in Pegu.

THAZI

This town, approx. 540 km from Rangoon, is a central traffic junction on the way to the north. Spend the night at the simple *THITAGU REST HOUSE** next to the point of departure for buses bound for Pagan. There are no restaurants in the area around the train station, only simple foodstalls. The guard will usher any boarding tourists to their reserved seats.

LEAVING THAZI
BY TRAIN

A 2nd class ticket to Rangoon (approx. 11 hrs.) costs 36 Kyat, 1st class (not on all trains) 88 Kyat, Upper Class 99 Kyat, Upper Class Sleeper (not on all trains) 136 Kyat. Trains depart around 8:45 and 20:40 h. Delays are not at all unusual. Buy your ticket in advance in Taunggyi or Pagan, otherwise you will not be allowed to board. At best, you may be allowed to stand in front of the toilet for the 11-hour trip.

BY PICK-UP / JEEP / BUS

It is better to take a direct bus or pickup to MANDALAY from PAGAN or TAUNGGYI. The pick-up and Datsunjeep stop is approx. 10 minutes from the railway station. For those arriving on the night train, they will already be waiting to pick you up and take you to where you want to go. It can take

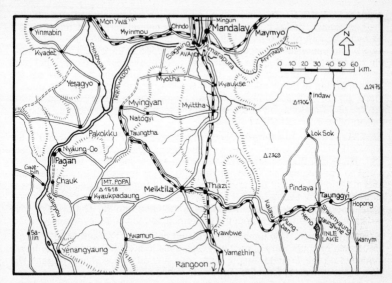

quite a while until they have a sufficient number of passengers, however, and the drivers rarely leave until their vehicles are bursting at the seams.

A ride to PAGAN via MEIKTILA will cost you 77 Kyat and take 6 hrs. It's 170 km to TAUNGGYI (Lake Inle), 55 Kyat, 6 hrs.

PAGAN

According to ancient Burmese chronicles, Pagan was founded in the 2nd century A.D. It was not until 1044, though, under King Anawratha, that the town reached its zenith and developed into one of the most important cities of the world. Had King Narathihpatis not been such a bad diplomat, Kublai Khan's armies may not have been ordered to besiege and ultimately destroy the city in 1287. Almost 5000 ruins, some of them restored, are still standing on an approx. 30km² area today. Unfortunately the ruins of Pagan, the largest archeological site in the entire South East Asian region, were partially destroyed by an earthquake in 1975. Visiting the gigantic temple city is quite an experience - a sunset seen from the Thatbyinnyu or the Gawdawpalin is particularly breathtaking. You will be gazing upon a seemingly endless sea of pagodas, the red bricks assuming a ruby-like quality in the setting sun, and a few of the white ruins glowing a bright silver.

NOTE: Even ruins are sacred Buddhist sites, and you have to take off your shoes before entering! You should at least visit the following temples:

ANANDA TEMPLE - This, the most highly venerated temple of Pagan, is also the best known. It was built around 1091. The central part of the temple has a perfectly square ground-plan, with each of the walls measuring 60 metres in length. All four walls have adjoining, gable-shaped entrances, giving the temple a perfect cross structure when seen from above. Six terraces, each one smaller than the preceding one, rise from the central structure. The square shikara on top of these merges with a Burmese stupa further up. The peak is made up of a gilded, umbrella-like structure. The building reaches a total height of 60 metres. There are four 10-metre statues in the interior, each depicting different incarnations of Buddha.

THATBYINNYU - This temple stands within the old town fortification and is the highest in all of Pagan (64 metres). It symbolizes the endless wisdom of Buddha. There is a Buddha statue gazing to the east in the upper part of the temple. The construction of Thatbyinnyu began in the middle of the 12th century and marked the advent of the Burmese style of temple architecture, which is characterized by two cubes set on top of each other. The two cubes are frequently separated by three terraces, as is the case with the Thatbyinnyu. You will have a wonderful view from the uppermost terrace in the evenings.

GAWDAWPALIN - This temple was erected between 1174 and 1178. The entire temple grounds were almost fully destroyed in the 1975 earthquake. It was modelled on the Ananda temple more than any other building in Pagan. The view of the Irrawaddy from the top terrace is beautiful.

PAHTOTHAMAYA - Built in the 10th century, this temple is still strongly influenced by the Mon architecture. Murals dating back to the Mon period decorate the interior.

MAHABODHI - This pagoda was modelled on an Indian temple in Bihar and is quite unique among Pagan's temple ruins.

There are several temple grounds in the south and southeast of Pagan that are worth a visit, but you'd be better off travelling to these by bicycle or some other form of transport.

SHWESANDAW - The cylindrical stupa and the five terraces leading up to it are a most impressive sight. A hair of Buddha's, seized by King Anawratha after the defeat of the Mon in 1057, is said to be embedded in one of the temple walls.

SULAMANI - The ground-plan and general style of this temple are vaguely reminiscent of the Thatbyinnyu. The many murals are much more recent, however - they were painted over the original temple murals by monks during the course of the last century.

DHAMMAYANGYI - Only the vestibules and the outer terraces of this temple can be explored - the interior was probably bricked up soon after construction.

HOTELS

The ac bungalows of the luxury hotel *THIRIPYITSAYA***** are set in a quiet, peaceful area, right by the Irrawaddy river. If you can't afford to spend the night here, you can at least come and

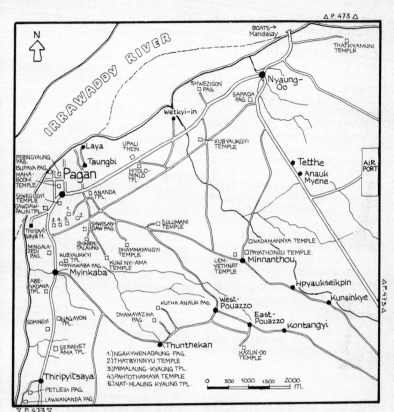

△ P.473 △

Map labels (as shown):

IRRAWADDY RIVER

BOATS→ Mandalay

THATKYAMUNI TEMPLE

SHWEZIGON PAG.

Nyaung-Oo

SAPADA PAG.

Wetkyi-in

KUBYAUKGYI TEMPLE

Laya

UPALI THEIN

Taungbi

Tetthe

Anauk Myene

AIR PORT

PEBINGYAUNG PAG.
BUPAYA PAG.
MAHA-BODHI TEMPLE

Pagan

HITILO-MINLO TPL.

ANANDA TPL.

SHWEGUGYI TEMPLE
GAWDAW-PALIN TPL.

1.
3. 4. 5. 2.

SHWESAN-DAW PAG.

SULUMANI TEMPLE

NADAMANNYA TEMPLE

Thinpyit-saya H.

SHINBIN-TALAUNG

DHAMMAYANGYI TEMPLE

PAYATHONZU TEMPLE

MINGALA-ZEDI PAG.

KUBYAUKGYI TPL.

KUNI NYI-AMA TEMPLE

LEM-YETHNAT TEMPLE

Minnanthou

MYINKABA PAG.

Myinkaba

Hpyaukseikpin

ABE-YADANA TPL.

KUTHA ANAUK PAG.

West-Pouazzo

Kunsinkye

SOMINGYI

NAGAYON TPL.

DHAMAYAZIKA PAG.

East-Pouazzo

Kontangyi

SEINNYET AMA TPL.

Thunthekan

KAZUN-OO TEMPLE

Thiripyitsaya

PETLEIK PAG.

LAWKANANDA PAG.

1.) NGAKYWENADAUNG PAG.
2.) THATBYINNYU TEMPLE
3.) MIMALAUNG -KYAUNG TPL.
4.) PAHTOTHAMAYA TEMPLE
5.) NAT-HLAUNG KYAUNG TPL.

0   500   1000   1500   2000 m.

△ P.473 △

▽ P.473 ▽

enjoy a cool Mandalay Beer in the evenings. You can exchange money here, too.

All other hotels can be found on the main road of new Pagan: The *CO-OPERATIVE INN**, diagonally across from the new museum, has a good restaurant and serves Mandalay Beer in the evenings. The *ZARNEE REST HOUSE** is at the road branching off to the new paved road.

Along the main road you'll find the *MOE MOE HOTEL**, *AUNG THA HAYA GUEST HOUSE**, *MIN CHAN MYIE GUEST HOUSE**, *BURMA REST HOUSE**, and the *MYA THI DA HOTEL** - all of the above charge the same rates and have similar furnishings.

The *IRRA IN**-**** is on the road leading to the Irrawaddy - peaceful, clean, friendly people.

FOOD

Travellers like hanging out at the *NATION RESTAURANT*, at the entrance of town, opposite Tourist Burma. Meals cost between 5 and 15 Kyat, good yoghurts are available. The vegetarian *MARIE MAN* restaurant is next door. The Burmese and Chinese dishes served at the *MAY YADANA* across the road are better, though. The place is owned by a friendly woman. The food served at the *CO-OPERATIVE* is also quite good. Excellent Burmese and Chinese food, reasonably priced and served by friendly people, is available at the *AYE YAKETHAR YAR* near the Irra Inn. If you've got a couple of Kyat to spare, treat yourself to a multi-course lunch at the *THIRIPYITSAYA*.

GENERAL INFORMATION

TOURIST BURMA - at the entrance to town, open daily from 8:00-20:00 h. You can also exchange money here.

MUSEUM - open from 9:00-16:30 h except for Mon and holidays.

ART GUIDE - you should definitely buy the 'Pictorial Guide to Pagan' for 40 Kyat (30 Kyat if you bargain well). Often not available, try to get it in Rangoon.

TRANSPORT - 4-5 people can get together and rent a horse-drawn carriage, a charming way to see more in the little time available. The cost is 10-20 Kyat an hour or approx. 60 Baht for the entire day. Carriages with English speaking guides cost 200 Kyat for 7 hrs. Bicycles for 10-15 Kyat a day, difficult to ride on the sandy and dusty roads. Jeeps approx. 30 Kyat per hour. A ride to Nyaung Oo in a carriage or a trishaw will cost you 15 Kyat.

STATE LACQUERWARE SCHOOL

SCHOOL - diagonally across from the Irra Inn. Open until 16:30 h daily. You can buy nice pieces of lacquerware opposite the Ananda temple.

LEAVING PAGAN
BY PLANE

The small Pagan airfield lies by the road leading to Kyaukpadaung from Nyaung Oo. Every now and then BAC sends down a small minibus free of charge. Taxis cost 10 Kyat. There is a daily flight to MANDALAY (30 minutes, 190 Kyat) and RANGOON (1 hour, 495 Kyat). You will have to fly via Mandalay if you wish to get to HEHO (380 Kyat).

BY BUS / TAXI-JEEP / PICK-UP All buses have to be booked through Tourist Burma. The fares have to be entered on your Money Declaration Form. Buses to TAUNGGYI cost 121 Kyat, to MANDALAY 66 Kyat (Coopbus) or 88 Kyat. Departure at 3:30 in the morning and 11:00 h, arrival (with a little luck) at 14:00 and 21:30 h.

In order to catch the train from Mandalay to Rangoon in THAZI, you'll have to catch one of the THAZI-bound pick-ups that stand in front of Tourist Burma and leave at around 2:00 in the morning and 13:30 h. The ride will cost you 77 Kyat per person. At least 10 people have to come along, and the drivers usually manage to squeeze in 15. There is no other way you can possibly be in Thazi in time for the morning train.

If you're forced to take public transport to Thazi or Mandalay because

---

PHOTOGRAPHS: *top:* Sule Pagode in the centre of Rangoon; *bottom left:* Festively clad boy; *bottom right:* Overloaded truck

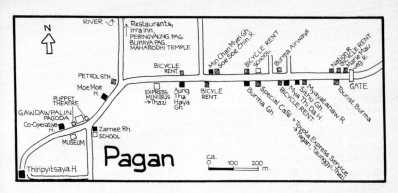

Pagan

the morning pick-up is booked up weeks in advance, here's the way to do it (we have been told that this method is now illegal!?): Catch one of the ancient, heavily loaded trucks to NYAUNG OO at 6:00 h (1 Kyat). From here catch a similar truck to KYAUK-PADAUNG (5 Baht) at 7:00 h. From here you can catch a pick-up to THAZI or MANDALAY (25 Kyat). The last Mandalay-bound pick-up leaves around 16:00 h. The trip will take you 10-12 hrs. Be prepared for 30-40 fellow travellers.

EXCURSIONS FROM PAGAN
THE VILLAGE OF THIRIPYITSAYA
This small village is approx. 6 km south of Pagan, on the Irrawaddy riverbank. You can still experience a genuine village atmosphere here; few tourists ever come by. The startlingly white LAWKANANDA PAGODA is on top of a nearby mountain. It used to be a reference point for ships sailing along the Irrawaddy. The road leading south from Pagan is difficult for cyclists, especially during the dry season, when fine sand and dust make bike-riding almost impossible. Stop by in *MYINKABA* along the way and pay a visit to Aung Myin's traditional lacquerware workshop.

MOUNT POPA

The 1500 metre Mount Popa is approx. 60 km southeast of Pagan, in Burma's hot, central plain. Once an active volcano, it is now considered the Mount Olympus of the Burmese Nats. The belief in these spirits, dating to back to pre-Buddhist times, is still as widely spread as ever in Burma, regardless of the state-religion-status Buddhism seems to have acquired. You'll have a wonderful view of the Pagan plain from the monastery on the peak. The fastest way to Mount Popa is to charter a jeep (350-400 Kyat). If you go by truck or pick-up you'll need a whole day for the entire trip.

PHOTOGRAPHS: *top left:* Gawdawpalin Pagoda, Pagan; *top right:* View from the U-Bein Bridge; *bottom:* Boy selling melons in Rangoon

TAUNGGYI

One of the prettiest trips you can make in this area is the one to Taunggyi, the capital of the Shan State. The town is on the edge of a 1550 metre plateau in the middle of the mountains, 170 km from THAZI, the closest large traffic junction. While the first 20 km from Thazi are still on level ground, the road soon starts going uphill. Not until you have passed NAMPANDET (65 km) - by which time you will also have reached the border of the Shan State - does it really get steep. Continue driving uphill for another 30 km and you'll reach KALAW at a height of 1400 metres. Once you've passed the small settlement you'll be back on the level ground of a raised plateau. After SHWENYAUNG there's only one steep road left to TAUNGGYI. 150,000 people inhabit the town on the big (=gyi) mountain (=Taung).

Much of the old, colonial atmosphere can still be felt in the area north of the seemingly endless, incredibly straight main road. The

CATHEDRAL for instance, which stands next to the sports field and the houses on the slope, seems strangely out of place.

There are pagodas on all of the surrounding hills. You will have a particularly nice view from the

PAGODA south of town, from where you will be able to see the settlement, the hinterland, and - the weather permitting - even Lake Inle. The pagoda is said to have the power to grant wishes. All other sights are in the vicinity of the main road. You should definitely go and see the

TAUNGGYI HOTEL, which is set in a beautiful park in the east of town, even if you're not staying there. The small, frequently closed

MUSEUM is nearby. Here you may be able to visit an ethnological and natural history exhibition, should the museum be open. The city's main attraction, however, is the

CENTRAL MARKET, where members of the hilltribes - even those from the more remote parts of the country - come to shop and offer their own wares for sale. The market is only held once every five days.

HOTELS
The old colonial hotel, *TAUNGGYI HOTEL***** (formerly the STRAND), has huge rooms with running, hot water (!). The restaurant is quite good but rather expensive. The Tourist Burma office is in the main lobby. This is the place to go for information, tickets, and exchanging money - friendly people. The other hotels in town are frequently booked out, e.g. the *SAN PYA*** (probably the best), the *MAY KYU***, and the *THI THANT GUEST HOUSE***. Have breakfast at the *SHWE TAIK CAFE,* near the marketplace and the main road. The *SHANGHAI* serves good food and beer.

LEAVING TAUNGGYI
BY PLANE
The daily flights from HEHO to RANGOON (460 Kyat) and MANDALAY (205 Kyat) are convenient but unfor-

tunately frequently booked up. The HEHO airstrip is 40 km west of Taunggyi. You can catch the Tourist Burma bus there for 15 Kyat.

BY TRAIN / BY PICK-UP

To RANGOON: Jeeps and pick-ups to SHWENYAUNG, the final stop of the railway at the road branching off to Lake Inle, cost 7 Kyat. Few trains leave from here, however. You'd probably be better off taking one of the incredibly overloaded pick-ups through the mountains to THAZI (170 km, 6 hrs., 55 Kyat). You can catch a train to Rangoon from here (11 hrs., 36 Kyat in the 2nd, 99 Kyat in the upper class).

Non-stop buses to PAGAN (121 Kyat) and MANDALAY (8 hrs., 143 Kyat) leave town regularly.

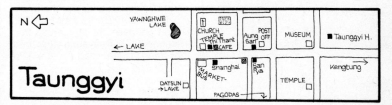

LAKE INLE

The famous lake (measuring 15 km in length and from 2 - 5 km in width) is in the middle of a huge, swampy area. It is rather difficult to find out what its actual size is, due to the lake merging with large, reedy areas on all sides.

Approx. 80,000 Intha live around and on Lake Inle. They had originally settled in Tenasserim, the Burmese part of the Malay peninsula. As they had no desire to fall victim to the seemingly endless Burmese-Thai wars, however, they moved to the Lake Inle region approx. 200 years ago. Their houses are built upon wooden stilts in the generally rather flat lake. The Intha cultivate tomatoes, aubergines, beans, and other vegetables on little floating islands of water hyacinth, reeds, and humus. In order to have their hands free while navigating through these floating gardens, they tie an oar to one of their feet. This traditional method of 'leg-rowing' is no longer as common as it used to be, though; these days many have enough money to be able to afford a noisy outboard motor-boat.

The road ends at *YAWNGHWE*, at the northern tip of the lake. There are many wooden buildings and temples in the area. The atmosphere is tranquil and rural, the climate pleasant. You can catch a boat to the 'floating' town of

YWAMA from here between 7:00 and 8:00 h for 20 Kyat. Chartering your own boat is much more expensive. The small town by the lake is criss-crossed by a number of canals. The houses face the water and are built upon wooden stakes. The floating market, held every day before noon, is particularly impressive. Pay a visit to the *PHAUNG DAW U PAGODA*. If you've chartered your own boat you can also visit the floating gardens and a nearby cigar factory.

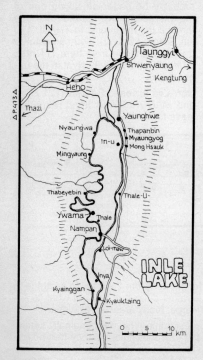

HOTELS

If you want to spend a night in Yawnghwe get out at Shwenyaung, before Taunggyi. The *INLE INN*** outside of the village, is something for people who love the rural life. Good food is served at the *FRIENDSHIP RESTAURANT*.

HOW TO GET THERE

You'll have to pay 7 Kyat for a pick-up and 110 Kyat for a taxi for the 27 km trip from Taunggyi to YAWNGHWE. Drive back down the steep road from Taunggyi to Shwenyaung. It is here that the 11 km road to the lake branches off.

KALAW

Lying between Taunggyi and Thazi, this beautiful settlement is rarely visited. Spend the night in the wonderfully located *KALAW HOTEL***. A big market is held every five days. Members of various hilltribes, particularly the Palaung, come to buy and sell. An excursion to the PINDAYA CAVES is unfortunately too dangerous to be recommended, and only rarely is one able to visit the surrounding Palaung villages. Ask for up-to-date information at the hotel desk.

MANDALAY

A whole day-trip on the train, this former capital of Burma is 650 km north of Rangoon. The country was ruled from here between 1857 and 1885. King Mindon was responsible for making an old prophecy come true:

When Buddha and his disciple Ananda visited the present-day Mandalay Hill, the Enlightened said that a large city would be founded here in the year 2400 of his faith (=1857 in the Christian era).

The city has been able to keep much of its fascinating, individual character to the present day. Horse-drawn carriages, jeeps, ancient buses, and trishaws are the only forms of public transportation. Life at the Irrawaddy is still much as it was during the days of Kipling. Women and girls wash their clothes in the river, children jump into its murky, brown water to cool off, and the ancient steamboats chug by at a lazy, unhurried pace.

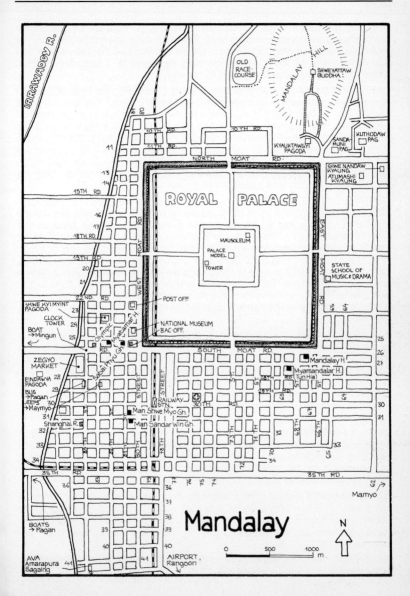

Mandalay

Spending a couple of days in Mandalay is worth it, as there are several places worth visiting in the surrounding area. One can even spend the night in the mountain village of Maymyo. Almost all the buildings of the 26th/30th Road and 81st/84th Street block were completely destroyed by a large fire in 1984. There are still great gaps in the road to this day.

Climb *MANDALAY HILL* on your first evening - not during the heat of the day! There are two staircases and one path that lead to the top. You will get to the easiest way up by taking bus no. 5 from the Mandalay Hotel. The bus stops directly at the main staircase. The second path leads past the Mandalay Palace and through a small village until it reaches the western side of the hill. From here you can hardly miss the staircase - it even has a roof. Once on top of the hill, you will have a spectacular view of the mountains of the Shan State in the east and the sun setting over the Irrawaddy in the west. Before climbing the hill, we would recommend paying a visit to the

KUTHODAW PAGODA, which is next to the southern staircase. The teachings of Buddha are inscribed upon large marble tablets that are distributed among the 729 small pagodas within the temple grounds - surely this must be the world's largest book. There are more temple grounds nearby. MANDALAY PALACE was completely destroyed in 1945, shortly before the end of World War II. King Mindon had the palace built of wood. Only the thick, outer walls, each measuring 1600 metres in length and the four of them forming a perfect square, were of stone. Part of the area is used by the Burmese army today. You can only visit the remains of the palace with a military escort. A wooden model in the centre of the ruin will give you an idea of what the palace used to look like.

The *ARAKAN PAGODA*, second-most sacred pagoda of Burma (second only to the Shwedagon itself) is 3 km south of town, by the road leading to Ava (buses 6 and 8). It is also known as the Mahamuni Pagoda. The 4 metre Mahamuni Buddha statue, decorated with layer upon layer of thin slivers of gold, is said to have been made during the lifetime of Buddha and to have been modelled on the Enlightened himself. A gong weighing 5 tons can be seen in the inner courtyard. Lacquerware as well as wood, bone, and ivory carvings are sold around the pagoda. The large, roofed

ZEGYO MARKET in the centre of town may not have an extensive variety of wares, but its atmosphere makes it a place well worth a longer visit. Although Burma is the most important gem-producing country in the world, the rubies and sapphires offered for sale here are usually third rate. The best stones are either exported or sold at the Diplomatic Store in Rangoon for US$. A

NIGHT MARKET is held from 18:00 h on 80th Street / 31st Road. Potential customers are often also seen as potential sellers, so be prepared for being asked what ware you have to offer - jeans, watches, calculators, jewelry, cosmetics, perfume etc. are extremely popular. From the market, take bus no. 2 down to the

IRRAWADDY (landing-place for boats to Mingun). A walk along the river-bank in the early evening is especially nice.

IRRAWADDY RIVER, MANDALAY

HOTELS

The *MANDALAY*****, on the corner of 26th Road / 67th Street, is the top hotel in town. Clean, quiet, and next to the palace, ac rooms cost around US$20. You will also find the Tourist Burma office here, the only place in town where you can legally exchange money and buy tickets.

You'll get better value at the *MYA MANDALAR**** (formerly the Tun Hia), just around the corner. Rooms of various standards are offered, most of them are frequently booked up, however.

The *SABAI PHYU REST HOUSE***** is on 81st Street, in between 25th and 26th Road. You will have a wonderful view of the entire city from the upper-floor rooms and the penthouse of the large, concrete building.

You will find a number of cheaper hotels in town, all of them **: *MAN SANDAR WIN,* no. 149, 31st Road, between 80th and 81st Street - friendly people. The *MANSHWEMYO,* no. 142, is opposite. Rather tacky, no mosquito nets. The *AUNG TI RI GUESTHOUSE* is on 31st Road, near 80th Street.

FOOD

Ignore the shabby exterior of the *SHANGHAI,* no. 172, 84th Street - good Chinese food is served here. The same can be said of the SHWE WAH, 80th Street, between 32nd and 33rd Road. You will find the *MANN RESTAURANT* near the Zegyo Market. The *OLYMPIC CAFE* is opposite. Tea, cakes, and filled pastries are served. Fruit juices, ice cream and milkshakes are available at the *NYLON ICE CREAM BAR* right next door. You will find the *MIN MIN RESTAURANT*, good Chinese food, just a couple of houses further on, between 26th and 27th Road. The Chinese food served at the *KAINKYI* on 29th Road, between 83rd and 84th Street is also good.

GENERAL INFORMATION

TOURIST BURMA - the office is in the luxurious Mandalay Hotel. Information and coupons are available from 8:00-20:00 h daily, tickets are only sold until 14:00 h.

MUSEUM - the Ministry of Culture has opened an Art Academy (dance performances) east of the palace walls. The old museum and the library have also been moved here (East Moat Road).

TRANSPORT - public buses cost between -.20 and 1 Kyat. No. 1 goes to the Mahamuni Pagoda; no. 2 to the landing place for Mingun; no. 4 and 5 to Mandalay Hill.

A short ride through town in a trishaw may cost up to 5 Kyat, longer rides cost up to 15 Kyat. A complete city-tour will cost you around 40 Kyat.

Horse-drawn carriages (tongas) may cost up to 20 Kyat, depending on the distance. A city-tour to all the important sights will cost you approx. 40 Kyat.

A day trip to Sagaing / Amarapura in a taxi costs 200 Kyat.

LEAVING MANDALAY
BY PLANE
You will find the BAC office on the corner of 25th Road / 80th Street. Free BAC buses travel to and from the airport from here. You can also catch the bus 11 for 50 Paise. Upon having arrived in Mandalay, immediately book the ticket for your next destination (PAGAN 190 Kyat, HEHO 205 Kyat, RANGOON 545 Kyat).

BY TRAIN
Again, tickets have to be bought at Tourist Burma. Trains to RANGOON leave at 7:00 and 18:15 h, 650 km, 2nd class 44 Kyat, 1st class (not on all trains) 98 Kyat, Upper Class 110 Kyat, and Upper Class Sleeper (not on all trains) 138 Kyat. We would suggest taking a bus if you're headed to TAUNGGYI or PAGAN.

BY BUS / TAXI-JEEP / PICK-UP
Buses and pick-ups leave for PAGAN at 4:00 in the morning (66 Kyat (Coop-bus) / 88 Kyat). Leave well in time - some ricksha drivers are slow on purpose. The first bus to TAUNGGYI leaves at 4:30 h (143 Kyat). Toyota pick-ups take approx. 8 hrs. and leave Mandalay at 5:30, 8:00, and 10:00 h. For information go to the Taunggyi Booking Office next to the Olympic Cafe.

BY RIVERBOAT
A Tourist Burma steamboat leaves the 35th Road landing place at 5:00 in the morning every Thur and Sun. It is meant to arrive in NYAUNG OO by 17:30 h (!!) - deck ticket 120 Kyat, cabin 160 Kyat including transfer, breakfast, and lunch. You will be separated from the local passengers, but it is a pleasant trip nevertheless. There is also a daily steamboat, but tourists are allegedly (?!) not allowed to travel on it any more - check up on this! Women selling fruit, eggs, and drinks come on board whenever the boat drops anchor along the way. 'White' tourists will find themselves besieged by women with coloured blankets, who are out to trade. The Irrawaddy's water-level sinks dramati-

cally during the weeks prior to the monsoon. It takes hours and sometimes even days for the trip to continue once the ship has run aground on a sandbank, something which happens quite frequently - we would not recommend doing the trip between February and June if you do not have much time to spare.

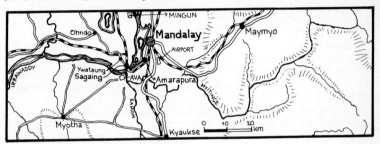

EXCURSIONS FROM MANDALAY
AMARAPURA

Bus no. 8 to Amarapura and Ava leaves from the market. Amarapura is 13 km south of Mandalay. It was Burma's capital and the centre of the silk-weaving industry from 1782 to 1857. Several pagodas, ruins, and some remains of the former city wall, all partially damaged by an earthquake, can still be viewed.

The wooden U BEIN BRIDGE in the south measures 1200 metres in length and goes across the TAUNGTHAMAN LAKE, which all but evaporates at the end of the dry season each year. The village leader, U Bein, had the bridge built of the wood of the former palace in Ava 200 years ago. The KYAUKTAW-GYI PAGODA, which was modelled on the Ananda Pagoda of Pagan, stands on the other side of the lake. The villages surrounding Amarapura are well-known for the silk they produce, and the nearby village of KYI TUN KHAT has become famous for producing bronze Buddha figures.

AVA

Ava became Burma's Royal city after the destruction of Pagan. Amarapura took over this role in 1782. Ava was also the name given to Burma by the Europeans until well into the last century. It is located on the river-bank, near the point at which the MYITNGE RIVER merges with the Irrawaddy. Take bus no. 8 from the market in Mandalay to the Ava-bridge (20 km), then walk down to the Myitnge river ferry. Horse-drawn carriages await you on the opposite bank. Ever since the 1930s, this has been the only bridge to cross the Irrawaddy river. Two of its 16 arches were destroyed by British troops during World War II, and it was almost 10 years before the bridge could be re-opened to traffic and the general public in 1954. The MAHA AUNGMYE BONZAN MONASTERY with its old tamarind trees and the northern part of the former CITY WALL is definitely worth a visit. You will find the so-called 'leaning tower of Ava', the NANMYIN TOWER, at the NORTHERN ENTRANCE. The upper parts of the tower once collapsed and the foundation subsequently sank due to an earthquake.

SAGAING

This town, 21 km southwest of Mandalay on the western bank of the Irrawaddy, was Burma's most important city from 1315-1365. The surrounding hills are literally covered with pagodas, stupas, and cave-temples. Almost 5000 monks live in the approx. 600 monasteries.

Silversmiths can be watched at work in the village of YWATAUNG, 1 km west of Sagaing. Another 10 km further west you'll come across Sagaing's most famous pagoda, the KAUNG MU DAW PAGODA.

MINGUN

Mingun is 12 km upstream from Mandalay. Boats leave more or less every hour, as soon as they are full, from the landing-place at the end of 26th Road. The ride is most enjoyable, 2.50 Kyat, 1-2 hrs. The last boat back to Mandalay leaves at 15:00 h.

The incomplete MINGUN PAGODA, which was once meant to become the largest temple in the whole world, is worth a visit. The model 600 metres south of the temple will give you an idea of how huge the pagoda was meant to become.

Nearby you will also be able to gaze upon the second largest bell in the whole world, which weighs a staggering 90 tons. You will find the HSINBYUME PAGODA 150 metres north of the landing place.

Tourist Burma sometimes organizes boat trips for 25 Kyat per person.

MAYMYO

This former British hill-station is 68 km from Mandalay and lies at an altitude 900 metres higher. The small and sleepy settlement has a definite colonial atmosphere - the clock tower by the main road still has Big Ben chimes after all these years. A visit to the

MORNING MARKET between 5:30 and 10:00 h is quite an experience. Shan, Lahu, Palaung, and other hilltribe members come to offer their wares. Good milkshakes with fresh strawberries are sold at the lower end of the market during the harvest season (Jan - March). All sorts of vegetables thrive up here in the cool mountain climate. We would suggest visiting the

BOTANICAL GARDENS, which cover an area of 175 hectares. Admission 0.5 Kyat. Walk downhill from the Maymyo Rest House and you'll find a

CHINESE TEMPLE. There are an unusually large number of churches, mosques, and Hindu temples in the settlement. Both the

ANIKASAN WATERFALL, approx. 11 km towards Mandalay, and the

WETWUN WATERFALL, 24 km away, are out of town.

Horse-drawn carriages, the only form of transportation in town, cost approx. 15 Kyat an hour.

The area controlled by the rebels (or insurgents, as they are officially called) begins behind Maymyo, which, incidentally, was named after Colonel May of the 5th Bengali Infantry Regiment. The most important city of the northern Shan State, LASHIO (off-limits to tourists), is just 300 km away from here. Note all the wares being smuggled to and from LASHIO on the train-ride back, which also offers a good opportunity to get to know some people from Burma and possibly even from other countries.

HOTELS
The *MAYMYO REST HOUSE***, formerly the Candacraig, has a refined atmosphere and serves good food. The evenings can be spent lounging about in front of the warm fireplace. Bicycles can be rented for 3 Kyat an hour. The *NANN MYAING HOTEL**** is relatively new, all rooms have a bathroom. Eat at the hotels - the food there is better than at the *SHANGHAI RESTAURANT*.

HOW TO GET THERE
Go to Tourist Burma for the coupons necessary for the jeep ride. A jeep from MANDALAY (29th Road) takes 2 hrs. and costs 22 Kyat. If you can't be bothered to wait around for the jeep to fill up, try to charter it for yourself for 150 - 170 Kyat. You will reach the mountains after 26 km. It is here that the road starts working its way uphill in 22 hairpin bends. You will have a wonderful view of the Mandalay plain after a total of 40 km.

The railway trip from Mandalay is more romantic (upper class 10.50 Kyat, 3 hrs., departure 5:00 in the morning). Try to be at the station by 4:00 h.

SUGGESTED READING

Many of the following books can be found in the large bookstores in Bangkok. You might also try the libraries of the foreign cultural institutes such as the British Council.

THAILAND

GENERAL INFORMATION

THAILAND IN THE 80's (various authors; Bangkok 1984). An officially published handbook - wide ranging and informative on country, people, economy, administration etc.

CONFLICT OR COMMUNICATION (reprint of various articles out of the magazine 'Business in Thailand', Bangkok 1980). An excellent introduction to the social structure of the country and the mentality of the people.

CULTURE SHOCK! THAILAND (Cooper, R. & N.; Times Books, Singapore 1982). Amusing and relaxed, this is a good aid for a better understanding of the Thais and for knowing how to behave as a 'farang'. A good book to buy and read during your stay in Thailand.

THE FIVE FACES OF THAILAND (Donner, Wolf; Hamburg 1978). The economic history of Thailand.

THE POLITICS OF HEROIN IN SOUTH EAST ASIA (McCoy, Alfred; New York 1973). A scrupulously researched book about the opium business in the Golden Triangle area and its neighbouring countries.

THAILAND - ITS PEOPLE, ITS SOCIETY, ITS CULTURE (Blanchard, W.; New Haven 1958). Introduction to the problems of Thailand.

THAILAND FROM THE AIR (Invernizzi, Luca / Cassio, Alberto; Bangkok 1984). Large format book with excellent photographs taken from a rather unusual visual angle.

THAILAND - SEVEN DAYS IN THE KINGDOM (Warren, William, and "50 of the World's Greatest Photographers", Singapore 1988). This beautiful, large format picture book full of stunning photography is the result of the joint efforts of 50 renowned international photographers who spent a week travelling around Thailand in 1987.

HISTORY / POLITICS

POPULAR HISTORY OF THAILAND (Jumsai, Manich; Bangkok). A historical text about the kings and wars of old Siam. The same author has also written a language guide, history of Thai literature, and an examination of Thai Buddhism.

THAILAND - A SHORT HISTORY (Wyatt, David; New Haven 1984). Excellent introduction to the history of Thailand from the pre-Thai period to our times.

THE MAKING OF SOUTH EAST ASIA (Coedes, George; Los Angeles 1966). Standard work on the early history of the South East Asian states.

KUKRIT PRAMOJ: HIS WIT AND WISDOM (Bangkok 1983). A critical survey of one of the most important Thai politicians in his speeches, writings, and interviews.

HISTORICAL ACCOUNTS

THE KINGDOM AND THE PEOPLE OF SIAM (Bowring,Sir John; New York 1969). A wide-ranging two volume work written by an English diplomat who travelled the country in 1855.

TEMPLES AND ELEPHANTS (Carl Bock, London 1884, reprint Bangkok 1985). Description of a journey from Bangkok to Chiang Mai under King Chulalongkorn.

VOYAGE TO SIAM (Tachard, Guy; London 1688; reprint Bangkok 1981).The account of an embassy made up of six Jesuits sent by King Louis XIV to King Narai.

A NARRATIVE OF A RESIDENCE IN SIAM (Neale, Frederick Arthur; London 1852; reprint Bangkok 1986).

AN ENGLISHMAN'S SIAMESE JOURNALS 1890 - 1893 (anonymous; reprint Bangkok 1986). The expedition of an English surveyor to the north of Thailand. Written by a keen observer.

SIAM ON THE MEINAM FROM THE GULF TO AYUTHIA (Sommerville, Maxwell; London 1897; reprint Bangkok 1985). Upon finding no guidebook with ready information to help him, the author sets out to write his own descriptive account of places he has visited.

LITERATURE

THAI-RAMAYANA (a translation by M.L.Manich Jumsai of the King Rama I version, Bangkok). There are several versions of this epic, beloved throughout South East Asia. The Thai version includes many of its own fairy tales and legends.

FOLK TALES OF THAILAND (Chaudhury, Roy P. C.; New Delhi 1976). Eighteen folk tales with an introduction concerning country and people.

SIAMESE DRAMA (Pira Sudham; Bangkok 1983). Short stories of a Thai modern author mainly concerned with village life in the Northeast.

TAW AND OTHER THAI STORIES (Draskau, Jennifer, ed. and transl.; Hong Kong 1975). Collection of short stories.

PEOPLE OF ESARN (Sudham, Pira; Bangkok 1987). Tales of life in north-eastern Thailand.

ETHNOLOGY

PEOPLE OF THE HILLS (Chaturabhand, Preecha; Bangkok 1980). Extremely readable descriptions of seven different hilltribes.

PEOPLES OF THE GOLDEN TRIANGLE (Lewis, Paul & Elaine; London 1984). Very comprehensive introduction to all hilltribes. Large format, many colour photographs.

HIGHLANDERS OF THAILAND (Mc Kinnon, Ed John; Bhrukhsari, Wanat; Kuala Lumpur 1983). A collection of essays on the hilltribes of northern Thailand, written by various social scientists.

BUDDHISM

UNDERSTANDING THAI BUDDHISM (Jumsai, M. L. Manich; Bangkok). Written in an out-of-date style, this book nevertheless contains all the necessary information.

A HISTORY OF BUDDHISM IN THAILAND (Nivat Dhani, Prince; Bangkok 1966).

A MEDITATOR'S DIARY. **A Western woman's unique experiences in Thailand monasteries** (Hamiltion-Merritt, Jane; London, Boston, Sydney 1976). Recommended for anyone who wants to gain a deeper insight into Buddhism and life in a Thai monastery.

ARTS

ART IN THAILAND: A BRIEF HISTORY (Subradradis Diskul, Prince; Bangkok).

THE IMAGE OF THE BUDDHA (Snellgrove, David L.; Paris 1978). The gigantic volume describes the development of Buddha images in all Asian countries in chronological and geographical order. Numerous illustrations and photographs.

THE HERITAGE OF THAI SCULPTURE (Boisselier, Jean; Weatherhill 1974). The most comprehensive standard work on Buddhist sculpture.

THE ARTS OF THAILAND (van Beek, Steve / Tettoni, Invernizzi; Hong Kong 1985). Impressive colour photography.

THE ART OF SUKHOTHAI (Stratton, Carol / McNair Scott, Miriam; Kuala Lumpur 1981).

A CONCISE HISTORY OF BUDDHIST ART IN THAILAND (Le May, Reginald; Tokyo 1963).

TRADITIONAL THAILAND, GLIMPSES OF A NATION'S CULTURE (Segaller, Denis; Hong Kong 1982).

NINE TEMPLES OF BANGKOK (Bruce, Helen; Bangkok 1960). History and background of important temples in Bangkok.

TRAVEL GUIDES

INSIGHT GUIDE THAILAND (Apa, Singapore 1983). A travel guide with nice pictures and extensive route descriptions. Few practical tips.

50 TRIPS THROUGH SIAM'S CANALS (Veran, Ch.; Bangkok 1979). For everyone who wants to explore the central part of Thailand by river boat. Due to the language difficulties, it's not easy even with the book.

THAILAND - A TRAVEL SURVIVAL KIT (Cummings, Joe; Melbourne 1987). A traveller book from the well known series.

THE SHELL GUIDE TO THE NATIONAL PARKS OF THAILAND (Dobias, Robert; Bangkok 1982). Description of all national parks with practical tips concerning climate and getting there. Many maps.

GUIDE TO THAILAND (Clarac, A ; Bangkok 1985). The most comprehensive art guide to Thailand, written by the former French ambassador to the country. Even remote areas are described. No practical information, though.

THE TRAVELER'S COMPLETE GUIDE TO PATTAYA & SOUTH-EASTERN THAILAND (van Beek, Steve; Hong Kong 1981). Practical route description for people using their own transportation.

GUIDE TO CHIANG MAI & NORTHERN THAILAND (Hoskin, John; Hong Kong 1984). Same kind of guide book.

PHUKET (Nichols, Fiona; Bangkok 1985). Beautiful photos, nice to look at but no practical information.

MAPS

THE LATEST THAILAND HIGHWAY MAP (ed. by the Roads Association of Thailand; Bangkok 1986). The most comprehensive road atlas of the country at the present time. Many city maps. English and Thai.

APA MAP 1:1,500,000 (Singapore 1987). Sights are marked. Based on a topographical map. Not always reliable!

ESSO MAP 1:2,000,000 (Bangkok 1986). Thai and English, main roads with distances in km, city map of Bangkok, city and road index.

BANGKOK STREET DIRECTORY (Bangkok 1984). 265 pp. street atlas of the capital. Thai and English. Bus stops and government offices.

MAP OF BANGKOK & MAP OF CHIANG MAI (Nancy Chandler; Bangkok). Nicely drawn and illustrated maps with interesting markets, shops, restaurants, sights etc.

LATEST TOUR'S GUIDE TO BANGKOK & THAILAND (Bangkok). To be recommended as all bus routes are included.

BURMA

GENERAL INFORMATION

BURMA - A PROFILE (Bixler, Norma; New York 1971). A remarkable general account.

WE THE BURMESE (Trager, Helen; New York 1969). Interesting description of the Burmese way and life.

BURMA THE GOLDEN (Klein, Wilhelm / Pfannmüller, Günter; Singapore 1982). Excellent colour photography by the authors of the Insight Guide. Large format.

HISTORY

A HISTORY OF MODERN BURMA (Cady, J.F.; Ithaca 1958). The standard introduction to the history of Burma since the 18th century.

BURMA (Hall, D. G. E.; London 1960).

HISTORY OF BURMA (Harvey, G. E.; London 1925 and 1967). Deals with ancient history up to the 19th century. Reprint was published in 1967.

JOURNAL OF HIS SECOND EMBASSY TO THE COURT OF AVA IN 1802 (Symes, Michael; reprint London 1955). Description and political background of the British embassy to the court of Ava. A great complement for a visit to the historical sites. Ava comes alive.

A NARRATIVE OF THE MISSION TO THE COURT OF AVA IN 1855 (Yule, Henry; reprint Kuala Lumpur 1968).

NOVELS

BURMESE DAYS (Orwell, George; London 1934, 1975). The best novel about the colonial twenties.

TRAVEL GUIDES

INSIGHT GUIDE BURMA (Klein, Wilhelm / Pfannmüller, Günter; Singapore 1981). Beautiful coffee-table guide. Hardly any practical information.

BURMA - A TRAVEL SURVIVAL KIT (Wheeler, Tony; Melbourne 1986) Practical tips in shoestring-style.

HISTORICAL SITES IN BURMA (Aung Thaw; Rangoon 1978). Recommended, although the quality of the photos is bad. Sold only in Burma (Diplomatic Store).

PICTORIAL GUIDE TO PAGAN (Rangoon 1975). Most comprehensive guide to Pagan and all temples.

GENERAL INDEX

MAPS

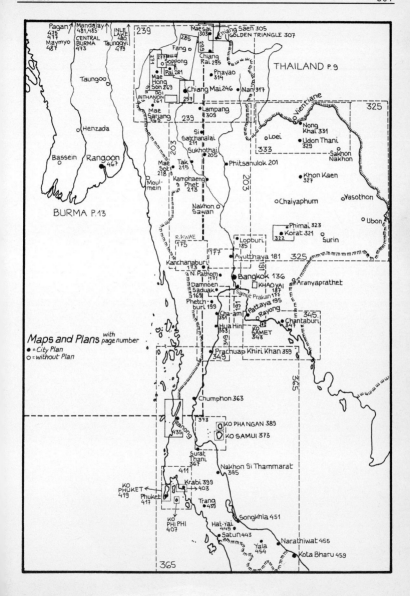

Maps and Plans with page number
● = City Plan
○ = without Plan